W9-CLL-658

Jeffersonian Democracy

((•—[Hear the Audio at myhistorylab.com

Do you have too much debt?

DURING THEIR FIRST WEEK IN COLLEGE, FRESHMEN RECEIVE ON average eight applications for credit cards. Credit card companies target college students because they have a lifetime to acquire debt—and pay it off. The average freshman in 2008 finished the year with a credit card debt of $2,038, while graduating seniors owed $4,138—up 44 percent since 2004. Many students cope with debt by cutting expenses, taking jobs, or skipping school, while some do not cope. A 2006 documentary film described the plight of two college students in Oklahoma who, awash in credit card debt, committed suicide.

Many college students incur debt responsibly, most often to pay for college. In 2008 the average college graduate owed $23,000, mostly for college loans. But this investment usually pays off—literally: College graduates on average earned $57,200, while individuals with only a high school education earned $31,300.

Many of the founders of the nation were also entangled in personal debt. In 1798 Robert Morris, the financier who had devised the funded debt to pay and equip George Washington's army, was imprisoned for personal debt. He languished in the Prune Street debtor's prison in Philadelphia for three years. Thomas Jefferson, on paper one of the richest men in Virginia, owner of thousands of acres of land and 200 slaves, was also plagued by debt. His financial woes mounted as he built additions to Monticello, his home, and acquired more books for his library, one of the finest in the nation. Creditors harassed him. "I am miserable till I shall owe not a shilling," he wrote in 1787. When he died, he was bankrupt. His slaves were sold to pay creditors.

Jefferson's antipathy toward debt influenced his ideas about government. He opposed federal expenditures because they could lead to indebtedness. A weak government, too, was less likely to restrict individual freedoms, a doctrine that endures to this day. Few presidents have left a deeper imprint. His parsimony sometimes left the nation vulnerable to foreigners, whether high-handed European rulers or pirate states in northern Africa. On a few occasions—such as the chance to acquire the Louisiana territory—he splurged, but soon recanted. On leaving office he urged his successor to pay off the federal deficit.[1]

---

[1]After the 3,000-volume Library of Congress was destroyed by fire in 1814, Madison persuaded Congress to purchase Jefferson's 6,000-volume library for $23,950. This helped pay some of Jefferson's debts. At the time, some politicians grumbled that Jefferson's library had been overvalued. Many of his books, after all, were pirated (published by printers who had not paid copyright fees), that era's equivalent of an "illegal download."

From Chapter 6 of *American Destiny: Narrative of a Nation*, Combined Volume, Fourth Edition. Mark C. Carnes and John A. Garraty. Copyright © 2012 by Pearson Education, Inc. Published by Pearson Prentice Hall. All rights reserved.

Jefferson Elected President

Once the furor over war and subversion subsided, public attention focused on the presidential contest between Adams and Jefferson. Because of his stand for peace, Adams personally escaped the brunt of popular indignation against the Federalist party. His solid qualities had a strong appeal to conservatives, and fear that the Republicans would introduce radical "French" social reforms did not disappear when the danger of war with France ended. Many nationalist-minded voters worried that the Republicans, waving the banner of states' rights, would weaken the strong government established by the Federalists. The economic progress stimulated by Hamilton's financial reforms also seemed threatened. When the electors' votes were counted in February 1801, however, the Republicans were discovered to have won narrowly, seventy-three to sixty-five.

But which Republican was to be president? The Constitution did not distinguish between presidential and vice presidential candidates; it provided only that each elector vote for two candidates, the one with the most votes becoming president and the runner-up vice president. The development of national political parties made this system impractical. The vice presidential candidate of the Republicans was Aaron Burr of New York, a former senator and a rival of Hamilton in law and politics. But Republican party solidarity had been perfect; Jefferson and Burr received seventy-three votes each. Because of the tie, the Constitution required that the House of Representatives (voting by states) choose between them.

In the House the Republicans could control only eight of the sixteen state delegations. On the first ballot Jefferson got these eight votes, one short of election, while six states voted for Burr. Two state delegations, being evenly split, lost their votes. Through thirty-five ballots the deadlock persisted; the Federalist congressmen, fearful of Jefferson's supposed radicalism, voted solidly for Burr.

In the end, Alexander Hamilton decided who would be the next president. Although he considered Jefferson "too much in earnest in his

ELECTORAL VOTE
TOTAL: 138

53% 73   47% 65

Democratic-Republican (Jefferson)
Federalist (J. Adams)

The Wild Election of 1800 The election of 1800 was arguably the weirdest in the nation's history. When the electors' votes were counted in February 1801, the Republicans won New York State—and, seemingly, the election, seventy-three to sixty-five. But which Republican was to be president? The Republican electors held to the party line: Jefferson and Burr each received seventy-three votes. Because of the tie, the Constitution required that the House of Representatives (voting by states) choose between them. Jefferson ultimately prevailed.

PEARSON CUSTOM LIBRARY

AMERICAN HISTORY

HIST 104
America in the 19th Century
CAYUGA COMMUNITY COLLEGE

PEARSON

Cover Art: Courtesy of Library of Congress and the Chicago History Museum; "Rocket at Cape Canaveral" courtesy of Pgiam/iStockphoto; "Saturn V Rocket" courtesy of Chad Purser/iStockphoto; "Dr. Martin Luther King, Jr. statue" courtesy of Carol Highsmith/Library of Congress; "Three Suffragists casting votes in New York City" courtesy of National Photo Company Collection/Library of Congress; "Governor Edwin P. Morrow signing the Anthony Amendment" courtesy of Library of Congress; "Woman operating machine in factory" courtesy of HultonArchive/iStockPhoto; "Woman in WWII uniform saluting in studio" courtesy of HultonArchive/iStockPhoto. Additional images courtesy of Comstock, Photodisc/Getty Images.

Copyright © 2013 by Pearson Learning Solutions

All rights reserved.

Permission in writing must be obtained from the publisher before any part of this work may be reproduced or transmitted in any form or by any means, electronic or mechanical, including photocopying and recording, or by any information storage or retrieval system.

Additional copyright information is included, where applicable, as a footnote at the beginning of each chapter.

Printed in the United States of America.

V092

Please visit our website at *www.pearsonlearningsolutions.com.*

Attention bookstores: For permission to return any unsold stock, contact us at *pe-uscustomreturns@pearson.com.*

Pearson Learning Solutions, 501 Boylston Street, Suite 900, Boston, MA 02116
A Pearson Education Company
www.pearsoned.com

ISBN 10: 1-269-23188-X
ISBN 13: 978-1-269-23188-6

Table of Contents

democracy" and "not very mindful of truth," he detested Burr. He exerted his considerable influence on Federalist congressmen on Jefferson's behalf. Finally, on February 17, 1801, Jefferson was elected. Burr became vice president.

To make sure that this deadlock would never be repeated, the Twelfth Amendment was drafted, providing for separate balloting in the Electoral College for president and vice president. This change was ratified in 1804, shortly before the next election.

The Federalist Contribution

On March 4, 1801, in the new national capital on the Potomac River named in honor of George Washington, Thomas Jefferson took the presidential oath and delivered his inaugural address. His goal was to recapture the simplicity and austerity—the "pure republicanism"—that had characterized "the spirit of '76." The new president believed that a revolution as important as that heralded by his immortal Declaration of Independence had occurred, and for once most of his political enemies agreed with him.

> •●•⊣Read the Document
> Thomas Jefferson, *First Inaugural Address* at
> **myhistorylab.com**

Jefferson erred, however, in calling this triumph a revolution. The real upheaval had been attempted in 1798; it was Federalist-inspired, and it failed. In 1800 the voters expressed a preference for individual freedom and limited national power. And Jefferson, despite Federalist fears that he would destroy the Constitution and establish a radical social order, presided instead over a regime that confirmed the great achievements of the Federalist era, chiefly, the creation and implementation of the Constitution itself.

What was most significant about the election of 1800 was that it was *not* a revolution. After a bitter contest, the Jeffersonians took power and proceeded to change the policy of the government. They did so peacefully. Thus American republican government passed a crucial test: Control of its machinery had changed hands in a democratic and orderly way. And only slightly less significant, the informal party system had demonstrated its usefulness. The Jeffersonians had organized popular dissatisfaction with Federalist policies, formulated a platform of reform, chosen leaders to put their plans into effect, and elected those leaders to office.

Thomas Jefferson: Political Theorist

Much as Jefferson worried that an indebted nation could become enslaved to its creditors, he feared banks because they, too, deprived debtors of true liberty. He believed *all* government a necessary evil at best, for by its nature it restricted the freedom of the individual. For this reason, he wanted the United States to remain a society of small independent farmers. Such a nation did not need much political organization.

Jefferson's main objection to Alexander Hamilton was that Hamilton wanted to commercialize and centralize the country; Hamilton embraced public debt so as to initiate public projects and promote investment. This Jefferson feared, for it would mean that financial speculators and creditors would acquire economic power. Moreover, a commercial economy would lead to the growth of cities, which would complicate society and hence require more regulation. "The mobs of great cities add just as much to the support of pure government," he said, "as sores do to the strength of the human body." Like Hamilton, he believed that city workers were easy prey for demagogues. "I consider the class of artificers as the panderers of vice, and the instruments by which the liberties of a country are usually overturned," he said. Like Hamilton, Jefferson thought human beings basically selfish. "Lions and tigers are mere lambs compared with men," he once said. Although he claimed to have some doubts about the subject, he suspected that blacks were "inferior to whites in the endowments both of body and mind." (Hamilton, who also owned slaves, stated flatly of blacks that "Their natural faculties are as good as ours.") Jefferson's pronouncements on race are yet more troubling in light of recent research, including DNA studies, that point to the likelihood that he fathered one or more children by Sally Hemings, one of his slaves.

●●●—|Read the Document
Memoirs of a Monticello Slave at **myhistorylab.com**

Jefferson as President

The novelty of the new administration lay in its style and its moderation. Both were apparent in Jefferson's inaugural address. The new president's opening remarks showed that he was neither a demagogue nor a firebrand. "The task is above my talents," he said modestly, "and . . . I approach it with . . . anxious and awful presentiments." The people had spoken, and their voice must be heeded, but the rights of dissenters must be respected. "All . . . will bear in mind this sacred principle," he said, "that though the will of the majority is in all cases to prevail, that will to be rightful must be reasonable; that the minority possess their equal rights, which equal law must protect, and to violate would be oppression."

Jefferson spoke at some length about specific policies. He declared himself against "entangling alliances" and for economy in government, and he promised to pay off the national debt, preserve the government's credit, and stimulate both agriculture and its "handmaid" commerce. His main stress was on the cooling of partisan passions: "Every difference of opinion is not a difference of principle. We have called by different names brethren of the same principle. We are all Republicans—we are all Federalists." And he promised the country "a wise and frugal Government which shall restrain men from injuring one another" and "leave them otherwise free to regulate their own pursuits."

●●●—|Read the Document
Reflections Upon Meeting Jefferson at **myhistorylab.com**

Jefferson quickly demonstrated the sincerity of his remarks. He saw to it that the whiskey tax and other Federalist excises were repealed, and he made sharp cuts in military and naval

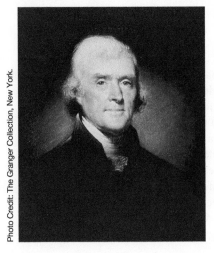

Photo Credit: The Granger Collection, New York.

This portrait of Thomas Jefferson, painted when he was thirty-seven years old, in 1800, the year before he was elected president, is considered an accurate likeness. Its artist, just twenty at the time, was the American painter, Rembrandt Peale. Rembrandt's father—the painter Charles Willson Peale—also named his other sons after painters: Rubens, Titian, Raphaelle, and Titian II.

expenditures to keep the budget in balance. The Naturalization Act of 1798 was repealed, and the old five-year residence requirement for citizenship restored. The Sedition Act and the Alien Act expired of their own accord in 1801 and 1802.

The changes were not drastic. Jefferson made no effort to tear down the fiscal structure that Hamilton had erected. "We can pay off his debt," the new president confessed, "but we cannot get rid of his financial system." Nor did the author of the Kentucky Resolves try to alter the balance of federal-state power.

Yet there was a different tone to the new regime. Jefferson had no desire to surround himself with pomp and ceremony; the excessive formality of the Washington and Adams administrations had been distasteful to him. From the moment of his election, he played down the ceremonial aspects of the presidency. He asked that he be notified of his election by mail rather than by a committee, and he would have preferred to have taken the oath at Charlottesville, near Monticello, his home, rather than at Washington. After the inauguration, he returned to his boardinghouse on foot and took dinner in his usual seat at the common table.

In the White House he often wore a frayed coat and carpet slippers, even to receive the representatives of foreign powers when they arrived. At social affairs he paid little heed to the status and seniority of his guests. During business hours congressmen, friends, foreign officials, and plain citizens coming to call took their turn in the order of their arrival. "The principle of society with us," Jefferson explained, "is the equal rights of all. . . . Nobody shall be above you, nor you above anybody, *pell-mell* is our law."

"Pell-mell" was also good politics, and Jefferson turned out to be a superb politician. He gave dozens of small stag dinner parties for congressmen, serving the food personally from a dumbwaiter connected with the White House kitchen. The guests, carefully chosen to make congenial groups, were seated at a round table to encourage general conversation, and the food and wine were first-class. These were ostensibly social occasions—shoptalk was avoided—yet they paid large political dividends. Jefferson learned to know every congressman personally, Democratic Republican and Federalist alike, and not only their political views but their strengths, their quirks, and their flaws as well. And he worked his personal magic on them, displaying the breadth of his knowledge, his charm and wit, and his lack of pomposity.

Jefferson made effective use of his close supporters in Congress and of Cabinet members as well, in persuading Congress to go along with his proposals. His state papers were models of reason, minimizing conflicts, stressing areas where all honest people must agree. After all, as he indicated in his inaugural address, nearly all Americans believed in having both a federal government and a republican system. No great principle divided them into irreconcilable camps. Jefferson set out to bring them all into *his* camp, and he succeeded so well in four years that when he ran for reelection against Charles Pinckney, he got 162 of the 176 electoral votes cast. Eventually even John Quincy Adams, son of the second president, became a Jeffersonian.

At the same time, Jefferson was anything but nonpartisan in the sense that Washington had been. His Cabinet consisted exclusively of men of his own party. He exerted almost continuous pressure on Congress to make sure that his legislative program was enacted into law. He did not remove many Federalist officeholders, and at one point he remarked ruefully that government officials seldom died and never resigned. But when he could, he used his power of appointment to reward his friends and punish his enemies.

Jefferson's Attack on the Judiciary

Although notably open-minded and tolerant, Jefferson had a few stubborn prejudices. One was against kings, another against the British system of government. A third was against judges, or rather, against entrenched judicial power. The biased behavior of Federalist judges during the trials under the Sedition Act had enormously increased this distrust, and it burst all bounds when the Federalist majority of the dying Congress rammed through the Judiciary Act of 1801.

The Judiciary Act created six new circuit courts, presided over by sixteen new federal judges and a small army of attorneys, marshals, and clerks. The expanding country needed the judges, but with the enthusiastic cooperation of President Adams, the Federalists made shameless use of the opportunity to fill all the new positions with conservative members of their own party. The new appointees were dubbed "midnight justices" because Adams had stayed up until midnight on March 3, his last day as president, feverishly signing their commissions.

The Republicans retaliated as soon as the new Congress met by repealing the Judiciary Act of 1801. But on taking office Jefferson had discovered that in the confusion of Adams's last hours, the commissions of a number of justices of the peace for the new District of Columbia had not been distributed. While these were small fry indeed, Jefferson was so angry that he ordered the commissions held up even though they had been signed by Adams.

One of the appointees, William Marbury, then petitioned the Supreme Court for a writ of mandamus (Latin for "we order") directing the new secretary of state, James Madison, to give him his commission.

The case of **Marbury v. Madison** (1803) placed Chief Justice John Marshall, one of Adams's "midnight" appointments, in an embarrassing position. Marbury had a strong claim; if Marshall refused to order Madison to give Marbury the job, everyone would say Marshall dared not stand up to Jefferson, and the prestige of the Court would suffer. If he ordered that Marbury be seated, however, he would place the Court in direct conflict with the President. Jefferson particularly disliked Marshall. He would probably tell Madison to ignore the order, and in the prevailing state of public opinion nothing could be done about it. This would be a still more staggering blow to the judiciary. If its decisions were ignored, would the Supreme Court have any purpose?

Marshall had studied law only briefly and had no previous judicial experience, but in this crisis he first displayed the genius that was to mark him as a great judge. By right Marbury should have his commission, Marshall announced. However, the Court could not require Madison to give it to him. Marbury's request for a court order had been based on an ambiguous clause in the Judiciary Act of 1789. That clause was unconstitutional, Marshall declared, and therefore void. Congress could not legally give the Supreme Court the right to issue such orders.

With the skill and foresight of a chess grand master, Marshall turned what had looked like a trap into a triumph. By sacrificing the pawn, Marbury, he established the power of the Supreme Court to invalidate federal laws that conflicted with the Constitution. Jefferson could not check him because Marshall had *refused* power instead of throwing an anchor ahead, as Jefferson had

Read the Document

Opinion of the Supreme Court for Marbury v. Madison at **myhistorylab.com**

feared. Yet he had certainly grappled a "further hold for future advances of power," and the president could do nothing to stop him.

The Marbury case made Jefferson more determined to strike at the Federalist-dominated courts. He decided to press for the impeachment of some of the more partisan judges. First he had the House of Representatives bring charges against District Judge John Pickering. Pickering was clearly deranged—he had frequently delivered profane and drunken harangues from the bench—and the Senate quickly voted to remove him. Then Jefferson went after a much larger fish, Samuel Chase, associate justice of the Supreme Court.

Chase had been prominent for decades and active in the affairs of the Continental Congress. Washington had named him to the Supreme Court in 1796, and he had delivered a number of important opinions. But his handling of cases under the Sedition Act had been outrageously high-handed. Defense lawyers had become so exasperated as to throw down their briefs in disgust at some of his prejudiced rulings. However, the trial demonstrated that Chase's actions had not constituted the "high crimes and misdemeanors" required by the Constitution to remove a judge. Even Jefferson became disenchanted with the efforts of some of his more extreme followers and accepted Chase's acquittal with equanimity.

The Barbary Pirates

The North African Arab states of Morocco, Algiers, Tunis, and Tripoli had for decades made a business of piracy, seizing vessels all over the Mediterranean and holding crews and passengers for ransom. The European powers found it simpler to pay them annual protection money than to crush them. Under Washington and Adams, the United States joined in the payment of this tribute; while large, the sums were less than the increased costs of insurance for shippers when the protection was not purchased.

Such spinelessness ran against Jefferson's grain. "When this idea comes across my mind, my faculties are absolutely suspended between indignation and impatience," he said. When the pasha of Tripoli tried to raise the charges, Jefferson balked. Tripoli then declared war in May 1801, and Jefferson dispatched a squadron to the Mediterranean.

But the pirates were not overwhelmed, and a major American warship, the frigate *Philadelphia*, had to be destroyed after running aground off the Tripolitan coast. The payment of tribute continued until 1815. Just the same, America, though far removed from the pirate bases, was the only maritime nation that tried to resist the blackmail. Although the war failed to achieve Jefferson's purpose of ending the payments, the pasha agreed to a new treaty more favorable to the United States, and American sailors, led by Commodore Edward Preble, won valuable experience.

The Louisiana Purchase

The major achievements of Jefferson's first term had to do with the American West, and the greatest by far was the **Louisiana Purchase**, the acquisition of the huge area between the Mississippi River and the Rocky Mountains. In a sense the purchase of this region, called Louisiana, was fortuitous, an accidental by-product of

See the Map
The Louisiana Purchase at
myhistorylab.com

This depicts New Orleans in 1803, when the city was acquired—along with much of the modern United States—in the Louisiana Purchase. It was known as the Crescent City because of the way it hugged a curved section of the Mississippi River. In 1803, New Orleans's population was about 8,000, including 4,000 whites, 2,700 slaves, and about 1,300 free "persons of color."
Source: P&S-1932.0018/Creator—Boqueto de Woieseri/Chicago History Museum.

European political adjustments and the whim of Napoleon Bonaparte. Certainly Jefferson had not planned it, for in his inaugural address he had expressed the opinion that the country already had all the land it would need "for a thousand generations." It was nonetheless the perfectly logical—one might almost say inevitable—result of a long series of events in the history of the Mississippi Valley.

Along with every other American who had even a superficial interest in the West, Jefferson understood that the United States must have access to the mouth of the Mississippi and the city of New Orleans or eventually lose everything beyond the Appalachians. "There is on the globe one single spot, the possessor of which is our natural and habitual enemy," he was soon to write. "It is New Orleans." Thus when he learned shortly after his inauguration that Spain had given Louisiana back to France, he was immediately on his guard. Control of Louisiana by Spain, a "feeble" country with "pacific dispositions," could be tolerated; control by a resurgent France dominated by Napoleon, the greatest military genius of the age, was entirely different.

Deeply worried, the president instructed his minister to France, Robert R. Livingston, to seek assurances that American rights in New Orleans would be respected and to negotiate the purchase of West Florida in case that area had also been turned over to France.

Jefferson's concern was well-founded; France was indeed planning new imperial ventures in North America. Immediately after settling its difficulties with the United States through the Convention of 1800, France signed a secret treaty with Spain, which returned Louisiana to France. Napoleon hoped to use this region as a breadbasket for the French West Indian sugar plantations, just as colonies like Pennsylvania and Massachusetts had fed the British sugar islands before the Revolution.

However, the most important French island, Saint Domingue (Hispaniola), at the time occupied entirely by the nation of Haiti, had slipped from French control. During the French Revolution, the slaves of the island had revolted. In 1793 they were granted personal freedom, but they fought on under the leadership of the "Black Napoleon," a self-taught genius named Toussaint L'Ouverture, and by 1801 the island was entirely in their hands. The original Napoleon, taking advantage of the slackening of war in Europe, dispatched an army of 20,000 men under General Charles Leclerc to reconquer it.

When Jefferson learned of the Leclerc expedition, he had no trouble divining its relationship to Louisiana. His uneasiness became outright alarm. In April 1802 he again urged Minister Livingston to attempt the purchase of New Orleans and Florida or, as an alternative, to buy a tract of land near the mouth of the Mississippi where a new port could be constructed. Of necessity, the mild-mannered, idealistic president now became an aggressive realist. "The day that France takes possession of New Orleans," he warned, "we must marry ourselves to the British fleet and nation."

In October 1802 the Spanish, who had not yet actually turned Louisiana over to France, heightened the tension by declaring that American boats plying the Mississippi could no longer deposit and store their goods in warehouses in New Orleans, the first step to exporting them to Europe. We now know that the French had no hand in this action, but it was beyond reason to expect Jefferson or the American people to believe it at the time. With the West clamoring for relief, Jefferson appointed his friend and

Photo Credit: © Bettmann/ CORBIS All Rights Reserved.

Toussaint L'Ouverture leading a revolt of slaves against the French in Haiti—the first and only successful slave rebellion in history.

disciple James Monroe minister plenipotentiary and sent him to Paris with instructions to offer up to $10 million for New Orleans and Florida. If France refused, he and Livingston should open negotiations for a "closer connection" with the British.

The tension broke before Monroe even reached France. General Leclerc's Saint Domingue expedition ended in disaster. Although Toussaint surrendered, Haitian resistance continued. Yellow fever raged through the French army; Leclerc himself fell to the fever, which wiped out practically his entire force.

When news of this calamity reached Napoleon early in 1803, he had second thoughts about reviving French imperialism in the New World. Without Saint Domingue, the wilderness of Louisiana seemed of little value. Napoleon was preparing a new campaign in Europe. He could no longer spare troops to recapture a rebellious West Indian island or to hold Louisiana against a possible British attack, and he needed money.

For some weeks the commander of the most powerful army in the world mulled the question without consulting anyone. Then, with characteristic suddenness, he made up his mind. On April 10 he ordered Foreign Minister Talleyrand to offer not merely New Orleans but all of Louisiana to the Americans. The next day Talleyrand summoned Livingston to his office on the rue du Bac and dropped this bombshell. Livingston was almost struck speechless but quickly recovered his composure. When Talleyrand asked what the United States would give for the province, he suggested the French equivalent of about $5 million. Talleyrand pronounced the sum "too low" and urged Livingston to think about the subject for a day or two.

Livingston faced a situation that no modern diplomat would ever have to confront. His instructions said nothing about buying an area almost as large as the entire United States, and there was no time to write home for new instructions. The offer staggered the imagination. Luckily, Monroe arrived the next day to share the responsibility. The two Americans consulted, dickered with the French, and finally agreed—they could scarcely have done otherwise—to accept the proposal. Early in May they signed a treaty. For 60 million francs—about $15 million—the United States was to have all of Louisiana.

No one knew exactly how large the region was or what it contained. When Livingston asked Talleyrand about the boundaries of the purchase, he replied, "I can give you no direction. You have made a noble bargain for yourselves, and I suppose you will make the most of it." Never, as the historian Henry Adams wrote, "did the United States government get so much for so little."

Napoleon's unexpected concession caused consternation in America, though there was never real doubt that the treaty would be ratified. Jefferson did not believe that the government had the power under the Constitution to add new territory or to grant American citizenship to the 50,000 residents of Louisiana by executive act, as the treaty required. He even drafted a constitutional amendment: "The province of Louisiana is incorporated with the United States and made part thereof." But his advisers convinced him that it would be dangerous to delay approval of the treaty until an amendment could be acted on by three-fourths of the states. Jefferson then suggested that the Senate ratify the treaty and submit an amendment afterward "confirming an act which the nation had not previously authorized." This idea was so obviously illogical that he quickly dropped it. Finally, he came to believe "that the less we say about constitutional difficulties the better." Since what he called "the good sense of our country" clearly wanted Louisiana, he decided to "acquiesce with satisfaction" while Congress overlooked the "metaphysical subtleties" of the problem and ratified the treaty.

Louisiana Purchase Jefferson bought the Louisiana region from Napoleon. No payments were made to the many Indians who had no idea that the world of their ancestors was owned by distant rulers.

Some of the more partisan Federalists, who had been eager to fight Spain for New Orleans, attacked Jefferson for undermining the Constitution. One such critic described Louisiana contemptuously as a "Gallo-Hispano-Indian" collection of "savages and adventurers." Even Hamilton expressed hesitation about absorbing "this new, immense, unbounded world," though he had dreamed of seizing still larger domains himself. In the end Hamilton's nationalism reasserted itself, and he urged ratification of the treaty, as did such other important Federalists as John Adams and John Marshall. It was ironic—and a man as perceptive as Hamilton must surely have recognized the irony—that the acquisition of Louisiana ensured Jefferson's reelection and further contributed to the downfall of the Federalists. The purchase was popular even in the New England bastions of that party. While the negotiations were progressing in Paris, Jefferson had written the following of partisan political affairs: "If we can settle happily the difficulties of the Mississippi, I think we may promise ourselves smooth seas during our time." These words turned out to be no more accurate than most political predictions, but the Louisiana Purchase drove another spike into the Federalists' coffin.

Read the Document
The Louisiana Purchase at **myhistorylab.com**

Read the Document
Fisher Ames on the Louisiana Purchase at **myhistorylab.com**

The Federalists Discredited

As the election of 1804 approached, the West and South were solidly for Jefferson, and the North was rapidly succumbing to his charm. The addition of new western states would soon further reduce New England's power in national affairs.

Photo Credit: Photo by Vincent Colabella Photography / Courtesy of JP Morgan Chase Archives.

These pistols were used in the duel between Aaron Burr and Alexander Hamilton. Before the duel Hamilton's lawyer drew up a contract specifying the terms: The duelists were to shoot at ten paces, and the barrels of the guns were to be no longer than 11 inches. Witnesses claimed that Hamilton never fired his fine pistol, but Burr took deadly aim, firing a .54-caliber ball that hit Hamilton in the chest. It ricocheted off his rib, punctured his liver, and lodged in his backbone. Hamilton died the next day.

So complete did the Republican triumph seem that a handful of diehard Federalists in New England began to think of secession. Led by former secretary of state Timothy Pickering, a group known as the Essex Junto organized in 1804 a scheme to break away from the Union and establish a "northern confederacy."

Even within the dwindling Federalist ranks the junto had little support. Nevertheless, Pickering and his friends pushed ahead, drafting a plan whereby, having captured political control of New York, they would take the entire Northeast out of the Union. Since they could not begin to win New York for anyone in their own ranks, they hit on the idea of supporting Vice President Aaron Burr, who was running against the "regular" Republican candidate for governor of New York. Although Burr did not promise to bring New York into their confederacy if elected, he encouraged them enough to win their backing. The foolishness of the plot was revealed in the April elections: Burr was overwhelmed by the regular Republican. The junto's scheme collapsed.

The incident, however, had a tragic aftermath. Hamilton had campaigned against Burr, whom he considered "an embryo Caesar." When he continued after the election to cast aspersions on Burr's character (not a very difficult assignment, since Burr, despite being a grandson of the preacher Jonathan Edwards, frequently violated both the political and sexual mores of the day), Burr challenged him to a duel. It was well known that Hamilton opposed dueling in principle, his own son having been slain in such an encounter, and he certainly had no need to prove his courage. But he believed that his honor was at stake. The two met with pistols on July 11, 1804, at Weehawken, New Jersey, across the Hudson from New York City. Hamilton made no effort to hit the challenger, but Burr took careful aim. Hamilton fell, wounded; he died the next day.

Thus a great, if enigmatic, man was cut off in his prime. His work, in a sense, had been completed, and his philosophy of government was being everywhere rejected, yet the nation's loss was large.

Lewis and Clark

While the disgruntled Federalists dreamed of secession, Jefferson was planning the exploration of Louisiana and the region beyond. He especially hoped to find a water route to connect the upper Mississippi or its tributaries with the Pacific Ocean. Early in 1803 he got $2,500 from Congress and obtained the permission of the French to send his exploring party across Louisiana. To command the expedition he appointed his private secretary, Meriwether Lewis, a young Virginian who had seen considerable service with the army in the West and who possessed, according to Jefferson, "a great mass of accurate information on all the subjects of nature." Lewis chose as his companion officer William Clark, another soldier (he had served with General Anthony Wayne at the Battle of Fallen Timbers) who had much experience in negotiating with Indians.

•••—Read the Document

Thomas Jefferson to Meriwether Lewis at **myhistorylab.com**

The country greeted the news of the explorers' return to St. Louis with delight. Besides locating several passes across the Rockies, Lewis and Clark had established friendly relations with a great many Indian tribes to whom they presented gifts, medals, American flags,

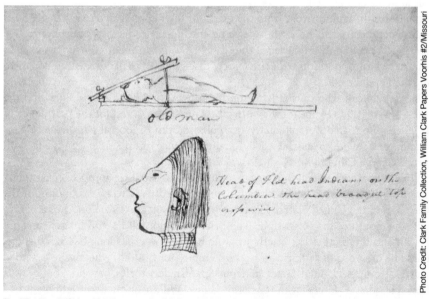

Photo Credit: Clark Family Collection, William Clark Papers Voorhis #2/Missouri Historical Society, St. Louis.

The "Flat Head" (Chinook) Indians acquired their name through shaping in infancy, as shown in a diagram from the Lewis and Clark journals. More remarkable to the explorers than the shape of the Indians' heads was the tribeswomen's open sexuality. "The young females are fond of the attention of our men and appear to meet the sincere approbation of their friends and connections for thus obtaining their favors," Captain Clark confided in his diary.

●━[Read the Document

Lewis and Clark Meet the Shoshone at
myhistorylab.com

and a sales talk designed to promote peace and the fur trade. They brought back a wealth of data about the country and its resources. The journals kept by members of the group were published and, along with their accurate maps, became major sources for scientists, students, and future explorers.

The success of the **Lewis and Clark expedition** did not open the gates of Louisiana very wide. Other explorers sent out by Jefferson accomplished far less. Thomas Freeman, an Irish-born surveyor, led a small party up the Red River but ran into a powerful Spanish force near the present junction of Arkansas, Oklahoma, and Texas and was forced to retreat. Between 1805 and 1807 Lieutenant Zebulon Pike explored the upper Mississippi Valley and the Colorado region. (He discovered but failed to scale the peak south of Denver that bears his name.) Pike eventually made his way to Santa Fe and the upper reaches of the Rio Grande,

●━[Watch the Video

Lewis and Clark: What Were They Trying to Accomplish? at
myhistorylab.com

but he was not nearly so careful and acute an observer as Lewis and Clark were and consequently brought back much less information. By 1808 fur traders based at St. Louis were beginning to invade the Rockies, and by 1812 there were 75,000 people in the southern section of the new territory, which was admitted to the Union that year as the state of Louisiana. The northern region lay almost untouched until much later.

The Burr Conspiracy

Republican virtue seemed to have triumphed, but Jefferson soon found himself in trouble at home and abroad.

In part his difficulties arose from the extent of the Republican victory. In 1805 his Federalist opponents had no useful ideas, no intelligent leadership, and no effective numbers. They held only a quarter of the seats in Congress. As often happens in such situations, lack of opposition weakened party discipline and encouraged factionalism among the Republicans.

The Republican who caused Jefferson the most trouble was Aaron Burr, and the president was partly to blame for the difficulty. After their contest for the presidency in 1801, Jefferson pursued Burr vindictively, depriving him of federal patronage in New York and replacing him as the 1804 Republican vice presidential candidate with Governor George Clinton, Burr's chief rival in the state.

While still vice president, Burr began to flirt with treason. He approached Anthony Merry, the British minister in Washington, and offered to "effect a separation of the Western part of the United States." His price was £110,000 and the support of a British fleet off the mouth of the Mississippi. The British did not fall in with his scheme, but Burr went ahead nonetheless. Exactly what he had in mind has long been in dispute. Certainly he dreamed of acquiring a western empire for himself; whether he intended to wrest it from the United States or from Spanish territories beyond Louisiana is unclear. He joined forces with General James Wilkinson, whom Jefferson had appointed governor of the Louisiana Territory and was secretly in the pay of Spain.

The opening of the Ohio and Mississippi valleys had not totally satisfied land-hungry westerners. In 1806 Burr and Wilkinson had no difficulty raising a small force at a place called Blennerhassett Island, in the Ohio River. Some six dozen men began to move downriver toward New Orleans under Burr's command. Whether the objective was New Orleans or some part of Mexico, the scheme was clearly illegal. For some reason, however—possibly because he was incapable of loyalty to anyone[2]—Wilkinson betrayed Burr to Jefferson at the last moment. Burr tried to escape to Spanish Florida but was captured in February 1807, brought to Richmond, Virginia, under guard, and charged with high treason.

Any president will deal summarily with traitors, but Jefferson's attitude during Burr's trial reveals the depth of his hatred. He "made himself a party to the prosecution," personally sending evidence to the United States attorney who was handling the case and offering blanket pardons to associates of Burr who would agree to turn state's evidence. In stark contrast, Chief Justice Marshall, presiding at the trial in his capacity as judge of the circuit court, repeatedly showed favoritism to the prisoner.

In this contest between two great men at their worst, Jefferson as a vindictive executive and Marshall as a prejudiced judge, the victory went to the judge. Organizing "a military assemblage," Marshall declared on his charge to the jury, "was not a levying of war." To "advise or procure treason" was not in itself treason. Unless two independent witnesses testified to an overt act of treason as thus defined, the accused should be declared innocent. The jury, deliberating only twenty-five minutes, found Burr not guilty.

The Burr affair was a blow to Jefferson's prestige; it left him more embittered against Marshall and the federal judiciary, and it added nothing to his reputation as a statesman.

Napoleon and the British

Jefferson's difficulties with Burr may be traced at least in part to the purchase of Louisiana, which, empty and unknown, excited the greed of men like Burr and Wilkinson. But problems infinitely more serious were also related to Louisiana.

Napoleon had jettisoned Louisiana to clear the decks before resuming the battle for control of Europe. This war had the effect of stimulating the American economy, for the warring powers needed American goods and American vessels. Shipbuilding boomed and foreign trade, which had quintupled since 1793, nearly doubled again between 1803 and 1805. By the summer of 1807, however, the situation had changed: An unusual stalemate had developed in the war.

In October 1805 Britain's Horatio Nelson demolished the combined Spanish and French fleets in the Battle of Trafalgar, off the coast of Spain. Napoleon, now at the summit of his powers, quickly redressed the balance, smashing army after army thrown against him by Great Britain's continental allies. By 1807 he was master of Europe, while the British controlled the seas around the Continent. Neither nation could strike directly at the other.

They therefore resorted to commercial warfare, striving to disrupt each other's economy. Napoleon struck first with his Berlin Decree (November 1806), which made "all commerce and correspondence" with Great Britain illegal. The British retaliated with a series of edicts called Orders in Council, blockading most continental ports and barring from them all foreign vessels unless they first stopped at a British port and paid customs duties. Napoleon then issued his Milan Decree (December 1807), declaring any vessel that submitted to the British rules "to have become English property" and thus subject to seizure.

---

[2]John Randolph said that "Wilkinson is the only man that I ever saw who was from the bark to the very core a villain."

Photo Credit: Werner Forman/Art Resource, N.Y.

American traders in the exchange at a port in China.

When war first broke out between Britain and France in 1792, the colonial trade of both sides had fallen largely into American hands because the danger of capture drove many belligerent merchant vessels from the seas. This commerce had engaged Americans in some devious practices.

For example, American merchants carried sugar from the French colony of Martinique first to the United States, a legal peacetime voyage under French mercantilism. Then they reshipped it to France as American sugar. Since the United States was a neutral nation and sugar was not contraband of war, the Americans expected the British to let their ships pass with impunity. Continental products likewise reached the French West Indies by way of United States ports, and the American government encouraged the traffic in both directions by refunding customs duties on foreign products reshipped within a year.

This underhanded commerce irritated the British. Thus just when Britain and France were cracking down on direct trade by neutrals, Britain determined to halt the American reexport trade, thereby gravely threatening American prosperity.

The Impressment Controversy

More dismaying were the cruel indignities being visited on American seamen by the British practice of **impressment**. Under British law any able-bodied subject could be drafted for service in the Royal Navy in an emergency. Normally, when the commander of a warship found himself shorthanded, he put into a British port and sent a "press gang" ashore to round up the necessary men in harborside pubs. When far from home waters, he might hail any passing British merchant ship and commandeer the necessary men, though this practice was understandably unpopular in British maritime circles. He might also stop a *neutral* merchant vessel on the high seas and remove any British subject. Since the United States owned by far the largest merchant fleet among the neutrals, its vessels bore the brunt of this practice.

Many British captains made little effort to be sure they were impressing British subjects. Furthermore, there were legal questions in dispute. When did an English immigrant become an American? When he was naturalized, the United States claimed. Never, the British retorted: "once an Englishman, always an Englishman."

The Jefferson administration conceded the right of the British to impress their own subjects from American merchant ships. When naturalized Americans were impressed, however, the administration was irritated, and when native-born Americans were taken, it became incensed. Impressment, Secretary of State Madison said in 1807, was "anomalous in principle . . . grievous in practice, and . . . abominable in abuse." Between 1803 and 1812 at least 5,000 sailors were snatched from the decks of United States vessels and forced to serve in the Royal Navy. Most of them—estimates run as high as three out of every four—were Americans.

The combination of impressment, British interference with the reexport trade, and the general harassment of neutral commerce instituted by both Great Britain and France would have perplexed the most informed and hardheaded of leaders, and in dealing with these problems Jefferson was neither informed nor hardheaded. He believed it much wiser to stand up for one's rights than to compromise, yet he hated the very thought of war. Perhaps, being a Southerner, he was less sensitive than he might have been to the needs of New England commercial interests. While the American merchant fleet passed 600,000 tons and continued to grow at an annual rate of over 10 percent, Jefferson kept only a skeleton navy on active service, despite the fact that the great powers were fighting a worldwide, no-holds-barred war. Instead of building a navy that other nations would have to respect, he relied on a tiny fleet of frigates and a swarm of gunboats that were useless against the Royal Navy—"a macabre monument," in the words of one historian, "to his hasty, ill-digested ideas" about defense.[3]

The Embargo Act

The frailty of Jefferson's policy became obvious once the warring powers began to attack neutral shipping in earnest. Between 1803 and 1807 the British seized more than 500 American ships, Napoleon more than 200. The United States could do nothing.

---

[3]The gunboats had performed effectively against the Barbary pirates, but Jefferson was enamored of them mainly because they were cheap. A gunboat cost about $10,000 to build, a big frigate over $300,000.

The Ograbme ("embargo" spelled backward), a snapping turtle drawn by cartoonist Alexander Anderson, frustrates an American tobacco smuggler.
Source: Collection of The New-York Historical Society, [Neg. No. 7278].

The ultimate in frustration came on June 22, 1807, off Norfolk, Virginia. The American forty-six-gun frigate *Chesapeake* had just left port for patrol duty in the Mediterranean. Among its crew were a British sailor who had deserted from HMS *Halifax* and three Americans who had been illegally impressed by the captain of HMS *Melampus* and had later escaped. The *Chesapeake* was barely out of sight of land when HMS *Leopard* (fifty-six guns) approached and signaled it to heave to. Thinking that *Leopard* wanted to make some routine communication, Captain James Barron did so. A British officer came aboard and demanded that the four "deserters" be handed over to him. Barron refused, whereupon as soon as the officer was back on board, *Leopard* opened fire on the unsuspecting American ship, killing three sailors. Barron had to surrender. The "deserters" were seized, and then the crippled *Chesapeake* was allowed to limp back to port.

The attack was in violation of international law, for no nation claimed the right to impress sailors from warships. The British government admitted this, though it delayed making restitution for years. The American press clamored for war, but the country had nothing to fight with. Jefferson contented himself with ordering British warships out of American territorial waters. However, he was determined to put a stop to the indignities being heaped on the flag by Great Britain and France. The result was the **Embargo Act**.

The Embargo Act prohibited all exports. American vessels could not clear for any foreign port, and foreign vessels could do so only if empty. Although the law was sure to injure the American economy, Jefferson hoped that it would work in two ways to benefit the nation. By keeping U.S. merchant ships off the seas, it would end all chance of injury to them and to the national honor. By cutting off American goods and markets, it would

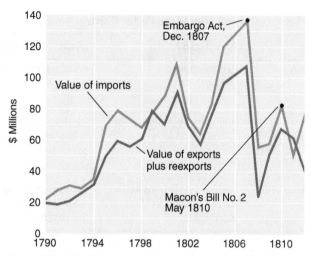

American Foreign Trade, 1790–1812 This graph shows the embargo's effects. The space between the upper (import) and the lower (export) line indicates a persistent foreign-trade deficit.

put great economic pressure on Britain and France to moderate policies toward American shipping.

Seldom has a law been so bitterly resented and resisted by a large segment of the public. It demanded of the maritime interests far greater sacrifices than they could reasonably be expected to make. Massachusetts-owned ships alone were earning over $15 million a year in freight charges by 1807, and Bay State merchants were making far larger gains from the buying and selling of goods. Foreign commerce was the most expansive force in the economy, the chief reason for the nation's prosperity. As John Randolph remarked in a typical sally, the administration was trying "to cure the corns by cutting off the toes."

The Embargo Act had catastrophic effects. Exports fell from $108 million in 1807 to $22 million in 1808, imports from $138 million to less than $57 million. Prices of farm products and manufactured goods reacted violently, seamen were thrown out of work, and merchants found their businesses disrupted.

Surely the embargo was a mistake. The United States ought either to have suffered the indignities heaped on its vessels for the sake of profits or, by constructing a powerful navy, made it dangerous for the belligerents to treat its merchant ships so roughly. Jefferson was too proud to choose the former alternative, too parsimonious to choose the latter. Instead he applied harsher and harsher regulations in a futile effort to accomplish his purpose. Jefferson refused to admit that the embargo was a fiasco and urge its repeal. Only in his last week in office did a leaderless Congress finally abolish it, substituting the Non-Intercourse Act, which forbade trade only with Great Britain and France and authorized the president to end the boycott against either power by proclamation when and if it stopped violating the rights of Americans.

Thus Jefferson's political career ended on a sour note. Several weeks after he had left office and returned to Monticello, he privately advised his successor, James Madison, to trust his own judgment to govern because the people readily succumbed to "the floating lies of the day."

Table 1   Jeffersonian Doctrine: Small Federal Government

Measure	Advantages	Disadvantages
Repealed whiskey and other taxes on imports (excise)	Reduced taxes	Lowered federal revenue
Curtailed military and naval spending	Reduction in federal debt	Weak navy: Foreign powers could "impress" American sailors and seize American ships
Embargo Act (1807): no export trade	End to humiliations at the hand of British and French warships	Collapse of foreign trade, weakening of economy, increased smuggling

Jeffersonian Democracy

Yet Jefferson completed the construction of the political institution known as the Republican party and the philosophy of government known as Jeffersonian democracy. In part his success was a matter of personality; he was perfectly in tune with the thinking of his times. The colonial American had practiced democracy without really believing in it, for example, the maintenance of property qualifications for voting in regions where nearly everyone owned property. Stimulated by the libertarian ideas of the Revolution, Americans were rapidly adjusting their beliefs to conform with their practices. However, it took Jefferson, possessed of the general prejudice in favor of the old-fashioned citizen rooted in the soil, yet deeply committed to majority rule, to oversee the transition.

Jefferson's marvelous talents as a writer help explain his success. He expounded his ideas in language that few people could resist. He had a remarkable facility for discovering practical arguments to justify his beliefs—as when he suggested that by letting everyone vote, elections would be made more honest because with large numbers going to the polls, bribery would become prohibitively expensive.

Jefferson prepared the country for democracy by proving that a democrat could establish and maintain a stable regime. The Federalist tyranny of 1798 was compounded of selfishness and stupidity, but it was also based in part on honest fears that an egalitarian regime would not protect the fabric of society from hotheads and crackpots. The impact of the French Revolution on conservative thinking in the mid-1790s cannot be overestimated. America had fought a seven-year revolution without executing a single Tory, yet during the few months that the Reign of Terror ravaged France, nearly 17,000 persons were officially put to death for political "crimes" and many thousands more were killed in civil disturbances. Worse, in the opinion of many, the French extremists had attempted to destroy Christianity, substituting for it a "cult of reason." Little wonder that many Americans feared that the Jeffersonians, lovers of France and of *liberté, égalité, fraternité*, would try to remodel American society in a similar way.

Jefferson calmed these fears. The most partisan Federalist was hard put to see a Robespierre, leader during the Reign of Terror in France, in the amiable Jefferson scratching out state papers at his desk or chatting with a Kentucky congressman at a

Photo Credit: *Storming of the Bastille on 14th July 1789* (oil on panel), French School, (18th century)/Musee de la Ville de Paris, Musee Carnavalet, Paris, France/The Bridgeman Art Library International.

The storming of the Bastille in 1789. After the crowd seizes the fortification, they tear it down, stone by stone.

"republican" dinner party. Furthermore, Jefferson accepted Federalist ideas on public finance, even learning to live with Hamilton's bank. As a good democrat, he drew a nice distinction between his own opinions and the wishes of the majority, which he felt must always take priority. Even in his first inaugural address he admitted that manufacturing and commerce were, along with agriculture, the "pillars of our prosperity," and he accepted the principle that the government should protect them when necessary from "casual embarrassments." During his term the country grew and prospered, the commercial classes sharing in the bounty along with the farmers so close to Jefferson's heart.

Thus Jefferson undermined the Federalists all along the line. They had said that the country must pay a stiff price for prosperity and orderly government, and they demanded prompt payment in full, both in cash (taxes) and in the form of limitations on human liberty. Under Jefferson these much-desired goals had been achieved cheaply and without sacrificing freedom. A land whose riches could only be guessed at had been obtained without firing a shot and without burdening the people with new taxes. Order without discipline, security without a large military establishment, prosperity without regulatory legislation, freedom without license—truly the Sage of Monticello appeared to have led his fellow Americans into a golden age.

Jefferson insisted that one of his chief accomplishments had been to reduce the national debt from $83 million to $57 million. Writing from Monticello shortly after leaving office, he urged his successors to eliminate the remainder. "The discharge of the public debt," he warned Treasury Secretary Gallatin, "is vital to the destinies of our government."

Yet Jefferson had also learned the perils of an inadequately funded government. His unwillingness to build a real navy had rendered the nation vulnerable to foreign states. Conversely, he had exulted in the purchase of Louisiana, and he backed modest proposals for spending federal money on roads, canals, and other projects that, according to his political philosophy, ought to have been left to the states and private individuals. Debt, Jefferson accepted, was sometimes good policy.

Milestones

1801	Judiciary Act of 1801 allows Adams to appoint many Federalist judges	1804–1806	Lewis and Clark explore West
	Jefferson is elected president	1806	Aaron Burr schemes to take land in West during Burr Conspiracy
1801–1805	U.S. wages war against Barbary pirates in North Africa	1806–1807	Napoleon issues Berlin and Milan decrees in order to disrupt British shipping and economy
1803	Supreme Court declares part of Judiciary Act of 1789 unconstitutional (*Marbury v. Madison*)	1807	HMS *Leopard* attacks USS *Chesapeake*
	Jefferson negotiates Louisiana Purchase with France		Embargo Act prohibits all exports
1804	Aaron Burr kills Alexander Hamilton in duel	1809	Non-Intercourse Act forbids trade with Great Britain and France
	Jefferson is reelected		

✓●─[Study and Review at www.myhistorylab.com

Review Questions

1. The Federalist vision of the nation largely prevailed during the 1790s. Why did it fade so rapidly during the 1800s? Was its decline caused by a failure of Federalist leadership or the successes of Jefferson?

2. What effect did the Napoleonic wars have on events in America? Why did Napoleon abandon his dreams of a French economic empire in the Americas?

3. What chief obstacle—literally—stood in the way of an all-water route across the United States connecting the Atlantic and Pacific Oceans?

4. The text asserts that the Embargo Act was "surely" a mistake, yet Jefferson was a savvy politician. How did he decide to propose it in the first place?

Key Terms

Embargo Act
impressment
Lewis and Clark expedition

Louisiana Purchase
Marbury v. Madison

National Growing Pains

((•—[Hear the Audio at myhistorylab.com

Does the government help you pay for college?

THE RECESSION THAT STRUCK IN 2008 HIT YOUNG ADULTS THE HARDEST. By the end of the year, less than half (46 percent) of those aged eighteen to twenty-four had jobs—the lowest rate on record.[1] Many of those who couldn't find jobs decided to go to college. This influx produced another record in 2008: More young adults ages eighteen to twenty-four were enrolled in either two- or four-year colleges than ever before. The chief enrollment increase was in community colleges, whose costs (tuition, fees, books and expenses) averaged $7,000, compared to four-year public colleges ($10,000) and four-year private colleges ($27,000).

But how could young people pay for college during a severe recession? The federal government provided the answer—through loans for college, chiefly Pell grants. By 2010, for example, nearly 8 million students received Pell grants averaging $3,700 with a maximum grant of $5,500.

That the federal government would one day play so profound a role in the lives of its people would have astonished the founding generation. Well into the nineteenth century, the federal government failed to generate much income. In 1809 its total revenue fell short of $8 million. Of that, $7 million came from taxes on imports (the tariff); the balance came mostly from the sale of federal lands and postage stamps. Without income from the tariff, the federal government could have done little more than deliver the mail.

From 1809 to 1828, Americans repeatedly expanded the role of the federal government. Armies and navies were raised to subdue the Indians and defend the nation from European predators; highways were built to encourage trade and promote settlement of the Louisiana territories. The federal budget tripled. The nation was growing, and the federal government grew with it. The tariff inevitably increased as well. The 1828 "**Tariff of Abominations**" was the highest to that time.

But the sharp increase in the tariff, and in the role of the federal government, sent shock waves through American society. As the tariff raised the price of manufactured goods, farmers had to pay more for clothing and farm implements. Worse, Britain and

---

[1]The federal government began tracking such data in 1948.

From Chapter 7 of *American Destiny: Narrative of a Nation*, Combined Volume, Fourth Edition. Mark C. Carnes and John A. Garraty. Copyright © 2012 by Pearson Education, Inc. Published by Pearson Prentice Hall. All rights reserved.

other foreign nations retaliated against high American tariffs by setting their own high tariffs on American imports—chiefly tobacco, cotton, wheat, and other foodstuffs mostly grown in the South and West. This angered southern farmers because it made their products more expensive—and so less desirable—in foreign markets.

The tariff pitted one section of the nation against another, especially North vs. South. The years from 1809 to 1828 were marked by growth and governmental expansion; but new problems—none more important than the question of slavery—loomed ever larger and more menacing.

Madison in Power

In his inaugural address, James Madison observed that the "present situation" of the United States was "full of difficulties" and that war continued to rage among European powers. Yet he assumed the presidency, he said, "with no other discouragement than what springs from my own inadequacy." The content of the speech was as modest as its delivery; virtually no one could hear it.

•→ Read the Document

Madison, *First Inaugural Address* at myhistorylab.com

Madison was narrower in his interests than Jefferson but in many ways a deeper thinker. He was more conscientious in the performance of his duties and more consistent in adhering to his principles. Ideologically, however, they were as close as two active and intelligent people could be. Madison had no better solution to offer for the problem of the hour than had Jefferson. The Embargo Act had failed and its successor, the Non-Intercourse Act, proved difficult to enforce—once an American ship left port, there was no way to prevent the skipper from steering for England or France. The British continued to seize American vessels.

Because prudent captains remained in port, trade stagnated. Federal revenue through the tariff declined. In 1809, Secretary of the Treasury Gallatin was alarmed by the growing federal deficit. He urged Representative Nathaniel Macon of North Carolina to introduce legislation to remove all restrictions on commerce with France and Britain. Known as Macon's Bill No. 2, it authorized the president to reapply the principle of non-intercourse to either of the major powers if the other should "cease to violate the neutral commerce of the United States." This bill became law in May 1810.

The volume of U.S. commerce with the British Isles zoomed to pre-embargo levels. The mighty British fleet controlled the seas. Napoleon therefore announced that he had repealed his decrees against neutral shipping, seemingly fulfilling the provisions of Macon's Bill No. 2. Madison, seeking concessions from Britain, closed American ports to British ships and goods. Napoleon, despite his announcement to the contrary, continued to seize American ships and cargoes whenever it suited his purposes.

The British refused to modify the Orders in Council. Madison could not afford either to admit that Napoleon had deceived him or to reverse American policy still another time. Reluctantly he came to the conclusion that unless Britain repealed the Orders, the United States must declare war.

Tecumseh and Indian Resistance

There were other reasons for war with Britain besides its violations of neutral rights. The Indians were again restive, and western farmers believed that the British in Canada were egging them on. This had been true in the past but was no longer the case in 1811 and 1812.

Photo Credit: (left and right) Public Domain. 198 Stephan Savoia/AP Wide World Photos.

As a young man Tecumseh was a superb hunter and warrior; his younger brother, Tenskwatawa, was awkward and inept with weapons; he accidentally gouged out his right eye with an arrow. In 1805 he had a religious vision, became known as "The Prophet," and inspired Tecumseh's warriors.

American domination of the southern Great Lakes region was no longer in question. Canadian officials had no desire to force a showdown between the Indians and the Americans, for that could have but one result. Aware of their own vulnerability, the Canadians wanted to preserve Indian strength in case war should break out between Great Britain and the United States.

Read the Document

Pennsylvania *Gazette*, "Indian hostilities" at **myhistorylab.com**

American political leaders tended to believe that Indians should be encouraged to become farmers and to copy the "civilized" ways of whites. However, no government had been able to control the frontiersmen, who by bribery, trickery, and force were driving the tribes back year after year from the rich lands of the Ohio Valley. General William Henry Harrison, governor of the Indiana Territory, kept constant pressure on them. He wrested land from one tribe by promising it aid against a traditional enemy, from another as a penalty for having murdered a white man, from others by corrupting a few chiefs. Harrison justified his sordid behavior by citing the end in view—that "one of the fairest portions of the globe" be secured as "the seat of civilization, of science, and of true religion." The "wretched savages" should not be allowed to stand in the path of this worthy objective. Unless something drastic was done, Harrison's aggressiveness, together with the corroding effects of white civilization, would soon obliterate the tribes.

Tecumseh, the Shawnee chief, made a bold and imaginative effort to reverse the trend by binding all the tribes east of the Mississippi into a great confederation. Traveling from the Wisconsin country to the Floridas, he persuaded tribe after tribe to join him.

To Tecumseh's political movement his brother Tenskwatawa, known as "The Prophet," added the force of a moral crusade. Instead of aping white customs, the Prophet said that Indians must give up white ways, white clothes, and white liquor and reinvigorate their own culture. Ceding lands to the whites must stop because the Great Spirit intended that the land be used in common by all.

The Prophet saw visions and claimed to be able to control the movement of heavenly bodies. Tecumseh, however, possessed true genius. A powerful orator and a great organizer, he had deep insight into the needs of his people. Harrison himself said of Tecumseh, "He is one of those uncommon geniuses which spring up occasionally to produce revolutions and overturn the established order of things." The two brothers made a formidable team. By 1811 thousands of Indians were organizing to drive the whites off Indian land.

With about a thousand soldiers, General Harrison marched against the brothers' camp at Prophetstown in Indiana. Tecumseh was away recruiting men, and the Prophet recklessly ordered an assault on Harrison's camp outside the village on November 7, 1811. When the white soldiers held their ground despite the Prophet's magic, the Indians lost confidence and fell back. Harrison then destroyed Prophetstown.

Unwilling as usual to admit that their own excesses were the chief cause of the trouble, the settlers directed their resentment at the British in Canada. "This combination headed by the Shawanese prophet is a British scheme," a resolution adopted by the citizens of Vincennes, Indiana, proclaimed. As a result, the cry for war with Great Britain rang along the frontier.

Depression and Land Hunger

Some westerners pressed for war because they were suffering an agricultural depression. The prices they received for their wheat, tobacco, and other products in the markets of New Orleans were falling, and they attributed the decline to the loss of foreign markets and the depredations of the British. American commercial restrictions had more to do with the western depression than the British, and in any case the slow and cumbersome transportation and distribution system that western farmers were saddled with was the major cause of their difficulties. But the farmers were no more inclined to accept these explanations than they were to absolve the British from responsibility for the Indian difficulties. If only the seas were free, they reasoned, costs would go down, prices would rise, and prosperity would return.

It was primarily because of Canada, nearby and presumably vulnerable, that westerners wanted war. President Madison probably regarded an attack on Canada as a way to force the British to respect neutral rights. Still more important in Madison's mind, if the United States conquered Canada, Britain's hope of obtaining food in Canada for its West Indian sugar islands would be shattered. Then it would have to end its hateful assaults and restrictions on American merchant ships or the islands' economy would collapse.

But westerners, and many easterners too, were more patriots than imperialists or merchants in 1811 and 1812. When the **War Hawks** (their young leaders in Congress) called for war against Great Britain, they did so because they saw no other way to defend the national honor and force repeal of the Orders in Council. The choice seemed to lie between war and surrender of true independence. As Madison put it, to bow to British policy would be to "recolonize" American foreign commerce.

Opponents of War

Large numbers of people, however, thought that a war against Great Britain would be a national calamity. No shipowner could view with equanimity the idea of taking on the largest navy in the world. Such persons complained sincerely enough about impressment and the Orders in Council, but war seemed worse to them by far. Self-interest led them to urge patience.

Such a policy would have been wise, for Great Britain did not represent a real threat to the United States. British naval officers were high-handed, officials in London complacent, British diplomats in Washington second-rate and obtuse. Yet language, culture, and strong economic ties bound the two countries. Napoleon, on the other hand, represented a tremendous potential danger. He had offhandedly turned over Louisiana, but even Jefferson, the chief beneficiary of his largesse, hated everything he stood for. Jefferson called Napoleon "an unprincipled tyrant who is deluging the continent of Europe with blood."

No one understood the Napoleonic danger to America more clearly than the British; part of the stubbornness and arrogance of their maritime policy grew out of their conviction that Napoleon was a threat to all free nations. The *Times* of London declared, "The Alps and the Apennines of America are the British Navy. If ever that should be removed, a short time will suffice to establish the headquarters of a [French] Duke-Marshal at Washington." Yet by going to war with Britain, the United States was aiding Napoleon.

What made the situation even more unfortunate was the fact that by 1812 conditions had changed in England in a way that made a softening of British maritime policy likely. A depression caused chiefly by the increasing effectiveness of Napoleon's Continental System was plaguing the country. Manufacturers, blaming the slump on the loss of American markets, were urging repeal of the Orders in Council. On June 23, after a change of ministries, the new foreign secretary, Lord Castlereagh, suspended the Orders. Five days earlier, alas, the United States had declared war.

The War of 1812

In the first phase of the war, 1812–1813, the United States attempted to invade Canada near Detroit, Buffalo, and Plattsburgh (New York); it failed. In the second phase, 1814, the British invaded the Chesapeake and burned Washington, DC. The final phase of the war occurred from November 1814 to early 1815, after the Treaty of Ghent was signed. British troops landed at the mouth of the Mississippi River and were defeated by General Andrew Jackson at New Orleans.

The illogic of the War Hawks in pressing for a fight was exceeded only by their ineffectiveness in planning and managing what would become the **War of 1812**. By what possible strategy could the ostensible objective of the war be achieved? To construct a navy capable of challenging the British fleet would have been the work of many years and a more expensive proposition than the War Hawks were willing to consider. Several hundred merchant ships lashed a few cannon to their decks and sailed off as privateers to attack British commerce. The navy's seven modern frigates, built during the war scare after the XYZ Affair, put to sea. But these forces could make no pretense of disputing Britain's mastery of the Atlantic.

For a brief moment the American frigates held center stage, for they were faster, tougher, larger, and more powerfully armed than their British counterparts. Barely two months after the declaration of war, Captain Isaac Hull of the USS *Constitution* chanced upon the HMS *Guerrière* mid-Atlantic, outmaneuvered the *Guerrière* brilliantly, and gunned it into submission. In October the USS *United States* caught the HMS *Macedonian* off the Madeiras, pounded it unmercifully at long range, and forced the British

Photo Credit: Stephan Savoia/AP Wide World Photos.

The USS *Constitution*, restored in 1997.

ship to surrender. The *Macedonian* was taken into New London as a prize; over a third of the 300-man crew were casualties, while American losses were but a dozen. Then, in December, the *Constitution*, now under Captain William Bainbridge, took on the British frigate *Java* off Brazil. "Old Ironsides" shot away *Java's* mainmast and reduced it to a hulk too battered for salvage.

These victories had little influence on the outcome of the war. The Royal Navy had thirty-four frigates, seven more powerful ships of the line, and dozens of smaller vessels. As soon as these forces could concentrate against them, the American frigates were immobilized, forced to spend the war gathering barnacles at their moorings while powerful British squadrons ranged offshore. The privateering merchantmen were more effective because they were so numerous; they captured more than 1,300 British vessels during the war. The best of them—vessels like the *America* and the *True-Blooded Yankee*—were redesigned, given more sail to increase their speed, and formidably armed. The *America* captured twenty-six prizes valued at more than a million dollars. The *True-Blooded Yankee* took twenty-seven vessels and destroyed seven more in a Scottish harbor.

Great Britain's one weak spot seemed to be Canada. The colony had but half a million inhabitants to oppose 7.5 million Americans. Only 2,257 British regulars guarded the long border from Montréal to Detroit. The Canadian militia was feeble, and many of its members, being American-born, sympathized with the "invaders." According to the War Hawk congressman Henry Clay of Kentucky, the West was one solid horde of ferocious frontiersmen, armed to the teeth and thirsting for Canadian blood. Yet such talk was mostly brag and bluster; when Congress authorized increasing the army by 25,000 men, Kentucky produced 400 enlistments.

American military leadership proved extremely disappointing. Madison showed poor judgment by relying on officers who had served with distinction in the Revolution. Instead of a concentrated strike against Canada's St. Lawrence River lifeline, which would have isolated Upper Canada, the generals planned a complicated three-pronged attack. It failed dismally. In July 1812 General William Hull, veteran of the battles of Trenton, Saratoga, and Monmouth and now governor of the Michigan Territory, marched forth with 2,200 men against the Canadian positions facing Detroit. Hoping that the Canadian militia would desert, he delayed his assault, only to find his communications threatened by hostile Indians led by Tecumseh. Hastily he retreated to Detroit, and when the Canadians, under General Isaac Brock, pursued him, he surrendered the fort without firing a shot! In October

Photo Credit: The Mariners' Museum, Newport News, VA.

In the heat of the Battle of Lake Erie, Perry had to abandon his flagship, the *Lawrence*, which had been shot to pieces by enemy fire. (Over three-fourths of the ship's crew were killed or wounded.) He was rowed to the *Niagara*, from which he directed the rest of the engagement.

another force attempted to invade Canada from Fort Niagara. After an initial success it was crushed by superior numbers, while a large contingent of New York militiamen watched from the east bank of the Niagara River, unwilling to fight outside their own state.

The third arm of the American "attack" was equally unsuccessful. Major General Henry Dearborn, who had fought honorably in the Revolution from Bunker Hill to Yorktown, but who had now grown so fat that he needed a specially designed cart to get from place to place, set out from Plattsburgh, New York, at the head of an army of militiamen. Their objective was Montréal, but when they reached the border, the troops refused to cross. Dearborn meekly marched them back to Plattsburgh.

Meanwhile, the British had captured Fort Michilimackinac in northern Michigan, and the Indians had taken Fort Dearborn (now Chicago), massacring eighty-five captives. Instead of sweeping triumphantly through Canada, the Americans found themselves trying desperately to keep the Canadians out of Ohio.

Stirred by these disasters, westerners rallied somewhat in 1813. General Harrison, the victor of Tippecanoe, headed an army of Kentuckians in a series of inconclusive battles against British troops and Indians led by Tecumseh. He found it impossible to recapture Detroit because a British squadron controlling Lake Erie threatened his communications. President Madison therefore assigned Captain Oliver Hazard Perry to the task of building a fleet to challenge this force. In September 1813, at Put-in-Bay near the western end of the lake, Perry destroyed the British vessels in a battle in which 85 of the 103 men on Perry's flagship were casualties. "We have met the enemy and

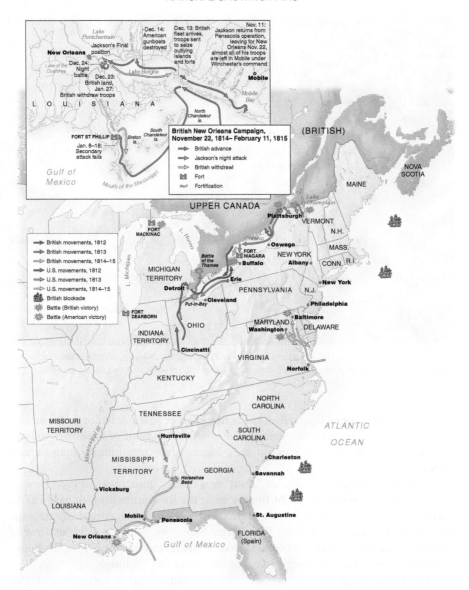

The War of 1812 In the first phase of the war, 1812–1813, the United States attempted to invade Canada near Detroit, Buffalo, and Plattsburgh (New York); it failed. In the second phase, 1814, the British invaded the Chesapeake and burned Washington, DC. The final phase of the war occurred from November 1814 to early 1815, after the Treaty of Ghent was signed. British troops landed at the mouth of the Mississippi River and were defeated by General Andrew Jackson at New Orleans.

they are ours," he reported. About a quarter of Perry's 400 men were blacks, which led him to remark that "the color of a man's skin" was no more an indication of his worth than "the cut and trimmings" of his coat. With the Americans in control of Lake Erie, Detroit became untenable for the British, and when they fell back, Harrison gave chase and defeated them at the Thames River, some 60 miles northeast of Detroit. Although little more than a skirmish, this battle had large repercussions. Tecumseh was among the dead and without him the Indians lost heart. But American attempts to win control of Lake Ontario and to invade Canada in the Niagara region were again thrown back. Late in 1813 the British captured Fort Niagara and burned the town of Buffalo. The conquest of Canada was as far from realization as ever.

The British fleet had intensified its blockade of American ports, extending its operations to New England waters previously spared to encourage the antiwar sentiments of local maritime interests. All along the coast, patrolling cruisers, contemptuous of Jefferson's puny gunboats, captured small craft, raided shore points to commandeer provisions, and collected ransom from port towns by threatening to bombard them. One captain even sent a detail ashore to dig potatoes for his ship's mess.

Britain Assumes the Offensive

Until 1814 the British put relatively little effort into the American war, being concerned primarily with the struggle against Napoleon. However, in 1812 Napoleon had invaded Russia and been thrown back; thereafter, one by one, his European satellites rose against him. Gradually he relinquished his conquests, and in April 1814 the Allies drove Napoleon from power. Then the British, free to strike hard at the United States, dispatched some 14,000 veterans to Canada.

By the spring of 1814 British strategists had devised a master plan for crushing the United States. One army, 11,000 strong, was to march from Montréal, tracing the route that General Burgoyne had followed to disaster in the Revolution. A smaller amphibious force was to make a feint at the Chesapeake Bay area, destroying coastal towns and threatening Washington and Baltimore. A third army was to assemble at Jamaica and sail to attack New Orleans and bottle up the West.

While the main British army was assembling in Canada, some 4,000 veterans under General Robert Ross sailed from Bermuda for the Chesapeake. After making a rendezvous with a fleet commanded by Vice Admiral Sir Alexander Cochrane and Rear Admiral Sir George Cockburn, which had been terrorizing the coast, they landed in Maryland at the mouth of the Patuxent River, southeast of Washington. A squadron of gunboats "protecting" the capital promptly withdrew upstream; when the British pursued, their commander ordered them blown up to keep them from being captured.

The British troops marched rapidly toward Washington. At Bladensburg, on the outskirts of the city, they came upon an army twice their number, commanded by General William H. Winder, a Baltimore lawyer who had already been captured and released by the British in the Canadian fighting. While President Madison and other officials watched, the British charged—and Winder's army turned tail almost without firing a shot. The British swarmed into the capital and put most public buildings to the torch. Before personally setting fire to the White House, Admiral Cockburn took one of the president's hats and a cushion from Dolley Madison's chair as souvenirs, and, finding the table set for dinner, derisively drank a toast to "Jemmy's health."

●◆●⌐Read the Document

Dolley Payne Madison to Lucy Payne Todd at **myhistorylab.com**

This was the sum of the British success. When they attempted to take Baltimore, they were stopped by a formidable line of defenses devised by General Samuel Smith, a militia officer. General Ross fell in the attack. The fleet then moved up the Patapsco

River and pounded Fort McHenry with its cannon, raining 1,800 shells upon it in a twenty-five-hour bombardment on September 13 and 14.

"The Star Spangled Banner"

While this attack was in progress, an American civilian, Francis Scott Key, who had been temporarily detained on one of the British ships, watched anxiously through the night. As twilight faded, Key had seen the Stars and Stripes flying proudly over the battered fort. During the night the glare of rockets and bursting of bombs proved that the defenders were holding out. Then, by the first light of the new day, Key saw again the flag, still waving over Fort McHenry. Drawing an old letter from his pocket, he dashed off the words to "The Star Spangled Banner," which, when set to music, was to become the national anthem of the United States.

To Key that dawn seemed a turning point in the war. He was roughly correct, for in those last weeks of the summer of 1814 the struggle began to move toward resolution. Unable to crack the defenses of Baltimore, the British withdrew to their ships; shortly after, they sailed to Jamaica to join the forces preparing to attack New Orleans.

The destruction of Washington had been a profound shock. Thousands came forward to enlist in the army. The new determination and spirit were strengthened by news from the northern front, where General Sir George Prevost had been leading the main British invasion force south from Montréal. At Plattsburgh, on the western shore of Lake Champlain, his 1,000 Redcoats came up against a well-designed defense line manned by 3,300 Americans under General Alexander Macomb. Prevost called up his

Photo Credit: The Granger Collection, New York.

The Bombardment of Fort McHenry by John Bower, with the Stars and Stripes flying over the fort (center). The British fleet fired 1,800 bombs and red-glaring incendiary rockets. The fort did not return fire because the British ships were beyond the range of its cannon. Although "The Star Spangled Banner" celebrates the "home of the brave," the defenders of Fort McHenry sensibly fled the ramparts and took cover below during the bombardment; they sustained only thirty casualties.

supporting fleet of four ships and a dozen gunboats. An American fleet of roughly similar strength under Captain Thomas Macdonough came forward to oppose the British. On September 11, in a brutal battle at point-blank range, Macdonough destroyed the British ships and drove off the gunboats. With the Americans now threatening his flank, Prevost lost heart and retreated to Canada.

The Treaty of Ghent

The war might as well have ended with the battles of Plattsburgh, Washington, and Baltimore, for later military developments had no effect on the outcome. Earlier in 1814 both sides had agreed to discuss peace terms. Commissioners were appointed and negotiations begun during the summer at Ghent, in Belgium.

The talks at Ghent were drawn out and frustrating. The British were in no hurry to sign a treaty, believing that their three-pronged offensive in 1814 would swing the balance in their favor. But news of the defeat at Plattsburgh modified their ambitions, and when the Duke of Wellington advised that from a military point of view they had no case for territorial concessions so long as the United States controlled the Great Lakes, they agreed to settle for *status quo ante bellum*, to leave things as they were before the war. The other issues, everyone suddenly realized, had simply evaporated. The mighty war triggered by the French Revolution seemed finally over. The seas were free to all ships,

> **Read the Document**
> *The Treaty of Ghent* at **myhistorylab.com**

and the Royal Navy no longer had need to snatch sailors from the vessels of the United States or of any other power. On Christmas Eve 1814 the treaty, which merely ended the state of hostilities, was signed. Although, like other members of his family, he was not noted for tact, John Quincy Adams rose to the spirit of the occasion. "I hope," he said, "it will be the last treaty of peace between Great Britain and the United States." And so it was.

The Hartford Convention

Before news of the treaty could cross the Atlantic, two events took place that had important effects but that would not have occurred had the news reached America more rapidly. The first was the **Hartford Convention**, a meeting of New England Federalists held in December 1814 and January 1815 to protest the war and to plan for a convention of the states to revise the Constitution.

Sentiment in New England had opposed the war from the beginning. The governor of Massachusetts titled his annual address in 1813 "On the Present Unhappy War," and the General Court went on record calling the conflict "impolitic, improper, and unjust." The Federalist party had been quick to employ the discontent to revive its fortunes. Federalist-controlled state administrations refused to provide militia to aid in the fight and discouraged individuals and banks from lending money to the hard-pressed national government. Trade with the enemy flourished as long as the British fleet did not crack down on New England ports, and goods flowed across the Canadian line in as great or greater volume as during Jefferson's embargo.

Their attitude toward the war made the Federalists even more unpopular with the rest of the country, and this in turn encouraged extremists to talk of seceding from the Union. After Massachusetts summoned the meeting of the Hartford Convention, the fear was widespread that the delegates would propose a New England Confederacy, thereby striking at the Union in a moment of great trial.

Luckily for the country, moderate Federalists controlled the convention. They approved a statement that in the case of "deliberate, dangerous and palpable infractions of the Constitution" a state has the right "to interpose its authority" to protect itself. This concept, similar to that expressed in the Kentucky and Virginia resolutions by the Republicans when they were in the minority, was accompanied by a list of proposed constitutional amendments designed to weaken the federal government, reduce Congress's power to restrict trade, and limit presidents to a single term.

Nothing formally proposed at Hartford was treasonable, but the proceedings were kept secret, and rumors of impending secession were rife. In this atmosphere came the news from Ghent of an honorable peace. The Federalists had been denouncing the war and predicting a British triumph; now they were discredited.

The Battle of New Orleans and the End of the War

Still more discrediting to Federalists was the second event that would not have happened had communications been more rapid: the Battle of New Orleans. During the fall of 1814 the British had gathered an army at Negril Bay in Jamaica, commanded by Major General Sir Edward Pakenham, brother-in-law of the Duke of Wellington. Late in November an armada of sixty ships set out for New Orleans with 11,000 soldiers. Instead of sailing directly up from the mouth of the Mississippi as the Americans expected, Pakenham approached the city by way of Lake Borgne, to the east. Proceeding through a maze of swamps and bayous, he advanced close to the city's gates before being detected. Early on the afternoon of December 23, three mud-spattered local planters burst into the headquarters of General Andrew Jackson, commanding the defenses of New Orleans, with the news.

For once in this war of error and incompetence the United States had the right man in the right place at the right time. After his Revolutionary War experiences, Jackson had studied law, then moved west, settling in Nashville, Tennessee. He served briefly in both houses of Congress and was active in Tennessee affairs. Jackson was a hard man and fierce-tempered, frequently involved in brawls and duels, but honest and, by western standards, a good public servant. When the war broke out, he was named major general of volunteers. Almost alone among nonprofessional troops during the conflict, his men won impressive victories, savagely crushing the Creek Indians in a series of battles in Alabama.

Following these victories, Jackson was assigned the job of defending the Gulf Coast against the expected British strike. Although he had misjudged Pakenham's destination, he was ready when the news of the British arrival reached him. "By the Eternal," he vowed, "they shall not sleep on our soil." "Gentlemen," he told his staff officers, "the British are below, we must fight them tonight."

While the British rested and awaited reinforcements, planning to take the city the next morning, Jackson rushed up men and guns. At 7:30 PM on December 23 he attacked, taking the British by surprise. But Pakenham's veterans rallied quickly, and the battle was inconclusive. With Redcoats pouring in from the fleet, Jackson fell back to a point five miles below New Orleans and dug in.

He chose his position wisely. On his right was the Mississippi, on his left an impenetrable swamp, to the front an open field. On the day before Christmas (while the commissioners in Ghent were signing the peace treaty), Jackson's army, which included a segregated unit of free black militiamen, erected an earthen parapet about ten yards behind a dry canal bed. Here the Americans would make their stand.

General Andrew Jackson, on the horse, exhorts his men to throw back the advancing British; they succeed, and Jackson becomes a war hero.

For two weeks Pakenham probed the American line. Jackson strengthened his defenses daily. At night, patrols of silent Tennesseans slipped out with knives and tomahawks to stalk British sentries. They called this grim business "going hunting." On January 8, 1815, Pakenham ordered an all-out frontal assault. The American position was formidable, but these were men who had defeated Napoleon. At dawn, through the lowland mists, the Redcoats moved forward with fixed bayonets. Pakenham assumed that the undisciplined Americans—about 4,500 strong—would run at the sight of bare steel.

The Americans did not run. Perhaps they feared the wrath of their commander more than enemy bayonets. Artillery raked the advancing British, and when the range closed to about 150 yards, the riflemen opened up. Jackson had formed his men in three ranks behind the parapet. One rank fired, then stepped down as another took its place. By the time the third had loosed its volley, the first had reloaded and was ready to fire again. Nothing could stand against this rain of lead. General Pakenham was wounded twice, then killed by a shell fragment while calling up his last reserves. During the battle a single brave British officer reached the top of the parapet. When retreat was finally sounded, the British had suffered almost 2,100 casualties, including nearly 300 killed. Thirteen Americans lost their lives, and fifty-eight more were wounded or missing.

Word of Jackson's magnificent triumph reached Washington almost simultaneously with the good news from Ghent. People found it easy to confuse the chronology and consider the war a victory won on the battlefield below New Orleans instead of the standoff it had been. Jackson became the "Hero of New Orleans"; his proud fellow citizens rated his military abilities superior to those of the Duke of Wellington. The nation rejoiced. One sour Republican complained that the Federalists of Massachusetts had fired off more powder and wounded more men celebrating the victory than they had during the whole course of the conflict. The Senate ratified the peace treaty unanimously, and the frustrations and failures of the past few years were forgotten. Moreover, American success in holding off Great Britain despite internal frictions went a long way toward convincing European nations that both the United States and its republican form of government were here to stay. The powers might accept these truths with less pleasure than the Americans, but accept them they did.

Anglo-American Rapprochement

There remained a few matters to straighten out with Great Britain, Spain, and Europe generally. Since no territory had changed hands at Ghent, neither signatory had reason to harbor a grudge. For years no serious trouble marred Anglo-American relations. The war had taught the British to respect Americans, if not to love them.

In this atmosphere the two countries worked out peaceful solutions to a number of old problems. American trade was becoming ever more important to the British, that of the sugar islands less so. In July 1815 they therefore signed a commercial convention ending discriminatory duties and making other adjustments favorable to trade. Boundary difficulties also moved toward resolution. At Ghent the diplomats had created several joint commissions to settle the disputed boundary between the United States and Canada. Many years were to pass before the line was finally drawn, but establishing the principle of defining the border by negotiation was important. In time, a line extending over 3,000 miles was agreed to without the firing of a single shot.

Immediately after the war the British reinforced their garrisons in Canada and began to rebuild their shattered Great Lakes fleet. The United States took similar steps. But both nations found the cost of rearming more than they cared to bear. When the United States suggested demilitarizing the lakes, the British agreed. The Rush-Bagot Agreement of 1817 limited each country to one 100-ton vessel armed with a single eighteen-pounder on Lake Champlain and another on Lake Ontario. The countries were to have two each for all the other Great Lakes.

Gradually, as an outgrowth of this decision, the entire border was demilitarized, a remarkable achievement. In the Convention of 1818 the two countries agreed to the forty-ninth parallel as the northern boundary of the Louisiana Territory between the Lake of the Woods and the Rockies, and to the joint control of the Oregon country for ten years. The question of the rights of Americans in the Labrador and Newfoundland fisheries, which had been much disputed during the Ghent negotiations, was settled amicably.

The Transcontinental Treaty

The acquisition of Spanish Florida and the settlement of the western boundary of Louisiana were also accomplished as an aftermath of the War of 1812, but in a far different spirit. Spain's control of the Floridas was feeble. West Florida had passed into American hands by 1813, and frontiersmen in Georgia were eyeing East Florida greedily. Indians struck frequently into Georgia from Florida, then fled to sanctuary across the line. American slaves who escaped across the border could not be recovered. In 1818 James Monroe, who had been elected president in 1816, ordered General

Andrew Jackson to clear raiding Seminole Indians from American soil and to pursue them into Florida if necessary. Seizing on these instructions, Jackson marched into Florida and easily captured two Spanish forts.

Although Jackson eventually withdrew from Florida, the impotence of the Spanish government made it obvious even in Madrid that if nothing were done, the United States would soon fill the power vacuum by seizing the territory. The Spanish minister in Washington, Luis de Onís, set out in December 1817 to negotiate a treaty with John Quincy Adams, Monroe's secretary of state. Adams pressed the minister mercilessly on the question of Louisiana's western boundary and eventually the minister agreed to accept a boundary that followed the Sabine, Red, and Arkansas Rivers to the Continental Divide and the forty-second parallel to the Pacific, thus abandoning Spain's claim to a huge area beyond the Rockies that had no connection at all with the Louisiana Purchase. The United States obtained Florida in return for a mere $5 million.

This **Transcontinental Treaty** was signed in 1819, although ratification was delayed until 1821. Most Americans at the time thought the acquisition of Florida the most important part of the treaty, but Adams, whose vision of America's future was truly continental, knew better. "The acquisition of a definite line of boundary to the [Pacific] forms a great epoch in our history," he recorded in his diary.

The Monroe Doctrine

Concern with defining the boundaries of the United States did not reflect a desire to limit expansion; rather, most Americans felt that quibbling and quarreling with foreign powers might prove a distraction from the great task of

Read the Document

Monroe Doctrine at **myhistorylab.com**

national development. The classic enunciation of this point of view, the completion of America's withdrawal from Europe, was the **Monroe Doctrine**.

Two separate strands met in this pronouncement. The first led from Moscow to Alaska and down the Pacific coast to the Oregon country. Beginning with the explorations of Vitus Bering in 1741, the Russians had maintained an interest in fishing and fur trading along the northwest coast of North America. In 1821 the czar extended his claim south to the fifty-first parallel and forbade the ships of other powers to enter coastal waters north of that point. This announcement was disturbing.

The second strand ran from the courts of the European monarchs to Latin America. Between 1817 and 1822 practically all of the region from the Rio Grande to the southernmost tip of South America had won its independence. Spain, former master of all the area except Brazil, was too weak to win it back by force, but Austria, Prussia, France, and Russia decided at the Congress of Verona in 1822 to try to regain the area for Spain in the interests of "legitimacy." There was talk of sending a large French army to South America. This possibility also caused grave concern in Washington.

To the Russian threat, Monroe and Secretary of State Adams responded with a terse warning: "The American continents are no longer subjects for any new European colonial establishments." This statement did not impress the Russians, but they had no intention of colonizing the region. In 1824 they signed a treaty with the United States abandoning all claims below the present southern limit of Alaska (54°40'; north latitude) and removing their restrictions on foreign shipping.

Photo Credit: © CORBIS All Rights Reserved.

HARBOUR of NEW ARCHANGEL in SITCA or NORFOLK SOUND.

The harbor of New Archangel in Sitka, Alaska, part of the Russian empire's expansive claims to North America.

The Latin American problem was more complex. The United States was not alone in its alarm at the prospect of a revival of French or Spanish power in that region. Great Britain, having profited greatly from the breakup of the mercantilist Spanish empire by developing a thriving commerce with the new republics, had no intention of permitting a restoration of the old order. But the British monarchy preferred not to recognize the new revolutionary South American republics, for England itself was only beginning to recover from a period of social upheaval as violent as any in its history. Bad times and high food prices had combined to cause riots, conspiracies, and angry demands for parliamentary reform.

In 1823 the British foreign minister, George Canning, suggested to the American minister in London that the United States and Britain issue a joint statement opposing any French interference in South America, pledging that they themselves would never annex any part of Spain's old empire, and saying nothing about recognition of the new republics. This proposal of joint action with the British was flattering to the United States but scarcely in its best interests. The United States had already recognized the new republics, and it had no desire to help Great Britain retain its South American trade. As Secretary Adams pointed out, to agree to the proposal would be to abandon the possibility of someday adding Cuba or any other part of Latin America to the United States. America should act independently, Adams urged.

Monroe heartily endorsed Adams's argument and decided to include a statement of American policy in his annual message to Congress in December 1823. "The American continents," he wrote, "by the free and independent condition which they have assumed and maintain, are henceforth not to be considered as subjects for future colonization by any European powers." Europe's political system was "essentially

The United States, 1819 As American settlers ventured farther westward, the United States government sought to extend the nation's boundaries, negotiating with Spain for control of Florida and border sections of the Southwest, and with Britain for the Oregon Country.

different" from that developing in the New World, and the two should not be mixed. The United States would not interfere with existing European colonies in North or South America and would avoid involvement in strictly European affairs, but any attempt to extend European control to countries in the hemisphere that had already won their independence would be considered, Monroe warned, "the manifestation of an unfriendly disposition toward the United States" and consequently a threat to the nation's "peace and safety."

This policy statement—it was not dignified with the title Monroe Doctrine until decades later—attracted little notice in Europe or Latin America and not much more at home. European statesmen dismissed Monroe's message as "arrogant" and "blustering," worthy only of "the most profound contempt." Latin Americans, while appreciating the intent behind it, knew better than to count on American aid in case of attack from European powers.

Nevertheless, the principles laid down by President Monroe so perfectly expressed the wishes of the people of the United States that when the country grew powerful enough to enforce them, there was little need to alter or embellish his pronouncement. However understood at the time, the doctrine may be seen as the final stage in the evolution of American independence.

From this perspective, the famous Declaration of 1776 merely began a process of separation and self-determination. The peace treaty ending the Revolutionary War was a further step, and Washington's Declaration of Neutrality in 1793 was another, demonstrating as it did the capacity of the United States to determine its own best interests despite the treaty of alliance with France. The removal of British troops from the northwest forts, achieved by the otherwise ignominious Jay Treaty, marked the next stage. Then the Louisiana Purchase made a further advance toward true independence by ensuring that the Mississippi River could not be closed to the commerce so vital to the development of the western territories.

The standoff War of 1812 ended any lingering British hope of regaining control of America, the Latin American revolutions further weakened colonialism in the Western Hemisphere, and the Transcontinental Treaty pushed the last European power from the path of westward expansion. Monroe's "doctrine" was a kind of public announcement that the sovereign United States had completed its independence and wanted nothing better than to be left alone to concentrate on its own development. Better yet, Europe should be made to allow the entire hemisphere to follow its own path.

The Era of Good Feelings

The person who gave his name to the so-called Monroe Doctrine was an unusually lucky man. James Monroe lived a long life in good health and saw close up most of the great events in the history of the young republic. At the age of 18 he shed his blood for liberty at the Battle of Trenton. He was twice governor of Virginia, a United States senator, and a Cabinet member. He was at various times the nation's representative in Paris, Madrid, and London. Elected president in 1816, his good fortune continued. The world was finally at peace, the country united and prosperous. A person of good feeling who would keep a steady hand on the helm and hold to the present course seemed called for, and Monroe possessed exactly the qualities that the times required. "He is a man whose soul might be turned wrongside outwards, without discovering a blemish," Jefferson said, and John Quincy Adams, a harsh critic of public figures, praised Monroe's courtesy, sincerity, and sound judgment.

By 1817 the divisive issues of earlier days had vanished. Monroe dramatized their disappearance by beginning his first term with a goodwill tour of New England, heartland of the opposition. The tour was a triumph. Everywhere the president was greeted with tremendous enthusiasm. After he visited Boston, once the headquarters and now the graveyard of Federalism, a Federalist newspaper, the *Columbian Centinel*, gave the age its name. Pointing out that the celebrations attending Monroe's visit had brought together in friendly intercourse many persons "whom party politics had long severed," it dubbed the times the **Era of Good Feelings**.

The people of the period had good reasons for thinking it extraordinarily harmonious. Peace, prosperity, liberty, and progress all flourished in 1817 in the United States. The heirs of Jefferson had accepted, with a mixture of resignation and enthusiasm, most of the economic policies advocated by the Hamiltonians.

The Jeffersonian balance between individual liberty and responsible government, having survived both bad management and war, had justified itself to the opposition. The new unity was symbolized by the restored friendship of Jefferson and John Adams. Although they continued to disagree vigorously about matters of philosophy and government, the bitterness between them disappeared entirely. By Monroe's day, Jefferson was writing long letters to "my dear friend," and receiving equally warm and voluminous replies. "Whether you or I were right," Adams wrote amiably to Jefferson, "Posterity must judge."

When political divisions appeared again, as they soon did, it was not because the old balance had been shaky. Few of the new controversies challenged Republican principles or revived old issues. Instead, these controversies were children of the present and the future, products of the continuing growth of the country. From 1790 to 1820, the area of the United States doubled, but very little of the Louisiana Purchase had been settled. More significant, the population of the nation had more than doubled, from 4 million to 9.6 million. The pace of the westward movement had also quickened; by 1820 the moving edge of the frontier ran in a long, irregular curve from Michigan to Arkansas.

New Sectional Issues

The War of 1812 and the depression that struck the country in 1819 had shaped many controversies. The tariff question was affected by both. Before the War of 1812 the level of duties averaged about 12.5 percent of the value of dutiable products, but to meet the added expenses occasioned by the conflict, Congress doubled all tariffs. In 1816, when the revenue was no longer needed, a new act kept duties close to wartime levels. Infant industries that had grown up during the years of embargo, non-intercourse, and war were able to exert considerable pressure. The act especially favored textiles because the British were dumping cloth in America at bargain prices in their attempt to regain lost markets. Unemployed workers and many farmers became convinced that prosperity would return only if American industry were shielded against foreign competition.

At first every section endorsed high duties, but with the passage of time the South rejected protection almost completely. Besides increasing the cost of nearly everything they bought, Southerners exported most of their cotton and tobacco and high duties on imports would limit the foreign market for southern staples by inhibiting international exchange. As this fact became clear, the West tended to divide on the tariff question: The Northwest and much of Kentucky, which had a special interest in protecting its considerable hemp production, favored high duties; the Southwest, where cotton was the major crop, favored low duties.

National banking policy was another important political issue affected by the war and the depression. Presidents Jefferson and Madison had managed to live with the Bank of the United States despite its dubious constitutionality, but its charter was not renewed when it expired in 1811. Aside from the constitutional question, the major opposition to recharter came from state banks eager to take over the business of the Bank for themselves. The fact that English investors owned most of the Bank's stock was also used as an argument against recharter.

Many more state banks were created after 1811, and most extended credit recklessly. When the British raid on Washington and Baltimore in 1814 sent panicky depositors scurrying to convert their deposits into gold or silver, the overextended financiers could not oblige them. All banks outside New England suspended specie payments; that is, they stopped exchanging their bank notes for hard money on demand.

Table 1 Key Sectional Issues

Issue	West	South	North
Favorite leaders	Henry Clay (Kentucky)	John Calhoun (South Carolina), William Crawford (Georgia), Andrew Jackson (Tennessee)	John Quincy Adams (Massachusetts), Daniel Webster (Massachusetts), Martin Van Buren (New York)
Should import taxes (tariffs) be high?	Yes and no, depending on the region	No, because high tariffs increased the cost of manufactured goods and harmed export trade (cotton, tobacco)	Yes, because manufacturers and factory workers wanted protection from inexpensive foreign-made products; the exception: New England, because high tariffs harmed trade
Should federal government support construction of roads and canals?	Yes, to reduce transportation costs of products from western farms	No, because this would require more federal revenue—and thus an increase in the tariff	Yes and no, depending on the locality
Should federally owned lands be sold as cheaply as possible?	Yes, because pioneers and farmers needed cheap land	No, because income from land sales would reduce the need for tariffs to raise money; and the products of cheap western farms would compete with southern farms	No, because cheap land in the west would drain off surplus labor and increase labor costs in the East
Should slavery be allowed in the new states being created in the West?	Yes and no, but generally yes because much of the West was economically tied to the South, which supported slavery	Yes, because slaveowners were moving into western regions and were entitled to keep their "property"	No, because new "slave states" would give the South more power in the Senate and because free labor could not fairly compete with a slave system

The shaded boxes indicate the critical issue for each region.

Paper money immediately fell in value; a paper dollar was soon worth only eighty-five cents in coin in Philadelphia, less in Baltimore. Government business also suffered from the absence of a national bank. In October 1814 Secretary of the Treasury Alexander J. Dallas submitted a plan for a second Bank of the United States, and after considerable wrangling over its precise form, the institution was authorized in April 1816.

The new Bank was much larger than its predecessor, being capitalized at $35 million. However, unlike Hamilton's creation, it was badly managed at the start. Its first president, William Jones, a former secretary of the treasury, allowed his institution to join in the irresponsible creation of credit. By the summer of 1818 the Bank's eighteen branches had issued notes in excess of ten times their specie reserves, far more than was prudent, considering the Bank's responsibilities. When depression struck the country in 1819, the Bank of the United States was as hard pressed as many of the state banks. Jones resigned.

The new president, Langdon Cheves of South Carolina, was as rigid as Jones had been permissive. During the bad times, when easy credit was needed, he pursued a policy of stern curtailment. The Bank thus regained a sound position at the expense of hardship to borrowers. "The Bank was saved," the contemporary economist William Gouge wrote somewhat hyperbolically, "and the people were ruined." Indeed, the bank reached a low point in public favor. Irresponsible state banks resented it, as did the advocates of hard money.

Regional lines were less sharply drawn on the Bank issue than on the tariff. Northern congressmen voted against the Bank fifty-three to forty-four in 1816—many of them because they objected to the particular proposal, not because they were against any national bank. Those from other sections favored it, fifty-eight to thirty. The collapse occasioned by the Panic of 1819 produced further opposition to the institution in the West.

Land policy in the West also caused sectional controversy. No one wished to eliminate the system of survey and sale, but there was continuous pressure to reduce the price of public land and the minimum unit offered for sale. The Land Act of 1800 set $2 an acre as the minimum price and 320 acres (a half section) as the smallest unit. In 1804 the minimum was cut to 160 acres, which could be had for about $80 down, roughly a quarter of what the average artisan could earn in a year.

Sectional attitudes toward the public lands were fairly straightforward. The West wanted cheap land; the North and South tended to look on the national domain as an asset that should be converted into as much cash as possible. Northern manufacturers feared that cheap land in the West would drain off surplus labor and force wages up, while southern planters were concerned about the competition that would develop when the virgin lands of the Southwest were put to the plow to make cotton. The West, however, was ready to fight to the last line of defense over land policy, while the other regions would usually compromise on the issue to gain support for their own vital interests.

The most divisive sectional issue was slavery. After the compromises affecting the "peculiar institution" made at the Constitutional Convention, it caused remarkably little conflict in national politics before 1819. Although the importation of blacks rose in the 1790s, Congress abolished the African slave trade in 1808 without major incident. As the nation expanded, free and slave states were added to the Union in equal numbers with Ohio, Indiana, and Illinois being balanced by Louisiana, Mississippi, and Alabama. In 1819 there were twenty-two states, eleven slave and eleven free. The expansion of slavery occasioned by the cotton boom led Southerners to support it more aggressively, which tended to irritate many Northerners, but most persons considered slavery mainly a local issue. To the extent that it was a national question, the North opposed it and the South defended it ardently. The West leaned toward the southern point of view, for in addition to the southwestern slave states, the Northwest was sympathetic, partly because much of its produce was sold on southern plantations and partly because at least half of its early settlers came from Virginia, Kentucky, and other slave states.

New Leaders

By 1824 the giants of the Revolutionary generation had completed their work. Washington, Hamilton, Franklin, Samuel Adams, Patrick Henry, and most of their peers were dead. John Adams (88), Thomas Jefferson (81), and James Madison (73) were passing their declining years quietly on their ancestral acres, full of memories and sage advice, but no longer active in national affairs. In every section new leaders had come forward, men shaped by the past but chiefly concerned with the present. Quite suddenly, between the war and the panic, they had inherited power. They would shape the future of the United States.

In the North, John Quincy Adams was the best-known of the new political leaders. Just completing his brilliant work as secretary of state under Monroe, highlighted by his negotiation of the Transcontinental Treaty and his design of the Monroe Doctrine, he had behind him a record of public service dating to the Confederation period.

Adams was farsighted, imaginative, hardworking, and extremely intelligent, but he was inept in personal relations. He had all the virtues and most of the defects

Samuel Morse, chiefly famous for his work on the telegraph and Morse code, was also a talented painter. His *House of Representatives* (1822–1823) shows the legislators at work at night, a symbolic expression of their commitment to the nation.

Source: Samuel F.B. Morse, *The House of Representatives*. 1822–23. oil on Canvas. 86 $7/8$ × 130 $5/8$. Corcoran Gallery of Art, Museum Purchase, Gallery Fund.

Eyes like "anthracite furnaces," the Scottish historian Thomas Carlyle remarked of Daniel Webster; this is the "Black Dan" portrait by Francis Alexander (1835).
Source: Hood Museum of Art, Dartmouth College, Hanover, New Hampshire, Gift of George C. Shattuck, Class of 1803.

of the puritan, being suspicious both of others and of himself. He suffered in two ways from being his father's child: As the son of a president he was under severe pressure to live up to the Adams name, and his father expected a great deal of him. When the boy was only seven, John Adams wrote the following to his wife: "Train [the children] to virtue. Habituate them to industry, activity, and spirit. Make them consider vice as shameful and unmanly. Fire them with ambition to be useful."

Like his father, John Quincy Adams was a strong nationalist. While New England still opposed high tariffs, he was at least open-minded on the subject. Unlike most easterners, he believed that the federal government should spend freely on roads and canals in the West. To slavery he was, like most New Englanders, personally opposed. As Monroe's second term drew toward its close, Adams seemed one of the most likely candidates to succeed him, and at this period his ambition to be president was his great failing. It led him to make certain compromises with his principles, which in turn plagued his oversensitive conscience and had a corrosive effect on his peace of mind.

Daniel Webster, a congressman from Massachusetts, was recognized as one of the coming leaders of New England. He owed much of his reputation to his formidable presence and his oratorical skill. Dark, broad-chested, large-headed, and craggy of brow, he projected a remarkable appearance of heroic power and moral strength. His thunderous voice, his resourceful vocabulary, and his manner—all backed by the mastery of every oratorical trick—made him unique.

New York's man of the future was a sandy-haired politico named Martin Van Buren. The Red Fox, as he was called, was one of the most talented politicians ever to play a part in American affairs. He was clever and hardworking, but his mind and his energy were always devoted to some political purpose. From 1812 to 1820 he served in the state legislature; in 1820 he was elected United States senator.

Van Buren had great charm and immense tact. By nature affable, he never allowed partisanship to mar his personal relationships with other leaders. The members of his political machine, known as the Albany Regency, were almost fanatically loyal to him, but even his enemies could seldom dislike him as a person.

The most prominent southern leader was William H. Crawford, Monroe's secretary of the treasury. After being elected to the Senate from Georgia, he became controversial. Many of his contemporaries considered him no more than a cynical spoilsman, although his administration of the treasury department was first-rate. Yet he had many friends. His ambition was vast, his power great. Fate, however, was about to strike Crawford a crippling blow.

John C. Calhoun, the other outstanding southern leader, was born in South Carolina in 1782 and graduated from Yale in 1804. After serving in the South Carolina legislature, he was elected to Congress in 1811. He took a strong nationalist position on all the issues of the day. In 1817 Monroe made him secretary of war.

Calhoun, a well-to-do planter, was devoted to the South and its institutions, but he took the broadest possible view of political affairs. John Quincy Adams, seldom charitable in his private opinions of colleagues (he called Crawford "a worm" and Henry Clay a "gamester" with an "undigested system of ethics"), praised Calhoun's "enlarged philosophic views" and considered him "above all sectional and factional prejudices."

The outstanding western leader of the 1820s was Henry Clay of Kentucky, one of the most charming and colorful of American statesmen. On the platform he ranked with Webster; behind the political scenes he was the peer of Van Buren. In every environment he was warm and open—what a modern political scientist might call a charismatic personality. Clay loved to drink, swear, tell tales, and play poker. He was a reasonable man, skilled at arranging political compromises, but he possessed a reckless streak: Twice in his career he challenged men to duels for having insulted him. Fortunately, all concerned were poor shots.

Clay was elected to Congress in 1810. He led the War Hawks in 1811 and 1812 and was Speaker of the House from 1811 to 1820 and from 1823 to 1825.

In the early 1820s he was just developing his **American System**. In return for eastern support of a policy of federal aid in the construction of roads and canals, the West would back the protective tariff. He justified this deal on the widest national grounds. America has a "great diversity of interests," ranging from agriculture and fishing to manufacturing, shipbuilding, and commerce. "The good of each . . . and of the whole should be carefully consulted. This is the only mode by which we can preserve, in full vigor, the harmony of the whole Union." Stimulating manufacturing, for example, would increase the demand for western raw materials, while western prosperity would lead to greater consumption of eastern manufactured goods.

Although himself a slaveowner, Clay called slavery the "greatest of human evils." He favored freeing the slaves and "colonizing" them in Africa, which could, he said, be accomplished gradually and at relatively minor cost.

The Missouri Compromise

The sectional concerns of the 1820s repeatedly influenced politics. The depression of 1819–1822 increased tensions by making people feel more strongly about the issues of the day. For example, manufacturers who wanted high tariffs in 1816 were more vehemently in favor of protection in 1820 when their business fell off. Even when economic conditions improved, geographic alignments on key issues tended to solidify.

One of the first and most critical of the sectional questions concerned the admission of Missouri as a slave state. When Louisiana entered the Union in 1812, the rest of the Louisiana Purchase was organized as the Missouri Territory. Building on a nucleus of Spanish and French inhabitants, the region west and north of St. Louis grew rapidly, and in 1817 the Missourians petitioned for statehood. A large percentage of the settlers—the population exceeded 60,000 by 1818—were Southerners who had moved into the valleys of the Arkansas and Missouri rivers. Since many of them owned slaves, Missouri would become a slave state.

The admission of new states had always been a routine matter in keeping with the admirable pattern established by the Northwest Ordinance. But during the debate on the Missouri Enabling Act in February 1819, Congressman James Tallmadge of New York introduced an amendment prohibiting "the further introduction of slavery" and providing that all slaves born in Missouri after the territory became a state should be freed at age 25.

While Tallmadge was merely seeking to apply in the territory the pattern of race relations that had developed in the states immediately east of Missouri, his amendment represented, at least in spirit, something of a revolution. The Northwest Ordinance had prohibited slavery in the land between the Mississippi and the Ohio, but that area had only a handful of slaveowners in 1787 and little prospect of attracting more. Elsewhere no effort to restrict the movement of slaves into new territory had been attempted. If one assumed (as whites always had) that the slaves themselves should have no say in the matter, it appeared democratic to

Read the Document
Missouri Enabling Act at myhistorylab.com

let the settlers of Missouri decide the slavery question for themselves. Nevertheless, the Tallmadge amendment passed the House, the vote following sectional lines closely. The Senate, however, resoundingly rejected it. The less populous southern part of Missouri was then organized separately as the Arkansas Territory, and an attempt to bar slavery there was stifled. The Missouri Enabling Act failed to pass before Congress adjourned.

When the next Congress met in December 1819, the Missouri issue came up at once. The vote on Tallmadge's amendment had shown that the rapidly growing North controlled the House of Representatives. Southerners thought it vital to preserve a balance in the Senate. Yet Northerners objected to the fact that Missouri extended hundreds of miles north of the Ohio River, which they considered slavery's natural boundary. Angry debate raged in Congress for months.

The debate did not turn on the morality of slavery or the rights of blacks. Northerners objected to adding new slave states because under the Three-Fifths Compromise these states would be overrepresented in Congress (60 percent of their slaves would be counted in determining the size of the states' delegations in the House of Representatives) and because they did not relish competing with slave labor. Since the question was political influence rather than the rights and wrongs of slavery, a compromise was worked out in 1820. Missouri entered the Union as a slave state and Maine, having been separated from Massachusetts, was admitted as a free state to preserve the balance in the Senate.

To prevent further conflict, Congress adopted the proposal of Senator Jesse B. Thomas of Illinois, that "forever prohibited" slavery in all other parts of the Louisiana Purchase north of 36°300' latitude, the westward extension of Missouri's southern boundary. Although this division would keep slavery out of most of the territory, Southerners accepted it cheerfully. The land south of the line, the present states of Arkansas and Oklahoma, seemed ideally suited for the expanded plantation economy, and most persons considered the treeless northern regions little better than a desert.

The **Missouri Compromise** did not end the crisis. When Missouri submitted its constitution for approval by Congress (the final step in the admission process), the document, besides authorizing slavery and prohibiting the emancipation of any slave without the consent of the owner, required the state legislature to pass a law barring free blacks and mulattos from entering the state "under any pretext whatever." This provision plainly violated Article IV, Section 2, of the U.S. Constitution: "The Citizens of each State shall be entitled to all Privileges and Immunities of Citizens in the several States." It did not, however, represent any more of a break with established racial patterns, North or South, than the Tallmadge amendment; many states east of Missouri barred free blacks without regard for the Constitution.

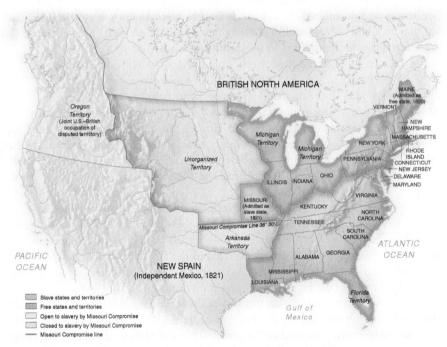

The Missouri Compromise, 1820 The Missouri Compromise admitted Missouri as a slave state, and Maine as a free state, retaining a balance in the Senate: Half of the nation's 24 states allowed slavery; half did not. The Compromise also drew an imaginary line along the 36°30' latitude (northern boundary of Arkansas): Slavery would be allowed in the lands to the south of the line.

Nevertheless, northern congressmen hypocritically refused to accept the Missouri constitution. Once more the debate raged. Again, since few Northerners cared to defend the rights of blacks, the issue was compromised. In March 1821 Henry Clay found a face-saving formula: Out of respect for the "supreme law of the land," Congress accepted the Missouri constitution with the demurrer that no law passed in conformity to it should be construed as contravening Article IV, Section 2.

Every thinking person recognized the political dynamite inherent in the Missouri controversy. The sectional lineup had been terrifyingly compact. Moreover, despite the timidity and hypocrisy of the North, everyone realized that the rights and wrongs of slavery lay at the heart of the conflict. "We have the wolf by the ears, and we can neither safely hold him, nor safely let him go," Jefferson wrote a month after Missouri became a state. The dispute, he said, "like a fire bell in the night, awakened and filled me with terror." Jefferson knew that the compromise had not quenched the flames ignited by the Missouri debates. "This is a reprieve only," he said. John Quincy Adams called it the "title page to a great tragic volume." Yet one could still hope that the fire bell was only a false alarm, that Adams's tragic volume would remain unread.

The Election of 1824

The tariff continued to divide the country. When a new, still higher tariff was enacted in 1824, the slave states voted almost unanimously against it, the North and Northwest in favor, and New England remained of two minds. Webster (after conducting a poll of business leaders before deciding how to vote) made a powerful speech against the act, but the measure passed without creating a major storm.

The presidential fight was waged on personal grounds, although the heat generated by the contest began the process of reenergizing party politics. Besides Calhoun the candidates were Andrew Jackson (hero of the battle of New Orleans), Crawford, Adams, and Clay. The maneuvering among them was complex, the infighting savage. In March 1824, Calhoun, who was young enough to wait for the White House, withdrew and declared for the vice presidency, which he won easily. Crawford, who had the support of many congressional leaders, seemed the likely winner, but he suffered a series of paralytic strokes that gravely injured his chances.

Despite the bitterness of the contest, it attracted relatively little public interest; barely a quarter of those eligible took the trouble to vote. In the Electoral College Jackson led with ninety-nine, Adams had eighty-four, Crawford forty-one, and Clay thirty-seven. Since no one had a majority, the contest was thrown into the House of Representatives, which, under the Constitution, had to choose from among the three leaders, each state delegation having one vote. By employing his great influence in the House, Clay swung the balance. Not wishing to advance the fortunes of a rival westerner like Jackson and feeling, with reason, that Crawford's health made him unavailable, Clay gave his support to Adams, who was thereupon elected.

John Quincy Adams as President

Adams, elected in 1824, hoped to use the national authority to foster all sorts of useful projects. He asked Congress for a federal program of internal improvements so vast that even Clay boggled when he realized its scope. He came out for aid to manufacturing and agriculture, for a national university, and even for a government astronomical observatory. For a nationalist of unchallengeable Jeffersonian origins like Clay or Calhoun to have pressed for so extensive a program would have been politically risky. For the son of John Adams to do so was disastrous; every doubter remembered his Federalist background and decided that he was trying to overturn the glorious "Revolution of 1800."

◆●●─| Read the Document

John Quincy Adams, *Inaugural Address* at **myhistorylab.com**

Adams proved to be his own worst enemy, for he was an inept politician. To persuade Americans, who were almost pathological on the subject of monarchy, to support his road building program, he cited with approval the work being done abroad by "the nations of Europe and . . . their rulers," which revived fears that all Adamses were royalists at heart. He was insensitive to the ebb and flow of public feeling; even when he wanted to move with the tide, he seldom managed to dramatize and publicize his stand effectively. Many Americans, for example, endorsed a federal bankruptcy law to protect poor debtors; Adams agreed, but instead of describing himself as a friend of debtors, he called for the "amelioration" of the "often oppressive codes relating to insolvency" and buried the recommendation at the tail end of a dull state paper.

Calhoun's *Exposition and Protest*

The tariff question added to the president's troubles. An increasingly powerful federal government required higher revenues—and higher duties—culminating in what became known as the record-high 1828 "Tariff of Abominations." This exacerbated sectional divisions.

Vice President Calhoun was especially upset; he believed that the new tariff would impoverish the South. His essay, *The South Carolina Exposition and Protest*, repudiated the nationalist philosophy he had previously championed.

The South Carolina legislature released this document to the country in December 1828, along with eight resolutions denouncing the protective tariff as unfair and unconstitutional. The theorist Calhoun, however, was not content with outlining the case against the tariff. His *Exposition* provided an ingenious defense of the right of the people of a state to reject a law of Congress. Starting with John Locke's revered concept of government as a contractual relationship, he argued that since the states had created the Union, logic dictated that they be the final arbiters of the meaning of the Constitution. If a special state convention, representing the sovereignty of the people, decided that an act of Congress violated the Constitution, it could interpose its authority and "nullify" the law within its boundaries. Calhoun did not seek to implement this theory in 1828, for he hoped that the next administration would lower the tariff and make nullification unnecessary.

The Meaning of Sectionalism

The sectional issues that occupied the energies of politicians and strained the ties between the people of the different regions were produced by powerful forces that actually bound the sections together. Growth caused differences that sometimes led to conflict, but growth itself was the product of prosperity. People were drawn to the West by the expectation that life would be better there, as more often than not it was, at least in the long run.

Another force unifying the nation was patriotism; the increasing size and prosperity of the nation made people proud to be part of a growing, dynamic society. Still another was the uniqueness of the American system of government and the people's knowledge that their immediate ancestors had created it. John Adams and Thomas Jefferson died on the same day, July 4, 1826, the fiftieth anniversary of the signing of the Declaration of Independence. People took this not as a remarkable coincidence, but as a sign from the heavens, an indication that God looked with favor on the American experiment. Many believed that patriotism and providence would transcend the intensifying sectionalism. They would be proven wrong.

John Lewis Krimmel's painting of the *Fourth of July in Centre Square Philadelphia* (1812). Note the diversity of those who've assembled to observe the festivities.

Source: Courtesy of the Pennsylvania Academy of Fine Arts, Philadelphia. Pennsylvania Academy purchase (from the estate of Paul Beck, Jr.).

Milestones

1808	James Madison is elected president	1816	James Monroe is elected president
1810	Macon's Bill No. 2 removes all restrictions on commerce with Britain and France	1817	Rush-Bagot Agreement limits American and British forces on Lake Champlain and Great Lakes
1811	Battle of Tippecanoe shatters Indian confederation	1819	United States signs Transcontinental Treaty with Spain
1812	James Madison is reelected president	1819–1822	United States experiences economic depression
	Congress declares war on Great Britain	1820	James Monroe is reelected president
	USS *Constitution* and *United States* win naval victories	1820–1821	Missouri Compromise closes Missouri Territory to slavery, but opens Arkansas Territory to slavery
1813	Captain Oliver Hazard Perry destroys British fleet in Battle of Lake Erie	1820–1850	Cities and manufacturing grow rapidly
	General William Henry Harrison defeats British in Battle of the Thames	1823	Monroe Doctrine says United States will consider future European colonization in Western Hemisphere a threat to American peace and safety
	Tecumseh dies at Battle of the Thames		
1814	British burn Washington, DC		
	Francis Scott Key writes "The Star Spangled Banner" during the bombardment of Fort McHenry	1824–1825	House of Representatives decides election of 1824 in favor of John Quincy Adams, leading to claims of a "corrupt bargain" with Henry Clay
	New England Federalists meet at Hartford Convention		
	Treaty of Ghent officially ends War of 1812	1828	Congress passes Tariff of Abominations, leading to nullification debate
1815	General Andrew Jackson defeats British at Battle of New Orleans		

✓●─[Study] and **Review** at **www.myhistorylab.com**

Review Questions

1. The period covered in this chapter saw a steady increase in federal power. During that time, the Democratic party, which opposed federal power, was dominant. What explains this seeming contradiction?

2. Before 1812, who sought war against the British and who opposed it? Why?

3. What accounted for the military reverses during the war and its one major success?

4. What factors led to the Missouri Compromise and what were its main provisions?

Key Terms

American System
Era of Good
   Feelings
Hartford
   Convention

Missouri
   Compromise
Monroe Doctrine
Tariff of
   Abominations

Transcontinental
   Treaty
War Hawks
War of 1812

Toward a National Economy

From Chapter 8 of *American Destiny: Narrative of a Nation*, Combined Volume, Fourth Edition. Mark C. Carnes and John A. Garraty. Copyright © 2012 by Pearson Education, Inc. Published by Pearson Prentice Hall. All rights reserved.

Toward a National Economy

((•─[Hear the Audio at myhistorylab.com

Are you wearing anything made in the United States?

IF YOU'RE WEARING SOCKS, THEY WERE LIKELY MADE IN DATANG, China, a small city near the Vietnamese border. Datang manufactures eight billion socks annually, about one-third of the world's output. Within Datang, companies specialize in different aspects of sock production: some buy yarn, dye it, or weave it into cloth; some sew in toes or heels; some press the socks or bind them with metal clips; some put socks into packages. Because of the huge scale and specialization, Datang manufactures a pair of socks for twenty-five cents, about half the cost of socks made in the United States.

That a single city provides socks for much of the world illustrates the global character of the modern economy. The emergence of a global economy has been going on for centuries. A global market for Asian spices was well-established at the time of Columbus, a reason for his voyage in 1492.

As late as the 1700s, American farmers still produced much of what they needed—food, soap, candles, clothing, and even their socks. Farm women working in their homes spun locally produced flax, wool, and cotton into thread and yarn; knitted the yarn into fabric; and sewed the pieces into socks.

But by the early 1800s the "Age of Homespun" was waning. Manufactured products, often produced in distant factories, increasingly supplanted home-made goods. Historians still debate whether the shift from rural self-sufficiency to a specialized market economy occurred over a few pivotal decades during the early 1800s or whether it evolved slowly, over a longer period of time.

Nearly all agree, though, that after 1810 a cluster of changes imparted a new dynamism to the American economy: the growing demand for high-quality, store-bought goods; the rise of the factory system; the recruitment and training of a cheap labor force; the emergence of corporations; the revival of the Southern economy based on slavery and cotton production; the development of improved transportation that facilitated the exchange of farm and factory goods; and the creation of legal structures that promoted economic growth.

By the mid-nineteenth century, most Americans had been contributors to and consumers of an economic system that, while not yet fully global, had become national in scope. Most Americans wore socks that were manufactured in a handful of cities in Massachusetts, New York, and Pennsylvania. Thus while political tendencies tended to pull the nation apart, especially the growing dispute over the future of slavery in the territories, Americans were becoming more interdependent economically.

Gentility and the Consumer Revolution

The democratic revolution that led to the founding of the American nation was accompanied by widespread emulation of aristocratic behavior. Sometimes the most ardent American democrats proved the most susceptible to the allure of European gentility. Thus young John Adams, while lampooning "the late Refinements in modern manners," nevertheless advised his future wife, Abigail, to be more attentive to posture: "You very often hang your Head like a Bulrush, and you sit with your legs crossed to the ruin of the figure." On his trip to Paris in 1778 on behalf of the Continental Congress, he denounced the splendor of the houses, furniture, and clothing. "I cannot help suspecting that the more Elegance, the less Virtue," he concluded. Yet despite the exigencies of war, on returning to America, Adams bought a three-story mansion and furnished it with Louis XV chairs and, among other extravagances, an ornate wine cooler from Vincennes.

Among aristocratic circles in Europe, gentility was the product of ancestry and cultivated style; but in America it was largely defined by possession of material goods. By the mid-eighteenth century the "refinement of America" had touched the homes of some Southern planters and urban merchants; but a half century later porcelain plates

Watch the Video

Coming of Age in 1833 (a great period of change/ reinvention in the world) at **myhistorylab.com**

Americans enshrined the simple life and a homespun equality; yet they coveted the cultural markers of aristocracy, such as imported porcelain tea services. This one, made in France, was given to Alexander Hamilton. Gentility spread, historian Richard Bushman writes, "because people longed to be associated with the 'best society.'"

Photo Credit: Paul Rocheleau.

made by English craftsman Josiah Wedgwood and mahogany washstands by Thomas Chippendale were appearing even in frontier communities. Americans were demanding more goods than such craftsmen could turn out. Everywhere producers sought to expand their workshops, hire and train more artisans, and acquire large stocks of materials and labor-saving machines.

But first they had to locate the requisite capital, find ways to supervise large numbers of workers, and discover how to get raw materials to factories and products to customers. The solutions to these problems, taken together, constituted the "market revolution" of the early nineteenth century. The "industrial revolution" came on its heels.

Birth of the Factory

By the 1770s British manufacturers, especially those in textiles, had made astonishing progress in mechanizing their operations, bringing workers together in buildings called factories where waterpower, and later steam, supplied the force to run new spinning and weaving devices that increased productivity and reduced labor costs.

Because machine-spun cotton was cheaper and of better quality than that spun by hand, producers in other countries were eager to adopt British methods. Americans had depended on Great Britain for such products until the Revolution cut off supplies; then the new spirit of nationalism gave impetus to the development of local industry. A number of state legislatures offered bounties to anyone who would introduce the new machinery. The British, however, guarded their secrets vigilantly. It was illegal to export any of the new machines or to send their plans abroad. Workers skilled in their construction and use were forbidden to leave the country. These restrictions were effective for a time; the principles on which the new machines were based were simple enough, but to construct workable models without plans was another matter. Although a number of persons tried to do so, it was not until Samuel Slater installed his machines in Pawtucket, Rhode Island, that a successful factory was constructed.

Slater, born in England, was more than a skilled mechanic. Attracted by stories of the rewards offered in the United States, he slipped out of England in 1789. Not daring to carry any plans, he depended on his memory and his mechanical sense for the complicated specifications of the necessary machines. Moses Brown brought Slater to Rhode Island to help run his textile-manufacturing operation. Working in secrecy with a carpenter who was "under bond not to steal the patterns nor disclose the nature of the work," Slater built and installed his machinery. In December 1790 the first American factory began production.

It was a humble beginning indeed. Slater's machines made only cotton thread, which Brown's company sold in its Providence store and "put out" to individual artisans, who, working for wages, wove it into cloth in their homes. The machines were tended by a labor force of nine children, for the work was simple and the pace slow. The young operatives' pay ranged from thirty-three to sixty-seven cents a week, about what a youngster could earn in other occupations. The factory was profitable from the start. Slater soon branched out on his own, and others trained by him opened their own establishments. By 1800 seven mills possessing 2,000 spindles were in operation; by 1815, after production had been stimulated by the War of 1812, there were 130,000 spindles turning in 213 factories.

Before long the Boston Associates, a group of merchants headed by Francis Cabot Lowell, added a new dimension to factory production. Beginning at Waltham, Massachusetts, where the Charles River provided the necessary waterpower, between 1813 and 1850 they revolutionized textile production. Some early factory owners had set up hand looms in their plants, but the weavers could not keep pace with the spinning jennies. After an extensive study of British mills, Lowell smuggled the plans for an efficient power loom into America. His Boston Manufacturing Company at Waltham, capitalized at $300,000, combined machine production, large-scale operation, efficient management, and centralized marketing procedures. It concentrated on the mass production of a standardized product.

●●●─[Read the Document

The Harbinger, "Female Workers at Lowell" at **myhistorylab.com**

Lowell's cloth, though plain and rather coarse, was durable and cheap. His profits averaged almost 20 percent a year during the Era of Good Feelings. In 1823 the Boston Associates began to harness the power of the Merrimack River, setting up a new $600,000 corporation at the sleepy village of East Chelmsford, Massachusetts (population 300), where there was a fall of thirty-two feet in the river. Within three years the town, appropriately renamed Lowell, had 2,000 inhabitants.

An Industrial Proletariat?

As machines displaced skilled labor, the ability of laborers to influence working conditions declined. If skilled, they either became employers and developed entrepreneurial and managerial skills, or they descended into the mass of wage earners. Simultaneously, the changing structure of production widened the gap between owners and workers and blurred the distinction between skilled and unskilled labor.

These trends might have been expected to generate hostility between workers and employers. To some extent they did. There were strikes for higher wages and to protest work speedups throughout the 1830s and again in the 1850s. Efforts to found unions and to create political organizations dedicated to advancing the interests of workers were also undertaken. But well into the 1850s Americans displayed less evidence of the class solidarity common among European workers.

Why America did not produce a self-conscious working class is a question that has long intrigued historians. Some historians argue that the existence of the frontier siphoned off displaced and dissatisfied workers. The number of urban laborers who went west could not have been large, but the fact that the expanding economy created many opportunities for laborers to rise out of the working class was surely another reason why so few of them developed strong class feelings.

Other historians believe that ethnic and racial differences kept workers from seeing themselves as a distinct class with common needs and common enemies. The influx of needy immigrants willing to accept almost any wage was certainly resented by native-born workers. The growing number of free blacks in Northern cities—between 1800 and 1830 the number tripled in Philadelphia and quadrupled in New York—also inhibited the development of a self-identified working class.

These answers help explain the relative absence of class conflict during the early stages of the industrial revolution in America, but so does the fact that conditions in

Slater's Mill, in Pawtucket, Rhode Island.
Source: N. Carter/North Wind Picture Archives.

the early shops and factories represented an improvement for the people who worked in them. This was the case with nearly all European immigrants, though less so for urban free blacks, since in the South many found work in the skilled trades.

Most workers in the early textile factories were drawn from outside the regular labor market. Relatively few artisan spinners and weavers became factory workers; indeed, some of them continued to work as they had, for it was many years before the factories could even begin to satisfy the ever-increasing demand for cloth. Nor did immigrants attend the new machines. Instead, the mill owners relied chiefly on women and children. They did so because machines lessened the need for skill and strength and because the labor shortage made it necessary to tap unexploited sources. By the early 1820s about half the cotton textile workers in the factories were under sixteen years of age.

Most people of that generation reasoned that the work was easy and that it kept youngsters busy at useful tasks while providing their families with extra income. Roxanna Foote, whose daughter, Harriet Beecher Stowe, wrote *Uncle Tom's Cabin*, came from a solid, middle-class family in Guilford, Connecticut. Nevertheless, she worked full-time before her marriage in her grandfather's small spinning mill. "This spinning-mill was a favorite spot," a relative recalled many years later. "Here the girls often received visitors, or read or chatted while they spun." Roxanna explained her daily regimen as a mill girl matter-of-factly: "I generally rise with the sun, and, after breakfast, take my wheel, which is my daily companion, and the evening is generally devoted to reading, writing, and knitting."

This seems like an idealized picture, or perhaps working for one's grandfather made a difference. Another young girl, Emily Chubbock, later a well-known writer, had a less pleasant recollection of her experience as an eleven-year-old factory hand earning

$1.25 a week: "My principal recollections . . . are of noise and filth, bleeding hands and aching feet, and a very sad heart." In any case, a society accustomed to seeing the children of fairly well-to-do farmers working full-time in the fields was not shocked by the sight of children working all day in mills. In factories where laborers were hired in family units, no member earned very much, but with a couple of adolescent daughters and perhaps a son of nine or ten helping out, a family could take home enough to live decently. For most working Americans, that was success enough.

Lowell's Waltham System: Women as Factory Workers

Instead of hiring children, the Boston Associates developed the "Waltham System" of employing young, unmarried women in their new textile mills. For a generation after the opening of the Merrimack Manufacturing Company in 1823, the thriving factory towns of Lowell, Chicopee, and Manchester provided the background for a remarkable industrial idyll. Young women came from farms all over New England to work for a year or two in the mills. They were lodged in company boardinghouses, which, like college dormitories, became centers of social life. Unlike modern college dormitories, the boardinghouses were strictly supervised; straitlaced New Englanders did not hesitate to permit their daughters to live in them. The regulations laid down by one company, for example, required that all employees "show that they are penetrated by a laudable love of temperance and virtue." "Ardent spirits" were banished from company property, and "games of hazard and cards" prohibited. A 10 PM curfew was strictly enforced.

The women earned between $2.50 and $3.25 a week, about half of which went for room and board. Some of the remainder they sent home, the rest (what there was of it) they could spend as they wished.

Most of these young women did not have to support themselves. They worked to save for a trousseau, to help educate a younger brother, or simply for the experience and excitement of meeting new people and escaping the confining environment of the farm. Anything but an industrial proletariat, they filled the windows of the factories with flowering plants, organized sewing circles, edited their own literary periodicals, and attended lectures on edifying subjects. That such activity was possible on top of a seventy-hour work week is a commentary on both the resiliency of youth and the leisurely pace of these early factories.

Life in the mills was nevertheless demanding. Although they made up 85 percent of the workforce, women were kept out of supervisory positions. In 1834 workers in several mills "turned out" to protest cuts in their wages and a hike in what they paid for board. This work stoppage did not force a reversal of management policy. Another strike two years later in response to a work speedup was somewhat more successful. But when a drop in prices in the 1840s led the owners to introduce new rules designed to increase production, workers lacked the organizational strength to block them. By then young women of the kind that had flocked to the mills in the 1820s and 1830s were beginning to find work as schoolteachers and clerks. Mill owners turned increasingly to Irish immigrants to operate their machines.

Read the Document

Regarding Life in the Mills at **myhistorylab.com**

Irish and German Immigrants

Between 1790 and 1820 the population of the United States had more than doubled to 9.6 million. The most remarkable feature of this growth was that it resulted almost entirely from natural increase. The birthrate in the early nineteenth century exceeded fifty per 1,000 population, a rate as high as that of any country in the world today. Fewer than 250,000 immigrants entered the United States between 1790 and 1820. European wars, the ending of the slave trade, and doubts about the viability of the new republic slowed the flow of humanity across the Atlantic to a trickle.

But soon after the final defeat of Napoleon in 1815, immigration picked up. In the 1820s, some 150,000 European immigrants arrived; in the 1830s, 600,000; and in the 1840s, 1.7 million. The 1850 census, the first to make the distinction, estimated that of the nation's population of 23 million, more than 10 percent were foreign-born. In the Northeast the proportion exceeded 15 percent.

Most of this human tide came from Germany and Ireland, but substantial numbers also came from Great Britain and the Scandinavian countries. As with earlier immigrants, most were drawn to America by what are called "pull" factors: the prospect of abundant land, good wages, and economic opportunity generally, or by the promise of political and religious freedom. But many came because of "push" factors: To stay where they were meant to face starvation. This was particularly true of those from Ireland, where a potato blight triggered the flight of tens of thousands. This Irish exodus continued; by the end of the century there were more people of Irish origin in America than in Ireland.

Once ashore in New York, Boston, or Philadelphia, most relatively prosperous immigrants pushed directly westward. Others found work in the new factory towns

Population Density, 1790 Then, as now, the most densely populated part of the nation was the coastal region from Virginia to Massachusetts.

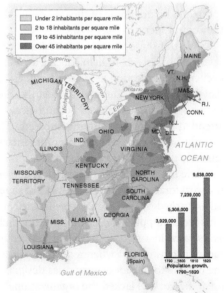

Population Density, 1820 The thirty years from 1790 to 1820 saw a sizable increase in population, especially along the Ohio and Mississippi River valleys.

along the route of the Erie Canal, in the lower Delaware Valley southeast of Philadelphia, or along the Merrimack River north of Boston. But most of the Irish immigrants, "the poorest and most wretched population that can be found in the world," one of their priests called them, lacked the means to go west. Like it or not, they had to settle in the eastern cities.

Viewed in historical perspective, this massive wave of immigration stimulated the American economy. In the short run, the influx of the 1830s and 1840s depressed living standards and strained the social fabric. For the first time the nation had acquired a culturally distinctive, citybound, and propertyless class. The poor Irish immigrants had to accept whatever wages employers offered them. By doing so they caused resentment among native workers—resentment exacerbated by the unfamiliarity of the Irish with city ways and by their Roman Catholic faith, which the Protestant majority associated with European authoritarianism and corruption.

The Persistence of the Household System

Since technology affected American industry unevenly, contemporaries found the changes difficult to evaluate. Interchangeable firing pins for rifles did not lead at once even to matching pairs of shoes. More than fifteen years passed after John Fitch built and launched the world's first regularly scheduled steamboat in 1790 before it was widely accepted. Few people in the 1820s appreciated how profound the impact of the factory system would be. The city of Lowell seemed remarkable and important but not necessarily a herald of future trends.

Yet in nearly every field apparently minor changes were being made. Beginning around 1815, small improvements in the design of waterwheels, such as the use of leather transmission belts and metal gears, made possible larger and more efficient machinery in mills and factories. Iron production advanced beyond the stage of the blacksmith's forge and the small foundry only slowly; nevertheless, by 1810 machines were stamping out nails at a third of the cost of the hand-forged type. At about this time the puddling process for refining pig iron made it possible to use coal for fuel instead of expensive charcoal.

Rise of Corporations

Mechanization required substantial capital investment, and capital was chronically in short supply. The modern method of organizing large enterprises, the corporation, was slow to develop. Between 1781 and 1801 only 326 corporations were chartered by the states, and only a few of them were engaged in manufacturing.

The general opinion was that only quasi-public projects, such as roads and waterworks, were entitled to the privilege of incorporation. Anyone interested in organizing a corporation had to obtain a special act of a state legislature. And even among businessmen there was a tendency to associate corporations with monopoly, with corruption, and with the undermining of individual enterprise. In 1820 the economist Daniel Raymond wrote, "The very object . . . of the act of incorporation is to produce inequality, either in rights, or in the division of property. Prima facie, therefore all money corporations are detrimental to national wealth. They are always created for the benefit of the rich. . . ." Such feelings help explain why as late as the 1860s most manufacturing was being done by unincorporated companies.

While the growth of industry did not suddenly revolutionize American life, it reshaped society in various ways. For a time it lessened the importance of foreign commerce. Some relative decline from the lush years immediately preceding Jefferson's embargo was no doubt inevitable, especially in the fabulously profitable reexport trade. But American industrial growth reduced the need for foreign products and thus the business of merchants. Only in the 1850s, when the wealth and population of the United States were more than three times what they had been in the first years of the century, did the value of American exports climb back to the levels of 1807. As the country moved closer to self-sufficiency (a point it never reached), nationalistic and isolationist sentiments were subtly augmented. During the embargo and the War of 1812 a great deal of capital had been transferred from commerce to industry; afterward new capital continued to prefer industry, attracted by the high profits and growing prestige of manufacturing. The rise of manufacturing affected farmers too, for as cities grew in size and number, the need to feed the populace caused commercial agriculture to flourish.

Cotton Revolutionizes the South

By far the most important indirect effect of industrialization occurred in the South, which soon began to produce cotton to supply the new textile factories of Great Britain and New England. Beginning in 1786, "sea-island" cotton was grown successfully in the mild, humid lowlands and offshore islands along the coasts of Georgia and South Carolina. This was a high-quality cotton, silky and long-fibered like the Egyptian kind. But its susceptibility to frost severely limited the area of its cultivation. Elsewhere in the South, "green-seed," or upland, cotton flourished, but this plant had little commercial value because the seeds could not be easily separated from the lint. When sea-island cotton was passed between two rollers, its shiny black seeds simply popped out; with upland cotton the seeds were pulled through with the lint and crushed, the oils and broken bits destroying the value of the fiber. To remove the seeds by hand was laborious; a slave working all day could clean scarcely a pound of the white fluff. This made it an uneconomical crop. In 1791 the usually sanguine Hamilton admitted in his *Report on Manufactures* that "the extensive cultivation of cotton can, perhaps, hardly be expected."

Early American cotton manufacturers used the sea-island variety or imported the foreign fiber, in the latter case paying a duty of 3 cents a pound. However, the planters of South Carolina and Georgia, suffering from hard times after the Revolution, needed a new cash crop. Rice production was not expanding, and indigo, the other staple of the area, had ceased to be profitable when it was no longer possible to claim the British bounty. Cotton seemed an obvious answer. Farmers were experimenting hopefully with varieties of the plant and mulling the problem of how upland cotton could be more easily deseeded.

Generations of American schoolchildren—and college students—have been taught that over the course of two weeks in 1793 Eli Whitney, a Yankee who had never seen a

In 2005 historian Angela Lakwete used this print as the cover of *Inventing the Cotton Gin: Machine and Myth in Antebellum America* to show that devices similar to that "invented" by Eli Whitney in 1793 had long been in use in the South. The human details in the image are revealing as well.

Photo Credit: © Bettmann/Corbis.

cotton plant, invented a machine that instantly revolutionized the production of cotton. His cotton gin (engine) consisted of a cylinder covered with rows of wire teeth rotating in a box filled with cotton. As the cylinder turned, the teeth passed through narrow slits in a metal grating. Cotton fibers were caught by the teeth and pulled through the slits. The seeds, too thick to pass through the openings, were left behind. A second cylinder, with brushes rotating in the opposite direction to sweep the cotton from the wires, prevented matting and clogging.

In fact, as the lithograph on this page suggests, Southern cotton planters had for decades used a roller gin, which operated according to similar principles—tugging cotton through meshed teeth to pull out seeds without harming the fibers. Many regarded Whitney's design as an improvement, but it took nearly three decades before it replaced the roller gins. The expansion of cotton production did not rise sharply until the 1820s.

Upland cotton would grow wherever there were 200 consecutive days without frost and twenty-four inches of rain. The crop engulfed Georgia and South Carolina and spread north into parts of Virginia. After Andrew Jackson defeated the southeastern Indians during the War of 1812, the rich "Black Belt" area of central Alabama and northern Mississippi and the delta region along the lower Mississippi River were rapidly taken over by the fluffy white staple. In 1821 Alabama alone raised 40,000 bales. Central Tennessee also became important cotton country.

Cotton stimulated the economy of the rest of the nation as well. Most of it was exported, the sale paying for much-needed European products. The transportation,

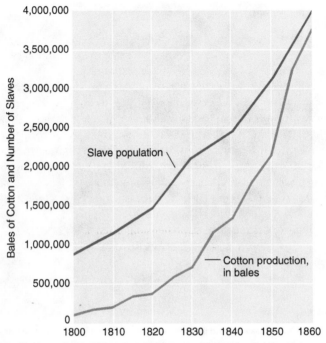

Cotton Production and Slave Population, 1800–1860 As the number of slaves increased, the production of cotton increased also.

insurance, and final disposition of the crop fell largely into the hands of Northern merchants, who profited accordingly. And the surplus corn and hogs of western farmers helped feed the slaves of the new cotton plantations. Cotton was the major force in the economy for a generation, beginning about 1815.

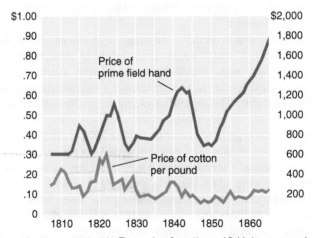

Prices for Cotton and for Slaves, 1802–1860 These prices for cotton and field slaves appear in New Orleans records. The left axis shows the price of cotton; the right, the price of a slave. The rising trend of slave prices (especially from 1850 to 1860), and a growing slave population, show the continuing profitability and viability of slavery up to 1860.

Revival of Slavery

Amid the national rejoicing over this prosperity, one aspect both sad and ominous was easily overlooked. Slavery, a declining or at worst stagnant institution in the decade of the Revolution, was revitalized in the following years.

Libertarian beliefs inspired by the Revolution ran into the roadblock of race prejudice as soon as some of the practical aspects of freedom for blacks became apparent. As disciples of John Locke, the Revolutionary generation had a deep respect for property rights; in the last analysis most white Americans placed these rights ahead of the personal liberty of black Americans. Forced abolition of slavery therefore attracted few recruits. Moreover, the rhetoric of the Revolution had raised the aspirations of blacks. Increasing signs of rebelliousness appeared among them, especially after the slave uprising in Saint Domingue, which culminated, after a great bloodbath, in the establishment of the black Republic of Haiti in 1804. This example of a successful slave revolt filled white Americans with apprehension. Their fears were irrational (Haitian blacks outnumbered whites and mulattos combined by seven to one), but nonetheless real. And fear led to repression; the exposure in 1801 of a plot to revolt in Virginia resulted in some three dozen executions even though no actual uprising had occurred.

The mood of the Revolutionary decade had led a substantial number of masters to free their slaves. Unfortunately this led many other whites to have second thoughts about ending slavery. "If the blacks see all of their color slaves, it will seem to them a disposition of Providence, and they will be content," a Virginia legislator claimed. "But if they see others like themselves free . . . they will repine." As the number of free blacks rose, restrictions on them were everywhere tightened.

In the 1780s many opponents of slavery began to think of solving the "Negro problem" by colonizing freed slaves in some distant region—in the western districts or perhaps in Africa. The colonization movement had two aspects. The first one was a manifestation of an embryonic black nationalism that reflected the disgust of black Americans with local racial attitudes and their interest in African civilization. Paul Cuffe, a Massachusetts Quaker, managed to finance the emigration of thirty-eight of his fellow blacks to British Sierra Leone in 1815, but few others followed. Most influential Northern blacks, the most conspicuous among them the Reverend Richard Allen, bishop of the African Methodist Church, opposed the idea vigorously.

The other colonization movement, led by whites, was paternalistic. Some white colonizationists genuinely abhorred slavery. Others could not stomach living with free blacks; to them colonization was merely a polite word for deportation. Most white colonizationists were conservatives who considered themselves realists.

The colonization idea became popular in Virginia in the 1790s, but nothing was achieved until after the founding of the **American Colonization Society** in 1817. The society purchased African land and established the Republic of Liberia. However, despite the cooperation of a handful of black nationalists and the patronage of many important white Southerners, including Presidents Madison and Monroe and Chief Justice Marshall, it accomplished little. Although some white colonizationists expected ex-slaves to go to Africa as Christian missionaries to convert and "civilize" the natives, few blacks wished to migrate to a land so alien to their own experience. Only about 12,000 went to Liberia, and the toll taken among them by tropical diseases was large. As late as 1850 the black American population of Liberia was only 6,000.

The cotton boom of the early nineteenth century acted as a brake on the colonization movement. As cotton production expanded, the need for labor in the South grew apace. The price of slaves doubled between 1795 and 1804. As it rose, the inclination of even the most kindhearted masters to free their slaves began to falter. Although the importation of slaves from abroad had been outlawed by all the states, perhaps 25,000 were smuggled into the country in the 1790s. In 1804 South Carolina reopened the trade, and between that date and 1808, when the constitutional prohibition of importation became effective, some 40,000 were brought in. Thereafter the miserable traffic in human beings continued clandestinely, though on a lesser scale.

The cotton boom triggered an internal trade in slaves that frequently ripped black families apart. While it had always been legal for owners to transport their own slaves to a new state if they were settling there, many states forbade, or at least severely restricted, interstate commercial transactions in human flesh. A Virginia law of 1778, for example, prohibited the importation of slaves for purposes of sale, and persons entering the state with slaves had to swear that they did not intend to sell them. Once cotton became important, these laws were either repealed or systematically evaded. There was a surplus of slaves in one part of the United States and an acute shortage in another. A migration from the upper South to the cotton lands quickly sprang up. Slaves from "free" New York and New Jersey and even from New England began to appear on the auction blocks of Savannah and Charleston. Early in the Era of Good Feelings, newspapers in New Orleans were carrying reports such as, "Jersey negroes appear to be particularly adapted to this market. . . . We have the right to calculate on large importations in the future, from the success which hitherto attended the sale."

The lot of African Americans in the Northern states was almost as bad as that of Southern free blacks. Except in New England, where there were few blacks to begin with, most were denied the vote, either directly or by extralegal pressures. They could not testify in court, intermarry with whites, obtain decent jobs or housing, or get even a rudimentary education. Most states segregated blacks in theaters, hospitals, churches, and on public transportation facilities. They were barred from hotels and restaurants patronized by whites.

Northern blacks could at least protest and try to convince the white majority of the injustice of their treatment. These rights were denied their Southern brethren. They could and did publish newspapers and pamphlets, organize for political action, and petition legislatures and Congress for redress of grievance—in short, they applied methods of peaceful persuasion in an effort to improve their position in society.

Roads to Market

Inventions and technological improvements were extremely important in the settlement of the West. On superficial examination, this may not seem to have been the case, for the hordes of settlers who struggled across the mountains immediately after the War of 1812 were no better equipped than their ancestors who had pushed up the eastern slopes in previous generations. Many plodded on foot over hundreds of miles, dragging crude carts laden with their meager possessions. More

See the Map

Expanding America and Internal Improvements at **myhistorylab.com**

This stagecoach has just passed over a solid road made of tree trunks, but it must now continue traveling across a dirt road. Already its wheels have sunk several inches into the mud.
Source: George Tattersall, English, 1817–1849 (active U.S. 1836), *Album of Western Sketches: Highways and Byeways of the Forest*, a Scene on "the Road", 1836. Pen and brown ink with brush and brown wash, heightened with white gouache, over graphite pencil, on gray paper. 21.0 x 29.8 cm (8 1/4 x 11 3/4 in.) Museum of Fine Arts, Boston. Gift of Maxim Karolik for the M. and M. Karolik Collection of American Watercolors and Drawings, 1800–1875, 56.400.11. Photograph © 2011 Museum of Fine Arts, Boston.

fortunate pioneers traveled on horseback or in heavy, cumbersome wagons, the best known being the canvas-topped Conestoga "covered wagons," pulled by horses or oxen.

In many cases the pioneers followed trails and roads no better than those of colonial days—quagmires in wet weather, rutted and pitted with potholes a good part of the year. When they settled down, their way of life was no more advanced than that of the Pilgrims. At first they were creatures of the forest, feeding on its abundance, building their homes and simple furniture with its wood, clothing themselves in the furs of forest animals. They usually planted the first crop in a natural glade; thereafter, year by year, they pushed back the trees with ax and saw and fire until the land was cleared. Until the population of the territory had grown large enough to support town life, settlers were as dependent on crude household manufacturers as any earlier pioneer.

The spread of settlement into the Mississippi Valley created challenges that required technological advances if they were to be met. In the social climate of that age in the United States, these advances were not slow in coming. Most were related to transportation, the major problem for westerners. Everyone recognized that an efficient transportation network would increase land values, stimulate domestic and foreign trade, and strengthen the entire economy. The Mississippi River and its tributaries provided a natural highway for western commerce and communication, but it was one that had grave disadvantages. Farm products could be floated down to New Orleans on rafts and flatboats, but the descent along the Ohio River from Pittsburgh to the Mississippi took at least a month. In any case, the natural flow of trade was between the East and West. That is why, from early in the westward movement, much attention was given to building roads linking the Mississippi Valley to the eastern seaboard.

Constructing decent roads over the rugged Appalachians was a formidable task. The steepest grades had to be reduced by cutting through hills and filling in low places, all without modern blasting and earth-moving equipment. Drainage ditches were essential if the roads were not to be washed out by the first rains, and a firm foundation of stones had to be provided if they were to stand up under the pounding of heavy wagons. The skills required for building roads of this quality had been developed in Great Britain and France, and the earliest American examples, constructed in the 1790s, were similar to good European highways. The first such road, connecting Philadelphia and Lancaster, Pennsylvania, opened to traffic in 1794.

Transportation and the Government

Most of the improved highways and many bridges were built as business ventures by private interests. Promoters charged tolls, the rates being set by the states. Tolls were collected at gates along the way; hinged poles suspended across the road were turned back by a guard after receipt of the toll. Hence these thoroughfares were known as turn-pikes, or simply pikes.

The profits earned by a few early turnpikes, such as the one between Philadelphia and Lancaster, caused the boom in private road building, but even the most fortunate of the turnpike companies did not make much money. Maintenance was expensive, and traffic spotty. (Ordinary public roads paralleling turnpikes were sometimes called "shunpikes" because penny-pinching travelers used them to avoid the tolls.) Some states bought stock to bolster weak companies, and others built and operated turnpikes as public enterprises. Local governments everywhere provided considerable support, for every town was eager to develop efficient communication with its neighbors.

Despite much talk about individual self-reliance and free enterprise, local, state, and national governments contributed heavily to the development of what in the jargon of the day were called "internal improvements." They served as "primary entrepreneurs," supplying capital for risky but socially desirable enterprises with the result that a fascinating mixture of private and public energy went into the building of these institutions. At the federal level even the parsimonious Jeffersonians became deeply involved. In 1808 Secretary of the Treasury Albert Gallatin drafted a comprehensive plan for constructing much-needed roads at a cost of $16 million. This proposal was not adopted, but the government poured money in an erratic and unending stream into turnpike companies and other organizations created to improve transportation.

Logically, the major highways, especially those over the mountains, should have been built by the national government. Strategic military requirements alone would have justified such a program. One major artery, the Old National Road, running from Cumberland, Maryland, to Wheeling, in western Virginia, was constructed by the United States between 1811 and 1818. In time it was extended as far west as Vandalia, Illinois. However, further federal road building was hampered by political squabbles in Congress, usually phrased in constitutional terms but in fact based on sectional rivalries and other economic conflicts. Thus no comprehensive highway program was undertaken in the nineteenth century.

While the National Road, the New York Pike, and other, rougher trails such as the Wilderness Road into the Kentucky country were adequate for the movement of settlers, they did not begin to answer the West's need for cheap and efficient transportation.

Wagon freight rates averaged at least thirty cents a ton-mile around 1815. At such rates, to transport a ton of oats from Buffalo to New York would have cost twelve times the value of the oats! To put the problem another way, four horses could haul a ton and a half of oats about eighteen or twenty miles a day over a good road. If they could obtain half their feed by grazing, the horses would still consume about fifty pounds of oats a day. It requires little mathematics to figure out how many pounds of oats would be left in the wagon when it reached New York City, almost 400 miles away.

Until the coming of the railroad, which was just being introduced in England in 1825, the cost of shipping bulky goods by land over the great distances common in America was prohibitive. Businessmen and inventors concentrated instead on improving water transport, first by designing better boats and then by developing artificial waterways.

Development of Steamboats

Rafts and flatboats were adequate for downstream travel, but the only practical solution to upstream travel was the steamboat. After John Fitch's work around 1790, a number of others made important contributions to the development of steam navigation. One early enthusiast was John Stevens, a wealthy New Jerseyite, who designed an improved steam boiler for which he received one of the first patents issued by the United States. Stevens got his brother-in-law, Robert R. Livingston, interested in the problem, and the latter used his political influence to obtain an exclusive charter to operate steamboats on New York waters. In 1802, while in France trying to buy New Orleans from Napoleon, Livingston got to know Robert Fulton, a young American artist and engineer who was experimenting with steam navigation, and agreed to finance his work. In 1807, after returning to New York, Fulton constructed the *North River Steam Boat*, famous to history as the *Clermont*.

The *Clermont* was 142 feet long, 18 feet abeam, and drew 7 feet of water. With its towering stack belching black smoke, its side wheels could push it along at a steady five miles an hour. Nothing about it was radically new, but Fulton brought the essentials—engine, boiler, paddle wheels, and hull—into proper balance and thereby produced an efficient vessel.

No one could patent a steamboat; soon the new vessels were plying the waters of every navigable river from the Mississippi east. After 1815 steamers were making the run from New Orleans as far as Ohio. By 1820 at least sixty vessels were operating between New Orleans and Louisville, and by the end of the decade there were more than 200 steamers on the Mississippi.

The day of the steamboat had dawned, and although the following generation would experience its high noon, even in the 1820s its major effects were clear. The great Mississippi Valley, in the full tide of its development, was immensely enriched. Produce poured down to New Orleans, which soon ranked with New York and Liverpool among the world's great ports. From 1816–1817, only 80,000 tons of freight was shipped down the Mississippi to New Orleans; but by 1840–1841, that freight arriving in New Orleans had increased to 542,000 tons. Upriver traffic was affected even more spectacularly. Freight charges plummeted, in some cases to a tenth of what they had been after the War of 1812. Around 1818 coffee cost sixteen cents a pound more in Cincinnati than in

New Orleans, a decade later less than three cents more. The Northwest emerged from self-sufficiency with a rush and became part of the national market.

Steamboats were far more comfortable than any contemporary form of land transportation, and competition soon led builders to make them positively luxurious. The *General Pike*, launched in 1819 and set the fashion. Marble columns, thick carpets, mirrors, and crimson curtains adorned its cabins and public rooms. Soon the finest steamers were floating palaces where passengers could dine, drink, dance, and gamble in luxury as they sped smoothly to their destinations. Yet raft and flatboat traffic increased. Farmers, lumbermen, and others with goods from upriver floated down in the slack winter season and returned in comfort by steamer after selling their produce and their rafts as well, for lumber was in great demand in New Orleans. Every January and February New Orleans teemed with westerners and Yankee sailors, their pockets jingling, bent on a fling before going back to work. The shops displayed everything from the latest Paris fashions to teething rings made of alligator teeth mounted in silver. During the carnival season the city became one great festival, where every human pleasure could be tasted, every vice indulged.

The Canal Boom

While the steamboat was conquering western rivers, canals were being constructed that further improved the transportation network. Since the midwestern rivers all emptied into the Gulf of Mexico, they did not provide a direct link with the eastern seaboard. If an artificial waterway could be cut between the great central valley and some navigable stream flowing into the Atlantic, all sections would profit immensely.

Canals were more expensive than roads, but so long as the motive power used in overland transportation was the humble horse, they offered enormous economic advantages to shippers. Because there is less friction to overcome, a team plodding along a towpath could pull a canal barge with a 100-ton load and make better time over long distances than it could pulling a single ton in a wagon on the finest road.

Although canals were as old as Egypt, only about 100 miles of them existed in the United States as late as 1816. Construction costs aside, in a rough and mountainous country canals presented formidable engineering problems. To link the Mississippi Valley and the Atlantic meant somehow circumventing the Appalachian Mountains. Most people thought this impossible.

Mayor DeWitt Clinton of New York believed that such a project was feasible in New York State. In 1810, while serving as state canal commissioner, he traveled across central New York and convinced himself that it would be practicable to dig a canal from Buffalo, on Lake Erie, to the Hudson River. The Mohawk Valley cuts through the Appalachian chain just north of Albany, and at no point along the route to Buffalo does the land rise more than 570 feet above the level of the Hudson. Marshaling a mass of technical, financial, and commercial information and using his political influence cannily, Clinton placed his proposal before the New York legislature. In its defense he was eloquent and farsighted:

> As an organ of communication between the Hudson, the Mississippi, the
> St. Lawrence, the great lakes of the north and west, and their tributary rivers,
> [the canal] will create the greatest inland trade ever witnessed. The most fertile

and extensive regions of America will avail themselves of its facilities for a market. All their surplus . . . will concentrate in the city of New York. . . . That city will, in the course of time, become the granary of the world, the emporium of commerce, the seat of manufactures, the focus of great moneyed operations. . . . And before the revolution of a century, the whole island of Manhattan, covered with habitations and replenished with a dense population, will constitute one vast city.

The legislators were convinced, and in 1817 the state began construction along a route 363 miles long, most of it across densely forested wilderness. At the time the longest canal in the United States ran less than twenty-eight miles!

The construction of the Erie Canal, as it was called, was a remarkable accomplishment. The chief engineer, Benjamin Wright, a surveyor-politician from Rome, New York, had had almost no experience with canal building. Fortunately, Wright proved to be a good organizer and a fine judge of engineering talent. He quickly spotted young men of ability among the workers and pushed them forward. One of his finds, Canvass White, was sent to study British canals. White became an expert on the design of locks; he also discovered an American limestone that could be made into waterproof cement, a vital product in canal construction that had previously been imported at a substantial price from England. Another of Wright's protégés, John B. Jervis, began as an axman, rose in two years to resident engineer in charge of a section of the project, and went on to become perhaps the outstanding American civil engineer of his time. Workers who learned the business digging the "Big Ditch" supervised the construction of dozens of canals throughout the country in later years.

The Erie, completed in 1825, was an immediate financial success. Together with the companion Champlain Canal, which linked Lake Champlain and the Hudson, it brought in over half a million dollars in tolls in its first year. Soon its entire $7 million cost had been recovered, and it was earning profits of about $3 million a year. The effect of this prosperity on New York State was enormous. Buffalo, Rochester, Syracuse, and half a dozen lesser towns along the canal flourished.

New York City: Emporium of the Western World

New York City had already become the largest city in the nation, thanks chiefly to its merchants who had established a reputation for their rapid and orderly way of doing business. In 1818 the Black Ball Line opened the first regularly scheduled freight and passenger service between New York and England. Previously shipments might languish in port for weeks while a skipper waited for additional cargo. Now merchants on both sides of the Atlantic could count on the Black Ball packets to move their goods between Liverpool and New York on schedule whether or not the transporting vessel had a full cargo. This improvement brought much new business to the port.

Now the canal cemented New York's position as the national metropolis. Most European-manufactured goods destined for the Mississippi Valley entered the country at New York and passed on to the West over the canal. The success of the Erie also sparked a nationwide canal-building boom. Most canals were constructed either by the states, as in the case of the Erie, or as "mixed enterprises" that combined public and private energies.

Nicolino V. Calyo's painting, *Burning of the Merchant's Exchange* (1835) in New York.
The entire block was rebuilt within a year.
Source: Museum of the City of New York.

No state profited as much from this construction as New York, for none possessed New York's geographic advantages. The rocky hills of New England discouraged all but fanatics. Canals were built connecting Worcester and Northampton, Massachusetts, with the coast, but they were financial failures. The Delaware and Hudson Canal, running from northeastern Pennsylvania across northern New Jersey and lower New York to the Hudson, was completed by private interests in 1828. It managed to earn respectable dividends by barging coal to the eastern seaboard, but it made no attempt to compete with the Erie for the western trade. Pennsylvania, desperate to keep up with New York, engaged in an orgy of construction. In 1834 it completed a complicated system, part canal and part railroad, over the mountains to Pittsburgh. This Mainline Canal cost a staggering sum for that day. With its 177 locks and cumbersome "inclined-plane railroad" it was slow and expensive to operate and never competed effectively with the Erie. Efforts in Maryland to link Baltimore with the West by water failed utterly.

Beyond the mountains there was even greater zeal for canal construction in the 1820s and still more in the 1830s. Once the Erie opened the way across New York, farmers in the Ohio country demanded that links be built between the Ohio River and the Great Lakes so that they could ship their produce by water directly to the East. Local feeder canals seemed equally necessary; with corn worth 20 cents a bushel at Columbus selling for 50 cents at Marietta, on the Ohio, the value of cheap transportation became obvious to Ohio farmers.

Even before the completion of the Erie, Ohio had begun construction of the Ohio and Erie Canal running from the Ohio River to Cleveland. Another, from Toledo to Cincinnati, was begun in 1832. Meanwhile, Indiana had undertaken the 450-mile Wabash and Erie Canal. These canals were well conceived, but the western states overextended themselves building dozens of feeder lines, trying, it sometimes seemed, to supply all farmers west of the Appalachians with water connections from their barns to the New York docks. Politics made such programs almost inevitable, for in order to win support for their pet projects, legislators had to back the schemes of their fellows. The result was frequently financial disaster. There was not enough traffic to pay for all the waterways that were dug. By 1844, $60 million in state "improvement" bonds were in default. Nevertheless, the canals benefited both western farmers and the national economy.

The Marshall Court

The most important legal advantages bestowed on business in the period were the gift of Chief Justice John Marshall. His particular combination of charm, logic, and forcefulness made the Court during his long reign remarkably submissive to his view of the Constitution. Marshall's belief in a powerful central government explains his tendency to hand down decisions favorable to manufacturing and business interests. He also thought that "the business community was the agent of order and progress" and tended to interpret the Constitution in a way that would advance its interests.

Many important cases came before the Court between 1819 and 1824, and in each one Marshall's decision was applauded by most of the business community. The cases involved two major principles: the "sanctity" of contracts and the supremacy of federal legislation over the laws of the states. Marshall shared the conviction of the Revolutionary generation that property had to be protected against arbitrary seizure if liberty was to be preserved. Contracts between private individuals and between individuals and the government must be strictly enforced, he believed, or chaos would result. He therefore gave the widest possible application to the constitutional provision that no state could pass any law "impairing the Obligation of Contracts."

●●●–[Read the Document

Martin v. Hunter's Lessee at myhistorylab.com

In **Dartmouth College v. Woodward** (1819), which involved an attempt by New Hampshire to alter the charter granted to Dartmouth by King George III in 1769, Marshall held that such a charter was a contract which could not be canceled or altered without the consent of both parties. The state had sought not to destroy the college but to change it from a private to a public institution, yet Marshall held that to do so would violate the contract clause.

Marshall's decisions concerning the division of power between the federal government and the states were even more important. The question of the constitutionality of a national bank, first debated by Hamilton and Jefferson, had not been submitted to the courts during the life of the first Bank of the United States. By the time of the second Bank there were many state banks, and some of them felt that their interests were threatened by the national institution. Responding to pressure from local banks, the Maryland legislature placed an annual tax of $15,000 on "foreign" banks, including the Bank of the United States! The Maryland branch of the Bank of the United States refused to pay, whereupon the state brought suit against its cashier, John W McCulloch. **McCulloch v. Maryland** was crucial to the Bank, for five other states had levied taxes on its branches, and others would surely follow suit if the Maryland law were upheld.

Marshall extinguished the threat. The Bank of the United States was constitutional, he announced in phrases taken almost verbatim from Hamilton's 1791 memorandum to Washington on the subject; its legality was implied in many of the powers specifically granted to Congress. Full "discretion" must be allowed Congress in deciding exactly how its powers "are to be carried into execution." Since the Bank was legal, the Maryland tax was unconstitutional. Marshall found a "plain repugnance" in the thought of "conferring on one government a power to control the constitutional measures of another." He put this idea in the simplest possible language: "The power to tax involves the power to destroy . . . the power to destroy may defeat and render useless the power to create." The long-range significance of the decision lay in its strengthening of the implied powers of Congress and its confirmation of the "loose" interpretation of the Constitution. By establishing the legality of the Bank, it also aided the growth of the economy.

In 1824 Marshall handed down an important decision involving the regulation of interstate commerce. This was the "steamboat case," ***Gibbons v. Ogden***. In 1815 Aaron Ogden, former U.S. senator and governor of New Jersey, had purchased the right to operate a ferry between Elizabeth Point, New Jersey, and New York City from Robert Fulton's backer, Robert R. Livingston, who held a New York monopoly of steamboat navigation on the Hudson. When Thomas Gibbons, who held a federal coasting license, set up a competing line, Ogden sued him. Ogden argued in effect that Gibbons could operate his boat on the New Jersey side of the Hudson but had no right to cross into New York waters. After complicated litigation in the lower courts, the case reached the Supreme Court on appeal. Marshall decided in favor of Gibbons, effectively destroying the New York monopoly. A state can regulate commerce that begins and ends in its own territory but not when the transaction involves crossing a state line; then the national authority takes precedence. "The act of Congress," he said, "is supreme; and the law of the state . . . must yield to it."

This decision threw open the interstate steamboat business to all comers, and since an adequate 100-ton vessel could be built for as little as $7,000, dozens of small operators were soon engaged in it. More important in the long run was the fact that in order

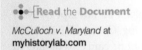

Read the Document

McCulloch v. Maryland at myhistorylab.com

to include the ferry business within the federal government's power to regulate interstate commerce, Marshall had given the word the widest possible meaning: "Commerce, undoubtedly, is traffic, but it is something more,—it is intercourse." By construing the "commerce" clause so broadly, he made it easy for future generations of judges to extend its coverage to include the control of interstate electric power lines and even radio and television transmission.

Many of Marshall's decisions aided the economic development of the country in specific ways, but his chief contribution lay in his broadly national view of economic affairs. When he tried consciously to favor business by making contracts inviolable, his influence was important but limited—and, as it worked out, impermanent. In the steamboat case and in *McCulloch v. Maryland*, where he was really deciding between rival property interests, his work was more truly judicial in spirit and far more lasting. In such matters his nationalism enabled him to add form and substance to Hamilton's vision of the economic future of the United States.

Marshall and his colleagues firmly established the principle of judicial limitation on the power of legislatures and made the Supreme Court a vital part of the American system of government. In an age plagued by narrow sectional jealousies, Marshall's contribution was of immense influence and significance, and on it rests his claim to greatness.

John Marshall died in 1835. Two years later, in the *Charles River Bridge* case, the court handed down another decision that aided economic development. The state of Massachusetts had built a bridge across the Charles River between Boston and Cambridge that drew traffic from an older, privately owned toll bridge nearby. Since no

Table 1   Supreme Court Decisions and Economic Growth

	Specific Issue	Marshall Court Ruled—	Economic Consequences
Dartmouth College v. Woodward (1819)	NH sought to revoke the charter of Dartmouth College, a private school, and turn it into a public institution	For Dartmouth College: Contracts cannot be overturned	Ensured the security and regularity of business agreements and protected property rights
McCullough v. Maryland (1819)	Maryland proposed to tax the Baltimore branch of the Bank of the United States; McCullough, cashier for the bank, refused to pay Maryland tax	For federal government: States cannot tax the federal government	Ensured the supremacy of federal government over states; also strengthened the Bank of the United States and promoted economic growth
Gibbons v. Ogden (1824)	NJ steamboat operator sought to run a ferry across the Hudson River between New Jersey and New York (City), challenging a company that had a New York monopoly on such ferries	For the competing ferry: States cannot make laws that impede interstate commerce	Encouraged interstate commerce and fully national markets
Charles River Bridge Case (1837)	Operators of a company that had a contract to run a ferry across the Charles River sued Massachusetts for building a bridge that ruined the company—thereby rendering its contract worthless	For Massachusetts: The needs of the community transcend contract rights (Note: Marshall had died by time of decision)	Promoted new economic initiatives

tolls were collected from users of the state bridge after construction costs were recovered, owners of the older bridge sued for damages on the ground that the free bridge made the stock in their company worthless. They argued that in building the bridge, Massachusetts had violated the contract clause of the Constitution.

The Court, however, now speaking through the new Chief Justice, Roger B. Taney, decided otherwise. The state had a right to place "the comfort and convenience" of the whole community over that of a particular company, Taney declared. "Improvements" that add to public "wealth and property" take precedence. Like most of the decisions of the Court that were made while Marshall was chief justice, the *Charles River Bridge* case advanced the interests of those who favored economic development. Whether they were pursuing political or economic advantage, the Americans of the early nineteenth century seemed committed to a policy of compromise and accommodation.

Milestones

1790	Samuel Slater sets up first American factory	1819	Chief Justice John Marshall asserts "sanctity" of contracts in *Dartmouth College v. Woodward*
1793	Eli Whitney is widely—but wrongly—credited for inventing the cotton gin		Chief Justice Marshall strengthens implied powers of Congress in *McCulloch v. Maryland* (Bank of United States)
1794	Philadelphia–Lancaster turnpike is built		
1807	Robert Fulton constructs the *North River Steam Boat* (the *Clermont*)	1824	Chief Justice Marshall defends supremacy of federal government over states in *Gibbons v. Ogden* (steamboat case)
1808	Constitutional prohibition of importation of slaves goes into effect		
1813	Boston Manufacturing Company opens in Waltham, Massachusetts	1825	Erie Canal is completed
1816	Second Bank of the United States is created	1837	Chief Justice Roger B. Taney rules in favor of the whole community over a particular company in *Charles River Bridge v. Warren Bridge*
1817	American Colonization Society is founded in order to establish Republic of Liberia for freed slaves		

✓●─[Study] and Review at **www.myhistorylab.com**

Review Questions

1. That we live in a global economy is obvious; Americans in the early 1800s similarly perceived that their economy was undergoing substantial changes. Historians chiefly debate whether this transformation from self-sufficient farms to a market economy was sudden—revolutionary—or whether it was more gradual. What evidence can be cited in support of both positions?
2. How did cotton "revolutionize" the South?
3. How did the Marshall Court stimulate economic development?

Key Terms

American Colonization Society
Dartmouth College v. Woodward

Gibbons v. Ogden
McCulloch v. Maryland

Jacksonian Democracy

Do you vote?

THE 2008 OBAMA CAMPAIGN BROUGHT THE INTERNET REVOLUTION TO American politics. By election night Obama had 7 million friends on Facebook and 1 million on MySpace. Some 137,573 followed his every move on Twitter ("Traveling through PA today & asking folks to vote for change!") Obama's YouTube site logged 15 million viewer-hours. Yet this high-tech media blitz had little impact on the young voters it was supposed to mobilize. Fewer than half of the registered voters aged eighteen to twenty-four cast ballots, an increase of only 2 percent over 2004. And the young-voter turnout (49 percent) remained below the turnout for all age groups—64 percent.

By contrast, the political revolution inaugurated by Andrew Jackson in 1828 energized voters like nothing before or since. Prior to 1828, only one in four eligible voters cast ballots on average during a presidential election. But Jackson transformed his supporters—called Jacksonians—into a well-structured Democratic party, built a rudimentary bureaucracy to manage its affairs, and appealed directly—and effectively—to masses of voters. In 1828 more than 1.1 million ballots were cast by 58 percent of the eligible voters, more than doubling the turnout of previous elections.

Jackson won in a landslide. During the next few decades, his opponents had little choice but to imitate his techniques and build a rival mass party—the Whigs. A new type of politics emerged, which some historians call the "Second American Party System." Its central feature was the mass mobilization of the electorate, characterized by a consistent turnout of over half of all voters.

Almost from the start, Jackson's more inclusive politics encountered new challenges and obstacles. Victorious campaign workers clamored for government jobs. Energized voters, seeking cheap land, ignored the plight of the Indians, not to mention legal rights secured by treaties. As more people voted, too, politicians were obliged to "represent" a vast electorate, which made it difficult to broker deals. Sectional tensions became more intractable. The new politics of democratic engagement were not without costs; within several decades, these would include civil war.

From Chapter 9 of *American Destiny: Narrative of a Nation*, Combined Volume, Fourth Edition. Mark C. Carnes and John A. Garraty. Copyright © 2012 by Pearson Education, Inc. Published by Pearson Prentice Hall. All rights reserved.

"Democratizing" Politics

At 11 AM on March 4, 1829, a bright sunny day, Andrew Jackson, hatless and dressed severely in black, left his quarters at Gadsby's Hotel. Accompanied by a few close associates, he walked up Pennsylvania Avenue to the Capitol. At a few minutes after noon he emerged on the East Portico with the justices of the Supreme Court and other dignitaries. Before a throng of more than 15,000 people he delivered an almost inaudible and thoroughly commonplace inaugural address and then took the presidential oath. The first man to congratulate him was Chief Justice Marshall, who had administered the oath. The second was "Honest George" Kremer, a Pennsylvania congressman who led the cheering crowd that brushed past the barricade and scrambled up the Capitol steps to wring the new president's hand.

●●▪ Read the Document

Jackson, *First Annual Message to Congress* at **myhistorylab.com**

Jackson shouldered his way through the crush, mounted a splendid white horse, and rode off to the White House. A reception had been announced, to which "the officially and socially eligible as defined by precedent" had been invited. As Jackson rode down Pennsylvania Avenue, the crowds that had turned out to see the Hero of New Orleans followed—on horseback, in rickety wagons, and on foot. Nothing could keep them out of the executive mansion, and the result was chaos. Jackson was pressed back helplessly as men tracked mud across valuable rugs and clambered up on delicate chairs to catch a glimpse of him. The White House shook with their shouts. Glassware splintered, furniture was overturned, women fainted.

Jackson was a thin old man despite his toughness, and soon he was in danger. Fortunately, friends formed a cordon and managed to extricate him through a rear door. The new president spent his first night in office at Gadsby's Hotel.

Jackson's inauguration, and especially this celebration in the White House, symbolized the triumph of "democracy," the achievement of place and station by "the common man." Having been taught by Jefferson that all men are created equal, the Americans of Jackson's day (conveniently ignoring black males, to say nothing of women, regardless of color) found it easy to believe that every person was as competent and as politically important as his neighbor.

The difference between **Jacksonian democracy** and the Jefferson variety was more one of attitude than of practice. Jefferson had believed that ordinary citizens could be educated to determine what was right. Jackson insisted that they knew what was right by instinct. Jefferson's pell-mell encouraged the average citizen to hold up his head; by the time of Jackson, the "common man" gloried in ordinariness and made mediocrity a virtue. The slightest hint of distinctiveness or servility became suspect. While most middle-class families could still hire people to do their cooking and housework, the word *servant* itself fell out of fashion, replaced by the egalitarian *help*.

The Founders had not foreseen all the implications of political democracy for a society like the one that existed in the United States. They believed that the ordinary man should have political power in order to protect himself against the superior man, but they assumed that the latter would always lead. The people would naturally choose the best men to manage public affairs. In Washington's day and even in Jefferson's this was generally the case, but the inexorable logic of democracy gradually produced a change. The new western states, unfettered by systems created in a less democratic age, drew up constitutions that eliminated property qualifications for voting and holding office. Many more public offices were made elective rather than appointive. The eastern states revised their own frames of government to accomplish the same purposes.

Even the presidency, designed to be removed from direct public control by the Electoral College, felt the impact of the new thinking. By Jackson's time only two states, Delaware and South Carolina, still provided for the choice of presidential electors by the legislature; in all others they were selected by popular vote. The system of permitting the congressional caucus to name the candidates for the presidency came to an end before 1828. Jackson and Adams were put forward by state legislatures, and soon thereafter the still more democratic system of nomination by national party conventions was adopted.

Certain social changes reflected a new way of looking at political affairs. The final disestablishment of churches further reveals the dislike of special privilege. The beginnings of the free-school movement, the earliest glimmerings of interest in adult education, and the slow spread of secondary education all bespeak a concern for improving the knowledge and judgment of the ordinary citizen. The rapid increase in the number of newspapers, their declining prices, and their ever-greater concentration on political affairs indicate an effort to bring political news to the common man's attention.

All these changes emphasized the idea that every citizen was equally important and the conviction that all should participate in government. Officeholders began to stress the fact that they were *representatives* as well as leaders and to appeal more openly and much more intensively for votes. The public responded. At each succeeding presidential election, more people went to the polls. Eight times as many people voted in 1840 as in 1824.

As voting became more important, so did competition among candidates, and this led to changes in the role and structure of political parties. Running campaigns and getting out the vote required money, people, and organized effort. Party managers, often holders of relatively minor offices, held rallies, staged parades, dreamed up catchy slogans, and printed broadsides, party newspapers, and ballots containing the names of the party's nominees for distribution to their supporters. Parties became powerful institutions that instilled loyalty among adherents.

1828: The New Party System in Embryo

The new system could scarcely have been imagined in 1825 while John Quincy Adams ruled over the White House; Adams was not well equipped either to lead King Mob or to hold it in check. Indeed, it was the battle to succeed Adams that caused the system to develop. The campaign began almost on the day of his selection by the House of Representatives. Jackson felt that he, the man who had received the largest number of votes, had been cheated of the presidency in 1824 by "the corrupt bargain" that he believed Adams had made with Henry Clay, and he sought vindication.

Relying heavily on his military reputation and on Adams's talent for making enemies, Jackson avoided taking a stand on issues where his views might displease one or another faction. The political situation thus became chaotic, one side unable to marshal support for its policies, the other unwilling to adopt policies for fear of losing support.

Photo Credit: *Rachel Donelson* by Ralph Earl, 1826. The Hermitage.

Rachel Jackson, wife of Andrew Jackson. At seventeen she had married Lewis Robards, but the marriage failed and after two years she returned to her family in Natchez, Mississippi. Robards sued for divorce in Virginia. Several months later, Rachel married Jackson in Mississippi, unaware that Robards would not finalize the divorce until a year later. In defending Rachel's honor from a charge of bigamy, Jackson killed a man in a duel. During the 1824 and 1828 presidential campaigns, critics denounced their marriage as immoral. Rachel died in December 1828, several weeks before her husband was inaugurated.

The campaign was disgraced by character assassination and lies of the worst sort. Administration supporters denounced Jackson as a bloodthirsty military tyrant, a drunkard, and a gambler. His wife Rachel, ailing and shy, was dragged into the campaign by an Adams pamphleteer who branded her a "convicted adulteress."

Furious, the Jacksonians (now calling themselves Democrats) replied in kind. Discovering that Adams had purchased a chess set and a billiard table for the White House, they accused him of squandering public money on gambling devices. They translated his long and distinguished public service into the statistic that he had received over the years a sum equal to $16 for every day of his life in government pay. The great questions of the day were largely ignored.

All this was inexcusable, and both sides must share the blame. But as the politicians noticed when the votes were counted, their efforts had certainly brought out the electorate. *Each* candidate received far more votes than all four candidates had received in the preceding presidential election.

The Jacksonian Appeal

Although Jackson's supporters liked to cast him as the political heir of Jefferson, he was in many ways like the conservative Washington: a soldier first, an inveterate speculator in western lands, the owner of a fine plantation and of many slaves, a man with few intellectual interests, and only sketchily educated.

Nor was Jackson quite the rough-hewn frontier character he sometimes seemed. True, he could not spell (again, like Washington), he possessed the unsavory habits of the tobacco chewer, and he had a violent temper. But his manners and lifestyle were those of a southern planter. "I have always felt that he was a perfect savage," Grace Fletcher Webster, wife of Senator Daniel Webster, explained. "But," she added, "his manners are very mild and gentlemanly." Jackson's judgment was intuitive yet usually

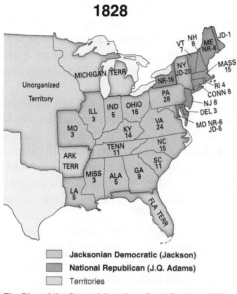

1828

MICHIGAN TERR

Unorganized
Territory

VT
7

NH
8

ME
NR-8

JD-1

NY
JD-20

NR-16

MASS
15

RI 4
CONN 8

PA
28

NJ 8

DEL 3

MD NR-6
JD-5

ILL
3

IND
5

OHIO
16

MO
3

KY
14

VA
24

ARK
TERR

TENN
11

NC
15

MISS
3

ALA
5

GA
9

SC
11

LA
5

FLA TERR

☐ Jacksonian Democratic (Jackson)
☐ National Republican (J.Q. Adams)
☐ Territories

The Rise of the Second American Party System, 1828
Jackson's enormous turnout in 1828 heralded a new era in
mass political participation. In the past, Federalists tended
to take New England, and Democrats, the South. But in
1832 Jackson shattered his fragmented opposition.

Andrew Jackson as president.

Photo Credit: © Bettmann/CORBIS All Rights Reserved.

sound; his frequent rages were often feigned, designed to accomplish some carefully thought-out purpose. Once, after scattering a delegation of protesters with an exhibition of wrath, he turned to an observer and said impishly, "They thought I was mad."

Whatever his personal convictions, Jackson stood as the symbol for a new, democratically oriented generation. That he was both a great hero and in many ways a most extraordinary person helps explain his mass appeal. He had defeated a mighty British army and killed many Indians, but he acted on hunches and not always consistently, put loyalty to old comrades above efficiency when making appointments, and distrusted "aristocrats" and all special privilege. Perhaps he was rich, perhaps conservative, but he was a man of the people, born in a frontier cabin, and familiar with the problems of the average citizen.

For these reasons Jackson drew support from every section and every social class: western farmers and southern planters, urban workers and bankers, and merchants. In this sense he was profoundly democratic. He believed in equality of opportunity, distrusted entrenched status of every sort, and rejected no free American because of humble origins or inadequate education.

The Spoils System

Jackson took office with the firm intention of punishing the "vile wretches" who had attacked him so viciously during the campaign. (Rachel Jackson died shortly after the election, and her devoted husband was convinced that the indignities heaped on her by

Adams partisans had hastened her decline.) The new concept of political office as a reward for victory seemed to justify a housecleaning in Washington. Henry Clay captured the fears of anti-Jackson government workers. "Among the official corps here there is the greatest solicitude and apprehension," he said. "The members of it feel something like the inhabitants of Cairo when the plague breaks out; no one knows who is next to encounter the stroke of death."

Eager for the "spoils," an army of politicians invaded Washington. Such invasions were customary, for the principle of filling offices with one's partisans was almost as old as the republic. However, the long lapse of time since the last real political shift, and the recent untypical example of John Quincy Adams, who rarely removed or appointed anyone for political reasons, made Jackson's policy appear revolutionary. His removals were not entirely unjustified, for many government workers had grown senile and others corrupt. Jackson was determined to root out the thieves. Even Adams admitted that some of those Jackson dismissed deserved their fate.

Aside from going along with the **spoils system** and eliminating crooks and incompetents, Jackson advanced another reason for turning experienced government employees out of their jobs: the principle of rotation. "No man has any more intrinsic right to official station than another," he said. Those who hold government jobs for a long time "are apt to acquire a habit of looking with indifference upon the public interests and of tolerating conduct from which an unpracticed man would revolt." By "rotating" jobholders periodically, more citizens could participate in the tasks of government, and the danger of creating an entrenched bureaucracy would be eliminated. The problem was that the constant replacing of trained workers by novices was not likely to increase the efficiency of the government. Jackson's response to this argument was typical: "The duties of all public officers are . . . so plain and simple that men of intelligence may readily qualify themselves for their performance."

Contempt for expert knowledge and the belief that ordinary Americans can do anything they set their minds to became fundamental tenets of Jacksonian democracy. To apply them to present-day government would be to court disaster, but in the early nineteenth century it was not so preposterous, because the role that government played in American life was simple and nontechnical.

President of All the People

President Jackson was not cynical about the spoils system. As a strong man who intuitively sought to increase his authority, the idea of making government workers dependent on him made excellent sense. His opponents had pictured him as a simple soldier fronting for a rapacious band of politicians, but he soon proved he would exercise his authority directly. Except for Martin Van Buren, the secretary of state, his Cabinet was not distinguished, and he did not rely on it for advice. He turned instead to an informal "Kitchen Cabinet," which consisted of the influential Van Buren and a few close friends. But these men were advisers, not directors; Jackson was clearly master of his own administration.

More than any earlier president, he conceived of himself as the direct representative of all the people and therefore the embodiment of national power. From Washington to John Quincy Adams, his predecessors together had vetoed only nine bills, all on the ground that they believed the measures unconstitutional. Jackson vetoed a dozen, some simply because he thought the legislation inexpedient. Yet he had no ambition to expand the scope of federal authority at the expense of the states. Basically he was a Jeffersonian; he favored a "frugal," constitutionally limited national government. Furthermore, he was a poor administrator, given to penny-pinching and lacking in imagination. His strong prejudices and his contempt for expert advice, even in fields such as banking where his ignorance was almost total, did him no credit and the country considerable harm.

Sectional Tensions Revived

In office Jackson had to say something about western lands, the tariff, and other issues. He tried to steer a moderate course, urging a slight reduction of the tariff and "constitutional" internal improvements. He suggested that once the rapidly disappearing federal debt had been paid off, the surplus revenues of the government might be "distributed" among the states.

So complex were the interrelations of sectional disputes that even these cautious proposals caused conflict. If the federal government turned its expected surplus over to the states, it could not afford to reduce the price of public land without going into the red. This disturbed westerners, notably Senator Thomas Hart Benton of Missouri, and western concern suggested to southern opponents of the protective tariff an alliance of South and West. The Southerners argued that a tariff levied only to raise revenue would increase the cost of foreign imports, bring more money into the treasury, and thus make it possible to reduce the price of public land.

The question came up in the Senate in December 1829, when Senator Samuel A. Foot of Connecticut suggested restricting the sale of government land. Benton promptly denounced the proposal. On January 19, 1830, Senator Robert Y. Hayne of South Carolina, a spokesman for Vice President Calhoun, supported Benton vigorously, suggesting an alliance of South and West based on cheap land and low tariffs. Daniel Webster then rose to the defense of northeastern interests, cleverly goading Hayne by accusing South Carolina of advocating disunionist policies. Responding to this attack, the South Carolinian launched into an impassioned exposition of the states' rights doctrine.

Webster then took the floor again and for two days, before galleries packed with the elite of Washington society, cut Hayne's argument to shreds. The Constitution was a compact of the American people, not merely of the states, he insisted, the Union perpetual and indissoluble. Webster made the states' rights position appear close to treason; his "second reply to Hayne" effectively prevented the formation of a West–South alliance and made Webster a presidential candidate.

Jackson: "The Bank . . . I Will Kill It!"

In the fall of 1832 Jackson was reelected president, handily defeating Henry Clay. The main issue in this election, aside from Jackson's personal popularity, was the president's determination to destroy the Second Bank of the United States. In this **Bank war**, Jackson won a complete victory, yet the effects of his triumph were anything but beneficial to the country.

After *McCulloch v. Maryland* had presumably established its legality and the conservative Langdon Cheves had gotten it on a sound footing, the Bank of the United States had flourished. In 1823 Cheves was replaced as president by Nicholas Biddle, who managed it brilliantly. A talented Philadelphian, Biddle realized that his institution could act as a rudimentary central bank, regulating the availability of credit throughout the nation by

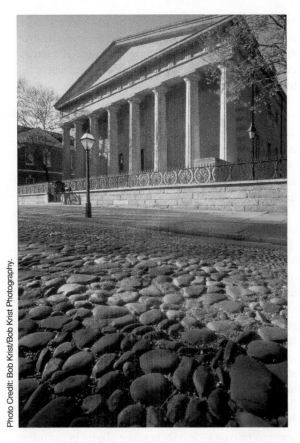

With its simple lines and perfect symmetry, the Second Bank of the United States was a symbol of Classical architecture. Jackson thought its internal workings were less simple and transparent.

Photo Credit: Bob Krist/Bob Krist Photography.

controlling the lending policies of the state banks. Small banks, possessing limited amounts of gold and silver, sometimes overextended themselves in making large amounts of bank notes available to borrowers in order to earn interest. All this paper money was legally convertible into hard cash on demand, but in the ordinary run of business people seldom bothered to convert their notes so long as they thought the issuing bank was sound.

Bank notes passed freely from hand to hand and from bank to bank in every section of the country. Eventually much of the paper money of the local banks came across the counter of one or another of the twenty-two branches of the Bank of the United States. By collecting these notes and presenting them for conversion into coin, Biddle could compel the local banks to maintain adequate reserves of gold and silver—in other words, make them hold their lending policies within bounds. "The Bank of the United States," he explained, "has succeeded in keeping in check many institutions which might otherwise have been tempted into extravagant and ruinous excesses."

Biddle's policies in the 1820s were good for the Bank of the United States (which earned substantial profits), for the state banks, and probably for the country. Pressures on local bankers to make loans were enormous. The nation had an insatiable need for capital, and the general mood of the people was optimistic. Everyone wanted to borrow, and everyone expected values to rise, as in general they did. But by making liberal loans to produce merchants, for example, rural bankers indirectly stimulated farmers to expand their output beyond current demand, which eventually led to a decline in prices and an agricultural depression. In every field of economic activity, reckless lending caused inflation and greatly exaggerated the ups and downs of the business cycle. (This lesson was hammered home to Americans during the financial meltdown of 2008, when lending for home mortgages spiraled out of control and the mortgage market crashed.)

Biddle's policies acted to stabilize the economy, and many interests, including a substantial percentage of state bankers, supported them. They also provoked a great deal of opposition. In part the opposition originated in pure ignorance: Distrust of paper money did not disappear, and people who disliked all paper saw the Bank as merely the largest (and thus the worst) of many bad institutions. At the other extreme, some bankers chafed under Biddle's restraints because by discouraging them from lending freely, he was limiting their profits.

Finally, some people objected to the Bank because it was a monopoly. Distrust of chartered corporations as agents of special privilege tended to focus on the Bank, which had a monopoly of public funds but was managed by a private citizen and controlled by a handful of rich men. Biddle's wealth and social position intensified this feeling. Like many brilliant people, he sometimes appeared arrogant. He was unused to criticism and disdainful of ignorant and stupid attacks, failing to see that they were sometimes the most dangerous.

Jackson's Bank Veto

This formidable opposition to the Bank was diffuse and unorganized until Andrew Jackson brought it together. When he did, the Bank was quickly destroyed. Jackson can be included among the ignorant enemies of the institution, a hard-money man suspicious of all commercial banking. "I think it right to be perfectly frank with you," he told Biddle in 1829. "I do not dislike your Bank any more than all banks. But ever since I read the history of the South Sea Bubble I have been afraid of banks."

Jackson's attitude dismayed Biddle. It also mystified him, since the Bank was the country's best defense against a speculative mania like the eighteenth-century South Sea Bubble, in which hundreds of naive British investors had been fleeced. Bankers usually *opposed* government restraints on lending. Almost against his will, Biddle found himself gravitating toward Clay and the new National Republican party, offering advantageous loans and retainers to politicians and newspaper editors in order to build up a following. Thereafter, events moved inevitably toward a showdown, for the president's combative instincts were easily aroused. "The Bank," he told Van Buren, "is trying to kill me, *but I will kill it!*"

Henry Clay, Daniel Webster, and other prominent National Republicans hoped to use the Bank controversy against Jackson. They reasoned that the institution was so important to the country that Jackson's opposition to it would undermine his popularity. They therefore urged Biddle to ask Congress to renew the Bank's charter. The charter would not expire until 1836, but by pressing the issue

> ◆●◆ Read the Document
> Jackson, *Veto of the Bank Bill* at **myhistorylab.com**

before the 1832 presidential election, they could force Jackson either to approve the recharter bill or to veto it (which would give candidate Clay a lively issue in the campaign). The banker yielded to this strategy and a recharter bill passed Congress early in July 1832. Jackson promptly vetoed it.

Jackson's message explaining why he had rejected the bill was immensely popular, but it adds nothing to his reputation as a statesman. Being a good Jeffersonian—and no friend of John Marshall—he insisted that the Bank was unconstitutional. (*McCulloch v. Maryland* he brushed aside, saying that as president he had sworn to uphold the Constitution as *he* understood it.) The Bank was inexpedient, he argued. A dangerous private monopoly that allowed a handful of rich men to accumulate "many millions" of dollars, the Bank was making "the rich richer and the potent more powerful."

Furthermore, many of its stockholders were foreigners: "If we must have a bank . . . it should be *purely American*."[1]

Buttressed by his election triumph, Jackson acted swiftly. He ordered the withdrawal of government funds from the Bank, but his own secretary of the treasury thought it unwise and refused to do so. Jackson replaced him with Attorney General Roger B. Taney, who had been advising him closely on Bank affairs. Taney carried out the order by depositing new federal receipts in seven state banks in eastern cities while continuing to meet government expenses with drafts on the Bank of the United States.

Set on winning the Bank war, Jackson lost sight of his fear of unsound paper money. Taney, however, knew exactly what he was doing. One of the state banks receiving federal funds was the Union Bank of Baltimore. Taney owned stock in this institution, and its president was his close friend. Little wonder that Jackson's enemies were soon calling the favored state banks "pet" banks.

When Taney began to remove the deposits, the government had $9,868,000 to its credit in the Bank of the United States; within three months the figure fell to about $4 million. Faced with the withdrawal of so much cash, Biddle had to contract his operations. He decided to exaggerate the contraction, pressing the state banks hard by presenting all their notes and checks that came across his counter for conversion into specie and drastically limiting his own bank's business loans. He hoped that the resulting shortage of credit would be blamed on Jackson and that it would force the president to return the deposits.

For a time the strategy appeared to be working. Paper money became scarce, specie almost unobtainable. A serious panic threatened. New York banks were soon refusing to make any loans at all. "Nobody buys; nobody can sell," a French visitor to the city observed. Petitions poured in on Congress. Worried and indignant delegations of businessmen began trooping to Washington seeking "relief." Clay, Webster, and John C. Calhoun thundered against Jackson in the Senate.

The president would not budge. "I am fixed in my course as firm as the Rocky Mountain," he wrote Vice President Van Buren. No "frail mortals" who worshiped "the golden calf" could change his mind. To others he swore he would sooner cut off his right arm and "undergo the torture of ten Spanish inquisitions" than restore the deposits. When delegations came to him, he roared, "Go to Nicholas Biddle . . . . Biddle has all the money!" And in the end—because he was right—business leaders began to take the old general's advice. Pressure on Biddle mounted swiftly, and in July 1834 he suddenly reversed his policy and began to lend money freely. The artificial crisis ended.

Jackson versus Calhoun

The Webster-Hayne debate had revived discussion of Calhoun's argument about nullification. Although southern-born, Jackson had devoted too much of his life to fighting for the entire United States to countenance disunion. Therefore, in April 1830,

---

[1]The country needed all the foreign capital it could attract. Foreigners owned only $8 million of the $35 million stock, and in any case they could not vote their shares.

when the states' rights faction invited him to a dinner to celebrate the anniversary of Jefferson's birth, he came prepared. The evening reverberated with speeches and toasts of a states' rights tenor, but when the president was called on to volunteer a toast, he raised his glass, fixed his eyes on John C. Calhoun, and said, "Our *Federal* Union: It must be preserved!" Calhoun took up the challenge at once. "The Union," he retorted, "next to our liberty, most dear!"

It is difficult to measure the importance of the animosity between Jackson and Calhoun in the crisis to which this clash was a prelude. Calhoun wanted very much to be president. He had failed to inherit the office from John Quincy Adams and had accepted the vice presidency again under Jackson in the hope of succeeding him at the end of one term, if not sooner, for Jackson's health was known to be frail. Yet Old Hickory showed no sign of passing on or retiring. Jackson also seemed to place special confidence in the shrewd Van Buren, who, as secretary of state, also had claim to the succession.

A silly social fracas in which Calhoun's wife appeared to take the lead in the systematic snubbing of Peggy Eaton, wife of the secretary of war, had estranged Jackson and Calhoun. (Peggy was supposed to have had an affair with Eaton while she was still married to another man, and Jackson, undoubtedly sympathetic because of the attacks he and Rachel had endured, stoutly defended her good name.) Then, shortly after the Jefferson Day dinner, Jackson discovered that in 1818, when he had invaded Florida, Calhoun, then secretary of war, had recommended to President Monroe that Jackson be summoned before a court of inquiry and charged with disobeying orders. Since Calhoun had repeatedly led Jackson to believe that he had supported him at the time, the revelation convinced the president that Calhoun was not a man of honor.

The personal difficulties are worth stressing because Jackson and Calhoun were not far apart ideologically except on the ultimate issue of the right of a state to overrule federal authority. Jackson was a strong president, but he did not believe that the area of national power was large or that it should be expanded. His interests in government economy, in the distribution of federal surpluses to the states, and in interpreting the powers of Congress narrowly were all similar to Calhoun's. Like most westerners, he favored internal improvements, but he preferred that local projects be left to the states.

Indian Removals

The president also took a states' rights position in the controversy that arose between the Cherokee Indians and Georgia. The Cherokee inhabited a region coveted by whites because it was suitable for growing cotton. Since most Indians preferred to maintain their tribal ways, Jackson pursued a policy of removing them from the path of white settlement. This policy seems heartless to modern critics, but since few Indians were willing to adopt the white way of life, most contemporary whites considered removal the only humane solution if the nation was to continue to expand. Jackson insisted that the Indians receive fair prices for their lands and that the government bear the expense of resettling them. He believed that moving them beyond the Mississippi would protect them from the "degradation and destruction to which they were rapidly hastening . . . in the States."

Many tribes resigned themselves to removal without argument. Between 1831 and 1833, some 15,000 Choctaw migrated from their lands in Mississippi to the region west of the Arkansas Territory.

In *Democracy in America*, the French writer Alexis de Tocqueville described "the frightful sufferings that attend these forced migrations," and he added sadly that the migrants "have no longer a country, and soon will not be a people." He vividly described a group of Choctaw crossing the Mississippi River at Memphis in the dead of winter:

> The cold was unusually severe; the snow had frozen hard upon the ground, and the river was drifting huge masses of ice. The Indians had their families with them, and they brought in their train the wounded and the sick, with children newly born and old men upon the verge of death. They possessed neither tents nor wagons, but only their arms and some provisions. I saw them embark to pass the mighty river, and never will that solemn spectacle fade from my remembrance. No cry, no sob, was heard among the assembled crowd; all were silent.

A few tribes, such as Black Hawk's Sac and Fox in Illinois and Osceola's Seminole in Florida, resisted removal and were subdued by troops. One Indian nation, the Cherokee, sought to hold on to their lands by adjusting to white ways. They took up farming and cattle raising, developed a written language, drafted a constitution, and tried to establish a state within a state in northwestern Georgia. Several treaties with the United States seemed to establish the legality of their government. But Georgia would not recognize the Cherokee Nation. It passed a law in 1828 declaring all Cherokee laws void and the region part of Georgia.

The Indians challenged this law in the Supreme Court. In *Cherokee Nation v. Georgia* (1831), Chief Justice John Marshall had ruled that the Cherokee were "not a foreign state, in the sense of the Constitution" and therefore could not sue in a U.S. court. However, in *Worcester v. Georgia* (1832), a case involving two missionaries to the Cherokee who had not procured licenses required by Georgia law, he ruled that the state could not control the Cherokee or their territory. Later, when a Cherokee named Corn Tassel, convicted in a Georgia court of the murder of another Indian, appealed on the ground that the crime had taken place in Cherokee territory, Marshall agreed and declared the Georgia action unconstitutional.

Photo Credit: George Catlin, *Osceola, the Black Drink, a warrior of Great Distinction*, 1838. Smithsonian American Art Museum/Art Resource, NY.

Jackson backed Georgia's position. No independent nation could exist within the United States, he insisted. Georgia thereupon hanged Corn Tassel. In 1838, after Jackson had left the White House, the United States forced 15,000 Cherokee to leave

Osceola had led the Seminole Indians' resistance to their forced removal from Florida to lands west of the Mississippi. He was seized during a truce parlay and imprisoned at Fort Moultrie, South Carolina. George Catlin, incensed by this treatment, became friends with Osceola and then painted this picture.

Osceola's Rebellion Osceola, a young warrior, refused to accept tribal elders' decision to cede Seminole land in Florida and move to Oklahoma. In 1835 he murdered the tribal leader who had accepted removal and spearheaded Seminole resistance. Seminole warriors, augmented by African Americans who had escaped from slavery, proved to be astute tacticians in guerrilla warfare. During the next seven years, the federal government spent $20 million, an immense sum, and lost 1,500 soldiers in the war to force the remaining Seminole from Florida. When Osceola hoisted a white flag to negotiate with federal officers, they seized him and put him in prison. He died shortly after George Catlin completed his portrait. Because of his courageous resistance and the treacherous manner of his capture, Osceola became famous after his death.

Georgia for Oklahoma. At least 4,000 of them died on the way; the route has been aptly named the **Trail of Tears**.

Jackson's willingness to allow Georgia to ignore decisions of the Supreme Court persuaded extreme southern states' righters that he would not oppose the doctrine of nullification should it be formally applied to a law of Congress. They deceived themselves egregiously. Jackson did not challenge Georgia because he approved of the state's position. He spoke of "the poor deluded . . . Cherokees" and called William Wirt, the distinguished lawyer who defended

See the Map

Native American Removal at myhistorylab.com

their cause, a "truly wicked" man. Jackson was not one to worry about being inconsistent. When South Carolina revived the talk of nullification in 1832, he acted in quite a different manner.

The Nullification Crisis

The proposed alliance of South and West to reduce the tariff and the price of land had not materialized, partly because Webster had discredited the South in the eyes of western patriots and partly because the planters of South Carolina and Georgia, fearing the competition of fertile new cotton lands in Alabama and Mississippi, opposed the rapid exploitation of the West almost as vociferously as northern manufacturers did. When a new tariff law was passed in 1832, it lowered duties much less than the Southerners desired. At once talk of nullifying it began to be heard in South Carolina.

In addition to the economic woes of the up-country cotton planters, the great planter-aristocrats of the rice-growing Tidewater, though relatively prosperous, were troubled by northern criticisms of slavery. In the rice region, blacks outnumbered whites two to one; it was the densest concentration of blacks in the United States. Usually controlled by overseers of the worst sort, the slaves seemed to their masters like savage beasts straining to rise up against their oppressors. In 1822 the exposure in Charleston of a planned revolt organized by Denmark Vesey, who had bought his freedom with money won in a lottery, had alarmed many whites. News of a far more serious uprising in Virginia led by the slave Nat Turner in 1831, just as the tariff controversy was coming to a head, added to popular concern. Radical South Carolinians saw protective tariffs and agitation against slavery as the two sides of one coin; against both aspects of what appeared to them the tyranny of the majority, nullification seemed the logical defense. Yield on the tariff, editor Henry L. Pinckney of the influential *Charleston Mercury* warned, and "abolition will become the order of the day."

Endless discussions of Calhoun's doctrine after the publication of his *Exposition and Protest* in 1828 had produced much interesting theorizing without clarifying the issue. Plausible at first glance, it was based on false assumptions: that the Constitution was subject to definitive interpretation; that one party could be permitted to interpret a compact unilaterally without destroying it; that a minority of the nation could reassume its sovereign independence but that a minority of a state could not.

President Jackson was in this respect Calhoun's exact opposite. The South Carolinian's mental gymnastics he brushed aside; intuitively he realized the central reality: If a state could nullify a law of Congress, the Union could not exist. "Tell . . . the Nullifiers from me that they can talk and write resolutions and print threats to their hearts'

Photo Credit: Samuel Barnard, *View along the East Battery, Charleston*, Yale University Art Gallery, Mabel Brady Garvan Collection.

View along the East Battery, Charleston by Samuel Bernard (1831). Many whites feared a slave uprising in South Carolina where African Americans outnumbered whites.

content," he warned a South Carolina representative when Congress adjourned in July 1832. "But if one drop of blood be shed there in defiance of the laws of the United States, I will hang the first man of them I can get my hands on to the first tree I can find."

The warning was not taken seriously in South Carolina. In October the state legislature provided for the election of a special convention, which, when it met, contained a solid majority of nullifiers. On November 24, 1832, the convention passed an ordinance of **nullification** prohibiting the collection of tariff duties in the state after February 1, 1833. The legislature then authorized the raising of an army and appropriated money to supply it with weapons.

Read the Document

South Carolina's Ordinance of Nullification at **myhistorylab.com**

Jackson quickly began military preparations of his own, telling friends that he would have 50,000 men ready to move in a little over a month. He also made a statesmanlike effort to end the crisis peaceably. First he suggested to Congress that it lower the tariff further. On December 10 he delivered a "Proclamation to the People of South Carolina." Nullification could only lead to the destruction of the Union: "The laws of the United States must be executed. I have no discretionary power on the subject. . . . Those who told you that you might peaceably prevent their execution deceived you." Old Hickory added sternly, "Disunion by armed force is *treason*. Are you really ready to incur its guilt?" If South Carolina did not back down, the president's threat to use force would mean civil war and possibly the destruction of the Union he claimed to be defending.

Calhoun sought desperately to control the crisis. By prearrangement with Senator Hayne, he resigned as vice president and was appointed to replace Hayne in the Senate, where he led the search for a peaceful solution. Having been defeated in his campaign for the presidency, Clay was a willing ally. In addition, many who admired Jackson nonetheless, as Van Buren later wrote, "distrusted his prudence," fearing that he would "commit some rash act." They believed in dealing with the controversy by discussion and compromise.

As a result, administration leaders introduced both a new tariff bill and a Force Bill granting the president additional authority to execute the revenue laws. Jackson was perfectly willing to see the tariff reduced but insisted that he was determined to enforce the law. As the February 1 deadline approached, he claimed that he could raise 200,000 men if needed to suppress resistance. "Union men, fear not," he said. "*The Union will be preserved.*"

Jackson's determination sobered the South Carolina radicals. Their appeal for the support of other southern states fell on deaf ears: All rejected the idea of nullification. The unionist minority in South Carolina added to the radicals' difficulties by threatening civil war if federal authority were defied.

Ten days before the deadline, South Carolina postponed nullification pending the outcome of the tariff debate. Then, in March 1833, Calhoun and Clay pushed a compromise tariff through Congress. As part of the agreement Congress also passed the Force Bill, mostly as a face-saving device for the president.

The compromise reflected the willingness of the North and West to make concessions in the interest of national harmony. And so the Union weathered the storm. Having stepped to the brink of civil war, the nation had drawn hastily back. The South Carolina legislature professed to be satisfied with the new tariff (in fact it made few immediate reductions, providing for a gradual lowering of rates over a ten-year period) and repealed the Nullification Ordinance. But the radical South Carolina planters were becoming convinced that only secession would protect slavery. The nullification fiasco had proved that they could not succeed without the support of other slave states. Thereafter they devoted themselves ceaselessly to obtaining it.

Boom and Bust

During 1833 and 1834 Secretary of the Treasury Taney insisted that the pet banks maintain large reserves. But other state banks began to offer credit on easy terms, aided by a large increase in their reserves of gold and silver resulting from causes unconnected with the policies of either the government or Biddle's Bank. A decline in the Chinese demand for Mexican silver led to increased exports of the metal to the United States, and the rise of American interest rates attracted English capital into the country. Heavy English purchases of American cotton at high prices also increased the flow of specie into American banks. These developments caused bank notes in circulation to jump from $82 million in January 1835 to $120 million in December 1836. Bank deposits rose even more rapidly.

Much of the new money flowed into speculation in land; a mania to invest in property swept the country. The increased volume of currency caused prices to soar 15 percent in six months, buoying investors' spirits and making them ever more optimistic about the future. By the summer of 1835 one observer estimated that in New York City, which had about 250,000 residents, enough house lots had been laid out and sold to support a population of 2 million. Chicago at this time had only 2,000 to 3,000 inhabitants, yet most of the land for twenty-five miles around had been sold and resold in small lots by speculators anticipating the growth of the area. Throughout the West farmers borrowed money from local banks by mortgaging their land, used the money to buy more land from the government, and then borrowed still more money from the banks on the strength of their new deeds.

So long as prices rose, the process could be repeated endlessly. In 1832, while the Bank of the United States still regulated the money supply, federal income from the sale of land was $2.6 million; in 1834 it was $4.9 million; and in 1835, $14.8 million. In 1836 it rose to $24.9 million, and the government found itself totally free of debt and with a surplus of $20 million!

Finally Jackson became alarmed by the speculative mania. In the summer of 1836 he issued the **Specie Circular,** which provided that purchasers must henceforth pay for public land in gold or silver. At once the rush to buy land came to a halt. As demand slackened, prices sagged. Speculators, unable to dispose of lands mortgaged to the banks, had to abandon them to the banks, but the banks could not realize enough on the foreclosed property to recover their loans. Suddenly the public mood changed. Commodity prices tumbled 30 percent between February and May. Hordes of depositors sought to withdraw their money in the form of specie, and soon the banks exhausted their supplies. Panic swept the country in the spring of 1837 as every bank in the nation was forced to suspend specie payments. The boom was over.

Major swings in the business cycle can never be attributed to the actions of a single person, however powerful, but there is no doubt that Jackson's war against the Bank exaggerated the swings of the economic pendulum, not so much by its direct effects as by the impact of the president's ill-considered policies on popular thinking. His Specie

Circular did not prevent speculators from buying land—at most it caused purchasers to pay a premium for gold or silver. But it convinced potential buyers that the boom was going to end and led them to make decisions that in fact ended it. Old Hickory's combination of impetuousness, combativeness, arrogance, and ignorance rendered the nation he loved so dearly a serious disservice.

The Jacksonians

Jackson's personality had a large impact on the shape and tone of American politics and thus with the development of the **second party system**. When he came to office, nearly everyone professed to be a follower of Jefferson. By 1836 being a Jeffersonian no longer meant much; what mattered was how one felt about Andrew Jackson. He had ridden to power at the head of a diverse political army, but he left behind him an organization with a fairly cohesive, if not necessarily consistent, body of ideas. This Democratic party contained rich citizens and poor, easterners and westerners, abolitionists as well as slaveholders. It was not yet a close-knit national organization, but the Jacksonians agreed on certain underlying principles. These included suspicion of special privilege and large business corporations, both typified by the Bank of the United States; freedom of economic opportunity, unfettered by private or governmental restrictions; absolute political freedom, at least for white males; and the conviction that any ordinary man is capable of performing the duties of most public offices.

Jackson's ability to reconcile his belief in the supremacy of the Union with his conviction that national authority should be held within narrow limits tended to make the Democrats the party of those who believed that the powers of the states should not be diminished. Tocqueville caught this aspect of Jackson's philosophy perfectly: "Far from wishing to extend Federal power," he wrote, "the president belongs to the party that wishes to limit that power."

Although the radical Locofoco[2] wing of the party championed the idea, nearly all Jacksonians, like their leader, favored giving the small man his chance—by supporting public education, for example, and by refusing to place much weight on a person's origin, dress, or manners. "One individual is as good as another" (for accuracy we must insert the adjective *white*) was their axiom. This attitude helps explain why immigrants, Catholics, and other minority groups usually voted Democratic. However, the Jacksonians showed no tendency either to penalize the wealthy or to intervene in economic affairs to aid the underprivileged. The motto "That government is best which governs least" graced the masthead of the chief Jacksonian newspaper, the *Washington Globe*, throughout the era.

Rise of the Whigs

The opposition to Jackson was far less cohesive. Henry Clay's National Republican party provided a nucleus, but Clay never dominated that party as Jackson dominated the Democrats. Its orientation was basically anti-Jackson. It was as though the

---

[2]A locofoco was a type of friction match. The name was first applied in politics when a group of New York Jacksonians used these matches to light candles when a conservative faction tried to break up their meeting by turning off the gaslights.

American people were a great block of granite from which some sculptor had just fashioned a statue of Jackson, the chips scattered about the floor of the studio representing the opposition.

While Jackson was president, the impact of his personality delayed the formation of a true two-party system, but as soon as he surrendered power, the opposition, taking heart, began to coalesce. Many Democrats could not accept the odd logic of Jacksonian finance. As early as 1834 they (together with the Clay element, the extreme states' righters who followed Calhoun, and other dissident groups) were calling themselves **Whigs**. The name harkened back to the Revolution. It implied patriotic distaste for too-powerful executives, expressed specifically as resistance to the tyranny of "King Andrew."

This coalition possessed great resources of wealth and talent. Anyone who understood banking was almost obliged to become a Whig unless he was connected with one of Jackson's "pets." Those spiritual descendants of Hamilton who rejected the administration's refusal to approach economic problems from a broadly national perspective also joined in large numbers. Those who found the coarseness and "pushiness" of the Jacksonians offensive were another element in the new party. The anti-intellectual and antiscientific bias of the administration (Jackson rejected proposals for a national university, an observatory, and a scientific and literary institute) drove many ministers, lawyers, doctors, and other well-educated people into the Whig fold.

The philosopher Ralph Waldo Emerson was no doubt thinking of these types when he described the Whigs as "the enterprizing, intelligent, well-meaning & wealthy part of the people," but Whig arguments also appealed to ordinary voters who were predisposed to favor strong governments that would check the "excesses" of unrestricted individualism.

Table 1   Second American Party System: Democrats and Whigs, 1828–1850s

	Democrats	Whigs
Leaders	Andrew Jackson, Martin Van Buren, John Calhoun, James Polk	Henry Clay, Daniel Webster
Key issue	For: "the common man"	Against: "King Andrew" (Jackson)
Bank of United States	Oppose	Favor
Federal support for internal improvements (roads, canals)	Oppose	Favor
Removal of Indians	Favor	Oppose
Tariffs	Favor low	Favor high
States' rights vs. strong central government	Endorse states' rights	Endorse strong federal government

The Whigs were slow to develop effective party organization. They had too many generals and not enough troops. The issues that defined the Whigs varied from one state to another. For the most part, the sole unifying principle was opposition to Jackson. Furthermore, they stood in conflict with the major trend of the age: the glorification of the common man.

Lacking a dominant leader in 1836, the Whigs relied on "favorite sons," hoping to throw the presidential election into the House of Representatives. Daniel Webster ran in New England. For the West and South, Hugh Lawson White of Tennessee, a former friend who had broken with Jackson, was counted on to carry the fight. General William Henry Harrison was supposed to win in the Northwest and to draw support everywhere from those who liked to vote for military heroes. This sorry strategy failed; Jackson's handpicked candidate, Martin Van Buren, won a majority of both the popular and the electoral votes.

Martin Van Buren: Jacksonianism without Jackson

Van Buren's brilliance as a political manipulator—the Red Fox, the Little Magician— has tended to obscure his statesmanlike qualities and his engaging personality. He made a powerful argument, for example, that political parties were a force for unity, not for partisan bickering. In addition, high office sobered him, and improved his judgment. He fought the Bank of the United States as a monopoly, but he also opposed irresponsible state banks. New York's Safety Fund System (requiring all banks to contribute to a fund) supervised by the state (to be used to redeem the notes of any member bank that failed) was established largely through his efforts. Van Buren believed in public construction of internal improvements, but he favored state rather than national programs, and he urged a rational approach: Each project must stand on its own as a useful and profitable public utility.

Van Buren had outmaneuvered Calhoun easily in the struggle to succeed Jackson, winning the old hero's confidence and serving him well. In 1832 he was elected vice president and thereafter was conceded to be the "heir apparent." In 1835 the Democratic National Convention unanimously nominated him for president.

((•—| **Hear** the **Audio**

Van Buren at
myhistorylab.com

Van Buren took office just as the Panic of 1837 struck the country. Its effects were frightening but short-lived. When the banks stopped converting paper money into gold and silver, they outraged conservatives but in effect eased the pressure on the money market: Interest rates declined and business loans again became relatively easy to obtain. In 1836, at the height of the boom in land sales, Congress had voted to "distribute" the new treasury surplus to the states, and this flow of money, which the states promptly spent, also stimulated the revival. Late in 1838 the banks resumed specie payments.

But in 1839 a bumper crop caused a sharp decline in the price of cotton. Then a number of state governments that had overextended themselves in road- and canal-building projects were forced to default on their debts. This discouraged investors, particularly foreigners. A general economic depression ensued that lasted until 1843.

Van Buren was not responsible for the panic or the depression, but his manner of dealing with economic issues was scarcely helpful. He saw his role as being concerned only with problems plaguing the government, ignoring the economy as a whole.

American Lives

Davy Crockett, the myth, is known better than the man, who was born David Crockett in 1786 in a cabin in hardscrabble east Tennessee. John Crockett, his father, borrowed money to buy cheap frontier land and seldom repaid his creditors. When a passing Dutchman said he needed help to drive his cattle to market in Virginia, John proposed he take on David as a "bound boy" to help out. David was twelve.

After delivering the cattle to Virginia, the driver declared that David's term of service was not over. The boy pretended to accept the arrangement, but after several weeks he sneaked away in a snowstorm; two months later he was back home in Tennessee.

The next fall his father enrolled David at a small country school. But after beating up another boy, he played hooky, fearing the wrath of the schoolmaster. When his father learned of his son's truancy, he came after the boy with a hickory stick. David hightailed it into the woods.

He was gone for over two years, wandering through Tennessee, North Carolina, Virginia, and Maryland. He moved from town to town "to see what sort of place it was, and what sort of folks lived there." He mostly did odd jobs on farms for twenty-five cents a day. When he showed up back home two years later, his father, near bankruptcy, bartered David's labor to settle the debts with various creditors.

Soon young Crockett's thoughts turned to girls, few of whom had much interest in such an uncouth boy. Crockett could not even write his name. So he broke free from his father and made his own deal with a local schoolteacher, bartering his labor for board and instruction. The arrangement lasted for six months, Crockett's only formal schooling.

Shortly afterward he attended a "stomp down"—a community-wide harvest festival with games, music, and dancing—where he met Polly Finley, "a very pretty" Irish girl. Within a few months they were married. Polly's parents gave the couple two cows. Crockett rented a nearby farm.

But Crockett proved to be a poor farmer. Time and again he fell into debt, lost his farm, and moved to cheaper land farther west. "I found that I was better at increasing my family than my fortune," he observed: He and his wife had three children. In 1813 they took possession of land deep in Creek territory, near the Alabama border.

The timing was poor. By then, the War of 1812 had spread to the frontier, as Tecumseh, the Indian leader, incited Indian uprisings throughout the West. In Alabama, Creeks attacked and overran Fort Mims, killing hundreds of soldiers and settlers. In response Crockett enlisted in the Tennessee militia. He served under

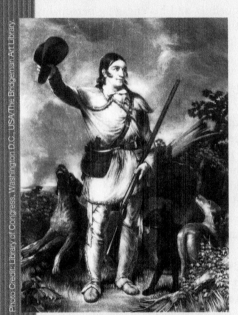

Photo Credit: Library of Congress, Washington D.C., USA/The Bridgeman Art Library.

This 1839 engraving of Davy Crockett was based on an earlier painting.

Andrew Jackson, participating in the slaughter of scores of Indians. "We shot them like dogs," Crockett noted.

After returning to Tennessee, he was elected magistrate for Lawrence County, a rough frontier district. Again, his farm failed; but the woodsy region was thick with game and Crockett was accurate with a long rifle. He killed deer, wolves, panthers, alligators and, in one winter alone, 105 bear. Soon tales of Crockett's hunting prowess spread throughout the region.

In 1821 Crockett was elected to the Tennessee legislature, the first of many victories. Once, accused of telling lies about an opponent, Crockett conceded that he had. But therein lay the difference, he explained, for he truthfully admitted his lies while his opponent did not. The crowd roared. In 1826 Crockett was elected to the House of Representatives.

Newspapermen delighted in the spectacle of the rough frontiersman in the nation's capital. They reported that at a White House dinner Crockett drank from the finger bowls and accused a waiter of trying to steal his food.

In Congress, Crockett's key issue—indeed, the only one he pursued with much passion—was cheap land for frontier farmers. "The rich require but little legislation," he said. "We should, at least occasionally, legislate for the poor." Such positions aligned him with the Jacksonian Democrats.

But in 1830 Crockett broke with Jackson over the removal of Indians from the South. Although Crockett readily acknowledged that he had fought to "kill up Indians," he thought it wrong that "the poor remnants of a once powerful people" should be driven from their homes. He voted against the Indian removal bill. In the next election Jackson, furious, campaigned against Crockett, who lost.

But by then his fame had spread. Newspaper editors seized on the story of the rough-hewn, bear-killing frontiersman. An 1831 play entitled *The Lion of the West,* based on Crockett, was performed in New York and London. Publishers found an eager audience for books about Crockett: some celebrated him, others lampooned him, but all exaggerated his exploits. The *Crockett Almanacs*—the first comic books—told of how Crockett rode his pet alligator up Niagara Falls, skinned Indians "the natural way, with his teeth," and indulged in insatiable and exotic sexual appetites. Tens of thousands were sold.

After seeing others make money off his celebrity, Crockett published several books of his own. In 1833 he was reelected to Congress. There was talk of his running for president on a Whig ticket, allowing that party to steal the "common man" claims of the Jacksonians. In 1835, however, Crockett was defeated for reelection to Congress by several hundred votes. Thereafter, always on the lookout for cheaper land, he told the voters of Tennessee, "you may all go to hell and I will go to Texas."

Several months later, toting his long rifle, Crockett rode into the Alamo in Texas, then a part of Mexico. Thirteen days later history caught up with the legend of Davy Crockett—and perhaps surpassed it.

Questions for Discussion
- Davy Crockett was arguably the first American to become famous for his fame. What explains the appeal of Crockett to Americans in the 1830s?
- Davy Crockett symbolized the frontier as violent, savage, and uncouth. How did his life sustain that image? And how did it undermine it?

"The less government interferes with private pursuits the better for the general prosperity," he pontificated. As Daniel Webster scornfully pointed out, Van Buren was following a policy of "leaving the people to shift for themselves," one that many Whigs rejected.

Van Buren's chief goal was finding a substitute for the state banks as a place to keep federal funds. He soon settled on the idea of "divorcing" the government from all banking activities. His independent treasury bill called for the construction of government-owned vaults where federal revenues could be stored until needed. To ensure absolute safety, all payments to the government were to be made in hard cash. After a battle that lasted until the summer of 1840, the Independent Treasury Act passed both the House and the Senate.

Opposition to the Independent Treasury Act had been bitter, and not all of it was partisan. Bankers and businessmen objected to the government's withholding so much specie from the banks because they needed all the hard money they could get to support loans that were the lifeblood of economic growth. It seemed irresponsible for the federal government to turn its back on the banks, which so obviously performed a semipublic function. These criticisms made good sense, but through a lucky combination of circumstances, the system worked reasonably well for many years.

By creating suspicion in the public mind, officially stated distrust of banks acted as a damper on their tendency to overexpand. No acute shortage of specie developed because heavy agricultural exports and the investment of much European capital in American railroads beginning in the mid-1840s brought in large amounts of new gold and silver. After 1849 the discovery of gold in California added another important source of specie. The supply of money and bank credit kept pace roughly with the growth of the economy, but through no fault of the government. "Wildcat" banks proliferated. Fraud and counterfeiting were common, and the operation of everyday business affairs was inconvenienced in countless ways. The disordered state of the currency remained a grave problem until corrected by Civil War banking legislation.

The Log Cabin Campaign

It was not his financial policy that led to Van Buren's defeat in 1840. The depression naturally hurt the Democrats, and the Whigs were far better organized than in 1836. The Whigs also adopted a different strategy. The Jacksonians had come to power on the coattails of a popular general whose views on public questions they concealed or ignored. They had maintained themselves by shouting the praises of the common man. Now the Whigs seized on these techniques and carried them to their logical—or illogical—conclusion. Not even bothering to draft a program, and passing over Clay and Webster, whose views were known and therefore controversial, they nominated General William Henry Harrison for president. To "balance" the ticket, the Whigs chose a former Democrat, John Tyler of Virginia, an ardent supporter of states' rights, as their vice presidential candidate.

The Democrats used the same methods as the Whigs and were equally well organized, but they had little heart for the fight. The best they could come up with was the fact that their vice presidential candidate, Richard Mentor Johnson, had killed Tecumseh, not merely defeated him. Van Buren tried to focus public attention on issues, but his voice could not be heard above the huzzahs of the Whigs.

A huge turnout (four-fifths of the eligible voters) carried Harrison to victory by a margin of almost 150,000. The electoral vote was 234 to 60.

The Whigs continued to repeat history by rushing to gather the spoils of victory. Washington was again flooded by office seekers, the political confusion was monumental. Harrison had no ambition to be an aggressive leader. He believed that Jackson had misused the veto and professed to put as much emphasis as had Washington on the principle of the separation of legislative and executive powers. This delighted the Whig leaders in Congress, who had had their fill of the "executive usurpation" of Jackson. Either Clay or Webster seemed destined to be the real ruler of the new administration, and soon the two were squabbling over their old general like sparrows over a crust.

At the height of their squabble, less than a month after his inauguration, Harrison fell gravely ill. Pneumonia developed, and on April 4 he died. John Tyler of Virginia, honest and conscientious but doctrinaire, became president of the United States. The political climate of the country was changed dramatically. Events began to march in a new direction.

Milestones

1828	Andrew Jackson is elected president	1831–1838	Chief Justice Marshall rules in Cherokees' favor in *Worcester v. Georgia*
1829	Crowds cause chaos at Jackson's White House inaugural reception		Jackson is reelected president
	Jackson relies on his "Kitchen Cabinet"	1833	Treasury Secretary Roger B. Taney orders Treasury funds removed from Bank of the United States
1830	Daniel Webster, in his "Second Reply to Hayne," calls Union perpetual and indissoluble		Calhoun and Clay push through Compromise Tariff
	Jackson vetoes the Maysville Road Bill	1836	Jackson issues Specie Circular to control speculation
1831	Nat Turner leads slave rebellion in Virginia		Martin Van Buren is elected president
	Chief Justice Marshall denies Cherokee rights in *Cherokee Nation v. Georgia*	1837–1838	Panic sweeps nation, ending boom
1831–1838	Southern Indians are removed to Oklahoma	1838	4,000 Cherokee die on Trail of Tears to Oklahoma
	South Carolina defends states' rights in Ordinance of Nullification	1840	"Log Cabin" Campaign is first to use "hoopla"
	Force Bill grants president authority to execute revenue laws		William Henry Harrison is elected president
	Jackson vetoes Bank Recharter Bill	1841	Harrison dies one month after inauguration; John Tyler becomes president

✓● Study and Review at www.myhistorylab.com

Review Questions

1. How did the Jacksonian Democrats agree with the principles of the Jeffersonian Democrats? How did they disagree?

2. How did Jackson generate so high a turnout in the election of 1828? How did the opponents of the Jacksonian Democrats respond to Jackson's success?

3. How did the Second Bank of the United States restrain local banks from loaning too much money? Why did President Jackson seek to "kill" the Bank of the United States? Was this policy wise?

4. Why did Jackson insist on the removal of Indians from the Southeast? Was the policy justified? Were there alternatives?

5. The Jacksonian Democrats stood for "states' rights" on many issues. Why did Jackson break so vociferously with fellow Democrat Calhoun's claim that states had the right to "nullify" federal laws with which they disagreed?

Key Terms

Bank war
Jacksonian democracy
nullification

second party system
Specie Circular
spoils system

Trail of Tears
Whigs

The Making of Middle-Class America

Hear the Audio at myhistorylab.com

Who is your family?

FEARS ABOUT A CRISIS IN THE FAMILY HAVE GENERATED HEADLINES since the early 1900s, when divorce rates began to rise. Nowadays defenders of the traditional family cite a set of familiar statistics: Nearly a third of all children are born to unwed mothers; half of all marriages end in divorce; a third of all families are headed by a single parent; more than half of all single mothers with children younger than six work outside the home. Some even redefine marriage itself. By 2010 state legislatures and judges in New Hampshire, Iowa, Massachusetts, Vermont, and Connecticut allowed same sex marriages. Yet when the issue was put directly to the electorate, the voters of thirty-five states rejected it.

If ever the traditional "ideal" prevailed in America, it was among white families in the 1820s and 1830s. Divorce was rare; the overwhelming majority of families had two parents; only one woman in fifteen worked outside the home.

Whether such families were "happier" or "stronger" than now is a different matter. Divorce was rare partly because so few could obtain it. South Carolina recognized no legal grounds for divorce. Many other states granted divorce only if a spouse committed adultery. Many couples thus endured loveless, unhappy marriages.

Nevertheless the family after 1820 was perceived as a new and dynamic force in American society. Middle-class women, especially those freed from the drudgery of farm chores, were especially influential. Sarah Hale, the leading female journalist of the era, pronounced women to be "God's appointed agents of morality." Such women organized religious revivals, spearheaded efforts to improve prisons and mental asylums, and campaigned for temperance, abolition, and women's rights. Young middle-class women, too, were avid readers, and their patronage stimulated publication of countless books and magazines. These women shaped society and culture even more directly by serving as teachers in the common schools that extended public education to much of the nation.

The reformers of the era decried the pessimism of their Calvinist forebears. Romanticism in the arts and literature affirmed that Americans and their institutions could—and would—grow and change for the better.

From Chapter 10 of *American Destiny: Narrative of a Nation*, Combined Volume, Fourth Edition. Mark C. Carnes and John A. Garraty. Copyright © 2012 by Pearson Education, Inc. Published by Pearson Prentice Hall. All rights reserved.

Tocqueville: Democracy in America

On May 12, 1831, two French aristocrats, Alexis de Tocqueville and Gustave de Beaumont, arrived in New York City from Le Havre. Their official purpose was to make a study of American prisons for the French government. But they really came, as Tocqueville explained, "to see what a great republic is like."

Tocqueville and Beaumont believed that Europe was passing from its aristocratic past into a democratic future. How better to prepare for the change, they believed, than by studying the United States, where democracy was already the "enduring and normal state" of the land. The visit provided the material for Tocqueville's classic *De la Démocratie en Amérique*, published in France in 1835 and a year later in an English translation. *Democracy in America* has been the starting point for virtually all subsequent writers who have tried to describe what Tocqueville called "the creative elements" of American institutions.

The gist of *Democracy in America* is contained in the book's first sentence: "No novelty in the United States struck me more vividly during my stay there than the equality of conditions." Tocqueville meant not that Americans lived in a state of total equality, but that the inequalities that did exist among white Americans were not enforced by institutions or supported by public opinion. "In America," he concluded, "men are nearer equality than in any other country in the world."

This sweeping generalization, however comforting to Americans then and since, is an oversimplification. Few modern students of Jacksonian America would accept it without qualification. In the 1830s and 1840s a wide and growing gap existed between the rich and poor in the eastern cities. According to one study, the wealthiest 4 percent of the population of New York controlled about half the city's wealth in 1828, about two-thirds in 1845. The number of New Yorkers worth $100,000 or more tripled in that period. A similar concentration of wealth was occurring in Philadelphia and Boston. Moreover, Tocqueville failed to observe the many poor people in Jacksonian America. Particularly in the cities, bad times forced many unskilled laborers and their families into dire poverty. Tocqueville took little notice of such inequalities, in part because he was so captivated by the theme of American equality.

Despite his blind spots, Tocqueville realized that America was undergoing some fundamental social changes. These changes, he wrote, were being made by "an innumerable crowd who are . . . not exactly rich nor yet quite poor [and who] have enough property to want order and

Rural versus Urban Population, 1820–1860 As the balance of rural and urban population began to shift during the years from 1820 to 1860, the number of cities with populations over 100,000 grew from one in 1820—New York—to nine in 1870, including southern and western cities like New Orleans and San Francisco.

not enough to excite envy." In his notes he put it even more succinctly: "The whole society seems to have turned into one middle class."

The Family Recast

Tocqueville was particularly struck by the character of the family. Americans, he wrote, showed an "equal regard" for husbands and wives, but defined their roles differently. This was made possible by the growth of the market economy, which undermined the importance of home and family as the unit of economic production. More and more people did their work in shops, in offices, or on factory floors. Whether a job was skilled or unskilled, white-collar or blue-collar, or strictly professional, it took the family breadwinner out of the house during working hours six days a week. This did not mean that the family necessarily ceased to be an economic unit. But the labor of the father and any children with jobs came home in the form of cash, thus at least initially in the custody of the individual earners. The social consequences of this change were enormous for the traditional "head of the family" and for his wife and children.

Because he was away so much, the husband had to surrender to his wife some of the power in the family that he had formerly exercised, if for no other reason than the fact that she was always there. Noah Webster explained that the ideal father's authority was "like the mild dominion of a limited monarch, and not the iron rule of an austere tyrant." It certainly explains why Tocqueville concluded that "a sort of equality reigns around the domestic hearth" in America.

◆◆◆ Read the Document

Carey, *Rules for Husbands and Wives* at **myhistorylab.com**

The new power and prestige that wives and mothers enjoyed were not obtained without cost. Since they were exercising day-to-day control over household affairs, they were expected to tend only to those affairs. Expanding their interest to other fields of human endeavor was frowned on. Where the typical wife had formerly been a partner in a family enterprise, she now left earning a living entirely to her husband. She was certainly not encouraged to have an independent career as, say, a lawyer or doctor. Time spent away from home or devoted to matters unrelated to

Lilly Martin Spencer's *Young Husband: First Marketing* (1854). Note that passersby are amused at this husband's inept attempt to do "women's work."

Source: *Young Husband: First Marketing,* 1854 by Lilly Martin Spencer. The Metropolitan Museum of Art, New York, NY, U.S.A. Image copyright © The Metropolitan Museum of Art.

the care of husband and family was, according to the new normative doctrine of "separate spheres," time misappropriated.

This trend widened the gap between the middle and lower classes. For a middle-class wife and mother to take a job or, still worse, to devote herself to any "frivolous" activity outside the home was considered a dereliction of duty. Such an attitude could not possibly develop in lower-class families where everyone had to work simply to keep food on the table.

Some women objected to the **Cult of True Womanhood**: By placing an ideal on so high a pedestal, all real women would fall short. Others escaped its more suffocating aspects by forming close friendships with other women. But most women, including

•◆•─[Read the Document

Beecher, from *A Treatise on Domestic Economy* at **myhistorylab.com**

such forceful proponents of women's rights as Hale and the educator Catharine Beecher, subscribed to the view that a woman's place was in the home. "The formation of the moral and intellectual character of the young is committed mainly to the female hand," Beecher wrote in *A Treatise on Domestic Economy for the Use of Young Ladies* (1841). "The mother forms the character of the future man."

Another reason for the shift in domestic influence from husbands to wives was that women began to have fewer children. People married later than in earlier periods. Long courtships and broken engagements were common, probably because prospective marriage partners were becoming more selective. On average, women began having their children two or three years later than their mothers had, and they stopped two or three years sooner. Apparently many middle-class couples made a conscious effort to limit family size, even when doing so required sexual abstinence.

As families became smaller, relations within them became more caring. Parents ceased to think of their children mostly as future workers. The earlier tendency even

•◆•─[Read the Document

Mother's Magazine at **myhistorylab.com**

among loving parents to keep their children at arm's length, yet within reach of the strap, gave way to more intimate relationships. Gone was the puritan notion that children possessed "a perverse will, a love of what's forbid," and with it the belief that parents were responsible for crushing all juvenile resistance to their authority. In its place arose the view described by Lydia Maria Child in *The Mother's Book* (1831) that children "come to us from heaven, with their little souls full of innocence and peace." Mothers "should not interfere with the influence of angels," Child advised her readers.

The Second Great Awakening

The basic goodness of children contradicted the Calvinist doctrine of infant damnation, to which most American Protestant churches formally subscribed. "Of all the impious doctrines which the dark imagination of man ever conceived," Bronson Alcott wrote in his journal, "the worst [is] the belief in original and certain depravity of infant nature." Alcott was far from alone in thinking infant damnation a "debased doctrine," despite its standing as one of the central tenets of orthodox Calvinism. Mothers enshrined infancy and childhood; they became increasingly active and vocal in church. They scathingly indicted the concept of infant damnation.

The inclination to set aside other Calvinist tenets, such as predestination, became more pronounced as a new wave of revivalism took shape in the 1790s. This **Second Great Awakening** began as a counteroffensive to the deistic thinking and other forms of "infidelity" that New England Congregationalists and southern Methodists alike identified with the French Revolution. Prominent New England ministers, who considered themselves traditionalists but also revivalists (men such as Yale's president, Timothy Dwight, and Dwight's student, the Reverend Lyman Beecher) placed less stress in their sermons on God's arbitrary power over mortals, and more on the promise of the salvation of sinners because of God's mercy and "disinterested benevolence." When another of Dwight's students, Horace Bushnell, declared in a sermon on "Christian nurture" in 1844 that Christian parents should prepare their children "for the skies," he meant that parents could contribute to their children's salvation.

Calvinism came under more direct assault from Charles Grandison Finney, probably the most effective of a number of charismatic Evangelists who brought the Second Great Awakening to its crest. In 1821 Finney abandoned a promising career as a lawyer and became an itinerant preacher. His most spectacular successes occurred during a series of revivals conducted in towns along the Erie Canal, a region Finney called "the burned-over district" because it had been the site of so many revivals before his own. From Utica, where his revival began in 1826, to Rochester, where it climaxed in 1831, he

Read the Document

Finney, *What a Revival of Religion Is* at **myhistorylab.com**

exhorted his listeners to take their salvation into their own hands. He insisted that people could control their own fate. He dismissed Calvinism as a "theological fiction." Salvation was available to anyone. But the day of judgment was just around the corner; there was little time to waste.

During and after Finney's efforts in Utica, conversions increased sharply. In Rochester, church membership doubled in six months. Elsewhere in the country, churches capitalized on the efforts of other Evangelists to fill their pews. In 1831 alone, church membership grew by 100,000, an increase, according to a New England minister, "unparalleled in the history of the church." The success of the Evangelists of the Second Great Awakening stemmed from the timeliness of their assault on Calvinist doctrine and even more from their methods. Finney, for example, consciously set out to be entertaining as well as edifying. The singing of hymns and the solicitation of personal testimonies provided his meetings with emotional release and human interest. Prominent among his innovations was the "anxious bench," where leading members of the community awaited the final prompting from within before coming forward to declare themselves saved.

Economic changes and their impact on family life also contributed to the Second Awakening. The growth of industry and commerce that followed the completion of the Erie Canal in 1825, along with the disappearance of undeveloped farmland, led hundreds of young men to leave family farms to seek their fortunes in Utica and other towns along the canal. There, uprooted, uncertain, and buffeted between ambition, hope, and anxiety, they found it hard to resist the comfort promised by the revivalists to those who were saved.

Women, and especially the wives of the business leaders of the community, felt particularly responsible for the Christian education of their children, which fell within

Lily Spenser Martin's painting, *Domestic Happiness* (1844), reflects the change in attitudes toward infants. Parents such as these could not believe that God had consigned their angelic babies to eternal damnation. Source: *Domestic Happiness*, 1849 (oil on canvas), Spencer, Lilly Martin (1827–1902)/Detroit Institute of Arts, USA/Gift of Dr. and Mrs. James Cleland Jr./The Bridgeman Art Library International.

their separate sphere. Many women had servants and thus had time and energy to devote to their own and their offsprings' salvation.

Paradoxically, this caused many of them to venture out of that sphere and in doing so they moved further out of the shadow of their husbands. They founded the Oneida County Female Missionary Society, an association that did most of the organizing and a good deal of the financing of the climactic years of the Second Awakening. The Female Missionary Society raised more than $1,000 a year (no small sum at that time) to support the revival in Utica, in its environs, and throughout the burned-over district.

Watch the Video
Evangelical Religion & Politics, Then and Now at **myhistorylab.com**

Apparently without consciously intending to do so, women challenged the authority of the paternalistic, authoritarian churches they so fervently embraced. Then, by mixtures of exhortation, example, and affection, they set out to save the souls of their loved ones, first their children and ultimately their husbands too.

The Era of Associations

Alongside the recast family and the "almost revolutionized" church, a third pillar of the emerging American middle class was the voluntary association. Unlike the other two, it had neither colonial precedents nor contemporary European equivalents. The voluntary association of early nineteenth-century America was unique. "In France," Tocqueville wrote of this phenomenon, "if you want to proclaim a truth or propagate some feeling . . . you would find the government or in England some territorial magnate." In America, however, "you are sure to find an association."

The leaders of these associations tended to be ministers, lawyers, or merchants, but the rank and file consisted of tradesmen, foremen, clerks, and especially their wives. Some of these associations were formed around a local cause that some townspeople wished to advance, such as the provision of religious instruction for orphaned children; others were affiliated with associations elsewhere for the purposes of combating some national evil, such as drunkenness. Some, such as the American Board of Commissioners of Foreign Missions, founded in Boston in 1810, quickly became large and complex enterprises. (By 1860 the board had sent 1,250 missionaries into the "heathen world" and raised $8 million to support them.) Others lasted only as long as it took to accomplish a specific good work, such as the construction of a school or a library.

In a sense the associations were assuming functions previously performed in the family, such as caring for old people and providing moral guidance to the young, but without the paternalistic discipline of the old way. They constituted a "benevolent empire," eager to make society over into their members' idea of how God wanted it to be.

Backwoods Utopias

Americans frequently belonged to several associations at the same time and more than a few made reform their life's work. The most adventuresome tested their reform theories by withdrawing from workaday American society and establishing experimental communities. The communitarian point of view aimed at "commencing a wholesale social reorganization by first establishing and demonstrating its principles completely on a small scale." The first communitarians were religious reformers. In a sense the Pilgrims fall into this category, along with a number of other groups in colonial times, but only in the nineteenth century did the idea flourish.

One of the most influential of the earlier communities were the **Shakers**, founded by an Englishwoman, Ann Lee, who came to America in 1774. Mother Ann, as she was called, saw visions that convinced her that Christ would come to earth again as a woman and that she was that woman. With a handful of followers she founded a community near Albany, New York. The group grew rapidly, and after Ann Lee's death in 1784 her movement continued to expand. By the 1830s her followers had established about twenty successful communities.

Watch the Video

Religious Troublemakers of the Nineteenth Century at **myhistorylab.com**

The Shakers practiced celibacy; believing that the millennium was imminent, they saw no reason for perpetuating the human race. Each group lived in a large Family House, the sexes strictly segregated. Property was held in common but controlled by a ruling hierarchy. So much stress was placed on equality of labor and reward and on voluntary acceptance of the rules, however, that the system does not seem to have been oppressive.

The Shaker religion, joyful and fervent, was marked by much group singing and dancing, which provided the members with emotional release from their tightly controlled regimen. An industrious, skillful people, they made a special virtue of simplicity; some of their designs for buildings and, especially, furniture achieved a classic beauty seldom equaled among untutored artisans. Despite their customs, the Shakers were universally tolerated and even admired.

The most important of the religious communitarians were the Mormons. A remarkable Vermont farm boy, Joseph Smith, founded the religion in western New York in the 1820s. Smith saw visions; he claimed to have discovered and translated an ancient text, the Book of Mormon, which described the adventures of a tribe of Israelites that had populated America from biblical times until their destruction in a great war in 400 CE. With a small band of followers, Smith established a community in Ohio in 1831. The Mormons' dedication and economic efficiency attracted large numbers of converts, but their unorthodox religious views and their exclusivism, a product of their sense of being a chosen people, caused resentment among unbelievers. The Mormons were forced to move first to Missouri and then back to Illinois, where in 1839 they founded the town of Nauvoo.

In 1839 Mary Cragin, 29, became a convert to John Humphrey Noyes's "communism of love" and persuaded her husband to move with her to the commune. In 1846, after having an affair with another member of the commune, she and Noyes developed an attachment. After a meeting of the church, Noyes proposed that he and Cragin's husband share each other's wives. In an understatement, he called the arrangement a "complex marriage."

Photo Credit: From the Collection of the Oneida Community Mansion House, Oneida, NY.

Nauvoo flourished—by 1844 it was the largest city in the state, with a population of 15,000—but once again the Mormons ran into local trouble. They quarreled among themselves, especially after Smith secretly authorized polygamy and a number of other unusual rites for members of the "Holy Order," the top leaders of the church.[1] They created a paramilitary organization, the Nauvoo Legion, headed by Smith, envisaging themselves as a semi-independent state within the Union. Smith announced that he was a candidate for president of the United States. Rumors circulated that the Mormons intended to take over the entire Northwest for their "empire." Once again local "gentiles" rose against them. Smith was arrested, then murdered by a mob.

Under a new leader, Brigham Young, the Mormons sought a haven beyond the frontier. In 1847 they marched westward, pressing through the mountains until they reached the desolate wilderness on the shores of the Great Salt Lake. There, at last, they established their Zion and began to make their truly significant impact on American history. Irrigation made the desert flourish, precious water wisely being treated as a community asset. Hard, cooperative, intelligently directed effort spelled growth and prosperity; more than 11,000 people were living in the area when it became part of the Utah Territory in 1850. In time the communal Mormon settlement broke down, but the religion has remained—known as the Church of Latter-Day Saints, a major force in the shaping of the West. The Mormon Church is still by far the most powerful single influence in Utah and is a thriving organization in many other parts of the United States and in Europe.

The religious communities had some influence on reformers who wished to experiment with social organization. When Robert Owen, a British **utopian** socialist who believed in economic as well as political equality and who considered competition debasing, decided to create an ideal community in America, he purchased the Rappite settlement at New Harmony, Indiana. Owen's advocacy of free love and "enlightened atheism" did not add to the stability of his group or to its popularity among outsiders. The colony was a costly failure.

The American followers of Charles Fourier, a French utopian socialist who proposed that society should be organized in cooperative units called phalanxes, fared

---

[1]One justification of polygamy, paradoxically, was that marriage was a sacred, eternal state. If a man remarried after his wife's death, eventually he would have two wives in heaven. Therefore why not on earth?

New England Roots of Utopian Communities The shaded section represents areas that were settled predominantly by people from New England. It suggests that communitarian sentiments were strongly influenced by New England culture.

better. Fourierism did not seek to tamper with sexual and religious mores. Its advocates included important journalists such as Horace Greeley of the *New York Tribune* and Parke Godwin of the *New York Evening Post*. In the 1840s several dozen Fourierist colonies were established in the northern and western states. Members worked at whatever tasks they wished and only as much as they wished. As might be expected, none of the communities lasted very long.

See the **Map**

Utopian Communities before the Civil War at **myhistorylab.com**

The Age of Reform

The communitarians were the most colorful of the reformers, their proposals the most spectacular. More effective, however, were the many individuals who took on themselves responsibility for caring for the physically and mentally disabled and for the rehabilitation of criminals. The work of Thomas Gallaudet in developing methods for educating deaf people reflects the spirit of the times. Gallaudet's school in Hartford, Connecticut, opened its doors in 1817; by 1851 similar schools for the deaf had been established in fourteen states.

Dr. Samuel Gridley Howe did similar work with the blind, devising means for making books with raised letters (Louis Braille's system of raised dots was not introduced until later in the century) that the blind could "read" with their fingers. Howe headed a school for the blind in Boston, the pioneering Perkins Institution, which opened in 1832. Of all that Charles Dickens observed in America, nothing so favorably impressed him as Howe's success in educating twelve-year-old Laura Bridgman, who was deaf, mute, and blind. Howe was also interested in trying to educate the mentally disabled and in other causes, including antislavery. "Every creature in human shape should command our respect," he insisted. "The strong should help the weak, so that the whole should advance as a band of brethren."

One of the most striking aspects of the reform movement was the emphasis reformers placed on establishing special institutions for dealing with social problems. In the colonial period, orphans, indigent persons, the insane, and the feebleminded were usually cared for by members of their own families or boarded in a neighboring household. They remained part of the community. Even criminals were seldom "locked away" for extended jail terms; punishment commonly consisted of whipping, being placed in stocks in the town square, or (for serious crimes) execution. But once persuaded that people were primarily shaped by their surroundings, reformers demanded that deviant and dependent members of the community be taken from their present corrupting circumstances and placed in specialized institutions where they could be trained or rehabilitated. Almshouses, orphanages, reformatories, prisons, and "lunatic asylums" sprang up throughout the United States like mushrooms in a forest after a summer rain.

Eastern State Penitentiary, opened in 1829 in Philadelphia, sought to reform prisoners by enforcing a solitary life to promote reflection.

Photo Credit: Albert Vecerka, 2001. Courtesy of Eastern State Penitentiary Historic Site, Philadelphia, PA.

The rationale for this movement was scientific; elaborate statistical reports attested to the benefits that such institutions would bring to both inmates and society as a whole. The motivating spirit of the founders of these asylums was humane, although many of the institutions seem anything but humane to the modern eye. The highly regarded Philadelphia prison system was based on strict solitary confinement, which was supposed to lead culprits to reflect on their sins and then reform their ways. The prison was literally a penitentiary, a place to repent. In fact, the system drove some inmates mad, and soon a rival Auburn system was introduced in New York State, which allowed for some social contact among prisoners and for work in shops and stone quarries. Absolute silence was required at all times. The prisoners were herded about in lockstep and punished by flogging for the slightest infraction of the rules. Regular "moral and religious instruction" was provided, which the authorities believed would lead inmates to reform their lives. Tocqueville and Beaumont, in their report on American prisons, concluded that the Philadelphia system produced "the deepest impression on the soul of the convict," while the Auburn system made the convict "more conformable to the habits of man in society."

The hospitals for mental patients were intended to cure inmates, not merely to confine them. The emphasis was on isolating them from the pressures of society; on order, quiet, routine; and on control—but not on punishment. The unfortunates were seen as *de*ranged; the task was to *ar*range their lives in a rational manner. In practice, shortages of trained personnel, niggardly legislative appropriations, and the inherent difficulty of managing violent and irrational patients often produced deplorable conditions in the asylums.

This situation led Dorothea Dix, a woman of almost saintlike selflessness, to devote thirty years of her life to a campaign to improve the care of the insane. She traveled to every state in the Union, and as far afield as Turkey and Japan, inspecting asylums and poorhouses. Insane persons in Massachusetts, she wrote in a memorial intended to shock state legislators into action, were being kept in cages and closets, *"chained, naked, beaten with rods, and lashed into obedience!"* Her reports led to some improvement in conditions in Massachusetts and other states, but in the long run the bright hopes of the reformers were never realized. Institutions founded to uplift the deviant and dependent all too soon became places where society's "misfits" might safely be kept out of sight.

"Demon Rum"

Women did much of the work in all antebellum reforms, but they were especially active in the **temperance movement**. The husband who squandered his earnings on booze, or who came home drunk and debauched, imperiled the family. Thus middle-class women who believed that a woman's place was in the home were obliged to take on a public role to protect the family.

Alcohol—"demon rum"—was perhaps foremost among those threats. By the 1820s Americans were consuming prodigious amounts of alcohol, more than ever before or since. Not that the colonists had been teetotalers. Liquor, mostly in the form of rum or hard apple cider, was cheap and everywhere available; taverns were an integral part of colonial society.

Watch the Video

Drinking & the Temperance Movement in Nineteenth-Century America at **myhistorylab.com**

There were alcoholics in colonial America, but because neither political nor religious leaders considered drinking dangerous, there was no alcohol "problem." Most doctors recommended the regular consumption of alcohol as healthy. John Adams, certainly the soul of propriety, drank a tankard of hard cider every day for breakfast. Dr. Benjamin Rush's *Inquiry into the Effects of Ardent Spirits* (1784), which questioned the medicinal benefits of alcohol, fell on deaf ears.

However, alcohol consumption increased markedly in the early years of the new republic, thanks primarily to the availability of cheap corn and rye whiskey distilled in the new states of Kentucky and Tennessee. In the 1820s the per capita consumption of hard liquor reached five gallons, well over twice what it is today. Since small children and many grown people did not drink that much, others obviously drank a great deal more.

The foundation of the American Temperance Union in 1826 signaled the start of a national crusade against drunkenness. Employing lectures, pamphlets, rallies, essay contests, and other techniques, the union set out to persuade people to "sign the pledge" not to drink liquor. Primitive sociological studies of the effects of drunkenness (reformers were able to show a high statistical correlation between alcohol consumption and crime) added to the effectiveness of the campaign.

Read the Document

Beecher, *Six Sermons on Intemperance* at **myhistorylab.com**

Revivalist ministers like Charles Grandison Finney argued that alcohol was one of the great barriers to conversion, which helps explain why Utica, a town of fewer than 13,000 residents in 1840, supported four separate temperance societies in that year. Employers all over the country also signed on, declaring their businesses henceforward to be "cold-water" enterprises. Soon the temperance movement claimed a million members.

The temperance people aroused bitter opposition, particularly after they moved beyond calls for restraint to demands for prohibition of all alcohol. German and Irish immigrants, for the most part Catholics, and also members of Protestant sects that used wine in their religious services, objected to being told by reformers that their drinking would have to stop. But by the early 1840s the reformers had secured legislation in many states that imposed strict licensing systems and heavy liquor taxes. Local option laws permitted towns and counties to ban the sale of alcohol altogether.

In 1851 Maine passed the first effective law prohibiting the manufacture and sale of alcoholic beverages. The leader of the campaign was Mayor Neal Dow of Portland, a businessman who became a prohibitionist after seeing the damage done by drunkenness among workers in his tannery. By 1855 a dozen other states had passed laws based on the Maine statute, and the nation's per capita consumption of alcohol had plummeted to two gallons a year.

The Abolitionist Crusade

No reform movement of this era was more significant, more ambiguous, or more provocative of later historical investigation than **abolitionism**—the drive to abolish slavery. That slavery should have been a cause of indignation to reform-minded Americans was inevitable. Humanitarians were outraged by the master's whip and by the practice of disrupting families. Democrats protested the denial of political and civil rights to slaves. Perfectionists of all stripes deplored the fact that slaves had no chance to improve themselves. However, well into the 1820s, the abolitionist cause attracted few followers because there seemed to be no way of getting rid of slavery short of revolution. While a few theorists argued that the Fifth Amendment, which provides that no one may be "deprived of life, liberty, or property, without due process of law," could be interpreted to mean that the Constitution outlawed slavery, the great majority believed that the institution was not subject to federal control.

Particularly in the wake of the Missouri Compromise, antislavery Northerners neatly compartmentalized their thinking. Slavery was wrong; they would not tolerate it in their own communities. But since the Constitution obliged them to tolerate it in states where it existed, they felt no responsibility to fight it. The issue was explosive enough even when limited to the question of the expansion of slavery into the territories. People who advocated any kind of forced abolition in states where it was legal were judged irresponsible in the extreme. Most critics of slavery therefore confined themselves to urging "colonization" or persuading slaveowners to treat their property humanely.

More provocative and less accommodating to local sensibilities were people such as William Lloyd Garrison of Massachusetts, who called for "immediate" abolition. When his extreme position made continued residence in Baltimore impossible, he returned to Boston, where in 1831 he established his own newspaper, *The Liberator*. "I am in earnest," he announced in the first issue. "I will not equivocate—I will not excuse—I will not retreat a single inch—and I will be heard."

Read the Document
Garrison, First Issue of *The Liberator* at myhistorylab.com

Garrison's position, and that espoused by the New England Anti-Slavery Society, which he organized in 1831, was absolutely unyielding: Slaves must be freed immediately and treated as equals; compensated emancipation was unacceptable, colonization unthinkable. Because the U.S. government countenanced slavery, Garrison refused to engage in political activity to achieve his ends. Burning a copy of the Constitution—that "agreement with hell"—became a regular feature at Society-sponsored public lectures.

Few white Americans found Garrison's line of argument convincing, and many were outraged by his confrontational tactics. In 1833 a Garrison meeting in New York City was broken up by colonizationists. Two years later a mob dragged Garrison through the streets of his own Boston. That same day a mob broke up the convention of the New York Anti-Slavery Society in Utica. In 1837 Elijah Lovejoy, a Garrisonian newspaper editor in Alton, Illinois, first saw his press destroyed by fire and then was himself murdered by a mob. When the proprietors of Philadelphia's Pennsylvania Hall booked an abolitionist meeting in 1838, a mob burned the hall to the ground to prevent the meeting from taking place.

In the wake of this violence some of Garrison's backers had second thoughts about his call for an immediate end to slavery. The wealthy New York businessmen Arthur and Lewis Tappan, who had subsidized *The Liberator*, turned instead to Theodore Dwight Weld, a young minister who was part of Charles Grandison Finney's "holy band" of revivalists. Weld and his followers spoke of "immediate" emancipation "gradually" achieved, and they were willing to engage in political activity to achieve that goal.

In 1840 the Tappans and Weld broke with Garrison over the issue of involvement in politics and the participation of female abolitionists as public lecturers. Garrison, mindful of women's central role in other reforms, supported the women. "The destiny of the slaves

THE MAKING OF MIDDLE-CLASS AMERICA

is in the hands of American women," he declared in 1833. Weld thought women lecturers would needlessly antagonize would-be supporters. The Tappans then organized the Liberty party, which nominated as its presidential candidate James G. Birney, a Kentucky slaveholder who had been converted to evangelical Christianity and abolitionism by Weld. Running on a platform of universal emancipation to be gradually brought about through legislation, Birney received only 7,000 votes.

Many blacks were abolitionists long before the white movement began to attract attention. In 1830 some fifty black antislavery societies existed, and thereafter these groups grew in size and importance, being generally associated with the Garrisonian wing. White abolitionists eagerly sought out black speakers, especially runaway slaves, whose heartrending accounts of their experiences aroused sympathies and who, merely by speaking clearly and with conviction, stood as living proof that blacks were neither animals nor fools.

The first prominent black abolitionist was David Walker, whose powerful *Appeal to the Coloured Citizens of the World* (1829) is now considered one of the roots of the modern black nationalist movement. Walker was born free and had experienced American racism extensively in both the South and the North. He denounced white talk of democracy and freedom as pure hypocrisy and predicted that when God finally brought justice to America white "tyrants will wish they were never born!"

Frederick Douglass, a former slave who had escaped from Maryland, was one of the most remarkable Americans of his generation. While a bondsman he had received a full portion of beatings and other indignities, but he had been allowed to learn to read and write and to master a trade, opportunities denied the vast majority of slaves.

Photo Credit: National Portrait Gallery, Smithsonian Institution/Art Resource, New York.

A photo of Frederick Douglass in 1847, having escaped from slavery nine years earlier. He attracted large audiences as an antislavery lecturer, though his white supporters worried that he neither looked nor sounded like a former slave. Lest audiences think him an imposter, William Lloyd Garrison counseled him to not sound too "learned." Another thought it would be better if he had "a little of the plantation in his speech." Douglass rejected such suggestions.

Settling in Boston, he became an agent of the Massachusetts Anti-Slavery Society and a featured speaker at its public meetings.

Douglass was a tall, majestically handsome man who radiated determination and indignation. Slavery, he told white audiences, "brands your republicanism as a sham, your humanity as a base pretense, your Christianity as a lie." In 1845 he published his *Narrative of the Life of Frederick Douglass*, one of the most gripping autobiographical accounts of a slave's life ever written. Douglass insisted that freedom for blacks required not merely emancipation but full equality, social and economic as well as political. Not many white Northerners accepted his reasoning, but few who heard him or read his works could afterward maintain the illusion that all blacks were dull-witted or resigned to inferior status.

Read the Document

Passages from *The Autobiography of Frederick Douglass* at **myhistorylab.com**

At first Douglass was, in his own words, "a faithful disciple" of Garrison, prepared to tear up the Constitution and destroy the Union to gain his ends. In the late 1840s, however, he changed his mind, deciding that the Constitution, created to "establish Justice, insure domestic Tranquility . . . and secure the Blessings of Liberty," as its preamble states, "could not well have been designed at the same time to maintain and perpetuate a system of rapine and murder like slavery." Thereafter he fought slavery and race prejudice from within the system, something Garrison was never willing to do.

Garrison's importance cannot be measured by the number of his followers, which was never large. Unlike more moderately inclined enemies of slavery, he recognized that abolitionism was a revolutionary movement, not merely one more middle-class reform. He also understood that achieving racial equality, not merely "freeing" the slaves, was the only way to reach the abolitionists' professed objective: full justice for blacks. And he saw clearly that few whites, even among abolitionists, believed that blacks were their equals.

Both Garrison's insights into the limits of northern racial egalitarianism and his blind contempt for southern whites led him to the conclusion that American society was rotten to the core. Thus he refused to make any concession to the existing establishment, religious or secular. He was hated in the North as much for his explicit denial of the idea that a constitution that supported slavery merited respect as for his implicit denial of the idea that a professed Christian who tolerated slavery for even an instant could hope for salvation. He was, in short, a perfectionist, a trafficker in moral absolutes who wanted his Kingdom of Heaven in the here and now. By contrast, most other American reformers were willing to settle for perfection on the installment plan.

Women's Rights

The question of slavery was related to another major reform movement of the era, the crusade for women's rights. Superficially, the connection can be explained in this way: Women were as likely as men to find slavery offensive and to protest against it. When they did so, they ran into even more adamant resistance: the prejudices of those who objected to abolitionists being reinforced by their feelings that women should not speak in public or participate in political affairs. Thus female abolitionists, driven by the urgencies of conscience, were almost forced to become advocates of women's rights. "We have good cause to be

Watch the Video

The Women's Rights Movement in Nineteenth-Century America at **myhistorylab.com**

Photo Credit: The Granger Collection, New York.

Single women worth at least 50 pounds were allowed to vote in New Jersey from 1775 to 1807.

grateful to the slave," the feminist Abby Kelley wrote. "In striving to strike his irons off, we found most surely, that we were manacled ourselves."

At a more profound level, the reference that abolitionists made to the Declaration of Independence to justify their attack on slavery radicalized women with regard to their own place in society. Were only all men created equal and endowed by God with unalienable rights? For many women the question was a consciousness-raising experience; they began to believe that, like African Americans, they were imprisoned from birth in a caste system, legally subordinated and assigned menial social and economic roles that prevented them from developing their full potentialities. Such women considered themselves in a sense worse off than blacks, who had at least the psychological advantage of confronting an openly hostile and repressive society rather than one concealed behind the cloying rhetoric of romantic love.

With the major exception of Margaret Fuller, whose book *Women in the Nineteenth Century* (1844) made a frontal assault on all forms of sexual discrimination, the leading advocates of equal rights for women began their public careers in the abolitionist movement. Among the first were Sarah and Angelina Grimké, South Carolinians who abandoned their native state and the domestic sphere to devote themselves to speaking out against slavery. Male objections to the Grimkés' activities soon made them advocates of women's rights. Similarly, the refusal of delegates to the World Anti-Slavery Convention held in London in 1840 to let women participate in their debates precipitated the decision of two American abolitionists, Lucretia Mott and Elizabeth Cady Stanton, to turn their attention to the women's rights movement.

As Lydia Child, a popular novelist noted, the subordination of women was as old as civilization. The attack on it came not because of any new discrimination but for the same reasons that motivated reformers against other forms of injustice: belief in progress, a sense of personal responsibility, and the conviction that institutions could be changed and that the time for changing them was limited.

When women sought to involve themselves in reform, they became aware of perhaps the most serious handicap that society imposed on them—the conflict between their roles as wives and mothers and their urge to participate in the affairs of the larger world. Elizabeth Cady Stanton has left a striking description of this dilemma. She lived in the 1840s in Seneca Falls, a small town in central New York. Her husband was frequently away on business; she had a brood of growing children and little domestic help. When, stimulated by her interest in abolition and women's rights, she sought to become active in the movements, her family responsibilities made it almost impossible even to read about them.

"I now fully understood the practical difficulties most women had to contend with," she recalled in her autobiography *Eighty Years and More* (1898):

> The general discontent I felt with woman's portion as wife, mother, housekeeper, physician, and spiritual guide, the chaotic condition into which everything fell without her constant supervision, and the wearied, anxious look of the majority of women, impressed me with the strong feeling that some active measures should be taken.

Active measures she took. Together with Lucretia Mott and a few others of like mind, she organized a meeting, the **Seneca Falls Convention** (July 1848), and drafted a Declaration of Sentiments patterned on the Declaration of Independence. "We hold these truths to be self-evident: that all men and women are created equal," it stated, and it went on to list the "injuries and usurpations" of men, just as Jefferson had outlined those of George III.

Read the Document
Stanton, *Declaration of Sentiments* at **myhistorylab.com**

From this seed the movement grew. During the 1850s a series of national conventions was held, and more and more reformers, including William Lloyd Garrison, joined the cause. Of the recruits, Susan B. Anthony was the most influential, for she was the first to see the need for thorough organization if effective pressure was to be brought to bear on male-dominated society. Her first campaign, mounted in 1854 and 1855 in behalf of a petition to the New York legislature calling for reform of the property and divorce laws, accumulated 6,000 signatures. But the petition did not persuade the legislature to act. Indeed, the feminists achieved very few practical results during the Age of Reform. Their leaders, however, were persevering types, most of them extraordinarily long-lived. Their major efforts lay in the future.

Despite the aggressiveness of many reformers and the extremity of some of their proposals, little social conflict blighted these years. Although Americans argued about everything from prison reform to vegetarianism, from women's rights to phrenology (a pseudoscience much occupied with developing the diagnostic possibilities of measuring the bumps on people's heads), they seldom came to blows. Even the abolitionist movement might not have caused serious social strife if the territorial expansion of the late 1840s had not dragged the slavery issue back into politics. When that happened, politics again assumed center stage, public discourse grew embittered, and the first great Age of Reform came to an end.

The Romantic View of Life

The spreading belief that human institutions were improving had a profound effect on the arts and literature. In the Western world, it gave rise to **romanticism**, a revolt against the bloodless logic of the Age of Reason. It was a noticeable if unnamed point of view in Germany, France, and England as early as the 1780s and in America a generation later; by the second quarter of the nineteenth century, few intellectuals were unmarked by it. "Romantics" believed that change and growth were the essence of life, for individuals and for institutions. They valued feeling and intuition over pure thought, and they stressed the differences between individuals and societies rather than the similarities. Ardent love of country characterized the movement; individualism, optimism, ingenuousness, and emotion were its bywords. Romanticism, too, drew much from the religious sensibilities of mothers. Children were innately good; pernicious influences led to their corruption.

The romantic way of thinking found its greatest American expression in **transcendentalism**, a New England creation that is difficult to describe because it emphasized the indefinable and the unknowable. It was a mystical, intuitive way of looking at life that subordinated facts to feelings. Its literal meaning was "to go beyond the world of the senses," by which the transcendentalists meant the material and observable world. To the transcendentalists, human beings were truly divine because they were part of nature, itself the essence of divinity. Peoples' intellectual capacities

Photo Credit: Frederic Edwin Church (American), 1826–1900). *Twilight in the Wilderness*, 1860. Oil on canvas; 101.6 × 162.6 cm. © The Cleveland Museum of Art. Mr. and Mrs. William H. Marlatt Fund 1965.233.

Frederic Edwin Church conveyed the romantic sensibility in *Twilight in the Wilderness* (1860). The clouds glow with religious portent, and their reflected light pervades Nature.

did not define their capabilities, for they could "transcend" reason by having faith in themselves and in the fundamental benevolence of the universe. Transcendentalists were complete individualists, seeing the social whole as no more than the sum of its parts. Organized religion, indeed all institutions, were unimportant if not counterproductive; what mattered was the single person and that people aspire, stretch *beyond* their known capabilities.

Emerson and Thoreau

The leading transcendentalist thinker was Ralph Waldo Emerson. Born in 1803 and educated at Harvard, Emerson became a minister, but in 1832 he gave up his pulpit, deciding that "the profession is antiquated." After traveling in Europe he settled in Concord, Massachusetts, where he had a long career as an essayist, lecturer, and sage.

Emerson's philosophy was at once buoyantly optimistic, rigorously intellectual, self-confident, and conscientious. In "The American Scholar," a notable address he delivered at Harvard in 1837, he urged Americans to put aside their devotion to things European and seek inspiration in their immediate surroundings. Emerson saw himself as pitting "spiritual powers" against "the mechanical powers and the mechanical philosophy of this time." The new industrial society of New England disturbed him profoundly.

Because he put so much emphasis on self-reliance, Emerson disliked powerful governments. "The less government we have the better," he said. In a sense he was the prototype of some modern alienated intellectuals, so repelled by the world as it was that he would not actively try to change it. Nevertheless he thought strong leadership essential. Emerson also had a strong practical streak. He made his living by lecturing, tracking tirelessly across the country, talking before every type of audience for fees ranging from $50 to several hundreds.

◆●◆─Read the Document
Emerson, *The Concord Hymn*
at **myhistorylab.com**

Closely identified with Emerson was his Concord neighbor Henry David Thoreau. After graduating from Harvard in 1837, Thoreau taught school for a time and helped out in a small pencil-making business run by his family. He was a strange man, content to absorb the beauties of nature almost intuitively, yet stubborn and individualistic to the point of selfishness. The hectic scramble for wealth that Thoreau saw all about him he found disgusting and alarming, for he believed it was destroying both the natural and the human resources of the country.

Like Emerson, Thoreau objected to many of society's restrictions on the individual. "That government is best which governs not at all," he said, surpassing both Emerson and the Jeffersonians. He was perfectly prepared to see himself as a majority of one. "When were the good and the brave ever in a majority?" Thoreau asked. "If a man does not keep pace with his companions," he wrote on another occasion, "perhaps it is because he hears a different drummer."

In 1845 Thoreau decided to put to the test his theory that a person need not depend on society for a satisfying existence. He built a cabin at Walden Pond on some property owned by Emerson and lived there alone for two years. The best fruit of this period was that extraordinary book *Walden* (1854). Superficially, *Walden* is the story of Thoreau's experiment, movingly and beautifully written. It is also an indictment of the social behavior of the average American, an attack on unthinking conformity, on subordinating one's own judgment to that of the herd.

Photo Credit: © Joseph Sohm; Chromosohm/ CORBIS All Rights Reserved.

Walden Pond, where Henry David Thoreau lived from 1845 to 1847: "I went to the woods because I wished to live deliberately, to front only the essential facts of life, and see if I could not learn what it had to teach, and not, when I came to die, to discover that I had not lived."

The most graphic illustration of Thoreau's confidence in his own values occurred while he was living at Walden. At that time the Mexican War was raging. Thoreau considered the war immoral because it advanced the cause of slavery. To protest, he refused to pay his Massachusetts poll tax. For this he was arrested and lodged in jail, although only for one night because an aunt promptly paid the tax for him. His essay "Civil Disobedience," explaining his view of the proper relation between the individual and the state, resulted from this experience. Like Emerson, however, Thoreau refused to participate in practical reform movements. "I love Henry," one of his friends said, "but I cannot like him; and as for taking his arm, I should as soon think of taking the arm of an elm tree."

Edgar Allan Poe

The work of all the imaginative writers of the period reveals romantic influences, and it is possibly an indication of the affinity of the romantic approach to American conditions that a number of excellent writers of poetry and fiction first appeared in the 1830s and 1840s. Edgar Allan Poe, one of the most remarkable, seems almost a caricature of the romantic image of the tortured genius. Poe was born in Boston in 1809, the son of poor actors who died before he was three years old. He was raised by a wealthy Virginian, John Allan.

Few persons as neurotic as Poe have been able to produce first-rate work. In college he ran up debts of $2,500 in less than a year and had to withdraw. He won an appointment to West Point but was discharged after a few months for disobedience and "gross neglect of duty." He was a lifelong alcoholic and an occasional taker of drugs. He married a child of thirteen.

Poe responded strongly to the lure of romanticism. His works abound with examples of wild imagination and fascination with mystery, fright, and the occult. If he did not invent the detective story, he perfected it; his tales "The Murders in the Rue Morgue" and "The Purloined Letter" stressed the thought processes of a clever detective in solving a mystery by reasoning from evidence.

Although dissolute in his personal life, when Poe touched pen to paper, he became a disciplined craftsman. The most fantastic passages in his works are the result of careful, reasoned selection; not a word, he believed, could be removed without damage to the whole. And despite his rejection of most of the values prized

An image of Edgar Allan Poe on a cigar box. In 1845, impoverished and an alcoholic, Poe was living in the "greatest wretchedness." His young wife was dying of tuberculosis. That same year he wrote, "The Raven," a poem about an ill-omened bird that intrudes on a young man's grief over the death of his beloved. "Take thy beak from out my heart," the man screams. Quoth the raven—famously—"Nevermore."

Photo Credit: Hulton Archive/ Getty Images.

by middle-class America, Poe was widely read in his own day. His poem "The Raven" won instantaneous popularity when it was published in 1845. Had he been a little more stable, he might have made a good living with his pen—but in that case he might not have written as he did.

Nathaniel Hawthorne

Another product of the prevailing romanticism was Nathaniel Hawthorne, born in 1804 in Salem, Massachusetts. When Hawthorne was a small child, his father died and his grief-stricken mother became a recluse. Left largely to his own devices, he grew to be a lonely, introspective person. Wandering about New England by himself in summertime, he soaked up local lore, which he drew on in writing short stories.

Hawthorne's early stories, originally published in magazines, were brought together in *Twice-Told Tales* (1837). They made excellent use of New England culture and history for background but were concerned chiefly with the struggles of individuals with sin, guilt, and especially the pride and isolation that often afflict those who place too much reliance on their own judgment. His greatest works were two novels written after the Whigs turned him out of his government job in 1849. *The Scarlet Letter* (1850), a grim yet sympathetic analysis of adultery, condemned not the woman, Hester Prynne, but the people who presumed to judge her. *The House of the Seven Gables* (1851) was a gripping account of the decay of an old New England family brought on by the guilty feelings of the current owners of the house, caused by the way their ancestors had cheated the original owners of the property.

Like Poe, Hawthorne was appreciated in his own day and widely read; unlike Poe, he made a modest amount of money from his work. Yet he was never very comfortable in the society he inhabited. He had no patience with the second-rate. And despite his success in creating word pictures of a somber, mysterious world, he considered America too prosaic a country to inspire good literature. "There is no shadow, no antiquity, no mystery, no picturesque and gloomy wrong, nor anything but a commonplace prosperity," he complained.

Herman Melville

In 1850, while Hawthorne was writing *The House of the Seven Gables*, his publisher introduced him to another writer who was in the midst of a novel. The writer was Herman Melville and the book, *Moby-Dick*. Hawthorne and Melville became good friends at once, for despite their dissimilar backgrounds, they had a great deal in common. Melville was a New Yorker, born in 1819, one of eight children of a merchant of distinguished lineage. His father, however, lost all his money and died when the boy was twelve. Melville left school at fifteen, worked briefly as a bank clerk, and in 1837 went to sea. For eighteen months, in 1841 and 1842, he was crewman on the whaler *Acushnet*. Then he jumped ship in the South Seas. For a time he lived among a tribe of cannibals in the Marquesas; later he made his way to Tahiti, where he idled away nearly a year. After another year at sea he returned to America in the fall of 1844.

Experience made Melville too aware of the evil in the world to be a transcendentalist. His dark view of human nature culminated in *Moby-Dick* (1851). This book, Melville said, was "broiled in hellfire." Against the background of a whaling voyage he dealt subtly and symbolically with the problems of good and evil, of courage and cowardice, of faith, stubbornness, and pride. In Captain Ahab, driven relentlessly to hunt down the huge white whale Moby Dick, which had destroyed his leg, Melville created one of the great figures of literature; in the book as a whole, he produced one of the finest novels written by an American, comparable to the best in any language.

As Melville's work became more profound, it lost its appeal to the average reader, and its originality and symbolic meaning escaped most of the critics. *Moby-Dick*, his masterpiece, received little attention and most of that unfavorable. He kept on writing until his death in 1891 but was virtually ignored. Only in the 1920s did the critics rediscover him and give him his merited place in the history of American literature.

Walt Whitman

Walt Whitman, whose *Leaves of Grass* (1855) was the last of the great literary works of this brief outpouring of genius, was the most romantic and by far the most distinctly American writer of his age. He was born on Long Island, outside New York City, in 1819. At thirteen he left school and worked for a printer; thereafter he held a succession of newspaper jobs in the metropolitan area.

◄●►─[Read the Document

Whitman, Preface to *Leaves of Grass* at **myhistorylab.com**

Although genuinely a "common man," thoroughly at home among tradesmen and laborers, he was surely not an ordinary man. During the early 1850s, while employed as a carpenter and composing the poems that made up *Leaves of Grass*, he regularly carried a book of Emerson in his lunch box. "I was simmering, simmering, simmering," he later recalled. "Emerson brought me to a boil." The transcendental idea that inspiration and aspiration are at the heart of all achievement captivated him. Poets could best

Some scholars regard Walt Whitman as a poet of nature, and others, a poet of the body—a reference to erotic lines such as: "Without shame the man I like knows and avows the deliciousness of his sex. Without shame the woman I like knows and avows hers." Whitman's Leaves of Grass had every leaf in nature, complained critic E. P. Whipple, except the fig leaf.

Photo Credit: The Granger Collection, New York.

express themselves, he believed, by relying uncritically on their natural inclinations without regard for rigid metrical forms.

Leaves of Grass consisted of a preface, in which Whitman made the extraordinary statement that Americans had "probably the fullest poetical nature" of any people in history, and twelve poems in free verse: rambling, uneven, appearing to most readers shocking both in the commonplace nature of the subject matter and the coarseness of the language. Emerson, Thoreau, and a few others saw a fresh talent in these poems, but most readers and reviewers found them offensive. Indeed, the work was so undisciplined and so much of it had no obvious meaning that it was easy to miss the many passages of great beauty and originality.

Part of Whitman's difficulty arose because there was much of the charlatan in his makeup; often his writing did not ring true. He loved to use foreign words and phrases, and since he had no more than a smattering of any foreign language, he sounded pretentious and sometimes downright foolish when he did so. In reality a sensitive, gentle person, he tried to pose as a great, rough character. (Later in his career he bragged of fathering no less than six illegitimate children, which was assuredly untrue.) He never married, and his work suggests that his strongest emotional ties were with men. Thomas Carlyle once remarked shrewdly that Whitman thought he was a big man because he lived in a big country.

Whitman's work was more authentically American than that of any contemporary. His egoism—he titled one of his finest poems "Song of Myself"—was tempered by his belief that he was typical of all humanity:

> I celebrate myself and sing myself
> And what I assume you shall assume,
> For every atom belonging to me as good belongs to you.

Source: Walt Whitman "Song of Myself."

He had a remarkable ear for rendering common speech poetically, for employing slang, and for catching the breezy informality of Americans and their faith in themselves:

> *Earth! you seem to look for something at my hands,*
> *Say, old top-knot, what do you want?*
> *I bequeath myself to the dirt to grow from the grass I love,*
> *If you want me again look for me under your boot-soles.*

Source: Walt Whitman "Song of Myself."

Because of these qualities and because in his later work, especially during the Civil War, he occasionally struck a popular chord, Whitman was never as neglected as Melville. When he died in 1892, he was, if not entirely understood, at least widely appreciated.

Reading and the Dissemination of Culture

As the population grew and became more concentrated, and as society, especially in the North, was permeated by a middle-class point of view, popular concern for "culture" in the formal sense increased. A largely literate people, committed to the idea of education but not generally well-educated, set their hearts on being "refined" and "cultivated." Industrialization made it easier to satisfy this new demand for culture, though the new machines also tended to make the artifacts of culture more stereotyped.

Improved printing techniques reduced the cost of books, magazines, and newspapers. In the 1850s one publisher sold a fifty-volume set of Sir Walter Scott for $37.50. The first penny newspaper was the *New York Sun* (1833), but James Gordon Bennett's *New York Herald*, founded in 1835, brought the cheap new journalism to perfection. The *Boston Daily Times* and the *Philadelphia Public Ledger* soon followed. The penny newspapers depended on sensation, crime stories, and society gossip to attract readers, but they covered important national and international news too.

The desire for knowledge and culture in America is well illustrated by the success of the mutual improvement societies known as **lyceums**. The movement began in Great Britain; in the United States its prime mover was Josiah Holbrook, an itinerant lecturer and sometime schoolmaster from Connecticut. Holbrook founded the first lyceum in 1826 at Millbury, Massachusetts; within five years there were over a thousand scattered across the country. The lyceums conducted discussions, established libraries, and lobbied for better schools. Soon they began to sponsor lecture series on topics of every sort. Many of the nation's political and intellectual leaders, such as Webster, Emerson, Melville, and Lowell, regularly graced their platforms. So did other less famous lecturers who in the name of culture pronounced on subjects ranging from "Chemistry Applied to the Mechanic Arts" to a description of the tombs of the Egyptian pharaohs.

Education for Democracy

Except on the edge of the frontier and in the South, most youngsters between the ages of five and ten attended a school for at least a couple of months of the year. These schools, however, were privately run and charged fees. Attendance was not required and fell off sharply once children learned to read and do their sums well enough to get along in day-to-day life. The teachers were usually young men waiting for something better to turn up.

All this changed with the rise of the common school movement. At the heart of the movement was the belief, widely expressed in the first days of the republic, that a government based on democratic rule must provide the means, as Jefferson put it, to "diffuse knowledge throughout the mass of the people." This meant free tax-supported schools that all children were expected to attend. It also came to mean that such an educational system should be administered on a statewide basis and that teaching should become a profession that required formal training.

The two most effective leaders of the common school movement were Henry Barnard and Horace Mann. Both were New Englanders, Whigs, trained in the law, and in other ways conservative types. They shared an unquenchable faith in the improvability of the human race through education. Mann drafted the 1837 Massachusetts law creating a state school board and then became its first secretary. Over the next decade Mann's annual reports carried the case for common schools to every corner of the land. Seldom given to understatement, Mann called common schools "the greatest discovery ever made by man." He encouraged young women to become teachers while commending them to school boards by claiming that they could get along on lower salaries than men.

Read the Document

Mann, *Report of the Massachusetts Board of Education* at **myhistorylab.com**

Young women heeded the call. By 1860, women comprised 78 percent of the common school teachers in Massachusetts, a trend that prefigured developments elsewhere. The influx of young women invigorated the common schools and brought to the enterprise the zeal of a missionary. Harriet Beecher Stowe, who once taught at the Hartford Seminary, explained that men teachers lacked the "patience, the long-suffering, and gentleness necessary to superintend the formation of character."

By the 1850s every state outside the South provided free elementary schools and supported institutions for training teachers. Many extended public education to include high schools, and Michigan and Iowa even established publicly supported colleges.

Historians differ in explaining the success of the common school movement. Some stress the arguments Mann used to win support from employers by appealing to their need for trained and well-disciplined workers. Others see the schools as designed to "Americanize" the increasing numbers of non-English and non-Protestant immigrants who were flooding into the country. (Supporting this argument is the fact that Catholic bishops in New York and elsewhere opposed laws requiring Catholic children to attend these "Protestant" schools and set up their own private, parochial schools.)

Still other scholars argue that middle-class reformers favored public elementary schools on the theory that they would instill the values of hard work, punctuality, and submissiveness to authority in children of the laboring classes. All these reasons played a part in advancing the cause of the common schools. Yet it remains the case that the most compelling argument for common schools was cultural; more effectively than any other institution, they brought Americans of different economic circumstances and ethnic backgrounds into early and mutually beneficial contact with one another. They served the two roles that Mann assigned to them: "the balance wheel of the social machinery" and "the great equalizer."

Watch the Video

Who Was Horace Mann and Why Are So Many Schools Named After Him? at **myhistorylab.com**

The State of the Colleges

Unlike common schools, with their democratic overtones, private colleges had at best a precarious place in Jacksonian America. For one thing, there were too many of them. Any

Watch the Video

What Was the Progressive Education Movement? at **myhistorylab.com**

town with pretensions of becoming a regional center felt it had to have a college. Ohio had twenty-five in the 1850s, and Tennessee sixteen. Many of these institutions were short-lived. Of the fourteen colleges founded in Kentucky between 1800 and 1850, only half were still operating in 1860.

The problem of supply was compounded by a demand problem—too few students. Enrollment at the largest, Yale, never topped 400 until the mid-1840s. On the eve of the Civil War the largest state university, North Carolina, had fewer than 500. Higher education was beyond the means of the average family. Although most colleges charged less than half the $55 tuition required by Harvard, that was still too much for most families. So desperate was the shortage that colleges accepted applicants as young as eleven and twelve and as old as thirty.

The typical college curriculum, dominated by the study of Latin and Greek, had almost no practical relevance except for future clergymen. The Yale faculty, most of them ministers, defended the classics as admirably providing for both "the discipline and the furniture of the mind," but these subjects commended themselves to college officials chiefly because they did not require costly equipment or a faculty that knew anything else. Professors spent most of their time in and out of the classroom trying to maintain a semblance of order, "to the exclusion of any great literary undertakings to which their choice might lead them," one explained. "Our country is yet too young for old professors," a Bostonian informed a foreign visitor in the 1830s, "and, besides, they are too poorly paid to induce first rate men to devote themselves to the business of lecturing. . . . We consider professors as secondary men."

Fortunately for the future of higher education, some college officials recognized the need for a drastic overhaul of their institutions. President Francis Wayland of Brown University used his 1842 address, "On the Present Collegiate System," to call for a thorough revamping of the curriculum to make it responsive to the economic realities of American society. This meant more courses in science, economics (where Wayland's own *Elements of Political Economy* might be used), modern history, and applied mathematics; and fewer in Hebrew, biblical studies, Greek, and ancient history.

Yale established a separate school of science in 1847, which it hoped would attract serious-minded students and research-minded professors. At Harvard, which also opened a scientific school, students were allowed to choose some of their courses and were compelled to earn grades as a stimulus to study. Colleges in the West and the South began to offer mechanical and agricultural subjects relevant to their regional economies. Oberlin enrolled four female students in 1837, and the first women's college, the Georgia Female College, opened its doors in 1839.

These reforms slowed the downward spiral of colleges; they did not restore them to the honored place they had enjoyed in the Revolutionary era. Of the first six presidents of the United States, only Washington did not graduate from college. Beginning in 1829, seven of the next eleven did not. In this Presidents Jackson, Van Buren, Harrison, Taylor, Fillmore, Lincoln, and Johnson were like 98 of every 100 white males, all blacks and Indians, and all but a handful of white women in mid-nineteenth-century America. Going to college had yet, in Wayland's words, to "commend itself to the good sense and patriotism of the American people."

Milestones

1774	Mother Ann Lee founds first Shaker community	1843	Dorothea Dix exposes treatment of the insane in *Memorial to the Legislature of Massachusetts*
1784	Dr. Benjamin Rush's *Inquiry into the Effects of Ardent Spirits* questions alcohol's benefits	1844	Margaret Fuller condemns sexual discrimination in *Women in the Nineteenth Century*
1826	American Temperance Union begins campaign against drunkenness		Nauvoo mob murders Joseph Smith
1829	Black abolitionist David Walker publishes *Appeal to the Coloured Citizens of the World*	1845	Frederick Douglass describes slave life in *Narrative of the Life of Frederick Douglass*
1830s	Second Great Awakening stresses promise of salvation	1847	Brigham Young leads Mormon migration to Great Salt Lake
	Prison reformers debate Auburn versus Philadelphia system	1848	Elizabeth Cady Stanton and Lucretia Mott organize Seneca Falls Convention and draft Declaration of Sentiments
1830–1850	Utopian communities flourish		
1830	Joseph Smith shares his "vision" in *Book of Mormon*	1850	Nathaniel Hawthorne publishes *The Scarlet Letter*
1831	Abolitionist William Lloyd Garrison founds *The Liberator* and New England Anti-Slavery Society	1851	Maine bans alcoholic beverages
			Herman Melville publishes *Moby-Dick*
1831–1832	Alexis de Tocqueville and Gustave de Beaumont tour America	1854–1855	Susan B. Anthony leads petition campaign against New York property and divorce laws
1832	Perkins Institution for the Blind opens in Boston	1854	Henry David Thoreau attacks conformity in *Walden*
1837	Illinois abolitionist Elijah Lovejoy is murdered	1855–1892	Walt Whitman publishes *Leaves of Grass* (various editions)
	Ralph Waldo Emerson delivers "The American Scholar" at Harvard		
	Horace Mann and Henry Barnard call for common schools		

✓●—[Study and Review at www.myhistorylab.com

Review Questions

1. The introduction to this chapter suggests that the "traditional" family was far more common in the mid-nineteenth century than nowadays. What were its strengths and limitations?

2. Many institutions were created during the years from 1820 to 1850; many remain a part of contemporary life. Prisons are an obvious example. What other institutions were established during this period that exist today? Does their persistence prove their value to society or the difficulty of eliminating outmoded institutions?

3. How did the changing attitudes toward marriage and children influence the rise of reform movements during the first half of the nineteenth century? How did the Great Awakening contribute to the social reforms of the era?

4. The campaign for women's rights and woman suffrage gained momentum during this period. Did these new ideas of women's roles in society stimulate the structural transformation of the family (fewer children, for example), or did the smaller families free women to undertake new initiatives such as reform and woman's suffrage?

5. Why did the great writers of the age—Emerson, Thoreau, Melville, Hawthorne, Whitman—fail to find large audiences?

Key Terms

abolitionism
Cult of True
    Womanhood
lyceums
romanticism

Second Great
    Awakening
Seneca Falls
    Convention
Shakers

temperance
    movement
transcendentalism
utopian

Westward Expansion

((•─Hear the Audio at myhistorylab.com

Has your family crossed borders?

IN 2010 ADRIANA CARILLO, A MEMBER OF THE MEXICAN SENATE, DERIDED
President Barack Obama's plans to strengthen the 700-mile fence between the United
States and Mexico. She explained that Spanish-speaking peoples, many of them of
Mexican descent, constituted a third of the population of New Mexico, California,
Texas, and Arizona. No fence, she declared, should separate the southwestern United
States and Mexico, a region bound by economic and cultural ties. On the other side of
the fence—literally and rhetorically—U.S. Senator Lamar Smith of San Antonio, Texas,
complained that Obama was not doing enough to stem the flood of illegal immigrants
into the United States.

As the debate raged, few noted that the United States had built the fence to prevent
Mexicans from passing into lands that had once belonged to Mexico. In 1821, when
Mexico secured its independence from Spain, the American Southwest became Mexican
territory. But the heavy influx of American settlers into the Mexican state of Texas
prompted Mexico to restrict further American immigration. Yet the "illegal" immigrants
kept coming into Texas; some talked of independence and in 1836 secured it by war. In
1845 Texas became part of the United States; California (1850), New Mexico (1912) and
Arizona (1912) would follow. Mexicans who entered the region were trespassing; in time,
they would become illegal immigrants.

The acquisition of the Southwest by the United States had several important (if unin-
tended) consequences. The most important concerned slavery. The annexation of Texas
as a slave state raised the question of slavery throughout the Southwest. Would the "peculiar institution" eventually span the entire continent, stretching all the way to California?
And, if the federal government disallowed slavery in some of the western regions, why not
all of them? A crisis of inconceivable dimensions loomed.

Tyler's Troubles

John Tyler, who became president in 1841 after the death of William Henry Harrison,
was a thin, rather delicate-appearing man. Courteous, tactful, and soft-spoken, he gave
the impression of being weak, an impression reinforced by his professed belief that the

From Chapter 11 of *American Destiny: Narrative of a Nation*, Combined Volume, Fourth Edition.
Mark C. Carnes and John A. Garraty. Copyright © 2012 by Pearson Education, Inc. Published by
Pearson Prentice Hall. All rights reserved.

president should defer to Congress in the formulation of policy. This was a false impression; John Tyler was stubborn and proud, and these characteristics combined with an almost total lack of imagination to make him worship consistency. He had turned away from Jackson because of the aggressive way the president had used his powers of appointment and the veto, but he also disagreed with Henry Clay and the northern Whigs about the Bank, protection, and federal internal improvements. Being a states' rights Southerner, he considered such measures unconstitutional. Nevertheless, he was prepared to cooperate with Clay as the leader of what he called the "more immediate representatives" of the people, the members of Congress. But he was not prepared to be Clay's puppet. He asked all of Harrison's Cabinet to remain in office.

Tyler and Clay did not get along, and for this Clay was chiefly to blame. He behaved in an overbearing manner that was out of keeping with his nature, probably because he resented having been passed over by the Whigs in 1840. He considered himself the real head of the Whig party and intended to exercise his leadership.

In Congress, Clay announced a comprehensive federal program that ignored Tyler's states' rights view of the Constitution. Most important was his plan to set up a new Bank of the United States. When Congress passed the new Bank bill, Tyler vetoed it. The entire Cabinet except Secretary of State Daniel Webster thereupon resigned in protest.

Abandoned by the Whigs, Tyler attempted to build a party of his own. He failed to do so, and for the remainder of his term the political squabbling in Washington was continuous.

The Webster-Ashburton Treaty

Webster's decision to remain in the Cabinet was motivated in part by his desire to settle the boundary between Maine and New Brunswick. The intent of the peace treaty of 1783 had been to award the United States all land in the area drained by rivers flowing into the Atlantic rather than into the St. Lawrence, but the wording was obscure and the old maps conflicting. In 1842 the British sent a new minister, Lord Ashburton, to the United States to try to settle all outstanding disputes. Ashburton and Webster easily worked out a compromise boundary. The British needed only a small part of the territory to build a military road connecting Halifax and Quebec. Webster, who thought any settlement desirable simply to eliminate a possible cause of war, willingly agreed.

Webster solved the problem of placating Maine and Massachusetts, both of which wanted every acre of the land in dispute, in an extraordinary manner. During the peace negotiations ending the Revolution, Franklin had marked the boundary between Maine and Canada on a map with a heavy red line, but no one could find the Franklin map. Webster obtained an old map of the area and had someone mark off in red a line that followed the British version of the boundary. He showed this document to representatives of Maine and Massachusetts, convincing them that they had better agree to his compromise before the British got wind of it and demanded the whole region! It later came out that the British had a true copy of the Franklin map, which showed that the entire area rightfully belonged to the United States.

Nevertheless, Webster's generosity made excellent sense. Lord Ashburton, gratified by having obtained the strategic territory, made concessions elsewhere along the Canadian and American border. British dependence on foreign foodstuffs was increasing; America's need for British capital was rising. War, or even unsettled affairs, would have injured vital business relations and produced no compensating gains. The **Webster-Ashburton Treaty** was regarded as a diplomatic triumph.

The Texas Question

The settlement with Great Britain won support in every section of the United States, but the same could not be said for Tyler's attempt to annex the Republic of Texas, for this involved the question of slavery. In the Transcontinental Treaty of 1819 with Spain the boundary of the United States had been drawn in such a way as to exclude Texas. This seemed unimportant at the time, yet within months of the treaty's ratification in February 1821, Americans led by Stephen F. Austin had begun to settle in the area. Almost simultaneously Mexico threw off the last vestiges of Spanish rule and secured its independence. Texas was now part of Mexico.

Cotton flourished on the fertile Texas plains, and for a time, the new Mexican authorities offered free land and something approaching local autonomy to groups of settlers from the United States. By 1830 there were some 20,000 white Americans in Texas, about 2,000 slaves, and only a few thousand Mexicans.

President John Quincy Adams had offered Mexico $1 million for Texas, and Jackson was willing to pay $5 million, but Mexico would not sell. Nevertheless, by the late 1820s, the flood of American settlers was giving the Mexican authorities second thoughts. The immigrants apparently felt no loyalty to Mexico. Most were Protestants, though Mexican law required that all immigrants be Catholics; few attempted to learn more than a few words of Spanish. When Mexico outlawed slavery in 1829, American settlers evaded the law by "freeing" their slaves and then signing them to lifetime contracts as indentured servants. In 1830 Mexico prohibited further immigration of Americans into Texas, though again the law proved impossible to enforce.

As soon as the Mexican government began to restrict them, the Texans began to seek independence. In 1835 a series of skirmishes escalated into a full-scale rebellion. The Mexican president, Antonio López de Santa Anna, marched north with over 5,000 soldiers to subdue the rebels. Late in February 1836 he reached San Antonio.

A force of 187 men under Colonel William B. Travis held the city. They took refuge behind the stout walls of a former mission called the Alamo. For nearly two weeks they held off Santa Anna's assaults, inflicting terrible casualties on the attackers. Finally, on March 6, the Mexicans breached and scaled the walls. Once

Read the Document

Travis, *Letter from the Alamo* at **myhistorylab.com**

inside they killed everyone, even the wounded. Among the dead were the legendary Davy Crockett and Jim Bowie, inventor of the Bowie knife. (See Re-Viewing the Past, *The Alamo*.)

After the Alamo and the slaughter of another garrison at Goliad, southeast of San Antonio, peaceful settlement of the dispute between Texas and Mexico was impossible. Meanwhile, on March 2, 1836, Texas had declared its independence. Sam Houston, a former congressman and governor of Tennessee and an experienced Indian fighter, was placed in charge of the rebel army. For a time Houston retreated before Santa Anna's troops, who greatly outnumbered his own. At the San Jacinto River he took a stand. On April 21, 1836, shouting "Forward! Charge! Remember the Alamo! Remember Goliad!" his troops routed the Mexican army, which soon retreated across the Rio Grande. In October, Houston was elected president of the Republic of Texas, and a month later a plebiscite revealed that an overwhelming majority favored annexation by the United States.

President Jackson hesitated. To take Texas might lead to war with Mexico. Assuredly it would stir up the slavery controversy. On his last day in office he recognized the republic, but he made no move to accept it into the Union, nor did his successor, Van Buren. Texas thereupon went its own way, which involved developing friendly ties with Great Britain. An independent Texas suited British tastes perfectly, for it could provide an alternative supply of raw cotton and a market for manufactures unfettered by tariffs.

Sam Houston—and his horse—earned this heroic tribute. At the Battle of San Jacinto, a musket ball shattered Houston's right ankle; his horse, hit by five bullets, fell dead.

Source: San Jacinto Museum of History, Houston.

These events caused alarm in the United States, especially among Southerners, who dreaded the possibility that a Texas dominated by Great Britain might abolish slavery. As a Southerner, Tyler shared these feelings; as a beleaguered politician, spurned by the Whigs and held in contempt by most Democrats, he saw in annexation a chance to revive his fortunes. When Webster resigned as secretary of state in 1843, Tyler replaced him with a fellow Virginian, Abel P. Upshur, whom he ordered to seek a treaty of annexation. The South was eager to take Texas, and in the West and even the Northeast the patriotic urge to add such a magnificent new territory to the national domain was great. Upshur negotiated a treaty in February 1844, but before he could sign it he was killed by the accidental explosion of a cannon on USS *Princeton* during a weapons demonstration.

To ensure the winning of Texas, Tyler appointed John C. Calhoun secretary of state. This was a blunder; by then Calhoun was so closely associated with the South and with slavery that his appointment alienated thousands of Northerners who might otherwise have welcomed annexation. Suddenly Texas became a hot political issue. Clay and Van Buren, who seemed assured of the 1844 Whig and Democratic presidential nominations, promptly announced that they opposed annexation, chiefly on the ground that it would probably lead to war with Mexico. With a national election in the offing, northern and western senators refused to vote for annexation, and in June the Senate rejected the treaty, 35 to 16. The Texans were angry and embarrassed, the British eager again to take advantage of the situation.

Watch the Video
The Annexation of Texas
at **myhistorylab.com**

Manifest Destiny

The Senate, Clay, and Van Buren had all misinterpreted public opinion. John C. Calhoun, whose world was so far removed from that of the average citizen, in this case anticipated the mood of the country.

After 200 years of westward expansion, Americans perceived their destined goal: *The whole continent was to be theirs!* A New York journalist, John L. O'Sullivan, captured the new mood in a sentence. Nothing must interfere, he wrote in 1845, with "the fulfillment of our *manifest destiny* to overspread the continent allotted by Providence for the free development of our yearly multiplying millions."

Read the Document
John O'Sullivan, *Annexation* at
myhistorylab.com

The expansion, stimulated by the natural growth of the population and by a revived flood of immigration, was going on in every section and with little regard for political boundaries. New settlers rolled westward in hordes to fulfill their **manifest destiny**. The politicians did not sense the new mood in 1844; even Calhoun, who saw the acquisition of Texas as part of a broader program, was thinking of balancing sectional interests rather than of national expansion.

Life on the Trail

The romantic myths attached by later generations to this mighty human tide have obscured the adjustments forced on the pioneers and focused attention on the least significant of the dangers they faced and the hardships they endured. For example, Indians could of course be deadly enemies, but pioneers were more likely to complain that

In *American Progress* (1872), John Gast depicts a feminized (and eroticized) America moving westward, a school book in one hand, a telegraph wire in the other. Confronted with the onslaught of "civilization," the buffalo flee and the Indians cringe.

Photo Credit: Courtesy of the Library of Congress.

the Indians they encountered were dirty, lazy, and pitiably poor than to worry about the danger of Indian attack.

The greater dangers were accidents on the trail, particularly to children, and also unsanitary conditions and exposure to the elements. "Going west" had always been laborious, but in the 1840s the distances covered were longer by far and the comforts and conveniences of "civilization" that had to be left behind, being more extensive than those available to earlier generations, tended to be more painful to surrender.

Travel on the plains west of the Mississippi was especially taxing for women. Some assumed tasks traditionally performed by men. "I keep close to my gun and dog," a woman from Illinois wrote in her diary. But most found the experience disillusioning. Guidebooks promised them that "regular exercise, in the open air . . . gives additional vigor and strength." But the books did not prepare women for collecting dried buffalo dung for fuel, for the heat and choking dust of summer, for the monotony, the dirt, the cramped quarters. Caring for an infant or a two-year-old in a wagon could be torture week after week on the trail.

California and Oregon

By 1840 many Americans had settled far to the west in California, which was unmistakably Mexican territory, and in the Oregon country, jointly claimed by the United States and Great Britain; and it was to these distant regions that the pioneers traveled in increasing numbers as the decade progressed. California was a sparsely settled land of some 7,000 Spanish-speaking ranchers and a handful of "Anglo" settlers from the United States. Until the 1830s, when their estates were broken up by the anticlerical Mexican government, twenty-one Catholic missions, stretching north from San Diego to San Francisco, controlled more than 30,000 Indian converts, who were little better off than slaves.

Oregon, a vaguely defined area between California and Russian Alaska, proved still more alluring to Americans. Captain Robert Gray had sailed up the Columbia River in 1792, and Lewis and Clark had visited the region on their great expedition. In 1811 John Jacob Astor's Pacific Fur Company had established trading posts on the Columbia. Two decades later Methodist, Presbyterian, and Catholic missionaries began to find their way into the Willamette Valley, a green land of rich soil, mild climate, and tall forests teeming with game. Gradually a small number of settlers followed, until by 1840 there were about 500 Americans in the Willamette area.

In the early 1840s, fired by the spirit of manifest destiny, the country suddenly burned with "Oregon fever." In dozens upon dozens of towns, societies were founded to collect information and organize groups to make the march to the Pacific. Land hunger (stimulated by glowing reports from the scene) drew the new migrants most powerfully, but the patriotic concept of manifest destiny gave the trek across the 2,000 miles of wilderness separating Oregon from the western edge of American settlement in Missouri the character of a crusade. In 1843 nearly 1,000 pioneers made the long trip.

The Oregon Trail began at the western border of Missouri and followed the Kansas River and the muddy Platte past Fort Laramie to the Rockies. It crossed the Continental Divide by the relatively easy South Pass, veered south to Fort Bridger (on Mexican soil), and then ran north and west through the valley of the Snake River and

Ada McColl gathers buffalo chips, used for fuel, in western Nebraska.
Source: Kansas State Historical Society.

eventually, by way of the Columbia, to Fort Vancouver, a British post guarding the entrance to the Willamette Valley.

Over this tortuous path wound the canvas-covered caravans with their scouts and their accompanying herds. Each group became a self-governing community on the march, with regulations democratically agreed on "for the

◄●►Read the Document

Geer, *Oregon Trail Journal* at myhistorylab.com

purpose of keeping good order and promoting civil and military discipline." Most of the travelers consisted of young families, some from as far away as the East Coast cities, more from towns and farms in the Ohio Valley. Few could be classified as poor because the cost of the trip for a family of four was about $600, no small sum at that time. (The faster and less fatiguing trip by ship around South America cost about $600 per person.)

For large groups Indians posed no great threat (though constant vigilance was necessary), but the five-month trip was full of labor, discomfort, and uncertainty. "It became so monotonous after a while that I would have welcomed an Indian fight if awake," one man wrote. And at the end lay the regular tasks of pioneering. The spirit of the trailblazers is caught in an entry from the diary of James Nesmith:

> Friday, October 27.—Arrived at Oregon City at the falls of the Willamette.
> Saturday, October 28.—Went to work.

Trails West The Old Spanish Trail was the earliest of the trails west. Part of it was mapped in 1776 by a Franciscan missionary. The Santa Fe Trail came into use after 1823. The Oregon Trail was pioneered by trappers and missionaries. The Mormon Trail was first traversed in 1847, while the Oxbow Route, developed under a federal mail contract, was used from 1858 to 1861.

Behind the dreams of the Far West as an American Eden lay the commercial importance of the three major West Coast harbors: San Diego, San Francisco, and the Strait of Juan de Fuca leading into Puget Sound. Eastern merchants considered these harbors the keys to the trade of the Orient. That San Diego and San Francisco were Mexican and the Puget Sound district was claimed by Great Britain only heightened their desire to possess them. As early as 1835, Jackson tried to buy the San Francisco region. Even Calhoun called San Francisco the future New York of the Pacific and proposed buying all of California from Mexico.

The Election of 1844

In the spring of 1844 expansion did not seem likely to affect the presidential election. The Whigs nominated Clay unanimously and ignored Texas in their party platform. When the Democrats gathered in convention at Baltimore in May, Van Buren appeared to have the nomination in his pocket. He too wanted to keep Texas out of the campaign. John C. Calhoun, however, was determined to make Texas a campaign issue.

That a politician of Van Buren's caliber, controlling the party machinery, could be upset at a national convention seemed unthinkable. But upset he was, for the southern delegates rallied round the Calhoun policy of taking Texas to save it for slavery. "I can beat Clay and Van Buren put together on this issue," Calhoun boasted. "They are behind the age." James K. Polk of Tennessee, who favored expansion, swept the convention.

Polk was a good Jacksonian; his supporters called him "Young Hickory." He opposed high tariffs and was dead set against establishing another national bank. But he believed in taking Texas. The Democratic platform demanded that Texas be "reannexed" (implying that it had been part of the Louisiana Purchase) and that all of Oregon be "reoccupied" (suggesting repeal of the joint occupation of the region with Great Britain, which had been agreed to in the Convention of 1818).

Texas was now in the campaign. When Clay sensed the new expansionist sentiment of the voters, he tried to hedge on his opposition to annexation, but by doing so he probably lost as many votes as he gained. The election was extremely close. The campaign followed the pattern established in 1840, with stress on parades, mass meetings, and slogans. Polk carried the country by only 38,000 of 2.7 million votes. In the Electoral College the vote was 170 to 105. Polk's victory was nevertheless taken as a mandate for expansion. Tyler promptly called on Congress to take Texas by joint resolution, which was done a few days before Tyler left the White House. Under the resolution, if the new state agreed, as many as four new states might be carved from its territory. Polk accepted this arrangement, and in December 1845 Texas became a state.

Polk as President

Polk was uncommonly successful in doing what he set out to do as president. He persuaded Congress to lower the tariff of 1842 and to restore the independent treasury. He opposed federal internal improvements and managed to have his way. He made himself the spokesman of American expansion by committing himself to obtaining, in addition to Texas, both Oregon and the great Southwest. Here again, he succeeded.

Oregon was the first order of business. In his inaugural address Polk stated the American claim to the entire region in the plainest terms, but he informed the British minister in Washington, Richard Pakenham, that he would accept a boundary following the forty-ninth parallel to the Pacific. Pakenham rejected this proposal without submitting it to London, and Polk thereupon decided to insist again on the whole area. When Congress met in December 1845, he asked for authority to give the necessary one year's notice for withdrawing from the 1818 treaty of joint occupation. Following considerable discussion, Congress complied and in May 1846 Polk notified Great Britain that he intended to terminate the joint occupation.

The British then decided to compromise. Officials of the Hudson's Bay Company had become alarmed by the rapid growth of the American settlement in the Willamette Valley. By 1845 some 5,000 people had poured into the region, whereas the country north of the Columbia contained no more than 750 British subjects. The company decided to shift its base from the Columbia to Vancouver Island. And British experts outside the company reported that the Oregon country could not possibly be defended in case of war. Thus, when Polk accompanied the one-year notice with a hint that he would again consider a compromise, the British foreign secretary, Lord Aberdeen, hastily suggested Polk's earlier proposal, dividing the Oregon territory along the forty-ninth parallel. Polk agreed. The treaty followed that line from the Rockies to Puget Sound, but Vancouver Island, which extends below the line, was left entirely to the British, so that both nations retained free use of the Strait of Juan de Fuca. Although some northern Democrats accused Polk of treachery because he had failed to fight for all of Oregon, the treaty so obviously accorded with the national interest that the Senate approved it by a large majority in June 1846. Polk was then free to take up the Texas question in earnest.

War with Mexico

One reason for the popularity of the Oregon compromise was that the country was already at war with Mexico and wanted no trouble with Great Britain. The **Mexican War** had broken out in large measure because of the expansionist spirit, and the confidence born of its overwhelming advantages of size and wealth certainly encouraged the United States to bully Mexico. In addition, Mexico had defaulted on debts owed the United States, which caused some people to suggest using force to obtain the money. But Mexican pride was also involved. Texas had been independent for the better part of a decade, and Mexico had made no serious effort to reconquer it; nevertheless, Mexico never recognized its independence and promptly broke off diplomatic relations when the United States annexed the republic.

Polk then ordered General Zachary Taylor into Texas to defend the border. However, the location of that border was in dispute. Texas claimed the Rio Grande; Mexico insisted that the boundary was the Nueces River, which emptied into the Gulf of Mexico about 150 miles to the north. Taylor reached the Nueces in July 1845 with about 1,500 troops and crossed into the disputed territory. He stopped on the southern bank at Corpus Christi, not wishing to provoke the Mexicans by marching to the Rio Grande.

In November, Polk sent an envoy, John Slidell, on a secret mission to Mexico to try to obtain the disputed territory by negotiation. He authorized Slidell to

The War with Mexico, 1846–1848 The war with Mexico required considerable coordination of far-flung military and naval operations.

cancel the Mexican debt in return for recognition of the annexation of Texas and acceptance of the Rio Grande boundary. The president also empowered Slidell to offer as much as $30 million if Mexico would sell the United States all or part of New Mexico and California.

It would probably have been to Mexico's advantage, at least in the short run, to have made a deal with Slidell. The area Polk wanted, lying in the path of American expansion, was likely to be engulfed as Texas had been, without regard for the actions of the American or Mexican governments. But the Mexican government refused to receive Slidell. Amid a wave of anti-American feeling, a military coup occurred and General Mariano Paredes, the new head of state, promptly reaffirmed his country's claim to all of Texas. Slidell returned to Washington convinced that the Mexicans would not give an inch until they had been "chastised."

Polk had already ordered Taylor to advance to the Rio Grande. By late March 1846 the army, which swelled to about 4,000, had taken up positions near the Mexican town of Matamoros. The Mexicans crossed the river on April 25 and attacked an American mounted patrol. They were driven back easily, but when news of the fighting reached Washington, Polk asked Congress to declare war. He treated the matter as a *fait accompli*: "War exists," he stated flatly. Congress accepted this reasoning and without actually declaring war voted to raise and supply an additional 50,000 troops.

From the first battle, the outcome of the Mexican War was never in doubt. At Palo Alto, north of the Rio Grande, 2,300 Americans scattered a Mexican force more than twice their number. Then, 1,700 Americans routed 7,500 Mexicans at Resaca de la Palma near what is now Brownsville, Texas. Fewer than 50 U.S. soldiers lost their lives in these engagements, while Mexican losses in killed, wounded, and captured exceeded 1,000. Within a week of the outbreak of hostilities, the Mexicans had been driven across the Rio Grande and General Taylor had his troops firmly established on the southern bank.

To the Halls of Montezuma

President Polk insisted not only on directing grand strategy but on supervising hundreds of petty details, down to the purchase of mules and the promotion of enlisted men. But he allowed party considerations to control his choice of generals. This partisanship caused unnecessary turmoil in army ranks. He wanted, as Thomas Hart Benton said, "a small war, just large enough to require a treaty of peace, and not large enough to make military reputations dangerous for the presidency."

◆●━[Read the Document

Thomas Corwin, *Against the Mexican War* at **myhistorylab.com**

Unfortunately for Polk, both Taylor and Winfield Scott, the commanding general in Washington, were Whigs. Polk, who tended to suspect the motives of anyone who disagreed with him, feared that one or the other would make political capital of his popularity as a military leader. The examples of his hero, Jackson, and of General Harrison loomed large in Polk's thinking.

Polk's attitude was narrow, almost unpatriotic, but not unrealistic. Zachary Taylor was not a brilliant soldier. He had joined the army in 1808 and made it his whole life. He cared so little for politics that he had never bothered to cast a ballot in an election. Polk believed that he lacked the "grasp of mind" necessary for high command, and

Photo Credit: West Point Museum Art Collection, United States Military Academy, West Point, New York.

American soldiers—some of them regulars in deep blue uniforms, others in buckskin cowboy outfits—fight in the streets to drive Mexicans from a Spanish mission in Monterrey, California, in 1846.

General Scott complained of his "comfortable, laborsaving contempt for learning of every kind." But Taylor commanded the love and respect of his men, and he knew how to deploy them in the field. He had won another victory against a Mexican force three times larger than his own at Buena Vista in February 1847.

The dust had barely settled on the field of Buena Vista when Whig politicians began to pay Taylor court. "Great expectations and great consequences rest upon you," a Kentucky politician explained to him. "People everywhere begin to talk of converting you into a political leader, when the War is done."

Polk's concern was heightened because domestic opposition to the war was growing. Many Northerners feared that the war would lead to the expansion of slavery. Others—among them an obscure Illinois congressman named Abraham Lincoln—felt that Polk had misled Congress about the original outbreak of fighting and that the United States was the aggressor. The farther from the Rio Grande one went in the United States, the less popular "Mr. Polk's war" became; in New England opposition was almost as widespread as it had been to "Mr. Madison's war" in 1812.

Polk's design for prosecuting the war consisted of three parts. First, he would clear the Mexicans from Texas and occupy the northern provinces of Mexico. Second, he would take possession of California and New Mexico. Finally, he would march on Mexico City. Proceeding west from the Rio Grande, Taylor swiftly overran Mexico's northern provinces. In June 1846, American settlers in the Sacramento Valley seized Sonoma and raised the Bear Flag of the Republic of California. Another group, headed by Captain John C. Frémont, leader of an American exploring party that happened to be in the area, clashed with the Mexican authorities around Monterey, California, and then joined with the Sonoma rebels. A naval squadron under Commodore John D. Sloat captured Monterey and San Francisco in July 1846, and a squadron of cavalry joined the other American units in mopping-up operations around San Diego and Los Angeles. By February 1847 the United States had won control of nearly all of Mexico north of the capital city.

The campaign against Mexico City was the most difficult of the war. Fearful of Taylor's growing popularity and entertaining certain honest misgivings about his ability to oversee a complicated campaign, Polk put Winfield Scott in charge of the offensive.

About Scott's competence no one entertained a doubt. But he seemed even more of a threat to the Democrats than Taylor, because he had political ambitions as well as military ability. In 1840 the Whigs had considered him for president. Scion of an old Virginia family, Scott was intelligent, even-tempered, and cultivated, if somewhat pompous. After a sound but not spectacular record in the War of 1812, he had added to his reputation by helping modernize military administration and strengthen the professional training of officers. On the record, and despite the politics of the situation, Polk had little choice but to give him this command.

Scott landed his army south of Veracruz, Mexico, on March 9, 1847, laid siege to the city, and obtained its surrender in less than three weeks with the loss of only a handful of his 10,000 men. Marching westward through hostile country, he maintained effective discipline, avoiding atrocities that might have inflamed the countryside against him. Finding his way blocked by well-placed artillery and a large army at Cerro Gordo, where the National Road rose steeply toward the central highlands, Scott outflanked the Mexican position and then carried it by storm, capturing more than 3,000 prisoners and much equipment. By mid-May he had advanced to Puebla, only eighty miles southeast of Mexico City.

After delaying until August for the arrival of reinforcements, he pressed on, won two hard-fought victories at the outskirts of the capital, and on September 14 hammered his way into the city. In every engagement the American troops had been outnumbered, yet they always exacted a far heavier toll from the defenders than they themselves were forced to pay. In the fighting on the edge of Mexico City, for example, Scott's army sustained about 1,000 casualties, for the Mexicans defended their capital bravely. But 4,000 Mexicans were killed or wounded in the engagements, and 3,000 (including eight generals, two of them former presidents of the republic) were taken prisoner. No less an authority than the Duke of Wellington, the conqueror of Napoleon, called Scott's campaign the most brilliant of modern times.

The Treaty of Guadalupe Hidalgo

Following the fall of Mexico City, the Mexican government was in turmoil. Polk had authorized payment of $30 million for New Mexico, upper and lower California, and the right of transit across Mexico's narrow isthmus of Tehuantepec. Now, observing the disorganized state of Mexican affairs, he began to consider demanding more territory and paying less for it. He recalled his chief negotiator, Nicholas P. Trist, who ignored the order. Trist realized that unless a treaty was arranged soon, the Mexican government might disintegrate, leaving no one in authority to sign a treaty. He dashed off a sixty-five-page letter to the president, in effect refusing to be recalled, and continued to negotiate. Early in February the **Treaty of Guadalupe Hidalgo** was completed. By its terms Mexico accepted the Rio Grande as the boundary of Texas and ceded New Mexico and upper California to the United States. In return the United States agreed to pay Mexico $15 million and to take on the claims of American citizens against Mexico, which by that time amounted to another $3.25 million.

When he learned that Trist had ignored his orders, the president ordered that he be fired from the State Department and placed under arrest. Yet Polk had no choice but to submit the treaty to the Senate, for to have insisted on more territory would have meant more fighting, and the war had become increasingly unpopular. The relatively easy military victory made some people ashamed that their country was crushing a weaker neighbor. Abolitionists, led by William Lloyd Garrison, called it an "invasion . . . waged solely for the detestable and horrible purpose of extending and perpetuating American slavery." The Senate, subject to the same pressures as the president, ratified the agreement by a vote of thirty-eight to fourteen.

The Fruits of Victory: Further Enlargement of the United States

See the **Map**

U.S. Territorial Expansion in the 1850s at **myhistorylab.com**

The Mexican War, won quickly and at relatively small cost in lives and money, brought huge territorial gains. The Pacific coast from south of San Diego to the forty-ninth parallel and all the land between the coast and the Continental Divide had become the property of the American people.

Immense amounts of labor and capital would have to be invested before this new territory could be made to yield its bounty, but the country clearly had the capacity to accomplish the job.

In this atmosphere came what seemed a sign from the heavens. In January 1848, while Scott's veterans rested on their victorious arms in Mexico City, a mechanic named James W. Marshall was building a sawmill on the American River in the Sacramento Valley east of San Francisco. One day, while supervising the deepening of the millrace, he noticed a few flecks of yellow in the bed of the stream. These he gathered up and tested. They were pure gold.

Other strikes had been made in California and been treated skeptically or as matters of local curiosity; since the days of Jamestown, too many pioneers had run fruitlessly in search of El Dorado, and too much fool's gold had been passed off as the real thing. Yet this discovery produced an international sensation. The gold was real and plentiful—$200 million of it was extracted in four years—but equally important was the fact that everyone was ready to believe the news. The **gold rush** reflected the heady confidence inspired by Guadalupe Hidalgo; it seemed the ultimate justification of manifest destiny. Surely an era of continental prosperity and harmony had dawned.

Slavery: Storm Clouds Gather

Prosperity came in full measure but harmony did not, for once again expansion brought the nation face to face with the divisive question of slavery. The future of this giant chunk of North America, most of it vacant, was soon to be determined—slave or free? The question, in one sense, seems hardly worth the national crisis it provoked. Slavery appeared to have little future in New Mexico and California, and none in Oregon. Why did the South fight so hard for the right to bring slaves into a region that seemed so poorly suited to their exploitation?

Slavery raised a moral question. Most Americans tried to avoid confronting this truth; as patriots they assumed that any sectional issue could be solved by compromise. However, while the majority of whites had little respect for blacks, slave or free, few persons, northern or southern, could look upon the ownership of one human being by another as simply an alternative form of economic organization and argue its merits as they would those of the protective tariff or a national bank. Twist the facts as they might, slavery was either right or it was wrong; being on the whole honest and moral, they could not, having faced that truth, stand by unconcerned while the question was debated.

Slavery had complicated the Texas problem from the start, and it beclouded the future of the Southwest even before the Mexican flag had been stripped from the staffs at Santa Fe and Los Angeles. The northern, Van Burenite wing of the Democratic party had become increasingly uneasy about the proslavery cast of Polk's policies, which were unpopular in that part of the country. Once it became likely that the war would bring new territory into the Union, these Northerners felt compelled to try to check the president and to assure their constituents that they would resist the admission of further slave territory. On August 8, 1846, during the debate on a bill appropriating money for the conduct of the war, Democratic Congressman David Wilmot of Pennsylvania introduced an amendment that provided "as an express and fundamental condition to the acquisition of any territory from the Republic of Mexico" that "neither slavery nor involuntary servitude shall ever exist in any part of said territory."

Southerners found the **Wilmot Proviso** particularly insulting. Nevertheless, it passed the House, where northern congressmen outnumbered southern. But it was defeated in the Senate, where Southerners held the balance. To counter the Proviso, Calhoun, once again serving as senator from South Carolina, introduced resolutions in 1846 arguing that Congress had no right to bar slavery from any territory; because territories belonged to all the states, slave and free, all should have equal rights in them. From this position it was only a step (soon taken) to demanding that Congress guarantee the right of slave owners to bring slaves into the territories and establish federal slave codes in the territories. Most Northerners considered this proposal as repulsive as Southerners found the Wilmot Proviso.

To resolve the territorial problem, two compromises were offered. One, eventually backed by President Polk, would extend the Missouri Compromise line to the Pacific. The majority of Southerners were willing to go along with this scheme, but most Northerners would no longer agree to the reservation of *any* new territory for slavery. The other possibility, advocated by Senator Lewis Cass of Michigan, called for organizing new territories without mention of slavery, thus leaving it to local settlers, through their territorial legislatures, to determine their own institutions. Cass's **popular sovereignty**, known more vulgarly as "squatter sovereignty," had the superficial merit of appearing to be democratic. Its virtue for the members of Congress, however, was that it allowed them to escape the responsibility of deciding the question themselves.

The Election of 1848

One test of strength occurred in August, before the 1848 presidential election. After six months of acrimonious debate, Congress passed a bill barring slavery from Oregon. The test, however, proved little. If it required half a year to settle the question for Oregon, how could an answer ever be found for California and New Mexico? Plainly the time had come, in a democracy, to go to the people. The coming presidential election seemed to provide an ideal opportunity.

The opportunity was missed. The politicians of the parties hedged, fearful of losing votes in one section or another. With the issues blurred, voters had no real choice. That the Whigs should behave in such a manner was perhaps to be expected. In 1848 they nominated Zachary Taylor for president, despite his lack of political sophistication and even after he had flatly refused to state his opinion on any current subject. The party offered no platform. Taylor's contribution to the campaign was so naive as to be pathetic. "I am a Whig, *but not an ultra Whig.* . . . If elected . . . I should feel bound to administer the government untrammeled by party schemes."

The Democratic party had little better to offer. All the drive and zeal characteristic of it in the Jackson period had gradually seeped away. Polk's espousal of Texas's annexation had driven many Northerners from its ranks. The party members finally nominated Lewis Cass, the father of popular sovereignty, but they did not endorse that or any other solution to the territorial question. The Van Buren wing of the Democratic party could not stomach Cass's willingness to countenance the extension of slavery into new territories. Combining with the antislavery Liberty party, they formed the **Free Soil party** and nominated Van Buren.

The Free Soil party polled nearly 300,000 votes, about 10 percent of the total, in a very dull campaign. Offered a choice between the honest ignorance of Taylor and the cynical opportunism of Cass, the voters—by a narrow margin—chose the former, Taylor receiving 1.36 million votes to Cass's 1.22 million. Taylor carried eight of the fifteen slave states and seven of the fifteen free states, proof that the sectional issue

AN AVAILABLE CANDIDATE.

Photo Credit: Getty Images Inc. – Hulton Archive Photos.

According to this Democratic cartoon, the only qualification of General Zachary Taylor, the Whig candidate for president in 1848, is that he killed many Mexicans.

had been avoided. The chief significance of the election was the growing strength of the antislavery forces; in the next decade, this would bring about the collapse of the second party system.

The Gold Rush

The question of slavery in the territories could no longer be deferred. The discovery of gold had brought an army of prospectors into California. By the summer of 1848 San Francisco had become almost a ghost town, and an estimated two-thirds of the adult males of Oregon had hastened south to the gold fields. After President Polk confirmed the "extraordinary character" of the strike in his annual message of December 1848, there was no containing the gold seekers. During 1849, some 25,000 Americans made their way to California from the East by ship; more than 55,000 others crossed the continent by overland routes. About 8,000 Mexicans, 5,000 South Americans, and numbers of Europeans joined the rush.

The rough limits of the gold country had been quickly marked out. For 150 miles and more along the western slope of the Sierra stretched the great mother lode. Along the expanse any stream or canyon, or any ancient gravel bed might conceal a treasure in nuggets, flakes, or dust. Between 1849 and 1860 about 200,000 people, nearly all of them males, crossed the Rockies to California and thousands more reached California by ship via Cape Horn. Disregarding justice and reason alike, the newcomers from the

Read the Document

Burrum, from *Six Months in the Gold Mines* at **myhistorylab.com**

East, as one observer noted, "regarded every man but a native [North] American as an interloper." They referred to people of Latin American origin as "greasers" and sought by law and by violence to keep them from mining for gold. Even the local Californians (now American citizens) were discriminated against. The few free blacks in California and the several thousand more who came in search of gold were treated no better. As for the far larger Indian population, it was almost wiped out. There were about 150,000 Indians in California in the mid-1840s but only 35,000 in 1860.

The ethnic conflict was only part of the problem. Rough, hard men, separated from women, lusted for gold in a strange, wild country where fortunes could be made in a day, gambled away in an hour, or stolen in an instant. The situation demanded the establishment of a territorial government. President Taylor appreciated this, and in his gruff, simple-hearted way he suggested an uncomplicated answer: Admit California directly as a state, letting the Californians decide for themselves about slavery. The rest of the Mexican cession could be formed into another state. No need for Congress, with its angry rivalries, to meddle at all, he believed. In this way the nation could avoid the divisive effects of sectional debate.

The Californians reacted favorably to Taylor's proposal. They were overwhelmingly opposed to slavery, though not for humanitarian reasons. On the contrary, they tended to look on blacks as they did Mexicans and feared that if slavery were permitted, white gold seekers would be disadvantaged. By October 1849 they had drawn up a constitution that outlawed slavery, and by December the new state government was functioning.

Taylor was the owner of a large plantation and more than 100 slaves; Southerners had assumed (without bothering to ask) that he would fight to keep the territories open to slavery. But being a military man, he was above all a nationalist; he disliked the divisiveness that partisan discussion of the issue was producing. Southerners were horrified by the president's reasoning. To admit California would destroy the balance between free and slave states in the Senate; to allow all the new land to become free would doom the South to wither in a corner of the country, surrounded by hostile free states. Radicals were already saying that the South would have to choose between secession and surrender. Taylor's plan played into the hands of extremists.

The Compromise of 1850

This was no longer a squabble over territorial governments. With the Union itself at stake, Henry Clay rose to save the day. He had been as angry and frustrated when the Whigs nominated Taylor as he had been when they passed him over for Harrison. Now, well beyond age seventy and in poor health, he put away his ambition and his resentment and for the last time concentrated his remarkable vision on a great, multifaceted national problem. On

●●●─[Read the Document

Clay, *Speech to the U.S. Senate* at **myhistorylab.com**

January 29, 1850, he laid his proposal, "founded upon mutual forbearance," before the Senate. A few days later he defended it on the floor of the Senate in the last great speech of his life.

California should be brought directly into the Union as a free state, he argued. The rest of the Southwest should be organized as a territory without mention of slavery: The Southerners would retain the right to bring slaves there, while in fact none would do so. "You have got what is worth more than a thousand Wilmot Provisos," Clay pointed out to his northern colleagues. "You have nature on your side." Empty lands in dispute along the Texas border should be assigned to the New Mexico Territory, Clay continued, but in exchange the United States should take over Texas's preannexation debts. The slave trade should be abolished in the District of Columbia (but not slavery itself), and a more effective federal fugitive slave law should be enacted and strictly enforced in the North.

Clay's proposals occasioned one of the most magnificent debates in the history of the Senate. Every important member had his say. Calhoun, perhaps even more than Clay, realized that the future of the nation was at stake and that his own days were numbered (he died four weeks later). He was so feeble that he could not deliver his speech himself. He sat impassive, wrapped in a great cloak, gripping the arms of his chair, while Senator James M. Mason of Virginia read it to the crowded Senate. Calhoun thought his plan would save the Union, but his speech was an argument for secession; he demanded that the North yield completely on every point, ceasing even to discuss the question of slavery. Clay's compromise was unsatisfactory; he himself had no other to offer. If you will not yield, he said to the northern senators, "let the States . . . agree to separate and part in peace. If you are unwilling we should part in peace, tell us so, and we shall know what to do."

Three days later, on March 7, Daniel Webster took the floor. He too had begun to fail. Years of heavy drinking and other forms of self-indulgence had taken their toll. The brilliant volubility and the thunder were gone, and when he spoke his face was bathed in sweat and there were strange pauses in his delivery. But his argument was lucid. Clay's proposals should be adopted. Since the future of all the territories had already been fixed by geographic and economic factors, the Wilmot Proviso was unnecessary. The North's constitutional obligation to yield fugitive slaves, he said, braving the wrath of New England abolitionists, was "binding in honor and conscience." The Union, he continued, could not be sundered without bloodshed. At the thought of that dread possibility, the old fire flared: "Peaceable secession!" Webster exclaimed, "Heaven forbid! Where is the flag of the republic to remain? Where is the eagle still to tower?" The debate did not end with the aging giants. Every possible viewpoint was presented, argued, rebutted, rehashed.

●◆─┤Read the Document

Webster, *Speech to the U.S. Senate* at **myhistorylab.com**

The majority clearly favored some compromise, but nothing could have been accomplished without the death of President Taylor on July 9, 1850. Obstinate, probably resentful because few people paid him half the heed they paid Clay and other prominent members of Congress, the president had insisted on his own plan to bring both California and New Mexico directly into the Union. When Vice President Millard Fillmore, who was a politician, not an ideologue, succeeded Taylor, the deadlock between the White House and Capitol Hill was broken.

In the Senate and then in the House, tangled combinations pushed through the separate measures, one by one. California became the thirty-first state. The rest of the Mexican cession was divided into two territories, New Mexico and Utah, each to be admitted to the Union when qualified, "with or without slavery as [its] constitution may prescribe." Texas received $10 million to pay off its debt in return for accepting a narrower western boundary. The slave trade in the District of Columbia was abolished as of January 1, 1851. The **Fugitive Slave Act** of 1793 was amended to provide for the appointment of federal commissioners with authority to issue warrants, summon posses, and compel citizens under pain of fine or imprisonment to assist in the capture of fugitives. Commissioners who decided that an accused person was a runaway received a larger fee than if they declared the person legally free. The accused could not testify in their own defense. They were to be returned to the South without jury trial merely on the submission of an affidavit by their "owner."

Only four senators and twenty-eight representatives voted for all these bills. The two sides did not meet somewhere in the middle as is the case with most compromises. Each bill passed because those who preferred it outnumbered those opposed. In general, the Democrats gave more support to the **Compromise of 1850** than the Whigs, but party lines never held firmly. In the Senate, for example, seventeen Democrats and fifteen Whigs voted to admit California as a free state. A large number of congressmen absented themselves when parts of the settlement unpopular in their home districts came to a vote; twenty-one senators and thirty-six representatives failed to commit themselves on the new fugitive slave bill.

●◆─┤Read the Document

The Fugitive Slave Act (1850) at **myhistorylab.com**

In this piecemeal fashion the Union was preserved. The credit belongs mostly to Clay, whose original conceptualization of the compromise enabled lesser minds to understand what they must do.

Missouri Compromise 1820	Compromise of 1850
Missouri admitted as slave state, Maine as free state	California admitted as free state
Slavery prohibited in balance of Louisiana Purchase territory north of 36°30'.	Texas (slave state) has its borders finalized
	Status of remainder of territory acquired from Mexico left undetermined
	Congress to enact Fugitive Slave Law to capture escaped slaves

Everywhere sober and conservative citizens sighed with relief. Mass meetings throughout the country "ratified" the result. Hundreds of newspapers gave the compromise editorial approval. In Washington patriotic harmony reigned. When Congress met again in December it seemed that party discord had been buried forever. "I have determined never to make another speech on the slavery question," Senator Stephen A. Douglas of Illinois told his colleagues. "Let us cease agitating, stop the debate, and drop the subject." If this were done, he predicted, the compromise would be accepted as a "final settlement." With this bit of wishful thinking the year 1850 passed into history.

The Alamo

Alamo, Pearl Harbor, 9/11: Each of these syllables has been seared into the national consciousness. Each galvanized Americans to go to war; and each has persisted in memory.

Two movies entitled *The Alamo* have influenced how Americans remember the event: John Wayne directed the 1960 movie by that name, and also starred in it as Davy Crockett. The second was a 2004 release by director John Lee Hancock. Both movies briskly establish the historical context: Mexico secures independence from Spain in 1821, with Texas as a state within the Mexican federation. Antonio Lopez de Santa Anna, a Mexican general who regarded himself as the "Napoleon of the West," becomes dictator of Mexico. The American settlers in Texas seize several of Santa Anna's garrisons, including the Alamo, a fortified Spanish mission near San Antonio.

Neither movie explains that, up to this time, Santa Anna had been razing Zacatecas, a Mexican state that had also opposed his rule. Early in 1836, though, he marched an army of several thousand soldiers north to crush the Texas rebels. Late in February, his advance units entered San Antonio and took up positions outside the Alamo. Both movies show the Texans sending riders to get reinforcements from the fledgling Texas government at Washington-on-the-Brazos, far to the east. There Sam Houston tried but failed to find a way to relieve the beleaguered garrison.

At the Alamo, the defenders, probably fewer than 200, were divided into three sets of volunteers and a fourth group, consisting of the "regular" soldiers of the Texas government, commanded by William B. Travis, a twenty-six-year-old cavalryman. One of the volunteer groups was led by Jim Bowie, an Indian fighter known for his long-bladed knife. David Crockett, the bear-hunter-turned-Congressman-turned-celebrity led the second group of volunteer fighters. The third group of volunteers consisted of

Mexicans seeking to restore the Mexican republic.

Both movies ended with the battle that began on March 6, the thirteenth day of the siege. Within an hour, resistance had been silenced. All of the defenders were dead; some 500–600 Mexicans were killed, many caught in their own crossfire as they converged upon the Alamo.

Both movies *mostly* adhere to these facts. The 1960 movie added many fanciful plot elements: John Wayne's Crockett spends his nights stealing Mexican cattle, destroying their cannon, and romancing their prettiest senorita. There is no evidence for any of this. Both movies also show Santa Anna pounding the Alamo with artillery fusillades. In fact, Santa Anna had no big cannon. Some of his generals urged him to postpone the attack until heavier cannon had arrived; they would reduce the Alamo to rubble, sparing the heavy losses of a frontal assault. (Santa Anna, eager for victory in battle, refused to wait.) The 1960 movie also contends, wrongly, that Bowie wanted to abandon the Alamo while Travis insisted on staying. In fact, both men thought it essential to hold the Alamo. Sam Houston, by contrast, thought it was unwise for the commanders to have allowed their men to be "forted up" and destroyed.

The main question—for historians and movie makers—concerns the motivations of the defenders. Why did they persist against impossible odds? Santa Anna had signaled his intention to take no prisoners—certainly reason enough to fight on—but there was an alternative. Until the final forty-eight hours or so, escape was possible. Messengers and even small groups of men slipped through Santa Anna's lines at night. Some historians contend that the defenders remained at their posts because they expected to be rescued, but the defenders of the Alamo were not fools. The impossibility of their situation was clear. Why, then, did most choose to remain and die?

Photo Credit: Getty Images Inc. - Michael Ochs Archives.

John Wayne as Crockett.

Photo Credit: Touchstone Pictures/ Courtesy Everett Collection.

Billy Bob Thornton as Crockett.

John Wayne's movie provided a simple answer. Wayne's Crockett is fighting for freedom: "Republic. I like the sound of that word. Means people can live free, talk free. Go or come, buy or sell. Republic is one of the words that makes you tight in the throat, same tightness he gets when his baby takes his first step.

Such words made sense to Wayne's audience in 1960s America, then embroiled in a "cold war" against Communism. Santa Anna, a "tyrannical ruler," was akin to Soviet Communism, and the defenders of the Alamo were freedom fighters. But this analogy makes little historical sense. Mexico had outlawed slavery while the Texas rebels drafted a constitution that legalized slavery and prohibited the immigration of free blacks. From that perspective, Mexico stood for freedom, Texas for slavery.

The 2004 movie offered an alternative explanation of the defenders' self-sacrifice, citing the words of Travis: "We will show the world what patriots are made of." This notion of a death for posthumous honor was most strikingly scripted in the character of Davy Crockett, played by Billy Bob Thornton. As the prospects for reinforcement fade, Thornton's Crockett muses about escaping:

> If it was just simple old me, David, from Tennessee, I might drop over the wall some night and take my chances. But this Davy Crockett feller, they are all watching him. He's been fightin' on this wall every day of his life.

This resonates with what we know about the real Crockett. Similarly, the actual Travis, who had abandoned his wife and neglected his children, wrote a letter before the final battle hoping that he would leave his boy "the proud recollection that he is the son of a man who died for his country."

Much the same could have been said of the others at the Alamo. Most had grown up beneath the long shadow of the Revolutionary generation that had fought and died to found a great nation. As the men of the Alamo looked upon a horizon darkened by enemy troops, they perhaps realized that their deaths would assure their own immortality. The Alamo would not be forgotten, although doubtless none could have imagined the malleability of memory centuries later.

Questions for Discussion

- How was the rebellion of the Texas settlers against Santa Anna comparable to the Founders' battle against the British in 1776? How did it differ?
- Why do some events and people leave a deep imprint upon subsequent generations?

Milestones

1835	Alamo falls to Santa Anna's Mexican army	1845	John L. O'Sullivan coins the expression *manifest destiny*
1836	Sam Houston routs Santa Anna at Battle of San Jacinto	1846	United States and Britain settle Oregon boundary dispute
1837	United States recognizes Republic of Texas	1846–1848	United States wages "Mr. Polk's War" with Mexico
1840	Richard Henry Dana describes voyage to California in *Two Years Before the Mast*	1846	House of Representatives adopts Wilmot Proviso prohibiting slavery in Mexican cession, but Senate defeats it
	William Henry Harrison is elected president	1847	General Winfield Scott captures Mexico City
1841	William Henry Harrison dies; Vice President John Tyler becomes president	1848	James W. Marshall discovers gold at Sutter's Mill, California
	Preemption Act grants "squatters' rights" in West		Treaty of Guadalupe Hidalgo brings United States huge territorial gains
1842	Webster-Ashburton Treaty determines Maine boundary		Zachary Taylor is elected president
1843	Oregon Trail opens	1850	Taylor dies; Vice President Millard Fillmore becomes president
1844	James K. Polk is elected president		Henry Clay's Compromise of 1850 preserves Union
1845	United States annexes Texas		

✓•⌐Study and Review at www.myhistorylab.com

Review Questions

1. From the Louisiana Purchase (1803) until the war with Mexico in 1845 the United States only added Florida (1819) to the national domain. But in the next three years, with the addition of Texas, California, and much of the Southwest, the nation increased in size 50 percent. What accounts for this sudden expansionism?

2. Why did the United States go to war with Mexico and what were its consequences politically?

3. How did the frontier undermine traditional gender roles? How did it reinforce those roles?

4. What was the relationship between slavery and manifest destiny?

Key Terms

Compromise of 1850
Free Soil party
Fugitive Slave Act
gold rush
manifest destiny

Mexican War
popular sovereignty
Treaty of Guadalupe Hidalgo

Webster-Ashburton Treaty
Wilmot Proviso

The Sections Go Their Own Ways

Hear the Audio at myhistorylab.com

What do you do when someone curses at you?

YOUR RESPONSE MAY DEPEND ON WHERE YOU'RE FROM. IN 2009 Malcolm Gladwell, author of the non-fiction bestseller *The Tipping Point*, described a psychology test in which researchers asked male students at the University of Michigan to complete questionnaires and, one-by-one, to take them to an office down a narrow corridor past a row of file cabinets. As each student neared the office, a researcher posing as a clerk opened a file drawer, forcing the student to squeeze past. As he did, the "clerk" slammed the drawer and muttered, "Asshole." The student, after delivering his questionnaire, was asked to provide a technician with a saliva sample. It turned out that the saliva of students from the South showed heightened levels of cortisol and testosterone—chemicals released as part of a person's fight response; but the saliva of students from northern states showed no such elevation. Gladwell regarded this as proof that cultural legacies persist "virtually intact" over many generations. Today's southern men, even though attending a northern university, were behaving much as had their great-great-grandfathers 180 years earlier. When confronted with a challenge to their honor, their psychic defenses readied them to fight, or so Gladwell contended.

This thesis is speculative: Over the past 200 years, countless peoples have washed over the regions of the United States; how distinctive cultural patterns could have been continually imprinted upon such different peoples is unclear. Yet nowadays many people still speak of distinctive regional cultures; and a glance at the political maps in this book illustrates the persistence of regional voting patterns: Over the past forty-six presidential elections, for example, Massachusetts and South Carolina have voted for the same candidate only thirteen times.

If regional cultural variations have become an enduring trait in American life, this was largely a consequence of changes that gained momentum during the three decades after 1830. Each section of the country was shaped by distinctive economic systems and workforces. Industrialization took hold of much of the Northeast, attracting immigrants who found work in factories in the burgeoning cities and factory towns. To the West, farming became more commercial and productive, attracting immigrant and other forms of free (if lowly paid) labor. The South was characterized in large part by the production of cash crops, especially cotton, and by its unwilling immigrants, the slaves.

From Chapter 12 of *American Destiny: Narrative of a Nation*, Combined Volume, Fourth Edition. Mark C. Carnes and John A. Garraty. Copyright © 2012 by Pearson Education, Inc. Published by Pearson Prentice Hall. All rights reserved.

But countervailing forces after 1830 also reduced the differences among regions. The Northeast and the West became economically interdependent, linked by an increasingly elaborate network of canals and railroads. The South, whose transportation infrastructure lagged, nevertheless benefited from the improvements in international transportation and trade. By the 1850s the nation remained divided—chiefly between the slave economy of the South and the nominally "free" labor of the North. But as the nation was knit together more tightly, the incompatibility of those diverse economic systems could no longer be ignored.

The South

The South was less affected than other sections by urbanization, European immigration, the transportation revolution, and industrialization. The region remained predominantly agricultural; cotton was still king, slavery the most distinctive southern institution. But important changes were occurring. Cotton continued to march westward, until by 1859 fully 1.3 million of the 4.3 million bales grown in the United States came from beyond the Mississippi. In the upper South, Virginia held its place as the leading tobacco producer, but states beyond the Appalachians were raising more than half the crop. The introduction of Bright Yellow, a mild variety of tobacco that grew best in poor soil, gave a great stimulus to production. The older sections of Maryland, Virginia, and North Carolina shifted to the kind of diversified farming usually associated with the Northeast. By 1849 the wheat crop of Virginia was worth twice as much as the tobacco crop.

The Economics of Slavery

The increased importance of cotton in the South strengthened the hold of slavery on the region. The price of slaves rose until by the 1850s a prime field hand was worth as much as $1,800, roughly three times the cost in the 1820s. While the prestige value of owning this kind of property affected prices, the rise chiefly reflected the increasing value of the South's agricultural output. "Crop value per slave" jumped from less than $15 early in the century to more than $125 in 1859.

In the cotton fields of the Deep South slaves brought several hundred dollars per head more than in the older regions; thus the tendency to sell them "down the river" continued. Mississippi took in some 10,000 slaves a year throughout the period; by 1830 the black population of the state exceeded the white. The westward shift of cotton cultivation was accompanied by the forcible transfer of more than a million African American slaves from the seaboard states to the dark, rich soil of regions watered by the Mississippi and Arkansas rivers and their tributaries. This "second great migration" of blacks far surpassed the original uprooting of blacks from Africa to the United States.

The impact of the trade on the slaves was frequently disastrous. Husbands were often separated from wives, and parents from children. This was somewhat less likely to happen on large, well-managed plantations than on small farms, but it was common enough everywhere. According to one study, one-third of all slave first "marriages" in the upper South were broken by forced separation and nearly half of all children were separated from at least one parent. Families were torn apart less frequently in the lower South, where far more slaves were bought than sold.

A woman in a net on a Congo shore. Although the importation of slaves was illegal after 1807, historians William Cooper and Thomas Terrill estimate in *The American South* (2009) that 50,000 were smuggled into the United States between 1808 and 1860.

Photo Credit: Musee de l'Homme/ Paris/RMN/Art Resource, NY.

As blacks became more expensive, the ownership of slaves became more concentrated. In 1860 only about 46,000 of the 8 million white residents of the slave states had as many as twenty slaves. When one calculates the cost of twenty slaves and the land to keep them profitably occupied, it is easy to understand why this figure is so small. The most efficient size of a plantation worked by gangs of slaves ranged between 1,000 and 2,000 acres. In every part of the South the majority of farmers cultivated no more than 200 acres, and in many sections fewer than 100 acres. On the eve of the Civil War only one white family in four in the South owned any slaves at all. A few large plantations and many small farms—this was the pattern.

There were few genuine economies of scale in southern agriculture. Small farmers grew the staple crops; and many of them owned a few slaves, often working beside them in the fields. These yeomen farmers were hardworking, self-reliant, and moderately prosperous, quite unlike the poor whites of the Appalachians who scratched a meager subsistence from substandard soils.

Well-managed plantations yielded annual profits of 10 percent and more, and, in general, money invested in southern agriculture earned at least a modest return. Considering the way the workforce was exploited, this is hardly surprising. Recent estimates indicate that after allowing for the cost of

◄●►─[Read the Document

Overseer's Report from Chicora Wood Plantation at **myhistorylab.com**

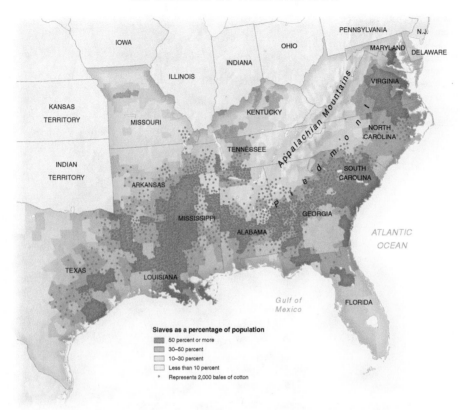

Cotton and Slaves in the South, 1860 Not surprisingly, the areas of greatest cotton production were also the areas with the highest proportion of slaves in the population. Note the concentrations of both in the Piedmont, the Alabama Black Belt, and the lower Mississippi Valley, and the relative absence of both in the Appalachian Mountains.

land and capital, the average plantation slave "earned" cotton worth $78.78 in 1859. It cost masters about $32 a year to feed, clothe, and house a slave. In other words, almost 60 percent of the product of slave labor was expropriated by the masters.

The South failed to develop locally owned marketing and transportation facilities, and for this slavery was at least partly responsible. In 1840 *Hunt's Merchant Magazine* estimated that it cost $2.85 to move a bale of cotton from the farm to a seaport and that additional charges for storage, insurance, port fees, and freight to a European port exceeded $15. Middlemen from outside the South commonly earned most of this money. New York capitalists gradually came to control much of the South's cotton from the moment it was picked, and a large percentage of the crop found its way into New York warehouses before being sold to manufacturers. The same middlemen supplied most of the foreign goods that the planters purchased with their cotton earnings.

Southerners complained about this state of affairs but did little to correct it. Capital tied up in the ownership of labor could not be invested in anything else, and social pressures in the South militated against investment in trade and commerce. Ownership of land and slaves yielded a kind of psychic income not available to any middleman. As one British visitor pointed out, the southern blacks were "a nonconsuming class." Still more depressing, under slavery the enormous reservoir of intelligence and skill that the blacks represented was almost entirely wasted. Many slave artisans worked on the plantations, and a few free blacks made their way in the South remarkably well, but the amount of talent unused, energy misdirected, and imagination smothered can only be guessed.

Foreign observers in New England frequently noted the alertness and industriousness of ordinary laborers and attributed this, justifiably, to the high level of literacy. Nearly everyone in New England could read and write. Correspondingly, the stagnation and inefficiency of southern labor could be attributed in part to the high degree of illiteracy, for over 20 percent of *white* Southerners could not read or write, another tragic squandering of human resources.

Antebellum Plantation Life

The "typical" plantation did not exist, but it is possible to describe, in a general way, what a medium-to-large operation employing twenty or more slaves was like in the two decades preceding the Civil War. Such a plantation was more like a small village than a northern-type agricultural unit, and in another way more like a self-sufficient colonial farm than a nineteenth-century commercial operation, although its major activity involved producing cotton or some other cash crop.

Slaveholding families were also quite different from northern families of similar status, in part because they were engaged in agriculture and in part because of their so-called peculiar institution. Husbands and wives did not function in separate spheres to nearly the same extent, although their individual functions were different and gender-related.

The master was in general charge and his word was law—the system was literally paternalistic. But his wife nearly always had immense responsibilities. Running the household meant supervising the servants (and sometimes punishing them, which often meant wielding a lash), nursing the sick, taking care of the vegetable and flower gardens, planning meals, and seeing to the education of her own children and the training of young slaves. It could also involve running the entire plantation on the frequent occasions when her husband was away on business. At the same time, her role entailed being a "southern lady": refined, graceful, and supposedly untroubled by worldly affairs.

The majority of the slaves of both sexes were field hands who labored on the land from dawn to dusk. Household servants and artisans, indeed any slave other than small children and the aged and infirm, might be called on for such labor when needed. Slave women were expected to cook for their own families and do other chores after working in the fields.

Children, free and slave, were cared for by slaves, the former by household servants, the latter usually by an elderly woman, perhaps with the help of a girl only a little older than the children. Infants were brought to their mothers in the fields for nursing several times a day, for after a month or two at most, slave mothers were required to go back to work. Slave children were not put to work until they were six or seven years old, and until they were about ten they were given only small tasks such as feeding the chickens or minding a smaller child. Black and white youngsters played together and were often cared for by the same nursemaid.

Read the Document

Harper, *The Slave Mother* at **myhistorylab.com**

Slave cabins were simple and crude; most consisted of a single room, dark, with a fireplace for cooking and heat. Usually the flooring was raised above ground level, though some were set on the bare earth. In 1827 Basil Hall, a British naval officer, reported that in a large South Carolina plantation, 140 slaves lived in twenty-eight cottages or huts. These were "uncommonly neat and comfortable, and might have shamed those of many countries I have seen." Yet Hall dismissed the claims of whites that slaves were happier than the peasantry of England. Slavery was, above all, a "humiliation" imposed upon "the whole mass of the labouring population" of the South.

The Sociology of Slavery

It is difficult to generalize about the peculiar institution because so much depended on the individual master's behavior. Although some ex-slaves told of masters who refused to whip them, Bennet Barrow of Louisiana, a harsh master, averaged one whipping a month. "The great secret of our success," another planter recalled years later, "was the great motive power contained in that little instrument." Overseers were commonly instructed to give twenty lashes for ordinary offenses, such as shirking work or stealing, and thirty-nine for more serious offenses, such as running away. Sometimes slaves were whipped to death; by 1821, however, all southern states had passed laws allowing a master to be charged with murder if he caused a slave's death from excessive punishment. Conviction normally resulted in a fine. In 1840 a South Carolina woman convicted of killing a slave was fined $214.28.

On balance, it is significant that the United States was the only nation in the Western Hemisphere where the slave population grew by natural increase. After the

Photo Credit: The Historic New Orleans Collection, Museum/Research Center, Acc. No. 1960.46.

This slave burial service, painted by John Antrobus in 1860, reflects an inversion of power relations, a slave preacher leads the mourners while the white overseer and the plantation owners watch uneasily, shunted (literally) to the sides.

ending of the slave trade in 1808, the black population increased at nearly the same rate as the white. Put differently, during the entire period from the founding of Jamestown to the Civil War, only a little more than half a million slaves were imported into the country, about 5 percent of the number of Africans carried by slavers to the New World. Yet in 1860 there were about 4 million blacks in the United States.

Most owners felt responsibilities toward their slaves, and slaves were dependent on and in some ways imitative of white values. However, powerful fears and resentments, not always recognized, existed on both sides. The plantation environment forced the two races to live in close proximity. From this circumstance could arise every sort of human relationship. One planter, using the appropriate pseudonym Clod Thumper, could write, "Africans are nothing but brutes, and they will love you better for whipping, whether they deserve it or not." Another, describing a slave named Bug, could say, "No one knows but myself what feeling I have for him. Black as he is we were raised together." One southern white woman tended a dying servant with "the kindest and most unremitting attention." Another, discovered crying after the death of a slave she had repeatedly abused, is said to have explained her grief by complaining that she "didn't have nobody to whip no more."

Slaves were without rights; they developed a distinctive way of life by attempting to resist oppression and injustice while accommodating themselves to the system. Their marriages had no legal status, but their partnerships seem to have been loving and stable. Even families whose members were sold to different masters often maintained close ties over considerable distances.

Slave religion, on the surface an untutored form of Christianity tinctured with some African infusions, seemed to most slave owners a useful instrument for teaching meekness and resignation and for providing harmless emotional release, which it sometimes was and did. However, religious meetings, secret and open, provided slaves with the opportunity to organize, which led at times to rebellions and more often to less drastic ways of resisting white domination. Religion also sustained the slaves' sense of their own worth as beings made in the image of God, and it taught them, therefore, that while human beings can be enslaved in body, their spirits cannot be enslaved without their consent.

((•─[Hear the Audio
When the Roll Is Called up Yonder at **myhistorylab.com**

•••─[Read the Document
A Catechism for Slaves at **myhistorylab.com**

Observing that slaves often seemed happy and were only rarely overtly rebellious, whites persuaded themselves that most blacks accepted the system without resentment and indeed preferred slavery to the uncertainties of freedom. There was much talk about "loyal and faithful servants." The Civil War, when slaves flocked to the Union lines once assured of freedom and fair treatment, would disabuse them of this illusion.

As the price of slaves rose and as northern opposition to the institution grew more vocal, the system hardened perceptibly. White Southerners made much of the danger of insurrection. When a plot was uncovered or a revolt took place, instant and savage reprisals resulted. In 1811, Charles Deslondes led a rebellion of several hundred slaves, armed with tools, who burned a handful of plantations and marched toward New Orleans before being routed by the United States Army. Over fifty slaves were slaughtered immediately; a tribunal of plantation owners ordered the execution of several dozen more. In 1822, after the conspiracy of Denmark Vesey was exposed by informers, thirty-seven slaves were executed and another thirty-odd deported, although no overt act of rebellion had occurred.

The Nat Turner revolt in Virginia in 1831 was the most sensational of the slave uprisings; fifty-seven whites lost their lives before it was suppressed. White Southerners treated runaways almost as brutally as rebels, although they posed no real threat to whites. The authorities tracked down fugitives with bloodhounds and subjected captives to merciless lashings.

◆●◆ Read the Document

Turner, *The Confessions of Nat Turner* at **myhistorylab.com**

After the Nat Turner revolt, interest in doing away with slavery vanished in the white South. The southern states made it increasingly difficult for masters to free their slaves; during 1859 only about 3,000 in a slave population of nearly 4 million were given their freedom.

Slavery did not flourish in urban settings, and cities did not flourish in societies where slavery was important. Most southern cities were small, and within them, slaves made up a small fraction of the labor force. The existence of slavery goes a long way toward explaining why the South was so rural and why it had so little industry. Slaves were much harder to supervise and control in urban settings. Individual slaves were successfully employed in southern manufacturing plants, but they made up only an insignificant fraction of the South's small industrial labor supply.

Southern whites considered the existence of free blacks undesirable, no matter where they lived. The mere fact that they could support themselves disproved the notion that African Americans were by nature childlike and shiftless, unable to work efficiently without white guidance. From the whites' point of view, free blacks set a bad example for slaves. In a petition calling for the expulsion of free blacks from the state, a group of South Carolinians noted that slaves

> continualy [sic] have before their eyes, persons of the same color . . . freed from the control of masters, working where they please, going where they please, and expend-ing their money how they please.

Many southern states passed laws aimed at forcing free blacks to emigrate, but these laws were not well enforced. There is ample evidence that the white people of, say, Maryland, would have liked to get rid of the state's large free-black population. Free blacks were barred from occupations in which they might cause trouble—no free black could be the captain of a ship, for example—and they were required by law to find a "respectable" white person who would testify as to their "good con-duct and character." But whites, who needed slave labor, did not try very hard to expel them.

Psychological Effects of Slavery

The injustice of slavery needs no proof; less obvious is the fact that it had a corrosive effect on the personalities of Southerners, slave and free alike. By "the making of a human being an animal without hope," the system bore heavily on all slaves' sense of their own worth. Some found the condition absolutely unbearable. They became the habitual runaways who collected whip scars like medals, the "loyal" servants who struck out in rage against a master knowing that the result would be certain death, and the leaders of slave revolts.

Table 1 Major Slave Rebellions

Rebellion	Year	Description	Backlash against slaves	Legislative response
New York Slave Revolt	1712	Several buildings burned; whites attacked	Twenty-one African Americans executed, including free blacks	Slaves prohibited from carrying firearms and free blacks from owning land; slave owners obliged to pay tax for freeing slaves
Gabriel's Rebellion	1800	Conspiracy to rebel near Richmond, Virginia	Over two dozen slaves hanged, including Gabriel	Restrictions placed on owner's right to free slaves; free blacks not allowed to congregate freely on Sundays
Deslondes' Rebellion	1811	Burned plantations near New Orleans	Nearly 100 slaves killed, including Deslondes	Restrictions on right of free blacks to congregate
Denmark Vesey's Rebellion	1822	Plot to free blacks, kill whites, flee to Haiti	Thirty-five slaves hanged, including Vesey	Municipal guard established in Charleston, South Carolina
Nat Turner's Rebellion	1831	Fifty-five whites killed in Virginia	Over 100 slaves killed, including Turner	Virginia legislature prohibited teaching literacy to blacks, slave and free alike, and required the presence of white ministers during slave religious meetings

Denmark Vesey of South Carolina, even after buying his freedom, could not stomach the subservience demanded of slaves by the system. When he saw Charleston slaves step into the gutter to make way for whites, he taunted them: "You deserve to remain slaves!" For years he preached resistance to his fellows, drawing his texts from the Declaration of Independence and the Bible and promising help from black Haiti. So vehemently did he argue that some of his followers claimed they feared Vesey more than their masters, even more than God. He planned his uprising for five years, patiently working out the details, only to see it aborted at the last moment when a few of his recruits lost their nerve and betrayed him. For Denmark Vesey, death was probably preferable to living with such rage as his soul contained.

Yet Veseys were rare. Most slaves appeared at least resigned to their fate. Many seemed even to accept the whites' evaluation of their inherent abilities and place in society. Of course in most instances it is impossible to know whether this apparent subservience was feigned in order to avoid trouble.

Slaves had strong family and group attachments and a complex culture of their own, maintained, so to speak, under the noses of their masters. By a mixture of subterfuge, accommodation, and passive resistance, they erected subtle defenses against exploitation, achieving a sense of community that helped sustain the psychic integrity of individuals. But slavery discouraged, if it did not extinguish, independent judgment and self-reliance.

American Lives

Isabella was born in 1797, or perhaps 1799, in Ulster County, New York. She was a slave. Her owner was Colonel Ardinburgh, a Dutch farmer, who grew tobacco, corn, and flax. Because he could make use of only a handful of slaves, he sold most of the slave children, including Isabella's brother and sister. When Ardinburgh died in 1807, his heirs sold his "slaves, horses, and other cattle" at auction. A local farmer of English descent bought Isabella for $100. Isabella's parents, too old to work, were freed. Destitute, they soon died.

Isabella, who spoke only Dutch, found herself at odds with her new English master and family. "If they sent me for a frying pan, not knowing what they meant, perhaps I carried them the pot hooks," she recalled. Once, for failing to obey an order she did not understand, her master whipped her with a bundle of rods, scarring her back permanently.

In 1810 she was sold to John Dumont, a farmer. Though she came to regard him "as a God," she claimed that his wife subjected her to cruel and "unnatural" treatment. What exactly transpired, she refused "from motives of delicacy" to say. In 1815 Dumont arranged for Isabella to marry another of his slaves. Isabella had no say in the matter. She had five children by him.

Isabella labored in the fields, sowing and harvesting crops. She also cooked and cleaned the house. In recognition of her diligence, Dumont promised to set her free on July 4, 1826, exactly one year prior to the date set by the New York State legislature to end slavery. But on the proposed date, Dumont reneged. Soon thereafter Isabella heard the voice of God tell her to leave. She picked up her baby and walked to the house of a neighbor. When Dumont showed up to bring her back, the neighbor paid him $25 for Isabella and the baby and set them free.

But Isabella learned that her five-year-old son, Peter, had been sold to a planter in Alabama, which had no provision for ending slavery. She angrily confronted the Dumonts, who scoffed at her concern for "a paltry nigger." "I'll have my child again," Isabella retorted. She consulted a Quaker lawyer. He filed suit in her behalf and won. In 1828 the boy was returned.

Now on her own, Isabella went to New York City, then awash in religious ferment. Isabella, whose views on religion were a complex amalgam of African folkways, spiritualism, temperance, and dietary asceticism, was attracted to various unorthodox religious leaders. The most curious of these was Robert Matthews, a bearded, thundering tyrant who claimed to be the Old Testament prophet Matthias. Matthews acquired a house in the town of Sing Sing, housed nearly a dozen converts, and ruled it with an iron hand. Isabella was among those who joined the commune. In 1834, local authorities, who had heard stories of sexual and other irregularities, arrested Matthews.

Isabella had by this time become a preacher. Tall and severe in manner, she jabbed at the air with bony fingers and demanded the obedience she had formerly given to others. She changed her name to Sojourner Truth, a messenger conveying God's true spirit, and embarked on a career of antislavery feminism.

Sojourner Truth

Photo Credit: The Granger Collection, New York.

Questions for Discussion

- In what ways did Sojourner Truth's life likely differ from that of a slave on a plantation in the Deep South?
- How did religion contribute to Sojourner Truth's self-empowerment?

These qualities are difficult enough to develop in human beings under the best of circumstances; when every element in white society encouraged slaves to let others do their thinking for them, to avoid questioning the status quo, to lead a simple life, many did so willingly enough. Was this not slavery's greatest shame?

●●●—Read the Document

Runaway Slave Advertisements
at **myhistorylab.com**

Whites, too, were harmed by the slave system. Associating working for others with servility discouraged many poor whites from hiring out to earn a stake. Slavery provided the weak, the shiftless, and the unsuccessful with a scapegoat that made their own miserable state easier to bear but harder to escape.

More subtly, the patriarchal nature of the slave system reinforced the already existing tendency toward male dominance over wives and children typical of the larger society. For men of exceptional character, the responsibilities of ownership could be ennobling, but for hotheads, alcoholics, or others with psychological problems, the power could be brutalizing, with terrible effects on the whole plantation community, whites and blacks alike.

Aside from its fundamental immorality, slavery caused basically decent people to commit countless petty cruelties. "I feel badly, got very angry and whipped Lavinia," one Louisiana woman wrote in her diary. "O! for government over my temper." But for slavery, she would surely have had better self-control. The finest white Southerners were often warped by the institution. Even those who abhorred slavery sometimes let it corrupt their thinking: "I consider the labor of a breeding woman as no object, and that a child raised every 2 years is of more profit than the crop of the best laboring man." This cold calculation came from the pen of Thomas Jefferson, author of the Declaration of Independence, a man who, it now seems likely, fathered at least one child by a slave.

Manufacturing in the South

Although the temper of southern society discouraged business and commercial activities, considerable manufacturing developed.

The availability of the raw material and the abundance of waterpower along the Appalachian slopes made it possible to manufacture textiles profitably. By 1825 a thriving factory was functioning at Fayetteville, North Carolina, and soon others sprang up elsewhere in North Carolina and in adjoining states. William Gregg's factory, at Graniteville, South Carolina, established in 1846, was employing about 300 people by 1850. An able propagandist as well as a good businessman, Gregg saw the textile business not only as a source of profit but also as a device for improving the lot of the South's poor whites. He worked hard to weaken the southern prejudice against manufacturing and made his plant a model of benevolent paternalism similar to that of the early mills of Lowell, Massachusetts. As with every other industry, however, southern textile manufacturing amounted to very little when compared with that of the North. While Gregg was employing 300 textile workers in 1850, the whole state of South Carolina had fewer than 900. In 1860 Lowell, Massachusetts had more spindles turning cotton into yarn than the entire South.

Less than 15 percent of all the goods manufactured in the United States in 1860 came from the South; the region did not really develop an industrial society. Its textile manufacturers depended on the North for machinery, for skilled workers and technicians, for financing, and for insurance. When the English geologist Charles Lyell visited New Orleans in 1846, he was astounded to discover that the thriving city supported not a single book publisher. Even a local guidebook that he purchased bore a New York imprint.

The Northern Industrial Juggernaut

The most obvious change in the North in the decades before the Civil War was the rapid growth of industry. The best estimates suggest that immediately after the War of 1812 the United States was manufacturing less than $200 million worth of goods annually. In 1859 the northeastern states alone produced $1.27 billion of the national total of almost $2 billion.

Manufacturing expanded in so many directions that it is difficult to portray or to summarize its evolution. The factory system made great strides. The development of rich anthracite coal fields in Pennsylvania was particularly important in this connection. The coal could be floated cheaply on canals to convenient sites and used to produce both heat for smelting and metalworking and steam power to drive machinery. Steam permitted greater flexibility in locating factories and in organizing work within them, and since waterpower was already being used to capacity, steam was essential for the expansion of output.

American industry displayed a remarkable receptivity to technological change. The list of inventions and processes developed between 1825 and 1850, included—besides such obviously important items as the sewing machine, the vulcanization of rubber, and the cylinder press—the screw-making machine, the friction match, the lead pencil, and an apparatus for making soda water.

By 1850 the United States led the world in the manufacture of goods that required the use of precision instruments, and in certain industries the country was well on the way toward modern mass production methods. American clocks, pistols, rifles, and locks were outstanding.

Industrial growth led to a great increase in the demand for labor. The effects, however, were mixed. Skilled artisans, technicians, and toolmakers earned good wages and found it relatively easy to set themselves up first as independent craftsmen, later as small manufacturers. The expanding frontier drained off much agricultural labor that might otherwise have been attracted to industry, and the thriving new towns of the West absorbed large numbers of eastern artisans of every kind. At the same time, the pay of an unskilled worker was never enough to support a family decently, and the new machines weakened the bargaining power of artisans by making skill less important.

Many other forces acted to stimulate the growth of manufacturing. Immigration increased rapidly in the 1830s and 1840s. By 1860 Irish immigrants alone made up more than 50 percent of the labor force of the New England mills. An avalanche of strong backs, willing hands, and keen minds descended on the country from Europe. European investors poured large sums into the booming American economy, and the savings of millions of Americans and the great hoard of new California gold added to the supply of capital. Improvements in transportation, population growth, the absence of internal tariff barriers, and the relatively high per capita wealth all meant an ever expanding market for manufactured goods.

A Nation of Immigrants

Rapid industrialization influenced American life in countless ways, none more significant than its effect on the character of the workforce and consequently on the structure of society. The jobs created by industrial expansion attracted European immigrants by the tens of thousands. It is a truism that America is a nation of immigrants—recall that even the ancestors of the Indians came to the New World from Asia.

Read the Document

Foreign Immigration at **myhistorylab.com**

But only with the development of nationalism, that is, with the establishment of the independent United States, did the word *immigrant*, meaning a foreign-born resident, come into existence.

The "native" population (native in this case meaning those whose ancestors had come from Europe rather than native Americans, the Indians) tended to look down on immigrants, and many of the immigrants, in turn, developed prejudices of their own. The Irish, for example, disliked blacks, with whom they often competed for work. Antiblack prejudice was less noticeable among other immigrant groups but by no means absent; most immigrants adopted the views of the local majority, which was often unfriendly to African Americans.

Social and racial rivalries aside, the infusion of unskilled immigrants into the factories of New England speeded the disintegration of the system of hiring young farm women. Already competition and technical advances in the textile industry were increasing the pace of the machines and reducing the number of skilled workers needed to run them. Fewer young farm women were willing to work under these conditions. Recent immigrants replaced the women in large numbers. By 1860 Irish immigrants alone made up more than 50 percent of the labor force in the New England mills.

How Wage Earners Lived

The influx of immigrants does not entirely explain the low standard of living of industrial workers during this period. Low wages and the crowding that resulted from the swift expansion of city populations produced slums that would make the most noisome modern ghetto seem a paradise. In New York tens of thousands of the poor lived in dark, rank cellars, those in the waterfront districts often invaded by high tides. Tenement houses rose back to back, each with many windowless rooms and often without heat or running water.

Out of doors, city life for the poor was almost equally squalid. Slum streets were littered with garbage and trash. Recreational facilities were almost nonexistent. Police and fire protection in the cities were pitifully inadequate. "Urban problems" were less critical than a century later only because they affected a smaller part of the population; for those who experienced them, they were, all too often, crushing.

In 1851 the editor Horace Greeley's *New York Tribune* published a minimum weekly budget for a family of five. The budget, which allowed nothing for savings, medical bills, recreation, or other amenities (Greeley did include 12 cents a week for newspapers), came to $10.37. Since the weekly pay of a factory hand seldom reached $5, the wives and children of most male factory workers also had to labor in the factories merely to survive. And child labor in the 1850s differed fundamentally

A girl stares blankly as the manager of an employment agency suggests her suitability as a maid or housekeeper. The lady, seated, ponders whether the girl will do. The sign on the wall reads, "Agent for Domestics: Warranted Honest." This painting is by William Henry Burr, 1849.
Source: Assession no. 1959.46 Collection of The New-York Historical Society.

from child labor in the 1820s. The pace of the machines had become much faster by then, and the working environment more debilitating.

Relatively few workers belonged to unions, but federations of craft unions sprang up in some cities, and during the boom that preceded the Panic of 1837, a National Trades Union representing a few northeastern cities managed to hold conventions. Early in the Jackson era, "workingmen's" political parties enjoyed a brief popularity, occasionally electing a few local officials. These organizations were made up mostly of skilled craftsmen, professional reformers, and even businessmen. They soon expired, destroyed by internal bickering over questions that had little or nothing to do with working conditions.

The depression of the late 1830s led to the demise of most trade unions. Nevertheless, skilled workers improved their lot somewhat in the 1840s and 1850s. The working day declined gradually from about twelve and a half hours to ten or eleven hours. Many states passed ten-hour laws and laws regulating child labor, but they were poorly enforced. Most states, however, enacted effective mechanic's lien laws, giving workers first call on the assets of bankrupt and defaulting employers, and the Massachusetts court's decision in the case of *Commonwealth v. Hunt* (1842), establishing the legality of labor unions, became a judicial landmark when other state courts followed the precedent.

The flush times of the early 1850s caused the union movement to revive. Many strikes occurred, and a few new national organizations appeared. However, most unions were local institutions, weak and with little control over their membership. The Panic of 1857 dealt the labor movement another body blow. Thus there was no trend toward the general unionization of labor between 1820 and the Civil War.

For this the workers themselves were partly responsible: Craftsmen took little interest in unskilled workers except to keep them down. Few common laborers considered themselves part of a permanent working class with different objectives from those of their employers. Although hired labor had existed throughout the colonial period, it was only with the growth of factories and other large enterprises that significant numbers of people worked for wages. To many people, wage labor seemed almost un-American, a violation of the republican values of freedom and independence that had triumphed in the Revolution. Jefferson's professed dislike of urban life was based in part on his fear that people who worked for wages would be so beholden to their employers that they could not act independently.

This republican value system, along with the fluidity of society, the influx of job-hungry immigrants, and the widespread employment of women and children in unskilled jobs made labor organization difficult. The assumption was that nearly anyone who was willing to work could eventually escape from the wage-earning class. "If any continue through life in the condition of the hired laborer," Abraham Lincoln declared in 1859, "it is . . . because of either a dependent nature which prefers it, or improvidence, folly, or singular misfortune."

Progress and Poverty

Any investigation of American society before the Civil War reveals a paradox that is obvious but difficult to resolve. The United States was a land of opportunity, a democratic society with a prosperous, expanding economy and few class distinctions. Its people had a high standard of living in comparison with the citizens of European countries. Yet within this rich, confident nation there existed a class of miserably underpaid and depressed unskilled workers, mostly immigrants, who were worse off materially than nearly any southern slave. In 1848 more than 56,000 New Yorkers, about a quarter of the population, were receiving some form of public relief. A police drive in that city in 1860 brought in nearly 500 beggars.

The middle-class majority seemed indifferent to or at best unaware of these conditions. Reformers conducted investigations, published exposés, and labored to help the victims of urbanization and industrialization. They achieved little. Great fires burned in these decades to release the incredible energies of America. The poor were the ashes, sifting down silent and unnoticed beneath the dazzle and the smoke. Industrialization produced poverty and riches (in Marxian terminology, a proletarian class and an aristocracy of capitalists).

Economic opportunities were great, and taxation was minimal. Little wonder that as the generations passed, the rich got richer. Industrialization accelerated the process and, by stimulating the immigration of masses of poor workers, skewed the social balance still further. By the mid-nineteenth century Americans were convinced that all men were equal, and indeed all *white* men had equal political rights. Socially and economically, however, the distances between top and bottom were widening. This situation endured for the rest of the century, and in some respects it still endures.

Foreign Commerce

Changes in the pattern of foreign commerce were less noticeable than those in manufacturing but were nevertheless significant. After increasing erratically during the 1820s and 1830s, both imports and exports leapt forward in the next twenty years. The nation remained primarily an exporter of raw materials and an importer of manufactured goods, and in most years it imported more than it exported. Cotton continued to be the most valuable export, in 1860 accounting for a record $191 million of total exports of $333 million. Despite America's own thriving industry, textiles still held the lead among imports, with iron products second. As in earlier days, Great Britain was both the best customer of the United States and its leading supplier.

The increase in the volume and value of trade and its concentration at larger ports had a marked effect on the construction of ships. By the 1850s the average vessel was three times the size of those built thirty years earlier. Startling improvements in design, culminating in the long, sleek, white-winged clipper ships, made possible speeds previously undreamed of. Appearing just in time to supply the need for fast transportation to the

Photo Credit: Niday Picture Library/Alamy Images.

The American clipper ship, *Red Jacket*, off Cape Horn, sails from Australia to Liverpool, England in 1854.

California gold fields, the clippers cut sailing time around Cape Horn to San Francisco from five or six months to three, the record of eighty-nine days being held jointly by *Andrew Jackson* and Donald McKay's famous *Flying Cloud*. To achieve such speeds, cargo capacity had to be sacrificed, making clippers uneconomical for carrying the bulky produce that was the mainstay of commerce. But for specialty goods, in their brief heyday the clippers were unsurpassed.

Steam Conquers the Atlantic

The reign of the clipper ship was short. Like so many other things, ocean commerce was being mechanized. Steamships conquered the high seas more slowly than the rivers because early models were unsafe in rough waters and uneconomical. A riverboat could take on fuel along its route, whereas an Atlantic steamer had to carry tons of coal across the ocean, thereby reducing its capacity for cargo. However, by the late 1840s, steamships were capturing most of the passenger traffic, mail contracts, and first-class freight. These vessels could not keep up with the clippers in a heavy breeze, but their average speed was far greater, especially on the westward voyage against the prevailing winds. Steamers were soon crossing the Atlantic in less than ten days.

The steamship, and especially the iron ship, which had greater cargo-carrying capacity and was stronger and less costly to maintain, took away the advantages that American shipbuilders had held since colonial times. American lumber was cheap, but the British excelled in iron technology. Although the United States invested about $14.5 million in subsidies for the shipping industry, the funds were not employed intelligently and did little good. In 1858 government efforts to aid shipping were abandoned.

The combination of competition, government subsidy, and technological advance drove down shipping rates from one cent to about a third of a cent. Transatlantic passengers could obtain the best accommodations on the fastest ships for under $200, good accommodations on slower packets for as little as $75.

Rates were especially low for European emigrants willing to travel to America on cargo vessels. By the 1840s at least 4,000 ships were engaged in carrying bulky American cotton and Canadian lumber to Europe. On their return trips with manufactured goods they had unoccupied space, which they converted into rough quarters for passengers. Conditions on these ships were crowded, gloomy, and foul. Frequently epidemics took a fearful toll among steerage passengers. On one crossing of the ship *Lark*, 158 of 440 passengers died of typhus.

Yet without this cheap means of transportation, thousands of poor immigrants would simply have remained at home. Bargain freight rates also help explain the clamor of American manufacturers for high tariffs, for transportation costs added relatively little to the price of European goods.

Canals and Railroads

Another dramatic change was the shift in the direction of the nation's internal commerce and its immense increase. From the time of the first settlers in the Mississippi Valley, the Great River had controlled the flow of goods from farm to market. The completion of the Erie Canal in 1825 heralded a shift. In 1830 there were 1,277 miles of canal in the United States; by 1840 there were 3,326 miles.

Each year saw more western produce moving to market through the canals. In 1845 the Erie Canal was still drawing over two-thirds of its west to east traffic from within New York, but by 1847, despite the fact that this local business held steady, more than half of its traffic came from west of Buffalo, and by 1851 more than two-thirds. The volume of western commerce over the Erie Canal in 1851 amounted to more than twenty times what it had been in 1836, while the value of western goods reaching New Orleans in this period increased only two and a half times.

The expanding traffic and New York's enormous share of it caused businessmen in other eastern cities whose canal projects had been unsuccessful to respond promptly when a new means of transport, the railroad, became available. The first railroads were built in England in the 1820s. In 1830 the first American line, the ambitiously named Baltimore and Ohio Railroad, carried 80,000 passengers over a thirteen-mile stretch of track. By 1833 Charleston, South Carolina, had a line reaching 136 miles to Hamburg, on the Savannah River. Two years later the cars began rolling on the Boston and Worcester Railroad. The Panic of 1837 slowed construction, but by 1840 the United States had 3,328 miles of track, equal to the canal mileage and nearly double the railroad mileage of all Europe.

The first railroads did not compete with the canals for intersectional traffic. The through connections needed to move goods economically over great distances materialized slowly. Of the 6,000 miles of track operating in 1848, nearly all lay east of the Appalachians, and little of it had been coordinated into railroad systems. The intention of most early builders had been to monopolize the trade of surrounding districts, not to establish connections with competing centers. Frequently, railroads used tracks of different widths deliberately to prevent other lines from tying into their tracks.

Between 1848 and 1852 railroad mileage nearly doubled. Three years later it had doubled again, and by 1860 the nation had 30,636 miles of track. During this extraordinary burst of activity, four companies drove lines of gleaming iron from the Atlantic seaboard to the great interior valley. In 1851 the Erie Railroad, the longest road in the world with 537 miles of track, linked the Hudson River north of New York City with Dunkirk on Lake Erie. Late the next year the Baltimore and Ohio reached the Ohio River at Wheeling, and in 1853 a banker named Erastus Corning consolidated eight short lines connecting Albany and Buffalo to form the New York Central Railroad. Finally, in 1858 the Pennsylvania Railroad completed a line across the mountains from Philadelphia to Pittsburgh.

In the states beyond the Appalachians, building went on at an even more feverish pace. By 1855 passengers could travel from Chicago or St. Louis to the east coast at a cost of $20 to $30, the trip taking, with luck, less than forty-eight hours. A generation earlier such a trip had required two to three weeks. Construction was slower in the South: Mississippi laid about 800 miles of track, and Alabama about 600.

Financing the Railroads

Railroad building required immense amounts of labor and capital at a time when many other demands for these resources existed. Immigrants or (in the South) slaves did most of the heavy work. Raising the necessary money proved a more complex task.

Private investors supplied about three-quarters of the money invested in railroads before 1860, more than $800 million in the 1850s alone. Much of this capital came from local merchants and businessmen and from farmers along the proposed rights-of-way. Funds were easy to raise because subscribers seldom had to lay out the full price of their stock at one time; instead they were subject to periodic "calls" for a percentage of their commitment as construction progressed. If the road made money, much of the additional mileage could be paid for out of earnings from the first sections built.

But many railroads that failed to find enough investors sought public money. Towns, counties, and the states themselves lent money to railroads and invested in their stock. Special privileges, such as exemption from taxation and the right to condemn property, were often granted, and in a few cases states built and operated roads as public corporations.

As with earlier internal improvement proposals, federal financial aid to railroads was usually blocked in Congress by a combination of eastern and southern votes. But in 1850 a scheme for granting federal lands to the states to build a line from Lake Michigan to the Gulf of Mexico passed both houses. The main beneficiary was the Illinois Central Railroad, which received a 200-foot right-of-way and alternate strips of land along the track one mile wide and six miles deep, a total of almost 2.6 million acres. By mortgaging this land and by selling portions of it to farmers, the Illinois Central raised nearly all the $23.4 million it spent on construction. The success of this operation led to additional grants of almost 20 million acres in the 1850s, benefiting more than forty railroads. Far larger federal grants were made after the Civil War, when the transcontinental lines were built.

Frequently, the capitalists who promoted railroads were more concerned with making money out of the construction of the lines than with operating them.

Others in the business were unashamedly crooked and avidly took advantage of the public passion for railroads. Some officials issued stock to themselves without paying for it and then sold the shares to gullible investors. Others manipulated the books of their corporations and set up special construction companies and paid them exorbitant returns out of railroad assets. These practices did not become widespread until after the Civil War, but all of them first sprang up in the decades preceding the war. At the same time that the country was first developing a truly national economy, it was also producing its first really big-time crooks.

Railroads and the Economy

The effects of so much railroad construction were profound. Although the main reason that farmers put more land under the plow was an increase in the price of agricultural products, the railroad helped determine just what land was used and how profitably it could be farmed. Much of the fertile prairie through which the Illinois Central ran had been available for settlement for many years before 1850, but development had been slow because it was remote from navigable waters and had no timber. In 1840 the three counties immediately northeast of Springfield had a population of about 8,500. They produced about 59,000 bushels of wheat and 690,000 bushels of corn. In the next decade the region grew slowly by the standards

●●●─[Read the Document

Senate Report on the Railroads at **myhistorylab.com**

of that day: The three counties had about 14,000 people in 1850 and produced 71,000 bushels of wheat and 2.2 million bushels of corn. Then came the railroad and with it an agricultural revolution. By 1860 the population of the three counties had soared to over 38,000, wheat production had topped 550,000 bushels, and corn 5.7 million bushels.

Access to world markets gave the farmers of the upper Mississippi Valley an incentive to increase output. Land was plentiful and cheap, but farm labor was scarce; consequently agricultural wages rose sharply, especially after 1850. New tools and machines appeared in time to ease the labor shortage. First came the steel plowshare, invented by John Deere, a Vermont-born blacksmith who had moved to Illinois in 1837. In 1839 Deere turned out ten such plows in his little shop in Moline, Illinois. By 1857 he was selling 10,000 a year.

Still more important was the perfection of the mechanical reaper, for wheat production was limited more by the amount that farmers could handle during the brief harvest season than by the acreage they could plant and cultivate. The major figure in the development of the reaper was Cyrus Hall McCormick. McCormick's horse-drawn reaper bent the grain against the cutting knife and then deposited it neatly on a platform, whence it could easily be raked into windrows. With this machine, two workers could cut fourteen times as much wheat as with scythes.

The railroad had an equally powerful impact on American cities. The eastern seaports benefited, and so did countless intermediate centers, such as Buffalo and Cincinnati. But no city was affected more profoundly by railroads than Chicago. In 1850 not a single line had

Railroads, 1860 Major trunk lines carrying long-distance traffic crisscrossed the area east of the Mississippi. The North had a more extensive rail grid than the South; the North and West were linked, while the South was not as tightly connected to the national economy.

reached there; five years later it was terminal for 2,200 miles of track and controlled the commerce of an imperial domain. By extending half a dozen lines west to the Mississippi, it drained off nearly all the river traffic north of St. Louis. The Illinois Central sucked the expanding output of the prairies into Chicago as well. Most of this freight went eastward over the new railroads or on the Great Lakes and the Erie Canal. Nearly 350,000 tons of shipping plied the lakes by 1855.

The railroads, like the textile industry, stimulated other kinds of economic activity. They transformed agriculture; both real estate values and the buying and selling of land increased whenever the iron horse puffed into a new district. The railroads spurred regional concentration of industry and an increase in the size of business units. Their insatiable need for capital stimulated the growth of investment banking. Their massive size required the creation of complex structures and the employment of salaried managers.

Agriculture, 1860 Cotton was central to the southern economy, while tobacco was the primary crop in Virginia, Tennessee, and Kentucky. Wheat was the key crop in the upper Midwest, and corn was grown nearly everywhere.

The proliferation of trunk lines and the competition of the canal system led to a sharp decline in freight and passenger rates. Cheap transportation had a revolutionary effect on western agriculture. Farmers in Iowa could now raise grain to feed the factory workers of Lowell and even of Manchester, England. Two-thirds of the meat consumed in New York City was soon arriving by rail from beyond the Appalachians. The center of American wheat production shifted westward to Illinois, Wisconsin, and Indiana. When the Crimean War (1853–1856) and European crop failures increased foreign demand, these regions boomed. Success bred success for farmers and for the railroads. Profits earned from carrying wheat enabled the roads to build feeder lines that opened up still wider areas to commercial agriculture and made it easy to bring in lumber, farm machinery, household furnishings, and the settlers themselves at low cost.

Railroads and the Sectional Conflict

Increased production and cheap transportation boosted the western farmer's income and standard of living. The days of isolation and self-sufficiency, even for the family on the edge of the frontier, rapidly disappeared. Pioneers quickly became operators of businesses and, to a far greater extent than their forebears, consumers, buying all sorts of manufactured articles that their ancestors had made for themselves or done without. These changes had their costs. Like southern planters, they now became dependent on middlemen and lost some of their feeling of self-reliance. Overproduction became a problem. Buying a farm began to require more capital, for as profits increased, so did the price of land. Machinery was an additional expense. The proportion of farm laborers and tenants increased.

The linking of the East and West had fateful effects on politics. The increased ease of movement from section to section and the ever more complex social and economic integration of the East and West stimulated nationalism and thus became a force for the preservation of the Union. Without the railroads and canals, Illinois and Iowa would scarcely have dared to side against the South in 1861. When the Mississippi ceased to be essential to them, citizens of the upper valley could afford to be more hostile to slavery and especially to its westward extension. Economic ties with the Northeast reinforced cultural connections.

The South might have preserved its influence in the Northwest if it had pressed forward its own railroad-building program. It failed to do so. There were many southern lines but nothing like a southern system. As late as 1856 one could get from Memphis to Richmond or Charleston only by very indirect routes. As late as 1859 the land-grant road extending the Illinois Central to Mobile, Alabama, was not complete, nor did any economical connection exist between Chicago and New Orleans.

This state of affairs could be accounted for in part by the scattered population of the South, the paucity of passenger traffic, the seasonal nature of much of the freight business, and the absence of large cities. Southerners placed too much reliance on the Mississippi: The fact that traffic on the river continued to be heavy throughout the 1850s blinded them to the precipitous rate at which their relative share of the nation's trade was declining. But the fundamental cause of the South's backwardness in railroad construction was the attitude of its leaders. Southerners of means were no more interested in commerce than in industry; their capital found other outlets.

The Economy on the Eve of Civil War

Between the mid-1840s and the mid-1850s the United States experienced one of the most remarkable periods of growth in the history of the world. Every economic indicator surged forward: manufacturing, grain and cotton production, population, railroad mileage, gold production, sales of public land. The building of the railroads stimulated business, and by making transportation cheaper, the completed lines energized the nation's economy. The American System that Henry Clay had dreamed of arrived with a rush just as Clay was passing from the scene.

Inevitably, this growth caused dislocations that were aggravated by the boom psychology that once again infected the popular mind. In 1857 there was a serious collapse. The return of Russian wheat to the world market after the Crimean War caused grain prices to fall. This checked agricultural expansion, which hurt the railroads and cut down on the demand for manufactures. Unemployment increased. Frightened depositors started runs on banks, most of which had to suspend specie payments.

People called this abrupt downturn the Panic of 1857. Yet the vigor of the economy was such that the bad times did not last long. The upper Mississippi Valley suffered most, for so much new land had been opened up that supplies of farm produce greatly exceeded demand. Elsewhere conditions improved rapidly.

The South, somewhat out of the hectic rush to begin with, was affected very little by the collapse of 1857, for cotton prices continued to be high. This gave planters the false impression that their economy was immune to such violent downturns. Some began to argue that the South would be better off out of the Union.

Before a new national upward swing could become well established, however, the sectional crisis between North and South shook people's confidence in the future. Then the war came, and a new set of forces shaped economic development.

Milestones

Year	Event	Year	Event
1808	Congress bans further importation of slaves	1840–1857	Economy surges during boom in manufacturing, railroad construction, and foreign commerce
1822	Thirty-seven slaves are executed when Denmark Vesey's "conspiracy" is exposed	1842	Massachusetts declares unions legal in *Commonwealth v. Hunt*
1825	Erie Canal is completed, connecting the East and the Midwest	1846	Elias Howe invents sewing machine
1830	Baltimore and Ohio Railroad begins operation	1850	Congress grants land to aid construction of Illinois Central Railroad
1831	Nat Turner's slave uprising kills fifty-seven whites	1854	Clipper ship *Flying Cloud* sails from New York to San Francisco in eighty-nine days
1837	Cyrus Hall McCormick invents reaper to harvest wheat	1857	Brief economic depression (Panic of 1857) collapses economy
1839	John Deere begins manufacturing steel plows		

✓● ┌Study┐ and **Review** at **www.myhistorylab.com**

Review Questions

1. This chapter explores two tendencies: an increasing economic and cultural gap between the South and the rest of the country; and a tighter integration of the nation through spreading transportation systems. In 1860, was the United States breaking into different economic and cultural systems, or did politicians exaggerate the significance of regional variations?

2. The harshness of the slave system was everywhere apparent. In what ways did slaves succeed in fashioning their own culture?

3. Southerners often insisted that immigrants who toiled in northern factories were subjected to far worse conditions than southern slaves. What arguments can be used to support and reject this thesis?

4. During these decades, southern cities sought militia units and armories to help defend against slave insurrections. Northern cities sought such protections to defend against industrial worker insurrections. Which was the greater threat?

The Coming of the Civil War

((•—[Hear the Audio at myhistorylab.com

Do you space out during political debates?

IN LATE JULY 2008 PRESIDENTIAL CANDIDATE JOHN MCCAIN, BEHIND IN the polls, ran a 30-second TV ad attacking Barack Obama. "He's the biggest celebrity in the world," the narrator declared, as the camera moved from Obama's beaming face to a crowd shouting, "Obama! Obama!" "But is he ready to lead?" the narrator intoned, with a quick cut to glamour shots of Britney Spears and Paris Hilton. Obama retaliated with an attack ad of his own: "John McCain. Same old politics. Same failed policies." By the time the 2008 campaign was over, Obama had placed 553,629 television ads, McCain 287,090. The great majority of these ads were negative.

Many pundits claimed that politics had devolved into little more than name-calling. It had been different 150 years earlier, they said, when Abraham Lincoln squared off against Stephen A. Douglas in a series of debates that framed the national discussion over slavery.

In fact, though, Lincoln and Douglas tore into each other. "Mr. Lincoln has not character enough for integrity and truth," Douglas declared in the first debate. Lincoln responded in kind: "I don't want to quarrel with him—to call him a liar—but when I come square up to him I don't know what else to call him."

If the tone of politics has changed little over the past century and a half, its substance is of an entirely different character. Each of the seven Lincoln-Douglas debates lasted three hours: For the first debate Douglas spoke for one hour. Lincoln's reply lasted ninety minutes, and Douglas concluded with another thirty minute speech. The order of speakers was reversed in subsequent debates. Such a debate nowadays is unimaginable. Most viewers would soon be reaching for the remote.

But during the 1850s audiences stood for hours to hear candidates debate the issues at the heart of this chapter: the morality of the Fugitive Slave Act; the accuracy of Harriet Beecher Stowe's description of slavery in *Uncle Tom's Cabin*; the question of whether "bleeding Kansas" should be admitted to the Union as a slave or free state; the Supreme Court's inflammatory decision in the Dred Scott case; John Brown's manic crusade to free the slaves by force. Most knew, or at least sensed, that the fate of the nation depended on the outcome of these debates. The drumbeat of words came faster

From Chapter 13 of *American Destiny: Narrative of a Nation*, Combined Volume, Fourth Edition. Mark C. Carnes and John A. Garraty. Copyright © 2012 by Pearson Education, Inc. Published by Pearson Prentice Hall. All rights reserved.

and louder. The din culminated in the superheated rhetoric of the 1860 presidential campaign and the secession of the South. Soon words would be drowned out by the roar of cannon.

Slave-Catchers Come North

The political settlement between the North and South that Henry Clay designed—the Compromise of 1850—lasted only four years. Its central provisions inevitably sparked controversy. Allowing new territories to decide the question of slavery themselves ensured that the issue would resurface. Americans continued to migrate westward by the thousands, and as long as slaveholders could carry their human property into federally controlled territories, northern resentment would smolder. The Fugitive Slave Act, another part of the Compromise of 1850, imposed fines for hiding or rescuing fugitive slaves. Abolitionists fought against the law and expanded the **underground railroad**, a secret network to help escaped slaves make their way to freedom.

When two Georgians came to Boston to reclaim William and Ellen Craft, admitted fugitives, a "vigilance committee" hounded them through the streets shouting "slave hunters, slave hunters," and forced them to return home empty-handed. The Crafts prudently—or perhaps in disgust—decided to leave the United States for

Watch the Video
Underground Railroad at
myhistorylab.com

Photo Credit: Courtesy of the Library of Congress.

This painting by Thomas S. Noble describes the story of Margaret Garner, a slave who escaped with her family across the frozen Ohio River to Cincinnati. When apprehended by slavecatchers, she killed her daughter rather than return her to slavery. Garner's story inspired Toni Morrison's Pulitzer Prize-winning novel *Beloved* (1987).

CANADA
MAINE
VERMONT
N.H.
MASS.
WISCONSIN
NEW YORK
CONN. R.I.
MICHIGAN
N.J.
PENNSYLVANIA
IOWA
INDIANA
OHIO
M.D.
DEL.
ILLINOIS
VIRGINIA
KENTUCKY
MISSOURI
TENNESSEE
NORTH
CAROLINA
ARKANSAS
SOUTH
CAROLINA
ATLANTIC
OCEAN
MISSISSIPPI
ALABAMA
GEORGIA
Counties with more
than 100 free blacks
Counties with more
than 2000 free blacks
LOUISIANA
FLORIDA
Gulf of
Mexico

Free Blacks in 1850 The existence of so many free blacks caused many slaves to question their own servitude and facilitated the attempts of others to escape from bondage.

England. Early in 1851 a Virginia agent captured Frederick "Shadrach" Jenkins, a waiter in a Boston coffeehouse. While Jenkins was being held for deportation, a mob of African Americans broke into the courthouse and hustled him off to Canada. That October a slave named Jerry, who had escaped from Missouri, was arrested in Syracuse, New York. Within minutes the whole town had the news. Crowds surged through the streets, and when night fell, a mob smashed into the building where Jerry was being held and spirited him away to safety in Canada.

●●●━[Read the Document

Drew, from *Narratives of Fugitive Slaves in Canada* at **myhistorylab.com**

Such incidents exacerbated sectional feelings. White Southerners accused the North of reneging on one of the main promises made in the Compromise of 1850, while the sight of harmless human beings being hustled off to a life of slavery disturbed many Northerners who were not abolitionists.

However, most white Northerners were not prepared to interfere with the enforcement of the Fugitive Slave Act themselves. Of the 332 blacks put on trial under the law, about 300 were returned to slavery, most without incident. Nevertheless, enforcing the law in the northern states became steadily more difficult.

Uncle Tom's Cabin

Tremendously important in increasing sectional tensions and bringing home the evils of slavery to still more people in the North was Harriet Beecher Stowe's novel *Uncle Tom's Cabin* (1852). Stowe was neither a professional writer nor an abolitionist, and she had almost no firsthand knowledge of slavery. But her conscience had been roused by the Fugitive Slave Act. In gathering material for the book, she depended heavily on abolitionist writers, many of whom she knew. *Uncle Tom's Cabin* was an enormous success: 10,000 copies were sold in a week, and 300,000 in a year. It was translated into dozens of languages. Dramatized versions were staged in countries throughout the world.

Read the Document
Stowe, *Uncle Tom's Cabin* at **myhistorylab.com**

Harriet Beecher Stowe was hardly a distinguished writer; it was her approach to the subject that explains the book's success. Her tale of the pious, patient slave Uncle Tom, the saintly white child Eva, and the callous slave driver Simon Legree appealed to an audience far wider than that reached by the abolitionists. She avoided the self-righteous, accusatory tone of most abolitionist tracts and did not seek to convert readers to belief in racial equality. Many of her southern white characters were fine, sensitive people, while the cruel Simon Legree was a transplanted Connecticut Yankee. There were many heart-rending scenes of pain, self-sacrifice, and heroism. The story proved especially effective on the stage: The slave Eliza crossing the frozen Ohio River to freedom, the death of Eva, Eva and Tom ascending to Heaven—these scenes left audiences in tears.

Watch the Video
Harriet Beecher Stowe & The Making of Uncle Tom's Cabin at **myhistorylab.com**

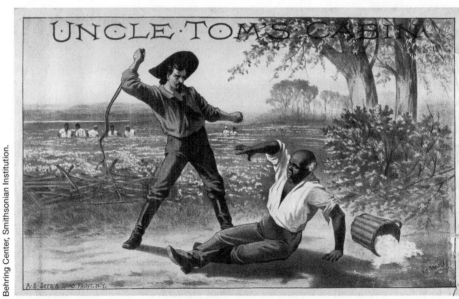

Photo Credit: Warsaw Collection of Business Americana - Theater, Archives Center, National Museum of American History, Behring Center, Smithsonian Institution.

Harriet Beecher Stowe's novel, *Uncle Tom's Cabin*, became a staple of the mid-nineteenth-century theater. This poster shows Simon Legree whipping a blameless Uncle Tom.

Southern critics pointed out, correctly enough, that Stowe's picture of plantation life was distorted, her slaves atypical. They called her a "coarse, ugly, long-tongued woman" and accused her of trying to "awaken rancorous hatred and malignant jealousies" that would undermine national unity. Most Northerners, having little basis on which to judge the accuracy of the book, tended to discount southern criticism as biased. In any case, *Uncle Tom's Cabin* raised questions that transcended the issue of accuracy. Did it matter if every slave was not as kindly as Uncle Tom, as determined as George Harris? What if only one white master was as evil as Simon Legree? No earlier white American writer had looked at slaves as people.

Uncle Tom's Cabin touched the hearts of millions. Some became abolitionists; others, still hesitating to step forward, asked themselves as they put the book down, "Is slavery just?"

Diversions Abroad: The "Young America" Movement

Clearly a distraction was needed to help keep the lid on sectional troubles. Some people hoped to find one in foreign affairs. The spirit of manifest destiny explains this in large part; once the United States had reached the Pacific, expansionists began to think of transmitting the dynamic, democratic U.S. spirit to other countries by aiding local revolutionaries, opening new markets, or perhaps even annexing foreign lands. This became known as the **Young America movement**, whose adherents were confident that democracy would triumph everywhere, even if by conquest.

One of those who dreamt of conquest was an adventurer named William Walker. In 1855 Walker, backed by an American company engaged in transporting migrants to California across Central America, seized control of Nicaragua and elected himself president. He was ousted two years later but made repeated attempts to regain control until, in 1860, when he died before a Honduran firing squad. There were reasons unrelated to slavery why Central America suddenly seemed important. The rapid development of California created a need for improved communication with the West Coast. A canal across Central America would cut weeks from the sailing time between New York and San Francisco. In 1850 Secretary of State John M. Clayton and the British minister to the United States, Henry Lytton Bulwer, negotiated a treaty providing for the demilitarization and joint Anglo-American control of any canal across the isthmus.

As this area assumed strategic importance to the United States, the desire to obtain Cuba grew stronger. In 1854 President Franklin Pierce instructed his minister to Spain to offer $130 million for the island. The State Department prepared a confidential dispatch suggesting that if Spain refused to sell Cuba, "the great law of self-preservation" might justify "wresting" it from Spain by force.

News of the dispatch—known as the **Ostend Manifesto**—leaked out, and it had to be published. Northern opinion was outraged by this "slaveholders' plot" to add another slave state to the Union. Europeans claimed to be shocked by such "dishonorable" and "clandestine" diplomacy. The government had to disavow the manifesto, and any hope of obtaining Cuba or any other territory in the Caribbean vanished.

The expansionist mood of the moment also explains President Fillmore's dispatching an expedition under Commodore Matthew C. Perry to try for commercial concessions in the isolated kingdom of Japan in 1854. Perry's expedition was a great success. The Japanese, impressed by American naval power, agreed to establish diplomatic relations. In 1858 an American envoy, Townsend Harris, negotiated a commercial treaty that opened to American ships six Japanese ports heretofore closed to foreigners. President Pierce's negotiation of a Canadian reciprocity treaty with Great Britain in 1854 and an unsuccessful attempt, also made under Pierce, to annex the Hawaiian Islands are further demonstrations of the assertive foreign policy of the period.

Stephen Douglas: "The Little Giant"

The most prominent spokesman of the Young America movement was Stephen A. Douglas. The senator from Illinois was the Henry Clay of his generation. Like Clay at his best, Douglas was able to see the needs of the nation in the broadest perspective. He held a succession of state offices before being elected to Congress in 1842 at the age of twenty-nine. After only two terms in the House, he was chosen to be a United States senator.

The foundations of Douglas's politics were expansion and popular sovereignty. He had been willing to fight for all of Oregon in 1846, and he supported the Mexican War to the hilt, in sharp contrast to his one-term Illinois colleague in Congress, Abraham Lincoln. That local settlers should determine their own institutions was, to his way of thinking, axiomatic. Since he believed that arguments over the future of slavery in the territories were a foolish waste of energy and time, he was convinced that natural conditions would keep the institution out of the West.

The main thing, he insisted, was to get on with the development of the United States. Let the nation build railroads, acquire new territory, expand its trade. He believed slavery "a curse beyond computation" for both blacks and whites, but he refused to admit that any moral issue was involved. He cared not, he boasted, whether slavery was voted up or voted down. This was not really true, but the question was interfering with the rapid exploitation of the continent. Douglas wanted it settled so that the country could concentrate on more important matters.

Douglas's success in steering the Compromise of 1850 through Congress added to his reputation. In 1851, he set out to win the Democratic presidential nomination, reasoning that since he was the brightest, most imaginative, and hardest-working Democrat around, he had every right to press his claim.

This brash aggressiveness proved his undoing. He expressed open contempt for James Buchanan and said of his other chief rival, Lewis Cass, who had won considerable fame while serving as minister to France, that his "reputation was beyond the C."

At the 1852 Democratic convention Douglas had no chance. Cass and Buchanan killed each other off, and the delegates finally chose a dark horse, Franklin Pierce of New Hampshire. The Whigs, rejecting the colorless Fillmore, nominated General Winfield Scott, who was known as "Old Fuss and Feathers" because of his "punctiliousness in dress and decorum." In the campaign both sides supported the Compromise of 1850. The Democrats won an easy victory, 254 electoral votes to 42.

So handsome a triumph seemed to ensure stability, but in fact it was a prelude to political chaos. The Whig party was crumbling fast. The "Cotton" Whigs of the South, alienated by the antislavery sentiments of their northern brethren, were flocking into the Democratic fold. In the North the Whigs, divided between an antislavery wing ("conscience Whigs") and another that was undisturbed by slavery, found themselves more and more at odds with each other. Congress fell overwhelmingly into the hands of proslavery southern Democrats, a development profoundly disturbing to northern Democrats as well as to Whigs.

The Kansas-Nebraska Act

Franklin Pierce appeared a youthful forty-eight years old when he took office. He was generally well-liked by politicians. His career had included service in both houses of Congress. Alcohol had become a problem for him in Washington, however, and in 1842 he had resigned from the Senate and returned home to try to best the bottle, a struggle in which he was successful. His law practice boomed,

See the **Map**

The Compromise of 1850 and the Kansas-Nebraska Act at **myhistorylab.com**

Photo Credit: The Granger Collection, New York.

This engraving of Franklin Pierce shows him on his horse during the Mexican War. In actuality, he did not remain there long. During one battle, Pierce was thrown from his horse and sustained pelvic and knee injuries. While leading his men the next day, he fainted. Another officer assumed that Pierce was drunk. For years, Whigs attacked Pierce's military record, calling him "hero of many a bottle."

and he added to his reputation by serving as a brigadier general during the Mexican War. Although his nomination for president came as a surprise, once made, it had appeared perfectly reasonable. Great things were expected of his administration, especially after he surrounded himself with men of all factions: To balance his appointment of a radical states' rights Mississippian, Jefferson Davis, as secretary of war, for example, he named a conservative Northerner, William L. Marcy of New York, as secretary of state.

Only a strong leader, however, can manage a ministry of all talents, and that President Pierce was not. The ship of state was soon drifting; Pierce seemed incapable of holding firm the helm.

This was the situation in January 1854 when Senator Douglas, chairman of the Committee on Territories, introduced what looked like a routine bill organizing the land west of Missouri and Iowa as the Nebraska Territory. Since settlers were beginning to trickle into the area, the time had arrived to set up a civil administration. But besides his expansionist motives, Douglas also acted because a territorial government was essential to railroad development. As a director of the Illinois Central line and as a land speculator, he hoped to make Chicago the terminus of a transcontinental railroad, but construction could not begin until the route was cleared of Indians and brought under some kind of civil control.

The railroad question aside, Nebraska would presumably become a free state, for it lay north of latitude 36°30' in a district from which slavery had been excluded by the Missouri Compromise. Under pressure from the Southerners, led by Senator David R. Atchison of Missouri, Douglas agreed first to divide the region into two territories, Kansas and Nebraska, and then—a fateful concession—to repeal the part of the Missouri Compromise that excluded slavery from land north of 36°30'. Whether the new territories should become slave or free, he argued, should be left to the decision of the settlers in accordance with the democratic principle of popular sovereignty. The fact that he might advance his presidential ambitions by making concessions to the South must have influenced Douglas too, as must the local political situation in Missouri, where slaveholders feared being "surrounded" on three sides by free states.

Douglas's miscalculation of northern sentiment was monumental. It was one thing to apply popular sovereignty to the new territories in the Southwest, but quite another to apply it to a region that had been part of the United States for half a century and free soil for thirty-four years. A group of abolitionist congressmen issued what they called their "Appeal of the Independent Democrats" (actually, all were Free Soilers and Whigs) denouncing the Kansas-Nebraska bill as "a gross violation of a sacred pledge" and calling for a campaign of letter writing, petitions, and public meetings to prevent its passage. The unanimity and force of the northern public's reaction was like nothing in America since the days of the Stamp Act and the Intolerable Acts.

But protests could not defeat the bill. Southerners in both houses backed it regardless of party. Douglas, at his best when under attack, pushed it with all his power. The authors of the "Appeal," he charged, were "the pure unadulterated representatives of Abolitionism, Free Soilism, [and] Niggerism." President Pierce added whatever force the administration could muster. As a result, the northern Democrats split and the **Kansas-Nebraska Act** was passed late in May 1854. In this manner the nation took the greatest single step in its march toward the abyss of secession and civil war.

The repeal of the Missouri Compromise struck the North like a slap in the face—at once shameful and challenging. Presumably the question of slavery in the territories had been settled forever; now, seemingly without justification, it had been reopened. On May 24, two days after the Kansas-Nebraska bill passed the House of Representatives, Anthony Burns, a slave who had escaped from Virginia by stowing away on a ship, was arrested in Boston. Massachusetts abolitionists brought suit against Burns's former master, charging false arrest. They also organized a protest meeting at which they inflamed the crowd into attacking the courthouse where Burns was being held. The mob broke into the building and a guard was killed, but federal marshals drove off the attackers.

President Pierce ordered the Boston district attorney to "incur any expense" to enforce the law. He also sent a federal ship to Boston to carry Burns back to Virginia. Thus Burns was returned to his master, but it required two companies of soldiers and 1,000 police and marines to get him aboard ship. As the grim parade marched past buildings festooned with black crepe, the crowd screamed "Kidnappers! Kidnappers!" at the soldiers. Estimates of the cost of returning this single slave to his owner ran as high as $100,000. A few months later, northern sympathizers bought Burns his freedom—for a few hundred dollars.

In previous cases Boston's conservative leaders, Whig to a man, had tended to hold back; after the Burns incident, they were thoroughly radicalized. "We went to bed one night old fashioned . . .Whigs," one of them explained, "and waked up stark mad Abolitionists."

Know-Nothings, Republicans, and the Demise of the Two-Party System

There were ninety-one free-state Democrats in the House of Representatives when the Kansas-Nebraska Act was passed, only twenty-five after the next election. With the Whig party already moribund, dissidents flocked to two new parties.

One was the American party, or **Know-Nothing party**, so called because it grew out of a secret society whose members used the password "I don't know." The Know-Nothings were primarily nativists—immigration was soaring in the early 1850s, and the influx of poor foreigners was causing genuine social problems. Crime was on the rise in the cities along with drunkenness and other "diseases of poverty."

Several emotion-charged issues related to the fact that a large percentage of the immigrants were Irish and German Catholics also troubled the Know-Nothings. Questions such as public financing of parochial schools, lay control of church policies, the prohibition of alcoholic beverages, and increasing the time before an immigrant could apply for citizenship (the Know-Nothings favored twenty-one years) were matters of major importance to them. Since these were divisive issues, the established political parties tried to avoid them—hence the development of the new party.

The American party was important in the South as well as in the North, and while most Know-Nothings disliked blacks and considered them inherently inferior beings, they tended to adopt the dominant view of slavery in whichever section they were located. In the North most opposed the Kansas-Nebraska Act.

Operating often in tacit alliance with the antislavery forces (dislike of slavery did not prevent many abolitionists from being prejudiced against Catholics and immigrants), the northern Know-Nothings won a string of local victories in 1854 and elected more than forty congressmen.

Far more significant in the long run was the formation of the Republican party, which was made up of former Free Soilers, Conscience Whigs, and "Anti-Nebraska" Democrats. The American party was a national organization, but the **Republican party** was purely sectional. It sprang up spontaneously throughout the Old Northwest and caught on with a rush in New England.

Republicans presented themselves as the party of freedom. They were not abolitionists (though most abolitionists were soon voting Republican), but they insisted that slavery be kept out of the territories. They believed that if America was to remain a land of opportunity, free white labor must have exclusive access to the West. Thus the party appealed not only to voters who disapproved of slavery, but also to those who wished to keep blacks—free or slave—out of their states. In 1854 the Republicans won more than a hundred seats in the House of Representatives and control of many state governments.

The Whig party had almost disappeared in the northern states and the Democratic party had been gravely weakened, but it was unclear how these two new parties would fare. The Know-Nothing party had the superficial advantage of being a nationwide organization, but where slavery was concerned, this was anything but advantageous. And many Northerners who disliked slavery were troubled by the harsh Know-Nothing policies toward immigrants and Catholics. If the Know-Nothings were in control, said former Whig congressman Abraham Lincoln in 1855, the Declaration of Independence would read "all men are created equal, except negroes, *and foreigners, and catholics.*"

"Bleeding Kansas"

The furor over slavery might have died down if settlement of the new territories had proceeded in an orderly manner. Almost none of the settlers who flocked to Kansas owned slaves and relatively few of them were primarily interested in the slavery question. Most had a low opinion of blacks. Like nearly all frontier settlers, they wanted land and local political office, lucrative government contracts, and other business opportunities.

When Congress opened the gates to settlement in May 1854, none of the land in the territory was available for sale. Treaties extinguishing Indian titles had yet to be ratified, and public lands had not been surveyed. In July Congress authorized squatters to occupy unsurveyed federal lands, but much of this property was far to the west of the frontier and practically inaccessible. The situation led to confusion over property boundaries, to graft and speculation, and to general uncertainty, thereby exacerbating the difficulty of establishing an orderly government.

The legal status of slavery in Kansas became the focus of all these conflicts. Both northern abolitionists and southern defenders of slavery were determined to have Kansas. They made of the territory first a testing ground and then a battlefield, thus exposing the fatal flaw in the Kansas-Nebraska Act and the idea of popular sovereignty. The law said that the people of Kansas were "perfectly free" to decide the slavery question. But the citizens of territories were not entirely free because territories were not sovereign political units. The Act had created a political vacuum, which its vague statement that the settlers must establish their domestic institutions "subject. . . to the Constitution" did not begin to fill. The virtues of the time-tested system of congressional control established by the Northwest Ordinance became fully apparent only when the system was discarded.

In November 1854 an election was held in Kansas to pick a territorial delegate to Congress. A large band of Missourians crossed over specifically to vote for a proslavery candidate and elected him easily. In March 1855 some 5,000 "border ruffians" again descended on Kansas and elected a territorial legislature. A census had recorded 2,905 eligible voters, but 6,307 votes were cast. The legislature promptly enacted a slave code and laws prohibiting abolitionist agitation. Antislavery settlers refused to recognize this regime and held elections of their own. By January 1856 two governments existed in Kansas: one based on fraud, the other extralegal.

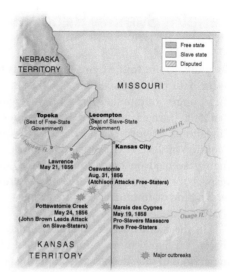

"Bleeding Kansas" In the late 1850s, one Kansas government (located in Topeka) abolished slavery; the other (located in Lecompton) legalized slavery. As proslavery settlers poured into Kansas from Missouri, and antislavery settlers from the North, clashes were inevitable.

By denouncing the free-state government located at Topeka, President Pierce encouraged the proslavery settlers to assume the offensive. In May, 800 of them sacked the antislavery town of Lawrence. An extremist named John Brown then took the law into his own hands in retaliation. By his reckoning, five Free Soilers had been killed by proslavery forces. In May 1856, together with six companions (four of them his sons), Brown stole into a settlement on Pottawatomie Creek in the dead of night. They dragged five unsuspecting men from their cabins and murdered them. This slaughter brought men on both sides to arms by the hundreds. Marauding bands came to blows and terrorized homesteads, first attempting to ascertain the inhabitants' position on slavery.

Brown and his followers escaped capture and were never indicted for the murders, but pressure from federal troops eventually forced him to go into hiding. He finally left Kansas in October 1856. By that time some 200 persons had lost their lives.

A certain amount of violence was normal in any frontier community, but it suited the political interests of the Republicans to make the situation in Kansas seem worse than it was. Exaggerated accounts of "bleeding Kansas" filled the pages of northern newspapers. The Democrats were also partly to blame, for although residents of nearby states often tried to influence elections in new territories, the actions of the border ruffians made a mockery of the democratic process.

However, the main responsibility for the Kansas tragedy must be borne by the Pierce administration. Under popular sovereignty the national government was supposed to see that elections were orderly and honest. Instead, the president acted as a partisan. When the first governor of the territory objected to the manner in which the proslavery legislature had been elected, Pierce replaced him with a man who backed the southern group without question.

Senator Sumner Becomes a Martyr for Abolitionism

As counterpoint to the fighting in Kansas there arose an almost continuous clamor in the halls of Congress. Epithets like "liar" were freely tossed about. Prominent in these angry outbursts was a new senator, Charles Sumner of Massachusetts. Brilliant, learned, and articulate, Sumner had made a name for himself in New England as a reformer interested in the peace movement, prison reform, and the abolition of slavery. His unyielding devotion to his principles was less praiseworthy than it seemed on casual examination, for it resulted from his complete lack of respect for the principles of others. Reform movements evidently provided him with a kind of emotional release; he became combative and totally lacking in objectivity when espousing a cause.

In the Kansas debates Sumner displayed an icy disdain for his foes. Colleagues threatened him with assassination, called him a "filthy reptile" and a "leper." He was impervious to such hostility. In the spring of 1856 he loosed a dreadful blast titled "The Crime Against Kansas." Characterizing administration policy as tyrannical, imbecilic, absurd, and infamous, he demanded that Kansas be admitted to the Union at once as a free state. Then he began a long and intemperate attack on both Douglas and the elderly Senator Andrew P. Butler of South Carolina, who was not present to defend himself.

SOUTHERN CHIVALRY — ARGUMENT versus CLUB'S.

In this cartoon Charles Sumner of Massachusetts is caned on the floor of the Senate by Preston Brooks of South Carolina.

Source: J. L. Magee, *Southern Chivalry-Argument Versus Clubs*, 1856. Lithograph. Weitenkampf Collection #745, Prints Collection: Miriam and Ira D. Wallach Division of Art, Prints and Photographs, The New York Public Library, Astor, Lenox, and Tilden Foundations.

Sumner described Butler as a "Don Quixote" who had taken "the harlot, slavery" as his mistress, and he spoke scornfully of "the loose expectoration" of Butler's speech. This was an inexcusable reference to the uncontrollable drooling to which the elderly senator was subject. While he was still talking, Douglas, who shrugged off most political name-calling as part of the game, was heard to mutter, "That damn fool will get himself killed by some other damn fool."

Such a "fool" quickly materialized in the person of Congressman Preston S. Brooks of South Carolina, a nephew of Senator Butler. Since Butler was absent from Washington, Brooks, who was probably as mentally unbalanced as Sumner, assumed the responsibility of defending his kinsman's honor. A southern romantic par excellence, he decided that caning Sumner would reflect his contempt more effectively than challenging him to a duel. Two days after the speech, Brooks entered the Senate as it adjourned. Sumner remained at his desk writing. Waiting until a talkative woman in the lobby had left so that she would be spared the sight of violence, Brooks then walked up to Sumner and rained blows on his head with a cane until Sumner fell, unconscious and bloody, to the floor. "I. . . gave him about 30 first-rate stripes," Brooks later boasted. "Towards the last he bellowed like a calf. I wore my cane out completely but saved the head which is gold." The physical damage suffered by Sumner was not life-threatening, but the incident so affected him psychologically that he was unable to return to his seat in Congress until 1859.

Both sides made much of this disgraceful incident. When the House censured him, Brooks resigned, returned to his home district, and was triumphantly reelected. A number of well-wishers sent him souvenir canes. Northerners viewed the affair as illustrating the brutalizing effect of slavery on southern whites and made a hero of Sumner.

Buchanan Tries His Hand

Such was the atmosphere surrounding the 1856 presidential election. The Republican party now dominated much of the North. It nominated John C. Frémont, "the Pathfinder," one of the heroes of the conquest of California during the war with Mexico. Frémont fit the Whig tradition of presidential candidates: a popular military man with almost no political experience. Unlike Taylor and Scott, however, he was articulate on the issue of slavery in the territories. Although citizens of diverse interests had joined the party, Republicans expressed their objectives in one simple slogan: "Free soil, free speech, and Frémont."

The Democrats cast aside the ineffectual Pierce, but they did not dare nominate Douglas because he had raised such a storm in the North. They settled on James Buchanan, chiefly because he had been out of the country serving as minister to Great Britain during the long debate over Kansas! The American party nominated former president Millard Fillmore, a choice the remnants of the Whigs endorsed.

In the campaign, the Democrats concentrated on denouncing the Republicans as a sectional party that threatened to destroy the Union. On this issue they carried the day. Buchanan won only a minority of the popular vote, but he had strength in every section. He got 174 electoral votes to Frémont's 114 and Fillmore's 8. The significant contest took place in the populous states just north of slave territory—Pennsylvania, Ohio, Indiana, and Illinois. Of these, Buchanan carried all but Ohio, although by narrow margins.

No one could say that James Buchanan lacked political experience. Elected to the Pennsylvania legislature in 1815 when he was only twenty-four years old, he served for well over twenty years in Congress and had served as minister to Russia, as secretary of state, and as minister to Great Britain.

Personally, Buchanan was a bundle of contradictions. Dignified in bearing and by nature cautious, he could consume enormous amounts of liquor without showing the slightest sign of inebriation. He wore a very high collar to conceal a scarred neck, and because of an eye defect he habitually carried his head to one side and slightly forward, which gave him, as his biographer says, "a perpetual attitude of courteous deference and attentive interest" that sometimes led individuals to believe they had won a greater share of his attention and support than was actually the case. In fact he was extremely stubborn and sometimes vindictive.

The Dred Scott Decision

Before Buchanan could fairly take the Kansas problem in hand, an event occurred that drove another deep wedge between North and South. Back in 1834 Dr. John Emerson of St. Louis joined the army as a surgeon and was assigned to duty at Rock Island, Illinois. Later he was transferred to Fort Snelling, in the Wisconsin Territory. In 1838 he returned to Missouri. Accompanying him on these travels was his body servant, Dred Scott, a slave. In 1846, after Emerson's death, Scott and his wife Harriet, whom he had married while in Wisconsin, brought suit in the Missouri courts for their liberty with the help of a friendly lawyer. They claimed that residence in Illinois, where slavery was barred under the Northwest Ordinance, and in the Wisconsin Territory, where the Missouri Compromise outlawed it, had made them free.

The future of Dred and Harriet Scott mattered not at all to the country or the courts; at issue was the question of whether Congress or the local legislatures had the power to outlaw slavery in the territories. After many years of litigation, the case reached the Supreme Court of the United States. On March 6, 1857, two days after Buchanan's inauguration, the high tribunal acted, issuing what is known as the **Dred Scott decision**. Free or slave, the Court declared, blacks were not citizens; therefore, Scott could not sue in a federal court. This was dubious legal logic because many blacks were accepted as citizens in some states when the Constitution was drafted and ratified, and Article IV, Section 2, says that "the citizens of each state shall be entitled to all privileges and immunities of citizens in the several states." But the decision settled Scott's fate.

However, the Court went further. Since the plaintiff had returned to Missouri, the laws of Illinois no longer applied to him. His residence in the Wisconsin Territory—this was the most controversial part of the decision—did not make him free because the Missouri Compromise was unconstitutional. According to the Bill of Rights (the Fifth Amendment), the federal government cannot deprive any person of life, liberty, or property without due process of law.[1] Therefore, Chief Justice Roger B. Taney reasoned, "an Act of Congress which deprives a person . . . of his liberty or property merely because he

Watch the Video
Dred Scott & The Crises that
led to the Civil War at
myhistorylab.com

---

[1]Some state constitutions had similar provisions, but the slave states obviously did not.

Dred Scott and his wife and children are featured on the cover of *Frank Leslie's Illustrated Newspaper*. Historian Joshua Brown argues in *Beyond the Lines* (2002) that this publication was the precursor to today's popular newsmagazines. Its plentiful pictures were made possible by the new technology of mass-produced wood engraving.

Photo Credit: MPI/Stringer/Hulton Archive/Getty Images.

came himself or brought his property into a particular Territory. . . could hardly be dignified with the name of due process of law." The Missouri Compromise had deprived Dr. Emerson of his "property"—his slaves—and thus was unconstitutional!

In addition to invalidating the already repealed Missouri Compromise, the decision threatened Douglas's principle of popular sovereignty, for if Congress could not exclude slaves from a territory, how could a mere territorial legislature do so? Until statehood was granted, slavery seemed as inviolate as freedom of religion or speech or any other civil liberty guaranteed by the Constitution. Where formerly freedom (as guaranteed in the Bill of Rights) was a national institution and slavery a local one, now, according to the Court, slavery was nationwide, excluded only where states had specifically abolished it.

•••• Read the Document
Opinion of the Supreme Court for Dred Scott v. Sanford at **myhistorylab.com**

The irony of employing the Bill of Rights to keep blacks in chains did not escape northern critics. Now slaves could be brought into the Minnesota Territory, even into Oregon. In his inaugural address Buchanan had urged the people to accept the forthcoming ruling, "whatever this may be," as a final settlement. Many assumed (indeed, it was true) that he had put pressure on the Court to act as it did and that he knew in advance of his speech what the decision would be. The Dred Scott decision convinced thousands that the South was engaged in an aggressive attempt to extend the peculiar institution so far that it could no longer be considered peculiar.

The Proslavery Lecompton Constitution

Kansas soon provided a test for northern suspicions. The proslavery leaders in Kansas had managed to convene a constitutional convention at Lecompton, but the Free Soil forces had boycotted the election of delegates. When this rump body drafted a proslavery constitution and then refused to submit it to a fair vote of all the settlers, Kansas governor Robert J. Walker denounced its work and hurried back to Washington to explain the situation to Buchanan.

The president refused to face reality. His prosouthern advisers were clamoring for him to "save" Kansas. Instead of rejecting the **Lecompton constitution**, he asked Congress to admit Kansas to the Union with this document as its frame of government.

Buchanan's decision brought him head-on against Stephen A. Douglas, and the repercussions of their clash shattered the Democratic party. Principle and self-interest forced Douglas to oppose the leader of his party. If he stood aside while Congress admitted Kansas, he not only would be abandoning popular sovereignty, but he would be committing political suicide as well. He was up for reelection to the Senate in 1858. All but one of the fifty-six newspapers in Illinois had declared editorially against the Lecompton constitution; if Douglas supported it, his defeat was certain. In a dramatic confrontation at the White House, he and Buchanan argued the question at length, tempers rising. Finally, the president tried to force him into line. "Mr. Douglas," he said, "I desire you to remember that no Democrat ever yet differed from an Administration of his own choice without being crushed." "Mr. President," Douglas replied contemptuously, "I wish you to remember that General Jackson is dead!" And he stalked out of the room.

Buchanan then compounded his error by putting tremendous political pressure on Douglas, cutting off his Illinois patronage on the eve of his reelection campaign. Of course Douglas persisted, openly joining the Republicans in the fight. Congress rejected the Lecompton bill.

Meanwhile, the extent of the fraud perpetrated at Lecompton became clear. In October 1857 a new legislature had been chosen in Kansas, antislavery voters participating in the balloting. It ordered a referendum on the Lecompton constitution in January 1858. This time the proslavery settlers boycotted the vote and the constitution was overwhelmingly rejected. When Buchanan persisted in pressing Congress to admit Kansas under the Lecompton constitution, Congress ordered another referendum. To slant the case in favor of approval, the legislators stipulated that if the constitution were voted down, Kansas could not be admitted into the Union until it had a population of 90,000. Nevertheless, the Kansans rejected it by a ratio of six to one.

The Emergence of Lincoln

Dissolution threatened the Union. To many Americans, Stephen A. Douglas seemed to offer the best hope of preserving it. For this reason unusual attention was focused on his campaign for reelection to the Senate in 1858. The importance of the contest and Douglas's national prestige put great pressure on the Republicans of Illinois to nominate someone who would make a good showing against him. The man they chose was Abraham Lincoln.

After a towering figure has passed from the stage, it is always difficult to discover what he was like before his rise to prominence. This is especially true of Lincoln, who changed greatly when power, responsibility, and fame came to him. Lincoln was not unknown in 1858, but his public career had not been distinguished. He was born in Kentucky in 1809, and the story of his early life can be condensed, as he once said himself, into a single line from Gray's *Elegy*: "The short and simple annals of the poor." His illiterate father, Thomas Lincoln, was a typical frontier wanderer. When Abraham was seven years old, the family moved to Indiana. In 1830 they pushed west again into southern Illinois. The boy received almost no formal schooling.

However, Lincoln had a good mind, and he was extremely ambitious.[2] In 1834, when barely twenty-five, he won a seat in the Illinois legislature as a Whig. Meanwhile, he studied law and was admitted to the bar in 1836.

Lincoln remained in the legislature until 1842, displaying a perfect willingness to adopt the Whig position on all issues. In 1846 he was elected to Congress. After one term in Congress, marked by his partisan opposition to Polk's Mexican policy, his political career petered out. He seemed fated to pass his remaining years as a small-town lawyer.

Even during this period Lincoln's personality was extraordinarily complex. His bawdy sense of humor and his endless fund of stories and tall tales made him a legend first in Illinois and then in Washington. He was thoroughly at home with toughs like the "Clary's Grove Boys" of New Salem and in the convivial atmosphere of a party caucus. But in a society where most men drank heavily, he never touched liquor. And he was subject to periods of profound melancholy. He wrote of himself in the early 1840s, "I am now the most miserable man living. If what I felt were equally distributed to the whole human family, there would not be one cheerful face on earth."

The revival of the slavery controversy in 1854 stirred Lincoln deeply. No abolitionist, he had tried to take a "realistic" view of the problem. The Kansas-Nebraska bill led him to see the moral issue more clearly. "If slavery is not wrong, nothing is wrong," he stated with the directness and simplicity of expression for which he later became famous. Yet unlike most Free Soilers, he did not blame the Southerners for slavery. "They are just what we would be in their situation," he confessed.

Thus Lincoln was at once compassionate toward the slave owner and stern toward the institution. "A house divided against itself cannot stand," he warned. "I believe this government cannot endure permanently half slave and half free." Without minimizing the difficulties or urging a hasty or ill-considered solution, Lincoln demanded that the people look toward a day, however remote, when not only Kansas but the entire country would be free.

---

[2]His law partner, William Herndon, said that Lincoln's ambition was "a little engine that knows no rest."

The Lincoln-Douglas Debates

As Lincoln developed these ideas his reputation grew. In 1855 he almost won the Whig nomination for senator. He became a Republican shortly thereafter, and in June 1856, at the first Republican National Convention, he received 110 votes for the vice-presidential nomination. He seemed the logical man to pit against Douglas in 1858. The Lincoln-Douglas debates were well-attended and widely reported, for the idea of a direct confrontation between candidates for an important office captured the popular imagination.

The choice of the next senator lay, of course, in the hands of the Illinois legislature. Technically, Douglas and Lincoln were campaigning for candidates for the legislature who were pledged to support them for the Senate seat. The two employed different political styles, each calculated to project a particular image. Douglas epitomized efficiency and success. Ordinarily he arrived in town in a private railroad car, to be met by a brass band, then to ride at the head of a parade to the appointed place.

Lincoln appeared before the voters as a man of the people. He wore ill-fitting black suits and a stovepipe hat that exaggerated his great height. He presented a worn and rumpled appearance, partly because he traveled from place to place on day coaches, accompanied by only a few advisers. When local supporters came to meet him at the station, he preferred to walk with them through the streets to the scene of the debate.

●●—[Read the Document

Douglas, *Debate at Galesburg, Illinois* at **myhistorylab.com**

Lincoln and Douglas maintained a high intellectual level in their speeches, but these were political debates. Both tailored their arguments to appeal to local audiences—more antislavery in the northern counties, more proslavery in the southern. They also tended to exaggerate their differences,

Photo Credit: Abraham Lincoln Presidential Library & Museum (ALPLM).

Abraham Lincoln speaks as Stephen Douglas gazes at the audience—mostly standing—during the debate in Charleston, Illinois in 1858, as painted by Robert Root.

which were not in fact enormous. Neither wanted to see slavery in the territories or thought it economically efficient, and neither sought to abolish it by political action or by force. Both believed blacks congenitally inferior to whites, although Douglas took more pleasure in expounding on supposed racial differences than Lincoln did.

Douglas's strategy was to make Lincoln look like an abolitionist. He accused the Republicans of favoring racial equality and refusing to abide by the decision of the Supreme Court in the Dred Scott case. Himself he pictured as a heroic champion of democracy, attacked on one side by the "black" Republicans and on the other by Buchanan supporters, yet ready to fight to his last breath for popular sovereignty.

Lincoln tried to picture Douglas as proslavery and a defender of the Dred Scott decision. "Slavery is an unqualified evil to the negro, to the white man, to the soil, and to the State," he said. "Judge Douglas," he also said, "is blowing out the moral lights around us, when he contends that whoever wants slaves has a right to hold them."

However, Lincoln often weakened the impact of his arguments, being perhaps too eager to demonstrate his conservatism. "All men are created equal," he would say on the authority of the Declaration of Independence, only to add, "I am not, nor ever have been, in favor of bringing about in any way the social and political equality of the white and black races." He opposed allowing blacks to vote, to sit on juries, to marry whites, even to be citizens. He predicted the "ultimate extinction" of slavery, but when pressed he predicted that it would not occur "in less than a hundred years at the least."

In the debate at Freeport, a town northwest of Chicago near the Wisconsin line, Lincoln asked Douglas if, considering the Dred Scott decision, the people of a territory could exclude slavery before the territory became a state. Unhesitatingly Douglas replied that they could, simply by not passing the local laws essential for holding blacks in bondage. "It matters not what way the Supreme Court may hereafter decide as to the abstract question," Douglas said. "The people have the lawful means to introduce or exclude it as they please, for the reason that slavery cannot exist. . . unless it is supported by local police regulations."

This argument saved Douglas in Illinois. The Democrats carried the legislature by a narrow margin, whereas it is almost certain that if Douglas had accepted the Dred Scott decision outright, the balance would have swung to the Republicans. But the so-called Freeport Doctrine cost him heavily two years later when he made his bid for the Democratic presidential nomination. "It matters not what way the Supreme Court may hereafter decide"—southern extremists would not accept a man who suggested that the Dred Scott decision could be circumvented, although in fact Douglas had only stated the obvious.

Probably Lincoln had not thought beyond the senatorial election when he asked the question; he was merely hoping to keep Douglas on the defensive and perhaps injure him in southern Illinois, where considerable proslavery sentiment existed. In any case, defeat did Lincoln no harm politically. He had more than held his own against one of the most formidable debaters in politics, and his distinctive personality and point of view had impressed themselves on thousands of minds. Indeed, the defeat revitalized his political career.

The campaign of 1858 marked Douglas's last triumph, Lincoln's last defeat. Elsewhere the elections in the North went heavily to the Republicans. When the old Congress reconvened in December, northern-sponsored economic measures (a higher tariff, the transcontinental railroad, river and harbor improvements, a free homestead bill) were all blocked by southern votes.

Whether the South could continue to prevent the passage of this legislation in the new Congress was problematical. In early 1859 even many moderate Southerners were uneasy about the future. The radicals, made panicky by Republican victories and their own failure to win in Kansas, spoke openly of secession if a Republican were elected president in 1860. Lincoln's "house divided" speech was quoted out of context, while Douglas's Freeport Doctrine added to southern woes. When Senator William H. Seward of New York spoke of an "irrepressible conflict" between freedom and slavery, white Southerners became still more alarmed.

John Brown's Raid

In October 1859, John Brown, the scourge of Kansas, made his second contribution to the unfolding sectional drama. Gathering a group of eighteen followers, white and black, he staged an attack on Harpers Ferry, Virginia, a town on the Potomac River upstream from Washington. Having boned up on guerrilla tactics, he planned to seize the federal arsenal there; arm the slaves, whom he thought would flock to his side; and then establish a black republic in the mountains of Virginia.

Simply by overpowering a few night watchmen, Brown and his men occupied the arsenal and a nearby rifle factory. They captured several hostages, one of them Colonel Lewis Washington, a great-grandnephew of George Washington. But no slaves came forward to join them. Federal troops commanded by Robert E. Lee soon trapped Brown's men in an engine house of the Baltimore and Ohio Railroad. After a two-day siege in which the attackers picked off ten of his men, Brown was captured.

After John Brown's capture, Emerson called him "a martyr" who would "make the gallows as glorious as the cross." Brown's principled radicalism found favor during the Depression decade of the 1930s. John Stewart Curry's mural, completed in 1943, depicted the demented John Brown in the pose of Christ on the cross. The image offended the Kansas legislature, which had commissioned Curry to portray Kansas history in a "sane and sensible manner."
Source: Kansas State Historical Society, Copy and Reuse Restrictions apply.

No incident so well illustrates the role of emotion and irrationality in the sectional crisis as does John Brown's raid. Over the years before his Kansas escapade, Brown had been a drifter, horse thief, a swindler, and several times a bankrupt, a failure in everything he attempted. After his ghastly Pottawatomie murders it should have been obvious to anyone that he was both a fanatic and mentally unstable: Some of the victims were hacked to bits with a broadsword. Yet numbers of high-minded Northerners, including Emerson and Thoreau, had supported Brown and his antislavery "work" after 1856. White Southerners reacted to Harpers Ferry with equal irrationality, some with a rage similar to Brown's. Dozens of hapless Northerners in the southern states were arrested, beaten, or driven off. One, falsely suspected of being an accomplice of Brown, was lynched.

Brown's fate lay in the hands of the Virginia authorities. Ignoring his obvious derangement, they charged him with treason, conspiracy, and murder. He was speedily convicted and sentenced to death by hanging.

Yet "Old Brown" had still one more contribution to make to the developing sectional tragedy. Despite the furor he had created, cool heads everywhere called for calm and denounced his attack. Most Republican politicians repudiated him. Even execution would probably not have made a martyr of Brown had he behaved like a madman after his capture. Instead, an enormous dignity descended on him as he lay in his Virginia jail awaiting death. Whatever his faults, he truly believed in racial equality. He addressed blacks who worked for him as "Mister" and arranged for them to eat at his table and sit with his family in church.

This conviction served him well in his last days. "If it is deemed necessary that I should forfeit my life for the furtherance of the ends of justice, and mingle my blood further with the blood of. . . millions in this slave country whose rights are disregarded by wicked, cruel, and unjust enactments," he said before the judge pronounced sentence, "I say, let it be done."

Read the Document

John Brown's Address Before Sentencing at **myhistorylab.com**

This John Brown, with his patriarchal beard and sad eyes, so apparently incompatible with the bloody terrorist of Pottawatomie and Harpers Ferry, led thousands in the North to ignore his past and treat him almost as a saint.

And so Brown, hanged on December 2, 1859, became to the North a hero and to the South a symbol of northern ruthlessness. Soon, as the popular song had it, Brown's body lay "a-mouldering in the grave," and the memory of his bloody act did indeed go "marching on."

The Election of 1860

By 1860 the nation was teetering on the brink of disunion. Radicals in the North and South were heedlessly provoking one another.

Extremism was more evident in the South, and to any casual observer that section must have seemed the aggressor in the crisis. Yet even in demanding the reopening of the African slave trade, southern radicals believed that they were defending themselves against attack. They felt surrounded by hostility. The North was growing at a much faster rate; if nothing was done, they feared, a flood of new free states would soon be able to amend the Constitution and emancipate the slaves. John Brown's raid, with its threat of an insurrection like Nat Turner's, reduced them to a state of panic.

Photo Credit: The Granger Collection, New York.

That politics was always a rough business is shown in this cartoon, which shows Lincoln, assisted by an African American (who carries a basket of liquor bottles) while Douglas is backed by some Irish pols, who have a basket overflowing with cash. John Breckinridge thumbs his nose at the combatants as he hustles up the hill toward the White House.

When legislatures in state after state in the South cracked down on freedom of expression, made the manumission of slaves illegal, banished free blacks, and took other steps that Northerners considered blatantly provocative, the advocates of these policies believed that they were only defending the status quo. Perhaps, by seceding from the Union, the South could raise a dike against the tide of abolitionism. Secession also provided an emotional release, a way of dissipating tension by striking back at criticism.

Stephen A. Douglas was probably the last hope of avoiding a rupture between North and South. But when the Democrats met at Charleston, South Carolina, in April 1860 to choose a presidential candidate, the southern delegates would not support him unless he promised not to disturb slavery in the territories. Indeed, they went further in their demands. The North, William L. Yancey of Alabama insisted, must accept the proposition that slavery was not merely tolerable but right. When southern proposals were voted down, most of the delegates from the Deep South walked out and the convention adjourned without naming a candidate.

In June the Democrats reconvened at Baltimore. Again they failed to reach agreement. The two wings then met separately, the Northerners nominating Douglas, the Southerners John C. Breckenridge of Kentucky, Buchanan's vice president. On the question of slavery in the territories, the Northerners promised to "abide by the decision of the Supreme Court," which meant, in effect, that they stood for Douglas's Freeport Doctrine. The Southerners announced their belief that neither Congress nor any territorial government could prevent citizens from settling "with their property" in any territory.

Meanwhile, the Republicans, who met in Chicago in mid-May, had drafted a platform attractive to all classes and all sections of the northern and western states.

Presidential Election, 1860 This map shows clearly the North-South electoral divide, and the fracturing of the Democratic party.

For manufacturers they proposed a high tariff, for farmers a homestead law providing free land for settlers. Internal improvements "of a National character," notably a railroad to the Pacific, should receive federal aid. No restrictions should be placed on immigration. As to slavery in the territories, the Republicans did not equivocate: "The normal condition of all the territory of the United States is that of freedom." Neither Congress nor a local legislature could "give legal existence to Slavery in any Territory."

In choosing a presidential candidate the Republicans displayed equally shrewd political judgment. Senator Seward was the front-runner, but he had taken too extreme a stand and appeared unlikely to carry the crucial states of Pennsylvania, Indiana, and Illinois. He led on the first ballot but could not get a majority. Then the delegates began to look closely at Abraham Lincoln. His thoughtful and moderate views on the main issue of the times and his formidable debating skills attracted many, and so did his political personality. "Honest Abe," the "Railsplitter," a man of humble origins (born in a log cabin), self-educated, self-made, a common man but by no means an ordinary man—the combination seemed unbeatable.

On the second ballot Lincoln drew shoulder to shoulder with Seward, on the third he was within two votes of victory. Before the roll could be called again, delegates began to switch their votes, and in a landslide, soon made unanimous, Lincoln was nominated.

A few days earlier the remnants of the American and Whig parties had formed the Constitutional Union party and nominated John Bell of Tennessee for president. "It is both the part of patriotism and of duty," they resolved, "to recognize no political principle

Table 1   Descent into War: The 1850s

Harriet Beecher Stowe's, *Uncle Tom's Cabin*	1852	Best-selling novel fuels abolitionist sentiment and enrages Southerners.
Kansas-Nebraska Act	1854	Opens Kansas and Nebraska Territories for settlement and repeals Missouri Compromise of 1820 by allowing residents to determine whether the new states would be slave or free.
Lecompton Constitution	1857	Proslavery constitution drafted by proslavery "government" of Kansas: It is accepted by President James Buchanan but rejected by Congress.
Dred Scott Case	1857	Supreme Court rules that Congress lacked the authority to ban slavery from the territories; slavery is legal everywhere unless states prohibit it.
John Brown's Raid at Harpers Ferry, Virginia	1859	Brown attacks federal arsenal in order to initiate slave rebellion; Brown's execution angers abolitionists; the martyrdom of Brown infuriates Southerners.
Election of 1860	1860	The Democrats, divided over slavery, disintegrate. Lincoln wins presidency but receives no electoral votes from South.

other than the Constitution of the country, the union of the states, and the enforcement of the laws." Ostrichlike, the Constitutional Unionists ignored the conflicts rending the nation. Only in the border states, where the consequences of disunion were sure to be most tragic, did they have any following.

With four candidates in the field, no one could win a popular majority, but it soon became clear that Lincoln was going to be elected. Breckenridge had most of the slave states in his pocket and Bell would run strong in the border regions, but the populous northern and western states had a majority of the electoral votes, and there the choice lay between the Republicans and the Douglas Democrats. In such a contest the Republicans, with their attractive economic program and their strong stand against slavery in the territories, were sure to come out on top.

Lincoln avoided campaigning and made no public statements. Douglas, recognizing the certainty of Lincoln's victory, accepted his fate and for the first time in his career rose above ambition. "We must try to save the Union," he said. "I will go South." In the heart of the Cotton Kingdom, he appealed to the voters to stand by the Union regardless of who was elected. He was the only candidate to do so; the others refused to remind the people that their election might result in secession and civil war.

When the votes were counted, Lincoln had 1.866 million, almost a million fewer than the combined total of his three opponents, but he swept the North and West, which gave him 180 electoral votes and the presidency. Douglas received 1.383 million votes, so distributed that he carried only Missouri and part of New Jersey. Breckenridge, with 848,000 popular votes, won most of the South; Bell, with 593,000, carried Virginia,

Tennessee, and Kentucky. Lincoln was thus a minority president, but his title to the office was unquestionable. Even if his opponents could have combined their popular votes in each state, Lincoln would have won.

The Secession Crisis

Only days after Lincoln's victory, the South Carolina legislature ordered an election of delegates to a convention to decide the state's future course. On December 20 the convention voted unanimously to secede, basing its action on the logic of Calhoun. "The State of South Carolina has resumed her position among the nations of the world," the delegates announced. By February 1, 1861, the six other states of the lower South had followed suit. A week later, at Montgomery, Alabama, a provisional government of the Confederate States of America was established. Virginia, Tennessee, North Carolina, and Arkansas did not leave the Union but announced that if the federal government attempted to use force against the Confederacy, they too would secede.

•◆•⌐Read the Document

South Carolina Declaration of the Causes of Secession at **myhistorylab.com**

Why were white Southerners willing to wreck the Union their forebears had put together with so much love and labor? No simple explanation is possible. Lincoln had assured them that he would respect slavery where it existed. The Democrats had retained control of Congress in the election; the Supreme Court was firmly in their hands as well. If the North did try to destroy slavery, secession would perhaps be a logical tactic, but why not wait until the threat materialized? To leave the Union meant abandoning the very objectives for which the South had been contending for over a decade: a share of the federal territories and an enforceable fugitive slave law.

One reason why the South rejected this line of thinking was the tremendous economic energy generated in the North, which seemed to threaten the South's independence.

Secession, white Southerners argued, would "liberate" the South and produce the kind of balanced economy that was proving so successful in the North. Moreover, the mere possibility of emancipation was a powerful force for secession. "We must either submit to degradation, and to the loss of property worth four billions," the Mississippi convention declared, "or we must secede."

Although states' rights provided the rationale for leaving the Union, and Southerners expounded the strict constructionist interpretation of the Constitution with great ingenuity, the economic and emotional factors were far more basic. The lower South decided to go ahead with secession regardless of the cost. "Let the consequences be what they may," an Atlanta newspaper proclaimed. "Whether the Potomac is crimsoned in human gore, and Pennsylvania Avenue is paved ten fathoms in depth with mangled bodies . . . the South will never submit."

Not every slave owner could contemplate secession with such bloodthirsty equanimity. Some believed that the risks of war and slave insurrection were too great. Others retained a profound loyalty to the United States. Many accepted secession only after the deepest examination of conscience. Lieutenant Colonel Robert E. Lee of Virginia was typical of thousands. "I see only that a fearful calamity is upon us," he wrote during the secession crisis. "There is no sacrifice I am not ready to

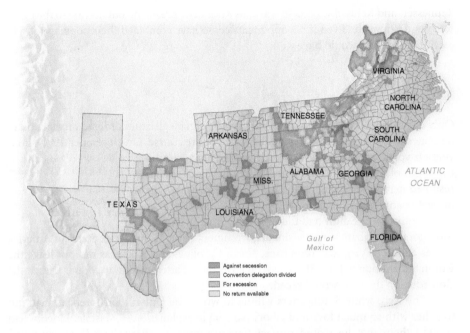

Against secession
Convention delegation divided
For secession
No return available

Secession of the South, 1860–1861 This map shows the minimal support for secession in the nonslave mountain areas of the Appalachians. The strong antisecession sentiment in the mountainous areas of Virginia eventually led several counties there to break from Virginia in 1863 and form the new state of West Virginia.

make for the preservation of the Union save that of honour. If a disruption takes place, I shall go back in sorrow to my people & share the misery of my native state."

In the North there was a foolish but understandable reluctance to believe that the South really intended to break away. President-elect Lincoln was inclined to write off secession as a bluff designed to win concessions he was determined not to make. He also showed lamentable political caution in refusing to announce his plans or to cooperate with the outgoing Democratic administration before his inauguration.

In the South there was an equally unrealistic expectation that the North would not resist secession forcibly. The "Yankees" were timid materialists who would neither bear the cost nor risk their lives to prevent secession. President Buchanan recognized the seriousness of the situation but professed himself powerless. Secession, he said, was illegal, but the federal government had no legal way to prevent it. He urged making concessions to the South yet lacked the forcefulness to take the situation in hand.

Of course he faced unprecedented difficulties. His term was about to run out—Lincoln's inauguration day was March 4—and since he could not commit to his successor, his influence was minuscule. Yet a bolder president would have denounced secession in uncompromising terms. Instead Buchanan vacillated between compromise and aimless drift.

Appeasers, well-meaning believers in compromise, and those prepared to fight to preserve the Union were alike—incapable of effective action. A group of moderates headed by Henry Clay's disciple, Senator John J. Crittenden of Kentucky, proposed a constitutional amendment in which slavery would be "recognized as existing" in all territories south of latitude 36°30'. Crittenden had a special reason for seeking to avoid a conflict. His oldest son was about to become a southern general, another son a northern general. His amendment also promised that no future amendment would tamper with the institution in the slave states and offered other guarantees to the South. But Lincoln refused to consider any arrangement that would open new territory to slavery. "On the territorial question," he wrote, "I am inflexible." The **Crittenden Compromise** got nowhere.

The new southern Confederacy set vigorously to work drafting a constitution, choosing Jefferson Davis as provisional president, seizing arsenals and other federal property within its boundaries, and preparing to dispatch diplomatic representatives to enlist the support of foreign powers. Buchanan bumbled helplessly in Washington. And out in Illinois, Abraham Lincoln juggled Cabinet posts and grew a beard.

Watch the Video
What Caused the Civil War? at
myhistorylab.com

Milestones

1850	Compromise of 1850 preserves Union; United States and Great Britain sign Clayton-Bulwer Treaty on interoceanic canal	1856	John Brown and followers murder five proslavery men in Pottawatomie Massacre
1851–1860	Northerners resist enforcement of Fugitive Slave Act		South Carolina's Preston Brooks canes Senator Charles Sumner of Massachusetts on Senate floor
1852	Harriet Beecher Stowe publishes *Uncle Tom's Cabin*, a novel depicting slavery		James Buchanan is elected president
	Franklin Pierce is elected president	1857	U.S. Supreme Court issues decision in Dred Scott case, declaring slaves are not citizens
1854	United States disavows secret Ostend Manifesto on Cuba		Panic of 1857 collapses economy
	Kansas-Nebraska Act repeals Missouri Compromise	1858	Abraham Lincoln loses Senate race to Stephen Douglas after Lincoln-Douglas Debates, but wins national attention
	Commodore Matthew Perry forces Japan to open its ports to U.S. trade	1859	John Brown raids Harpers Ferry, Virginia, arsenal
	Senate ratifies Gadsden Purchase of Mexican territory	1860	Abraham Lincoln is elected president
1855	William Walker seizes power in Nicaragua		South Carolina secedes from Union
1856–1858	Proslavery forces oppose Free Soilers in "Bleeding Kansas" Territory	1861	Seven southern states establish Confederate States of America
			Lincoln rejects Crittenden Compromise, last peaceful attempt to save Union

✓●─[Study] and **Review** at **www.myhistorylab.com**

Review Questions

1. The introduction to this chapter claims that Americans in the 1850s paid close attention to the issues that culminated in the election of Lincoln and the secession of the South. If political agitation can precipitate such anger and even war, is it always a good thing? Can there be such a thing as too much democracy—too much "popular sovereignty"? Should leaders refrain from raising questions that will elicit passionate responses?

2. What events during the 1850s reduced the prospects of finding a political compromise between North and South?

3. Were the economic divisions—free vs. slave labor—more consequential than the moral ones—freedom vs. slavery?

4. The 1858 Lincoln-Douglas debate largely turned on Lincoln's assertion that the United States could not endure half-slave and half-free. But for over seventy years, Douglas replied, the United States under the Constitution had done just that; compromise remained a possibility. Who was right?

Key Terms

Crittenden Compromise

Dred Scott decision

Kansas-Nebraska Act

Know-Nothing party

Lecompton constitution

Ostend Manifesto

Republican party

underground railroad

Young America movement

The War to Save the Union

((•—[Hear the Audio at myhistorylab.com

Are you a Northerner or a Southerner?

ON FEBRUARY 22, 2006, SUNNI MUSLIMS OVERWHELMED THE CARETAKER and staff of the Mosque of the Golden Dome in Samarra, sixty miles north of Baghdad, Iraq. The mosque was among the most revered Shiite shrines in the Middle East, visited by more than a million Muslims each year. Sunni and Shiite Muslims differed in their interpretation of Islam. Sunni insurgents placed explosives at the base of the dome and left the building. Moments later, an explosion collapsed the dome, shattering its 72,000 golden tiles. By sunset, Shiite militiamen had destroyed twenty-seven Sunni mosques and killed three imams—Islamic holy men. Over the next twelve months, the violence escalated, resulting in the deaths of over 34,000 Iraqi civilians. "The gates of hell are open in Iraq," declared Amr Moussa, head of the Arab League.

In 2009 President Barack Obama visited Iraq after a spate of bombings had destroyed another Shiite shrine and killed scores of Muslims. Obama called on Iraqis to end "this senseless violence."

But no civil war makes much sense, as Americans learned in 1861. Then, brother fought brother; men intent on destroying each other prayed to the same God. The horrors of the war eclipsed any good that might attend victory, or so it seemed.

The U.S. Civil War moved forward, impelled by its own terrible momentum. The first inconclusive battle led to others. More men were called to arms, often against their will. Farms and factories were diverted to the war effort. Lincoln emancipated some slaves to weaken the South. The strains of the war fractured the political consensus. When the guns at last fell silent, a half million men lay dead, and millions more were casualties. While touring a hospital ward after another gruesome battle, President Lincoln despaired at the horror of it all. "If there is a place worse than hell, I am in it."

Lincoln's Cabinet

The nomination of Lincoln had succeeded brilliantly for the Republicans, but was his election a good thing for the country? Honest Abe was a clever politician who had spoken well about the central issue of the times, but would he act decisively in this crisis? People

From Chapter 14 of *American Destiny: Narrative of a Nation,* Combined Volume, Fourth Edition. Mark C. Carnes and John A. Garraty. Copyright © 2012 by Pearson Education, Inc. Published by Pearson Prentice Hall. All rights reserved.

remembered uneasily that he had never held executive office, that his congressional career had been short and undistinguished. When he finally uprooted himself from Springfield in February 1861, his occasional speeches en route to Washington were vague, almost flippant. Some people thought it downright cowardly that he let himself be spirited in the dead of night through Baltimore, where feeling against him ran high.

Everyone waited tensely to see whether Lincoln would oppose secession with force, but Lincoln seemed concerned only with organizing his Cabinet. The final slate was not ready until the morning of inauguration day, March 4, and shrewd observers found it alarming, for the new president had chosen to construct a "balanced" Cabinet representing a wide range of opinion instead of putting together a group of harmonious advisers who could help him face the crisis.

William H. Seward, the secretary of state, was the ablest and best known of the appointees. Despite his reputation for radicalism, Seward hoped to conciliate the South and was thus in bad odor with the radical wing of the Republican party. In time Seward proved himself Lincoln's strong right arm, but at the start he underestimated the president and expected to dominate him. Senator Salmon P. Chase, an antislavery leader from Ohio whom Lincoln named secretary of the treasury, represented the radicals. Chase was humorless and vain but able; he detested Seward. Many of the president's other selections worried thoughtful people.

Lincoln's inaugural address was conciliatory but firm. Southern institutions were in no danger from his administration. Secession, however, was illegal, and the Union "perpetual." "A husband and wife may be divorced," Lincoln said, "but the different parts of our country cannot." His tone was calm and warm. His concluding words catch the spirit of the inaugural perfectly:

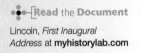

Read the Document

Lincoln, *First Inaugural Address* at **myhistorylab.com**

> I am loath to close. We are not enemies, but friends. We must not be enemies. Though passion may have strained, it must not break, our bonds of affection. The mystic chords of memory, stretching from every battlefield and patriot grave to every living heart . . . will yet swell the chorus of the Union when again touched, as surely they will be, by the better angels of our nature.

Fort Sumter: The First Shot

While denying the legality of secession, Lincoln had not decided what to do next. The Confederates had seized most federal property in the Deep South. Lincoln admitted frankly that he would not attempt to reclaim this property. However, two strongholds, Fort Sumter, on an island in Charleston harbor, and Fort Pickens, at Pensacola, Florida, were still in loyal Union hands. Most Republicans did not want to surrender them without a show of resistance. To do so, one wrote, would be to convert the American eagle into a "debilitated chicken."

Yet to reinforce the forts might mean bloodshed that would make reconciliation impossible. After weeks of indecision, Lincoln took the moderate step of sending a naval expedition to supply the beleaguered Sumter garrison with food. Unwilling to permit this, the Confederates opened fire on the fort on April 12 before the supply ships arrived. After holding out for thirty-four hours, Major Robert Anderson and his men surrendered.

Photo Credit: Courtesy of the Library of Congress.

This lithograph by Currier and Ives gives an erroneous impression of the "battle." Major Robert Anderson, commander of Ft. Sumter, did not want to expose his men to the looping mortar shells and artillery of the Confederates, so he manned only the cannon on the lowest floor, just above the water. The top two levels of guns were seldom fired.

The attack precipitated an outburst of patriotic indignation in the North. Lincoln issued a call for 75,000 volunteers; his request prompted Virginia, North Carolina, Arkansas, and Tennessee to secede. After years of crises and compromises, the nation chose to settle the great quarrel between the sections by force of arms.

Lincoln took the position that secession was a rejection of democracy. If the South could refuse to abide by the result of an election in which it had freely participated, then everything that monarchists and other conservatives had said about the instability of republican governments would be proved true. "The central idea of secession is the essence of anarchy," he said. The United States must "demonstrate to the world" that "when ballots have been fairly and constitutionally decided, there can be no successful appeal except to ballots themselves, at succeeding elections."

This was the proper ground to take. A war against slavery would not have been supported by a majority of Northerners. Slavery was the root cause of secession but not of the North's determination to resist secession, which resulted from the people's commitment to the Union. Although abolition was to be one of the major results of the Civil War, the war was fought for nationalistic reasons, not to destroy slavery. Lincoln made this plain when he wrote in response to an editorial by Horace Greeley urging immediate emancipation: "I would save the Union. . . . If I could save the Union without freeing any slave, I would do it; and if I could save it by freeing all the slaves, I would do it; and if I could do it by freeing some and leaving others alone, I would also do that." He added, however, "I intend no modification of my oft-expressed personal wish that all men, everywhere, could be free."

The Blue and the Gray

In any test between the United States and the Confederacy, the former possessed tremendous advantages. There were more than 20 million people in the northern states (excluding Kentucky and Missouri, where opinion was divided) but only 9 million in the South, including 3.5 million slaves whom the whites hesitated to trust with arms. The North's economic capacity to wage war was even more preponderant. It was manufacturing nine times as much as the Confederacy (including 97 percent of the nation's firearms) and had a far larger and more efficient railroad system than the South. Northern control of the merchant marine and the navy made possible a blockade of the Confederacy, a particularly potent threat to a region so dependent on foreign markets.

The Confederates discounted these advantages. Many doubted that public opinion in the North would sustain Lincoln if he attempted to meet secession with force. Northern manufacturers needed southern markets, and merchants depended heavily on southern business. Many western farmers still sent their produce down the Mississippi. War would threaten the prosperity of all these groups, Southerners maintained. Should the North try to cut Europe off from southern cotton, the European powers, particularly Great Britain, would descend on the land in their might, force open southern ports, and provide the Confederacy with the means of defending itself forever. Moreover, the South provided nearly three-fourths of the world's cotton, essential for most textile mills. "You do not dare to make war on cotton," Senator Hammond of South Carolina had taunted his northern colleagues in 1858. "No power on earth dares to make war upon it. Cotton is king."

The Confederacy also counted on certain military advantages. The new nation need only hold what it had; it could fight a defensive war, less costly in men and material and of great importance in maintaining morale and winning outside sympathy. Southerners would be defending not only their social institutions but also their homes and families.

Luck played a part too; the Confederacy quickly found a great commander, while many of the northern generals in the early stages of the war proved either bungling or indecisive. In battle after battle

Why did these young volunteers of the First Virginia Militia join the Confederate army in 1861? "It is better to spend our all in defending our country than to be subjugated and have it taken away from us," one explained, a sentiment that appeared often in the letters of Confederate soldiers. Soldiers on both sides believed that their cause was righteous.

Photo Credit: Cook Collection, Valentine Richmond History Center.

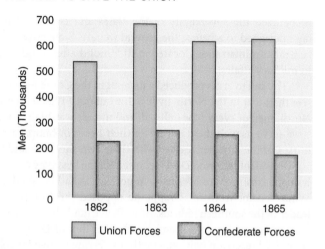

Men Present for Service during the Civil War From 1862 to 1864, the North had twice as many soldiers as the South; by 1865, the North had over three times more than the South.

Union armies were defeated by forces of equal or smaller size. There was little to distinguish the enlisted men of the two sides. Both, conscious of their forefathers of 1776, fought for liberty, though they interpreted the concept in different ways.

Both sides faced massive difficulties in organizing for a war long feared but never properly anticipated. After southern defections, the regular Union army consisted of only 13,000 officers and enlisted men, far too few to absorb the 186,000 who had joined the colors by early summer, much less the additional 450,000 who had volunteered by the end of the year. Recruiting was left to the states, each being assigned a quota; there was little central organization. Unlike later conflicts in which men from all parts of the country were mixed in each regiment, Civil War units were recruited locally. Few knew even the rudiments of soldiering. The hastily composed high command, headed by the elderly Winfield Scott, debated grand strategy endlessly while regimental commanders lacked decent maps of Virginia.

Read the Document

Davis, *Address to the Provisional Congress* at **myhistorylab.com**

Lincoln's strength lay in his ability to think problems through. When he did, he acted unflinchingly. Anything but a tyrant by nature, he boldly exceeded the conventional limits of presidential power in the emergency: expanding the army without congressional authorization, suspending the writ of habeas corpus (which entitles those seized by the government to go before a court to see if their arrest were warranted), even emancipating the slaves when he thought military necessity demanded that action. Yet he also displayed remarkable patience and depth of character: He would willingly accept snubs and insults in order to advance the cause.

Gradually Lincoln's stock rose—first with men like Seward, who saw him close up and experienced both his steel and his gentleness, and then with the people at large, who sensed his compassion, his humility, and his wisdom. He was only fifty-two when he became president, and already people were calling him Old Abe. Before long they would call him Father Abraham.

The Confederacy faced far greater problems than the North, for it had to create an entire administration under pressure of war with the additional handicap of the states' rights philosophy to which it was committed. The Confederate constitution explicitly recognized the sovereignty of the states and contained no broad authorization for laws designed to advance the general welfare. State governments repeatedly defied the central administration, located at Richmond after Virginia seceded, even with regard to military affairs.

The call to arms produced a turnout in the Confederacy perhaps even more impressive than that in the North; by July 1861 about 112,000 men were under arms. As in the North, men of every type enlisted, and morale was high. Some wealthy recruits brought slave servants with them to care for their needs in camp, cavalrymen supplied their own horses, and many men arrived with their own shotguns and hunting rifles.

President Jefferson Davis represented the best type of southern planter, noted for his humane treatment of his slaves. In politics he had pursued a somewhat unusual course. While senator from Mississippi, he opposed the Compromise of 1850 and became a leader of the southern radicals. After Pierce made him secretary of war, however, he took a more nationalistic position, one close to that of Douglas. After the 1860 election he supported secession only reluctantly, preferring to give Lincoln a chance to prove that he meant the South no harm.

Davis was courageous, industrious, and intelligent, but he was too reserved and opinionated to make either a good politician or a popular leader. As president he devoted too much time to details, failed to delegate authority, and (unlike Lincoln) was impatient with garrulous and dull-witted people, types political leaders frequently have to deal with. Being a graduate of West Point, he fancied himself a military expert, but he was a mediocre military thinker. Unlike Lincoln, he quarreled frequently with his subordinates, held grudges, and allowed personal feelings to distort his judgment.

The Test of Battle: Bull Run

"Forward to Richmond!" "On to Washington!" Such shouts propelled the armies into battle long before either was properly trained. On July 21 at Manassas Junction, Virginia, some twenty miles below Washington, on a branch of the Potomac called Bull Run, 30,000 Union soldiers under General Irvin McDowell attacked a roughly equal force of Confederates commanded by the "Napoleon of the South," Pierre G. T. Beauregard. McDowell swept back the Confederate left flank. Victory seemed sure. Then a Virginia brigade under Thomas J. Jackson rushed to the field by rail from the Shenandoah Valley in the nick of time and checked the advance.

See the Map
The Civil War, Part I: 1861–1862 at myhistorylab.com

The Southerners then counterattacked, driving the Union soldiers back. As often happens with green troops, retreat quickly turned to rout. McDowell's men fled toward the defenses of Washington, abandoning their weapons, stumbling through lines of supply wagons, trampling foolish sightseers who had come out to watch the battle. Panic engulfed Washington. Richmond exulted. Both sides expected the northern capital to fall within hours.

The inexperienced southern troops were too disorganized to follow up their victory. Casualties on both sides were light, and the battle had little direct effect on anything but morale. Southern confidence soared, while the North began to realize how immense the task of subduing the Confederacy would be.

Eighteen-year-olds were the largest age group in the first year of the war in both armies. Soldiers were universally called "the boys"; and officers, even in their thirties, were called "old men." One of the most popular war songs was "Just Before the Battle, Mother."

Photo Credit: Courtesy of the Library of Congress.

After Bull Run, Lincoln devised a broader, more systematic strategy for winning the war. The navy would clamp a tight blockade on all southern ports. In the West Union generals made plans to gain control of the Mississippi. (This was part of General Scott's **Anaconda Plan**, designed to starve the South into submission.) More important, a new army would be mustered at Washington to invade Virginia. Congress promptly authorized the enlistment of 500,000 three-year volunteers. To lead this army and—after General Scott's retirement in November—to command the Union forces, Lincoln appointed a thirty-four-year-old major general, George B. McClellan.

McClellan was the North's first military hero. After graduating from West Point second in his class in 1846, he had served in the Mexican War. During the Crimean War he spent a year in the field, talking with British officers and studying fortifications. He was a talented administrator and organizer. He liked to concoct bold plans and dreamed of striking swiftly at the heart of the Confederacy to capture Richmond, Nashville, even New Orleans. Yet he was sensible enough to insist on massive logistic support, thorough training for the troops, iron discipline, and meticulous staff work before making a move.

Paying for the War

After Bull Run, this policy was exactly right. By the fall of 1861 a real army was taking shape along the Potomac: disciplined, confident, adequately supplied. Northern shops and factories were producing guns, ammunition, wagons, uniforms, shoes, and the countless other supplies needed to fight a great war. Most manufacturers operated on a small scale, but with the armed forces soon wearing out 3 million pairs of shoes and 1.5 million uniforms a year and with men leaving their jobs by the hundreds of thousands to fight, the tendency of industry to mechanize and to increase the size of the average manufacturing unit became ever more pronounced.

At the beginning of the war Secretary of the Treasury Salmon P. Chase underestimated how much it would cost. He learned quickly. In August 1861 Congress passed an income tax law and assessed a direct tax on the states. Loans amounting to $140 million were authorized. As the war dragged on and expenses mounted, new excise taxes on every imaginable product and service were passed, and still further borrowing was necessary. In 1863 the banking system was overhauled.

During the war the federal government borrowed a total of $2.2 billion and collected $667 million in taxes, slightly over 20 percent of its total expenditures. These unprecedented large sums proved inadequate. Some debts were repaid by printing paper money unredeemable in coin. About $431 million in **greenbacks**—the term distinguished this fiat money from the redeemable yellowback bills—were issued during the conflict. Public confidence in all paper money vacillated with each change in the fortunes of the Union armies, but by the end of the war the cost of living in the North had doubled.

Politics as Usual

Partisan politics was altered by the war but not suspended. The secession of the southern states left the Republicans with large majorities in both houses of Congress. Most Democrats supported measures necessary for the conduct of the war but objected to the way the Lincoln administration was conducting it. The sharpest conflicts came when slavery and race relations were under discussion. The Democrats adopted a conservative stance, as reflected in the slogan "The Constitution as it is; the Union as it was; the Negroes where they are." The Republicans divided into Moderate and Radical wings. Political divisions on economic issues such as tariffs and land policy tended to cut across party lines and, so far as the Republicans were concerned, to bear little relation to slavery and race. As the war progressed, the Radical faction became increasingly influential.

In 1861 the most prominent Radical senator was Charles Sumner, finally recovered from his caning by Preston Brooks and brimful of hatred for slaveholders. In the House, Thaddeus Stevens of Pennsylvania was the rising power. Sumner and Stevens were uncompromising on all questions relating to slaves; they insisted not merely on abolition but on granting full political and civil rights to blacks. Moderate Republicans objected vehemently to treating blacks as equals and opposed making abolition a war aim, and even many of the so-called **Radical Republicans** disagreed with Sumner and Stevens on race relations. Senator Benjamin Wade of Ohio, for example, was a lifelong opponent of slavery, yet he disliked blacks (whom he called by a racial slur). But prejudice, he maintained, gave no one the right "to do injustice to anybody"; he insisted that blacks were at least as intelligent as whites and were entitled not merely to freedom but to full political equality.

At the other end of the political spectrum stood the so-called Peace Democrats. These **Copperheads** (apparently a reference to a time when some hard-money Democrats wore copper pennies around their necks) opposed all measures in support of the war. They hoped to win control of Congress and force a negotiated peace. Few were actually disloyal, but their activities at a time when thousands of men were risking their lives in battle infuriated many Northerners.

The most notorious domestic foe of the administration was the Peace Democrat Congressman Clement L. Vallandigham of Ohio, who was sent to prison by a military court. There were two rebellions in progress, Vallandigham claimed, "the Secessionist Rebellion" and "the Abolitionist Rebellion." "I am against both," he added. But Lincoln ordered him released and banished to the Confederacy. Once at liberty Vallandigham moved to Canada, from which refuge he ran unsuccessfully for governor of Ohio.

"Perish offices," he once said, "perish life itself, but do the thing that is right." In 1864 he returned to Ohio. Although he campaigned against Lincoln in the presidential election, he was not arrested. Lincoln was no dictator.

Behind Confederate Lines

The South also revised its strategy after Bull Run. Although it might have been wiser to risk everything on a bold invasion of the North, President Davis relied primarily on a strong defense to wear down the Union's will to fight. In 1862 the Confederate Congress passed a conscription act that permitted the hiring of substitutes and exempted many classes of people (including college professors, druggists, and mail carriers) whose work could hardly have been deemed essential. A provision deferring one slave owner or overseer for every plantation of twenty or more slaves led many to grumble about "a rich man's war and a poor man's fight."

Finance was the Confederacy's most vexing problem. The blockade made it impossible to raise much money through tariffs. The Confederate Congress passed an income tax together with many excise taxes but all told they covered only 2 percent of its needs by taxation. The most effective levy was a tax in kind, amounting to one-tenth of each farmer's production. The South borrowed as much as it could ($712 million), even mortgaging cotton undeliverable because of the blockade, in order to gain European credits. But it relied mainly on printing paper currency; over $1.5 billion poured from the presses during the war. Considering the amount issued, this currency held its value well until late in the war, when the military fortunes of the Confederacy began to decline. Then the bottom fell out, and by early 1865 the Confederate dollar was worth less than 2 cents in gold.

Outfitting the army strained southern resources to the limit. Large supplies of small arms (some 600,000 weapons during the entire war) came from Europe through the blockade, along with other valuable military supplies. As the blockade became more efficient, however, it became increasingly difficult to obtain European goods. The Confederates did manage to build a number of munitions plants, and they captured huge amounts of northern arms. No battle was lost because of a lack of guns or other military equipment, although shortages of shoes and uniforms handicapped the Confederate forces on some occasions.

Foreign policy loomed large in Confederate thinking, for the "cotton is king" theory presupposed that the great powers would break any northern blockade to get cotton for their textile mills. Southern expectations were not realized, however. The European nations would have been delighted to see the United States broken up, but none was prepared to support the Confederacy directly. The attitude of Great Britain was decisive.

The cutting off of cotton did not hit the British as hard as the South had hoped. They had a large supply on hand when the war broke out, and when that was exhausted, alternative sources in India and Egypt took up part of the slack. Furthermore, British crop failures necessitated the importation of large amounts of northern wheat, providing a powerful reason for not antagonizing the United States. The fact that most ordinary people in Great Britain favored the North also influenced British policy.

War in the West: Shiloh

After Bull Run no battles were fought until early 1862. Then, while McClellan continued his deliberate preparations to attack Richmond, important fighting occurred far to the west. Most of the Plains Indians sided with the Confederacy, principally because of their resentment of the federal government's policies toward them. White settlers from Colorado to California were mostly Unionists. In March 1862 a Texas army advancing beyond Santa Fe clashed with a Union force in the Battle of Glorieta Pass. The battle was indecisive, but a Union unit destroyed the Texans' supply train. The Texans felt compelled to retreat to the Rio Grande, thus ending the Confederate threat to the Far West.

Meanwhile, far larger Union forces, led by a shabby, cigar-smoking West Pointer named Ulysses S. Grant, had invaded Tennessee from a base at Cairo, Illinois. Making effective use of armored gunboats, Grant captured Fort Henry and Fort Donelson, strongholds on the Tennessee and Cumberland rivers, taking 14,000 prisoners. Next he marched toward Corinth, Mississippi, an important railroad junction.

To check Grant's advance, the Confederates massed 40,000 men under Albert Sidney Johnston. On April 6, while Grant slowly concentrated his forces, Johnston struck suddenly at Shiloh, twenty miles north of Corinth. Some Union soldiers were caught half-dressed, others in the midst of brewing their morning coffee. A few died in their blankets. "We were more than surprised," one Illinois officer later admitted. "We were astonished." However, Grant's men stood their ground. At the end of a day of ghastly carnage the Confederates held the advantage, but fresh Union troops poured in during the night, and on the second day of battle the tide turned. The Confederates fell back toward Corinth, exhausted and demoralized.

Grant, shaken by the unexpected attack and appalled by his losses, allowed the enemy to escape. This cost him the fine reputation he had won in capturing Fort Henry and Fort Donelson. He was relieved of his command. Although Corinth eventually fell and New Orleans was captured by a naval force under the command of Captain David Farragut, Vicksburg, key to control of the Mississippi, remained firmly in Confederate hands. A great opportunity had been lost.

Shiloh had other results. The staggering casualties shook the confidence of both belligerents. More Americans fell there in two days than in all the battles of the Revolution, the War of 1812, and the Mexican War combined. Union losses exceeded 13,000 out of 63,000 engaged; the Confederates lost 10,699, including General Johnston. Technology in the shape of more accurate guns that could be fired far more rapidly than the muskets of earlier times and more powerful artillery were responsible for the carnage. Gradually the generals began to reconsider their tactics and to experiment with field fortifications and other defensive measures. And the people, North and South, stopped thinking of the war as a romantic test of courage and military guile.

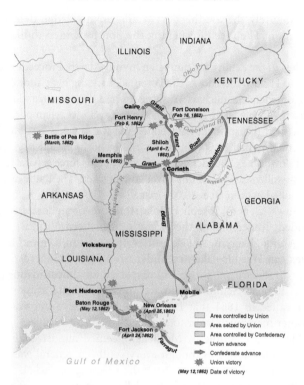

Battles in the West The Anaconda Plan called for the North to gain control of the Mississippi River. To that end, in the spring of 1862 Grant seized western Kentucky and Tennessee and won a major battle at Shiloh, just north of Corinth. Farragut, attacking by sea from the Gulf of Mexico, moved up the mouth of the Mississippi, seizing New Orleans and Baton Rouge. But the South retained Vicksburg: The Confederacy had not been sliced in two.

McClellan: The Reluctant Warrior

In Virginia, General McClellan, after unaccountable delays, was finally moving against Richmond. Instead of trying to advance across the difficult terrain of northern Virginia, he transported his army by water to the tip of the peninsula formed by the York and James rivers in order to attack Richmond from the southeast. After the famous battle on March 9, 1862, between the USS *Monitor* and the Confederate *Merrimack*, the first fight in history between armored warships, control of these waters was securely in northern hands.

While McClellan's plan alarmed many congressmen because it seemed to leave Washington relatively unprotected, it simplified the problem of keeping the army supplied in hostile country. But McClellan now displayed the weaknesses that eventually ruined his career. His problems were both intellectual and psychological. Basically he approached tactical questions in the manner of a typical eighteenth-century general. He considered war a kind of gentlemanly contest in which maneuver, guile, and position determined victory. He believed it more important to capture Richmond than to destroy the army protecting it. With their capital in northern hands, surely the Southerners would acknowledge defeat and agree to return to the Union. The idea of crushing the South seemed to him wrongheaded and uncivilized.

McClellan began the Peninsular campaign in mid-March. Proceeding deliberately, he floated an army of 112,000 men down the Potomac. Landing near Yorktown, he prepared to besiege the Confederates, much as Washington had done against Cornwallis in 1781. But in early May the Confederate army slipped away and McClellan pursued them nearly to Richmond. A swift thrust might have ended the war quickly, but McClellan delayed, despite the fact that he had 80,000 men in striking position and large reserves. As he pushed forward slowly, the Confederates caught part of his force separated from the main body by the rain-swollen Chickahominy River and attacked. The Battle of Seven Pines was indecisive yet resulted in more than 10,000 casualties.

At Seven Pines, General Joseph E. Johnston, the Confederate commander, was severely wounded; leadership of the Army of Northern Virginia then passed to Robert E. Lee. Although a reluctant supporter of secession, Lee was a superb soldier. During the Mexican War his gallantry under fire inspired General Scott to call him the bravest man in the army. He also had displayed an almost instinctive mastery of tactics. Admiral Raphael Semmes, who accompanied Scott's army on the march to Mexico City, recalled in 1851 that Lee "seemed to receive impressions intuitively, which it cost other men much labor to acquire."

Lee was McClellan's antithesis. McClellan seemed almost deliberately to avoid understanding his foes, acting as though every southern general was a genius. Lee, a master psychologist on the battlefield, took the measure of each Union general and devised his tactics accordingly. Where McClellan was complex, egotistical, perhaps even unbalanced, Lee was courtly, tactful, and entirely without McClellan's vainglorious belief that he was a man of destiny. Yet on the battlefield Lee's boldness skirted the edge of foolhardiness.

To relieve the pressure on Richmond, Lee sent General "Stonewall" Jackson, soon to be his most trusted lieutenant, on a diversionary raid in the Shenandoah Valley, west of Richmond and Washington. Jackson struck swiftly at scattered Union forces in the region, winning a number of battles and capturing vast stores of equipment. Lincoln dispatched 20,000 reserves to the Shenandoah to check him—to the dismay of McClellan, who wanted the troops to attack Richmond from the north. But after Seven Pines, Lee ordered Jackson back to Richmond. While Union armies streamed toward the valley, Jackson slipped stealthily between them. On June 25 he reached Ashland, directly north of the Confederate capital.

Before that date McClellan had possessed clear numerical superiority yet had only inched ahead; now the advantage lay with Lee, and the very next day he attacked. From June 25 to July 1 (the Seven Days' Battles) Lee repeatedly struck different parts of McClellan's lines. The full weight of his force never hit the northern army at any one time. Nevertheless, the shock was formidable. McClellan, who excelled in defense, fell back, his lines intact, exacting a fearful toll. Under difficult conditions he managed to transfer his troops to a new base on the James River at Harrison's Landing, where the guns of the navy could shield his position. Again the loss of life was terrible: Northern casualties totaled 15,800, and those of the South nearly 20,000 in the Seven Days' Battle for Richmond.

●●—[Read the Document

McClellan to Abraham Lincoln (July 7, 1862) at myhistorylab.com

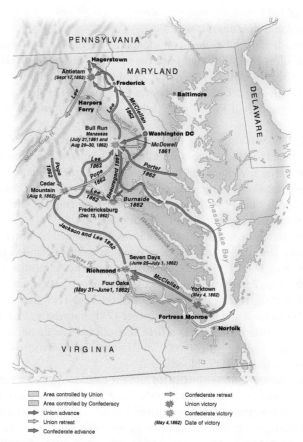

War in the East, 1861–1862 In the spring of 1862, McClellan seized Yorktown on the Virginia Peninsula (Peninsular Campaign). But he failed to take Richmond and his army was recalled to the Potomac. That fall, McClellan halted Lee's northern advance into Maryland at Antietam. By the end of 1862, the situation in the East was much as it had been a year earlier, except for the nearly 100,000 casualties.

Lee Counterattacks: Antietam

McClellan was still within striking distance of Richmond, in an impregnable position with secure supply lines and 86,000 soldiers ready to resume battle. Lee had absorbed heavy losses without winning any significant advantage. Yet Lincoln was exasperated with McClellan for having surrendered the initiative and, after much deliberation, reduced his authority by placing him under General Henry W. Halleck. Halleck called off the Peninsular campaign and ordered McClellan to move his army from the James to the Potomac, near Washington. He was to join General John Pope, who was gathering a new army between Washington and Richmond.

If McClellan had persisted and captured Richmond, the war might have ended and the Union been restored without the abolition of slavery, since at that point the North was still fighting for union, not for freedom for the slaves. By prolonging the war, Lee inadvertently enabled it to destroy slavery along with the Confederacy, though no one at the time looked at the matter this way.

For the president to have lost confidence in McClellan was understandable. Nevertheless, to allow Halleck to pull back the troops was a bad mistake. When they withdrew, Lee seized the initiative. With typical decisiveness and daring, he marched rapidly north. Late in August his Confederates drove General Pope's confused troops from the same ground, Bull Run, where the first major engagement of the war had been fought.

While McClellan was regrouping the shaken Union Army, Lee once again took the offensive. He realized that no number of individual southern triumphs could destroy the enormous material advantages of the North. Unless some dramatic blow, delivered on northern soil, persuaded the people of the United States that military victory was impossible, the South would surely be crushed in the long run. Lee therefore marched rapidly northwest around the defenses of Washington.

Acting with even more than his usual boldness, Lee divided his army of 60,000 into a number of units. One, under Jackson, descended on weakly defended Harpers Ferry, capturing more than 11,000 prisoners. Another pressed as far north as Hagerstown, Maryland, nearly to the Pennsylvania line. McClellan pursued with his usual deliberation until a captured dispatch revealed to him Lee's dispositions. Then he moved a bit more swiftly, forcing Lee to stand and fight on September 17 at Sharpsburg, Maryland, between the Potomac and Antietam Creek. On a field that offered Lee no room to maneuver, 70,000 Union soldiers clashed with 40,000 Confederates. When darkness fell, more than 22,000 lay dead or wounded on the bloody field.

Although casualties were evenly divided and the Confederate lines remained intact, Lee's position was perilous. His men were exhausted. McClellan had not yet thrown in his reserves, and new federal units were arriving hourly. A bold northern general would have continued the fight without respite through the night. One of ordinary aggressive-ness would have waited for first light and then struck with every soldier who could hold a rifle, for with the Potomac at his back, Lee could not retreat under fire without inviting disaster. McClellan, however, did nothing. For an entire day, while Lee scanned the field in futile search of some weakness in the Union lines, he held his fire. That night the Confederates slipped back across the Potomac into Virginia.

Lee's invasion had failed; his army had been badly mauled; the gravest threat to the Union in the war had been checked. But McClellan had let victory slip through his fingers. Soon Lee was back behind the defenses of Richmond, rebuilding his army.

Once again, this time finally, Lincoln dismissed McClellan from his command.

The Emancipation Proclamation

Antietam, though hardly the victory he had hoped for, gave Lincoln the excuse he needed to take a step that changed the character of the war decisively. When the fight-ing started, fear of alienating the border states was reason enough for not making emancipation of the slaves a war aim. Lincoln even insisted on enforcing the Fugitive Slave Act for this reason. However, pressures to act against the South's "peculiar insti-tution" mounted steadily. Slavery had divided the nation; now it was driving Northerners to war within themselves. Love of country led them to fight to save the

Union, but fighting aroused hatreds and caused many to desire to smash the enemy. Sacrifice, pain, and grief made abolitionists of many who had no love for blacks—they sought to free the slave only to injure the master.

To make abolition an object of the war might encourage the slaves to revolt, but Lincoln disclaimed this objective. Nevertheless, the possibility existed. Already the slaves seemed to be looking to the North for freedom: Whenever Union troops invaded Confederate territory, slaves flocked into their lines.

As the war progressed, the Radical faction in Congress gradually chipped away at slavery. In April 1862 the Radicals pushed through a bill abolishing slavery in the District of Columbia; two months later another measure outlawed it in the territories; in July the Confiscation Act "freed" all slaves owned by persons in rebellion against the United States. In fighting for these measures and in urging general emancipation, some Radicals made statements harshly critical of Lincoln; but while he carefully avoided being identified with them or with any other faction, the president was never very far from their position. He resisted emancipation because he feared it would divide the country and injure the war effort, not because he personally disapproved. Indeed, he frequently cited Radical pressure as an excuse for doing what he wished to do on his own.

Photo Credit: The Granger Collection, New York.

When Union troops pushed toward Richmond in June of 1862, these slaves crossed the Rappahonnock River heading north toward freedom. But McClellan's offensive failed and the Union army withdrew to Washington. Whether these slaves made it to Maryland in time is unknown.

Lincoln would have preferred to see slavery done away with by state law, with compensation for slave owners and federal aid for former slaves willing to leave the United States. He tried repeatedly to persuade the loyal slave states to adopt this policy, but without success. By the summer of 1862 he was convinced that for military reasons and to win the support of liberal opinion in Europe, the government should make abolition a war aim. "We must free the slaves or be ourselves subdued," he explained to a member of his Cabinet. He delayed temporarily, fearing that a statement in the face of military reverses would be taken as a sign of weakness. The "victory" at Antietam Creek gave him his opportunity, and on September 22 he made public the **Emancipation Proclamation**. After January 1, 1863, it said, all slaves in areas in rebellion against the United States "shall be then, thenceforward, and forever free."

Read the Document

The Emancipation Proclamation at myhistorylab.com

No single slave was freed directly by Lincoln's announcement, which did not apply to the border states or to those sections of the Confederacy, like New Orleans and Norfolk, Virginia, already controlled by federal troops. The proclamation differed in philosophy, however, from the Confiscation Act in striking at the institution, not at the property of rebels. Henceforth every Union victory would speed the destruction of slavery without regard for the attitudes of individual masters.

Southerners considered the Emancipation Proclamation an incitement to slave rebellion—as one of them put it, an "infamous attempt to . . . convert the quiet, ignorant, and dependent black son of toil into a savage incendiary and brutal murderer." Most antislavery groups thought it did not go far enough. Lincoln "is only stopping on the edge of Niagara, to pick up a few chips," one abolitionist declared. "He and they will go over together." Foreign opinion was mixed: Liberals tended to applaud, conservatives to react with alarm or contempt.

As Lincoln anticipated, the proclamation had a subtle but continuing impact in the North. Its immediate effect was to aggravate racial prejudices. Millions of whites disapproved of slavery yet abhorred the idea of equality for blacks. David Wilmot, for example, insisted that his famous proviso was designed to preserve the territories for whites rather than to weaken slavery, and as late as 1857 the people of Iowa had rejected black suffrage by a vote of 49,000 to 8,000.

The Democrats spared no effort to make political capital of these fears and prejudices even before Lincoln's Emancipation Proclamation, and they made large gains in the 1862 election, especially in the Northwest. So strong was antiblack feeling that most of the Republican politicians who defended emancipation did so with racist arguments. Far from encouraging southern blacks to move north, they claimed, the ending of slavery would lead to a mass migration of northern blacks to the South.

When the Emancipation Proclamation began actually to free slaves, the government pursued a policy of "containment," that is, of keeping the former slaves in the South. Panicky fears of an inundation of blacks subsided in the North. Nevertheless, emancipation remained a cause of social discontent. In March 1863, volunteering having fallen off, Congress passed the Conscription Act. The law applied to all men between ages twenty and forty-five, but it allowed draftees to hire substitutes and even to buy exemption for $300, provisions that were patently unfair to the poor. During the remainder of the war 46,000 men were actually drafted, whereas 118,000 hired substitutes, and another 161,000 "failed to report." Conscription represented an enormous expansion of national authority, since in effect it gave the government the power of life and death over individual citizens.

The Draft Riots

After the passage of the Conscription Act, draft riots erupted in a number of cities. By far the most serious disturbance occurred in New York City in July 1863. Many workers resented conscription in principle and were embittered by the $300 exemption fee (which represented a year's wages). The idea of being forced to risk their lives to free slaves who would then, they believed, compete with them for jobs infuriated them. On July 13 a mob attacked the office where the names of conscripts were being drawn. For four days the city was an inferno. Public buildings, shops, and private residences were put to the torch. What began as a protest against the draft became an assault on blacks and the well-to-do. It took federal troops and the temporary suspension of the draft in the city to put an end to the rioting. By the time order was restored more than a hundred people had lost their lives.

Most white Northerners did not surrender their comforting belief in black inferiority, and Lincoln was no exception. Yet Lincoln was evolving. He talked about deporting freed slaves to the tropics, but he did not send any there. And he began to receive black leaders in the White House and to allow black groups to hold meetings on the grounds.

Many other Americans were changing too. The brutality of the New York riots horrified many white citizens. Over $40,000 was swiftly raised to aid the victims, and some conservatives were so appalled by the Irish rioters that they began to talk of giving blacks the vote.

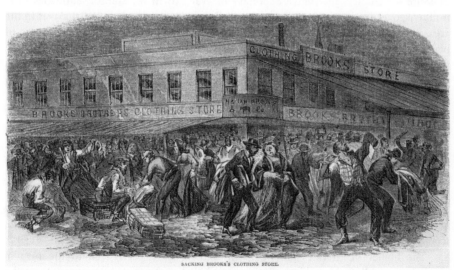

SACKING BROOKS'S CLOTHING STORE.

This lithograph of the New York draft riots, 1863, shows that although the rioters mainly targeted blacks, they also attacked homes and businesses of prominent Republicans: Brooks Brothers, Horace Greeley's newspaper, and the *Times*.

Photo Credit: The Granger Collection, New York.

The Emancipated People

To blacks, both slave and free, the Emancipation Proclamation served as a beacon. Even if it failed immediately to liberate one slave or to lift the burdens of prejudice from one black back, it stood as a promise of future improvement. "I took the proclamation for a little more than it purported," Frederick Douglass recalled in his autobiography, "and saw in its spirit a life and power far beyond its letter." Lincoln was by modern standards a racist, but his most militant black contemporaries respected him deeply. Douglass said of him, "Lincoln was not . . . either our man or our model. In his interests, in his association, in his habits of thought and in his prejudices, he was a white man." Nevertheless, Douglass described Lincoln as "one whom I could love, honor, and trust without reserve or doubt."

As for the slaves of the South, after January 1, 1863, whenever the "Army of Freedom" approached, they laid down their plows and hoes and flocked to the Union lines in droves. Such behavior came as a shock to the owners. "[The slaves] who loved us best—as we thought—were the first to leave us," one planter mourned. Talk of slave "ingratitude" increased. Instead of referring to their workers as "servants" or "my black family," many owners began to describe them as "slaves" or "niggers."

African American Soldiers

A revolutionary shift occurred in white thinking about using black men as soldiers. Although they had fought in the Revolution and in the Battle of New Orleans during the War of 1812, a law of 1792 barred blacks from the army. During the early stages of the rebellion, despite the eagerness of thousands of free blacks to enlist, the prohibition remained in force. By 1862, however, the need for manpower was creating pressure for change. In August Secretary of War Edwin M. Stanton authorized the military government of the captured South Carolina sea islands to enlist slaves in the area. After the Emancipation Proclamation specifically authorized the enlistment of blacks, the governor of Massachusetts moved to organize a black regiment, the famous Massachusetts 54th. (See Re-Viewing the Past, *Glory*.) Swiftly thereafter, other states began to recruit black soldiers, and in May 1863 the federal government established a Bureau of Colored Troops to supervise their enlistment. By the end of the war one soldier in eight in the Union army was black.

Enlisting so many black soldiers changed the war from a struggle to save the Union to a kind of revolution. "Let the black man . . . get an eagle on his button and a musket on his shoulder," wrote Frederick Douglass, "and there is no power on earth which can deny that he has won the right to citizenship."

At first black soldiers received only $7 a month, about half what white soldiers were paid. But they soon proved themselves in battle; of the 178,000 who served in the Union army, 37,000 were killed, a rate of loss about 40 percent higher than that among white troops. The Congressional Medal of Honor was awarded to twenty-one blacks.

The higher death rates among black soldiers were partly due to the fury of Confederate soldiers. Many black captives were killed on the spot. After overrunning the garrison of Fort Pillow on the Mississippi River, the Confederates massacred several dozen black soldiers, along with their white commander. Lincoln was tempted to order reprisals, but he and his advisers realized that to do so would have been both morally wrong (two wrongs never make a right) and likely to lead to still more atrocities. "Blood can not restore blood," Lincoln said in his usual direct way.

Read the **Document**

Letter from a Free Black Volunteer to the *Christian Recorder* (1864) at **myhistorylab.com**

Antietam to Gettysburg

It was well that Lincoln seized on Antietam to release his proclamation; had he waited for a more impressive victory, he would have waited nearly a year. To replace McClellan, he chose General Ambrose E. Burnside, best known to history for his magnificent side-whiskers (originally called burnsides, later, at first jokingly, sideburns). Burnside was a good corps commander, but he lacked the self-confidence essential to anyone who takes responsibility for major deci-

See the **Map**

The Civil War, Part II: 1863–1865 at **myhistorylab.com**

sions. He knew his limitations and tried to avoid high command, but patriotism and his sense of duty compelled him, when pressed, to accept leadership of the Army of the Potomac. He prepared to march on Richmond.

Unlike McClellan, Burnside was aggressive—too aggressive. He planned to ford the Rappahannock River at Fredericksburg. Supply problems and bad weather delayed him until mid-December, giving Lee time to concentrate his army in impregnable positions behind the town. Although he had more than 120,000 men against Lee's 75,000, Burnside should have called off the attack when he saw Lee's advantage; instead he ordered the troops forward. Crossing the river over pontoon bridges, his divisions occupied Fredericksburg. Then, in wave after wave, they charged the Confederate defense line while Lee's artillery riddled them from nearby Marye's Heights.

On December 14, the day following this futile assault, General Burnside, tears streaming down his cheeks, ordered the evacuation of Fredericksburg. Shortly thereafter General Joseph Hooker replaced him.

Unlike Burnside, "Fighting Joe" Hooker was ill-tempered, vindictive, and devious. He proved no better than his predecessor, but his failings were more like McClellan's than Burnside's. By the spring of 1863 he had 125,000 men ready for action. Late in April he forded the Rappahannock and quickly concentrated at Chancellorsville, about ten miles west of Fredericksburg. His army outnumbered the Confederates by more than two to one; he should have forced a battle at once. Instead he delayed, and while he did, Lee sent Jackson's corps of 28,000 men across tangled countryside to a position directly athwart Hooker's unsuspecting flank. At 6 PM on May 2, Jackson attacked.

Completely surprised, the Union right crumbled, brigade after brigade overrun before it could wheel to meet Jackson's charge. At the first sound of firing, Lee had struck along the entire front to impede Union troop movements. If the battle had begun earlier in the day, the Confederates might have won a decisive victory; as it happened, nightfall brought a lull, and the next day the Union troops rallied and held their ground. Heavy fighting continued until May 5, when Hooker abandoned the field and retreated in good order behind the Rappahannock.

Gettysburg Campaign, 1863 As Lee's main army advanced north, Meade paralleled his movements to the east, preventing Lee from attacking Baltimore or Philadelphia. When the armies converged at Gettysburg, Lee was for the first time soundly defeated. Jeb Stuart, Lee's calvalry commander, had been marauding to the east and missed the decisive engagement.

Chancellorsville cost the Confederates dearly, for their losses, in excess of 12,000, were almost as heavy as the North's and harder to replace. They also lost Stonewall Jackson, struck down by the bullets of his own men while returning from a reconnaissance. Nevertheless, the Union army had suffered another fearful blow to its morale.

Lee knew that time was still on the side of the North; to defend Richmond was not enough. Already federal troops in the West were closing in on Vicksburg, threatening to cut Confederate communications with Arkansas and Texas. Now was the time to strike, while the morale of the North was at low ebb. With 75,000 soldiers he crossed the Potomac again, a larger Union force dogging his right flank. By late June his army had fanned out across southern Pennsylvania in a fifty-mile arc from Chambersburg to the Susquehanna. Gray-clad soldiers ranged fifty miles *northwest* of Baltimore, within ten miles of Harrisburg, Pennsylvania.

As Union soldiers had been doing in Virginia, Lee's men destroyed property and commandeered food, horses, and clothing wherever they could find them. They even seized a number of blacks and sent them south to be sold as slaves. On July 1 a Confederate division looking for shoes in the town of Gettysburg clashed with two brigades of Union cavalry northwest of the town. Both sides sent out calls for reinforcements. Like iron filings drawn to a magnet, the two armies converged. The Confederates won control of the town, but the Union army, now commanded by General George G. Meade, took a strong position on Cemetery Ridge, a hook-shaped stretch of high ground just to the south. Lee's men occupied Seminary Ridge, a parallel position.

On this field the fate of the Union was probably decided. For two days the Confederates attacked Cemetery Ridge, pounding it with the heaviest artillery barrage ever seen in America and sweeping bravely up its flanks in repeated assaults. During General George E. Pickett's famous charge, a handful of his men actually reached the Union lines, but reserves drove them back. By nightfall on July 3 the Confederate army was spent, the Union lines unbroken.

The following day was the Fourth of July. The two weary forces rested on their arms. Had the Union army attacked in force, the Confederates might have been crushed, but just as McClellan had hesitated after Antietam, Meade let opportunity pass. On July 5 Lee retreated to safety. For the first time he had been clearly bested on the field of battle.

Lincoln Finds His General: Grant at Vicksburg

On Independence Day, a day after Gettysburg, federal troops won another great victory far to the west. When General Halleck was called east in July 1862, Ulysses S. Grant resumed command of the Union troops. Grant was one of the most controversial officers in the army. During the Mexican War he served well, but when he was later assigned to a lonely post in the West, he took to drink and was forced to resign his commission. Thereafter he was by turns a farmer, a real estate agent, and a clerk in a leather goods store. In 1861, approaching age forty, he seemed well into a life of frustration and mediocrity.

The war gave him a second chance. Back in service, however, his reputation as a ne'er-do-well and his unmilitary bearing worked against him, as did the heavy casualties suffered by his troops at Shiloh. Yet the fact that he knew how to manage a large army and win battles did not escape Lincoln. According to tradition, when a gossip tried to poison the president against Grant by referring to his drinking, Lincoln retorted that if he knew what brand Grant favored, he would send a barrel of it to some of his other generals.

Grant's major aim was to capture Vicksburg, a city of tremendous strategic importance. Together with Port Hudson, a bastion north of Baton Rouge, Louisiana, it guarded a 150-mile stretch of the Mississippi. The river between these points was inaccessible to federal gunboats. So long as Vicksburg remained in southern hands, the trans-Mississippi region could send men and supplies to the rest of the Confederacy.

Vicksburg sits on a bluff overlooking a sharp bend in the river. When it proved unapproachable from either the west or the north, Grant devised an audacious scheme for getting at it from the east. He descended the Mississippi from Memphis to a point a few miles north of the city. Then, leaving part of his force behind to create the impression that he planned to attack from the north, he crossed the west bank and slipped quickly southward. Recrossing the river below Vicksburg, he abandoned his communications and supply lines and struck at Jackson, the capital of Mississippi. In a series of swift engagements his troops captured Jackson, cutting off the army of General John C. Pemberton, defending Vicksburg, from other Confederate units. Turning next on Pemberton, Grant defeated him in two decisive battles, Champion's Hill and Big Black River, and drove him inside the Vicksburg fortifications. By mid-May the city was under siege. Grant applied relentless pressure, and on July 4 Pemberton surrendered. With Vicksburg in Union hands, federal gunboats could range the entire length of the Mississippi. Texas and Arkansas were for all practical purposes lost to the Confederacy.

Vicksburg Campaign Unable to seize Vicksburg by direct assualt, Grant swept to the south, crossed the Mississippi near Port Gibson, and then took Vicksburg from the east.

Lincoln had disliked Grant's plan for capturing Vicksburg. Now he generously confessed his error and placed Grant in command of all federal troops west of the Appalachians. Grant promptly took charge of the fighting around Chattanooga, Tennessee, where Confederate advances, beginning with the Battle of Chickamauga (September 19–20), were threatening to develop into a major disaster for the North. Shifting corps commanders and bringing up fresh units, he won another decisive victory at Chattanooga in a series of battles ending on November 25, 1863. This cleared the way for an invasion of Georgia. Suddenly this unkempt man emerged as the military leader the North had been so desperately seeking. In March 1864 Lincoln summoned him to Washington, named him lieutenant general, and gave him supreme command of the armies of the United States.

Economic and Social Effects, North and South

Although much blood would yet be spilled, by the end of 1863 the Confederacy was on the road to defeat. Northern military pressure, gradually increasing, was eroding the South's most precious resource: manpower. An ever-tightening naval blockade was reducing its economic strength. Shortages developed that, combined with the flood of currency pouring from the presses, led to drastic inflation. By 1864 an officer's coat cost $2,000 in Confederate money, cigars sold for $10 each, butter was $25 a pound, and flour went for $275 a barrel. Wages rose too, but not nearly as rapidly.

The southern railroad network was gradually wearing out, the major lines maintaining operations only by cannibalizing less vital roads. Imported products such as coffee disappeared; even salt became scarce. Efforts to increase manufacturing were only moderately successful because of the shortage of labor, capital, and technical knowledge. In general, southern prejudice against centralized authority prevented the Confederacy from making effective use of its scarce resources.

In the North, after a brief depression in 1861 caused by the uncertainties of the situation and the loss of southern business, the economy flourished: Government purchases greatly stimulated certain lines of manufacturing, the railroads operated at close to capacity and with increasing efficiency, the farm machinery business boomed because so many farmers left their fields to serve in the army, and bad harvests in Europe boosted agricultural prices.

Congress passed a number of economic measures long desired but held up in the past by southern opposition. The **Homestead Act (1862)** gave 160 acres to any settler who would farm the land for five years. The Morrill Land Grant Act of the same year provided the states with land at the rate of 30,000 acres for each member of Congress to support state agricultural colleges. Various tariff acts raised the duties on manufactured goods to an average rate of 47 percent in order to protect domestic manufacturers from foreign competition. The Pacific Railway Act (1862) authorized subsidies in land and money for the construction of a transcontinental railroad. And the National Banking Act of 1863 gave the country, at last, a uniform currency.

Although the economy grew, it did so more slowly during the 1860s than in the decades preceding and following. Prices soared beginning in 1862, averaging about 80 percent over the 1860 level by the end of the war. As in the South, wages did not keep pace. This did not make for a healthy economy. As the war dragged on and the continuing inflation eroded purchasing power, resentment on the part of workers deepened. During the 1850s iron molders, cigar makers, and some other skilled workers had formed national unions. This trend continued through the war years. There were many strikes. Inflation and shortages encouraged speculation and fostered a selfish, materialistic attitude toward life. Many contractors took advantage of wartime confusion to sell the government shoddy goods. By 1864 cotton was worth $1.90 a pound in New England. It could be had for twenty cents a pound in the South. Although it was illegal to traffic in the staple across the lines, unscrupulous operators did so and made huge profits.

Yet the war undoubtedly hastened industrialization and laid the basis for many other aspects of modern civilization. It posed problems of organization and planning, both military and civilian, that challenged the talents of creative persons and thus led to a more complex and efficient economy. The mechanization of production, the growth of large corporations, the creation of a better banking system, and the emergence of business leaders attuned to these conditions would surely have occurred in any case, for industrialization was under way long before the South seceded. Nevertheless, the war greatly speeded all these changes.

Civilian participation in the war effort was far greater than in earlier conflicts. Some churches split over the question of emancipation, but in North and South, church directors took the lead in recruitment drives and in charitable activities aimed at supporting the armed forces. In the North a Christian Commission raised the money and coordinated the personnel needed to provide Union soldiers with half a million Bibles, several million religious tracts, and other books, along with fruit, coffee, and spare clothing.

Women in Wartime

Many southern women took over the management of farms and small plantations when their menfolk went off to war. Others became volunteer nurses, and after an initial period of resistance, the Confederate army began to enlist women in the medical corps. At least two female nurses, Captain Sally Tompkins and Kate Cumming, left records of their experiences that throw much light on how the wounded were treated during the war. Other southern women worked as clerks in newly organized government departments.

Southern "ladyhood" more generally was yet another casualty of the war. The absence or death of husbands or other male relations changed attitudes toward gender roles. When her husband obeyed a military order to abandon Atlanta to the advancing Union armies, Julia Davidson, about to give birth, denounced the "men of Atlanta" for having "run and left Atlanta" and their homes. Such women learned to fend for themselves. "Necessity," Davidson later wrote her husband, would "make a different woman of me."

Large numbers of women also contributed to the northern war effort. As in the South, farm women went out into fields to plant and harvest crops, aided in many instances by new farm machinery. Many others took jobs in textile factories; in establishments making shoes, uniforms, and other supplies for the army; and in government agencies. But as was usually the case, the low wages traditionally paid women acted as a brake on wage increases for their male colleagues.

Besides working in factories and shops and on farms, northern women, again like their southern counterparts, aided the war effort more directly. Elizabeth Blackwell, the

Photo Credit: Lauren Cook Wike/Mr. Jackson K. Doane, Sr.

Photo Credit: Used with Permission of Documenting the American South, The University of North Carolina at Chapel Hill Libraries.

Harry T. Buford
1st Lt Indpt Scouts C.S.A

Sarah Rosetta Wakeman, a.k.a. Private Lyons Wakeman of the 153rd Regiment of New York, and Janeta Velasquez, a.k.a. Lt. Harry T. Buford of the Confederate army, disguised themselves as men to fight.

first American woman doctor of medicine, had already founded the New York Infirmary for Women and Children. After war broke out she helped set up what became the U.S. **Sanitary Commission**, an organization of women similar to the Christian Commission dedicated to improving sanitary conditions at army camps, supplying hospitals with volunteer nurses, and raising money for medical supplies. Many thousands of women volunteers took part in Sanitary Commission and related programs.

An additional 3,000-odd women served as regular army nurses during the conflict. At the start the high command of both armies resisted the efforts of women to help, but necessity and a grudging recognition of the competence of these women gradually brought the generals around. Clara Barton, a schoolteacher and government clerk, was among the first women to dress wounds at forward stations on the battlefield. After she ran out of bandages at Antietam, she dressed wounds with green corn leaves. The chief surgeon declared her to be "the angel of the battlefield." The "proper sphere" of American women was expanding, another illustration of the modernizing effect of the war.

◆●◆ Read the Document

Barton, *Memoirs About Medical Life at the Battlefield* at **myhistorylab.com**

Grant in the Wilderness

Grant's strategy as supreme commander was simple, logical, and ruthless. He would attack Lee and try to capture Richmond, Virginia. General William Tecumseh Sherman would drive from Chattanooga toward Atlanta, Georgia. Like a lobster's claw,

Toward Lee's Surrender in Virginia, 1864–1865
During the final year of the war in the East, Grant kept driving toward Richmond, and Lee kept blocking his way, like two whirling wrestlers locked in a hold. His army battered and bloodied, Lee surrendered at Appomattox Courthouse on April 9, 1865.

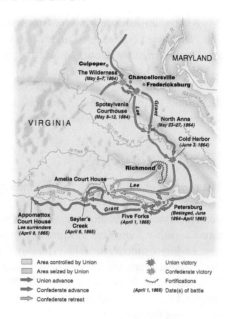

the two armies could then close to crush all resistance. Early in May 1864 Grant and Sherman commenced operations, each with more than 100,000 men.

Grant marched the Army of the Potomac directly into the tangled wilderness area south of the Rappahannock, where Hooker had been routed a year earlier. Lee, having only 60,000 men, forced the battle in the roughest possible country, where Grant found it difficult to make efficient use of his larger force. For two days (May 5–6) the Battle of the Wilderness raged. When it was over, the North had sustained another 18,000 casualties, far more than the Confederates. But unlike his predecessors, Grant did not fall back after being checked, nor did he expose his army to the kind of devastating counterattack at which Lee was so expert. Instead he shifted his troops to the southeast, attempting to outflank the Confederates. Divining his intent, Lee rushed his divisions southeastward and disposed them behind hastily erected earthworks in well-placed positions around Spotsylvania Court House. Grant attacked. After five more days, at a cost to the Union army of another 12,000 men, the Confederate lines were still intact.

Grant had grasped the fundamental truth that the war could be won only by grinding the South down beneath the weight of numbers. His own losses of men and equipment could be replaced; Lee's could not. When critics complained of the cost, he replied doggedly that he intended to fight on in the same manner if it took all summer. Once more he pressed southeastward in an effort to outflank the enemy. At Cold Harbor, nine miles from Richmond, he found the Confederates once more in strong defenses. He attacked. It was a battle as foolish and nearly as one-sided as General Pakenham's assault on Jackson's line outside New Orleans in 1815. "At Cold Harbor," the forthright Grant confessed in his memoirs, "no advantage whatever was gained to compensate for the heavy losses we sustained."

Sixty thousand casualties in less than a month! The news sent a wave of dismay through the North. There were demands that "Butcher" Grant be removed from command. Lincoln, however, stood firm. Although the price was fearfully high, Grant was gaining his objective. At Cold Harbor, Lee had to fight without a single regiment in general reserve while Grant's army was larger than at the start of the offensive. When Grant next swung around his flank, striking south of the James River toward Petersburg, Lee had to rush his troops to that city to hold him.

As the Confederates dug in, Grant put Petersburg under siege. Soon both armies had constructed complicated lines of breastworks and trenches, running for miles in a great arc south of Petersburg, much like the fortifications that would be used in France in World War I. Methodically the Union forces extended their lines, seeking to weaken the Confederates and cut the rail connections supplying Lee's troops and the city of Richmond. Grant could not overwhelm him, but by late June, Lee was pinned to earth. Moving again would mean having to abandon Richmond.

Sherman in Georgia

The summer of 1864 saw the North submerged in pessimism. The Army of the Potomac held Lee at bay but appeared powerless to defeat him. In Georgia, General Sherman inched forward methodically against the wily Joseph E. Johnston, but when he tried a direct assault at Kennesaw Mountain on June 27, he was thrown back with heavy casualties. In July Confederate raiders under General Jubal Early dashed suddenly across the Potomac from the Shenandoah Valley to within five miles of Washington before being turned back. A draft call for 500,000 additional men did not improve the public temper. Huge losses and the absence of a decisive victory were taxing the northern will to continue the fight.

In June, Lincoln had been renominated on a National Union ticket, with the Tennessee Unionist Andrew Johnson, a former Democrat, as his running mate. He was under attack not only from the Democrats, who nominated General McClellan and came out for a policy that might almost be characterized as peace at any price, but also from the Radical Republicans, many of whom had wished to dump him in favor of Secretary of the Treasury Chase.

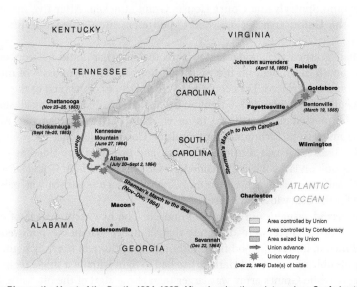

Sherman Pierces the Heart of the South, 1864–1865 After slogging through tenacious Confederate resistance in the Appalachians, Sherman finally broke through and seized Atlanta in September, 1864; he then marched "to the sea" to Savannah and in 1865 drove north through South Carolina and into North Carolina.

Table 1 Turning Points in the War

Pivotal Battles	Date	Outcome	Consequence
Ft. Sumter	April, 1861	Confederates fire on Ft. Sumter; Union garrison surrenders	Civil War commences
First Bull Run	July, 1861	Confederate victory	Northerners sobered, Southerners exhilarated; no swift ending to war likely
Shiloh	April, 1862	Tactical Union victory	23,000 casualties stagger everyone: Was the war worth such a high cost?
Antietam	September, 1862	Lee's advance northward halted	Lincoln, confidence regained, issues Emancipation Proclamation freeing slaves in rebel areas
Chancellorsville	May, 1863	Lee defeats Union army that had crossed into Virginia	Emboldened by victory, Lee invades North in search of decisive victory
Gettysburg	July, 1863	Confederate defeat; Lee retreats to Virginia	Confederate hopes dashed
Vicksburg	July, 1863	Grant seizes control of lower Mississippi River	Texas and Arkansas cut off from the Confederacy
Wilderness and Cold Harbor	May and June, 1864	Lee inflicts staggering losses on Union troops	Though criticized as a butcher, Grant perseveres, backed by Lincoln: War becomes battle of attrition
Sherman's March	November, 1864 through March, 1865	Sherman drives through Georgia and South Carolina	Demoralizes South
Siege of Petersburg	June 1864 through April 1865	Lee's defenses exhausted	South surrenders

Then, almost overnight, the whole atmosphere changed. On September 2, General Sherman's army fought its way into Atlanta. When the Confederates countered with an offensive northward toward Tennessee, Sherman did not follow. Instead he abandoned his communications with Chattanooga and marched unopposed through Georgia, "from Atlanta to the sea."

Sherman was in some ways like Grant. He was a West Pointer who resigned his commission only to fare poorly in civilian occupations. Back in the army in 1861, he suffered a brief nervous breakdown. After recovering he fought well under Grant at Shiloh and the two became close friends. "He stood by me when I was crazy," Sherman later recalled, "and I stood by him when he was drunk." Far more completely than most military men of his generation, Sherman believed in total war—in appropriating or destroying everything that might help the enemy continue the fight.

The march through Georgia had many objectives besides conquering territory. One obvious one was economic, the destruction of southern resources. "[We] must make old and young, rich and poor feel the hard hand of war," Sherman said.

Another object of Sherman's march was psychological. "If the North can march an army right through the South," he told General Grant, Southerners will take it "as proof positive that the North can prevail." This was certainly true of Georgia's blacks, who flocked to the invaders by the thousands, women and children as well as men, all cheering mightily when the soldiers put their former masters' homes to the torch. "They pray and shout and mix up my name with Moses," Sherman explained.

Sherman's victories staggered the Confederacy and the anti-Lincoln forces in the North. In November the president was easily reelected, 212 electoral votes to 21. The country was determined to carry on the struggle.

At last the South's will to resist began to crack. Sherman entered Savannah on December 22, having denuded a strip of Georgia sixty miles wide. Early in January 1865 he marched northward, leaving behind "a broad black streak of ruin and

Read the Document

Sherman, *The March Through Georgia* at **myhistorylab.com**

desolation—the fences all gone; lonesome smoke-stacks, surrounded by dark heaps of ashes and cinders, marking the spots where human habitations had stood." In February his troops captured Columbia, South Carolina. Soon they were in North Carolina, advancing relentlessly. In Virginia, Grant's vise grew tighter day by day while the Confederate lines became thinner and more ragged.

Photo Credit: Courtesy of the Library of Congress.

These photos are of Lincoln, when he became president, and shortly before he was assassinated.
Source: (left) ICHi-20265/Photo by Alexander Hesler/Chicago Historical Society.

To Appomattox Court House

On March 4 Lincoln took the presidential oath and delivered his second inaugural address. Photographs taken at about this time show how four years of war had marked him. Somehow he had become both gentle and steel-tough, both haggard and inwardly calm. With victory sure, he spoke for tolerance, mercy, and reconstruction. "Let us judge not," he said after stating again his personal dislike of slavery, "that we be not judged." He urged all Americans to turn without malice to the task of mending the damage and to make a just and lasting peace between the sections.

Now the Confederate troops around Petersburg could no longer withstand the federal pressure. Desperately Lee tried to pull his forces back to the Richmond and Danville Railroad at Lynchburg, but the swift wings of Grant's army enveloped them. Richmond fell on April 3. With fewer than 30,000 men to oppose Grant's 115,000, Lee recognized the futility of further resistance. On April 9 he and Grant met by prearrangement at Appomattox Court House.

It was a scene at once pathetic and inspiring. Lee was noble in defeat; Grant, despite his rough-hewn exterior, was sensitive and magnanimous in victory. "I met you once before, General Lee, while we were serving in Mexico," Grant said after they had shaken hands. "I have always remembered your appearance, and I think I should have recognized you anywhere." They talked briefly of that earlier war, and then, acting on Lincoln's instructions, Grant outlined his terms. All that would be required was that the Confederate soldiers lay down their arms. They could return to their homes in peace. When Lee hinted that his men would profit greatly if allowed to retain possession of their horses, Grant agreed to let them do so.

Winners, Losers, and the Future

And so the war ended in 1865. It had cost the nation more than 600,000 lives, nearly as many as in all other American wars combined. The story of one of the lost thousands must stand for all, Union and Confederate. Jones Budbury, a tall, nineteen-year-old redhead, was working in a Pennsylvania textile mill when the war broke out, and he enlisted at once. His regiment first saw action at Bull Run. He took part in McClellan's Peninsular campaign. He fought at Second Bull Run, at Chancellorsville, and at Gettysburg. A few months after Gettysburg he was wounded in the foot and spent some time in an army hospital. By the spring of 1864 he had risen through the ranks to first sergeant and his hair had turned gray. In June he was captured and sent to Andersonville military prison, near Macon, Georgia, but he fell ill and the Confederates released him. In March 1865 he was back with his regiment in the lines besieging Richmond. On April 6, three days before Lee's surrender, Jones Budbury was killed while pursuing Confederate units near Sayler's Creek, Virginia.

The war also caused enormous property losses, especially in the Confederacy. All the human and material destruction explains the corrosive hatred and bitterness that the war implanted in millions of hearts. The corruption, the gross materialism, and the selfishness generated by wartime conditions were other disagreeable by-products of the conflict. Such sores fester in any society, but the Civil War bred conditions that inflamed and multiplied them. The war produced many examples of

Glory

Glory (1989) tells the story of the 54th Massachusetts Volunteer Infantry, a black regiment, from its establishment in the fall of 1862 through its attack on Fort Wagner, South Carolina, on July 18, 1863.

"Historical accuracy," director Edward Zwick declared, was "the goal of everyone involved in the production." Filmmakers commonly make such assertions, but Zwick proved that he had attended to the historical record. The peak of Shaw's cap was dyed the exact shade of medium green used by officers of the Massachusetts 54th; and when shoes were distributed to the recruits, there were no "lefts" or "rights": Shoes were to shape themselves to either foot from wear.

Zwick's evident commitment to history makes his deviations all the more interesting. The movie begins with a panoramic shot of rolling hills, dotted with tents. Fog blankets the valley and softens the morning light. Then the quiet is shattered by explosions: Soldiers hasten to form ranks, trot toward a battlefield, and charge across it, a young officer in the vanguard. (He is Captain Robert Gould Shaw, played by Matthew Broderick.) The attackers are decimated. Shaw is hit and loses consciousness.

Shaw is sent home to Boston to convalesce. At a reception, Governor Andrew offers the young officer command of the Massachusetts 54th, a black regiment being raised in Boston. Shaw hesitates for a moment. Then he confers privately with another officer, who is appalled.

"I knew how much you'd like to be a colonel, but a colored regiment?"

"I'm gonna do it," Shaw replies.

"You're not serious."

"Yeah."

These scenes contain truths without being entirely truthful. Governor Andrew did offer the commission and Shaw accepted it. But at the time Shaw was in Virginia. Andrew, in Boston, conveyed it through Shaw's father and young Shaw initially refused. Zwick has compressed the story chronologically, squeezing weeks into minutes; and he has

rearranged it geographically to enable Andrew and young Shaw to meet. Such modifications are common in "reel history," and these do not impair historical understanding.

But *Glory* deviates from the historical record in more significant ways. It suggests, for example, that the Massachusetts 54th was composed mostly of former slaves. In fact, most of its volunteers were from northern states and had never been slaves.

The fiction that they had been slaves, however, made it possible for Zwick to examine a larger truth. Of the 178,000 blacks who served in the Union army, fewer than one-fifth were from the North; the great majority *were* former slaves. Nearly 100,000 were recruited from Louisiana, Mississippi, or Tennessee, among the first states occupied by the Union army. *Glory* thus merges the story of the free blacks of the Massachusetts 54th with that of former slaves who were recruited from the Deep South.

Zwick exploited the dramatic potential of the latter groups. How did slaves respond when, having just received their freedom, they were placed under the absolute power of white officers?

Glory develops the question chiefly through the character of Trip (Denzel Washington), a former slave who hates all whites, including Shaw. Shaw illuminates the other side of the question. An abolitionist, he reluctantly decides that former slaves must be whipped (literally) into shape. When Trip sneaks off one night and is captured for desertion, Shaw orders him flogged. When Trip's back is bared, Shaw sees that it is laced with scars from whippings by slave masters. During the flogging, Trip fixes Shaw with a hateful stare, a powerful scene that underscores the movie's central irony: To end slavery, Shaw has become Trip's master while Trip has again become a slave.

Whatever its dramatic merits, the scene is ahistorical. In 1861 Congress had outlawed flogging in the military. Disobedient soldiers were tied in a crouched position, or they were

Matthew Broderick as Robert Gould Shaw, and Denzel Washington as the former slave recruit Trip, in the movie *Glory*.

suspended by their thumbs, toes just touching the ground.

Physical punishment was, in fact, one of the chief sources of contention between ex-slave soldiers and white officers. "I am no slave to be driven," one black recruit informed a brutish commander. When an officer of the 38th Colored Infantry tied a black recruit up by the thumbs, his friends cut him down and forced the officers back with bayonets: "No white son of a bitch can tie a man up here," they declared. The blacks were charged with mutiny and several were executed, an incident that shows that former slaves did not willingly submit to army discipline tainted with racism. Though African Americans constituted only 8 percent of the Union army, 80 percent of those executed for mutiny were black. Many white officers, as the movie suggests, did assert that former slaves must be treated as slaves.

Could such soldiers—black recruits and white officers alike—have been good ones? The movie answers the question by recreating the actual attack on Fort Wagner, the first step in the offensive on Charleston. It shows the blacks of the Massachusetts 54th marching to the front of the line, and forming up along a narrow beach. On Shaw's command, they charge forward. Unlike the white troops in the opening scene, the blacks follow him to the ramparts; when he falls, they continue onward until they are wiped out.

Were the actual soldiers of the Massachusetts 54th as courageous as those in the movie? Shortly after the battle, Lieutenant Iredell Jones, a Confederate officer, reported,

"The negroes fought gallantly, and were headed by as brave a colonel as ever lived." Of the 600 members of the 54th Massachusetts, 40 percent were casualties on that day, an extraordinarily high ratio. But did ex-slaves fight as courageously as the free blacks of the 54th? The answer to this question came not at Fort Wagner, but at other, less publicized battles. A few weeks earlier, for example, several companies of the Louisiana (Colored) Infantry, composed of former slaves who had been in the army only for several weeks, fought off a furious Confederate assault at Milliken's Bend near Vicksburg. The Confederate general was astonished when whites in the Union army fled but the blacks held their ground despite sustaining staggering casualties—45 percent—the highest of any single battle in the war.

Thus while *Glory* is a fictional composite—of free black and ex-slave recruits, and of the assault on Fort Wagner and Milliken's Bend—it conveys a broader truth about black soldiers. Howell Cobb, a Confederate senator from Georgia, declared, "If the black can make a good soldier, our whole system of government is wrong." *Glory* shows that although white officers and black recruits did not form a harmonious team, they together proved that slavery was doomed.

Questions for Discussion
- Was conscription during the Civil War a form of slavery?
- Would free blacks or former slaves more likely have been the better soldiers?

Photo Credit: Photofest.

Photo Credit: Everett Collection.

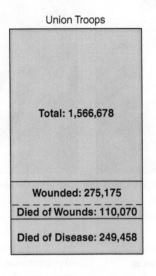

Casualties of the Civil War The Union death rate was 23 percent, the Confederate 24 percent. Twice as many soldiers were killed by disease as were killed by bullets.

Union Troops

Total: 1,566,678

Wounded: 275,175

Died of Wounds: 110,070

Died of Disease: 249,458

Confederate Troops

Total: 1,082,119

Wounded: 100,000

Died of Wounds: 94,000

Died of Disease: 164,000

charity, self-sacrifice, and devotion to duty as well, yet if the general moral atmosphere of the postwar generation can be said to have resulted from the experiences of 1861 to 1865, the effect overall was bad.

What had been obtained at this price? Slavery was dead. Paradoxically, while the war had been fought to preserve the Union, after 1865 the people tended to see the United States not as a union of states but as a nation. After Appomattox, secession was almost literally inconceivable. In a strictly political sense, as Lincoln had predicted from the start, the northern victory heartened friends of republican government and democracy throughout the world. A better-integrated society and a more technically advanced and productive economic system also resulted from the war.

The Americans of 1865 estimated the balance between cost and profit according to their individual fortunes and prejudices. Only the wisest realized that no final accounting could be made until the people had decided what to do with the fruits of victory. That the physical damage would be repaired no one could reasonably

The Meaning of the Civil War for Americans at **myhistorylab.com**

doubt; that even the loss of human resources would be restored in short order was equally apparent. But would the nation make good use of the opportunities the war had made available? What would the former slaves do with freedom? How would whites, northern and southern, react to emancipation? To what end would the new technology and social efficiency be directed? Would the people be able to forget the recent past and fulfill the hopes for which so many brave soldiers had given their "last full measure of devotion"?

Milestones

1861	Confederates attack Fort Sumter; Lincoln calls for 75,000 volunteers	1862	Lincoln's Emancipation Proclamation frees slaves in "areas of rebellion"
	First Battle of Bull Run (Virginia) boosts Confederate morale		Congress passes Homestead, Morrill Land Grant, and Pacific Railway acts
	Lincoln appoints George B. McClellan Union commander	1863	Congress passes Conscription and National Banking acts
	Supreme Court rules against Lincoln's suspension of habeas corpus in *Ex parte Merryman*		Federal troops subdue draft riots in New York City
1862	Confederate Congress passes Conscription Act		Union army defeats Confederates at turning point Battle of Gettysburg, Pennsylvania
	USS *Monitor* defeats Confederate *Merrimack* in first battle between ironclads		Union siege and capture of Vicksburg, Mississippi, gives Union control of entire Mississippi River
	Battle of Shiloh, Tennessee, leaves 23,000 dead, wounded, or missing	1864	Grant pushes deep into Virginia in costly Battles of the Wilderness, Spotsylvania Court House, and Cold Harbor
	Robert E. Lee assumes command of Confederate Army of Northern Virginia		Sherman captures Atlanta, Georgia; marches to sea; captures Savannah
	Lee and Stonewall Jackson defeat huge Union army at Seven Days' Battle for Richmond		Lincoln is reelected president
		1864–1865	Grant takes Petersburg, Virginia, after ten-month siege
	Lee and Jackson defeat Union army at Second Battle of Bull Run	1865	Sherman captures Columbia, South Carolina
	Lee's northern advance is stopped at Battle of Antietam; 22,000 casualties		Lee surrenders to Grant at Appomattox Court House, Virginia

✓ •─[Study and Review at www.myhistorylab.com

Review Questions

1. The introduction to this chapter notes that civil wars, in retrospect, often seem senseless. If the American people had known in advance the terrible cost of its civil war, would it have been fought? Why did each side think it could win?

2. Dwight D. Eisenhower, U.S. general during World War II and subsequently President, once declared that "every war is going to astonish you in the way it occurred and the way it is carried out." What were the astonishing aspects of the Civil War?

3. How did Lincoln's war aims evolve? What were the reasons for and consequences of Lincoln's Emancipation Proclamation?

4. What factors on the home front influenced the course of war?

5. Table 1 summarizes the "turning points" during the Civil War. Which one was the most important?

6. How did the Civil War strengthen the American nation? Was the nation stronger after the war than before?

Key Terms

Anaconda Plan
Copperheads
Emancipation Proclamation
greenbacks

Homestead Act (1862)
Radical Republicans
Sanitary Commission

Reconstruction and the South

((•●─[Hear the Audio at myhistorylab.com

Has your family overcome adversity?

WITH NEARLY $3 BILLION IN ASSETS, OPRAH WINFREY IS THE RICHEST self-made woman in America. Her great-great-grandfather, Constantine Winfrey, was an illiterate slave in Sanford, Mississippi. On gaining his freedom in 1865, he owned little more than a strong back and a knowledge of cotton farming. But within fifteen years, he had learned to read and write and was owner of several farms and over 100 acres of land.

Whoopi Goldberg, another prominent black woman TV host and actress, is the great-great-granddaughter of William Washington and Elsa Tucker, slaves who were living in Alachua County, Florida when Lee surrendered at Appomattox. Over the next decade, the couple fulfilled the demanding provisions of the Southern Homestead Act, passed by the Republican-dominated Congress in 1866.

Chris Rock, comedian and actor, is the great-great-grandson of Julius Caesar Tingman, a slave in South Carolina. In March 1865, a few weeks after Sherman had marched through South Carolina, Tingman joined the U.S. Colored Troops in the Union army. Three years later, at the age of twenty-four, he was elected to the "reconstructed" South Carolina legislature.

Such accounts add another dimension to the usual narrative of the Reconstruction era (1865–1877). The period began with the liberal readmission of southern states to the Union as proposed by Lincoln and his successor, Andrew Johnson. Once readmitted, southern states restricted the rights of former slaves through a series of "**Black Codes.**" A furious Republican Congress overturned white southern rule through a series of laws and constitutional amendments that empowered former slaves—and their Republican allies. A white backlash, often violent, followed Republican rule.

•●─[Read the Document
The Mississippi Black Code, at myhistorylab.com

Ultimately, white political power was restored, and a corrupt bargain secured the presidency for the Republican, Hayes. When Hayes removed Union troops from the South in 1877, Reconstruction was over.

Deprived of federal assistance, former slaves were obliged to make do on their own. Many failed. Only 10 percent of freed slaves acquired farms. But the ancestors of Oprah Winfrey, Whoopi Goldberg, Chris Rock, and many others prove that *some* former slaves succeeded, almost entirely through their own efforts. Harvard historian Louis Henry

From Chapter 15 of *American Destiny: Narrative of a Nation*, Combined Volume, Fourth Edition. Mark C. Carnes and John A. Garraty. Copyright © 2012 by Pearson Education, Inc. Published by Pearson Prentice Hall. All rights reserved.

Gates, Jr., whose *In Search of Our Roots* (2009) recounted their stories and many similar ones, hoped that someday such accounts would move history "from our kitchens or parlors into the texts, ultimately changing the official narrative of American history itself." This chapter describes the era's bitter wrangles and recriminations, its political failures and disappointments, but it also shows that many survived and even flourished during these difficult years.

The Assassination of Lincoln

On April 5, 1865, Abraham Lincoln visited Richmond. The fallen capital lay in ruins, sections blackened by fire, but the president was able to walk the streets unmolested and almost unattended. Everywhere African Americans crowded around him worshipfully; some fell to their knees as he passed, crying "Glory, Hallelujah," hailing him as a messiah. Even white townspeople seemed to have accepted defeat without resentment.

A few days later, in Washington, Lincoln delivered an important speech on Reconstruction, urging compassion and open-mindedness. On April 14 he held a Cabinet meeting at which postwar readjustment was considered at length. That evening, while Lincoln was watching a performance of the play *Our American Cousin* at Ford's Theater, an actor, John Wilkes Booth, slipped into his box and shot him in the back of the head with a small pistol. Early the next morning, without having regained consciousness, Lincoln died.

Photo Credit: CORBIS-NY.

Richmond, Virginia lies in ruins in April, 1865 at the time of Lincoln's visit—and a few days before his assassination.

The murder was part of a complicated plot organized by die-hard pro-Southerners. One of Booth's accomplices went to the home of Secretary of State William Seward and stabbed him—Seward recovered from his wounds. A third conspirator, assigned to kill Vice President Andrew Johnson, changed his mind and fled Washington. Seldom have fanatics displayed so little understanding of their own interests, for with Lincoln perished the South's best hope for a mild peace. After his body had been taken home to Illinois, the national mood hardened; apparently the awesome drama was still unfolding—retribution and a final humbling of the South were inevitable.

Presidential Reconstruction

Despite its bloodiness, the Civil War had caused less intersectional hatred than might have been expected. The legal questions related to bringing the defeated states back into the Union, however, were extremely complex. Since Southerners believed that secession was legal, logic should have compelled them to argue that they were out of the Union and would thus have to be formally readmitted. Northerners should have taken the contrary position, for they had fought to prove that secession was illegal. Yet the people of both sections did just the opposite. Senator Charles Sumner and Congressman Thaddeus Stevens, who in 1861 had been uncompromising expounders of the theory that the Union was indissoluble, now insisted that the Confederate states had "committed suicide" and should be treated like "conquered provinces."

The process of readmission began in 1862, when Lincoln reappointed provisional governors for those parts of the South that had been occupied by federal troops. On December 8, 1863, he issued a proclamation setting forth a general policy. With the exception of high Confederate officials and a few other special groups, all Southerners could reinstate themselves as United States citizens by taking a simple loyalty oath. When, in any state, a number equal to 10 percent of those voting in the 1860 election had taken this oath, they could set up a state government. Under this **Ten Percent Plan**, such governments had to be republican in form, must recognize the "permanent freedom" of the slaves, and must provide for black education. The plan, however, did not require that blacks be given the right to vote.

President Andrew Johnson poses regally with carefully manicured fingernails. Although Johnson hated southern aristocrats, he sometimes craved their approval.

Photo Credit: Arthur Stumpf, *Andrew Johnson*, 1808–1875. National Portrait Gallery, Smithsonian Institution/Art Resource, NY.

The Ten Percent Plan reflected Lincoln's lack of vindictiveness and his political wisdom. He realized that any government based on such a small minority of the population would be, as he put it, merely "a tangible nucleus which the remainder . . . may rally around as fast as it can," a sort of puppet regime, like the paper government established in those sections of Virginia under federal control.[1] The regimes established under this plan in Tennessee, Louisiana, and Arkansas bore, in the president's mind, the same relation to finally reconstructed states that an egg bears to a chicken. "We shall sooner have the fowl by hatching it than by smashing it," he remarked. He knew that eventually representatives of the southern states would again be sitting in Congress, and he wished to lay the groundwork for a strong Republican party in the section. Yet he realized that Congress had no intention of seating representatives from the "10 percent" states at once.

The Radicals in Congress disliked the Ten Percent Plan, partly because of its moderation and partly because it enabled Lincoln to determine Union policy toward the recaptured regions. In July 1864 they passed the **Wade-Davis Bill**, which provided for constitutional conventions only after a majority of the others in a southern state had taken a loyalty oath. Confederate officials and anyone who had "voluntarily borne arms against the United States" were barred from voting in the election or serving at the convention. Besides prohibiting slavery, the new state constitutions would have to repudiate Confederate debts. Lincoln disposed of the Wade-Davis Bill with a pocket veto and that's where matters stood when Andrew Johnson became president following the assassination.

Lincoln had picked Johnson for a running mate in 1864 because he was a border-state Unionist Democrat and something of a hero as a result of his courageous service as military governor of Tennessee. His political strength came from the poor whites and yeomen farmers of eastern Tennessee, and he was fond of extolling the common man and attacking "stuck-up aristocrats."

Johnson was a Democrat, but because of his record and his reassuring penchant for excoriating southern aristocrats, the Republicans in Congress were ready to cooperate with him. "Johnson, we have faith in you," said Senator Ben Wade, author of the Wade-Davis Bill, the day after Lincoln's death. "By the gods, there will be no trouble now in running the government!"

Johnson's reply, "Treason must be made infamous," delighted the Radicals, but the president proved temperamentally unable to work with them. Like Randolph of Roanoke, his antithesis intellectually and socially, opposition was his specialty; he soon alienated every powerful Republican in Washington.

Radical Republicans listened to Johnson's diatribes against secessionists and the great planters and assumed that he was anti-southern. Nothing could have been further from the truth. He had great respect for states' rights and he shared most of his poor white Tennessee constituents' contempt of blacks. "Damn the negroes, I am fighting these traitorous aristocrats, their masters," he told a friend during the war. "I wish to God," he said on another occasion, "every head of a family in the United States had one slave to take the drudgery and menial service off his family."

The new president did not want to injure or humiliate all white Southerners. He issued an amnesty proclamation only slightly more rigorous than Lincoln's. It assumed, correctly

---

[1] By approving the separation of the western counties that had refused to secede, this government had provided a legal pretext for the creation of West Virginia in 1863.

enough, that with the war over most southern voters would freely take the loyalty oath; thus it contained no 10 percent clause. More classes of Confederates, including those who owned taxable property in excess of $20,000, were excluded from the general pardon. By the time Congress convened in December 1865, all the southern states had organized governments, ratified the **Thirteenth Amendment** abolishing slavery, and elected senators and representatives. Johnson promptly recommended these new governments to the attention of Congress.

Republican Radicals

Peace found the Republicans in Congress no more united than they had been during the war. A small group of "ultra" Radicals were demanding immediate and absolute civil and political equality for blacks; they should be given, for example, the vote, a plot of land, and access to a decent education. Senator Sumner led this faction. A second group of Radicals, headed by Thaddeus Stevens in the House and Ben Wade in the Senate, agreed with the ultras' objectives but were prepared to accept half a loaf if necessary to win the support of less radical colleagues.

Nearly all Radicals distinguished between the "natural" God-given rights described in the Declaration of Independence, and social equality. The moderate Republicans wanted to protect the former slaves from exploitation and guarantee their basic rights but were unprepared to push for full political equality. A handful of Republicans sided with the Democrats in support of Johnson's approach, but all the rest insisted at least on the minimal demands of the moderates. Thus Johnsonian Reconstruction was doomed.

Johnson's proposal had no chance in Congress for reasons having little to do with black rights. The Thirteenth Amendment had the effect of increasing the representation of the southern states in Congress because it made the Three-fifths Compromise meaningless. Henceforth those who had been slaves would be counted as whole persons in apportioning seats in the House of Representatives. If Congress seated the Southerners, the balance of power might swing to the Democrats. To expect the Republicans to surrender power in such a fashion was unrealistic. Former Copperheads gushing with extravagant praise for Johnson put them instantly on guard.

Congress Rejects Johnsonian Reconstruction

The Republicans in Congress rejected Johnsonian Reconstruction. Quickly they created a joint committee on Reconstruction, headed by Senator William P. Fessenden of Maine, a moderate, to study the question of readmitting the southern states.

The committee held public hearings that produced much evidence of the mistreatment of blacks. Colonel George A. Custer, stationed in Texas, testified: "It is of weekly, if not of daily occurrence that Freedmen are murdered." The nurse Clara Barton told a gruesome tale about a pregnant woman who had been brutally whipped. Others described the intimidation of blacks by poor whites. The hearings strengthened the Radicals, who had been claiming all along that the South was perpetuating slavery under another name.

President Johnson's attitude speeded the swing toward the Radical position. While the hearings were in progress, Congress passed a bill expanding and extending the **Freedmen's Bureau**, which had been established in March 1865 to care for refugees. The bureau, a branch of the war department, was already exercising considerable coercive and supervisory power in the South. Now Congress sought to add to its authority in order to protect the black population. Although the bill had wide support, Johnson vetoed it, arguing that it was an unconstitutional extension of military authority in peacetime. Congress then passed a Civil Rights Act that, besides declaring specifically that blacks were citizens of the United States, denied the states the power to restrict their rights to testify in court, to make contracts for their labor, and to hold property. In other words, it put teeth in the Thirteenth Amendment.

Once again the president refused to go along, although his veto was sure to drive more moderates into the arms of the Radicals. On April 9, 1866, Congress repassed the Civil Rights Act by a two-thirds majority, the first time in American history that a major piece of legislation became law over the veto of a president. This event marked a revolution in the history of Reconstruction. Thereafter Congress, not President Johnson, had the upper hand.

In the clash between the president and Congress, Johnson was his own worst enemy. His language was often intemperate, his handling of opponents inept, his analysis of southern conditions incorrect. He had assumed that the small southern farmers who made up the majority in the Confederacy shared his prejudices against the planter class. They did not, as their choices in the postwar elections demonstrated.

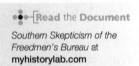

Read the Document

Southern Skepticism of the Freedmen's Bureau at **myhistorylab.com**

The president also misread northern opinion. He believed that Congress had no right to pass laws affecting the South before southern representatives had been readmitted to Congress. However, in the light of the refusal of most southern whites to grant any real power or responsibility to the freedmen (an attitude that Johnson did not condemn), the public would not accept this point of view. Johnson placed his own judgment over that of the overwhelming majority of northern voters, and this was a great error, morally and tactically. By encouraging white Southerners to resist efforts to improve the lot of blacks, Johnson played into the hands of the Radicals.

The Radicals encountered grave problems in fighting for their program. Northerners might object to the Black Codes and to seating "rebels" in Congress, but few believed in racial equality. Between 1865 and 1868, Wisconsin, Minnesota, Connecticut, Nebraska, New Jersey, Ohio, Michigan, and Pennsylvania all rejected bills granting blacks the vote.

The Radicals were in effect demanding not merely equal rights for freedmen but extra rights; not merely the vote but special protection of that right against the pressure that southern whites would surely apply to undermine it. This idea flew in the face of conventional American beliefs in equality before the law and individual self-reliance. Such protection would involve interference by the federal government in local affairs, a concept at variance with American practice. Events were to show that the Radicals were correct—that what amounted to a political revolution in state–federal relations was essential if blacks were to achieve real equality. But in the climate of that day their proposals encountered bitter resistance, and not only from white Southerners.

Thus, while the Radicals sought partisan advantage in their battle with Johnson and sometimes played on war-bred passions in achieving their ends, they were taking large political risks in defense of genuinely held principles.

The Fourteenth Amendment

In June 1866 Congress submitted to the states a new amendment to the Constitution. The **Fourteenth Amendment** was, in the context of the times, a truly radical measure. Never before had newly freed slaves been granted significant political rights. For example, in the British Caribbean sugar islands, where slavery had been abolished in the 1830s, stiff property qualifications and poll taxes kept freedmen from voting. The Fourteenth Amendment was also a milestone along the road to the centralization of political power in the United States because it reduced the power of all the states. In this sense it confirmed the great change wrought by the Civil War: the growth of a more complex, more closely integrated social and economic structure requiring closer national supervision. Few people understood this aspect of the amendment at the time.

Read the Document

13th, 14th, and 15th Amendments at **myhistorylab.com**

First the amendment supplied a broad definition of American citizenship: "All persons born or naturalized in the United States, and subject to the jurisdiction thereof, are citizens of the United States and of the State wherein they reside." Obviously this included blacks. Then it struck at discriminatory legislation like the Black Codes: "No State shall make or enforce any law which shall abridge the privileges or immunities of citizens of the United States; nor shall any State deprive any person of life, liberty, or property, without due process of law." The next section attempted to force the southern states to permit blacks to vote. If a state denied the vote to any class of its adult male citizens, its representation was to be reduced proportionately. Under another clause, former federal officials who had served the Confederacy were barred from holding either state or federal office unless specifically pardoned by a two-thirds vote of Congress. Finally, the Confederate debt was repudiated.

While the amendment did not specifically outlaw segregation or prevent a state from disenfranchising blacks, the southern states would have none of it. Without them the necessary three-fourths majority of the states could not be obtained.

President Johnson vowed to make the choice between the Fourteenth Amendment and his own policy the main issue of the 1866 congressional elections. He embarked on "a swing around the circle" to rally the public to his cause. He failed dismally. Northern women objected to the implication in the amendment that black men were more fitted to vote than white women, but a large majority of northern voters was determined that African Americans must have at least formal legal equality. The Republicans won better than two-thirds of the seats in both houses, together with control of all the northern state governments. Johnson emerged from the campaign discredited, the Radicals stronger and determined to have their way. The southern states, Congressman James A. Garfield of Ohio said in February 1867, have "flung back into our teeth the magnanimous offer of a generous nation. It is now our turn to act."

The Reconstruction Acts

Had the southern states been willing to accept the Fourteenth Amendment, coercive measures might have been avoided. Their recalcitrance and continuing indications that local authorities were persecuting blacks finally led to the passage, on March 2, 1867, of the First Reconstruction Act. This law divided the former Confederacy—exclusive of Tennessee, which had ratified the Fourteenth Amendment—into five military districts, each controlled by a major general. It gave these officers almost dictatorial power to protect the civil rights of "all persons," maintain order, and supervise the administration of justice. To rid themselves of military rule, the former states were required to adopt new state constitutions guaranteeing blacks the right to vote and disenfranchising broad classes of ex-Confederates. If the new constitutions proved satisfactory to Congress, and if the new governments ratified the Fourteenth Amendment, their representatives would be admitted to Congress and military rule ended. Johnson's veto of the act was easily overridden.

Although drastic, the Reconstruction Act was so vague that it proved unworkable. Military control was easily established. But in deference to moderate Republican views, the law had not spelled out the process by which the new constitutions were to be drawn up. Southern whites preferred the status quo, even under army control, to enfranchising blacks and retiring their own respected leaders. They made no effort to follow the steps laid down in the law. Congress therefore passed a second act, requiring the military authorities to register voters and supervise the election of delegates to constitutional conventions. A third act further clarified procedures.

See the Map
Reconstruction at myhistorylab.com

Still white Southerners resisted. The laws required that the constitutions be approved by a majority of the registered voters. Simply by staying away from the polls, whites prevented ratification in state after state. At last, in March 1868, a full year after the First Reconstruction Act, Congress changed the rules again. The constitutions were to be ratified by a majority of the voters. In June 1868 Arkansas, having fulfilled the requirements, was readmitted to the Union, and by July a sufficient number of states had ratified the Fourteenth Amendment to make it part of the Constitution. But it was not until July 1870 that the last southern state, Georgia, qualified to the satisfaction of Congress.

Congress Supreme

To carry out this program in the face of determined southern resistance required a degree of single-mindedness over a long period seldom demonstrated by an American legislature. The persistence resulted in part from the suffering and frustrations of the war years. The refusal of the South to accept the spirit of even the mild reconstruction designed by Johnson goaded the North to ever more overbearing efforts to bring the ex-Confederates to heel. President Johnson's stubbornness also influenced the Republicans. They became obsessed with the need to defeat him. The unsettled times and the large Republican majorities, always threatened by the possibility of a Democratic resurgence if "unreconstructed" southern congressmen were readmitted, sustained their determination.

These considerations led Republicans to attempt a kind of grand revision of the federal government, one that almost destroyed the balance between judicial, executive, and legislative power established in 1789. A series of measures passed between 1866 and 1868 increased the authority of Congress over the army, over the process of amending the Constitution, and over Cabinet members and lesser appointive officers. Even the Supreme Court was affected. Its size was reduced and its jurisdiction over civil rights cases limited. Finally, in a showdown caused by emotion more than by practical considerations, the Republicans attempted to remove President Johnson from office.

The chief issue was the Tenure of Office Act of 1867, which prohibited the president from removing officials who had been appointed with the consent of the Senate without first obtaining Senate approval. In February 1868 Johnson "violated" this act by dismissing Secretary of War Edwin M. Stanton, who had been openly in sympathy with the Radicals for some time. The House, acting under the procedure set up in the Constitution for removing the president, promptly impeached him before the bar of the Senate, Chief Justice Salmon P. Chase presiding.

In the trial, Johnson's lawyers easily established that he had removed Stanton only in an effort to prove the Tenure of Office Act unconstitutional. They demonstrated that the act did not protect Stanton to begin with, since it gave Cabinet members tenure "during the term of the President by whom they may have been appointed," and Stanton had been appointed in 1862, during Lincoln's first term!

Nevertheless the Radicals pressed the charges (eleven separate articles) relentlessly. Tremendous pressure was applied to the handful of Republican senators who were unwilling to disregard the evidence.

Seven of them resisted to the end, and the Senate failed by a single vote to convict Johnson. This was probably fortunate. The trial weakened the presidency, but if Johnson had been forced from office on such flimsy grounds, the independence of the executive might have been permanently undermined. Then the legislative branch would have become supreme.

The Fifteenth Amendment

The failure of the impeachment did not affect the course of Reconstruction. The president was acquitted on May 16, 1868. A few days later, the Republican National Convention nominated General Ulysses S. Grant for the presidency. At the Democratic convention Johnson had considerable support, but the delegates nominated Horatio Seymour, a former governor of New York. In November Grant won an easy victory in the Electoral College, 214 to 80, but the popular vote was close: 3 million to 2.7 million. Although he would probably have carried the Electoral College in any case, Grant's margin in the popular vote was supplied by southern blacks enfranchised under the Reconstruction acts, about 450,000 of whom supported him. A majority of white voters probably preferred Seymour. Since many citizens undoubtedly voted Republican because of personal admiration for General Grant, the election statistics suggest that a substantial white majority opposed the policies of the Radicals.

The Reconstruction acts and the ratification of the Fourteenth Amendment achieved the purpose of enabling black Southerners to vote. The Radicals, however, were

Photo Credit: Private Collection/Photo © Christie's Images/ The Bridgeman Art Library.

Thomas Waterman Wood, a Northerner, painted this hopeful interpretation of Reconstruction, *His First Vote* (1868).

not satisfied; despite the unpopularity of the idea in the North, they wished to guarantee the right of blacks to vote in every state. Another amendment seemed the only way to accomplish this objective, but passage of such an amendment appeared impossible. The Republican platform in the 1868 election had smugly distinguished between blacks voting in the South.

However, after the election had demonstrated how important the black vote could be, Republican strategy shifted. Grant had carried Indiana by fewer than 10,000 votes and lost New York by a similar number. If blacks in these and other closely divided states had voted, Republican strength would have been greatly enhanced.

Suddenly Congress blossomed with suffrage amendments. After considerable bickering over details, the **Fifteenth Amendment** was sent to the states for ratification in February 1869. It forbade all the states to deny the vote to anyone "on account of race, color, or previous condition of servitude." Once again nothing was said about denial of the vote on the basis of sex, which caused feminists, such as Elizabeth Cady Stanton, to be even more outraged than they had been by the Fourteenth Amendment.

Most southern states, still under federal pressure, ratified the amendment swiftly. The same was true in most of New England and in some western states. Bitter battles were waged in Connecticut, New York, Pennsylvania, and the states immediately north of the Ohio River, but by March 1870 most of them had ratified the amendment and it became part of the Constitution.

When the Fifteenth Amendment went into effect, President Grant called it "the greatest civil change and . . . the most important event that has occurred since the nation came to life." The American Anti-Slavery Society formally dissolved itself, its work apparently completed. "The Fifteenth Amendment confers upon the African race the care of its own destiny," Radical Congressman James A. Garfield wrote proudly after the amendment was ratified.

"Black Republican" Reconstruction: Scalawags and Carpetbaggers

The Radicals had at last succeeded in imposing their will on the South. Throughout the region former slaves had real political influence; they voted, held office, and exercised the "privileges" and enjoyed the "immunities" guaranteed them by the Fourteenth Amendment. Nearly all voted Republican.

The spectacle of blacks not five years removed from slavery in positions of power and responsibility attracted much attention. But the real rulers of the "black Republican" governments were white: the **scalawags**—Southerners willing to cooperate with the Republicans because they accepted the results of the war and wished to advance their own interests—and the **carpetbaggers**—Northerners who went to the South as idealists to help the freed slaves as employees of the federal government, or more commonly as settlers hoping to improve themselves.

Although scalawags were by far the more numerous, the carpetbaggers were a particularly varied lot. Most had mixed motives for coming south and personal gain was certainly among them. But so were opposition to slavery and the belief that blacks deserved to be treated decently and given a chance to get ahead in the world.

Many northern blacks became carpetbaggers: former Union soldiers, missionaries from northern black churches, and also teachers, lawyers, and other members of the small northern black professional class. Many of these became officeholders, but like southern black politicians their influence was limited.

That blacks should fail to dominate southern governments is certainly understandable. They lacked experience in politics and were mostly poor and uneducated. They were nearly everywhere a minority. Those blacks who held office during Reconstruction tended to be better educated and more prosperous than most southern blacks.

In South Carolina and elsewhere, blacks proved in the main to be able and conscientious public servants. Even at the local level, where the quality of officials was usually poor, there was little difference in the degree of competence displayed by white and black officeholders. In power, the blacks were not vindictive; by and large they did not seek to restrict the rights of ex-Confederates.

Not all black legislators and administrators were paragons of virtue. In South Carolina, despite their control of the legislature, they broke up into factions repeatedly and failed to press for laws that would improve the lot of poor black farm workers. Waste and corruption were common during Reconstruction governments. Half the budget of Louisiana in some years went for salaries and "mileage" for representatives and their staffs. A South Carolina legislator was voted an additional $1,000 in salary after he lost that sum betting on a horse race.

However, the corruption must be seen in perspective. The big thieves were nearly always white; blacks got mostly crumbs. Furthermore, graft and callous disregard of the public interest characterized government in every section and at every level during the decade after Appomattox. Big-city bosses in the North embezzled sums that dwarfed the most brazen southern frauds. The New York City Tweed Ring probably made off with more money than all the southern thieves, black and white, combined. While the

Photo Credit: The Granger Collection, New York.

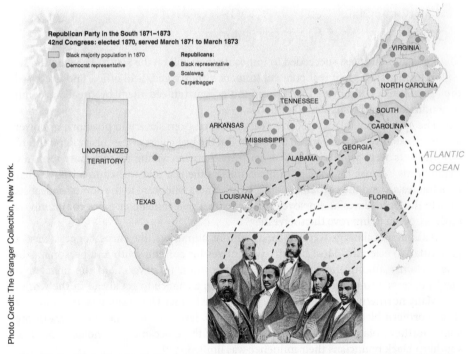

Republicans Win in Deep South The six black members of the House of Representatives in 1871 are from left to right: Benjamin Turner, Robert De Large, Josiah Wells, Jefferson Long, Joseph Rainey, Robert Brown Elliott. Each is linked to his district; the member in the blue coat—center—is not connected to a "black" dot. A special Republican primary replaced him with a scalawag.

evidence does not justify the southern corruption, it suggests that the unique features of Reconstruction politics—black suffrage, military supervision, and carpetbagger and scalawag influence—do not explain it.

In fact, the Radical southern governments accomplished a great deal. They spent money freely but not entirely wastefully. Tax rates zoomed, but the money financed the repair and expansion of the South's dilapidated railroad network, rebuilt crumbling levees, and expanded social services. Before the Civil War, southern planters possessed a disproportionate share of political as well as economic power, and they spent relatively little public money on education and public services of all kinds.

During Reconstruction an enormous gap had to be filled, and it took money to fill it. The Freedmen's Bureau made a major contribution. Northern religious and philanthropic organizations also did important work. Eventually, however, the state governments established and supported hospitals, asylums, and systems of free public education that, while segregated, greatly benefited everyone, whites as well as blacks. Much state money was also spent on economic development: land reclamation, repairing and expanding the war-ravaged railroads, maintaining levees.

Watch the Video
The Schools that the Civil War & Reconstruction created at **myhistorylab.com**

The Ravaged Land

The South's grave economic problems complicated the rebuilding of its political system. The section had never been as prosperous as the North, and wartime destruction left it desperately poor by any standard. In the long run the abolition of slavery released immeasurable quantities of human energy previously stifled, but the immediate effect was to create confusion. Freedom to move without a pass, to "see the world," was one of the former slaves' most cherished benefits of emancipation. Understandably, many at first equated legal freedom with freedom from having to earn a living, a tendency reinforced for a time by the willingness of the Freedmen's Bureau to provide rations and other forms of relief in war-devastated areas. Most, however, soon accepted the fact that they must earn a living; a small plot of land of their own ("40 acres and a mule") would complete their independence.

This objective was forcefully supported by the relentless Congressman Thaddeus Stevens, whose hatred of the planter class was pathological. "The property of the chief rebels should be seized," he stated. If the lands of the richest "70,000 proud, bloated and defiant rebels" were confiscated, the federal government would obtain 394 million acres. Every adult male ex-slave could easily be supplied with 40 acres. The beauty of his scheme, Stevens insisted, was that "nine-tenths of the [southern] people would remain untouched." Dispossessing the great planters would make the South "a safe republic," its lands cultivated by "the free labor of intelligent citizens." If the plan drove the planters into exile, "all the better."

Although Stevens's figures were faulty, many Radicals agreed with him. "We must see that the freedmen are established on the soil," Senator Sumner declared. "The great plantations, which have been so many nurseries of the rebellion, must be broken up, and the freedmen must have the pieces." Stevens, Sumner, and others who wanted to give land to the freedmen weakened their case by associating it with the idea of punishing the former rebels; the average American had too much respect for property rights to support a policy of confiscation.

The former slaves had either to agree to work for their former owners or strike out on their own. White planters, influenced by the precipitous decline of sugar production in Jamaica and other Caribbean islands that had followed the abolition of slavery there, expected freed blacks to be incapable of self-directed effort. If allowed to become independent farmers, they would either starve to death or descend into barbarism. Of course the blacks did neither. True, the output of cotton and other southern staples declined precipitously after slavery was abolished. Observers soon came to the conclusion that a free black produced much less than a slave had produced. "You can't get only about two-thirds as much out of 'em now as you could when they were slaves," an Arkansas planter complained.

View the Image
Five Generations of a Slave Family at **myhistorylab.com**

However, the decline in productivity was not caused by the inability of free blacks to work independently. They simply chose no longer to work like slaves. They let their children play instead of forcing them into the fields. Mothers devoted more time to childcare and housework, less to farm labor. Elderly blacks worked less.

Noting these changes, white critics spoke scornfully of black laziness and shiftlessness. "You cannot make the negro work without physical compulsion," was the common view. Even General Oliver O. Howard, head of the Freedmen's Bureau, used the phrase "wholesome compulsion" in describing the policy of forcing blacks to sign exploitive labor contracts. Moreover, studies show that emancipated blacks earned almost 30 percent more than the value of the subsistence provided by their former masters.

Sharecropping and the Crop-Lien System

Before the passage of the Reconstruction acts, plantation owners tried to farm their land with gang labor, the same system as before, only now paying wages to the former slaves. But blacks did not like working for wages because it kept them under the direction of whites and thus reminded them of slavery. They wanted to be independent, to manage not merely their free time but their entire lives for themselves.

Quite swiftly, a new agricultural system known as **sharecropping** emerged. Instead of cultivating the land by gang labor as in antebellum times, planters broke up their estates into small units and established on each a black family. The planter provided housing, agricultural implements, draft animals, seed, and other supplies, and the family provided labor. The crop was divided between them, usually on a fifty-fifty basis. If the landlord supplied only land and housing, the laborer got a larger share. This was called share tenancy.

Read the Document
A Sharecrop Contract at **myhistorylab.com**

Sharecropping gave blacks the day-to-day control of their lives that they craved and the hope of earning enough to buy a small farm. Many former slaves succeeded, as evidenced by the accounts narrated at the outset of this chapter. Oprah Winfrey's great-great-grandfather bought several plots of land and eventually moved a schoolhouse to his property so that black children in Sanford, Mississippi, could get an education. But not all managed to climb the first rungs into the middle class. As late as 1880 blacks owned less than 10 percent of the agricultural land in the South, although they made up more than half of the region's farm population.

Many white farmers in the South were also trapped by the sharecropping system and by white efforts to keep blacks in a subordinate position. New fencing laws kept them from grazing livestock on undeveloped land, a practice common before the Civil War. But the main cause of southern rural poverty for whites as well as for blacks was the lack of enough capital to finance the sharecropping system. Like their colonial ancestors, the landowners had to borrow against October's harvest to pay for April's seed. Thus the **crop-lien system** developed.

Under the crop-lien system, both landowner and sharecropper depended on credit supplied by local bankers, merchants, and storekeepers for everything from seed, tools, and fertilizer to overalls, coffee, and salt. Crossroads stores proliferated, and a new class of small merchants appeared. The prices of goods sold on credit were high, adding to the burden borne by the rural population. The small southern merchants were almost equally victimized by the system, for they also lacked capital, bought goods on credit, and had to pay high interest rates.

Seen in broad perspective, the situation is not difficult to understand. The South, drained of every resource by the war, was competing for funds with the North and West, both vigorous and expanding and therefore voracious consumers of capital. Reconstruction, in the literal sense of the word, was accomplished chiefly at the expense of the standard of living of the producing classes. The crop-lien system and the small

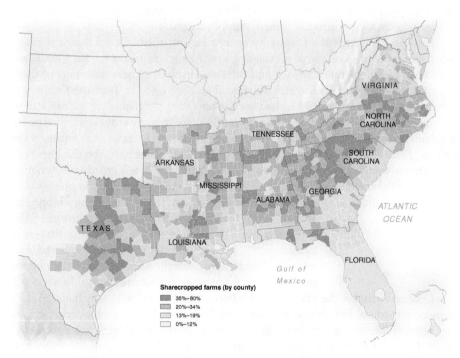

Sharecropping, 1880 Sharecropping became especially common in areas outside of the cotton belt—eastern Texas, upland Alabama, and North Carolina.

storekeeper were only agents of an economic process dictated by national, perhaps even worldwide, conditions.

Compared with the rest of the country, progress was slow. Just before the Civil War cotton harvests averaged about 4 million bales. During the conflict, output fell to about half a million, and the former Confederate states did not enjoy a 4-million-bale year again until 1870. In contrast, national wheat production in 1859 was 175 million bushels and in 1878, 449 million. About 7,000 miles of railroad were built in the South between 1865 and 1879; in the rest of the nation nearly 45,000 miles of track were laid.

But in the late 1870s, cotton production revived. It soon regained, and thereafter long retained, its title as "king" of the southern economy. This was true in large measure because of the crop-lien system.

The White Backlash

Radical southern governments could sustain themselves only as long as they had the support of a significant proportion of the white population, for except in South Carolina and Louisiana, the blacks were not numerous enough to win elections alone. The key to survival lay in the hands of the wealthy merchants and planters, mostly former Whigs. People of this sort had nothing to fear from black economic competition. Taking a broad view, they could see that improving the lot of the former slaves would benefit all classes.

Southern white Republicans used the Union League of America, a patriotic club founded during the war, to control the black vote. Employing secret rituals, exotic symbols, and other paraphernalia calculated to impress unsophisticated people, they enrolled the freedmen in droves and marched them to the polls en masse.

Powerless to check the League by open methods, dissident Southerners established a number of secret terrorist societies, bearing such names as the **Ku Klux Klan**, the Knights of the White Camelia, and the Pale Faces. The most notorious of these organizations was the Klan, which originated in Tennessee in 1866. At first it was purely a social club, but by 1868 it had been taken over by vigilante types dedicated to driving blacks out of politics, and it was spreading rapidly across the South. Sheet-clad nightriders roamed the countryside, frightening the impressionable and chastising the defiant. Klansmen, using a weird mumbo jumbo and claiming to be the ghosts of Confederate soldiers, spread horrendous rumors and published broadsides designed to persuade the freedmen that it was unhealthy for them to participate in politics.

When intimidation failed, the Klansmen resorted to force. After being whipped by one group in Tennessee, a recently elected justice of the peace reported, "They said they had nothing particular against me . . . but they did not intend any nigger to hold office." In hundreds of cases the KKK murdered their opponents, often in the most gruesome manner.

Read the Document

Accounts from Victims of the Ku Klux Klan at myhistorylab.com

Congress struck at the Klan with three **Force Acts** (1870–1871), which placed elections under federal jurisdiction and imposed fines and prison sentences on persons convicted of interfering with any citizen's exercise of the franchise. Troops were dispatched to areas where the Klan was strong, and by 1872 the federal authorities had arrested enough Klansmen to break up the organization.

Nevertheless the Klan contributed substantially to the destruction of Radical regimes in the South. Its depredations weakened the will of white Republicans (few of whom really believed in racial equality), and it intimidated many blacks. The fact that the army had to be called in to suppress it was a glaring illustration of the weakness of the Reconstruction governments.

Gradually it became respectable to intimidate black voters. Beginning in Mississippi in 1874, terrorism spread through the South. Instead of hiding behind masks and operating in the dark, these terrorists donned red shirts, organized into military companies, and paraded openly. Mississippi redshirts seized militant blacks and whipped them publicly. Killings were frequent. When blacks dared to fight back, heavily armed whites put them to rout. In other states similar results followed.

Before long the blacks learned to stay home on election day. One by one, "Conservative" parties—Democratic in national affairs—took over southern state governments. Intimidation was only a partial explanation of this development. The increasing solidarity of whites, northern and southern, was equally significant.

The North had subjected the South to control from Washington while preserving state sovereignty in the North itself. In the long run this discrimination proved unworkable. Many Northerners had supported the Radical policy only out of irritation with President Johnson. After his retirement their enthusiasm waned. The war was fading into the past and with it the worst of the anger it had generated.

Northern voters could still be stirred by references to the sacrifices Republicans had made to save the Union and by reminders that the Democratic party was the organization of rebels, Copperheads, and the Ku Klux Klan. "If the Devil himself were at the helm of the ship of state," wrote the novelist Lydia Maria Child in 1872, "my conscience would not allow me to aid in removing him to make room for the Democratic party." Yet emotional appeals could not convince Northerners that it was still necessary to maintain a large army in the South. In 1869 the occupying forces were down to 11,000 men. After Klan disruption and intimidation had made a farce of the 1874 elections in Mississippi, Governor Ames appealed to Washington for help. President Grant's attorney general, Edwards Pierrepont, refused to act. "The whole public are tired out with these autumnal outbreaks in the South," he told Ames. "Preserve the peace by the forces of your own state."

Nationalism was reasserting itself. Had not Washington and Jefferson been Virginians? Was not Andrew Jackson Carolina-born? Since most Northerners had little real love or respect for African Americans, their interest in racial equality flagged once they felt reasonably certain that blacks would not be re-enslaved if left to their own devices in the South.

Another, much subtler force was also at work. The prewar Republican party had stressed the common interest of workers, manufacturers, and farmers in a free and mobile society, a land of equal opportunity where all could work in harmony. Southern whites had insisted that laborers must be disciplined if large enterprises were to be run efficiently. By the 1870s, as large industrial enterprises developed in the northern states, the thinking of business leaders changed—the southern argument began to make sense to them, and they became more sympathetic to the southern demand for more control over "their" labor force.

An 1872 Grant campaign poster of "Our Three Great Presidents" at best got it about two-thirds right.

Photo Credit: The Granger Collection, New York.

Grant as President

Other matters occupied the attention of northern voters. The expansion of industry and the rapid development of the West, stimulated by a new wave of railroad building, loomed more important to many than the fortunes of the former slaves. Beginning in 1873, when a stock market panic struck at public confidence, economic difficulties plagued the country and provoked another debate over the tariff.

Grant's most serious weakness as president was his failure to deal effectively with economic and social problems, what injured him and the Republicans most was his inability to cope with government corruption. The worst of the scandals did not become public knowledge during Grant's first term. However, in 1872 Republican reformers, alarmed by rumors of corruption and disappointed by Grant's failure to press for civil service reform, organized the Liberal Republican party and nominated Horace Greeley, the able but eccentric editor of the *New York Tribune*, for president.

The Liberal Republicans were mostly well-educated, socially prominent types—editors, college presidents, economists, along with a sprinkling of businessmen and politicians. Their liberalism was of the laissez-faire variety; they were for low tariffs and sound money, and against what they called "class legislation," meaning measures benefiting particular groups, whether labor unions or railroad companies or farm organizations. Nearly all had supported Reconstruction at the start, but by the early 1870s most were including southern blacks among the special interests that ought to be left to their own devices. Their observation of urban corruption and of unrestricted immigration led them to disparage universal suffrage, which, one of them said, "can only mean in plain English the government of ignorance and vice."

The Democrats also nominated Greeley in 1872, although he had devoted his political life to flailing the Democratic party in the *Tribune*. That surrender to expediency, together with Greeley's temperamental unsuitability for the presidency, made the campaign a fiasco for the reformers. Grant triumphed easily, with a popular majority of nearly 800,000.

Nevertheless, the defection of the Liberal Republicans hurt the Republican party in Congress. In the 1874 elections, no longer hampered as in the presidential contest by Greeley's notoriety and Grant's fame, the Democrats carried the House of Representatives. It was clear that the days of military rule in the South were ending. By the end of 1875 only three southern states—South Carolina, Florida, and Louisiana—were still under Republican control.

The Republican party in the South was "dead as a doornail," a reporter noted. He reflected the opinion of thousands when he added, "We ought to have a sound sensible republican . . . for the next President as a measure of safety; but only on the condition of absolute noninterference in Southern local affairs, for which there is no further need or excuse."

The Disputed Election of 1876

Against this background the presidential election of 1876 took place. Since corruption in government was the most widely discussed issue, the Republicans passed over their most attractive political personality, the dynamic James G. Blaine, Speaker of the House of Representatives, who had been connected with some chicanery involving railroad securities. Instead they nominated Governor Rutherford B. Hayes of Ohio, a former general with an untarnished reputation. The Democrats picked Governor Samuel J. Tilden of New York, a wealthy lawyer who had attracted national attention for his part in breaking up the Tweed Ring in New York City.

In November early returns indicated that Tilden had carried New York, New Jersey, Connecticut, Indiana, and all the southern states, including Louisiana, South Carolina, and Florida, where Republican regimes were still in control. This seemed to give him 203 electoral votes to Hayes's 165, and a popular plurality in the neighborhood of 250,000 out of more than 8 million votes cast. However, Republican leaders had anticipated the possible loss of Florida, South Carolina, and Louisiana and were prepared to use their control of the election machinery in those states to throw out sufficient Democratic ballots to alter the results if doing so would change the national outcome. Realizing that the electoral votes of those states were exactly enough to elect their man, they telegraphed their henchmen on the scene, ordering them to go into action. The local Republicans then invalidated Democratic ballots in wholesale lots and filed returns showing Hayes the winner. Naturally the local Democrats protested vigorously and filed their own returns.

The Constitution provides (Article II, Section 1) that presidential electors must meet in their respective states to vote and forward the results to "the Seat of the Government." There, it adds, "the President of the Senate shall, in the Presence of the Senate and House of Representatives, open all the Certificates, and the Votes shall then be counted." But who was to do the counting? The House was Democratic, the Senate Republican; neither would agree to allow the other to do the job. On January 29, 1877, scarcely a month before inauguration day, Congress created an electoral commission to decide the disputed cases. The commission consisted of five senators (three Republicans and two Democrats), five representatives (three Democrats and two Republicans), and five justices of the Supreme Court (two Democrats, two Republicans, and one "independent" judge, David Davis).

Since it was a foregone conclusion that the others would vote for their party no matter what the evidence, Davis would presumably swing the balance in the interest of fairness.

But before the commission met, the Illinois legislature elected Davis senator. He had to resign from the Court and the commission. Since independents were rare even on the Supreme Court, no neutral justice was available to replace him. The vacancy went to Associate Justice Joseph P. Bradley of New Jersey, a Republican.

Evidence presented before the commission revealed a disgraceful picture of corruption. On the one hand, in all three disputed states Democrats had clearly cast a majority of the votes; on the other, it was unquestionable that many blacks had been forcibly prevented from voting.

In truth, both sides were shamefully corrupt. The governor of Louisiana was reported

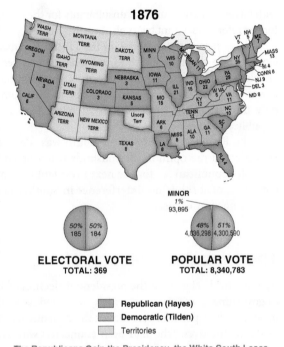

1876

ELECTORAL VOTE
TOTAL: 369

50% 185 | 50% 184

POPULAR VOTE
TOTAL: 8,340,783

MINOR 1% 93,895

48% 4,036,298 | 51% 4,300,590

Republican (Hayes)
Democratic (Tilden)
Territories

The Republicans Gain the Presidency, the White South Loses the Union Army, 1877 By 1876 white Democrats had regained political control in much of the South, giving Tilden 203 electoral votes to the Republican Hayes's 185. But Republican election officials in South Carolina, Florida, and Louisiana invalidated thousands of Democratic votes, which seemingly gave the election to Tilden. In 1877 a congressional commission finalized a deal giving the presidency to Hayes, who would withdraw the Union army from the South.

willing to sell his state's electoral votes for $200,000. The Florida election board was supposed to have offered itself to Tilden for the same price. "That seems to be the standard figure," Tilden remarked ruefully.

The Democrats had some hopes that Justice Bradley would be sympathetic to their case, for he was known to be opposed to harsh Reconstruction policies. On the eve of the commission's decision in the Florida controversy, he was apparently ready to vote in favor of Tilden. But the Republicans subjected him to tremendous political pressure. When he read his opinion on February 8, it was for Hayes. Thus, by a vote of eight to seven, the commission awarded Florida's electoral votes to the Republicans.

Grant, a Republican and a Union war hero, won easily in 1868 and 1872 because ex-Confederates, many of whom had voted Democratic, were barred from the polls. By 1876, however, white Democrats had regained political control in much of the South, creating the electoral stalemate that led to the Compromise of 1877.

The rest of the proceedings was routine. The commission assigned all the disputed electoral votes (including one in Oregon where the Democratic governor had seized on a technicality to replace a single Republican elector with a Democrat) to Hayes.

Democratic institutions, shaken by the South's refusal to go along with the majority in 1860 and by the suppression of civil rights during the rebellion, and further weakened by military intervention and the intimidation of blacks in the South during Reconstruction, seemed now a farce. According to Tilden's campaign manager, angry Democrats in fifteen states, chiefly war veterans, were readying themselves to march on Washington to force the inauguration of Tilden. Tempers flared in Congress, where some spoke ominously of a filibuster that would prevent the recording of the electoral vote and leave the country, on March 4, with no president at all.

The Compromise of 1877

Forces for compromise had been at work behind the scenes in Washington for some time. Although northern Democrats threatened to fight to the last ditch, many southern Democrats were willing to accept Hayes if he would promise to remove the troops and allow the southern states to manage their internal affairs by themselves. Ex-Whig planters and merchants who had reluctantly abandoned the carpetbag governments and who sympathized with Republican economic policies hoped that by supporting Hayes they might contribute to the restoration of the two-party system that had been destroyed in the South during the 1850s.

Tradition has it that a great compromise between the sections was worked out during a dramatic meeting at the Wormley Hotel[2] in Washington on February 26. Actually the negotiations were drawn out and informal, and the Wormley conference was but one of many. With the tacit support of many Democrats, the electoral vote was counted by the president of the Senate on March 2, and Hayes was declared elected, 185 votes to 184.

Like all compromises, the **Compromise of 1877** was not entirely satisfactory; like most, it was not honored in every detail. Hayes recalled the last troops from South Carolina and Louisiana in April. He appointed a former Confederate general, David M. Key of Tennessee, postmaster general and delegated to him the congenial task of finding Southerners willing to serve their country as officials of a Republican administration. But the alliance of ex-Whigs and northern Republicans did not flourish; the South remained solidly Democratic. The major significance of the compromise, one of the great intersectional political accommodations of American history, was that it ended Reconstruction and inaugurated a new political order in the South. More than the Constitutional amendments and federal statutes, this new regime would shape the destinies of the four million freedmen.

For many former slaves, this future was to be bleak. Forgotten in the North, manipulated and then callously rejected by the South, rebuffed by the Supreme Court, voiceless in national affairs, they and their descendants were condemned in the interests of sectional harmony to lives of poverty, indignity, and little hope. But many other former slaves managed to thrive during the last third of the nineteenth century. Their hard work, discipline, and financial savvy elevated them into a property-owning middle class whose existence—more than Union armies—marked the end of slavery.

Watch the Video

The Promise and Failure of Reconstruction at **myhistorylab.com**

---

[2]Ironically, the hotel was owned by James Wormley, reputedly the wealthiest black person in Washington.

Table 1 Two Phases of Reconstruction: 1863–1877

Phase	Measure	Consequence
1. Presidential Reconstruction: Accommodation with white South		
	Lincoln's Ten-Percent Plan (1863)	Re-admits Southern states when 10 percent of 1860 voters profess loyalty to Union
	Lincoln vetoes Wade-Davis Bill (1864)	Retains 10 percent "easy-admission" policy
	Andrew Johnson pardons many Confederates and recommends admission of all former Confederate states	By 1866, all southern states are readmitted
	Southern states pass Black Codes (1864–1865) sharply restricting rights of former slaves	Outrages Republicans
2. Radical Reconstruction: Republicans gain power in Congress		
	Thirteenth Amendment (1865)	Ends Slavery
	Freedmen's Bureau (1865) established as branch of war department	Promotes education and economic opportunities for former slaves and destitute whites
	Congress passes Civil Rights Act over Johnson's veto (1866)	Republicans in Congress dominate federal government Washington
	Reconstruction Act of 1867	Divides South into five military districts, each under command of Union general
	Tenure of Office Act (1867)	Prohibits president from removing high officials
	Johnson impeached for firing Secretary of State Stanton	Johnson is tried but not removed from office

Table 1   Two Phases of Reconstruction: 1863–1877 (Continued)

Fourteenth Amendment (passed 1866, ratified 1868)	Requires that all citizens have "equal protection" of laws
Republican Grant elected president (1868)	Further increases Republican domination
Fifteenth Amendment (passed 1869, ratified 1870)	Prohibits voting restrictions on basis of race
Force Acts (1870-1871)	Federal control of elections in South

Milestones

1863	Lincoln announces "Ten Percent Plan" for Reconstruction
1865	Federal government sets up Freedmen's Bureau to ease transition from slavery to freedom
	General Lee surrenders at Appomattox Court House
	Abraham Lincoln is assassinated
	Andrew Johnson becomes president
	Johnson issues amnesty proclamation
	States ratify Thirteenth Amendment abolishing slavery
1865–1866	Southern states enact Black Codes
1866	Civil Rights Act passes over Johnson's veto
	Johnson campaigns for his Reconstruction policy
1867	First Reconstruction Act puts former Confederacy under military rule
	Tenure of Office Act protects Senate appointees
1868	House of Representatives impeaches Johnson
1868	Fourth Reconstruction Act requires a majority of Southern voters to ratify state constitutions
	Senate acquits Johnson
	States ratify Fourteenth Amendment extending rights to freed slaves
	Ulysses S. Grant is elected president
	Ku Klux Klan uses intimidation and force throughout South
1870	States ratify Fifteenth Amendment granting black suffrage
1870–1871	Force Act destroys Ku Klux Klan
1872	Liberal Republican party nominates Horace Greeley for president
	Grant is reelected president
1876	Rutherford B. Hayes runs against Samuel Tilden in disputed presidential election
1877	Electoral Commission awards disputed votes to Rutherford B. Hayes who becomes president
	Hayes agrees to Compromise of 1877 ending Reconstruction

✓ ●─☐ Study and Review at www.myhistorylab.com

Review Questions

1. The introduction to this chapter—which cites the success of some randomly-chosen figures during Reconstruction—can be easily dismissed: Extraordinary people can prevail against any odds. What gains did most former slaves achieve during Reconstruction? Which federal policies and actions promoted their prospects?

2. What strategies did white Southerners use to control slaves after the Thirteenth Amendment had ended slavery?

3. Why did the Republicans in Congress disagree with Lincoln? With Andrew Johnson? In what sense did the Republican Congress come to "dominate" the political process?

4. What were the economic consequences of Reconstruction?

5. How did Reconstruction come to an end?

Key Terms

Black Codes
carpetbaggers
Compromise
 of 1877
crop-lien system
Fifteenth
 Amendment
Force Acts

Fourteenth
 Amendment
Freedmen's
 Bureau
Ku Klux Klan
Radical
 Republicans
scalawags

sharecropping
Ten Percent Plan
Thirteenth
 Amendment
Wade-Davis Bill

The Conquest of the West

((•—[Hear the Audio at myhistorylab.com

Do you live on land stolen from Indians?

IN 2010 THE CENSUS BUREAU REPORTED THAT BUFFALO COUNTY, South Dakota was the poorest in the nation, with well over half its residents below the poverty level. Buffalo County contains the Crow Creek Indian reservation. Six of the other ten poorest counties in the nation also consist of Indian reservations. Nationwide, nearly a quarter of all Indians live in poverty, twice the national average.

In 1988 Congress proposed to alleviate the plight of Native Americans with the Indian Gaming Regulatory Act. It allowed tribes to own casinos and other gambling operations. Within two decades, over 200 tribes had built 360 casinos and gaming establishments. By 2009, annual revenue from Indian casinos exceeded $25 billion, twice as much as the combined income of the National Football League (NFL) and Major League Baseball.

But little of the casino revenue has flowed to the poorest reservations. Foxwoods in Connecticut, the largest casino in the United States, generates about $1 billion annually, a windfall for the tiny Mashantucket Pequot tribe. But the Little Big Horn Casino, located in southeastern Montana near the battlefield where Custer lost his scalp, yielded a profit of only $100 a month during its first year of operation. Half of all reservation Indians live in Montana, Nevada, North and South Dakota, and Oklahoma, far from potential throngs of gamblers; those Indians remain mired in poverty.

Events that transformed the West after 1865 determined the plight of most Indians today. Ranchers and farmers acquired more Indian land. Railroad construction destabilized the habitat that sustained Indian life, especially the grazing lands of the buffalo, and brought still more settlers. The discovery of new deposits of gold, silver, and other valuable minerals caused miners and prospectors to swarm over and onto Indian lands. The federal government pushed Indians onto reservations, often on land unsuitable for cultivation, and sent troops to harass those who refused to abandon nomadic life. The new civilization that emerged in the West was increasingly controlled and organized by large-scale business enterprises.

By the turn of the twentieth century, the economic foundations of tribal life had been destroyed; relief, when it finally arrived many decades later, came in the form of slot machines. That so many Native Americans overcame the legacy of this past is testimony to their own initiative, and to traditional cultures characterized by both perseverance and adaptation.

From Chapter 16 of *American Destiny: Narrative of a Nation*, Combined Volume, Fourth Edition. Mark C. Carnes and John A. Garraty. Copyright © 2012 by Pearson Education, Inc. Published by Pearson Prentice Hall. All rights reserved.

The West after the Civil War

Although the image of the West as the land of great open spaces is accurate enough, after the Civil War the region contained several bustling cities. San Francisco, with a population approaching 250,000 in the late 1870s, had long outgrown its role as a rickety boomtown where the forty-niners bought supplies and squandered whatever wealth they had sifted from the streams of the Sierras. Though still an important warehouse and supply center, it had become the commercial and financial heart of the Pacific Coast and a center of light manufacturing, food processing, and machine shops. Denver, San Antonio, and Salt Lake City were far smaller, but growing rapidly and equally "urban."

Beginning in the mid-1850s a steady flow of Chinese migrated to the United States, most of them to the West Coast. About four or five thousand a year came, until the negotiation of the Burlingame Treaty of 1868, the purpose of which was to provide cheap labor for railroad construction crews. Thereafter the annual influx more than doubled, although before 1882 it exceeded 20,000 only twice. When the railroads were completed and the Chinese began to compete with native workers, a great cry of resentment went up on the west coast. Riots broke out in San Francisco in 1877. Chinese workers were called "groveling worms," "more slavish and brutish than the beasts that roam the fields." The California constitution of 1879 denied the right to vote to any "native of China" along with idiots, the insane, and persons convicted of "any infamous crime."

When Chinese immigration increased in 1882 to nearly 40,000, the protests reached such a peak that Congress passed the **Chinese Exclusion Act**, prohibiting all Chinese immigration for ten years. Later legislation extended the ban indefinitely.

Nevertheless, many parts of the West had as large a percentage of foreign-born residents as the populous eastern states—nearly a third of all Californians were foreign-born, as were more than 40 percent of Nevadans and more than half the residents of Idaho and Arizona. There were, of course, large populations of Spanish-speaking Americans of Mexican origin all over the Southwest. Chinese and Irish laborers were pouring into California by the thousands, and there were substantial numbers of Germans in Texas. Germans, Scandinavians, and other Europeans were also numerous on the High Plains east of the Rockies.

The Plains Indians

For 250 years the Indians had been driven back steadily, yet on the eve of the Civil War they still inhabited roughly half the United States. By the time of Hayes's inauguration, however, the Indians had been shattered as independent peoples, and in another decade the survivors were penned up on reservations, the government committed to a policy of extinguishing their way of life.

In 1860 the survivors of most of the eastern tribes were living peacefully in Indian Territory, what is now Oklahoma. In California the forty-niners had made short work of many of the local tribes. Elsewhere in the West—in the deserts of the Great Basin between the Sierras and the Rockies, in the mountains themselves, and on the semiarid, grass-covered plains between the Rockies and the edge of white civilization in eastern Kansas and Nebraska—nearly a quarter of a million Indians dominated the land.

In Charles Russell's *Trail of the Iron Horse* (1910) the steel rails stretch nearly to the sun, while wispy brushstrokes depict the Indians almost as ghosts.

Photo Credit: The Granger Collection, New York.

By far the most important lived on the High Plains. From the Blackfoot of southwestern Canada and the Sioux of Minnesota and the Dakotas to the Cheyenne of Colorado and Wyoming and the Comanche of northern Texas, the plains tribes possessed a generally uniform culture. All lived by hunting the hulking American bison, or buffalo, which ranged over the plains by the millions.

Although they seemed the epitome of freedom, pride, and self-reliance, the Plains Indians had begun to fall under the sway of white power. They eagerly adopted the products of the more technically advanced culture—cloth, metal tools, weapons, and cheap decorations. However, the most important thing the whites gave them had nothing to do with technology: It was the horse.

Horses thrived on the plains and so did their masters. Mounted Indians could run down buffalo instead of stalking them on foot. They could move more easily over the country and fight more effectively too. They could acquire and transport more possessions and increase the size of their tepees, for horses could drag heavy loads.

The Indians also adopted modern weapons: the cavalry sword, which they particularly admired, and the rifle. Both added to their effectiveness as hunters and fighters. However, like the whites' liquor and diseases, horses and guns caused problems. The buffalo herds began to diminish, and warfare became bloodier and more frequent.

After the start of the gold rush the need to link the East with California meant that the tribes were pushed aside. Deliberately the government in Washington prepared the way. In 1851 Thomas Fitzpatrick—an experienced mountain man, a founder of the Rocky Mountain Fur Company, scout for the first large group of settlers to Oregon in 1841 and for American soldiers in California during the Mexican War, and now an Indian agent—summoned a great "council" of the tribes. About 10,000 Indians, representing nearly all the plains tribes, gathered that September at Horse Creek, thirty-seven miles east of Fort Laramie, in what is now Wyoming.

In the Fort Laramie Treaty of 1851, Fitzpatrick persuaded each tribe to accept definite limits to its hunting grounds. In return the Indians were promised gifts and annual payments. This policy, known as "concentration," was designed to cut down on intertribal warfare and—far more important—to enable the government to negotiate separately with each tribe. It was the classic strategy of divide and conquer.

Although it made a mockery of diplomacy to treat Indian tribes as though they were European powers, the United States maintained that each tribe was a sovereign nation, to be dealt with as an equal in solemn treaties. Both sides knew that this was not the case. When Indians agreed to meet in council, they were tacitly admitting defeat. They seldom drove hard bargains or broke off negotiations. Moreover, tribal chiefs had only limited power; young braves frequently refused to respect agreements made by their elders.

Indian Wars

The government showed little interest in honoring agreements with Indians. No sooner had the Kansas-Nebraska bill become law than the Kansas, Omaha, Pawnee, and Yankton Sioux tribes began to feel pressure for further concessions of territory. A gold rush into Colorado in 1859 sent thousands of greedy prospectors across the plains to drive the Cheyenne and Arapaho from land guaranteed them in 1851. By 1860 most of Kansas and Nebraska had been cleared. Thus it happened that in 1862, after federal troops had been pulled out of the West for service against the Confederacy, most of the Plains Indians rose up against the whites. For five years intermittent but bloody clashes kept the entire area in a state of alarm.

This was guerrilla warfare, with all its horror and treachery. In 1864 a party of Colorado militia under the command of Colonel J. M. Chivington fell on an unsuspecting Cheyenne community at Sand Creek and killed several hundred Indians. General Nelson A. Miles called this "Chivington massacre" the "foulest and most unjustifiable crime in the annals of America."

Photo Credit: Courtesy, History Colorado (FC40432).

Robert Lindneux's *The Battle of Sand Creek*, 1864. Lindneux, born in 1871, did not witness what transpired at Sand Creek, Colorado. But although he used "battle" in the title of his painting, he depicted a massacre. "Kill and scalp all, big and little," Colonel J. M. Chivington, a minister in private life, told his men. The American flag (center right) was doubtless included as irony.

In turn the Indians slaughtered dozens of isolated white families, ambushed small parties, and fought many successful skirmishes against troops and militia. They achieved their most notable triumph in December 1866, when the Oglala Sioux, under their great chief Red Cloud, wiped out a party of eighty-two soldiers under Captain W. J. Fetterman. Red Cloud fought ruthlessly, but only when goaded by the construction of the Bozeman Trail, a road through the heart of the Sioux hunting grounds in southern Montana.[1]

Read the Document
Red Cloud's Speech at **myhistorylab.com**

In 1867 the government tried a new strategy. The "concentration" policy had evidently not gone far enough. All the Plains Indians would be confined to two small reservations, one in the Black Hills of the Dakota Territory, the other in Oklahoma, and forced to become farmers. At two great conclaves held in 1867 and 1868 at Medicine Lodge Creek and Fort Laramie, the principal chiefs yielded to the government's demands and signed the 1868 Treaty of Fort Laramie.

Many Indians refused to abide by these agreements. With their whole way of life at stake, they raged across the plains like a prairie fire—and were almost as destructive.

That a relative handful of "savages," without central leadership, could hold off the cream of the army, battle-hardened in the Civil War, can be explained by the fact that the U.S. Army, usually with fewer than 20,000 soldiers, had to operate over a million square miles. Few Indian leaders were capable of organizing a campaign or following up an advantage. But the Indians made superb guerrillas. Every observer called them the best cavalry soldiers in the world. Armed with stubby, powerful bows capable of driving an arrow clear through a bull buffalo, they were a fair match for troops equipped with carbines and Colt revolvers.

If one concedes that no one could reverse the direction of history or stop the invasion of Indian lands, then some version of the "small reservation" policy would probably have been best for the Indians. Had they been guaranteed a reasonable amount of land and adequate subsidies and allowed to maintain their way of life, they might have accepted the situation and ceased to harass the whites.

Whatever chance that policy had was weakened by the government's poor administration of Indian affairs. In dealing with Indians, nineteenth-century Americans displayed a grave insensitivity. After 1849 the Department of the Interior supposedly had charge of tribal affairs. Most of its agents systematically cheated the Indians. "No branch of the national government is so spotted with fraud, so tainted with corruption . . . as this Indian Bureau," Congressman Garfield charged in 1869.

At about this time a Yale paleontologist, Othniel C. Marsh, who wished to dig for fossils on the Sioux reservation, asked Red Cloud for permission to enter his domain. The chief agreed on condition that Marsh, whom the Indians called Big Bone Chief, take back with him samples of the moldy flour and beef that government agents were supplying to his people. Appalled by what he saw on the reservation, Professor Marsh took the rotten supplies directly to President Grant and prepared a list of charges against the agents.

In 1874 gold was discovered in the Black Hills Indian reservation. By the next winter thousands of miners had invaded the reserved area. Already alarmed by the

---

[1]Fetterman had boasted that with eighty cavalrymen he could ride the entire length of the Bozeman Trail. When he tried, however, he blundered into an ambush.

Indian Wars, 1860–1890 The frequent battles, involving nearly all tribes, show that the Indians did not cede their lands: The lands were taken in battle.

approach of crews building the Northern Pacific Railroad, the Sioux once again went on the warpath. Joining with nontreaty tribes to the west, they concentrated in the region of the Bighorn River, in southern Montana Territory.

The summer of 1876 saw three columns of troops in the field against them. The commander of one column, General Alfred H. Terry, sent ahead a small detachment of the Seventh Cavalry under Colonel George A. Custer with orders to locate the Indians' camp and then block their escape route into the inaccessible Bighorn Mountains. Grossly underestimating the number of the Indians, Custer decided to attack directly with his tiny force of 264 men. At the Little Bighorn late in June he found himself surrounded by 2,500 Sioux under Rain-in-the-Face, Crazy Horse, and Sitting Bull. He and all his men died on the field.

Because it was so one-sided, "Custer's Last Stand" was not a typical battle, although it may be taken as symbolic of the Indian warfare of the period in the sense that it was characterized by bravery, foolhardiness, and a tragic waste of life. The battle greatly heartened the Indians, but it did not gain them their cause. That autumn, short of rations and hard-pressed by overwhelming numbers of soldiers, they surrendered and returned to the reservation.

The Destruction of Tribal Life

Thereafter, the fighting slackened. For this the building of transcontinental railroads and the destruction of the buffalo were chiefly responsible. Thousands of buffalo were butchered to feed the gangs of laborers engaged in building the Union Pacific Railroad. Thousands more fell before the guns of sportsmen. Buffalo hunting became a fad, and a brisk demand developed for buffalo rugs and mounted buffalo heads. Railroads made the Army a far more efficient force. Troops and supplies could be moved swiftly when trouble with the tribes erupted. The lines also contributed to the decimation of the buffalo by running excursion trains for hunters.

The discovery in 1871 of a way to make commercial use of buffalo hides completed the tragedy. In the next three years about 9 million head were killed; after another decade the animals were almost extinct. No more efficient way could have been found for destroying the Plains Indians. The disappearance of the bison left them starving and homeless.

By the 1880s, the advance of whites into the plains had become, in the words of one congressman, as irresistible "as that of Sherman's to the sea." Greed for land lay behind the pressure, but large numbers of disinterested people, including most of those who deplored the way the Indians had been treated in the past, believed that the only practical way to solve the "Indian problem" was to persuade the Indians to abandon their tribal culture and live on family farms. The "wild" Indian must be changed into a "civilized" member of "American" society.

To accomplish this goal Congress passed the **Dawes Severalty Act of 1887**. Tribal lands were to be split up into individual allotments. To keep speculators from wresting the allotments from the Indians while they were adjusting to their new way of life, the land could not be disposed of for twenty-five years. Funds were to be appropriated for educating and training the Indians, and those who accepted allotments—took up residence "separate from any tribe," and "adopted the habits of civilized life"— were to be granted U.S. citizenship.

◆━Read the Document

Secretary of the Interior's Report on Indian Affairs at **myhistorylab.com**

A mound of buffalo skulls. In 1870 an estimated 30 million buffalo roamed the plains; by 1900, there were fewer than 1,000. During an eight-month period between 1867 and 1868, William F. Cody (Buffalo Bill) killed 4,280 buffalo, which fed construction crews for the Union Pacific railroad. Tourists also took up buffalo hunting, often shooting them from trains. The depletion of the buffalo, which provided the Plains Indians with meat and hides, was a major source of conflict with whites.

Photo Credit: Courtesy of the Burton Historical Collection, Detroit Public Library.

The sponsors of the Severalty Act thought they were effecting a fine humanitarian reform. "We must throw some protection over [the Indian]," Senator Henry L. Dawes declared. "We must hold up his hand." But no one expected all the Indians to accept allotments at once, and for some years little pressure was put on any to do so.

The Dawes Act had disastrous results in the long run. It assumed that Indians could be transformed into small agricultural capitalists by an act of Congress. It shattered what was left of the Indians' culture without enabling them to adapt to white ways. Moreover, unscrupulous white men tricked many Indians into leasing their allotments for a pittance, and local authorities often taxed Indian lands at excessive rates. In 1934, the government returned to a policy of encouraging tribal ownership of Indian lands.

The story of U.S.-Indian relations in the nineteenth century concludes, predictably, with a sad coda. In 1890 the Teton Sioux, suffering from cold and hunger, took heart from the words of Wovoka, a prophet, who had said that the whites would disappear if the Sioux performed their "ghost dance" rituals. When the Ghost Dance movement spread, federal military authorities resolved to stamp it out. On December 14 they attempted to arrest Chief Sitting Bull, a legendary Sioux warrior. When he resisted, shots rang out and Sitting Bull was killed. His people left the reservation at Pine Ridge and fled into the Badlands. The soldiers pursued them and the Indians surrendered. As they were

Table 1   Key Federal Policies Affecting Indians

Policy	Year	Provisions	Consequences
Indian Removal Bill	1830	Indians surrender land east of Mississippi to settle in Oklahoma and elsewhere	Forcible removal of Indians from South
Treaty of Fort Laramie	1851	Indian tribes establish tribal boundaries over shared hunting grounds and ensure safe passage of westward-bound settlers through Indian territory	Discourages concerted action among Indian tribes; settlers encroach on Indian lands
Railroad land grants	1850–1871	Gives railroads lands to lay track throughout the West	Promotes settlement and further encroachment; hastens demise of buffalo
Treaty of Fort Laramie	1868	Concentrates Indians in reservations in the Dakotas and Oklahoma	Dissident Indians commence open warfare against U.S. government
Dawes Severalty Act	1887	Breaks Indian lands into small plots for Indian families or sale to whites	Weakens tribal authority; causes loss of Indian land
Indian Reorganization Act	1934	Rescinds Dawes	Increases tribal authority
Indian Gaming Regulatory Act	1988	Allows tribes to run federally regulated casinos and gambling operations	Generates huge revenue for a handful of eastern tribes, and little for the rest

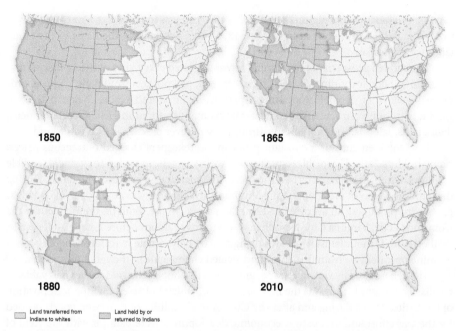

1850

1865

1880

2010

Land transferred from Indians to whites   Land held by or returned to Indians

Loss of Indian Lands, 1850–2010 This chapter describes the specific government policies, economic tendencies, and specific treaties that wrested land from the Indians. But the simplest explanation is that an aggressive, acquisitive, and militarily powerful people craved the West and they took it.

being disarmed, however, a scuffle broke out and the troops opened fire. Some 150 Sioux were killed, including many women and children. Thirty federal soldiers also died during the fighting at Wounded Knee.

The Lure of Gold and Silver in the West

The natural resources of the nation were exploited in these decades even more ruthlessly and thoughtlessly than were its human resources. From the mid-1850s to the mid-1870s thousands of gold-crazed prospectors fanned out through the Rockies, panning every stream and hacking furiously at every likely outcropping from the Fraser River country of British Columbia to Tucson in southern Arizona, from the eastern slopes of the Sierras to the Great Plains.

Gold and silver were scattered throughout the area, though usually too thinly to make mining profitable. Whenever anyone made a "strike," prospectors, the vast majority utterly without previous experience but driven by what a mining journal of the period called an "unhealthy desire" for sudden wealth, flocked to the site. For a few months the area teemed with activity. Then, usually, expectations faded in the light of reality: high prices, low yields, hardship, violence, and deception. A few found significant wealth, the rest only backbreaking labor and disappointment—that is, until tales of another strike sent them dashing feverishly across the land on another golden chase.

In June 1859 came the finds in Nevada, where the famous **Comstock Lode** yielded ores worth nearly $4,000 a ton. In 1861, while men in the settled areas were laying down their tools to take up arms, the miners were racing to the Idaho panhandle, hoping to become millionaires overnight. The next year the rush was to the Snake River valley, then in 1863 and 1864 to Montana. In 1874 to 1876 the Black Hills in the heart of the Sioux lands were inundated.

The sudden prosperity of the mining towns attracted every kind of shady character—according to one forty-niner "rascals from Oregon, pickpockets from New York, accomplished gentlemen from Europe, interlopers from Lima and Chile, Mexican thieves, gamblers from no particular spot, and assassins manufactured in Hell." Gambling dens, dance halls, saloons, and brothels mushroomed wherever precious metal was found.

Law enforcement was a constant problem. Storekeepers charged outrageous prices; claim holders "salted" worthless properties with nuggets in order to swindle gullible investors. Ostentation characterized the successful, mere swagger those who failed. During the administration of President Grant, Virginia City, Nevada, was at the peak of its vulgar prosperity, producing an average of $12 million a year in ore. Built on the richness of the Comstock Lode, Virginia City, Nevada had twenty-five saloons before it had 4,000 people. By the 1870s its mountainside site was disfigured by ugly, ornate mansions where successful mine operators ate from fine china and swilled champagne as though it were water.

Though marked by violence, fraud, greed, and lost hopes, the gold rushes had valuable results. The most obvious was the new metal itself, which bolstered the financial position of the United States during and after the Civil War. Quantities of European goods needed for the war effort and for postwar economic development were paid for with the yield of the new mines. Gold and silver also caused a great increase of interest in the West. A valuable literature appeared, part imaginative, part reportorial, describing the mining camps and the life of the prospectors. These works fascinated contemporaries. Mark Twain's *Roughing It* (1872), based in part on his experiences in the Nevada mining country, is the most famous example of this literature.

The mines also speeded the political organization of the West. Colorado and Nevada became territories in 1861, Arizona and Idaho in 1863, and Montana in 1864. Although Nevada was admitted before it had 60,000 residents, most of these territories did not become states for decades. But because of the miners, the framework for future development was early established.

Farmers Struggle to Keep Up

While miners were extracting the mineral wealth of the West, others were snapping up the region's choice farmland. Presumably the Homestead Act of 1862 was supposed to make it easier for poor families to acquire farms, thereby ending the reign of the speculator and the large landholder. The West, land reformers had assumed, would soon be dotted with 160-acre family farms.

They were doomed to disappointment. Most landless Americans were too poor to become farmers even when they could obtain land without cost. The expense of moving a family to the ever-receding frontier exceeded the means of many. As for the industrial workers for whom the free land was supposed to provide a "safety valve," they had neither the skills nor the inclination to become farmers. Homesteaders usually came from districts not far removed from frontier conditions.

The first settlers in western Kansas, Nebraska, and the Dakotas took up land along the rivers and creeks, where they found enough timber for home building, fuel, and fencing. Later arrivals had to build houses of the tough prairie sod and depend on hay, sunflower stalks, and buffalo dung for fuel.

Frontier farm families had always had to work hard and endure the hazards of storm, drought, and insect plagues, along with isolation and loneliness. But all these burdens were magnified on the prairies and the High Plains. Life was particularly hard for farm women, who, in addition to childcare and housework, performed endless farm chores.

Farming as Big Business

Immediately after the Civil War, Congress reserved 47.7 million acres of public land in the South for homesteaders, stopping all cash sales in the region. But in 1876 this policy was reversed and the land thrown open. Speculators flocked to the feast in such numbers that the Illinois Central Railroad ran special trains from Chicago to Mississippi and Louisiana.

The flat immensity of the land, combined with newly available farm machinery and the development of rail connections with the East, encouraged the growth of enormous corporation-controlled "bonanza" farms.

Bonanza farmers could buy supplies wholesale and obtain concessions from railroads and processors, but even the biggest organizations could not cope with prolonged drought, and most of the bonanza outfits failed in the dry years of the late 1880s. Those wise farmers who diversified their crops and cultivated their land intensively fared better in the long run, although even they could not hope to earn a profit in really dry years.

Despite the hazards of plains agriculture, the region became the breadbasket of America in the decades following the Civil War. By 1889 Minnesota topped the nation in wheat production, and ten years later four of the five leading wheat states lay west of the Mississippi. The plains also accounted for heavy percentages of the nation's other cereal crops, together with immense quantities of beef, pork, and mutton.

Like other exploiters of the nation's resources, farmers took whatever they could from the soil with little heed for preserving its fertility and preventing erosion. The consequent national loss was less apparent because it was diffuse and slow to assume drastic proportions, but it was nonetheless real.

Western Railroad Building

Further exploitation of land resources by private interests resulted from the government's policy of subsidizing western railroads. Here was a clear illustration of the conflict between the idea of the West as a national heritage to be disposed of to deserving citizens and the concept of the region as a cornucopia pouring forth riches to be gathered up and carted off. When it came to a choice between giving a particular tract to railroads or to homesteaders, the homesteaders nearly always lost out. On the other hand, the swift development of western railroads was essential if farmers, miners, and cattle ranchers were to prosper.

Unless the government had been willing to build the transcontinental lines itself—and this was unthinkable in an age dominated by belief in individual exploitation—some system of subsidy was essential. Private investors would not hazard the huge sums needed to lay tracks across hundreds of miles of rugged, empty country when traffic over the road could not possibly profit for many years. Most voters were wary of entrusting the dispensing of large sums to politicians. Grants of land seemed a sensible way of financing construction. The method avoided direct outlays of public funds, for the companies could pledge the land as security for bond issues or sell it directly for cash.

Federal land grants to railroads began in 1850 with those allotted to the Illinois Central. Over the next two decades about 49 million acres were given to various lines

Chinese work on a railway in the Far West. "Without them," Leland Stanford, president of the Central Pacific Railroad said, "it would be impossible to complete the western portion of this great national highway." Some Chinese were drawn from the gold fields farther north, and others were imported from China, under five-year contracts with the railroads, which paid them $10 or $12 a month.

Photo Credit: Huntington Library/ SuperStock, Inc.

indirectly in the form of grants to the states, but the most lavish gifts of the public domain were those made directly to builders of intersectional trunk lines. These roads received more than 155 million acres, although about 25 million acres reverted to the government because some companies failed to lay the required miles of track. About 75 percent of this land went to aid the construction of four transcontinental railroads: the Union Pacific–Central Pacific line, running from Nebraska to San Francisco, completed in 1869; the Atchison, Topeka, and Santa Fe, running from Kansas City to Los Angeles by way of Santa Fe and Albuquerque, completed in 1883; the Southern Pacific, running from San Francisco to New Orleans by way of Yuma and El Paso, completed in 1883; and the Northern Pacific, running from Duluth, Minnesota, to Portland, Oregon, completed in 1883.

The Pacific Railway Act of 1862 established the pattern for these grants. It gave the builders of the Union Pacific and Central Pacific railroads five square miles of public land on each side of their right-of-way for each mile of track laid. The land was allotted in alternate sections, forming a pattern like a checkerboard: the squares of one color representing railroad property, the other government property. Presumably this arrangement benefited the entire nation since half the land close to the railroad remained in public hands.

However, whenever grants were made to railroads, the adjacent government lands were not opened to homesteaders—on the theory that free land in the immediate vicinity of a line would prevent the road from disposing of its properties at good prices. In addition to the land granted the railroads, a wide zone of "indemnity" lands was reserved to allow the roads to choose alternative sites to make up for lands that settlers had already taken up within the checkerboard. Thus, homesteading was in fact prohibited near land-grant railroads. More than twenty years after receiving its immense grant, the Northern Pacific was still attempting to keep homesteaders from filing in the indemnity zone. President Cleveland finally put a stop to this in 1887, saying that he could find "no evidence" that "this vast tract is necessary for the fulfillment of the grant."

Historians have argued at length about the fairness of the land-grant system. Land-grant lines encouraged the growth of the West by advertising their property widely and by providing cheap transportation for prospective settlers and efficient shipping services for farmers. They were required by law to carry troops and handle government business free or at reduced rates, which saved the government millions over the years. At the same time the system imposed no effective restraints on how the railroads used the funds raised with federal aid. Being able to lay track with money obtained from land grants, the operators tended to be extravagant and often downright corrupt.

The construction of the Central Pacific in the 1860s illustrates how the system encouraged extravagance. The line was controlled by four businessmen: Collis P. Huntington, Leland Stanford, Mark Hopkins, and Charles Crocker. The Central Pacific and the Union Pacific were given, in addition to their land grants, loans in the form of government bonds—from $16,000 to $48,000 for each mile of track laid, depending on the difficulty of the terrain. The two competed with each other for the subsidies, the Central Pacific building eastward from Sacramento, the Union Pacific westward from Nebraska. They put huge crews to work grading and laying track, bringing up supplies over the already completed road. The Union Pacific employed Civil War veterans and Irish immigrants, while the Central employed Chinese immigrants.

This plan favored the Union Pacific. While the Central Pacific was inching up the gorges and granite of the mighty Sierras, the Union Pacific was racing across the level plains laying 540 miles of track between 1865 and 1867. Once beyond the Sierras, the Central Pacific would have easy going across the Nevada–Utah plateau country, but by then it might be too late to prevent the Union Pacific from making off with most of the government aid.

Crocker managed the Central Pacific construction crews. He wasted huge sums by working through the winter in the High Sierras. In 1866, over the most difficult terrain, he laid twenty-eight miles of track, at a cost of more than $280,000 a mile. Experts later estimated that 70 percent of this sum could have been saved had speed not been a factor.

Crocker's Herculean efforts paid off. The mountains were conquered, and then the crews raced across the Great Basin to Salt Lake City and beyond. The meeting of the rails—the occasion of a national celebration—took place at Promontory, north of Ogden, Utah, on May 10, 1869. Leland Stanford drove the final ceremonial golden spike with a silver hammer.[2] The Union Pacific had built 1,086 miles of track, the Central 689 miles.

In the long run the wasteful way in which the Central Pacific was built hurt the road severely. It was ill-constructed, over grades too steep and around curves too sharp, and burdened with debts that were too large. Such was the fate of nearly all the railroads constructed with the help of government subsidies.

The only transcontinental railroad built without land grants was the Great Northern, running from St. Paul, Minnesota, to the Pacific. Spending private capital, its guiding genius, James J. Hill, was compelled to build economically and to plan carefully. As a result, his was the only transcontinental line to weather the depression of the 1890s without going into bankruptcy.

---

[2]A mysterious "San Francisco jeweler" passed among the onlookers, taking orders for souvenir watch chains that he proposed to make from the spike at $5 each.

NAT LOVE

Nat Love, a slave, was born on a plantation in Davidson County, Tennessee sometime in 1854. Nat's father was a foreman on the plantation; his mother milked cows, cooked, and operated a loom.

After the Civil War, Love's father rented twenty acres from his former master. Nat spent Sundays at a horse farm, where he learned how to ride. Soon he was earning ten cents for every colt he "broke."

When Nat's father died, the family's circumstances became dire. He and his siblings went shoeless and their clothes were in tatters. Nat longed to escape from it all and see the world. His opportunity came when he won a horse in a raffle. In February 1869, he set out for the frontier. He was fifteen years old.

Months later, he arrived in Dodge City, Kansas, "a typical frontier city, with a great many saloons, dance halls, and gambling houses, and very little of anything else." At a camp outside of town, he asked a group of cowboys for a job. Eager to have some fun with the black "tenderfoot," they agreed if he could prove he could ride; then they put him on the wildest horse in camp. Love clung to the bucking bronco, much to everyone's astonishment. The boss hired him at $30 a month. He also gave Nat a saddle, a Colt 45 pistol and a new name—"Love" being unsuitable for a cowboy. Nat was now "Red River Dick."

Three days after the cowboys left Dodge, they were attacked by mounted Indians. "When I saw them coming after us and heard their blood curdling yell, I was too badly scared to run," Love recalled. Before the Indians were driven away by gunfire, they had killed one cowboy and made off with most of the horses and provisions. Love and the others walked to Texas.

Love then served with outfits that drove cattle to grazing ranges and markets throughout the West. Every spring and fall the ranchers staged a great roundup, driving in all the cattle to a central place, separating them by the brands, and culling steers for shipment to market. Love specialized as a brand reader. He "cut out" those belonging to his employer and drove them back to that herd.

Love's life was filled with adventure. In 1876, while Love was driving 500 steers from the Rio Grande to a ranch in the Shoshone mountains of Wyoming, Indians attacked and stampeded the cattle. The battle raged through the night. By morning, several score Indians were dead, most of them trampled by cattle. Another time, Love broke up a robbery of a Union Pacific railroad station.

After he won a roping and riding competition in Deadwood, South Dakota, "Red River Dick" became known as "Deadwood Dick." Shortly afterward he was shot by Indians and captured. When he recovered, the chief offered him his daughter in marriage along with 100 ponies. Dick pretended to go along with the marriage, but then stole a horse and escaped.

By the late 1880s, the heyday of the cowboy had ended. Now railroads hauled cattle from the grazing ranges to slaughterhouses in Kansas City, Omaha, Chicago, and St. Louis. In 1889, Dick went to Denver and got married. The following year he found a job as a porter on the Pullman Railroad cars. He died in 1921.

Question for Discussion
■ Which factors perhaps promoted racial equality among ranch hands?

Nat Love, posed here with the requisite implements, claimed to have been the "Deadwood Dick" on whom a series of novels was based.

Text Credit: *Life and Adventures of Nat Love, Better Known in the Cattle Country as "Deadwood Dick," by Himself; a True History of Slavery Days, Life on the Great Cattle Ranges and on the Plains of the "Wild and Woolly" West*, Los Angeles 1907.

Photo Credit: The Granger Collection

The Cattle Kingdom

While miners were digging out the mineral wealth of the West and railroaders were taking possession of much of its land, another group was exploiting endless acres of its grass. For twenty years after the Civil War cattlemen and sheep raisers dominated huge areas of the High Plains, making millions of dollars by grazing their herds on lands they did not own.

Watch the Video
Cowboys and Cattle at **myhistorylab.com**

The lack of markets and transportation explains why cattle, which existed in southern Texas by the millions, were lightly regarded. But conditions were changing. Industrial growth in the East was causing an increase in the urban population and a consequent rise in the demand for food. At the same time, the expansion of the railroad network made it possible to move cattle cheaply over long distances. As the iron rails inched across the plains, astute cattlemen began to do some elementary figuring. Longhorns could be had locally for $3 and $4 a head. In the northern cities they would bring ten times that much, perhaps even more. Why not round them up and herd them northward to the railroads, allowing them to feed along the way on the abundant grasses of the plains? The land was unoccupied and owned by the federal government. Anyone could drive cattle across it without paying a fee or asking anyone's permission.

In 1867 the drovers, inspired by a clever young Illinois cattle dealer named Joseph G. McCoy and other entrepreneurs, led their herds across unsettled grasslands to the Kansas Pacific line at Abilene, Kansas. They earned excellent profits, and during the next five years about 1.5 million head made the "long drive" over the Chisholm Trail to Abilene, where they were sold to ranchers, feedlot operators, and the agents of eastern meatpackers. Other shipping points sprang up as the railroads pushed westward.

Read the Document
Chisholm Trail at **myhistorylab.com**

According to the best estimates 10 million head were driven north before the practice ended in the mid-1880s. (For the story of one cowboy, see the American Lives essay on "Nat Love.")

Open-Range Ranching

Soon cattlemen discovered that the hardy Texas stock could survive the winters of the northern plains. Attracted by the apparently limitless forage, they began to bring up herds to stock the vast regions where the buffalo had so recently roamed. By 1880 some 4.5 million head had spread across the sea of grass that ran from Kansas to Montana and west to the Rockies.

The prairie grasses offered ranchers a bonanza almost as valuable as the gold mines. Open-range ranching required actual ownership of no more than a few acres along some watercourse. In this semiarid region, control of water enabled a rancher to dominate all the surrounding area back to the divide separating his range from the next stream without investing a cent in the purchase of land. His cattle, wandering freely on the public domain, fattened on grass owned by all the people, were to be turned into beefsteak and leather for the profit of the rancher.

Theoretically, anyone could pasture stock on the open range, but without access to water it was impossible to do so. "I have 2 miles of running water," a cattleman said in testifying before the Public Land Commission. "That accounts for my ranch being where it is. The next water from me in one direction is 23 miles; now no man can have a ranch between these two places. I have control of the grass, the same as though I owned it." In the late 1870s one Colorado cattle baron controlled an area roughly the size of Connecticut and Rhode Island even though he owned only 105 small parcels that totaled about 15,500 acres.

With the demand for meat rising and transportation cheap, princely fortunes could be made in a few years. Capitalists from the East and from Europe began to pour funds into the business. Soon large outfits such as the Nebraska Land and Cattle Company, controlled by British investors, and the Union Cattle Company of Wyoming, a $3 million corporation, dominated the business, just as large companies had taken over most of the important gold and silver mines.

Unlike other exploiters of the West's resources, cattle ranchers did not at first injure or reduce any public resource. Grass eaten by their stock annually renewed itself; droppings from the animals enriched the soil. Furthermore, ranchers poached on the public domain because there was no reasonable way for them to obtain legal possession of the large areas necessary to raise cattle on the plains. Federal land laws made no allowance for the special conditions of the semiarid West.

A system to take account for those conditions was soon devised by Major John Wesley Powell, later the director of the United States Geological Survey. His *Report on the Lands of the Arid Region of the United States* (1879) suggested that western lands be divided into three classes: irrigable lands, timber lands, and "pasturage" lands. On the pasturage lands the "farm unit" ought to be at least 2,560 acres (four sections), Powell urged. Groups of these units should be organized into "pasturage districts" in which the ranchers "should have the right to make their own regulations for the division of lands, the use of the water . . . and for the pasturage of lands in common or in severalty."

Barbed-Wire Warfare

Congress refused to change the land laws in any basic way, and this had two harmful effects. First, it encouraged fraud: Those who could not get title to enough land honestly turned to subterfuge. The Desert Land Act (1877) allowed anyone to obtain 640 acres in the arid states for $1.25 an acre provided the owner irrigated part of it within three years. Since the original claimant could transfer the holding, the ranchers set their cowboys and other hands to filing claims, which were then signed over to them. Over 2.6 million acres were taken up under the act, and according to the best estimate, 95 percent of the claims were fraudulent—no sincere effort was made to irrigate the land.

Second, overcrowding became a problem that led to serious conflicts, even killings, because no one had uncontestable title to the land. The leading ranchers banded together in cattlemen's associations to deal with overcrowding and with such problems as quarantine regulations, water rights, and thievery. In most cases these associations devised effective and sensible rules, but their functions would better have been performed by the government.

To keep other ranchers' cattle from those sections of the public domain they considered their own, the associations and many individuals began to fence huge areas. This was possible only because of the invention in 1874 of barbed wire by Joseph F. Glidden, an

Illinois farmer. By the 1880s thousands of miles of the new fencing had been strung across the plains, often across roads and in a few cases around entire communities. "Barbed-wire wars" resulted, fought by rancher against rancher, cattleman against sheepman, herder against farmer. Posted signs gave dire warnings to trespassers. "The Son of a Bitch who opens this fence had better look out for his scalp," one such sign announced, another fine statement of the philosophy of the age.

By stringing so much wire the cattlemen were unwittingly destroying their own way of doing business. On a truly open range, cattle could fend for themselves, instinctively finding water during droughts, drifting safely downwind before blizzards. Barbed wire prevented their free movement. During winter storms these slender strands became as lethal as high-tension wires: the drifting cattle piled up against them and died by the thousands.

The boom times were ending. Overproduction was driving down the price of beef; expenses were on the rise; many sections of the range were badly overgrazed. The dry summer of 1886 left the stock in such poor condition as winter approached that the *Rocky Mountain Husbandman* urged its readers to sell their cattle despite the prevailing low prices rather than "endanger the whole herd by having the range overstocked."

Some ranchers took this advice; those who did not made a fatal error. Winter that year arrived early and with unparalleled fury. Blizzards raged and temperatures plummeted far below zero. Cattle crowded into low places only to be engulfed in giant snowdrifts; barbed wire took a fearful toll. When spring finally came, the streams were choked with rotting carcasses. Between 80 and 90 percent of all cattle on the range were dead.

That cruel winter finished open-range cattle-raising. The large companies were bankrupt; many independent operators became discouraged and sold out. When the industry revived, it was on a smaller, more efficiently organized scale. The fencing movement continued, but now ranchers enclosed only the land they actually owned. It then became possible to bring in pedigreed bulls to improve the breed. Cattle-raising, like mining before it, ceased to be an adventure in rollicking individualism and became a business.

By the late 1880s the bonanza days of the West were over. No previous frontier had caught the imagination of Americans so completely as the Great West, with its heroic size, its awesome emptiness, its massive, sculptured beauty. Most of what Walter Prescott Webb, author of the classic study *The Great Plains* (1931) called the "primary windfalls" of the region—the furs, the precious metals, the forests, the cattle, and the grass—had been snatched up by first comers and by individuals already wealthy. Big companies were taking over all the West's resources. The frontier was no more.

But the frontier never existed except as an intellectual construction among white settlers and those who wrote about them. To the Indians, the land was simply home. The "conquest of the frontier" was thus an appealing evasion: It transformed

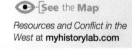
See the **Map**

Resources and Conflict in the West at **myhistorylab.com**

the harmful actions and policies of the nation into an expression of human progress, the march westward of "civilization."

"Civilization," though, was changing. The nation was becoming more powerful, richer, and larger, and its economic structure more complex and diversified as the West yielded its treasures. But the East, and especially eastern industrialists and financiers, were increasingly dominating the economy of the entire nation.

Milestones

1859	Discovery of the Comstock Lode lures miners west	1877	U.S. troops capture Chief Joseph of Nez Percé after 1,000-mile retreat
1864	Chivington massacre of Cheyenne	1878	Timber and Stone Act favors lumber companies
1869	Union Pacific Railroad completed	1879	Major Powell's *Report on the Lands of the Arid Region* suggests division of West
	Board of Indian Commissioners established		
1873	Timber Culture Act encourages western forestation	1882	Chinese Exclusion Act bans Chinese immigrant workers for ten years
1876	Sioux slaughter Custer's cavalry at Battle of Little Bighorn	1886–1887	Blizzards end open-range ranching
1877	Desert Land Act favors ranchers	1887	Dawes Severalty Act splits tribal lands

✓ ● Study and Review at www.myhistorylab.com

Review Questions

1. The text suggests that if federal policy had been more tolerant, there would have been no need to drive Indians from so much of their land. What alternative policies might have succeeded and how?

2. In The *Comanche Empire* (2009), historian Pekka Hamalainen insists that the Comanche themselves managed to forge a mighty empire. Maps showing the steady loss of Indian lands deprive the Indians of their "agency" in history. In what ways did Indians leave their own imprint upon this period?

3. How did the treatment of African Americans during the last third of the nineteenth century compare with that of Indians?

4. The West has exerted a powerful hold on the American imagination. What explains the popularity of western themes in American life? How does the history compare with the popular image?

Key Terms

Chinese Exclusion Act
Comstock Lode

Dawes Severalty Act of 1887

An Industrial Giant Emerges

((•─┤Hear the Audio at myhistorylab.com

Do you save money at big box stores?

IN 2010 WALMART, WITH 2.1 MILLION EMPLOYEES, WAS THE LARGEST corporation in the history of the world. Its revenues of $405 billion exceeded the gross domestic product of Sweden and Saudi Arabia. The company's clout made it a frequent target of popular satire. A 2008 episode of *The Simpsons* was set at "Sprawl-Mart," where Homer was offered a job as Executive Greeter. "Is there a chance for advancement?" he asks. "No," the manager says. "You get to work overtime without us paying you extra."

Real-world critics of Walmart leveled similar charges. A labor union website described Walmart as a "death star" that "destroys all other economic activity in its path." Others complained that many Walmart employees qualified for public assistance.

In 2009 Walmart, whose motto is "Save Money Live Better," claimed that it saved $3,100 per American household. Former CEO Lee Scott credited Walmart with having "democratized consumption" in the United States by enabling "working-class families to buy former luxuries like inexpensive flat-screen televisions, down comforters and porterhouse steaks." A retailer helps society best by lowering prices, or so the company contended.

The debate over the human costs of corporate efficiencies echoes the one that accompanied the rise of powerful industrial combinations during the last third of the nineteenth century. Then, the power of the railroads enabled them to bring substantial benefits to thousands of communities; but this power also enabled the railroads to ruin those who opposed their will. Industrial corporations followed suit, especially in steel, iron, oil, and electricity, providing millions with new and improved products at lower prices. But the industrial behemoths also controlled political processes and often exploited workers. Reformers and labor leaders denounced this concentration of wealth and power. Some advocated regulation; others called for revolution. Then as now, defenders of big business pointed out its benefits: new technology, better products, lower prices.

The question remains: Does the efficiency generated by economic concentration justify its threat to smaller businesses and communities—and to democratic institutions?

From Chapter 17 of *American Destiny: Narrative of a Nation*, Combined Volume, Fourth Edition. Mark C. Carnes and John A. Garraty. Copyright © 2012 by Pearson Education, Inc. Published by Pearson Prentice Hall. All rights reserved.

Essentials of Industrial Growth

When the Civil War began, the country's industrial output, while important and increasing, did not approach that of major European powers. By the end of the century the United States had become far and away the colossus among world manufacturers, dwarfing the production of Great Britain and Germany. The world had never seen such a remarkable example of rapid economic growth. The value of American manufactured products rose from $1.8 billion in 1859 to over $13 billion in 1899.

American manufacturing flourished for many reasons. New natural resources were discovered and exploited steadily, thereby increasing opportunities. These opportunities, in turn, attracted the brightest and most energetic of a vigorous and expanding population. The growth of the country added constantly to the size of the national market, and protective tariffs shielded that market from foreign competition. Foreign capital, however, entered the market freely, in part because tariffs kept out so many foreign goods.

The dominant spirit of the time encouraged businessmen to maximum effort by emphasizing progress, yet it also produced a generation of Robber Barons. The energetic search for wealth led to corrupt business practices such as stock manipulation, bribery, and cutthroat competition and ultimately to "combinations in restraint of trade," a kind of American euphemism for monopoly.

The period witnessed rapid advances in basic science, and technicians created a bountiful harvest of new machines, processes, and power sources that increased productivity in many industries and created new industries as well. Agriculture was transformed by improved harvesters and binding machines, and combines capable of threshing and bagging 450 pounds of grain a minute. An 1886 report of the Illinois Bureau of Labor Statistics claimed that "new machinery has displaced fully 50 percent of the muscular labor formerly required to do a given amount of work in the manufacture of agricultural implements." Of course that also meant that many farm families were "displaced" from their homes and livelihoods, and it made farmers dependent on the vagaries of distant markets and powerful economic forces they could not control.

As a result of improvements in the milling of grain, packaged cereals appeared on the American breakfast table. The commercial canning of food, spurred by the "automatic line" canning factory, expanded so rapidly that by 1887 a writer in *Good Housekeeping* could say, "Housekeeping is getting to be ready made, as well as clothing." The Bonsack cigarette-rolling machine created a new industry that changed the habits of millions. George B. Eastman created still another with his development of mass-produced, roll photographic film and the simple but efficient Kodak camera. The perfection of the typewriter by the Remington company in the 1880s revolutionized office work. But even some of these inventions were mixed blessings. The harm done by cigarettes, for example, needs no explanation.

Railroads: The First Big Business

In 1866, returning from his honeymoon in Europe, thirty-year-old Charles Francis Adams Jr., (great-grandson of John Adams and grandson of John Quincy Adams), full of ambition and ready, as he put it, to confront the world "face to face," looked about in search of a career. "Surveying the whole field," he later explained, "I fixed on the railroad system as the most developing force and the largest field of the day, and determined to attach myself to it." Adams's judgment was acute: For the next twenty-five years the

Photo Credit: © Tony Aruza/CORBIS All Rights Reserved.

The Union Railroad Station in Montgomery, Alabama, was designed by Henry Hobson Richardson, the nation's foremost architect in the late nineteenth century. Richardson borrowed ideas from the past, including arches that evoked ancient Rome. The building's massiveness and horizontal lines suggested the power and reach of the railroads: the American empire as built on steel rails.

railroads were probably the most significant element in American economic development, railroad executives the most powerful people in the country.

Railroads were important first as an industry in themselves. Fewer than 35,000 miles of track existed when Lee laid down his sword at Appomattox. In 1875 railroad mileage exceeded 74,000 and the skeleton of the network was complete. Over the next two decades the skeleton was fleshed out. In 1890 the mature but still-growing system took in over $1 billion in passenger and freight revenues. (The federal government's income in 1890 was only $403 million.) The value of railroad properties and equipment was more than $8.7 billion. The national railroad debt of $5.1 billion was almost five times the national debt of $1.1 billion. By 1900 the nation had 193,000 miles of track.

The emphasis in railroad construction after 1865 was on organizing integrated systems. The lines had high fixed costs: taxes, interest on their bonds, maintenance of track and rolling stock, and salaries of office personnel. A short train with half-empty cars required almost as many workers and as much fuel to operate as a long one jammed with freight or passengers. To earn profits the railroads had to carry as much traffic as possible. They therefore spread out feeder lines to draw business to their main lines the way the root network of a tree draws water into its trunk.

Before the Civil War, passengers and freight could travel by rail from beyond Chicago and St. Louis to the Atlantic coast, but only after the war did true interregional trunk lines appear. In 1867 the New York Central passed into the hands of "Commodore" Cornelius Vanderbilt, who had made a large fortune in the shipping business. Vanderbilt already controlled lines running from Albany to New York City; now he merged these properties with the New York Central. In 1873 he integrated the Lake Shore and Michigan

Southern into his empire and two years later the Michigan Central. At his death in 1877 the New York Central operated a network of over 4,500 miles of track between New York City and most of the principal cities of the Midwest.

While Vanderbilt was putting together the New York Central complex, Thomas A. Scott was fusing roads to Cincinnati, Indianapolis, St. Louis, and Chicago to his Pennsylvania Railroad, which linked Pittsburgh and Philadelphia. In 1871 the Pennsylvania line obtained access to New York; soon it reached Baltimore and Washington. By 1869 another important system, the Erie, extended from New York to Cleveland, Cincinnati, and St. Louis. Soon thereafter it too tapped the markets of Chicago and other cities. In 1874 the Baltimore and Ohio rail line also obtained access to Chicago.

The Civil War had highlighted the need for thorough railroad connections in the South. Shortly after the conflict the Chesapeake and Ohio opened a direct line from Norfolk, Virginia, to Cincinnati, Ohio. By the late 1880s, the Richmond and West Point Terminal Company controlled an 8,558-mile network. Like other southern trunk lines such as the Louisville and Nashville and the Atlantic Coast Line, this system was controlled by northern capitalists.

The trunk lines interconnected and thus had to standardize many of their activities. This in turn led to the standardization of other aspects of life. The present system of time zones was developed in 1883 by the railroads. The standard track gauge (four feet eight and one-half inches) was established in 1886. Standardized car coupling and braking mechanisms, standard signal systems, even standard methods of accounting were essential to the effective functioning of the network.

The lines sought to work out fixed rates for carrying different types of freight, charge more for valuable manufactured goods than for bulky products like coal or wheat, and they agreed to permit rate concessions to shippers when necessary to avoid hauling empty cars. In other words, they charged what the traffic would bear. However, by the 1880s the men who ran the railroads had come to recognize the advantages of cooperating with one another to avoid "senseless" competition. Railroad management was becoming a kind of profession, with certain standard ways of doing things, its own professional journals, and with regional organizations such as the Eastern Trunk Line Association and the Western Traffic Association.

To speed the settlement of new regions, the land-grant railroads sold land cheaply and on easy terms, for sales meant future business as well as current income. They offered reduced rates to travelers interested in buying farms and set up "bureaus of immigration" that distributed brochures describing the wonders of the new country. Their agents greeted immigrants at the eastern ports and tried to steer them to railroad property. They sent agents who were usually themselves immigrants—often ministers—all over Europe to recruit prospective settlers.

See the **Map**

Railroads & New Transportation Systems at **myhistorylab.com**

Iron, Oil, and Electricity

The transformation of iron manufacturing affected the nation almost as much as railroad development. Output rose from 920,000 tons in 1860 to 10.3 million tons in 1900, but the big change came in the development of ways to mass-produce steel. In its pure form (wrought iron) the metal is tough but relatively pliable: It bends under great stresses.

Ordinary cast iron, which contains large amounts of carbon and other impurities, is hard but brittle. Steel, which contains 1 or 2 percent carbon, combines the hardness of cast iron with the toughness of wrought iron. For nearly every purpose—structural girders for bridges and buildings, railroad track, machine tools, boiler plate, barbed wire—steel is immensely superior to other kinds of iron.

But steel was so expensive that it could not be used for bulky products until the invention in the 1850s of the Bessemer process, perfected independently by Henry Bessemer, an Englishman, and William Kelly of Kentucky. Bessemer and Kelly discovered that a stream of air directed into a mass of molten iron caused the carbon and other impurities to combine with oxygen and burn off. When measured amounts of carbon, silicon, and manganese were added, the brew became steel. What had been a rare metal could now be produced by the hundreds and thousands of tons. In 1870, 77,000 tons of steel were manufactured; by 1890, that had expanded to nearly 5 million tons. Such growth would have been impossible without the huge supplies of iron ore in the United States and the coal necessary to fire the furnaces that refined it.

Pittsburgh, surrounded by vast coal deposits, became the iron and steel capital of the country, the Minnesota ores reaching it by way of steamers on the Great Lakes and rail lines from Cleveland. Other cities in Pennsylvania and Ohio were important producers, and a separate complex, centering on Birmingham, Alabama, developed to exploit local iron and coal fields.

The petroleum industry expanded even more spectacularly than iron and steel. Edwin L. Drake drilled the first successful well in Pennsylvania in 1859. During the Civil War,

This 1900 photograph of steel factories at night in Duquesne, near Pittsburgh, was tinted by hand.
Source: North Wind Picture Archives.

production ranged between 2 million and 3 million barrels a year. By 1890 the figure had leaped to about 50 million barrels.

Before the invention of the gasoline engine and the automobile, the most important petroleum product was kerosene, which was burned in lamps. Refiners heated crude oil in large kettles and, after the volatile elements had escaped, condensed the kerosene in coils cooled by water. The heavier petroleum tars were discarded.

Technological advances came rapidly. By the early 1870s, refiners had learned how to "crack" petroleum by applying high temperatures to the crude oil in order to rearrange its molecular structure, thereby increasing the percentage of kerosene yielded. By-products such as naphtha, gasoline (used in vaporized form as an illuminating gas), rhigolene (a local anesthetic), cymogene (a coolant for refrigerating machines), and many lubricants and waxes began to appear on the market. At the same time a great increase in the supply of crude oil drove prices down.

These circumstances put a premium on refining efficiency. Larger plants using expensive machinery and employing skilled technicians became more important. In the mid-1860s only three refineries in the country could process 2,000 barrels of crude oil a week; a decade later plants capable of handling 1,000 barrels a day were common.

Two other important new industries were the telephone and electric light businesses. Both were typical of the period, being products of technical advances and intimately related to the growth of a high-speed, urban civilization that put great stress on communication. The telephone was invented in 1876 by Alexander Graham Bell, who had been led to the study of acoustics through his interest in the education of the deaf. The invention soon proved its value. By 1900 there were almost 800,000 telephones in the country, twice the total for all Europe. The American Telephone and Telegraph Company, a consolidation of over 100 local systems, dominated the business.

When the Western Union Telegraph Company realized the importance of the telephone, it tried for a time to compete with Bell by developing a machine of its own. The man it commissioned to devise this machine was Thomas A. Edison, but Bell's patents proved unassailable. Edison had already made a number of contributions toward solving what he called the "mysteries of electrical force," including a multiplex telegraph capable of sending four messages over a single wire at the same time. At Menlo Park, New Jersey, he built the prototype of the modern research laboratory, where specific problems could be attacked on a mass scale by a team of trained specialists. During his lifetime he took out more than 1,000 patents dealing with machines as varied as the phonograph, the motion-picture projector, the storage battery, and the mimeograph.

Edison's most significant achievement was the incandescent lamp, or electric lightbulb. Others before him had experimented with the idea of producing light by passing electricity through a filament in a vacuum. Always, however, the filaments quickly burned out.

●●●─ Read the Document

Edison, *The Success of the Electric Light* at **myhistorylab.com**

Edison tried hundreds of fibers before producing, in 1879, a carbonized filament that would glow brightly in a vacuum tube for as long as 170 hours without crumbling. At Christmastime he decorated the grounds about his laboratory with a few dozen of the new lights. People flocked by the thousands to see this miracle of the "Wizard of Menlo Park." The inventor boasted that soon he would be able to illuminate entire towns, even great cities like New York.

He was true to his promise. In 1882 his Edison Illuminating Company opened a power station in New York City and began to supply current for lighting to eighty-five consumers, including the *New York Times* and the banking house of J.P. Morgan and Company. Soon central stations were springing up everywhere until, by 1898, there were about 3,000 in the country.

The substitution of electric for steam power in factories was as liberating as that of steam for waterpower before the Civil War. Small, safe electric motors replaced dangerous and cumbersome mazes of belts and wheels. The electric power industry expanded rapidly. By the early years of the twentieth century almost 6 billion kilowatt-hours of electricity were being produced annually. Yet this was only the beginning.

Competition and Monopoly: The Railroads

During the post–Civil War era, expansion in industry went hand in hand with concentration. The principal cause of this trend, aside from the obvious economies resulting from large-scale production and the growing importance of expensive machinery, was the downward trend of prices after 1873. The deflation, which resulted mainly from the failure of the money supply to keep pace with the rapid increase in the volume of goods produced, affected agricultural goods as well as manufactures, and it lasted until 1896 or 1897.

Contemporaries believed that they were living through a "great depression." That label is misleading, for output expanded almost continuously, and at a rapid rate, until 1893, when production slumped and a true depression struck the country. Falling prices, however, kept a steady pressure on profit margins, and this led to increased production and thus to intense competition for markets.

According to the classical economists, competition advanced the public interest by keeping prices low and ensuring the most efficient producer the largest profit. Up to a point it accomplished these purposes in the years after 1865, but it also caused side effects that injured both the economy and society as a whole. Railroad managers, for instance, found it impossible to enforce "official" rate schedules and maintain their regional associations once competitive pressures mounted. In 1865 it had cost from ninety-six cents to $2.15 per 100 pounds, depending on the class of freight, to ship goods from New York to Chicago. In 1888 rates ranged from thirty-five cents to seventy-five cents.

Competition cut deeply into railroad profits, causing the lines to seek desperately to increase volume. It did so chiefly by reducing rates still more, on a selective basis. The competition gave rebates (secret reductions below the published rates) to large shippers in order to capture their business. Giving discounts to those who shipped in volume made economic sense: It was easier to handle freight in carload lots than in smaller units. So intense was the battle for business, however, that the railroads often made concessions to big customers far beyond what the economics of bulk shipment justified.

Railroad officials disliked rebating but found no way to avoid the practice. In extreme cases the railroads even gave large shippers drawbacks, which were rebates on the business of the shippers' competitors. Besides rebating, railroads issued passes to favored shippers, built sidings at the plants of important companies without charge, and gave freely of their landholdings to attract businesses to their territory.

To make up for losses forced on them by competitive pressures, railroads charged higher rates at waypoints along their tracks where no competition existed. Frequently it cost more to ship a product a short distance than a longer one. Rochester, New York, was served only by the New York Central. In the 1870s it cost thrity cents to transport a barrel of flour from Rochester to New York City, a distance of 350 miles. At the same time flour could be shipped from Minneapolis to New York, a distance of well over 1,000 miles, for only twenty cents a barrel.

Although cheap transportation stimulated the economy, few people benefited from cutthroat competition. Small shippers—and all businessmen in cities and towns with limited rail outlets—suffered; railroad discrimination speeded the concentration of industry in large corporations located in major centers. The instability of rates even troubled interests like the midwestern flour millers who benefited from the competitive situation, for it hampered planning. Nor could manufacturers who received rebates be entirely happy, since few could be sure that some other producer was not getting a larger reduction.

Probably the worst sufferers were the railroads themselves. The loss of revenue resulting from rate cutting, combined with inflated debts, put most of them in grave difficulty when faced with a downturn in the business cycle. In 1876 two-fifths of all railroad bonds were in default; three years later sixty-five lines were bankrupt.

Since the public would not countenance bankrupt railroads going out of business, these companies were placed in the hands of court-appointed receivers. The receivers, however, seldom provided efficient management and had no funds at their disposal for new equipment.

During the 1880s the major railroads responded to these pressures by building or buying lines in order to create interregional systems. These were the first giant corporations, capitalized in the hundreds of millions of dollars. Their enormous cost led to another wave of bankruptcies when a true depression struck in the 1890s.

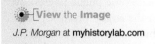
J.P. Morgan at myhistorylab.com

The consequent reorganizations brought most of the big systems under the control of financiers, notably J. Pierpont Morgan and such other private bankers as Kuhn, Loeb of New York and Lee, Higginson of Boston.

Critics called the reorganizations "Morganizations." Representatives of the bankers sat on the board of every line they saved and their influence was predominant. They consistently opposed rate wars, rebating, and other competitive practices. In effect, control of the railroad network became centralized, even though the companies maintained their separate existences and operated in a seemingly independent manner. When Morgan died in 1913, "Morgan men" dominated the boards of the New York Central; the Erie; the New York, New Haven, and Hartford; the Southern; the Pere Marquette; the Atchison, Topeka, and Santa Fe; and many other lines.

Competition and Monopoly: Steel

The iron and steel industry was also intensely competitive. Despite the trend toward higher production, demand varied erratically from year to year, even from month to month. In good times producers built new facilities, only to suffer heavy losses when demand declined. The forward rush of technology put a tremendous emphasis on efficiency; expensive plants quickly became obsolete. Improved transportation facilities allowed manufacturers in widely separated places to compete with one another.

The kingpin of the industry was Andrew Carnegie. Carnegie was born in Scotland and came to the United States in 1848 at the age of twelve. His first job, as a bobbin boy

This early 1900 photograph shows how steel mills spread along the riverfront of Pittsburgh, Pennsylvania.

Photo Credit: Private Collection/The Bridgeman Art Library.

in a cotton mill, brought him $1.20 a week, but his talents perfectly fitted the times and he rose rapidly: to Western Union messenger boy, to telegrapher, to private secretary, to railroad manager. He saved his money, made some shrewd investments, and by 1868 had an income of $50,000 a year.

At about this time he decided to specialize in the iron business. Carnegie possessed great talent as a salesman, boundless faith in the future of the country, an uncanny knack of choosing topflight subordinates, and enough ruthlessness to survive in the iron and steel jungle. Where other steel men built new plants in good times, he preferred to expand in bad times, when it cost far less to do so.

Carnegie grasped the importance of technological improvements. Slightly skeptical of the Bessemer process at first, once he became convinced of its practicality he adopted it enthusiastically. In 1875 he built the J. Edgar Thomson Steel Works, named after a president of the Pennsylvania Railroad, his biggest customer. He employed chemists and other specialists and was soon making steel from iron oxides that other manufacturers had discarded as waste. He was a merciless competitor. Carnegie sold rails by paying "commissions" to railroad purchasing agents, and he was not above reneging on a contract if he thought it profitable and safe to do so.

By 1890 the Carnegie Steel Company dominated the industry, and its output increased nearly tenfold during the next decade. Profits soared. Alarmed by his increasing control of the industry, the makers of finished steel products such as barbed wire and tubing considered pooling their resources and making steel themselves. Carnegie, his competitive temper aroused, threatened to manufacture wire, pipes, and other finished products. A colossal steel war seemed imminent.

However, Carnegie longed to retire in order to devote himself to philanthropic work. He believed that great wealth entailed social responsibilities and that it was a disgrace to die rich. When J.P. Morgan approached him through an intermediary with an offer to buy him out, he assented readily. In 1901 Morgan put together United States Steel, the "world's first billion-dollar corporation." This combination included all the Carnegie properties, the Federal Steel Company (Carnegie's largest competitor), and such important fabricators of finished products as the American Steel and Wire Company, the American Tin Plate Company, and the National Tube Company. Vast reserves of Minnesota iron ore and a fleet of Great Lakes ore steamers were also included. U.S. Steel was capitalized at $1.4 billion, about twice the value of its component properties but not necessarily an overestimation of its profit-earning capacity. The owners of Carnegie Steel received $492 million, of which $250 million went to Carnegie himself.

●●●━[Read the Document
Carnegie, *Wealth* at
myhistorylab.com

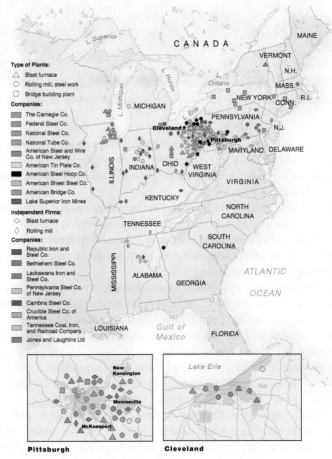

Firms Incorporated into U.S. Steel J.P. Morgan's consolidation that created U.S. Steel.

Competition and Monopoly: Oil

The pattern of fierce competition leading to combination and monopoly is well illustrated by the history of the petroleum industry. Irresistible pressures pushed the refiners into a brutal struggle to dominate the business. Production of crude oil, subject to the uncertainties of prospecting and drilling, fluctuated constantly and without regard for need. In general, output surged far ahead of demand.

By the 1870s the chief oil-refining centers were Cleveland, Pittsburgh, Baltimore, and the New York City area. Of these Cleveland was the fastest growing, chiefly because the New York Central and Erie railroads competed fiercely for its oil trade and the Erie Canal offered an alternative route.

The Standard Oil Company of Cleveland, founded in 1870 by a thirty-one-year-old merchant named John D. Rockefeller, emerged as the giant among the refiners. Rockefeller exploited every possible technical advance and employed fair means and foul to persuade competitors either to sell out or to join forces. By 1879 he controlled 90 percent of the nation's oil-refining capacity along with a network of oil pipelines and large reserves of petroleum in the ground.

Standard Oil emerged victorious from the competitive wars because Rockefeller and his associates were the toughest and most imaginative fighters as well as the most efficient refiners in the business. In addition to obtaining from the railroads a 10 percent rebate and drawbacks on its competitors' shipments, Standard Oil cut prices locally to force small independents to sell out or face ruin. Since kerosene was sold in grocery stores, Standard supplied its own outlets with meat, sugar, and other products at artificially low prices to help crush the stores that handled other brands of kerosene. The company employed spies to track down the customers of independents and offer them oil at bargain prices. Bribery was also a Standard practice; the reformer Henry Demarest Lloyd quipped that the company had done everything to the Pennsylvania legislature except refine it.

Although a bold planner and a daring taker of necessary risks, Rockefeller was far too orderly and astute to enjoy the free-swinging battles that plagued his industry. Born in an upstate New York village in 1839, he settled in Cleveland in 1855 and became a produce merchant. During the Civil War he invested in a local refinery and by 1865 was engaged full time in the oil business.

Having achieved his monopoly, Rockefeller stabilized and structured it by creating a new type of business organization, the trust. Standard Oil was an Ohio corporation, prohibited by local law from owning plants in other states or holding stock in out-of-state corporations. As Rockefeller and his associates took over dozens of companies with facilities scattered across the country, serious legal and managerial difficulties arose. How could these many organizations be integrated with Standard Oil of Ohio?

A Pennsylvania lawyer named Samuel C. T. Dodd came up with an answer to this question in 1879.[1] The stock of Standard of Ohio and of all the other companies that the Rockefeller interests had swallowed up was turned over to nine trustees, who were empowered to "exercise general supervision" over all the properties. In exchange, stockholders received trust certificates, on which dividends were paid. This seemingly simple device brought order to the petroleum business. Competition almost

---

[1]The trust formula was not "perfected" until 1882.

disappeared, prices steadied, and profits skyrocketed. By 1892 John D. Rockefeller was worth over $800 million.

The Standard Oil Trust was not a corporation. It had no charter, indeed no legal existence at all. For many years few people outside the organization knew that it existed. The form they chose persuaded Rockefeller and other Standard Oil officials that without violating their consciences, they could deny under oath that Standard Oil of Ohio owned or controlled other corporations "directly or indirectly through its officers or agents." The trustees controlled these organizations—and Standard of Ohio too!

After Standard Oil's duplicity was revealed during a New York investigation in 1888, the word *trust*, formerly signifying a fiduciary arrangement for the protection of the interests of individuals incompetent or unwilling to guard them themselves, became a synonym for monopoly. However, from the company's point of view, monopoly was not the purpose of the trust—that had been achieved before the device was invented. Centralization of the management of diverse and far-flung operations in the interest of efficiency was its chief function.

Competition and Monopoly: Retailing and Utilities

That utilities such as the telephone and electric lighting industries tended to form monopolies is not difficult to explain, for in such fields competition involved costly duplication of equipment and, particularly in the case of the telephone, loss of service efficiency. However, competitive pressures were strong in the early stages of their development. Since these industries depended on patents, Bell and Edison had to fight mighty battles in the courts with rivals seeking to infringe on their rights. A patent, Edison said bitterly, was "simply an invitation to a lawsuit."

The pattern of competition leading to dominance by a few great companies was repeated in many businesses. In life insurance an immense expansion took place after the Civil War. High-pressure salesmanship prevailed; agents gave rebates to customers by shaving their own commissions; companies stole crack agents from their rivals and raided new territories. They sometimes invested as much as 96 percent of the first year's premiums in obtaining new business. By 1900, after three decades of fierce competition, three giants dominated the industry—Equitable, New York Life, and Mutual Life, each with approximately $1 billion of insurance in force.

Watch the Video
Rural Free Delivery Mail at
myhistorylab.com

American Ambivalence to Big Business

The expansion of industry and its concentration in fewer and fewer hands changed the way many people felt about the role of government in economic and social affairs. On the one hand, they professed to believe strongly in a government policy of noninterference, or **laissez-faire**. " 'Things regulate themselves' . . . means, of course, that God regulates them by his general laws," Professor Francis Bowen of Harvard wrote in his *American Political Economy* (1870).

Certain intellectual currents encouraged this type of thinking. Charles Darwin's *The Origin of Species* was published in 1859, and by the 1870s his theory of evolution was beginning to influence opinion in the United States. That nature had ordained a kind of inevitable progress, governed by the natural selection of those individual organisms best

Photo Credit: Courtesy of the Library of Congress.

A sneeze is captured on film—the first copyrighted movie (1894). In 1889 Thomas A. Edison conceived of a machine that would do for the eye what the phonograph did for the ear. Over the next two years, Edison invented two separate devices—a camera to take a rapid sequence of pictures and a machine to view them, called a kinetoscope. In 1893 he developed reliable film for his camera. The motion picture industry was born.

adapted to survive in a particular environment, seemed eminently reasonable to most Americans, for it fitted well with their own experiences. "Let the buyer beware; that covers the whole business," the sugar magnate Henry O. Havemeyer explained to an investigating committee. "You cannot wet-nurse people from the time they are born until the time they die. They have to wade and get stuck, and that is the way men are educated."

This reasoning was similar to that of the classical economists and was thus at least as old as Adam Smith's *Wealth of Nations* (1776). But it appeared to supply a hard scientific substitute for Smith's "invisible hand" as an explanation of why free competition advanced the common good.

Yale professor William Graham Sumner sometimes used the survival-of-the-fittest analogy in teaching undergraduates. "Professor," one student asked Sumner, "don't you believe in any government aid to industries?" "No!" Sumner replied, "It's root, hog, or die." The student persisted: "Suppose some professor of political science came along and took your job away from you. Wouldn't you be sore?" "Any other professor is welcome to try," Sumner answered promptly. "If he gets my job, it is my fault. My business is to teach the subject so well that no one can take the job away from me." Sumner's argument described what came to be known as **social Darwinism,** the belief that the activities of people, that is, their business and social relationships, were governed by the Darwinian principle that "the fittest" will always "survive" if allowed to exercise their capacities without restriction.

But the fact that Americans disliked powerful governments in general and strict regulation of the economy in particular had never meant that they objected to all government activity in the economic sphere. Banking laws, tariffs, internal-improvement legislation, and the granting of public land to railroads are only the most obvious of the economic regulations enforced in the nineteenth century by both the federal government and the states. Americans saw no contradiction between government activities of this type and the free enterprise philosophy.

The growth of huge industrial and financial organizations and the increasing complexity of economic relations frightened people yet made them at the same time greedy for more of the goods and services the new society was turning out. To many, the great new corporations and trusts resembled Frankenstein's monster—marvelous and powerful but a grave threat to society.

To some extent public fear of the industrial giants reflected concern about monopoly—much as some people today worry that Walmart may drive other retailers out of business. If Standard Oil dominated oil refining, it might raise prices inordinately at vast cost to consumers.

Far more important in causing resentment was the fear that the monopolists were destroying economic opportunity and threatening democratic institutions. It was not the wealth of tycoons like Carnegie and Rockefeller and Morgan so much as their influence that worried people. "The belief is common," wrote Charles Francis Adams's brother Henry as early as 1870, "that the day is at hand when corporations . . . will ultimately succeed in directing government itself."

Table 1   Defenders of Economic Consolidation

Defenders	Occupation	Argument
J. Pierpont Morgan	Wall Street financier	Excessive competition was wasteful and unstable; stable growth and efficiency required large business combinations
William Graham Sumner	Yale professor	Large corporations were those that were "fittest"—best-suited to prevail in the Darwinian world of capitalism
Andrew Carnegie	Steel manufacturer	Large corporations generated wealth, which could be channeled into charitable and other worthy causes

As criticism mounted, business leaders rose to their own defense. Rockefeller described in graphic terms the chaotic conditions that plagued the oil industry before the rise of Standard Oil: "It seemed absolutely necessary to extend the market for oil . . . and also greatly improve the process of refining so that oil could be made and sold cheaply, yet with a profit. We proceeded to buy the largest and best refining concerns and centralized the administration of them with a view to securing greater economy and efficiency." Carnegie, in an essay published in 1889, insisted that the concentration of wealth was necessary if humanity was to progress, softening this "Gospel of Wealth" by insisting that the rich must use their money "in the manner which . . . is best calculated to produce the most beneficial results for the community."

The voices of the critics were louder if not necessarily more influential. Many clergymen denounced unrestrained competition, which they considered un-Christian. The new class of professional economists tended to repudiate laissez-faire. State aid, Richard T. Ely of Johns Hopkins University wrote, "is an indispensable condition of human progress."

Reformers: George, Bellamy, Lloyd

The popularity of a number of radical theorists reflects public feeling in the period. In 1879 Henry George, a California journalist, published *Progress and Poverty*, a forthright attack on the uneven distribution of wealth in the United States. George argued that labor was the true and only source of capital. Observing the speculative fever of the West, which enabled landowners to reap profits merely by holding property while population increased, George proposed a property tax that would confiscate this "unearned increment." George's "single tax," as others called it, would bring in so much money that no other taxes would be necessary, and the government would have plenty of funds to establish badly needed social and cultural services. Single tax clubs sprang up throughout the nation, and *Progress and Poverty* became a best-seller.

Even more spectacular was the reception afforded *Looking Backward, 2000–1887*, a utopian novel written in 1888 by Edward Bellamy. This text, which sold over a million copies in its first few years, described a future America that was completely socialized, all economic activity carefully planned. Bellamy compared nineteenth-century

Edward Bellamy, author of the utopian novel *Looking Backward* (1888). Bellamy's socialism worried many. *The Household Encyclopedia* (1892) included this photograph of Bellamy in a section on phrenology, the "science" of ascertaining a person's character and intellectual traits from the shape of his or her cranium. Referring to Bellamy's, it concluded, "Large perceptive faculties; defective reasoning powers."

Photo Credit: © Bettmann/CORBIS All Rights Reserved.

●●●─[Read the Document

Bellamy, from *Looking Backward* at **myhistorylab.com**

society to a lumbering stagecoach upon which the favored few rode in comfort while the mass of the people hauled them along life's route. The trend toward consolidation would continue, he predicted, until one monster trust controlled all economic activity. At this point everyone would realize that nationalization was essential.

A third influential attack on monopoly was that of Henry Demarest Lloyd, whose *Wealth Against Commonwealth* appeared in 1894. Lloyd, a journalist of independent means, devoted years to preparing a denunciation of the Standard Oil Company. Marshaling masses of facts and vivid examples of Standard's evildoing, he assaulted the trust at every point. In his zeal, Lloyd sometimes distorted and exaggerated the evidence; his forceful but uncomplicated arguments and his copious references to official documents made *Wealth Against Commonwealth* utterly convincing to thousands. The book was more than an attack on Standard Oil. Lloyd denounced the application of Darwin's concept of survival of the fittest to economic and social affairs, and he condemned laissez-faire policies as leading directly to monopoly.

The popularity of these books indicates that the trend toward monopoly in the United States worried many. But despite the drastic changes suggested in their pages, none of these writers questioned the underlying values of the middle-class majority. They insisted that reform could be accomplished without serious inconvenience to any individual or class.

Most of their millions of readers did not seriously consider trying to apply the reformers' ideas. Henry George ran for mayor of New York City in 1886 and lost narrowly to Abram S. Hewitt, a wealthy iron manufacturer, but even if he had won, he would have been powerless to apply the single tax to metropolitan property. The national discontent was apparently not as profound as the popularity of these works might suggest.

Reformers: The Marxists

By the 1870s the ideas of European socialists were beginning to penetrate the United States, and in 1877 a Socialist Labor party was founded. The first serious attempt to explain the ideas of German political philosopher Karl Marx to Americans was Laurence Gronlund's *The Cooperative Commonwealth*, which was published in 1884, two years before Marx's *Das Kapital* was translated into English.

Capitalism, Gronlund claimed, contained the seeds of its own destruction. The state ought to own all the means of production. Competition was "Established Anarchy," middlemen were "parasites," speculators "vampires." Yet like other harsh critics of that day, Gronlund expected the millennium to arrive in a peaceful, indeed orderly manner. The movement could accommodate "representatives of all classes," even "thoughtful" middlemen parasites.

The leading voice of the Socialist Labor party, Daniel De Leon, editor of the party's weekly publication, *The People*, was a different type. He was born in the West Indies, son of a Dutch army doctor stationed in Curaçao, and educated in Europe. He emigrated to the United States in the 1870s, where he was progressively attracted by the ideas of Henry George, then Edward Bellamy and the Knights of Labor, and finally Marx. While personally mild-mannered and kindly, when he put pen to paper he became a doctrinaire revolutionary. He excoriated American labor unions in *The People*, insisting that industrial workers could improve their lot only by adopting socialism and joining the

Table 2 Reformers Oppose Economic Consolidation

Reformers	Publication	Argument
Henry George	Author, *Progress and Poverty* (1879)	Labor was the source of wealth; but investors made money from *capital and property.* Governments should tax property, to help redistribute the unearned income of the wealthy.
Edward Bellamy	Author, *Looking Backward* (1888)	The trend toward industrial concentration would culminate in the government owning everything: an era of prosperity, stability, and cooperative planning would ensue.
Henry Demarest Lloyd	Author, *Wealth Against Commonwealth* (1894)	Concentration of power in corporations inevitably led to monopoly; the government must step in to prevent corporations from becoming behemoths.
Laurence Gronlund	Author, *The Cooperative Commonwealth* (1884)	Capitalism, including corporations, was doomed, as Marx had predicted; but the collapse of capitalism would not require a violent revolution.
Daniel De Leon	Editor, Socialist Labor, *The Weekly*	Capitalism, though doomed, would not fall without a fight; violent revolution was inevitable.

Socialist Labor party. He paid scant attention, however, to the practical needs or even to the opinions of rank-and-file working people. In 1891 he was the Socialist Labor party's candidate for governor of New York.

The Government Reacts to Big Business: Railroad Regulation

Political action related to the growth of big business came first on the state level and dealt chiefly with the regulation of railroads. Even before the Civil War, a number of New England states established railroad commissions to supervise lines within their borders; by the end of the century, twenty-eight states had such boards.

Strict regulation was largely the result of agitation by the **National Grange of the Patrons of Husbandry.** The Grange, founded in 1867 by Oliver H. Kelley, was created to provide social and cultural benefits for isolated rural communities. As it spread and grew in influence—fourteen states had Granges by 1872 and membership reached 800,000 in 1874—the movement became political too. "Granger" candidates won control of a number of state legislatures in the West and South. Granger-controlled legislatures established "reasonable" maximum rates and outlawed "unjust" discrimination. The legislature also set up a commission to enforce the laws and punish violators.

The railroads protested, insisting that they were being deprived of property without due process of law. In *Munn v. Illinois* (1877), a case that involved a grain elevator whose owner had refused to comply with a state warehouse act, the Supreme Court upheld the constitutionality of this kind of act. Any business that served a public interest, such as a railroad or a grain warehouse, was subject to state control, the justices ruled. Legislatures might fix maximum charges; if the charges seemed unreasonable to the parties concerned, they should direct their complaints to the legislatures or to the voters, not to the courts.

Regulation of the railroad network by the individual states was inefficient, and in some cases the commissions were incompetent and even corrupt. When the Supreme Court, in the case of *Wabash, St. Louis & Pacific Railroad v. Illinois* (1886), declared unconstitutional an Illinois regulation outlawing the long-and-short-haul evil, federal action became necessary. The railroad had charged twenty-five cents per 100 pounds for shipping goods from Gilman, Illinois, to New York City but only fifteen cents to ship goods from Peoria, which was eighty-six miles farther from New York. Illinois judges had held this to be illegal, but the Supreme Court decided that Illinois could not regulate interstate shipments.

Congress filled the gap created by the *Wabash* decision in 1887 by passing the **Interstate Commerce Act**. All charges made by railroads "shall be reasonable and just," the act stated. Rebates, drawbacks, the long-and-short-haul evil, and other competitive practices were declared unlawful, and so were their monopolistic counterparts—pools and traffic-sharing agreements. Railroads were required to publish

●●—[Read the Document

Interstate Commerce Act at
myhistorylab.com

A farmer with a pitchfork, wearing a hat identifying him as a Granger, warns of an oncoming railroad train. But the American people—one reads a newspaper, another smokes a cigar, but most doze—are oblivious of the danger that will soon crush them.

Photo Credit: The Granger Collection, New York.

schedules of rates and forbidden to change them without due public notice. Most important, the law established an Interstate Commerce Commission (ICC), the first federal regulatory board, to supervise the affairs of railroads, investigate complaints, and issue cease and desist orders when the roads acted illegally.

The new commission had less power than the law seemed to give it. It could not fix rates; it could only bring the roads to court when it considered rates unreasonably high. Such cases could be extremely complicated; applying the law "was like cutting a path through a jungle." With the truth so hard to determine and the burden of proof on the commission, the courts in nearly every instance decided in favor of the railroads.

Nevertheless, by describing so clearly the right of Congress to regulate private corporations engaged in interstate commerce, the Interstate Commerce Act challenged the philosophy of laissez-faire. Later legislation made the commission more effective. The commission also served as the model for a host of similar federal administrative authorities, such as the Federal Communications Commission (1934).

The Government Reacts to Big Business: The Sherman Antitrust Act

As with railroad legislation, the first antitrust laws originated in the states, but they were southern and western states with relatively little industry, and most of the statutes were vaguely worded and ill-enforced. Federal action came in 1890 with the passage of the **Sherman Antitrust Act**. Any combination "in the form of trust or otherwise" that was "in restraint of trade or commerce among the several states, or with foreign nations" was declared illegal. Persons forming such combinations were subject to fines of $5,000 and a year in jail. Individuals and businesses suffering losses because of actions that violated the law were authorized to sue in the federal courts for triple damages.

Where the Interstate Commerce Act sought to outlaw the excesses of competition, the Sherman Act was supposed to restore competition. If businessmen joined together to "restrain" (monopolize) trade in a particular field, they should be punished and their deeds undone. "The great thing this bill does," Senator George Frisbie Hoar of Massachusetts explained, "is to extend the common-law principle . . . to international and interstate commerce." This was important because the states ran into legal difficulties when they tried to use the common law to restrict corporations engaged in interstate activities.

The Supreme Court quickly emasculated the Sherman Act. In *United States v. E. C. Knight Company* (1895) it held that the American Sugar Refining Company had not violated the law by taking over a number of important competitors. Although the Sugar Trust now controlled about 98 percent of all sugar refining in the United States, it was not restraining trade. "Doubtless the power to control the manufacture of a given thing involves in a certain sense the control of its disposition," the Court said in one of the greatest feats of judicial understatement of all time. "Although the exercise of that power may result in bringing the operation of commerce into play, it does not control it, and affects it only incidentally and indirectly."

If the creation of the Sugar Trust did not violate the Sherman Act, it seemed unlikely that any other combination of manufacturers could be convicted under the law. However, in several cases in 1898 and 1899 the Supreme Court ruled that agreements to fix prices or divide markets did violate the Sherman Act. These decisions precipitated a wave of

**Table 3 Major Congressional and Supreme Court Decisions
Concerning Corporations**

Case/Act	Year	Decision/Action	Consequence
Munn v. Illinois	1877	State legislatures can regulate economic enterprises	Expansion of state powers against powerful corporations and trusts
Wabash, St. Louis & Pacific Railroad v. Illinois	1886	State legislatures can NOT regulate interstate economic activity; only federal government can do that	Congress passes Interstate Commerce Act 1887, regulating railroad behavior
Interstate Commerce Act	1887	Federal government can regulate railroad rates and practices	Sets precedent for federal intervention in national economic matters
Sherman Antitrust Act	1890	The federal government can break up economic enterprises that are so big and powerful that they have a monopoly	Originally used to weaken labor unions; eventually allows government to break up large corporations
United States v. E. C. Knight	1895	Huge corporations that dominated markets can not be broken up if they do not also behave badly	Weakens Sherman Antitrust Act

outright mergers in which a handful of large companies swallowed up hundreds of smaller ones. Presumably mergers were not illegal. When, some years after his retirement, Andrew Carnegie was asked by a committee of the House of Representatives to explain how he had dared participate in the formation of the U.S. Steel Corporation, he replied, "Nobody ever mentioned the Sherman Act to me that I remember."

The Labor Union Movement

At the time of the Civil War only a small percentage of the American workforce was organized, and most union members were cigarmakers, printers, carpenters, and other skilled artisans, not factory hands. Aside from ironworkers, railroad workers, and miners, few industrial laborers belonged to unions. Nevertheless the union was the workers' response to the big corporation: a combination designed to eliminate competition for jobs and to provide efficient organization for labor.

After 1865 the growth of national craft unions, which had been stimulated by labor dissatisfaction during the Civil War, quickened perceptibly. In 1866 a federation of these organizations, the National Labor Union, was founded and by the early 1870s many new trades, notably in railroading, had been unionized.

Most of the leaders of these unions were visionaries who were out of touch with the practical needs and aspirations of workers. They opposed the wage system, strikes, and anything that increased the laborers' sense of being members of the working class. A major objective was the formation of worker-owned cooperatives.

Far more remarkable was the **Knights of Labor**, a curious organization founded in 1869 by a group of Philadelphia garment workers headed by Uriah S. Stephens. Like so many labor organizers of the period, Stephens was a reformer of wide interests rather than a man dedicated to the specific problems of industrial workers. He, his successor Terence V. Powderly, and many other leaders of the Knights would have been thoroughly at home in the labor organizations of the Jacksonian era. Like the Jacksonians, they supported political objectives that had no direct connection with working conditions, such as currency reform and the curbing of land speculation. They rejected the idea that workers must resign themselves to remaining wage earners. By pooling their resources, working people could advance up the economic ladder and enter the capitalist class. The leading Knights saw no contradiction between their denunciation of "soulless" monopolies and "drones" like bankers and lawyers and their talk of "combining all branches of trade in one common brotherhood." Such muddled thinking led the Knights to attack the wage system and to frown on strikes as "acts of private warfare."

View the Image
Terence Powderly at Knights of Labor Convention at **myhistorylab.com**

If the Knights had one foot in the past, they also had one foot in the future. They supported some startlingly advanced ideas. Rejecting the traditional grouping of workers by crafts, they developed a concept closely resembling modern industrial unionism. They welcomed blacks, women, and immigrants, and they accepted unskilled workers as well as artisans. The eight-hour day was one of their basic demands, their argument being that increased leisure would give workers time to develop more cultivated tastes and higher aspirations. Higher pay would inevitably follow.

Between 1882 and 1886 successful strikes by local "assemblies" against western railroads, including one against the hated Jay Gould's Missouri Pacific, brought recruits by the thousands. The membership passed 42,000 in 1882, 110,000 in 1885, and in 1886 it soared beyond the 700,000 mark. Alas, sudden prosperity was too much for the Knights. Its national leadership was unable to control local groups. A number of poorly planned strikes failed dismally, and the public was alienated by sporadic acts of violence and intimidation. Disillusioned recruits began to drift away.

Circumstances largely fortuitous caused the collapse of the organization. By 1886 the movement for the eight-hour day had gained wide support among workers, including many who did not belong to unions. Several hundred thousand were on strike in various parts of the country by May of that year. In Chicago, a center of the eight-hour movement, about 80,000 workers were involved, and a small group of anarchists was trying to take advantage of the excitement to win support.

When a striker was killed in a fracas at the McCormick Harvesting Machine Company, the anarchists called a protest meeting on May 4, at Haymarket Square. Police intervened to break up the meeting, and someone—his identity was never established—hurled a bomb into their ranks. Seven policemen were killed and many others injured.

The American Federation of Labor

Although the anarchists were the immediate victims of the resulting public indignation and hysteria, organized labor, especially the Knights, suffered heavily. No tie between the Knights and the bombing could be established, but the union had been closely connected with the eight-hour agitation, and the public tended to associate it with violence and radicalism. Its membership declined as suddenly as it had risen, and soon it ceased to exist as a force in the labor movement.

The Knights' place was taken by the **American Federation of Labor (AFL),** a combination of national craft unions established in 1886. In a sense the AFL was a reactionary organization. Its principal leaders, Adolph Strasser and Samuel Gompers of the Cigarmakers Union, were, like the founders of the Knights of Labor, originally interested in utopian social reforms. They even toyed with the idea of forming a workers' political party. Experience, however, soon led them to concentrate on organizing skilled workers and fighting for "bread-and-butter" issues such as higher wages and shorter hours.

Strasser and Gompers paid great attention to building a strong organization of dues-paying members committed to unionism as a way of improving their lot. Rank-and-file AFL members were naturally eager to win wage increases and other benefits, but most also valued their unions for the companionship they provided, the sense of belonging to a group. Unions were a kind of club as well as a means of defending and advancing their members' material interests.

The chief weapon of the federation was the strike, which it used to win concessions from employers and to attract recruits. Gompers, president of the AFL almost continuously from 1886 until his death in 1924, encouraged workers to make "intelligent use of the ballot" in order to advance their interests. The federation avoided direct involvement in politics. "I have my own philosophy and my own dreams," Gompers once told a left-wing French politician, "but first and foremost I want to increase the workingman's welfare year by year. . . . The French workers waste their economic force by their political divisions."

On November 11, 1887, four anarchists were hanged in Chicago on charges they had thrown a bomb that had killed policemen at the Haymarket demonstration. The *Chicago Tribune* reported that after nooses were placed around the men's necks, and white hoods over their heads, "for a moment or two the men stood like ghosts." "Long live anarchy" one shouted.

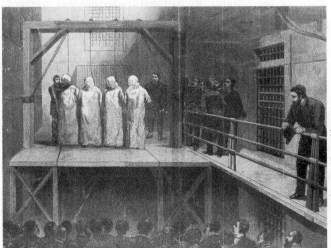

Photo Credit: Chicago History Museum.

Gompers's approach to labor problems produced solid, if unspectacular, growth for the AFL. Unions with a total of about 150,000 members formed the federation in 1886. By 1892 the membership had reached 250,000, and in 1901 it passed the million mark.

Labor Militancy Rebuffed

The stress of the AFL on the strike weapon reflected rather than caused the increasing militancy of labor. Workers felt themselves threatened from all sides: the growing size and power of their corporate employers; the substitution of machines for human skills; the invasion of foreign workers willing to accept substandard wages. At the same time they had tasted some of the material benefits of industrialization and had learned the advantages of concerted action.

The average employer behaved like a tyrant when dealing with his workers: He discharged them arbitrarily when they tried to organize unions; he hired scabs to replace strikers; he frequently failed to provide the most rudimentary protection against injury on the job. Some employers, Carnegie for example, professed to approve of unions, but almost none would bargain with labor collectively. To do so, they argued, would be to deprive workers of their freedom to contract for their own labor in any way they saw fit.

The industrialists of the period were not all ogres; they were as alarmed by the rapid changes of the times as their workers, and since they had more at stake materially, they were probably more frightened by the uncertainties. Deflation, technological change, and intense competition kept even the most successful under constant pressure.

The thinking of most employers was remarkably confused. They considered workers who joined unions "disloyal," and at the same time they treated labor as a commodity to be purchased as cheaply as possible. When labor was scarce, employers resisted demands for higher wages by arguing that the price of labor was controlled by its productivity; when it was plentiful, they justified reducing wages by referring to the law of supply and demand.

Thus capital and labor were often spoiling for a fight, frequently without fully understanding why. When labor troubles developed, they tended to be bitter, even violent. In 1877 a great railroad strike convulsed much of the nation. It began on the Baltimore and Ohio system in response to a wage cut and spread to other eastern lines and then throughout the West until about two-thirds of the railroad mileage of the country had been shut down. Violence broke out, rail yards were put to the torch, and dismayed and frightened businessmen formed militia companies to patrol the streets of Chicago and other cities. Eventually President Hayes sent federal troops to the trouble spots to restore order, and the strike collapsed. There had been no real danger of revolution, but the violence and destruction of the strike had been without precedent in America.

The disturbances of 1877 were a response to a business slump, those of the next decade a response to good times. Twice as many strikes occurred in 1886 as in any previous year. Even before the Haymarket bombing centered the country's attention on labor problems, the situation had become so disturbing that President Grover Cleveland, in the first presidential message devoted to labor problems, had urged Congress to create a voluntary arbitration board to aid in settling labor disputes— a remarkable suggestion for a man of Cleveland's conservative, laissez-faire approach to economic issues.

In 1892 a violent strike broke out among silver miners at Coeur d'Alene, Idaho, and a far more important clash shook Andrew Carnegie's Homestead steel plant near Pittsburgh when strikers attacked 300 private guards brought in to protect strikebreakers. Seven guards were killed at Homestead and the rest forced to "surrender" and march off ignominiously. The Homestead affair was part of a struggle between capital and labor in the steel industry. Steel producers insisted that the workers were holding back progress by resisting technological advances, while the workers believed that the company was refusing to share the fruits of more efficient operation fairly. The strike was precipitated by the decision of company officials to crush the union at all costs. The final defeat, after a five-month walkout, of the 24,000-member Amalgamated Association of Iron and Steel Workers, one of the most important elements in the AFL, destroyed unionism as an effective force in the steel industry and set back the progress of organized labor all over the country.

As in the case of the Haymarket bombing, the activities of radicals on the fringe of the dispute turned the public against the steelworkers. The boss of Homestead was Henry Clay Frick, a tough-minded foe of unions who was determined to "teach our employees a lesson." Frick made the decision to bring in strikebreakers and to employ Pinkerton detectives to protect them. During the course of the strike, Alexander Berkman, an anarchist, burst into Frick's office and attempted to assassinate him. Frick was only slightly wounded, but the attack brought him much sympathy and unjustly discredited the strikers.

The most important strike of the period took place in 1894. It began when the workers at George Pullman's Palace Car factory outside Chicago walked out in protest against wage cuts. Some Pullman workers belonged to the American Railway Union, headed by Eugene V. Debs. After the strike had dragged along for weeks, the union voted to refuse to handle trains with Pullman sleeper cars. The union was perfectly willing to handle mail trains, but the owners refused to run trains unless they were made up of a full complement of cars.

When Pullman cars were added to mail trains, the workers refused to move them. The resulting railroad strike tied up trunk lines running in and out of Chicago. The railroad owners appealed to President Cleveland to send troops to preserve order. On the pretext that the soldiers were needed to ensure the movement of the mails, Cleveland agreed. When Debs defied a federal injunction to end the walkout, he was jailed for contempt and the strike was broken.

Whither America, Whither Democracy?

Each year more of the nation's wealth and power seemed to fall into fewer hands. As with the railroads, other industries were being influenced, if not completely dominated, by bankers. The firm of J.P. Morgan and Company controlled many railroads; the largest steel, electrical, agricultural machinery, rubber, and shipping companies; two life insurance companies; and a number of banks. By 1913 Morgan and the Rockefeller National City Bank group between them could name 341 directors to 112 corporations worth over $22.2 billion. The "Money Trust," a loose but potent fraternity of financiers, seemed fated to become the ultimate monopoly.

Centralization unquestionably increased efficiency, at least in industries that used a great deal of expensive machinery to turn out goods for the mass market, and in those where close coordination of output, distribution, and sales was important. The public benefited immensely from the productive efficiency of the new empires. Living standards rose.

The crushing of the Pullman strike demonstrated the power of the courts to break strikes by issuing injunctions. And the courts seemed only concerned with protecting the interests of the rich and powerful. Particularly ominous for organized labor was the fact that the federal government based its request for the injunction that broke the strike on the Sherman Antitrust Act, arguing that the American Railway Union was a combination in restraint of trade. An indirect result of the Pullman strike was that while serving his sentence for contempt, Eugene Debs was visited by a number of prominent socialists who sought to convert him to their cause. One gave him a copy of Karl Marx's *Capital*, which he found too dull to finish, but he did read *Looking Backward* and *Wealth Against Commonwealth*. In 1897 he became a socialist.

Milestones

1859	First oil well is drilled in Pennsylvania	1886	Craft unions found American Federation of Labor (AFL)
	Charles Darwin publishes *The Origin of Species*	1887	Interstate Commerce Act regulates railroads
1868	Carnegie Steel Company is formed		
1869	George Westinghouse invents air brake	1888	Edward Bellamy publishes utopian *Looking Backward*
	Garment workers found Knights of Labor	1889	Philanthropist Andrew Carnegie publishes "Gospel of Wealth"
1870–1890	Railroad trunk lines are completed	1890	Sherman Antitrust Act outlaws monopolies
1876	Alexander Graham Bell invents telephone	1892	Seven Pinkerton guards are killed in Homestead steel strike
1877	Great railroad strike convulses nation		General Electric Company is formed
	Munn v. Illinois upholds state regulatory laws	1894	Eugene V. Debs leads American Railway Union in Pullman strike
1879	Thomas Edison invents electric light bulb		Henry Demarest Lloyd condemns laissez-faire in *Wealth Against the Commonwealth*
	Reformer Henry George publishes *Progress and Poverty*		
1884	Marxist Laurence Gronlund publishes *The Cooperative Commonwealth*	1895	*U.S. v. E.C. Knight Company* weakens Sherman Act
1886	Anarchists clash with police in Chicago's Haymarket bombing	1901	J.P. Morgan forms U.S. Steel, "world's first billion-dollar corporation"

✓●—[Study] and **Review** at **www.myhistorylab.zzcom**

Review Questions

1. The introduction asked whether the benefits of economic concentration outweighed its social and political costs. List the benefits and costs: Which argument is stronger?

2. What factors contributed to the nation's extraordinarily rapid industrial growth during the last third of the nineteenth century?

3. What technological developments had the greatest economic impact? Greatest social impact?

4. Who were the major critics of economic concentration in the late nineteenth century and how did they differ?

5. How did Congress respond to critics of monopoly? How did the Supreme Court respond to attempts to regulate the economy?

Key Terms

American Federation of Labor (AFL)
Interstate Commerce Act
Knights of Labor

laissez-faire
National Grange of the Patrons of Husbandry

Sherman Antitrust Act
social Darwinism

American Society in the Industrial Age

Hear the Audio at myhistorylab.com

Have you been kicked out of a mall?

THE MALL OF AMERICA OUTSIDE MINNEAPOLIS, MINNESOTA, IS THE largest enclosed mall in the United States. It is also the nation's most popular tourist destination, visited by 42.5 million people in 2009.

This mall, like many others, was also once a popular hangout for young people. On Friday and Saturday nights, as many as 10,000 teenagers would gather there. But this practice ended in 1996, when the Mall of America instituted a 6:00 PM weekend curfew for teenagers under sixteen unless accompanied by an adult. Since then, hundreds of malls have adopted similar curfews.

Teenagers, who in 2009 bought $170 billion in merchandise, spend much of their free time in malls—over fifty minutes a day on the average. Many resent the curfews. Malls insist that as privately owned enterprises, they are exempt from First Amendment protections, such as freedom of speech and the right to assemble. Malls are not public property.

Yet recent malls have been designed to evoke the public spaces of the nineteenth-century city. The Mall of America includes an exhibition gallery, amusement park, wedding chapel, assembly hall, school, medical clinic, and a central "Rotunda" for staging "public events" ranging from gardening shows to Hulk Hogan wrestling matches.

In the late nineteenth century, city life was played out in spaces that really were public. Factory workers walked to work along crowded streets or jammed into streetcars or subways. Courting couples strolled through shopping districts or public parks. Children played in streets. "Little Italy" or "Chinatown" provided exotic attractions for all. Amusement parks and sporting events drew huge throngs.

But city life was not for all. In 1900, 50 percent more Americans lived in rural areas than in urban areas—even when "urban" was generously defined as holding more than 2,500 people. Why, asked sociologist Henry Fletcher in 1895, do "large masses of people, apparently against their own interests," abandon the nation's healthful and sociable rural areas and crowd into the nation's disease-ridden, anonymous cities?

Nineteenth-century cities, though noisy, chaotic, and often ill-governed, exerted a peculiar fascination. In cities, workers, even immigrants and young women, could more

From Chapter 18 of *American Destiny: Narrative of a Nation*, Combined Volume, Fourth Edition. Mark C. Carnes and John A. Garraty. Copyright © 2012 by Pearson Education, Inc. Published by Pearson Prentice Hall. All rights reserved.

easily find jobs. Housing was cheap. Urban problems were daunting, but the immense aggregation of peoples and their resources constituted a limitless potential for uplift and reform.

Middle-Class Life

"This middle-class country had got a middle-class president, at last," Ralph Waldo Emerson had noted with satisfaction when Lincoln took office in 1861. Lincoln, in contrast to the presidents who had been wealthy planters or businessmen or high-ranking military men, was a self-made man who embraced middle-class values. Middle-class culture took the best aspects of romanticism—the enshrinement of human potential, the restless striving for personal betterment, the zest for competition and excitement—and tempered them with a passion for self-control and regularity.

But the Civil War sapped middle-class culture of its reforming zeal. The vital energy that invigorated antebellum reforms and had impelled the North to war became dissipated by that war. Afterwards, middle-class Americans focused their energies on building

The Breakfast (1911), by William McGregor Paxton, shows a middle-class husband, absorbed in the newspaper and in the world beyond the home. His wife, in a gorgeous dress, sits—very much a "bird in a gilded cage," the title of a popular song in 1900. The servant girl, face unseen, cleans up the cage.

Source: *The Breakfast*, William McGregor Paxton, American, 1911 The Metropolitan Museum of Art, New York, NY, U.S.A. Image copyright ©The Metropolitan Museum of Art.

institutions. American society and culture underwent a process of "incorporation," as the predominant form of the business world seeped deep into the American consciousness.

No institution was more central to middle-class life than the family. After the Civil War, it lost some of its moral fervor but gained a new substantiality. Increasingly family life was defined in terms of tangible goods. Modern scholars have often indicted this "culture of consumption" for its superficiality, a criticism commonly aired by patrician elites at the time. But no attack on middle-class culture and its conspicuous consumption surpassed the venom of Thorstein Veblen's *Theory of the Leisure Class* (1899). Veblen contended that consumers derived little real pleasure from their big homes and gaudy purchases; they were simply showing off their wealth. No one was ever satisfied with their wealth because everyone else was scrambling to get ahead of them. Everyone wanted more.

Middle-class people regarded the matter differently. They conceived of the family as a refuge from the increasingly chaotic and unsavory aspects of urban life: A beautiful house that was filled with books, paintings, and musical instruments would inculcate the finer sensibilities and elevate the minds of its occupants. Better for children to find stimulation at home than to visit the vice districts or unsupervised amusements downtown. The abundant material culture of the "Victorian age" reflected not its superficiality but its solidity.

Skilled and Unskilled Workers

Wage earners, too, were drawn to urban areas. They felt the full force of the industrial tide, being affected in countless ways—some beneficial, others unfortunate. As manufacturing became more important, the number of manufacturing workers increased nearly ten-fold, from around 600,000 in 1860 to nearly 5 million in 1890. While workers lacked much sense of solidarity, they exerted a far larger influence on society at the turn of the century than they had in the years before the Civil War.

More efficient methods of production enabled them to increase their output, making possible a rise in their standard of living. The working day still tended to approximate the hours of daylight, but it was shortening perceptibly by the 1880s, at least in many occupations. In 1860 the average had been eleven hours, but by 1880 only one worker in four labored more than ten hours and radicals were beginning to talk about eight hours as a fair day's work.

Industrialization created problems for workers beyond the obvious one of earning enough money to support themselves. By and large, skilled workers improved their positions relatively, despite the increased use of machinery. Furthermore, when machines took the place of human skills, jobs became monotonous. Mechanization undermined both the artisans' pride and their bargaining power with employers. As expensive machinery became more important, the worker seemed of necessity less important. Machines controlled the pace of work and its duration. The time clock regulated the labor force more rigidly than the most exacting foreman. The length of the workday may have declined, but the pace of work and the danger involved in working around heavy, high-speed machinery increased accordingly.

Another problem for workers was that industrialization tended to accentuate swings of the business cycle. On the upswing something approaching full employment

This girl ran four spinning machines in a cotton mill in Whitnel, North Carolina. Only four feet, three inches tall, she earned forty-eight cents a day. Photographer Lewis Hine hoped that pictures such as this one (1908) would generate public support for child labor laws.

Photo Credit: Lewis W. Hine/Gerge Eastman House/Getty Images - Creative Express.

existed, but in periods of depression unemployment became a problem that affected workers without regard for their individual abilities. It is significant that the word *unemployment* (though not, of course, the condition itself) was a late-nineteenth-century invention.

Working Women

Women continued to supply a significant part of the industrial working force. But now many more of them were working outside their homes; the factory had almost completely replaced the household as the seat of manufacturing.[1] Such women had no choice but to leave the "domestic sphere" to make a living. Textile mills and "the sewing trades" absorbed a large percentage of women, but in all fields women were paid substantially lower wages than men.

●●─[Read the Document

Massachusett Bureau of Statistics of Labor at **myhistorylab.com**

Women found many new types of work in these years. They made up the overwhelming majority of salespersons and cashiers in the big new department stores. Store managers considered women more polite, easier to control, and more honest than male workers, all qualities especially valuable in the huge emporiums.

Educated, middle-class women also dominated the new profession of nursing that developed alongside the expanding medical profession and the establishment of large urban hospitals. To nearly all doctors, to most men, and indeed to many women of that day, nursing seemed the perfect female profession since it required the same characteristics that women were thought to have by nature: selflessness, cleanliness, kindliness, tact, sensitivity, and submissiveness to male control. Typical was this remark of a contemporary authority: "Since God could not care for all the sick, he made women to nurse." Why it had not occurred to God to make more women physicians, or for that matter members of other prestigious professions like law and the clergy, this man did not explain, probably because it had not occurred to him either.

Middle-class women did replace men as teachers in most of the nation's grade schools, and they also replaced men as clerks and secretaries and operators of the new typewriters in government departments and in business offices. Most men with

---

[1]However, at least half of all working women were domestic servants.

the knowledge of spelling and grammar that these positions required had better opportunities and were uninterested in office work, so women high school graduates, of whom there was an increasing number, filled the gap.

Working-Class Family Life

Early social workers who visited the homes of industrial laborers in this period reported enormous differences in the standard of living of people engaged in the same line of work, differences related to such variables as health, intelligence, the wife's ability as a homemaker, the degree of the family's commitment to middle-class values, and pure luck. Some families spent most of their income on food; others saved substantial sums even when earning no more than $400 or $500 a year. Family incomes varied greatly among workers who received similar hourly wages, depending on the steadiness of employment and on the number of family members holding jobs.

Consider the cases of two families headed by railroad brakemen. One man brought home only $360 to house and feed a wife and eight children. Here is the report of a state official who interviewed the family: "Clothes ragged, children half-dressed and dirty. They all sleep in one room regardless of sex. . . . The entire concern is as wretched as could be imagined. Father is shiftless. . . . Wife is without ambition or industry."

The other brakeman and his wife had only two children, and he earned $484 in 1883. They owned a well-furnished house, kept a cow, and raised vegetables for home consumption. Although they were far from rich, they managed to put aside enough for insurance, reading matter, and a few small luxuries.

Working-Class Attitudes

Social workers and government officials made many efforts in the 1880s and 1890s to find out how working people felt about all sorts of matters connected with their jobs. Their reports reveal a wide spectrum of opinion. To the question, asked of two Wisconsin carpenters, "What new laws, in your opinion, ought to be enacted?" one replied, "Keep down strikes and rioters. Let every man attend to his own business." But the other answered, "Complete nationalization of land and all ways of transportation. Burn all government bonds. A graduated income tax. . . . Abolish child labor and [pass] any other act that capitalists say is wrong."

Every variation of opinion between these extremes was expressed by working people in many sections and in many kinds of work. In 1881 a female textile worker in Lawrence, Massachusetts, said to an interviewer, "If you will stand by the mill, and see the people coming out, you will be surprised to see the happy, contented look they all have."

Despite such remarks and the general improvement in living standards, it is clear, if only from the large number of bitter strikes of the period, that there was a considerable dissatisfaction among industrial workers. Writing in 1885, the labor leader Terence V. Powderly reported that "a deep-rooted feeling of discontent pervades the masses."

The discontent had many causes. For some, poverty was still the chief problem, but for others, rising aspirations triggered discontent. Workers were confused about their destiny; the tradition that no one of ability need remain a hired hand died hard. They wanted to believe their bosses and the politicians when those worthies voiced the old slogans about a classless society and the community of interest of capital and labor. The rich were growing richer and more people were growing rich, but ordinary workers were better off too. However, the gap between the very rich and the ordinary citizen was widening. "The tendency . . . is toward centralization and aggregation," the Illinois Bureau of Labor Statistics reported in 1886. "This involves a separation of the people into classes, and the permanently subordinate status of large numbers of them."

Working Your Way Up

Americans in the late nineteenth century believed their society offered great opportunities for individual advancement, and to prove it they pointed to men like Andrew Carnegie and to other poor boys who accumulated large fortunes. How general was the rise from rags to riches (or even to modest comfort) is another question.

Americans had been on the move, mostly, of course, in a westward direction, since the colonial period, but studies of census records show that there was considerable geographic mobility in urban areas throughout the last half of the nineteenth century and into the twentieth. Most investigations reveal that only about half the people recorded in one census were still in the same place ten years later. The nation had a vast reservoir of rootless people. For many, the way to move up in the world was to move on.

In most of the cities studied, mobility was accompanied by some economic and social improvement. On the average, about a quarter of the manual laborers traced rose to middle-class status during their lifetimes, and the sons of manual laborers were still more likely to improve their place in society. In New York City about a third of the Italian and Jewish immigrants of the 1890s had risen from unskilled to skilled jobs a decade later.

Such progress was primarily the result of the economic growth the nation was experiencing and of the energy and ambition of the people, native-born and immigrant alike, who were pouring into the cities in such numbers. The public education system gave an additional boost to the upwardly mobile.

The history of American education after about 1870 reflects the impact of social and economic change. Although Horace Mann, Henry Barnard, and others had laid the foundations for state-supported school systems in the 1840s and 1850s, most of these systems became compulsory only after the Civil War, when the growth of cities provided the concentration of population and financial resources necessary for economical mass education. In the 1860s about half the children in the country were getting some formal education, but this did not mean that half the children were attending school at any one time. Sessions were short, especially in rural areas, and many teachers were poorly trained. President Calvin Coolidge noted in his autobiography that the one-room school he attended in rural Vermont in the 1880s was open only in slack seasons when the twenty-odd students were not needed in the fields. "Few, if any, of my teachers reached the standard now required," he wrote, adding that his own younger sister had obtained a teaching certificate and actually taught a class when she was only twelve.

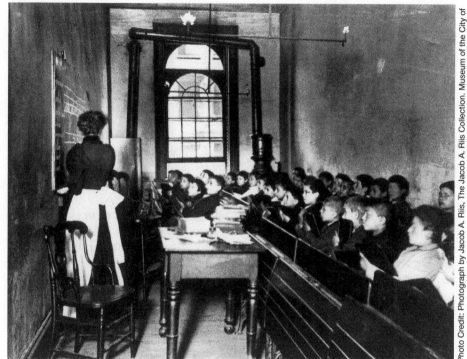

Photo Credit: Photograph by Jacob A. Riis, The Jacob A. Riis Collection. Museum of the City of New York.

Jacob Riis's photograph of a class on the Lower East Side of New York City. At Riis's death, Theodore Roosevelt called him "the staunchest, most efficient, friend the children of New York City have ever had."

Thereafter, steady growth and improvement took place. Attendance in the public schools increased from 6.8 million in 1870 to 15.5 million in 1900, a remarkable expansion even when allowance is made for the growth of the population. More remarkable still, during a time when prices were declining steadily, public expenditures for education nearly quadrupled. A typical elementary school graduate, at least in the cities, could count on having studied, besides the traditional "Three Rs," history, geography, a bit of science, drawing, and physical training.

Secondary education was still assumed to be only for those with special abilities and youths whose families did not require that they immediately become breadwinners. As late as 1890 fewer than 300,000 of the 14.3 million children attending public and private schools had progressed beyond the eighth grade and nearly a third of these were attending private institutions.

Education certainly helped young people to rise in the world, but progress from rags to real riches was far from common. Carnegies were rare. A study of the family backgrounds of 200 late-nineteenth-century business leaders revealed that nearly all of them grew up in well-to-do middle-class families. They were far better educated than the general run, and most were members of one or another Protestant church.

The unrealistic expectations inspired by the rags-to-riches myth more than the absence of real opportunity probably explains why so many workers, even when expressing dissatisfaction with life as it was, continued to subscribe to such middle-class values as hard work and thrift—that is, they continued to hope.

The "New" Immigration

Industrial expansion increased the need for labor, and this in turn powerfully stimulated immigration. Between 1866 and 1915 about 25 million foreigners entered the United States. Industrial growth alone does not explain the influx. The launching in 1858 of the English liner *Great Eastern*, which was nearly 700 feet from stem to stern and weighed about 19,000 tons, opened a new era in transatlantic travel. Although most immigrants traveled in steerage, which was cramped and almost totally lacking in anything that could be considered an amenity, the Atlantic crossing, once so hazardous, became safe and speedy with the perfection of the steamship. Competition between the great packet lines such as Cunard, North German Lloyd, and Holland-America drove down the cost of the passage, and advertising by the lines further stimulated traffic.

"Push" pressures as well as these "pull" factors had much to do with the new patterns of immigration. Improvements in transportation produced unexpected and disruptive changes in the economies of many European countries. Cheap wheat from the United States, Russia, and other parts of the world poured into Europe, bringing disaster to farmers throughout Europe. The spreading industrial revolution and the increased use of farm machinery led to the collapse of the peasant economy of central and southern Europe. For rural inhabitants this meant the loss of self-sufficiency, the fragmentation of landholdings, unemployment, and for many the decision to make a new start in the New World.

While immigrants continued to people the farms of America, industry absorbed an ever-increasing number of the newcomers. In 1870 one industrial worker in three was foreign-born. When congressional investigators examined twenty-one major industries

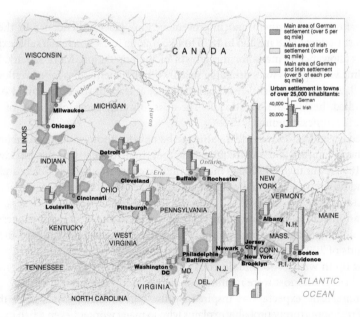

German and Irish Settlement in the Northeastern United States, 1870 In 1870, New York was the greatest immigrant city; its Irish population dwarfed that of Philadelphia or Boston. Its German population, too, greatly exceeded that of "German" cities such as Milwaukee and Chicago.

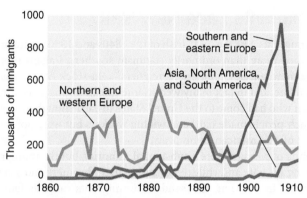

Immigration, 1860–1910 In this graph, Germany is counted as a part of northern and western Europe. Note the new immigration from southern and eastern Europe in the early 1900s.

early in the new century, they discovered that well over half of the labor force had not been born in the United States.

Before 1882, when—in addition to the Chinese—criminals, and persons adjudged mentally defective or liable to become public charges were excluded, entry into the United States was almost unrestricted. Indeed, until 1891 the Atlantic coast states, not the federal government, exercised whatever controls were imposed on newcomers. Even when federally imposed, medical inspection was perfunctory. Public health officials boasted that with "one glance" at each arrival, the inspectors could "take in six details, namely the scalp, face, neck, hands, gait and general condition, both mental and physical." Only those who failed this "test" were examined more closely. On average, only one immigrant in fifty was ultimately rejected.

Private agencies, philanthropic and commercial, served as a link between the new arrivals and employers looking for labor. Until the Foran Act of 1885 outlawed the practice, a few companies brought in skilled workers under contract, advancing them passage money and collecting it in installments from their paychecks, a system somewhat like the indentured servitude of colonial times. Numerous nationality groups assisted (and sometimes exploited) their compatriots by organizing "immigrant banks" that recruited labor in the old country, arranged transportation, and then housed the newcomers in boardinghouses in the United States while finding them jobs.

Beginning in the 1880s, the spreading effects of industrialization in Europe caused a shift in the sources of American immigration from northern and western to southern and eastern sections of the continent. In 1882, 789,000 immigrants entered the United States; more than 350,000 came from Great Britain and Germany, only 32,000 from Italy, and fewer than 17,000 from Russia. In 1907—the all-time peak year, with 1,285,000 immigrants— Great Britain and Germany supplied fewer than half as many as they had twenty-five years earlier, while the **new immigration** from southern and eastern Europe was supplying eleven times as many as then. Up to 1880, only about 200,000 southern and eastern Europeans had migrated to America. Between 1880 and 1910, approximately 8.4 million arrived.

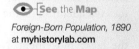

New Immigrants Face New Nativism

The "new" immigrants, like the "old" Irish of the 1840s and 1850s, were mostly peasants. They also seemed more than ordinarily clannish; southern Italians typically called all people outside their families *forestieri*, "foreigners." Old-stock Americans thought them harder to assimilate, and in fact many were. Some Italian immigrants, for example, were unmarried men who had come to the United States to earn enough money to buy a farm back home. Such people made hard and willing workers but were not much concerned with being part of an American community.

These "birds of passage" were a substantial minority, but the immigrant who saved in order to bring his wife and children or his younger brothers and sisters to America was more typical. In addition, thousands of immigrants came as family groups and intended to remain. Some, like the eastern European Jewish migrants, were refugees who were almost desperately eager to become Americans, although of course they retained and nurtured much of their traditional culture.

Many "older" Americans concluded, wrongly but understandably, that the new immigrants were incapable of becoming good citizens and should be kept out. During the 1880s, large numbers of social workers, economists, and church leaders, worried by the problems that arose when so many poor immigrants flocked into cities already bursting at the seams, began to believe that some restriction should be placed on the incoming human tide.

Social Darwinists and people obsessed with pseudoscientific ideas about "racial purity" also found the new immigration alarming. Misunderstanding the findings of the new science of genetics, they attributed the social problems associated with mass immigration to supposed physiological characteristics of the newcomers. Forgetting that earlier Americans had accused pre–Civil War Irish and German immigrants of similar deficiencies, they decided that the peoples of southern and eastern Europe were racially inferior to "Nordic" and "Anglo-Saxon" types and ought to be kept out.

Workers, fearing the competition of people with low living standards and no bargaining power, spoke out against the "enticing of penniless and unapprised

Looking Backward at Immigrant Origins at **myhistorylab.com**

immigrants . . . to undermine our wages and social welfare." In 1883 the president of the Amalgamated Iron and Steel Workers told a Senate committee that Hungarian, Polish, Italian, and other immigrants "can live where I think a decent man would die; they can live on . . . food that other men would not touch." A Wisconsin iron worker put it this way: "Immigrants work for almost nothing and seem to be able to live on wind—something I can not do."

Employers were not disturbed by the influx of people with strong backs willing to work hard for low wages. Nevertheless, by the late 1880s many employers were alarmed about the supposed radicalism of the immigrants. The Haymarket bombing focused attention on the handful of foreign-born extremists in the country and loosed a flood of unjustified charges that "anarchists and communists" were dominating the labor movement. **Nativism**, which had grown in the 1850s under the Know-Nothing banner and faded during the Civil War, now flared up again, and for similar reasons. Denunciations of "longhaired, wild-eyed, bad-smelling, atheistic, reckless foreign wretches," of "Europe's human and inhuman rubbish" crowded the pages of the nation's press.

These nativists, again like the pre–Civil War variety, disliked Catholics and other minority groups more than immigrants as such. The largest nativist organization of the period, the American Protective Association, founded in 1887, existed primarily to resist what its members called "the Catholic menace." The Protestant majority treated "new" immigrants as underlings, tried to keep them out of the best jobs, and discouraged their efforts to climb the social ladder. This prejudice functioned only at the social and economic level. But nowhere in America did prejudice lead to interference with religious freedom in the narrow sense. And neither labor leaders nor important industrialists, despite their misgivings about immigration, took a broadly antiforeigner position.

After the Exclusion Act of 1882 and the almost meaningless 1885 ban on importing contract labor, no further restrictions were imposed on immigration until the twentieth century. Strong support for a literacy test for admission developed in the 1890s, pushed by a new organization, the Immigration Restriction League. Since there was much more illiteracy in the southeastern quarter of Europe than in the northwestern, such a test would discriminate without seeming to do so on national or racial grounds. A literacy test bill passed both houses of Congress in 1897, but President Cleveland vetoed it. Such a "radical departure" from the "generous and free-handed policy" of the past, Cleveland said, was unjustified. He added, perhaps with tongue in cheek, that a literacy requirement would not keep out "unruly agitators," who were only too adept at reading and writing.

The Expanding City and Its Problems

Industrialization does not entirely explain the growth of nineteenth-century cities. All the large American cities began as commercial centers, and the development of huge metropolises like New York and Chicago would have been impossible without the national transportation network. But by the final decades of the century, the expansion of industry had become the chief cause of city growth. Thus the urban concentration continued; in 1890 one person in three lived in a city, by 1910 nearly one in two.

A steadily increasing proportion of the urban population was made up of immigrants. In 1890 the foreign-born population of Chicago almost equaled the total population of Chicago in 1880; a third of all Bostonians and a quarter of all Philadelphians were immigrants; and four out of five residents of New York City were either foreign-born or the children of immigrants.

After 1890 the immigrant concentration became even more dense. The migrants from eastern and southern Europe lacked the resources to travel to the agriculturally developing regions. As the concentration progressed it fed upon itself, for all the eastern cities developed many ethnic neighborhoods, in each of which immigrants of one nationality congregated. Lonely, confused, often unable to speak English, the Italians, the Greeks, the Polish and Russian Jews, and other immigrants tended to settle where their predecessors had settled.

Although ethnic neighborhoods were crowded, unhealthy, and crime-ridden, and many of the residents were desperately poor, they were not ghettos in the European sense, for those who lived there were not compelled by law to remain. Thousands "escaped" yearly to better districts. American ghettos were places where hopes and ambitions were fulfilled, where people worked hard and endured hardships in order to improve their own and their children's lot.

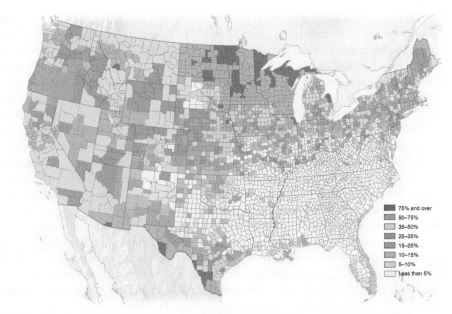

Percent of Foreign-Born Whites and Native Whites of Foreign or Mixed Parentage in Total Population, by Counties, 1910 In 1910, the South had the lowest proportion of immigrants; in Minnesota, Wisconsin, North Dakota, Massachusetts, Connecticut, Rhode Island, in the regions bordering Mexico, and in parts of the Rocky Mountains, over half of the population was immigrant.

Observing the immigrants' attachment to "foreign" values and institutions, numbers of "natives" accused the newcomers of resisting Americanization and blamed them for urban problems. The immigrants were involved in these problems, but the rapidity of urban expansion explains the troubles associated with city life far more fully than the high percentage of foreigners.

Teeming Tenements

The cities were suffering from growing pains. Sewer and water facilities frequently could not keep pace with skyrocketing needs. By the 1890s the tremendous growth of Chicago had put such a strain on its sanitation system that the Chicago River had become virtually an open sewer, and the city's drinking water contained such a high concentration of germ-killing chemicals that it tasted like creosote. In the 1880s all the sewers of Baltimore emptied into the sluggish Back Basin, and according to the journalist H. L. Mencken, every summer the city smelled "like a billion polecats." Fire protection became less and less adequate, garbage piled up in the streets faster than it could be carted away, and the streets themselves crumbled beneath the pounding of heavy traffic. Urban growth proceeded with such speed that new streets were laid out more rapidly than they could be paved. Chicago had more than 1,400 miles of dirt streets in 1890.

Substandard living quarters aggravated other evils such as disease and the disintegration of family life, with its attendant mental anguish, crime, and juvenile delinquency. The bloody New York City riots of 1863, though sparked by dislike of the Civil War draft

Impoverished immigrant families, like the one in this 1889 Jacob Riis photograph, often lived in tiny windowless rooms in crowded tenement districts. Riis devised a "flash bulb" for indoor photographs in poorly illuminated rooms like this one.
Source: Jacob A. Riis, *In Poverty Gap: An English Coal-Heaver's Home.* Courtesy of Museum of the City of New York.

and of blacks, reflected the bitterness and frustration of thousands jammed together amid filth and threatened by disease. A citizens' committee seeking to discover the causes of the riots expressed its amazement after visiting the slums "that so much misery, disease, and wretchedness can be huddled together and hidden . . . unvisited and unthought of, so near our own abodes."

New York City created a Metropolitan Health Board in 1866, and a state tenement house law the following year made a feeble beginning at regulating city housing. The magazine *Plumber and Sanitary Engineer* sponsored a contest to pick the best design for a **tenement**. The winner of the competition was James E. Ware, whose plan for a "dumbbell" apartment house managed to crowd from twenty-four to thirty-two four-room apartments on a plot of ground only 25 by 100 feet.

The unhealthiness of the tenements was notorious. No one knows exactly, but as late as 1900 about three-quarters of the residents of New York City's Lower East Side lacked indoor toilets and had to use backyard outhouses to relieve themselves.

View the Image
New York City Tenements
at myhistorylab.com

One noxious corner became known as the "lung block" because of the prevalence of tuberculosis among its inhabitants. In 1900 three out of five babies born in one poor district of Chicago died before their first birthday.

Slums bred criminals—the wonder was that they did not breed more. They also drove well-to-do residents into exclusive sections and to the suburbs. From Boston's

Beacon Hill and Back Bay to San Francisco's Nob Hill, the rich retired into their cluttered mansions and ignored conditions in the poorer parts of town.

The Cities Modernize

Gradually the basic facilities of urban living were improved. Streets were paved, first with cobblestones and wood blocks and then with smoother, quieter asphalt. Gaslight, then electric arc lights, and finally Edison's incandescent lamps brightened the cities after dark, making law enforcement easier, stimulating night life, and permitting factories and shops to operate after sunset.

Urban transportation underwent enormous changes. Until the 1880s, horse-drawn cars running on tracks set flush with the street were the main means of urban public transportation. In 1860 New York City's horsecars were carrying about 100,000 passengers a day. But horsecars had serious drawbacks. Enormous numbers of horses were needed, and feeding and stabling the animals was costly. Their droppings (ten pounds per day per horse) became a major source of urban pollution. That is why the invention of the electric trolley car in the 1880s put an end to horsecar transportation. Trolleys were cheaper and less unsightly than horsecars and quieter than steam-powered trains.

A retired naval officer, Frank J. Sprague, installed the first practical electric trolley line in Richmond, Virginia, in 1887–1888. At once other cities seized on the trolley. Lines soon radiated outward from the city centers, bringing commuters and shoppers from the residential districts to the business district. Without them the big-city department stores could not have flourished as they did. By 1895 some 850 lines were busily hauling city dwellers over 10,000 miles of track, and mileage tripled in the following decade. As with other new enterprises, ownership of street railways quickly became centralized until a few big operators controlled the trolleys of more than 100 eastern cities and towns.

Streetcars changed the character of big-city life. Before their introduction urban communities were limited by the distances people could conveniently walk to work. The "walking city" could not easily extend more than twenty-one-and-a-half miles from its center. Streetcars increased this radius to six miles or more, which meant that the area of the city expanded enormously. Dramatic population shifts resulted as the better-off moved away from the center in search of air and space, abandoning the crumbling, jam-packed older neighborhoods to the poor. Thus economic segregation speeded the growth of ghettos. Older peripheral towns that had maintained some of the self-contained qualities of village life were swallowed up, becoming metropolitan centers.

As time passed, each new area, originally peopled by rising economic groups, tended to become crowded and then deteriorated. By extending their tracks beyond the developed areas, the streetcar companies further speeded suburban growth because they assured developers, bankers, builders, and middle-class home buyers of efficient transport to the center of town. By keeping fares low (five cents a ride was standard) the lines enabled poor people to "escape" to the countryside on holidays.

Leisure Activities: More Fun and Games

By bringing together large numbers of people, cities made possible many kinds of social activity difficult or impossible to maintain in rural areas. Cities remained unsurpassed as centers of artistic and intellectual life. New York was the outstanding example, as seen in its many theaters and in the founding of the American Museum of Natural History (1870), the Metropolitan Museum of Art (1870), and the Metropolitan Opera (1883), but other cities were equally hospitable to such endeavors. Boston's Museum of Fine Arts, for example, was founded in 1870 and the Boston Symphony in 1881.

Read the Document
Fox, from *Coney Island Frolics*
at **myhistorylab.com**

Of course less sophisticated forms of recreation also flourished in the urban environment. From 1865 to 1885 the number of breweries in Massachusetts quadrupled. It is only a slight exaggeration to say that in crowded urban centers there was a saloon on every corner; during the last third of the century the number of saloons in the country tripled. Saloons were strictly male working-class institutions, usually decorated with pictures and other mementos of sports heroes, the bar perhaps under the charge of a retired pugilist.

Calvinist-inspired opposition to sports as a frivolous waste of valuable time was steadily evaporating, replaced among the upper and middle classes by the realization that games like golf and tennis were "healthy occupation[s] for mind and body." Bicycling became a fad, both as a means of getting from place to place in the ever-expanding cities and as a form of exercise and recreation.

The postwar era also saw the first important development of spectator sports, again because cities provided the concentrations of population necessary to support them. Curious relationships developed between upper- and working-class interests and between competitive sports as pure enjoyment for players and spectators and sports as something to bet on. Horse racing had strictly upper-class origins, but racetracks attracted huge crowds of ordinary people more intent on picking a winner than on improving the breed.

Professional boxing offers an even better example. It was in a sense a hobby of the rich, who sponsored favorite gladiators, offered prizes, and often wagered large sums on the matches. But the audiences were made up overwhelmingly of young working-class males, from whose ranks most of the fighters emerged. The gambling and also the brutality of the bloody, bare-knuckle character of the fights caused many communities to outlaw boxing, a fact that added to the appeal of the sport for some.

Three major team games—baseball, football, and basketball—developed in something approaching their modern form during the last quarter of the century. Various forms of what became baseball were played long before that time. Organized teams, in most cases made up of upper-class amateurs, first emerged in the 1840s, but the game only became truly popular during the Civil War, when it was a major form of camp recreation for the troops.

After the war professional teams began to appear (the first, the Cincinnati Red Stockings, paid players between $800 and $1,400 for the season), and in 1876 teams in eight cities formed the National League. The American League followed in 1901. After a brief period of rivalry, the two leagues made peace in 1903, the year of the first World Series.

Organized play led to codification of the rules and improvements in technique and strategy: for example, the development of "minor" leagues; impartial umpires calling balls and strikes and ruling on close plays; the use of catcher's masks and padded gloves; the invention of various kinds of curves and other erratic pitches (often enhanced by "doctoring" the ball). As early as the 1870s, baseball was being called "the national game" and losing all upper-class connotations. Important games

Photo Credit: Rue des Archives/The Granger Collection.

Luna Park at Coney Island was a vast living theater in which the strollers were both spectators and actors.
At night, a quarter of a million electric lights turned Luna Park into what its designer, Frederic Thompson, called
"a different world—a dream world, perhaps a nightmare world—where all is bizarre and fantastic."

attracted crowds in the tens of thousands; betting became a problem. Despite its urban origins, its broad green fields and dusty base paths gave the game a rural character that only recently has begun to fade away.

Nobody "invented" baseball, but both football and basketball owe their present form to individuals. James Naismith's invention of basketball is undisputed. In 1891, while a student at a YMCA school, he attached peach baskets to the edge of an elevated running track in the gymnasium and drew up what are still the basic rules of the game. The first basketball was a soccer ball. The game was popular from the start, but because it was played indoors it was not an important spectator sport until much later.

Football was not created by one person in the way that basketball was; it evolved out of English rugby. For many decades it remained almost entirely a college sport (and thus played almost entirely by upper- and middle-class types). Organized collegiate sports dated back to before the Civil War; the first intercollegiate matches were rowing races between Harvard and Yale students. The first intercollegiate football game occurred when Rutgers defeated Princeton in 1869, and by the 1880s college football had become extremely popular.

Much of the game's modern character, however, was the work of Walter Camp, the athletic director and football coach of Yale. Camp cut the size of teams from fifteen to eleven, and he invented the scrimmage line, the four-down system, and the key position of quarterback. He publicized the game in a series of books, ranging from *How to Coach a Team* (1886) to *Jack Hall at Yale* (1909). Camp's prestige was such that when he named his first All-American team after the 1889 season, no one challenged his judgment. Well into the twentieth century, the players that Camp selected were the All-Americans.

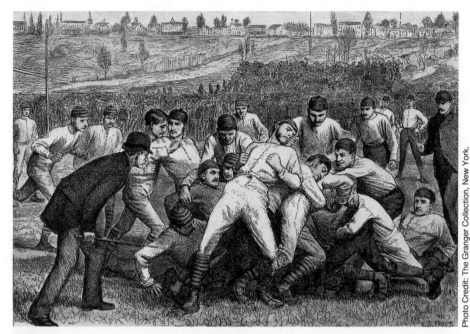

Photo Credit: The Granger Collection, New York.

A football game pits Yale and Princeton in 1879. The field was not lined or bounded, and play consisted mostly of disorganized scrums.

Spectator sports had little appeal to women at this time and indeed for decades thereafter. And few women participated in organized athletics. Sports were "manly" activities; a woman might ride a bicycle, play croquet, and perhaps play a little tennis, but to display any concentrated interest in excelling in a sport was considered unfeminine.

Christianity's Conscience and the Social Gospel

The modernization of the great cities was not solving most of the social problems of the slums. As this fact became clear, a number of urban religious leaders began to take a hard look at the situation. Traditionally, American churchmen had insisted that where sin was concerned there were no extenuating circumstances. To the well-to-do they preached the virtues of thrift and hard work; to the poor they extended the possibility of a better existence in the next world; to all they stressed one's responsibility for one's own behavior—and thus for one's own salvation. Such a point of view brought meager comfort to residents of slums. Consequently, the churches lost influence in the poorer sections. Furthermore, as better-off citizens followed the streetcar lines out from the city centers, their church leaders followed them.

In New York, seventeen Protestant congregations abandoned the depressed areas of Lower Manhattan between 1868 and 1888. Catering thereafter almost entirely to middle-class and upper-class worshippers, the pastors tended to become even more conservative. No more strident defender of reactionary ideas existed than the pastor of Brooklyn's fashionable Plymouth Congregational Church, Henry Ward Beecher. Beecher, a younger brother of Harriet Beecher Stowe, the author of *Uncle Tom's Cabin*, attributed poverty to the improvidence of laborers who, he claimed, squandered their wages on liquor and tobacco. "No man in this land suffers from poverty," he said, "unless it be more than his fault—unless it be his sin." The best check on labor unrest was a plentiful supply of cheap immigrant labor, he told President Hayes. Unions were "the worst form of despotism and tyranny in the history of Christendom."

An increasing proportion of the residents of the blighted districts were Catholics, and the Roman church devoted much effort to distributing alms, maintaining homes for orphans and old people, and other forms of social welfare. But church leaders seemed unconcerned with the social causes of the blight; they were deeply committed to the idea that sin and vice were personal, while poverty was an act of God. They deplored the rising tide of crime, disease, and destitution among their coreligionists, yet they failed to see the connection between these evils and the squalor of the slums. "Intemperance is the great evil we have to overcome," wrote the president of the leading Catholic charitable organization, the Society of St. Vincent de Paul. "It is the source of the misery for at least three-fourths of the families we are called upon to visit and relieve."

The conservatism of most Protestant and Catholic clergymen did not prevent some earnest preachers from working directly to improve the lot of the city poor. Some followed the path blazed by Dwight L. Moody, a lay evangelist who became famous throughout America and Great Britain in the 1870s. A gargantuan figure weighing nearly 300 pounds, Moody conducted a vigorous campaign to persuade the denizens of the slums to cast aside their sinful ways. He went among them full of enthusiasm and God's love and made an impact no less powerful than that of George Whitefield during the Great Awakening of the eighteenth century or Charles Grandison Finney in the first part of the nineteenth. The evangelists founded mission schools in the slums and tried to provide spiritual and recreational facilities for the unfortunate. They were prominent in the establishment of American branches of the YMCA (1851) and the Salvation Army (1880).

However, many evangelists paid little heed to the causes of urban poverty and vice, believing that faith in God would enable the poor to transcend the material difficulties of

Photo Credit: The Granger Collection, New York.

Dwight L. Moody, a lay preacher, saw the church he had built destroyed by the Chicago fire of 1871. But the fire also intensified his faith. His conversational manner appealed to working people, and his adherence to the literal word of the Bible provided them with an anchor in a sea of change.

life. For a number of Protestant clergymen who had become familiar with the slums, a different approach seemed called for. Slum conditions caused the sins and crimes of the cities; the wretched human beings who committed them could not be blamed, these ministers argued. They began to preach a **Social Gospel** that focused on improving living conditions rather than on saving souls. If people were to lead pure lives, they must have enough to eat, decent homes, and opportunities to develop their talents. Social Gospelers advocated civil service reform, child labor legislation, regulation of big corporations, and heavy taxes on incomes and inheritances.

The most influential preacher of the Social Gospel was probably Washington Gladden. At first, Gladden, who was raised on a Massachusetts farm, had opposed all government interference in social and economic affairs, but his experiences as a minister in Springfield, Massachusetts, and Columbus, Ohio, exposed him to the realities of life in industrial cities, and his views changed. In *Applied Christianity* (1886) and in other works he defended laborers' right to organize and strike and denounced the idea that supply and demand should control wage rates. He favored factory inspection laws, strict regulation of public utilities, and other reforms.

Nothing so well reveals the receptivity of the public to the Social Gospel as the popularity of Charles M. Sheldon's novel *In His Steps* (1896), one of America's all-time best-sellers. Sheldon, a minister in Topeka, Kansas, described what happened in the mythical city of Raymond when a group of leading citizens decided to live truly Christian lives, asking themselves "What would Jesus do?" before adopting any course of action. Naturally the tone of Raymond's society was immensely improved, but basic social reforms followed quickly. The Rectangle, a terrible slum area, "too dirty, too coarse, too sinful, too awful for close contact," became the center of a great reform effort. One of Raymond's "leading society heiresses" undertook a slum clearance project, and a concerted attack was made on drunkenness and immorality. The moral regeneration of the entire community was soon accomplished.

The Settlement Houses

Although millions read *In His Steps*, its effect, and that of other Social Gospel literature, was merely inspirational. On the practical level, a number of earnest souls began to grapple with slum problems by organizing what were known as **settlement houses**. These were community centers located in poor districts that provided guidance and services to all who would use them. The settlement workers, most of them idealistic, well-to-do young people, lived in the houses and were active in neighborhood affairs.

The prototype of the settlement house was London's Toynbee Hall, founded in the early 1880s; the first American example was the Neighborhood Guild, opened on the Lower East Side of New York in 1886 by Dr. Stanton Coit. By the turn of the century 100 had been established, the most famous being Jane Addams's Hull House in Chicago (1889), Robert A. Woods's South End House in Boston (1892), and Lillian Wald's Henry Street Settlement in New York (1893).

The settlement workers tried to interpret American ways to the new immigrants and to create a community spirit in order to teach, in the words of one of them, "right living through social relations." Unlike most charity workers, who acted out of a sense of upper-class responsibility toward the unfortunate, they expected to benefit morally

Table 1 Reformers and the Urban Poor

Person	Occupation	Action	Consequences
Jacob Riis, Lewis Hine	Photojournalists	Increased public awareness of poor immigrants' living conditions	Stimulated reform movements
Horace Mann	Educator	Favored state laws that supported public education	Increased proportion of young people in school
Dwight L. Moody	Lay evangelist	Encouraged people to consult the Bible for moral guidance and refrain from vice	Promoted spread of YMCA (1850) and Salvation Army (1880) in immigrant districts
Washington Gladden	Congregationalist minister	Persuaded people that they are obliged as Christians to improve conditions in the slums	Advanced the "social gospel"
Jane Addams, Robert Woods, and Lillian Wald	Settlement house organizers	Showed immigrants and impoverished people how to cope with urban conditions	Constructed playgrounds and provided social clubs, day-care centers, and schools

and intellectually themselves by experiencing a way of life far different from their own and by obtaining "the first-hand knowledge the college classroom cannot give."

Settlement workers soon discovered that practical problems absorbed most of their energies. They agitated for tenement house laws, the regulation of the labor of women and children, and better schools. They employed private resources to establish playgrounds in the slums, along with libraries, classes in everything from child nutrition and home management to literature and arts and crafts, social clubs, and day-care centers. When they observed that many poor families were so occupied with the struggle to survive that they were neglecting or even abandoning their children, they tried to place the children in foster homes in the country.

In Boston Robert A. Woods organized clubs to get the youngsters of the South End off the streets, helped establish a restaurant where a meal could be had for five cents, acted as an arbitrator in labor disputes, and lobbied for laws tightening up the franchises of public utility companies. In Chicago Jane Addams developed an outstanding cultural program that included classes in music and art and an excellent "little theater" group. Hull House soon boasted a gymnasium, a day nursery, and several social clubs. Addams also worked tirelessly and effectively for improved public services and for social legislation of all kinds. She even got herself appointed garbage inspector in her ward and hounded local landlords and the garbage contractor until something approaching decent service was established.

A few critics considered the settlement houses mere devices to socialize the unruly poor by teaching them the "punctilios of upper-class propriety," but almost everyone appreciated their virtues. By the end of the century the Catholics, laggard in entering the arena of practical social reform, were joining the movement, partly because they were losing many communicants to socially minded Protestant churches. The first Catholic-run settlement house was founded in 1898 in an Italian district of New York. Two years later Brownson House in Los Angeles, catering chiefly to Mexican immigrants, threw open its doors.

With all their accomplishments, the settlement houses seemed to be fighting a losing battle. "Private beneficence," Jane Addams wrote of Hull House, "is totally inadequate to deal with the vast numbers of the city's disinherited." Much as a tropical forest grows faster than a handful of men armed with machetes can cut it down, so the slums, fed by an annual influx of hundreds of thousands, blighted new areas more rapidly than settlement house workers could clean up old ones. It became increasingly apparent that the wealth and authority of the state must be brought to bear in order to keep abreast of the problem.

Civilization and Its Discontents

As the nineteenth century died, the majority of the American people, especially those comfortably well-off, the residents of small towns, the shopkeepers, and some farmers and skilled workers, remained confirmed optimists and uncritical admirers of their civilization. However, blacks, immigrants, and others who failed to share equitably in the good things of life, along with a growing number of humanitarian reformers, found little to cheer about and much to lament in their increasingly industrialized society. Giant monopolies flourished despite federal restrictions. The gap between rich and poor appeared to be widening while the slum spread its poison and the materially successful made a god of their success. Human values seemed in grave danger of being crushed by impersonal forces typified by the great corporations.

In 1871 Walt Whitman, usually so full of extravagant praise for everything American, had called his fellow countrymen the "most materialistic and money-making people ever known":

> I say we had best look our times and lands searchingly in the face, like a physician diagnosing some deep disease. Never was there, perhaps, more hollowness of heart than at present, and here in the United States.

By the late 1880s a well-known journalist could write to a friend, "The wheel of progress is to be run over the whole human race and smash us all." Others noted an alarming jump in the national divorce rate and an increasing taste for all kinds of luxury. "People are made slaves by a desperate struggle to keep up appearances," a Massachusetts commentator declared, and the economist David A. Wells expressed concern over statistics showing that heart disease and mental illness were on the rise. These "diseases of civilization," Wells explained, were "one result of the continuous mental and nervous activity which modern high-tension methods of business have necessitated."

Wells was a prominent liberal, but pessimism was no monopoly of liberals. A little later, Senator Henry Cabot Lodge of Massachusetts, himself a millionaire, complained of the "lawlessness" of "the modern and recent plutocrat" and his "disregard of the rights of others." Lodge spoke of "the enormous contrast between the sanguine mental attitude prevalent in my youth and that, perhaps wiser, but certainly darker view, so general today." His one-time Harvard professor, Henry Adams, was still more critical of the way his contemporaries had become moneygrubbers. "All one's friends," he complained, along with church and university leaders and other educated people, "had joined the banks to force submission to capitalism."

Of course intellectuals often tend to be critical of the world they live in, whatever its nature; Thoreau denounced materialism and the worship of progress in the 1840s as vigorously as any late-nineteenth-century prophet of gloom. But the voices of the dissatisfied were rising. Despite the many benefits that industrialization had made possible, it was by no means clear around 1900 that the American people were really better off under the new dispensation.

That the United States was fast becoming a modern nation no one disputed. Physician George M. Beard contended that "modern civilization" overloaded the human nervous system the way burning too many of Thomas Edison's lightbulbs overloaded an electrical circuit. On the other hand, Edward Bellamy saw the future as a "paradise of order, equity, and felicity." Most took a more balanced view, believing that the modern world encompassed new possibilities as well as perils. The future beckoned, and yet it also menaced.

Milestones

Year	Event	Year	Event
1858	English launch transatlantic liner *Great Eastern*	1885	Foran Act outlaws importing contract skilled labor
1870	Metropolitan Museum of Art and American Museum of Natural History open in New York City	1887	Nativists found American Protective Association
1876	Eight teams form National Baseball League	1888	Richmond, Virginia, opens first urban electric streetcar system
1880	American branch of Salvation Army is founded	1889	Jane Addams founds Hull House
1880s	New immigration begins		Yale's Walter Camp names first All-American football team
1882	John L. Sullivan wins heavyweight boxing championship	1890s	Louis Sullivan's skyscrapers rise
	Exclusion Act bans Chinese immigrants	1890	Jacob Riis publishes *How the Other Half Lives*
1883	Roebling completes Brooklyn Bridge	1896	Charles M. Sheldon asks "What would Jesus do?" in best-selling *In His Steps*
		1897	Cleveland vetoes Congress's literacy test bill

✓●⌐Study and Review at www.myhistorylab.com

Review Questions

1. The introduction to this chapter contrasts the appeal of cities in the late nineteenth century with their failures and limitations. Did people move into cities because they had no choice or because they wanted to do so? Were their lives better or worse in doing so?

2. What is the relationship between the rise of industry and economic consolidation to the rapid growth of cities described in this chapter?

3. How did the influx of immigrants into the cities affect relations among ethnic groups? Between immigrants and "natives"—nonimmigrant Americans?

4. How did the new forms of amusement and leisure differ from those in earlier, predominantly rural settings?

5. Which urban problems were most acute and what different solutions were proposed by the leading religious figures and social reformers?

Key Terms

nativism
new immigration
settlement houses

Social Gospel
tenement

Intellectual and Cultural Trends in the Late Nineteenth Century

From Chapter 19 of *American Destiny: Narrative of a Nation*, Combined Volume, Fourth Edition.
Mark C. Carnes and John A. Garraty. Copyright © 2012 by Pearson Education, Inc. Published by
Pearson Prentice Hall. All rights reserved.

Intellectual and Cultural Trends in the Late Nineteenth Century

((•—|Hear the Audio at myhistorylab.com

Is winning everything?

IN 2010 THE STATE OF CALIFORNIA CUT FUNDING FOR THE UNIVERSITY of California at Berkeley by several hundred million dollars, raised student fees 10 percent, and forced faculty and staff to take unpaid furloughs. Despite this, the university covered the nearly $6.4 million deficit generated by its intercollegiate athletics program. Campus supporters of the football program noted that two-thirds of the top NCAA football teams ran even larger deficits; the average was about $8 million.

Although some of Berkeley's faculty endorsed an "Academics First" petition, others applauded the chancellor's decision to pursue "competitive excellence" in all aspects of campus life. Berkeley's football team was mandated to compete "at the top levels of the Pacific Ten conference and in postseason and national championship play." To that end, Berkeley paid its head coach $1.5 million, about average for a Division I head coach.

This insistence on winning intercollegiate football originated in the late nineteenth century. At that time, a few colleges decided to pay coaches, recruited star prep school athletes, and charged spectators to watch the games. The game became faster and rougher. Soon the spectacle attracted huge audiences. Action often got out of hand and, lacking satisfactory protective equipment, many football players sustained serious injuries; each year, some were killed.

In 1892, William Rainey Harper, president of the University of Chicago, defended the high cost of winning football. "If the world can afford to sacrifice lives for commercial gain"—a reference to the victims of industrial accidents—"it can more easily afford to make similar sacrifices on the altar of vigorous and unsullied manhood." In 1896 Massachusetts Senator Henry Cabot Lodge told Harvard students that "the injuries incurred on the playing-field are part of the price which the English-speaking race has paid for being world-conquerors."

The rise of football in the 1890s symbolized a profound transformation in cultural and intellectual life. The religious sensibilities and gentlemanly precepts of an earlier age were yielding to a tougher, "more manly" mind-set. Life was a struggle, Darwin had proclaimed, in which the fittest prevailed and the losers vanished. In this "competition" for survival, power trounced sentiment. Ideas were valuable not because they espoused truths or evinced beauty, but because they left an imprint on the world. Art and literature functioned not to transcend life or prettify it but to lay bare its grim reality. This stern ethos unsettled many but also invigorated those who yearned to confront the world as it was.

Colleges and Universities

Industrialization altered the way Americans thought at the same time that it transformed their ways of making a living. Technological advances revolutionized the communication of ideas more drastically than they did the transportation of goods or the manufacture of steel. The materialism that permeated American attitudes toward business also affected contemporary education and literature, while Charles Darwin's theory of evolution influenced American philosophers, lawyers, and historians profoundly. This was especially true of the nation's institutions of higher education.

Between 1878 and 1898, the number of colleges and universities increased from about 350 to 500, and the student body roughly tripled. Despite this growth, less than 2 percent of the college-age population attended college, but the aspirations of the nation's youth were rising, and more and more parents had the financial means necessary for fulfilling them.

More significant than the expansion of the colleges were the alterations in their curricula and in the atmosphere permeating the average campus. In 1870 most colleges remained what they had been in the 1830s: small, limited in their offerings, and intellectually stagnant. Thereafter, change came like a flood tide: State universities proliferated; the federal government's land-grant program in support of training in "agriculture and the mechanic arts," established under the Morrill Act of 1862, came into its own; wealthy philanthropists poured fortunes into old institutions and founded new ones; educators introduced new courses and adopted new teaching methods; professional schools of law, medicine, education, business, journalism, and other specialties increased in number.

Read the Document

The Morrill Act at **myhistorylab.com**

In the forefront of reform was Harvard, the oldest and most prestigious college in the country. In the 1860s it possessed an excellent faculty, but teaching methods were antiquated and the curriculum had remained almost unchanged since the colonial period. In 1869, however, a dynamic president, the chemist Charles W. Eliot, undertook a transformation of the college. Eliot introduced the elective system, gradually eliminating required courses and expanding offerings in such areas as modern languages, economics, and the laboratory sciences.

An even more important development in higher education was the founding of Johns Hopkins in 1876. This university was one of many established in the period by wealthy industrialists; its benefactor, the Baltimore merchant Johns Hopkins, had made his fortune in the Baltimore and Ohio Railroad. Its distinctiveness, however, was due to the vision of Daniel Coit Gilman, its first president.

Gilman modeled Johns Hopkins on the German universities, where meticulous research and freedom of inquiry were the guiding principles. In staffing the institution, he sought scholars of the highest reputation, scouring Europe as well as America in his search for talent and offering outstanding men high salaries for that time—up to $5,000 for a

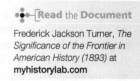

Read the Document

Frederick Jackson Turner, *The Significance of the Frontier in American History (1893)* at **myhistorylab.com**

A physics lecture, circa 1890, at the University of Michigan. Note that women are segregated from men; but in the men's section white and black men are sitting together. Many of the Morrill Act universities admitted women.

Photo Credit: Bentley Historical Library, University of Michigan.

professor, roughly ten times the income of a skilled artisan. Johns Hopkins specialized in graduate education. In the generation after its founding, it churned out a remarkable percentage of the most important scholars in the nation, including Woodrow Wilson in political science, John Dewey in philosophy, Frederick Jackson Turner in history, and John R. Commons in economics.

State and federal aid to higher education expanded rapidly. The Morrill Act, granting land to each state at a rate of 30,000 acres for each senator and representative, provided the endowments that gave many important modern universities, such as Illinois, Michigan State, and Ohio State, their start. While the federal assistance was earmarked for specific subjects, the land-grant colleges offered a full range of courses, and all received additional state funds. The land-grant universities adopted new ideas quickly. They were coeducational from the start, and most developed professional schools and experimented with extension work and summer programs.

Typical of the better state institutions was the University of Michigan, which reached the top rank among the nation's universities during the presidency of James B. Angell (1871–1909). Like Eliot at Harvard, Angell expanded the undergraduate curriculum and strengthened the law and medical schools. He encouraged graduate studies, seeking to make Michigan "part of the great world of scholars," and sought ways in which the university could serve the general community.

Important advances were made in women's higher education. Beginning with Vassar College, which opened its doors to 300 women students in 1865, the opportunity for young women to pursue serious academic work gradually expanded. Wellesley and Smith, both founded in 1875, completed the so-called Big Three women's colleges. Together with the already established Mount Holyoke (1837), and with Bryn Mawr (1885), Barnard (1889), and Radcliffe (1893), they became known as the Seven Sisters.

Not all the changes in higher education were beneficial. The elective system led to superficiality; students gained a smattering of knowledge of many subjects and mastered none. For example, 55 percent of the Harvard class of 1898 took elementary courses and no others during their four years of study. Intensive graduate work often produced narrowness of outlook and research monographs on trivial subjects. Attempts to apply the scientific method in fields such as history and economics often enticed students into making smug (and preposterous) claims to objectivity and definitiveness.

The gifts of rich industrialists sometimes came with strings, and college boards of trustees tended to be dominated by businessmen who sometimes attempted to impose their own social and economic beliefs on faculty members. Although few professors lost their positions because their views offended trustees, at many institutions trustees exerted constant nagging pressures that limited academic freedom and scholarly objectivity. At state colleges, politicians often interfered in academic affairs, even treating professorships as part of the patronage system.

As the number of college graduates increased, and as colleges ceased being primarily training institutions for clergymen, the influence of alumni on educational policies began to make itself felt, not always happily. Campus social activities became more important. Fraternities proliferated. Interest in organized sports first appeared as a laudable outgrowth of the general expansion of the curriculum, but soon athletic contests were playing a role all out of proportion to their significance. After football evolved as the leading intercollegiate sport (over 50,000 attended the Yale-Princeton game in 1893), it became a source of revenue that many colleges dared not neglect. Since students, alumni, and the public demanded winning teams, college administrators stooped to subsidizing student athletes, in extreme cases employing players who were not students at all. One exasperated college president quipped that the BA degree was coming to mean Bachelor of Athletics.

Watch the Video
College Football (1903) at myhistorylab.com

Thus higher education reflected American values, with all their strengths and weaknesses. A complex society required a more professional and specialized education for its youth; the coarseness and the rampant materialism and competitiveness of the era inevitably found expression in the colleges and universities.

Revolution in the Social Sciences

In the social sciences a close connection existed between the practical issues of the age and the achievements of the leading thinkers. The application of the theory of evolution to every aspect of human relations, the impact of industrialization on society—such topics were of intense concern to American economists, sociologists, and historians. An understanding of Darwin increased the already strong interest in studying the development of institutions and their interactions with one another. Controversies over trusts, slum conditions, and other problems drew scholars out of their towers and into practical affairs.

Among the economists something approaching a revolution took place in the 1880s. The classical school, which maintained that immutable natural laws governed all human behavior and which used the insights of Darwin only to justify unrestrained competition and laissez-faire, was challenged by a group of young economists who argued that as times changed, economic theories and laws must be modified in order to remain relevant. Richard T. Ely, another of the scholars who made Johns Hopkins a font of new ideas in the 1880s, summarized the thinking of this group in 1885. "The state [is] an educational and ethical agency whose positive aid is an indispensable condition of human progress," Ely proclaimed. Laissez-faire was outmoded and dangerous. Economic problems were basically moral problems; their solution required "the united efforts of Church, state and science." The proper way to study these problems was by analyzing actual conditions, not by applying abstract laws or principles.

This approach produced the so-called institutionalist school of economics, whose members made detailed, on-the-spot investigations of labor unions, sweatshops, factories, and mines. The study of institutions would lead both to theoretical insights and to practical social reform, they believed. John R. Commons, one of Ely's students at Johns Hopkins and later professor of economics at the University of Wisconsin, was the outstanding member of this school. His ten-volume *Documentary History of American Industrial Society* (1910–1911) reveals the institutionalist approach at its best.

A similar revolution struck sociology in the mid-1880s. Prevailing opinion up to that time rejected the idea of government interference with the organization of society. The influence of the English social Darwinist, Herbert Spencer, who objected even to public schools and the postal system, was immense. Spencer and his American disciples, among them Edward L. Youmans, editor of *Popular Science Monthly*, twisted the ideas of Darwin to mean that society could be changed only by the force of evolution, which moved with cosmic slowness. "You and I can do nothing at all," Youmans told the reformer Henry George. "It's all a matter of evolution. Perhaps in four or five thousand years evolution may have carried men beyond this state of things."

Read the Document

Herbert Spencer, Social Darwinism at **myhistorylab.com**

Progressive Education

Traditionally, American teachers had emphasized the three Rs and relied on strict discipline. Yet new ideas were attracting attention. According to a German educator, Johann Friedrich Herbart, teachers could best arouse the interest of their students by relating new information to what they already knew; good teaching called for professional training, psychological insight, enthusiasm, and imagination, not merely facts and a birch rod. At the same time, evolutionists were pressing for a kind of education that would help children to "survive" by adapting to the demands of their rapidly changing urban environment.

Forward-looking educators seized on these ideas because dynamic social changes were making the old system increasingly inadequate. Settlement house workers discovered that slum children needed training in handicrafts, citizenship, and personal hygiene as much as in reading and writing. They were appalled by the local schools, which suffered from the same diseases—filth, overcrowding, rickety construction—that plagued the tenements, and by school systems that were controlled by machine politicians who doled out teaching positions to party hacks and other untrained persons. They argued that school playgrounds, nurseries, kindergartens, and adult education programs were essential in communities where most women worked and many people lacked much formal education. The philosopher who summarized and gave direction to these forces was John Dewey, a professor at the University of Chicago. Dewey was concerned with the implications of evolution—indeed, of all science—for education.

"Education," Dewey insisted in *The School and Society* (1899), was "the fundamental method of social progress and reform." To seek to improve conditions merely by passing laws was "futile." Moreover, in an industrial society the family no longer performed many of the educational functions it had carried out in an agrarian society. Farm children learn about nature, about work, about human character in countless ways denied to children in cities. The school can fill the gap by becoming "an embryonic community . . . with types of occupations that reflect the life of the larger society." At the same time, education should center on the child, and new information should be related to what the child already knows. Finally, the school should become an instrument for social reform.

The School and Society created a stir, and Dewey immediately assumed leadership of what in the next generation was called progressive education. Although the gains made in public education before 1900 were more quantitative than qualitative and the philosophy dominant in most schools was not very different at the end of the century from that prevailing in Horace Mann's day, change was in the air. The best educators of the period were full of optimism, convinced that the future was theirs.

Law and History

Even jurisprudence, by its nature conservative and rooted in tradition, felt the pressure of evolutionary thought. In 1881 Oliver Wendell Holmes Jr. published *The Common Law.* Rejecting the ideas that judges should limit themselves to the mechanical explication of statutes and that law consisted only of what was written in law books, Holmes argued that "the felt necessities of the time" rather than precedent should determine the rules by which people are governed. "The life of the law has not been logic; it has been experience," he wrote.

Holmes went on to a long and brilliant judicial career, during which he repeatedly stressed the right of the people, through their elected representatives, to deal with contemporary problems in any reasonable way, unfettered by outmoded conceptions of the proper limits of government authority. Like the societies they regulated, laws should evolve as times and conditions changed, he said.

The new approach to knowledge did not always advance the cause of liberal reform. Historians in the graduate schools became intensely interested in studying the origins and evolution of political institutions. They concluded, after much "scientific" study of old charters and law codes, that the roots of democracy were to be found in the customs of the ancient tribes of northern Europe. This theory of the "Teutonic origins" of democracy, which has since been thoroughly discredited, fitted well with the prejudices of people of British stock, and it provided ammunition for those who favored restricting immigration and for those who argued that blacks were inferior beings.

Out of this work, however, came an essentially democratic concept, the frontier thesis of Frederick Jackson Turner, still another scholar trained at Johns Hopkins. Turner's essay "The Significance of the Frontier in American History" (1893) argued that the frontier experience, through which every section of the country had passed, had affected the thinking of the people and the shape of American institutions. The isolation of the frontier and the need during each successive westward advance to create civilization anew, Turner wrote, account for the individualism of Americans and the democratic character of their society. Nearly everything unique in our culture could be traced to the existence of the frontier, he claimed.

Turner, and still more his many disciples, made too much of his basic insights. Life on the frontier was not as democratic as Turner believed, and it certainly does not "explain" American development as completely as he said it did. Nevertheless, his work showed how important it was to investigate the evolution of institutions, and it encouraged historians to study social and economic, as well as purely political, subjects. If the

American Lives

In 1885, severe depression gripped twenty-five-year-old Charlotte Perkins Stetson. "Every morning the same helpless waking," she confided in her journal. "Retreat impossible, escape impossible." She had married the previous year and had just given birth to a daughter. But the infant gave her no pleasure. "I would hold her close—that lovely child!—and instead of love and happiness, feel only pain. The tears ran down my breast." Over the next few years, her depression worsened. She feared she was approaching "the edge of insanity."

Charlotte's life had not been easy. Shortly after she was born, her father abandoned the family. He visited every couple of years, and occasionally sent a check, but Charlotte, her brother, and her mother lacked regular income and lived with relatives, moving frequently. "What I do know is that my childhood had no father," she wrote. Charlotte's relationship with her mother was not much better. Shattered by her husband's abandonment, she refused to cuddle Charlotte as an infant lest the child become dependent on affection. They never were close. When she was an adolescent, Charlotte and her mother lived in a cooperative run by a spiritualist, a woman who claimed to communicate with spirits. One day Charlotte saw her taking grapes that were meant for the whole group. The woman accused Charlotte of thinking evil thoughts about her. Charlotte's mother insisted that Charlotte apologize for her thoughts; Charlotte refused. "And what are you going to do about it?" she taunted. Her mother hit her. At that moment, "I was born," Charlotte recalled. "Neither she, nor any one, could *make* me do anything."

Charlotte devised a stern regimen to ensure her future independence. Every day she ran a mile and educated herself by drawing, reading, and writing. Never would she depend on anyone— especially a man. "I am not domestic and I don't want to be," she told a female confidante.

Her resolve weakened when she was courted by an aspiring young writer. They married and the baby soon followed. Charlotte's bouts of depression became more frequent and incapacitating. Finally she agreed to consult with neurologist S. Weir Mitchell,

Charlotte Perkins Stetson, shortly after her marriage, wrote, "You were called to serve humanity, and you cannot serve yourself. No good as a wife, no good as a mother, no good at anything. And you did it yourself!"

Photo Credit: The Granger Collection, New York.

the nation's foremost expert on neurasthenia, a disease that especially afflicted well-to-do young women. Its chief symptoms were depression, listlessness, and invalidism.

Mitchell believed that women's nervous systems were attuned to childbearing and childrearing. Women who pursued education and careers would exhaust their nervous energy and become neurasthenic. Charlotte's condition, Mitchell assured her, resulted from her intellectual labors. His prescription was simple:

> Live as domestic a life as possible. Have your child with you all the time. Lie down an hour after each meal. Have but two hours' intellectual life a day. And never touch pen, brush, or pencil as long as you live.

For a time, Charlotte accepted his regimen. "I went home, followed those directions rigidly for months, and came perilously close to losing my mind," she noted. Then she decided to "cast off Dr. Mitchell bodily" and "do exactly as I pleased."

She separated from her husband, took her child to Pasadena, California, and wrote essays, editorials, and fiction.

In 1890 she finished "The Yellow Wallpaper," a story about a young wife who, suffering from depression, was confined by her doctor-husband to bed in an upstairs room, with servants tending to her every need. As she endlessly stared at her surroundings, the designs on the wallpaper changed shape; a figure appeared and wandered in and out of her consciousness. The wallpaper then grew bars that locked her into the room. Unable to escape through the bars, the woman chewed at the bed, fleeing ultimately into madness. The story was well-received as a literary horror story reminiscent of Edgar Allan Poe.

Having at last purged Mitchell from her psyche, Charlotte wrote incessantly and supported herself by giving lectures. She developed close and even intimate relationships with several women. When she sent her daughter to live with her father, newspapers denounced her for neglecting woman's proper function. Then she fell in love with Houghton Gilman, who accepted her refusal to embrace domesticity. "I *must not* focus on 'home duties' and entangle myself with them," she told him. They married in 1900.

Charlotte's first book, *Women and Economics* (1898), was a work of extraordinary creativity. A thoroughgoing Social Darwinist, Charlotte explained that marriage was founded on women's economic subjugation. Marx was wrong: Gender, not class, was the fundamental social distinction. The most important revolution would promote women's independence by allowing them to work outside the home.

In this and subsequent books and articles, Charlotte Perkins Gilman insisted that the domestic ideal had deprived society of women's creativity and ideas. Her own life was a case in point. With only four years of education, none after the age of fifteen, she achieved economic independence through her own heroic effort. Lacking alternative child-care arrangements, she sent her young child to live with her father so that she could pursue her life and work as an intellectual. The decision would psychologically scar both her and her daughter, but her work anticipated many of the themes of modern feminism.

claims of the new historians to objectivity and definitiveness were absurdly overstated, their emphasis on thoroughness, exactitude, and impartiality did much to raise standards in the profession.

Realism in Literature

When what Mark Twain called the Gilded Age began, American literature was dominated by the romantic mood. All the important writers of the 1840s and 1850s, except Hawthorne, Thoreau, and Poe, were still living. Longfellow stood at the height of his fame, and the lachrymose Susan Warner—"tears on almost every page"—continued to turn out stories in the style of her popular *The Wide, Wide World.* Romanticism, however, had lost its creative force; much of the popular writing in the decade after 1865 was sentimental trash pandering to the preconceptions of middle-class readers. Magazines like the *Atlantic Monthly* overflowed with stories about fair ladies worshiped from afar by stainless heroes, women coping selflessly with drunken husbands, and poor but honest youths rising through various combinations of virtue and diligence to positions of wealth and influence. Most writers of fiction tended to ignore the eternal conflicts inherent in human nature and the social problems of the age; polite entertainment and pious moralizing appeared to be their only objectives.

The patent unreality, even dishonesty, of contemporary fiction eventually caused a reaction. The most important forces giving rise to the Age of Realism were those that were transforming every other aspect of American life: industrialism, with its associated complexities and social problems; the theory of evolution, which made people more aware of the force of the environment and the basic conflicts of existence; the new science, which taught dispassionate, empirical observation. Novelists undertook the examination of social problems such as slum life, the conflict between capital and labor, and political corruption. They created multidimensional characters, depicted persons of every social class, used dialect and slang to capture the flavor of particular types, and fashioned painstaking descriptions of the surroundings into which they placed their subjects. The romantic novel did not disappear. General Lew Wallace's *Ben Hur* (1880) and Frances Hodgson Burnett's *Little Lord Fauntleroy* (1886) were best-sellers. But by 1880 realism was the point of view of the finest literary talents in the country.

Mark Twain

While it was easy to romanticize the West, that region lent itself to the realistic approach. Almost of necessity, novelists writing about the West described coarse characters from the lower levels of society and dealt with crime and violence. The outstanding figure of western literature, the first great American realist, was Mark Twain.

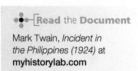

Read the Document

Mark Twain, *Incident in the Philippines (1924)* at **myhistorylab.com**

Twain, whose real name was Samuel L. Clemens, was born in 1835. He grew up in Hannibal, Missouri, on the banks of the Mississippi. After mastering the printer's trade and working as a riverboat pilot, he went west to Nevada in 1861. The wild, rough life of Virginia City fascinated him, but prospecting got him nowhere, and he became a reporter for the *Territorial Enterprise*. Soon he was publishing humorous stories about the local life under the nom de plume Mark Twain. In 1865, while working in California, he wrote "The Celebrated Jumping Frog of Calaveras County," a story that brought him national recognition. A tour of Europe and the Holy Land in 1867 to 1868 led to *The Innocents Abroad* (1869), which made him famous.

Twain's greatness stemmed from his keen reportorial eye and ear, his eagerness to live life to the full, his marvelous sense of humor, and his ability to be at once in society and outside it, and to love humanity yet be repelled by human vanity and perversity. He epitomized the zest and adaptability of his age and also its materialism. No contemporary pursued the almighty dollar more zealously. An inveterate speculator, he made a fortune with his pen and lost it in foolish business ventures.

Read the Document
Mark Twain, from *The Gilded Age* at myhistorylab.com

He was equally at home and equally successful on the Great River of his childhood, in the mining camps, and in the eastern bourgeois society of his mature years. But every prize slipped through his fingers. Twain died a dark pessimist, surrounded by adulation yet alone, an alien and a stranger in the land he loved and knew so well.

Whether directly, as in *The Innocents Abroad* and in his fascinating account of the world of the river pilot, *Life on the Mississippi* (1883), or when transformed by his imagination in works of fiction such as *Tom Sawyer* (1876) and *A Connecticut Yankee in King Arthur's Court* (1889), Mark Twain always put much of his own experience and feeling into his work. A story, he told a fellow author, "must be written with the blood out of a man's heart." His innermost confusions, the clash between his recognition of the pretentiousness and meanness of human beings and his wish to be accepted by society, added depths and overtones to his writing that together with his comic genius give it last-

Read the Document
Mark Twain, *To the Person Sitting in Darkness (1901)* at myhistorylab.com

ing appeal. He could not rise above the sentimentality and prudery of his generation entirely, for these qualities were part of his nature. He never dealt effectively with sexual love, for example, and often—even in *Huckleberry Finn*—contrived to end his tales on absurdly optimistic notes that ring false after so many brilliant pages portraying life as it is. On balance Twain's achievement was magnificent. Rough and uneven like the man himself, his works catch more of the spirit of the age he named than those of any other writer.

William Dean Howells

Twain's realism was far less self-conscious than that of his longtime friend William Dean Howells. Like Twain, Howells, who was born in Ohio in 1837, had little formal education. He learned the printer's trade from his father and became a reporter for the *Ohio State Journal*. After the Civil War he worked briefly for *The Nation* in New York and then moved to Boston, where he became editor of the *Atlantic Monthly*. In 1886 he returned to New York as editor of *Harper's*.

A long series of novels and much literary criticism poured from Howells's pen over the next thirty years. While he insisted on treating his material honestly, he was not at first a critic of society, being content to write about what he called "the smiling aspects" of life. Realism to Howells meant concern for the complexities of

In 1891 William Dean Howells championed the poetry of Emily Dickinson: "This poetry is as characteristic of our life as our business enterprise, our political turmoil, our demagogism, or our millionaires." Yet few of her poems appeared during her lifetime; arguably the most important poet of her age was unknown to that age.

Photo Credit: The Granger Collection, New York.

individual personalities and faithful description of the genteel, middle-class world he knew best.

Besides a sharp eye and an open mind, Howells had a real social conscience. Gradually he became aware of the problems that industrialization had created. In 1885, in *The Rise of Silas Lapham*, he dealt with some of the ethical conflicts faced by businessmen in a competitive society. The harsh public reaction to the Haymarket bombing in 1886 stirred him, and he threw himself into a futile campaign to prevent the execution of the anarchist suspects. Thereafter he moved rapidly toward the left. In *A Hazard of New Fortunes* (1890), he attempted to portray the whole range of metropolitan life, weaving the destinies of a dozen interesting personalities from diverse sections and social classes.

His own works were widely read, and Howells was also the most influential critic of his time. He encouraged many important young American novelists, among them Stephen Crane, Theodore Dreiser, Frank Norris, and Hamlin Garland.

Some of these writers went far beyond Howells's realism to what they called naturalism. Many, like Twain and Howells, began as newspaper reporters. Working for a big-city daily in the 1890s was sure to teach anyone a great deal about the dark side of life. Naturalist writers believed that the human being was essentially an animal, a helpless creature whose fate was determined by environment. Their world was Darwin's world—mindless, without mercy or justice. They wrote chiefly about the most primitive emotions—lust, hate, and greed. In *Maggie, A Girl of the Streets* (1893), Stephen Crane described the seduction, degradation, and eventual suicide of a young woman, all set against the background of a sordid slum; in *The Red Badge of Courage* (1895), he captured the pain and humor of war. In *McTeague* (1899), Frank Norris told the story of a brutal, dull-witted dentist who murdered his greed-crazed wife with his bare fists.

Such stuff was too strong for Howells, yet he recognized its importance and befriended the younger writers in many ways. He found a publisher for *Maggie* after it had been rejected several times, and he wrote appreciative reviews of the work of Garland and Norris. Even Theodore Dreiser, who was contemptuous of Howells's writings and considered him hopelessly middle-class in point of view, appreciated his aid and praised his influence on American literature. Dreiser's first novel, *Sister Carrie* (1900), treated sex so forthrightly that it was withdrawn after publication.

Henry James

Henry James was very different in spirit and background from the tempestuous naturalists. Born to wealth, reared in a cosmopolitan atmosphere, twisted in some strange way while still a child and unable to achieve satisfactory relationships with women, James spent most of his mature life in Europe, writing novels, short stories, plays, and volumes of criticism. He was preeminently a realist, determined, as he once said, "to leave a multitude of pictures of my time" for the future to contemplate.

James dealt with social issues such as feminism and the difficulties faced by artists in the modern world, but he subordinated them to his interest in his subjects as individuals. *The American* (1877) told the story of the love of a wealthy American in Paris for a French noblewoman who rejected him because her family disapproved of his commercial background. *The Portrait of a Lady* (1881) described the disillusionment of an intelligent woman married to a charming but morally bankrupt man and her eventual decision to remain with him nonetheless. *The Bostonians* (1886) was a complicated and psychologically sensitive study of the varieties of female behavior in a seemingly uniform social situation.

James's reputation, greater today than in his lifetime, rests more on his highly refined accounts of the interactions of individuals and their environment and his masterful commentaries on the novel as a literary form than on his ability as a storyteller. Few major writers have been more long-winded, more prone to circumlocution. Yet few have been so dedicated to their art, possessed of such psychological penetration, or so successful in producing a large body of important work.

Realism in Art

American painters responded to the times as writers did, but with this difference: Despite the new concern for realism, the romantic tradition retained its vitality. Preeminent among the realists was Thomas Eakins, who was born in Philadelphia in 1844. Eakins studied in Europe in the late 1860s and was influenced by the great realists of the seventeenth century, Velasquez and Rembrandt. Returning to America in 1870, he passed the remainder of his life teaching and painting in Philadelphia.

The scientific spirit of the age suited Eakins perfectly. He mastered human anatomy; some of his finest paintings, such as *The Gross Clinic* (1875), are graphic illustrations of surgical operations. He was an early experimenter with motion pictures, using the camera to capture exactly the attitudes of human beings and animals in action. Like his friend Walt Whitman, whose portrait is one of his greatest achievements, Eakins gloried in the ordinary. But he had none of Whitman's weakness for self-delusion. His portraits are monuments to his integrity and craftsmanship: Never would he touch up a likeness to please his sitter.

Winslow Homer, a Boston-born painter best known for his brilliant watercolors, was also influenced by realist ideas. Homer was a lithographer as well as a master of the watercolor medium, yet he had had almost no formal training. During the Civil War, he worked as an artist-reporter for *Harper's Weekly*, and he continued to do magazine illustrations for some years thereafter. He roamed America, painting

Photo Credit: 1990.19.1 Thomas Eakins, *The Swimming Hole*. Oil on canvas, 1885. Purchased by Friends of Art, Fort Worth Art Association, 1925; acquired by the Amon Carter Museum, 1990, from the Modern Art Museum of Fort Worth through grants and donations from Amon G. Carter Foundation, the Sid W. Richardson Foundation, the Anne Burnett and Charles Tandy Foundation, Capital Cities/ABC Foundation, Fort Worth Star-Telegrapm, The R. D. and Joan Dale Hubbard Foundation and the people of Fort Worth.

Thomas Eakins's interest in science was as great as his interest in art. In the early 1880s he collaborated with photographer Eadweard Muybridge in serial-action photographic experiments and later devised a special camera for his anatomical studies. The accompanying picture (top) was taken with the Marey wheel. The impact of Eakins's photographic experiments is evident in *The Swimming Hole* (bottom), painted in 1883. At that time Eakins was director of the art school at the Pennsylvania Academy of the Fine Arts.
Source: (top) Philadelpia Museum of Art. Gift of Charles Bregler.

scenes of southern farm life, Adirondack campers, and, after about 1880, magnificent seascapes and studies of fishermen and sailors.

The careers of Eakins and Homer show that the late-nineteenth-century American environment was not uncongenial to first-rate artists. Nevertheless, at least two major American painters abandoned native shores for Europe. One was James A. McNeill Whistler, whose portrait of his mother, which he called *Arrangement in Grey and Black*, is probably the most famous canvas ever painted by an American. Whistler left the United States in 1855 when he was twenty-one and spent most of his life in Paris and London. "I shall come to America," he announced grandly, "when the duty on works of art is abolished!"

Whistler made a profession of eccentricity, but he was a talented and versatile artist. Spare and muted in tone, his paintings are more interesting as precise arrangements of color and space than as images of particular objects; they had considerable influence on the course of modern art.

The second important expatriate artist was Mary Cassatt, daughter of a wealthy Pittsburgh banker and sister of Alexander J. Cassatt, who was president of the Pennsylvania Railroad around the turn of the century. She went to Paris as a tourist and dabbled in art like many conventional young socialites, then was caught up in the impressionist movement and decided to become a serious painter. Her work is more French than American and was little appreciated in the United States before World War I.

The Pragmatic Approach

The theory of evolution posed an immediate challenge to religion: If Darwin was correct, the biblical account of the creation was apparently untrue and the idea that the human race had been formed in God's image was highly unlikely. A bitter controversy erupted, described by President Andrew D. White of Cornell in *The Warfare of Science with Theology in Christendom* (1896). While millions continued to believe in the literal truth of the Bible, among intellectuals, lay and clerical, victory went to the evolutionists because, in addition to the arguments of the geologists and the biologists, scholars were throwing light on the historical origins of the Bible, showing that its words were of human rather than divine inspiration.

If the account of the creation in Genesis could not be taken literally, the Bible remained a repository of wisdom and inspiration. Such books as John Fiske's *The Outlines of Cosmic Philosophy* (1874) provided religious persons with the comforting thesis that evolution, while true, was merely God's way of ordering the universe—as the liberal preacher Washington Gladden put it, "a most impressive demonstration of the presence of God in the world."

The effects of Darwinism on philosophy were less dramatic but in the end more significant. Fixed systems and eternal truths were difficult to justify in a world that was constantly evolving. By the early 1870s a few philosophers had begun to reason that ideas and theories mattered little except when applied to specifics.

"Nothing justifies the development of abstract principles but their utility in enlarging our concrete knowledge of nature," wrote Chauncey Wright, secretary of the American Academy of Arts and Sciences. This startling philosophy, known as **pragmatism**, was further developed by William James, brother of the novelist. James was one of the most remarkable persons of his generation. His *Principles of Psychology* (1890) may be said to have established that discipline as a modern science. His *Varieties of Religious Experience* (1902), which treated the subject from both psychological and philosophical points of view, helped thousands of readers

Table 1 Key Figures and Intellectual Currents

Intellectual	Chief Accomplishment	Major Ideas
Charles W. Eliot	Elective system at Harvard	Encouraged development of college majors and hiring of specialized faculty
Daniel Coit Gilman	Graduate education at Johns Hopkins	Brought German standards of research to the United States
Richard Ely	Founded "institutional school of economics"	Challenged theorists who focused on markets and advocated laissez-faire governmental policy
John Dewey	*The School and Society* (1899)	Insisted that meaningful social change was impossible without educational change
Oliver Wendell Holmes, Jr.	*The Common Law* (1881)	Demonstrated that law was not founded on historical precedent; legal principles evolved with society
Frederick Jackson Turner	"The Significance of the Frontier in American History" (1893)	Frontier conditions explained the individualism and democracy that characterized American society
Mark Twain	*Huckleberry Finn* (1884)	Lampooned the sentimentality and hypocrisy of Victorian culture
Charlotte Perkins Gilman	*Women and Economics* (1898)	Maintained that society was unjustly built upon women's economic dependence on men; social change depended on women finding meaningful paid work
William Dean Howells	*A Hazard of New Fortunes* (1890)	Promoted a realistic, nonsentimental look at society
Henry James	*The Portrait of a Lady* (1881)	Showed how literature could probe the depths and complexities of human relationships
Thomas Eakins	*The Gross Clinic* (1875)	Applied realistic perspectives to art
William James	*The Principles of Psychology* (1890)	Contended that the will, as influenced by psychological factors, was an independent force in human affairs

reconcile their religious faith with their increasing knowledge of psychology and the physical universe.

James's wide range and his verve and imagination as a writer made him by far the most influential philosopher of his time. He rejected the deterministic interpretation of Darwinism and all other one-idea explanations of existence. Belief in free will was one of his axioms; environment might influence survival, but so did the *desire* to survive, which existed independent of surrounding circumstances. Even truth was relative; it did not exist in the abstract but *happened* under particular circumstances. What a person thought helped to make thought occur, or come true. The mind, James wrote in a typically vivid phrase, has "a vote" in determining truth. Religion was true, for example, because people were religious.

Pragmatism brought Americans face-to-face with somber problems. While relativism made them optimistic, it also bred insecurity, for there could be no certainty, no comforting reliance on any eternal value in the absence of absolute truth. Pragmatism also seemed to suggest that the end justified the means, that what worked was more important than what ought to be. At the time of James's death in 1910, the *Commercial and Financial Chronicle* pointed out that the pragmatic philosophy was helpful to businessmen in making decisions. By emphasizing practice at the expense of theory, the new philosophy encouraged materialism, anti-intellectualism, and other unlovely aspects of the American character. And what place had conventional morality in such a system? Perhaps pragmatism placed too much reliance on the free will of human beings, ignoring their capacity for selfishness and self-delusion.

The people of the new century found pragmatism a heady wine. They would quaff it freely and enthusiastically—down to the bitter dregs.

The Knowledge Revolution

Improvements in public education and the needs of an increasingly complex society for every type of intellectual skill caused a veritable revolution in how knowledge was discovered, disseminated, and put to use. Nothing so well illustrates the desire for new information as the rise of the Chautauqua movement, founded by John H. Vincent, a Methodist minister, and Lewis Miller, an Ohio manufacturer of farm machinery. Vincent had charge of Sunday schools for the Methodist church. In 1874 he and Miller organized a two-week summer course for Sunday school teachers on the shores of Lake Chautauqua in New York. Besides instruction, they offered good meals, evening songfests around the campfire, and a relaxing atmosphere—all for $6 for the two weeks.

The forty young teachers who attended were delighted with the program, and soon the leafy shore of Lake Chautauqua became a city of tents each summer as thousands poured into the region from all over the country. The founders expanded their offerings to include instruction in literature, science, government, and economics. Famous authorities, including, over the years, six presidents of the United States, came to lecture to open-air audiences on every subject imaginable. Eventually Chautauqua supplied speakers to reading circles throughout the country; it even offered correspondence courses leading over a four-year period to a diploma, the program designed, in Vincent's words, to give "the college outlook" to persons who had not had the opportunity to obtain a higher education. Books were written specifically for the program, and a monthly magazine, the *Chautauquan*, was published.

Still larger numbers profited from the proliferation of public libraries. By the end of the century nearly all the states supported libraries. Private donors, led by the steel industrialist Andrew Carnegie, contributed millions to the cause. In 1900 over 1,700 libraries in the

The first commercially successful typewriter, manufactured in quantity beginning in 1874. It used the QWERTY keyboard found on later typewriters—and eventually found on computer keyboards.

Photo Credit: © SSPL/The Image Works.

United States had collections of more than 5,000 volumes.

Publishers tended to be conservative, but reaching the masses meant lowering intellectual and cultural standards, appealing to emotions, and adopting popular, sometimes radical, causes. Cheap, mass-circulation papers had first appeared in the 1830s and 1840s, the most successful being the *Sun*, the *Herald*, and the *Tribune* in New York; the *Philadelphia Public Ledger*; and the *Baltimore Sun*. None of them much exceeded a circulation of 50,000 before the Civil War. The first publisher to reach a truly massive audience was Joseph Pulitzer, a Hungarian-born immigrant who made a first-rate paper of the *St. Louis Post-Dispatch*. In 1883 Pulitzer bought the *New York World*, a sheet with a circulation of perhaps 20,000. Within a year he was selling 100,000 copies daily, and by the late 1890s the *World*'s circulation regularly exceeded 1 million.

Growth and ferment also characterized the magazine world. In 1865 there were about 700 magazines in the country, and by the turn of the century more than 5,000. Until the mid-1880s, few of the new magazines were in any way unusual. A handful of serious periodicals, such as the *Atlantic Monthly*, *Harper's*, and the *Century*, dominated the field. They were staid in tone and conservative in politics. Although they had great influence, none approached mass circulation because of the limited size of the upper-middle-class audience they aimed at.

Popular magazines rarely discussed the great issues that preoccupied intellectuals—the impact of Darwinism on law, sociology, and anthropology; the theories of John Dewey and the progressive educators; the import of realism in literature and art; the implications of pragmatism to psychology, philosophy, and theology. But some phenomena—such as the mania for college football—pressed forward because they represented so powerful a convergence of popular culture and intellectual trends.

Milestones

1862	Morrill Act establishes land-grant colleges	1886	William Dean Howells becomes editor of *Harper's*
1865	Vassar College is founded for women	1889	Edward W. Bok becomes editor of the *Ladies' Home Journal*
1869	Charles W. Eliot becomes Harvard's president	1890	William James publishes *Principles of Psychology*
1874	Chautauqua movement begins	1893	Frederick Jackson Turner publishes "Significance of the Frontier in American History"
1876	Johns Hopkins University is founded to specialize in graduate education		
1881	Oliver Wendell Holmes Jr. publishes *The Common Law*	1895	William Randolph Hearst purchases the *New York Journal*
	Henry James publishes *The Portrait of a Lady*	1898	Charlotte Perkins Gilman publishes *Women and Economics*
1883	Joseph Pulitzer purchases *New York World*	1899	John Dewey publishes *The School and Society*
1884	Mark Twain publishes *Huckleberry Finn*		
1886	Ottmar Mergenthaler invents linotype machine		

✓•⎯Study and Review at **www.myhistorylab.com**

Review Questions

1. The introductory essay argues that football was embraced by colleges and universities in the late nineteenth century because it reflected hard-nosed Darwinian concepts. What other aspects of late-nineteenth-century intellectual and cultural life were influenced by Darwinism? What intellectual trends and movements rejected social Darwinism?

2. What institutional developments transformed higher education during the last third of the nineteenth century?

3. How was popular culture at odds with intellectual trends in literature and the arts?

4. How did pragmatism—the belief that ideas must be judged by their consequences—challenge earlier outlooks on philosophy and morality?

Key Terms

pragmatism

From Smoke-Filled Rooms to Prairie Wildfire: 1877–1896

From Chapter 20 of *American Destiny: Narrative of a Nation*, Combined Volume, Fourth Edition.
Mark C. Carnes and John A. Garraty. Copyright © 2012 by Pearson Education, Inc. Published by
Pearson Prentice Hall. All rights reserved.

From Smoke-Filled Rooms to Prairie Wildfire: 1877–1896

((•—[Hear the Audio at myhistorylab.com

Did you vote for an American Idol?

ON MAY 20, 2009, TWENTY-THREE-YEAR-OLD GUITAR-STRUMMING Kris Allen captivated the audience of *American Idol* with his rendition of Keith Urban's "Kiss a Girl" and Bill Withers's "Ain't No Sunshine." By receiving a majority of the nearly 100 million "votes"—by telephone and text message—Allen became the *American Idol* for 2009.

Although pundits had for years grumbled that Americans cared more about pop stars on *American Idol* than about their president, this may not have been true in 2009. The producers of the show did not release the exact number of votes for Allen, but they did say the vote was close; probably he received no more than 55 million. Six months earlier, presidential candidates Barack Obama and John McCain received more votes than Allen, with 69 million and 60 million respectively.

A better comparison is of voter turnout for presidential elections nowadays and during the late nineteenth century. Since 1946, fewer than half of the eligible voters have on the average voted in presidential elections. By contrast, over three-fourths of eligible voters did so in presidential campaigns from 1876 to 1896—the highest rates in the nation's history.

This puzzles scholars, because the issues of that time seem inconsequential: Civil War soldiers' pensions, the tariff, paper money vs. gold and silver coins, and civil service reform. Perhaps the most volatile issue—the plight of former slaves—never attracted much notice because most politicians looked the other way. The other key issue—the minimal role of the federal government in the nation's industrial ascent—went without saying and, being unsaid, generated little controversy.

Why, then, did so many people vote? Local issues seem to have loomed large in most people's thinking. Public health, municipal services, and corruption all dominated the headlines. Then, during the 1890s, a nationwide industrial depression crushed many local manufacturing firms, just as an agricultural crisis was sweeping through the midsection of the nation.

Because the nation had become more tightly integrated, these economic upheavals jolted nearly every community. National policy and local issues converged, culminating in the extraordinary election of 1896, which brought over 80 percent of the electorate to the polls. In these years, politics had become the greatest show around.

Congress Ascendant

A succession of weak presidents occupied the White House during the last quarter of the nineteenth century. Although the impeachment proceedings against Andrew Johnson had failed, Congress dominated the government. Within Congress, the Senate generally overshadowed the House of Representatives. Critics called the Senate a "rich man's club," and it did contain many millionaires. However, the true sources of the Senate's influence lay in the long tenure of many of its members (which enabled them to master the craft of politics), in the fact that it was small enough to encourage real debate, and in its long-established reputation for wisdom, intelligence, and statesmanship.

The House of Representatives, on the other hand, was one of the most disorderly and inefficient legislative bodies in the world.

Desks slammed; members held private conversations, hailed pages, shuffled from place to place, clamored for the attention of the Speaker—and all the while some poor orator tried to discuss the question of the moment. Speaking in the House, one writer said, was like trying to address the crowd on a passing Broadway bus from the curb in front of the Astor House in New York. On one occasion in 1878 the adjournment of the House was held up for more than twelve hours because most of the members of an important committee were too drunk to prepare a vital appropriations bill for final passage.

The fundamental division between Democrats and Republicans was sectional, a result of the Civil War. The South, after the political rights of blacks had been drastically circumscribed, became heavily Democratic. Most of New England was solidly Republican. Elsewhere the two parties stood in fair balance, although the Republicans tended to have the advantage. A preponderance of the well-to-do, cultured Northerners were Republicans. Perhaps in reaction to this concentration, immigrants, Catholics, and other minority groups—except for blacks—tended to vote Democratic. But the

An 1887 cartoon indicting the Senate for closely attending to the Big (read, fat) Trusts rather than to the needs of the public (whose "entrance" to the Senate is "closed"). Drawn by Joseph Keppler, a caricaturist who was born and trained in Germany, this type of grotesque satire greatly influenced late-nineteenth-century American comic arts.

Photo Credit: The Granger Collection, New York.

numerous exceptions weakened the applicability of these generalizations. German and Scandinavian immigrants usually voted Republican; many powerful business leaders supported the Democrats.

The bulk of the people—farmers, laborers, shopkeepers, white-collar workers—distributed their ballots fairly evenly between the two parties in most elections; the balance of political power after 1876 was almost perfect. Between 1856 and 1912 the Democrats elected a president only twice (1884 and 1892), but most contests were extremely close. Majorities in both the Senate and the House fluctuated continually. Between 1876 and 1896 the "dominant" Republican party controlled both houses of Congress and the presidency at the same time for only a single two-year period.

Recurrent Issues

Four questions obsessed politicians in these years. One was the "bloody shirt." The term, which became part of the language after a Massachusetts congressman dramatically displayed to his colleagues in the House the bloodstained shirt of an Ohio carpetbagger who had been flogged by terrorists in Mississippi, referred to the tactic of reminding the electorate of the northern states that the men who had precipitated the Civil War had been Democrats. Should Democrats regain power, former rebels would run the government and undo all the work accomplished at such sacrifice during the war. "Every man that endeavored to tear down the old flag," a Republican orator proclaimed in 1876, "was a Democrat. Every man that tried to destroy this nation was a Democrat. . . . The man that assassinated Abraham Lincoln was a Democrat. . . . Soldiers, every scar you have on your heroic bodies was given you by a Democrat." And every scoundrel or incompetent who sought office under the Republican banner waved the bloody shirt in order to divert the attention of northern voters from his own shortcomings. The technique worked so well that many decent candidates could not resist the temptation to employ it in close races.

Waving the bloody shirt was related intimately to the issue of the rights of African Americans. Throughout this period Republicans vacillated between trying to build up their organization in the South by appealing to black voters—which required them to make sure that blacks in the South could vote—and trying to win conservative white support by stressing economic issues such as the tariff.

The tariff was another perennial issue in post–Civil War politics. Despite considerable loose talk about free trade, almost no one in the United States except for a handful of professional economists, believed in eliminating duties on imports. Manufacturers desired protective tariffs to keep out competing products, and a majority of their workers were convinced that wage levels would fall if goods produced by cheap foreign labor entered the United States untaxed. Congressman William McKinley of Ohio stated the majority opinion in the clearest terms: high tariffs foster the growth of industry and thus create jobs. "Reduce the tariff and labor is the first to suffer," he said.

The tariff could have been a real political issue because American technology was advancing so rapidly that many industries no longer required protection from foreign competitors. The Democrats professed to believe in moderation, yet whenever party leaders tried to revise the tariff downward, Democratic congressmen from Pennsylvania, New York, and other industrial states sided with the Republicans. Many Republicans endorsed tariff reform in principle, but when particular schedules came up for discussion, most of them demanded the highest rates for industries in their own districts and traded votes shamelessly with colleagues representing other interests in order to get what they wanted. Every new tariff bill became an occasion for logrolling, lobbying, and outrageous politicking rather than for sane discussion and careful evaluation of the public interest.

A third political question in this period was currency reform. During the Civil War, the government, faced with obligations it could not meet by taxing or borrowing, suspended specie payments and issued about $450 million in paper money, originally printed in green ink. This currency, called greenbacks, did not command the full confidence of a people accustomed to money readily convertible into gold or silver. Greenbacks seemed to encourage inflation, for how could one trust the government not to print them in wholesale lots to avoid passing unpopular tax laws? Thus, when the war ended, strong sentiment developed for withdrawing the greenbacks from circulation and returning to a bullion standard—to coining money from silver and gold.

In fact, beginning during Reconstruction, prices declined sharply. The deflation increased the real income of bondholders and other creditors but injured debtors. Farmers were particularly hard-hit, for many of them had borrowed heavily during the wartime boom to finance expansion.

Many groups supported some kind of currency inflation. However, the major parties refused to confront each other over the currency question. While Republicans professed to be the party of sound money, most western Republicans favored expansion of the currency. Conservative Democrats favored deflation as much as Republicans did. Under various administrations steps were taken to increase or decrease the amount of money in circulation, but the net effect on the economy was not significant.

The final major political issue of these years was civil service reform. As American society grew larger and more complex, the government necessarily took on more functions. The need for professional administration increased. Corruption flourished; waste and inefficiency were the normal state of affairs.

Every honest observer could see the need for reform, but the politicians refused to surrender the power of dispensing government jobs to their lieutenants without regard for their qualifications. They argued that patronage was the lifeblood of politics, that parties could not function without armies of loyal political workers, and that the workers expected and deserved the rewards of office when their efforts were crowned with victory at the polls. When reformers suggested establishing the most modest kind of professional, nonpartisan civil service, politicians of both parties subjected them to every kind of insult and ridicule even though both the Democratic and Republican parties regularly wrote civil service reform planks into their platforms.

Party Politics: Sidestepping the Issues

With the Democrats invincible in the South and the Republicans predominant in New England and most of the states beyond the Mississippi, the outcome of presidential elections was usually determined in a handful of populous states: New York (together with its satellites, New Jersey and Connecticut), Ohio, Indiana, and Illinois. In every presidential election, Democrats and Republicans concentrated their heaviest guns on these states. Of the eighteen Democrats and Republicans nominated for president in the nine elections between 1868 and 1900, only three were not from New York, Ohio, Indiana, or Illinois, and all three lost.

With so much depending on so few, the level of political morality was abysmal. Mudslinging, character assassination, and plain lying were standard practice; bribery was routine. Drifters and other dissolute citizens were paid in cash—or more often in free drinks—to vote the party ticket. The names of persons long dead were solemnly inscribed in voting registers, their suffrages exercised by impostors.

Lackluster Presidents: From Hayes to Harrison

The leading statesmen of the period were disinterested in important contemporary questions, powerless to influence them, or content with things the way they were. Consider the presidents.

Rutherford B. Hayes, president from 1877 to 1881, came to office with a distinguished record. He attended Kenyon College and Harvard Law School before settling down to practice in Cincinnati. Although he had a family to support, he volunteered for service in the Union army within weeks after the first shell fell on Fort Sumter. "A just and necessary war," he called it in his diary. "I would prefer to go into it if I knew I was to die . . . than to live through and after it without taking any part."

In 1864 he was elected to Congress; four years later he became governor of Ohio, serving three terms altogether. The Republicans nominated him for president in 1876 because of his reputation for honesty and moderation, and his election, made possible by the Compromise of 1877, seemed to presage an era of sectional harmony and political probity.

Outwardly Hayes had a sunny disposition; inwardly, in his own words, he was sometimes "nervous to the point of disaster." Despite his geniality, he was utterly without political glamour. He played down the tariff issue. On the money question he was conservative. He approved the resumption of gold payments in 1879 and vetoed bills to expand the currency. He accounted himself a civil service reformer, being opposed to the collection of political contributions from federal officeholders.

Hayes complained about the South's failure to treat blacks decently after the withdrawal of federal troops, but he took no action. He worked harder for civil service reform, yet failed to achieve the "thorough, rapid, and complete" change he had promised. In most matters, he was content to "let the record show that he had made the requests."

Hayes's successor, James A. Garfield, fought at Shiloh and later at Chickamauga. In 1863 he won a seat in Congress, where his oratorical and managerial skills brought him to prominence in the affairs of the Republican party.

Garfield had been a compromise choice at the 1880 Republican convention. His election precipitated a great battle over patronage, the new president standing in a sort of no-man's land between contending factions within the party. In July 1881 an unbalanced office-seeker named Charles J. Guiteau shot Garfield in the Washington railroad station. The president died on September 19.

The assassination of Garfield elevated Chester A. Arthur to the presidency. A New York lawyer and abolitionist, Arthur became an early convert to the Republican party and rose rapidly in its local councils. In 1871 Grant gave him the juiciest political plum in the country, the collectorship of the Port of New York, which he held until removed by Hayes in 1878 for refusing to keep his hands out of party politics.

The vice presidency was the only elective position that Arthur had ever held. Before Garfield's death, he had paid little attention to questions like the tariff and

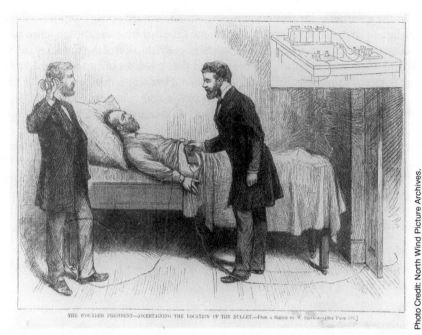

THE WOUNDED PRESIDENT—ASCERTAINING THE LOCATION OF THE BULLET.—From a Sketch by W. Shinkle.—[See Page 376.]

James A. Garfield lies mortally wounded. After failing to locate the bullet, surgeons called in Alexander Graham Bell, the famous inventor. Bell conceived of a device, pictured here, that anticipated the mine detector. Bell's machine failed to locate the bullet, however, perhaps because the metal bed springs interfered with its operation. Garfield died, either from the bullet or the surgeon's unsuccessful attempts to extricate it.

Photo Credit: North Wind Picture Archives.

monetary policy, being content to take in fees ranging upward of $50,000 a year as collector of the port and to oversee the operations of the New York customs office, with its hordes of clerks and laborers. Of course, Arthur was an unblushing defender of the spoils system, though in fairness it must be said that he was personally honest and an excellent administrator.

The tragic circumstances of his elevation to the presidency sobered Arthur. Although he was a genial, convivial man, perhaps overly fond of good food and flashy clothes, he comported himself with dignity as president. He handled patronage matters with restraint, and he gave at least nominal support to the movement for civil service reform, which had been strengthened by the public's indignation at the assas-

> **Read the Document**
> *Pendleton Civil Service Act* at **myhistorylab.com**

sination of Garfield. In 1883 Congress passed the **Pendleton Act**, "classifying" about 10 percent of all government jobs and creating the bipartisan Civil Service Commission to administer competitive examinations for these positions. The law made it illegal to force officeholders to make political contributions and empowered the president to expand the list of classified positions at his discretion.

The election of 1884 brought the Democrat Grover Cleveland to the White House. Cleveland grew up in western New York. After studying law, he settled in Buffalo. Although somewhat lacking in the social graces and in intellectual pretensions, he had a basic integrity that everyone recognized; when a group of reformers sought a candidate for mayor in 1881, he was a natural choice. His success in Buffalo led to his election as governor of New York in 1882.

In the governor's chair his no-nonsense attitude toward public administration end-eared him to civil service reformers at the same time that his basic conservatism pleased businessmen. When he vetoed a popular bill to force a reduction of the fares charged by the New York City elevated railway on the ground that it was an unconstitutional violation of the company's franchise, his reputation soared. Here was a man who cared more for principle than for the adulation of the multitude, a man who was courageous, honest, hardworking, and eminently sound. The Democrats nominated him for president in 1884.

The election revolved around personal issues, for the platforms of the parties were almost identical. On the one hand, the Republican candidate, the dynamic James G. Blaine, had an immense following, but his reputation had been soiled by the publica-tion of the "Mulligan letters," which connected him with the corrupt granting of congressional favors to the Little Rock and Fort Smith Railroad. On the other hand, it came out during the campaign that Cleveland, a bachelor, had fathered an illegitimate child. Instead of debating public issues, the Republicans chanted the ditty,

> *Ma! Ma! Where's my pa?*
> *Gone to the White House,*
> *Ha! Ha! Ha!*

to which the Democrats countered,

> *Blaine, Blaine, James G. Blaine,*
> *The continental liar from the State of Maine.*

Blaine lost more heavily in the mudslinging than Cleveland, whose quiet courage in saying "Tell the truth" when his past was brought to light contrasted favorably with Blaine's glib and unconvincing denials. A significant group of eastern Republicans, known as **mugwumps,** campaigned for the Democrats.[1] However, Blaine ran a strong race against a general pro-Democratic trend; Cleveland won the election by fewer than 25,000 votes. The change of 600 ballots in New York would have given that state, and the presidency, to his opponent.

Cleveland had little imagination and too narrow a conception of his powers and duties to be a dynamic president. He could defend a position against heavy odds, yet he lacked flexibility. He took a fairly broad view of the powers of the federal government, but he thought it unseemly to put pressure on Congress, believing in "the entire independence of the executive and legislative branches."

Toward the end of his term Cleveland bestirred himself and tried to provide constructive leadership on the tariff question. The government was embarrassed by a large revenue surplus, which Cleveland hoped to reduce by cutting the duties on necessities and on raw materials used in manufacturing. He devoted his entire annual message of December 1887 to the tariff, thereby focusing public attention on the subject. When worried Democrats reminded him that an election was coming up and that the tariff might cause a rift in the organization, he replied simply, "What is the use of being elected or re-elected, unless you stand for something?"

In that contest, Cleveland obtained a plurality of the popular vote, but his opponent, Benjamin Harrison, grandson of President William Henry Harrison, carried most of

---

[1]The mugwumps considered themselves reformers, but on social and economic questions nearly all of them were very conservative. They were sound-money proponents and advocates of laissez-faire. Reform to them consisted almost entirely of doing away with corruption and making the government more efficient.

President Grover Cleveland and Frances Folsom in 1888. The couple had married two years earlier; he was 48, and she, 21, the youngest First Lady. Her popularity blunted criticisms that Cleveland, a bachelor, had earlier fathered an illegitimate child. When he lost the 1888 election, his wife predicted that she would return as First Lady. Four years later, she did.

the key northeastern industrial states by narrow margins, thereby obtaining a comfortable majority in the electoral college, 233 to 168.

Although intelligent and able, Harrison was too reserved to make a good politician. During the Civil War he fought under Sherman at Atlanta and won a reputation as a stern, effective disciplinarian. In 1876 he ran unsuccessfully for governor of Indiana, but in 1881 was elected to the Senate.

Harrison believed ardently in protective tariffs. His approach to fiscal policy was conservative, though he was freehanded in the matter of veterans' pensions. Harrison professed to favor civil service reform, but fashioned an unimpressive record on the question. He appointed the vigorous young reformer Theodore Roosevelt to the Civil Service Commission and then proceeded to undercut him systematically. Before long the frustrated Roosevelt was calling the president a "cold blooded, narrow minded, prejudiced, obstinate, timid old psalm singing Indianapolis politician."

Under Harrison, Congress distinguished itself by expending, for the first time in a period of peace, more than $1 billion in a single session. It raised the tariff to an all-time high. The Sherman Antitrust Act was also passed.

Harrison had little to do with the fate of any of these measures. The Republicans lost control of Congress in 1890, and two years later Grover Cleveland swept back into power, defeating Harrison by more than 350,000 votes.

African Americans in the South after Reconstruction

Perhaps the most important issue of the last quarter of the nineteenth century was the fate of the former slaves after the withdrawal of federal troops from the South. Shortly after his inauguration in 1877, President Hayes made a goodwill tour of the South and he urged blacks to trust southern whites. That same year Governor Wade Hampton of South Carolina proposed to "secure to every citizen, the lowest as well

View the Image
Harrison and Morton Campaign Ad
at **myhistorylab.com**

as the highest, black as well as white, full and equal protection in the enjoyment of all his rights under the Constitution."

But the pledge was not kept. By December, Hayes was sadly disillusioned. "By state legislation, by frauds, by intimidation, and by violence of the most atrocious character, colored citizens have been deprived of the right of suffrage," he wrote in his diary. However, he did nothing to remedy the situation. Frederick Douglass called Hayes's policy "sickly conciliation."

Hayes's successors in the 1880s did no better. "Time is the only cure," President Garfield said, thereby confessing that he had no policy at all. President Arthur gave federal patronage to antiblack groups in an effort to split the Democratic South. In 1887 President Cleveland explained to a correspondent why he opposed "mixed [integrated] schools." Expert opinion, the president said, believed "that separate schools were of much more benefit for the colored people." Hayes, Garfield, and Arthur were Republicans, and Cleveland a Democrat; party made little difference. Both parties subscribed to hypocritical statements about equality and constitutional rights, and neither did anything to implement them.

For a time blacks were not totally disenfranchised in the South. Rival white factions tried to manipulate them, and corruption flourished as widely as in the machine-dominated wards of the northern cities. In the 1890s, however, the southern states, led by Mississippi, began to deprive blacks of the vote despite the Fifteenth Amendment. Poll taxes raised a formidable economic barrier, one that also disenfranchised many poor whites. Literacy tests completed the work; a number of states provided a loophole for illiterate whites by including an "understanding" clause whereby an illiterate person could qualify by demonstrating an ability to explain the meaning of a section of the state constitution when an election official read it to him. Blacks who attempted to take the test were uniformly declared to have failed it.

In Louisiana, 130,000 blacks voted in the election of 1896. Then the law was changed. In 1900 only 5,000 votes were cast by blacks. "We take away the Negroes' votes," a Louisiana politician explained, "to protect them just as we would protect a little child and prevent it from injuring itself with sharp-edged tools." Almost every Supreme Court decision after 1877 that affected blacks somehow nullified or curtailed their rights. The **civil rights cases** (1883) declared the Civil Rights Act of 1875 unconstitutional. Blacks who were refused equal accommodations or privileges by hotels, theaters, and other privately owned facilities had no recourse at law, the Court announced. The Fourteenth Amendment guaranteed their civil rights against invasion by the states, not by individuals.

Finally, in *Plessy v. Ferguson* (1896), the Court ruled that even in places of public accommodation, such as railroads and, by implication, schools, segregation was legal as

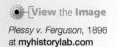

Plessy v. Ferguson, 1896
at **myhistorylab.com**

long as facilities of equal quality were provided: "If one race be inferior to the other socially, the Constitution of the United States cannot put them upon the same plane." In a noble dissent in the Plessy case, Justice John Marshall Harlan protested this line of argument. "Our Constitution is color-blind," he said. "The two races in this country are indissolubly linked together, and the interests of both require that the common government of all shall not permit the seeds of race hatred to be planted under the sanction of law."

Most Northerners supported the government and the Court. Newspapers presented a stereotyped, derogatory picture of blacks, no matter what the circumstances. Northern magazines, even high-quality publications such as *Harper's*, *Scribner's*, and the *Century*, repeatedly made blacks the butt of crude jokes.

A cartoon from *Judge* magazine in 1892 depicts Ku Klux Klansmen barring a black voter from the polls.

The restoration of white rule abruptly halted the progress in public education for blacks that the Reconstruction governments had made. Church groups and private foundations such as the Peabody Fund and the Slater Fund, financed chiefly by northern philanthropists, supported black schools after 1877. Among them were two important experiments in vocational training, Hampton Institute and Tuskegee Institute.

These schools had to overcome considerable resistance and suspicion in the white community; they survived only because they taught a docile philosophy, preparing students to accept second-class citizenship and become farmers and craftsmen. Since proficiency in academic subjects might have given the lie to the southern belief that blacks were intellectually inferior to whites, such subjects were avoided.

Booker T. Washington: A "Reasonable" Champion for African Americans

Since nearly all contemporary biologists, physicians, and other supposed experts on race were convinced that African Americans were inferior, white Americans generally accepted black inferiority as fact. By denying blacks decent educational opportunities and good jobs, the dominant race could use the blacks' resultant ignorance and poverty to justify the inferior facilities offered them.

Southern blacks reacted to this deplorable situation in a variety of ways. Some sought redress in racial pride and what would later be called black nationalism. Some became so disaffected that they tried to revive the African colonization movement. "Africa is our home," insisted Bishop Henry M. Turner, a huge, plainspoken man who had served as an army chaplain during the war and as a member of the Georgia legislature during Reconstruction. Another militant, T. Thomas Fortune, editor of the New York *Age* and founder of the Afro-American League (1887), called on blacks to demand full civil rights, better schools, and fair wages and to fight against discrimination of every sort. "Let us stand up like men in our own organization," he urged. "If others use . . . violence to combat our peaceful arguments, it is not for us to run away from violence."

For a time, militancy and black separatism won few adherents among southern blacks. For one thing, life was better than it had been under slavery. Segregation actually helped southern blacks who became barbers, undertakers, restaurateurs, and shopkeepers because whites were reluctant to supply such services to blacks. According to the most conservative estimates, the living standard of the average southern black more than doubled between 1865 and 1900. But this only made many southern whites more vindictive.

This helps explain the tactics of Booker T. Washington, one of the most extraordinary Americans of that generation. Washington had been born a slave in Virginia in 1856. Laboriously he obtained an education, supporting himself while a student by working as a janitor. In 1881, with the financial help of northern philanthropists, he founded Tuskegee Institute in Alabama. His experiences convinced Washington that blacks must lift themselves up by their own bootstraps but that they must also accommodate themselves to white prejudices. A persuasive speaker and a brilliant fund-raiser, he soon developed a national reputation as a "reasonable" champion of his race.

In 1895 Washington made a now-famous speech to a mixed audience at the Cotton States International Exposition in Atlanta. To the blacks he said, "Cast down your bucket where you are," by which he meant stop fighting segregation and second-class citizenship and concentrate on learning useful skills. Progress up the social and economic ladder would come not from "artificial forcing" but from self-improvement.

Photo Credit: The Granger Collection, New York.

Booker T. Washington in his office at Tuskegee Institute, 1900. Washington chose a policy of accommodation. Washington did not urge blacks to accept inferiority and racial slurs but to ignore them. His own behavior was indeed subtle, even devious. In public he minimized the importance of civil and political rights. Behind the scenes he lobbied against restrictive measures, marshaled large sums of money to fight test cases in the courts, and worked hard in northern states to organize the black vote and make sure that black political leaders got a share of the spoils of office.

Washington asked the whites of what he called "our beloved South" to lend the blacks a hand in their efforts to advance themselves. If you will do so, he promised, you will be "surrounded by the most patient, faithful, law-abiding, and unresentful people that the world has seen."

This **Atlanta Compromise** delighted white Southerners and won Washington financial support in every section of the country. He became one of the most powerful men in the United States, consulted by presidents, in close touch with business and philanthropic leaders, and capable of influencing in countless unobtrusive ways the fate of millions of blacks.

Blacks responded to the compromise with mixed feelings. Accepting Washington's approach might relieve them of many burdens and dangers. But Washington was asking them to give up specific rights in return for vague promises of future help. The cost was high in surrendered personal dignity and lost hopes of obtaining real justice.

Washington's career illustrates the dilemma that American blacks have always faced: the choice between confrontation and accommodation. This choice was particularly difficult in the late nineteenth century.

City Bosses

Outside of the South, the main issue concerned municipal government.

The immigrants who flocked into American cities in the 1880s and early 1890s were largely of peasant stock, and having come from societies unacquainted with democracy, they had no experience with representative government. The tendency of urban workers to move frequently in search of better jobs further lessened the likelihood that they would develop political influence independently.

Furthermore, the difficulties of life in the slums bewildered and often overwhelmed newcomers, both native- and foreign-born. Hopeful, but passive and naive, they could hardly be expected to take a broad view of social problems when so beset by personal ones. This enabled shrewd urban politicians to take command of the city masses and march them in obedient phalanxes to the polls.

Most city machines were loose-knit neighborhood organizations headed by ward bosses, not tightly geared hierarchical bureaucracies ruled by a single leader. "Big Tim" Sullivan of New York's Lower East Side and "Hinky Dink" Kenna of Chicago were typical of the breed. Sullivan, Kenna, and others like them performed many useful services for people they liked to think of as their constituents. They found jobs for new arrivals and distributed food and other help to all in bad times. Anyone in trouble with the law could obtain at least a hearing from the ward boss, and often, if the crime was minor or due to ignorance, the difficulty was quietly "fixed" and the culprit was sent off with a word of caution. Informally, probably without consciously intending to do so, the bosses educated the immigrants in the complexities of American civilization, helping them to leap the gulf between the almost medieval society of their origins and the modern industrial world.

The price of such aid was unquestioning political support, which the bosses converted into cash. In New York, Sullivan levied tribute on gambling, had a hand in the liquor business, and controlled the issuance of peddlers' licenses. When he died in 1913, he was reputedly worth $1 million. Yet he and others like him were immensely popular; 25,000 grieving constituents followed Big Tim's coffin on its way to the grave.

The more visible and better-known city bosses played even less socially justifiable roles than the ward bosses. Their principal technique for extracting money from the public till was the kickback. To get city contracts, suppliers were made to pad their bills and, when paid for their work with funds from the city treasury, turn over the excess to the politicians. Similarly, operators of streetcar lines, gas and electricity companies, and other public utilities were compelled to pay huge bribes to obtain favorable franchises.

The most notorious of the nineteenth-century city bosses was William Marcy Tweed, whose "Tweed Ring" extracted tens of millions of dollars from New York City during the brief period of 1869–1871. He was swiftly jailed!

Despite their welfare work and their popularity, most bosses were essentially thieves. Efforts to romanticize them as the Robin Hoods of industrial society grossly distort the facts. However, the system developed and survived because too many middle-class city dwellers were indifferent to the fate of the poor. Except during occasional reform waves, few tried to check the rapaciousness of the politicos.

Many substantial citizens shared at least indirectly in the corruption. The owners of tenements were interested in crowding as many rent payers as possible into their buildings. Utility companies seeking franchises preferred a system that enabled them to buy favors. Honest citizens who had no selfish stake in the system and who were repelled by the sordidness of city government were seldom sufficiently concerned to do anything about it.

Many so-called urban reformers resented the boss system mainly because it gave political power to people who were not "gentlemen" or, as one reformer put it, to a "proletarian mob" of "illiterate peasants, freshly raked from Irish bogs, or Bohemian mines, or Italian robber nests."

Crops and Complaints

The vacuity of American politics may well have stemmed from the complacency of the middle-class majority. The country was growing; no foreign enemy threatened it; the poor were mostly recent immigrants, blacks, and others with little influence, who were easily ignored by those in comfortable circumstances. However, one important group in society suffered increasingly as the years rolled by: the farmers. Out of their travail came the force that finally, in the 1890s, brought American politics face to face with the problems of the age.

After the Civil War most farmers did well, but in the 1890s disaster struck. First came a succession of dry years and poor harvests. Then farmers in Australia, Canada, Russia, and Argentina took advantage of improvements in transportation to sell their produce in European markets that had relied on American foodstuffs. The price of wheat fell to about sixty cents a bushel. Cotton, the great southern staple, which sold for more than thirty cents a pound in 1866 and fifteen cents in the early 1870s, at times in the 1890s fell below six cents.

The tariff on manufactured goods appeared to aggravate the farmers' predicament, and so did the domestic marketing system, which enabled a multitude of middlemen to gobble up a large share of the profits of agriculture. The shortage of credit, particularly in the South, was an additional burden.

The downward swing of the business cycle in the early 1890s completed the devastation. Settlers who had paid more for their lands than they were worth and borrowed money at high interest rates to do so found themselves squeezed relentlessly. Thousands lost their farms and returned eastward, penniless and dispirited.

The Populist Movement

The agricultural depression triggered a new outburst of farm radicalism, the Alliance movement. Alliances were organizations of farmers' clubs, most of which had sprung up during the bad times of the late 1870s. The first Knights of Reliance group was founded in 1877 in Lampasas County, Texas. As the Farmers' Alliance, this organization gradually expanded in northeastern Texas, and after 1885 it spread rapidly throughout the cotton states. Alliance leaders stressed cooperation. Their co-ops bought fertilizer and other supplies in bulk and sold them at fair prices to members. They sought to market their crops cooperatively but could not raise the necessary capital from banks, with the result that some of them began to question the workings of the American financial and monetary system. They became economic and social radicals in the process.

Although the state alliances of the Dakotas and Kansas joined the Southern Alliance in 1889, for a time local prejudices and conflicting interests prevented the formation of a single national organization. But the farm groups emerged as a potent force in the 1890 elections.

In the South, Alliance-sponsored gubernatorial candidates won in Georgia, Tennessee, South Carolina, and Texas; eight southern legislatures fell under Alliance control, and forty-four representatives and three senators committed to Alliance objectives were sent to Washington. In the West, Alliance candidates swept Kansas, captured a majority in the Nebraska legislature, and accumulated enough seats in Minnesota and South Dakota to hold the balance of power between the major parties.

Such success, coupled with the reluctance of the Republicans and Democrats to make concessions to their demands, encouraged Alliance leaders to create a new national party. By uniting southern and western farmers, they succeeded in breaking the sectional barrier erected by the Civil War. If they could recruit industrial workers, perhaps a real political revolution could be accomplished. In February 1892, farm leaders, representatives of the Knights of Labor, and various professional reformers met at St. Louis. They organized the **People's (Populist) party**, and issued a call for a national convention to meet at Omaha in July.

That convention nominated General James B. Weaver of Iowa for president and drafted a platform that called for a graduated income tax and national ownership of railroads, the telegraph, and telephone systems. It also advocated a "subtreasury" plan that would permit farmers to keep nonperishable crops off the market when prices were low. Under this proposal the government would make loans in the form of greenbacks to farmers, secured by crops held in storage in federal ware-

•◆•⎯Read the Document

The People's Party Platform at **myhistorylab.com**

houses. When prices rose, the farmers could sell their crops and repay the loans. To combat deflation further, the platform demanded the unlimited coinage of silver and an increase in the money supply "to no less than $50 per capita."

To make the government more responsive to public opinion, the Populists urged the adoption of the initiative and referendum procedures and the election of U.S. senators by popular vote. To win the support of industrial workers, their platform denounced the use of Pinkerton detectives in labor disputes and backed the eight-hour day and the restriction of "undesirable" immigration.

The Populists saw themselves not as a persecuted minority but as a victimized majority betrayed by what would a century later be called the establishment. They were at most ambivalent about the free enterprise system, and they tended to attribute social and

In Kansas in 1893 a Populist governor and a Populist-controlled Senate invalidated the election of some Republicans in the Kansas House of Representatives, giving the Populists control of that body, too. The displaced Republicans, denied seats, smashed their way into the capitol building with this sledgehammer and ousted the Populists, who decided to meet in a separate building. Each proclaimed itself to be the true legislature and passed its own laws. Eventually the Kansas Supreme Court decided in favor of the Republican legislature and disbanded the Populist gathering. Source: Kansas State Historical Society.

economic injustices not to built-in inequities in the system but to nefarious conspiracies organized by selfish interests in order to subvert the system.

The appearance of the new party was the most exciting and significant aspect of the presidential campaign of 1892, which saw Harrison and Cleveland refighting the election of 1888. The Populists put forth a host of colorful spellbinders: Tom Watson,

●●●—[Read the Document

Mary Elizabeth Lease, the Populist Crusader at **myhistorylab.com**

a Georgia congressman whose temper was such that on one occasion he administered a beating to a local planter with the man's own riding crop; William A. Peffer, a senator from Kansas whose long beard and grave demeanor gave him the look of a Hebrew prophet; "Sockless Jerry" Simpson of Kansas, unlettered but full of grassroots shrewdness and wit, a former Greenbacker, and an admirer of the single tax doctrine of Henry George; and Ignatius Donnelly, the "Minnesota Sage," who claimed to be an authority on science, economics, and Shakespeare.

In the one-party South, Populist strategists sought to wean black farmers away from the ruling Democratic organization. Southern black farmers had their own Colored Farmers' Alliance, and even before 1892 their leaders had worked closely with the white alliances. Of course, the blacks would be useless to the party if they could not vote; therefore, white Populist leaders opposed the southern trend toward disfranchising African Americans and called for full civil rights for all.

The results proved disappointing. Tom Watson lost his seat in Congress, and Donnelly ran a poor third in the Minnesota gubernatorial race. The Populists did sweep Kansas. They elected numbers of local officials in other western states and cast over a million votes for General Weaver. But the effort to unite white and black farmers in the South failed miserably. Conservative Democrats, while continuing with considerable success to attract black voters, played on racial fears, insisting that the Populists sought to undermine white supremacy. Since most white Populists saw the alliance with blacks as at best a marriage of convenience, this argument had a deadly effect. Elsewhere, even in the old centers of the Granger movement, the party made no significant impression.

Mary Elizabeth Lease was a prominent Populist, noted for her rallying cry to "raise less corn and more hell."
Source: Kansas State Historical Society.

By standing firmly for conservative financial policies, Cleveland attracted considerable Republican support and won a solid victory over Harrison in the electoral college, 277 to 145. Weaver received twenty-two electoral votes.

Showdown on Silver

One conclusion that politicians reached after analyzing the 1892 election was that the money question, particularly the controversy over the coinage of silver, was of paramount interest to the voters. Despite the wide-ranging appeal of the Populist platform, most of Weaver's strength came from the silver-mining states.

In truth, the issue of gold versus silver was superficial; the important question was what, if anything, should be done to check the deflationary spiral. The declining price level benefited people with fixed incomes and injured most others. Industrial workers profited from deflation except when depression caused unemployment.

By the early 1890s, discussion of federal monetary policy revolved around the coinage of silver. Traditionally, the United States had been on a bimetallic standard. Both gold and silver were coined, the number of grains of each in the dollar being adjusted periodically to reflect the commercial value of the two metals. The discovery of numerous gold mines in

California in the 1840s and 1850s depressed the price of gold relative to silver. By 1861, a silver dollar could be melted down and sold for $1.03. No miner took silver to the mint to be stamped into coin. In a short time, silver dollars were withdrawn and only gold dollars circulated. However, an avalanche of silver from the mines of Nevada and Colorado gradually depressed the price until, around 1874, it again became profitable for miners to coin their bullion. Alas, when they tried to do so, they discovered that the Coinage Act of 1873, taking account of the fact that no silver had been presented to the mint in years, had demonetized the metal.

Silver miners denounced this as the "Crime of '73." Inflationists joined them in demanding a return to bimetallism. They knew that if more dollars were put into circulation, the value of each dollar would decline; that is, prices and wages would rise. Conservatives, still fighting the battle against inflationary greenback paper money, resisted strongly. The result was a series of compromises. In 1878 the **Bland-Allison Silver Purchase Act** authorized the buying of between $2 million and $4 million of silver a month at the market price, but this had little inflationary effect because the government consistently purchased the minimum amount. The commercial price of silver continued to fall. In 1890 the **Sherman Silver Purchase Act** required the government to buy 4.5 million *ounces* of silver monthly, but in the face of increasing supplies the price of silver fell still further. By 1894, a silver coin weighed thirty-two times more than a gold one.

Photo Credit: Everett Collection, Inc.

L. Frank Baum, author of *The Wonderful Wizard of Oz* (1900) and a fan of William Jennings Bryan, perhaps wrote his story as an allegory of the 1896 election. Dorothy, wearing "silver" slippers (in the original), follows a "yellow brick road" (gold) on a crusade to free the Munchkins (the oppressed little people) from the Wicked Witch of the East (the rapacious corporations and financiers). Liberation is to come in Emerald City (greenbacks) through the intervention of a kindly, but ultimately ineffective wizard (Bryan). Only the entire people—Dorothy and entourage—can prevail against wickedness. Judy Garland starred as Dorothy in the film version of *The Wizard of Oz* (1939).

The compromises satisfied no one. Silver miners grumbled because their bullion brought in only half what it had in the early 1870s. Debtors noted angrily that because of the general decline in prices, the dollars they used to meet their obligations were worth more than twice as much as in 1865. Advocates of the gold standard feared that unlimited silver coinage would be authorized, "destroying the value of the dollar."

The Depression of 1893

Both the silverites and "gold bugs" warned of economic disaster if their policies were not followed. Then, in 1893, after the London banking house of Baring Brothers collapsed, a financial panic precipitated a worldwide industrial depression. In the United States hundreds of cotton mills and iron foundries closed, never to reopen. During the harsh winter of 1893–1894, millions were without jobs.

President Cleveland believed that the controversy over silver had caused the depression by shaking the confidence of the business community and that all would be well if the country returned to a single gold standard. He summoned a special session of Congress, and by exerting immense political pressure he obtained the repeal of the Sherman Silver Purchase Act in October 1893. All that this accomplished was to split the Democratic party, its southern and western wings deserting him almost to a man.

During 1894 and 1895, while the nation floundered in the worst depression it had ever experienced, a series of events further undermined public confidence. In the spring of 1894 several "armies" of the unemployed, the most imposing led by Jacob S. Coxey, an eccentric Ohio businessman, marched on Washington to demand relief. Coxey wanted the government to undertake a program of federal public works and other projects to hire unemployed workers to build roads.

When Coxey's group of demonstrators, perhaps 500 in all, reached Washington, he and two other leaders were arrested for trespassing on the grounds of the Capitol. Their followers were dispersed by club-wielding policemen. This callous treatment convinced many Americans that the government had little interest in the suffering of the people, an opinion strengthened when Cleveland, in July 1894, used federal troops to crush the Pullman strike.

The next year the Supreme Court handed down several reactionary decisions. In *United States v. E. C. Knight Company* it refused to employ the Sherman Antitrust Act to break up the Sugar Trust. The Court also denied a writ of habeas corpus to Eugene V. Debs of the American Railway Union, who was languishing in prison for disobeying a federal injunction during the Pullman strike.

On top of these indications of official conservatism came a desperate financial crisis. Throughout 1894 the Treasury's supply of gold dwindled as worried citizens exchanged greenbacks (now convertible into gold) for hard money and foreign investors cashed in large amounts of American securities. The government tried to sell bonds for gold to bolster the reserve, but the gold reserve continued to melt away. Early in 1895 it touched a low point of $41 million.

At this juncture a syndicate of bankers headed by J. P. Morgan turned the tide by underwriting a $62 million bond issue, guaranteeing that half the gold would come from Europe. This caused a great public outcry; the spectacle of the nation being saved from bankruptcy by a private banker infuriated millions.

As the presidential election of 1896 approached, the major parties found it impossible to continue straddling the money question. The Populist vote had increased by 42 percent

Table 1   The Supreme Court Supports Racial Segregation and Corporate Power

Civil Rights Cases	1883	Overturned Civil Rights Act of 1875	Limited Fourteenth Amendment to protecting blacks from deprivation of rights by *states*; allowed individuals to do so
Plessy v. Ferguson	1896	Upheld principle of "separate but equal" in public accommodations	Allowed southern states and municipalities to pass laws enforcing separation of whites and blacks
U.S. v. E.C. Knight Co.	1895	Refused to break up the Sugar Trust for being a monopoly	Rendered the Sherman Antitrust Act of 1890 nearly meaningless
In Re Debs	1895	Refused to free Eugene V. Debs, president of the American Railway Union who had been jailed for leading a strike	Enabled the government to use injunctions to stop strikes, thereby depriving union leaders of the chance to plead their case in court

in the 1894 congressional elections. Southern and western Democratic leaders feared that they would lose their following unless Cleveland was repudiated. Western Republicans, led by Senator Henry M. Teller of Colorado, were threatening to bolt to the Populists unless their party came out for silver coinage. After a generation of political equivocation, the major parties had to face an important issue squarely.

The Republicans, meeting to choose a candidate at St. Louis in June 1896, announced for the gold standard. "We are unalterably opposed to every measure calculated to debase our currency or impair the credit of our country," the platform declared. "We are therefore opposed to the free coinage of silver. . . . The existing gold standard must be maintained." The party then nominated Ohio's William McKinley for president. McKinley, best known for his staunch advocacy of the protective tariff yet highly regarded by labor, was expected to run strongly in the Midwest and the East.

The Democratic convention met in July in Chicago. The pro-gold Cleveland element made a hard fight, but the silverites swept them aside. The high point came when a youthful Nebraskan named William Jennings Bryan spoke for silver against gold, for western farmers against the industrial East.

"Burn down your cities and leave our farms," he said, "and your cities will spring up again as if by magic; but destroy our farms and the grass will grow in the streets of every city in the country." He ended with a marvelous figure of speech that set the tone for the coming campaign. "You shall not press down upon the brow of labor this crown of thorns," he warned, bringing his hands down suggestively to his temples. "You shall not crucify mankind upon a cross of gold!" Dramatically, he extended his arms to the side, the very figure of the crucified Christ.

The convention promptly adopted a platform calling for "the free and unlimited coinage of both silver and gold at the present legal ratio of 16 to 1" and went on to nominate Bryan, who was barely thirty-six, for president.

This action put tremendous pressure on the Populists. If they supported the Democrat Bryan, they risked losing their party identity; if they nominated another candidate, they would ensure McKinley's election. In part because the delegates could not find a person of stature willing to become a candidate against Bryan, the Populist convention nominated him, seeking to preserve the party identity by substituting Watson for the Democratic vice-presidential nominee, Arthur Sewall of Maine.

The Election of 1896

Never did a presidential campaign raise such intense emotions. The Republicans from the silver-mining states swung solidly behind Bryan. But many solid-money Democrats, especially in the Northeast, refused to accept the decision of the Chicago convention. Many others adopted the policy of Governor David B. Hill of New York, who said, "I am a Democrat still—very still." The extreme gold bugs, calling themselves National Democrats, nominated their own candidate, seventy-nine-year-old Senator John M. Palmer of Illinois. Palmer ran only to injure Bryan. "Fellow Democrats," he announced, "I will not consider it any great fault if you decide to cast your vote for William McKinley."

At the start the Republicans seemed to have everything in their favor. Bryan's youth and relative lack of political experience—two terms in the House—contrasted unfavorably with McKinley's distinguished war record, his long service in Congress and as governor of Ohio, and his reputation for honesty and good judgment. The severe depression operated in favor of the party out of power, although by repudiating Cleveland the Democrats escaped much of the burden of explaining away his errors. The newspapers came out almost unanimously for the Republicans. The Democrats had very little money and few well-known speakers to fight the campaign.

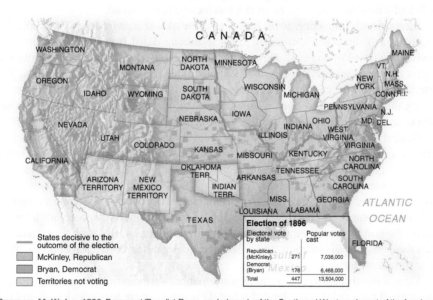

Bryan vs. McKinley, 1896 Democrat/Populist Bryan carried much of the South and West, and most of the farming regions of the plains. But he failed to win over enough industrial workers to take states in the North.

But Bryan proved a formidable opponent. Casting aside tradition, he took to the stump personally, traveling 18,000 miles and making over 600 speeches. He was one of the greatest of orators, projecting an image of absolute sincerity without appearing fanatical or argumentative. At every major stop on his tour, huge crowds assembled.

Read the Document

William Jennings Bryan, *Cross of Gold* Speech at **myhistorylab.com**

His energy was amazing, and his charm and good humor were unfailing. Everywhere he hammered away at the money question. Yet he did not totally neglect other issues. He was defending, he said, "all the people who suffer from the operations of trusts, syndicates, and combines."

View the Image

McKinley and Hobart Campaign Poster at **myhistorylab.com**

McKinley's campaign was managed by a new type of politician, Marcus "Mark" Alonzo Hanna, an Ohio businessman. In a sense Hanna was a product of the Pendleton Civil Service Act. When deprived of the contributions of officeholders, the parties turned to business for funds, and Hanna was one of the first leaders with a foot in both camps. Politics fascinated him, and despite his wealth and wide interests, he was willing to labor endlessly at the routine work of political organization.

Before most Republicans realized how effective Bryan was on the stump, Hanna perceived the danger and sprang into action.

Certain that money was the key to political power, he raised an enormous campaign fund. When businessmen hesitated to contribute, he pried open their purses by a combination of persuasiveness and intimidation. Banks and insurance companies were "assessed" a percentage of their assets, big corporations a share of their receipts, until some $3.5 million had been collected.

Hanna disbursed these funds with efficiency and imagination. He sent 1,500 speakers into the doubtful districts and blanketed the land with 250 million pieces of campaign literature, printed in a dozen languages. "He has advertised McKinley as if he were a patent medicine," Theodore Roosevelt, never at a loss for words, exclaimed.

Incapable of competing with Bryan as a swayer of mass audiences, McKinley conducted a "front-porch campaign." This technique dated from the first Harrison-Cleveland election, when Harrison regularly delivered off-the-cuff speeches to groups of visitors representing special interests or regions in his hometown of Indianapolis. The system conserved the candidate's energies and enabled him to avoid the appearance of seeking the presidency too openly—which was still considered bad form—and at the same time allowed him to make headlines throughout the country.

Guided by the masterful Hanna, McKinley brought the front-porch method to perfection. Superficially the proceedings were delightfully informal. From every corner of the land, groups representing various regions, occupations, and interests descended on McKinley's unpretentious frame house in Canton, Ohio. Gathering on the lawn—the grass was soon reduced to mud, the fence stripped of pickets by souvenir hunters—the visitors paid their compliments to the candidate and heard him deliver a brief speech, while beside him on the porch his aged mother and adoring invalid wife listened with rapt attention. Then there was a small reception, during which the delegates were given an opportunity to shake their host's hand.

Despite the air of informality, these performances were carefully staged. The delegations arrived on a tightly coordinated schedule worked out by McKinley's staff and the railroads, which operated cut-rate excursion trains to Canton from all over the nation.

William Jennings Bryan's "Cross of Gold" speech inspired this cartoonist's caricature of it as "plagiarized from the Bible." Bryan's speech in favor of bimetallism was, in fact, studded with religious references. He described the unlimited coinage of silver and gold as a "holy cause" supported by those who built churches "where they praise their Creator."

THE SACRILEGIOUS CANDIDATE.

Photo Credit: Culver Pictures, Inc.

McKinley was fully briefed on the special interests and attitudes of each group, and the speeches of delegation leaders were submitted in advance. Often his secretary amended these remarks, and on occasion McKinley wrote the visitors' speeches himself. His own talks were carefully prepared, each calculated to make a particular point. All were reported fully in the newspapers. Thus without moving from his doorstep, McKinley met thousands of people from every section of the country.

These tactics worked admirably. On election day McKinley collected 271 electoral votes to Bryan's 176, the popular vote being 7,036,000 to 6,468,000.

The Meaning of the Election

During the campaign, some frightened Republicans had laid plans for fleeing the country if Bryan were elected, and belligerent ones, such as Theodore Roosevelt, then police commissioner of New York City, readied themselves to meet the "social revolutionaries" on the battlefield. Victory sent such people into transports of joy. Most conservatives concluded that the way of life they so fervently admired had been saved for all time.

However heartfelt, such sentiments were not founded on fact. With workers standing beside capitalists and with the farm vote split, it cannot be said that the election divided the nation class against class or that McKinley's victory saved the country from revolution.

Far from representing a triumph for the status quo, the election marked the coming of age of modern America. The battle between gold and silver, which everyone had considered so vital, had little real significance. The inflationists seemed to have been beaten, but new discoveries of gold in Alaska and South Africa and improved methods of extracting gold from low-grade ores soon led to a great expansion of the money supply. In any case, within two decades the system of basing the volume of currency on bullion had been abandoned. Bryan and the "political" Populists who supported him, supposedly the advance agents of revolution, were oriented more toward the past than the future; their ideal was the rural America of Jefferson and Jackson.

McKinley, for all his innate conservatism, was capable of looking ahead toward the new century. His approach was national where Bryan's was basically parochial. Though never daring and seldom imaginative, McKinley was able to deal pragmatically with current problems. Before long, as the United States became increasingly an exporter of manufactures, he would even modify his position on the tariff. And no one better reflected the spirit of the age than Mark Hanna, the outstanding political realist of his generation. Far from preventing change, the outcome of the election of 1896 made possible still greater changes as the United States moved into the twentieth century.

Milestones

1872	Ulysses Grant is reelected president	1890	Sherman Silver Purchase Act requires government silver purchase
1873	Congress suspends the coining of silver ("Crime of '73")	1890–1900	Blacks are deprived of the vote in the South
1876	Rutherford B. Hayes is elected president	1892	People's (Populist) party is founded
1877	Farmers' Alliance movement is founded		Cleveland is elected president a second time
1878	Bland-Allison Act authorizes government silver purchases	1893	Sherman Silver Purchase Act is repealed
1879	Specie payments resume	1893	Panic of 1893 causes industrial depression
1880	James Garfield is elected president		
1881	Garfield is assassinated; Grover Cleveland becomes president	1894	Coxey's Army marches to Washington to demand relief
1881	Booker T. Washington founds Tuskegee Institute for blacks	1895	Supreme Court declares federal income tax unconstitutional (*Pollock v. Farmers' Loan and Trust Company*)
1883	Pendleton Act creates Civil Service Commission		
	Supreme Court Overturns Civil Rights Act of 1875 in the civil rights cases		Booker T. Washington urges self-improvement in Atlanta Compromise Speech
1884	Republicans support Democrats during Mugwump Movement		J. P. Morgan raises $62 million in gold for the U.S. Treasury
	Grover Cleveland is elected president		
1887	Interstate Commerce Act regulates railroad rates	1896	William Jennings Bryan delivers "Cross of Gold" speech
	Cleveland delivers tariff message		William McKinley is elected president
1888	Benjamin Harrison is elected president		
	Englishman James Bryce analyzes American politics in *The American Commonwealth*		Supreme Court upholds "separate but equal" in *Plessy v. Ferguson*

✓●─[Study and Review at **www.myhistorylab.com**

Review Questions

1. The introduction to this text suggests that Americans from 1877 to 1896 were as enthralled with politics as Americans are today with *American Idol*. And yet the chapter contends that the major parties took similar positions on the major issues. What explains the high voter turnouts of the era?

2. How did the urban bosses respond to the challenges confronting the cities?

3. How did the decisions of the Supreme Court aggravate race relations and give rise to political protest? What strategies did African American leaders consider in response to increased segregation?

4. Why did such a seemingly dull issue as currency reform generate such passion, culminating in William Jennings Bryan's crusade against "a cross of gold" in 1896? Why did the Populists fail to win the support of northern labor, and thus the election?

5. How has populism fared among historians? How is populism regarded by politicians today? Why?

Key Terms

Atlanta Compromise
Bland-Allison Silver
    Purchase Act
civil rights cases

mugwumps
Pendleton Act
People's (Populist)
    party

Plessy v. Ferguson
Sherman Silver
    Purchase Act

The Age of Reform

From Chapter 21 of *American Destiny: Narrative of a Nation*, Combined Volume, Fourth Edition.
Mark C. Carnes and John A. Garraty. Copyright © 2012 by Pearson Education, Inc. Published by
Pearson Prentice Hall. All rights reserved.

The Age of Reform

Are college students apathetic?

SOME THINK SO. IN 2007 *NEW YORK TIMES* COLUMNIST THOMAS Friedman proposed that they be known as Generation Q—for Quiet. That generation, he reported, was "too quiet, too online, for its own good, and for the country's own good."

In 2010 Gabrielle Grow, a senior at the University of California at Davis, offered an explanation in the *Huffington Post*: "From those who deem us apathetic, we have not only inherited a country up to its neck in debt but a society and lifestyle in which we are constantly expected to outperform each other... [An] intense course load combined with little free time leaves little room for political inquiry or investigation."

Other students challenged Friedman's stereotype through civic engagement of the old-fashioned sort, by rolling up their sleeves and helping out. In a 2009 UCLA survey, two-thirds of college seniors reported that they "occasionally" or "frequently" performed volunteer work. Over three-fourths said that they voted in the 2008 presidential election. In 2009 AmeriCorps, a federally sponsored public-service plan, received twice as many applications from college graduates as the previous year. That same year, more than 168,000 college students worked for Habitat for Humanity, far more than a decade earlier.

Today's college-age volunteers in many ways resemble their counterparts during the "age of reform" a century ago. Then, large numbers of young adults worked to improve society in various ways. They investigated tenements, factories, schools, municipal governments, and consumer goods. They promoted legislation to protect children from exploitative employers and to secure voting rights for women. They advocated conservation of natural resources. They swelled the ranks of the Socialist party, the Progressive party, and of more radical movements. In response to this sea change among younger voters, the Republican and Democratic parties embraced reforms that earlier generations had regarded as wild-eyed radicalism.

Roots of Progressivism

The progressives were never a single group seeking a single objective. The movement sprang from many sources. One was the fight against corruption and inefficiency in government, which began with the Liberal Republicans of the Grant era and was

Photo Credit: Culver Pictures, Inc.

Orchard Street, a tenement in lower Manhattan in New York City. The unpaved street, ankle-deep in mud, is lined with garbage. But while reformers deplored life in such slums, many who lived there enjoyed the sociability of the congested streets.

continued by the mugwumps of the 1880s. The struggle for civil service reform was only the first skirmish in this battle; the continuing power of corrupt political machines and the growing influence of large corporations and their lobbyists on municipal and state governments outraged thousands of citizens and led them to seek ways to make the machinery of government at all levels responsive to the majority rather than to special-interest groups.

Progressivism also had roots in the effort to regulate and control big business, which characterized the Granger and Populist agitation of the 1870s and 1890s. The failure of the Interstate Commerce Act to end railroad abuses and of the Sherman Antitrust Act to check the growth of large corporations became increasingly apparent after 1900. The return of prosperity after the depression of the 1890s encouraged reformers by removing the fear, so influential in the 1896 presidential campaign, that an assault on the industrial giants might lead to the collapse of the economy.

Between 1897 and 1904 the trend toward concentration in industry accelerated. Such new giants as Amalgamated Copper (1899), U.S. Steel (1901), and International Harvester (1902) attracted most of the attention, but even more alarming were the overall statistics. In a single year (1899) more than 1,200 firms were absorbed in mergers, the resulting combinations being capitalized at $2.2 billion. By 1904 there were 318 industrial combinations in the country with an aggregate capital of $7.5 billion. People who considered bigness inherently evil demanded that the huge new "trusts" be broken up or at least strictly controlled.

America was becoming more urban, more industrial, more mechanized, more centralized—in short, more complex. This trend put a premium on efficiency and cooperation. It seemed obvious to the progressives that people must become more socially minded, and the economy more carefully organized.

By attracting additional thousands of sympathizers to the general cause of reform, the return of prosperity after 1896 fueled the progressive movement. Good times made people more tolerant and generous. As long as profits were on the rise, the average employer did not object if labor improved its position too. Middle-class Americans who had been prepared to go to the barricades in the event of a Bryan victory in 1896 became conscience-stricken when they compared their own comfortable circumstances with those of the "huddled masses" of immigrants and native-born poor.

Giant industrial and commercial corporations undermined not so much the economic well-being as the ambitions and sense of importance of the middle class. The growth of large labor organizations worried such types. In general, character and moral values seemed less influential; organizations—cold, impersonal, heartless—were coming to control business, politics, and too many other aspects of life.

The middle classes could support reform measures without feeling that they were being very radical because they were resisting change and because the intellectual currents of the time harmonized with their ideas of social improvement and the welfare state. The new doctrines of the social scientists, the Social Gospel religious leaders, and the philosophers of pragmatism provided a salubrious climate for progressivism. Many of the thinkers who had formulated these doctrines in the 1880s and 1890s turned to the task of putting them into practice in the new century. Their number included the economist Richard T. Ely, the philosopher John Dewey, and the Baptist clergyman Walter Rauschenbusch, a civic reformer who wrote many books extolling the Social Gospel.

The Muckrakers

As the diffuse progressive army gradually formed its battalions, a new journalistic fad brought the movement into focus. For many years magazines had been publishing articles discussing current political, social, and economic problems. In the fall of 1902, *McClure's* began two particularly hard-hitting series of articles, one on Standard Oil by Ida Tarbell, the other on big-city political machines by Lincoln Steffens. When the editor, S. S. McClure, decided to include in the January 1903 issue an attack on labor gangsterism in the coal fields along with installments of the Tarbell and Steffens series, he called attention to the circumstance in a striking editorial.

Something was radically wrong with the "American character," McClure wrote. These articles showed that large numbers of American employers, workers, and politicians were fundamentally immoral. Lawyers were becoming tools of big business, judges were permitting evildoers to escape justice, the churches were materialistic, and educators seemed incapable of understanding what was happening.

McClure's editorial caused a sensation. The issue sold out quickly. Thousands of readers found their own vague apprehensions brought into focus. Some became active in progressive movements; still more lent passive support.

Other editors jumped to adopt the McClure formula. A small army of professional writers soon flooded the periodical press with denunciations of the insurance business, the drug business, college athletics, prostitution, sweatshop labor, political corruption, and dozens of other subjects. This type of article inspired Theodore Roosevelt, with his gift for vivid language, to compare the journalists to "the Man with the Muck-Rake" in John Bunyan's *Pilgrim's Progress*, whose attention was so fixed on the filth at his feet that he could not notice the "celestial crown" that was offered him in exchange. Roosevelt's characterization grossly misrepresented the literature of exposure, but the label *muckraking* was thereafter affixed to the type. Despite its literal connotations, **muckraker** became a term of honor.

The Progressive Mind

Unlike many earlier reformers, progressives believed that the source of society's evils lay in the structure of its institutions, not in the weaknesses or sinfulness of individuals. Therefore local, state, and national government must be made more responsive to the will of citizens who stood for the traditional virtues. In the South, many people who considered themselves progressives even argued that poll taxes and other measures designed to deny blacks the vote were reforms because they discouraged a class of people they considered unthinking and shiftless from voting.

When government had been thus reformed, then it must act; whatever its virtues, laissez-faire was obsolete. Businessmen, especially big businessmen, must be compelled to behave fairly, their acquisitive drives curbed in the interests of justice and equal opportunity for all. The weaker elements in society—women, children, the poor, the infirm—must be protected against unscrupulous power.

Despite its fervor and democratic rhetoric, progressivism was paternalistic, moderate, and often softheaded. Typical reformers of the period oversimplified complicated issues and treated their personal values as absolute standards of truth and morality. Thus progressives often acted at cross-purposes; at times some were even at war with themselves. This accounts for the diffuseness of the movement.

The progressives never challenged the fundamental principles of capitalism, nor did they attempt a basic reorganization of society. They would have little to do with the socialist brand of reform. Many progressives were anti-immigrant, and only a handful had anything to offer blacks, surely the most exploited group in American society.

A good example of the relatively limited radicalism of most progressives is offered by the experiences of progressive artists. Early in the century a number of painters, including Robert Henri, John Sloan, and George Luks, tried to develop a distinctively American style. They turned to city streets and the people of the slums for their models, and they depended more on inspiration and inner conviction than on careful craftsmanship to achieve their effects.

These artists of the **Ashcan School** were individualists, yet they supported political and social reform and were caught up in the progressive movement. Sloan was a socialist; Henri claimed to be an anarchist. Most saw themselves as rebels. But artistically the Ashcan painters were not very advanced. Their idols were long-dead European masters such as Hogarth, Goya, and Daumier. They were uninfluenced by the outburst of post-impressionist activity then taking place in Europe. To their dismay, when they included canvases by Matisse, Picasso, and other European artists in a show of their own works at the Sixty-Ninth Regiment Armory in New York City in 1913, the "advanced" Europeans got all the attention.

THE VERDICT

Photo Credit: Courtesy of the Library of Congress.

In 1900, Ashcan artist George Luks portrayed corporate monopolies and franchises as a monster preying on New York City.

"Radical" Progressives: The Wave of the Future

The hard times of the 1890s and the callous reactions of conservatives to the victims of that depression pushed many toward Marxian socialism. In 1900 the labor leader Eugene V. Debs ran for president on the Socialist ticket. He polled fewer than 100,000 votes. When he ran again in 1904 he got more than 400,000, and in later elections still more. Labor leaders hoping to organize unskilled workers in heavy industry were increasingly frustrated by the craft orientation of the American Federation of Labor, and some saw in socialism a way to win rank-and-file backing.

In 1905 Debs, William "Big Bill" Haywood of the Western Federation of Miners, Mary Harris "Mother" Jones (a former organizer for the United Mine Workers), Daniel De Leon of the Socialist Labor party, and a few others organized a new union: the **Industrial Workers of the World (IWW)**. The IWW was openly anticapitalist. The preamble to its constitution began: "The working class and the employing class have nothing in common."

But the IWW never attracted many ordinary workers. Haywood, its most prominent leader, was usually a general in search of an army. His forte was attracting attention to spontaneous strikes by unorganized workers, not the patient recruiting of workers and the pursuit of practical goals. In 1912 he was closely involved in a bitter and, at times, bloody strike of textile workers in Lawrence, Massachusetts, which was settled with some benefit to the strikers; he was also involved in a failed strike the following winter and spring by silk workers in Paterson, New Jersey.

Other "advanced" European ideas affected the thinking and behavior of some important progressive intellectuals. Sigmund Freud's psychoanalytical theories attracted numbers of Americans. Many picked up enough of the vocabulary of psychoanalysis to discourse impressively about the significance of slips of the tongue, sublimation, and infant sexuality.

Some saw in Freud's ideas reason to effect a "revolution of manners and morals" that would have shocked (or at least embarrassed) Freud, who was personally quite conventional. They advocated easy divorce, trial marriage, and doing away with the double standard in all matters relating to sex. They rejected Victorian reticence and what they incorrectly identified as "puritan" morality out of hand, and they called for programs of sex education, especially the dissemination of information about methods of birth control.

Most large cities boasted groups of these "bohemian" thinkers, by far the most famous being the one centered in New York City's Greenwich Village. The dancer Isadora Duncan, the photographer Alfred Stieglitz, the novelist Floyd Dell, several of the Ashcan artists, and the playwright Eugene O'Neill rubbed shoulders with Big Bill Haywood of the IWW, the anarchist Emma Goldman, the psychoanalyst A. A. Brill, the militant feminist advocate of birth control Margaret Sanger, Max Eastman, and John Reed, a young Harvard graduate who was soon to become famous for his eyewitness account of the Russian Revolution in *Ten Days That Shook the World*.

Goldman, Haywood, Sanger, and a few others in this group were genuine radicals who sought basic changes in bourgeois society, but most of the Greenwich Village intellectuals were as much concerned with aesthetic as social issues. Nearly all of them came from middle-class backgrounds. They found the far-different world of the Italian and Jewish immigrants of the Village and its surrounding neighborhoods charming. But they did not become involved in the immigrants' lives the way the settlement house workers did. Their influence on their own times, therefore, was limited. They are historically important, however, because many of them were genuinely creative people and because many of the ideas and practices they advocated were adopted by later generations.

The creative writers of the era, applying the spirit of progressivism to the realism they had inherited from Howells and the naturalists, tended to adopt an optimistic tone. The poet Ezra Pound, for example, at this time talked grandly of an American renaissance and fashioned a new kind of poetry called imagism, which, while not appearing to be realistic, rejected all abstract generalizations and concentrated on concrete word pictures to convey meaning. "Little" magazines and experimental theatrical companies sprang to life by the dozen, each convinced that it would revolutionize its art. The poet Carl Sandburg, the best-known representative of the Chicago school, denounced the local plutocrats but sang the praises of the city they had made: "Hog Butcher for the World," "City of the Big Shoulders."

Most writers eagerly adopted Freudian psychology without understanding it. Freud's teachings seemed only to mean that they should cast off the restrictions of Victorian prudery; they ignored his essentially dark view of human nature. Theirs was an "innocent rebellion," exuberant and rather muddleheaded.

Rural Socialism Socialist strength extended far beyond the cities. Socialists in rural areas called for tenants to be allowed to work on state-owned plots of land. In 1912, Socialist candidates received nearly half the vote in southern Oklahoma.

EMMA GOLDMAN

In January 1886 a sixteen-year-old Jewish girl named Emma Goldman arrived in New York City from St. Petersburg, Russia, where her parents ran a grocery store. As soon as immigration officials had approved her entry into the United States, she hurried on to Rochester, New York, where her half-sister lived. Like most immigrants she expected the United States to be a kind of paradise on earth.

After moving in with her half-sister's family, Emma got a job in a factory sewing coats and earning $2.50 a week. She paid her sister $1.50 a week for room and board and spent sixty cents a week to get to her job. But when she asked her employer for more money he told her to "look for work elsewhere." She found a job at another factory that paid $4 a week.

In 1887 she married Jacob Kirshner, another Russian immigrant, but they soon divorced. In 1889 she took up with a group of radicals, most of them either socialists or anarchists. By this time Goldman was herself an ardent anarchist, convinced by her experiences that *all* governments repressed individual freedom and should be abolished.

In New York Emma fell in love with another Russian-born radical, Alexander Berkman. They started a kind of commune. Emma worked at home sewing shirts. Alexander found a job making cigars. They never married.

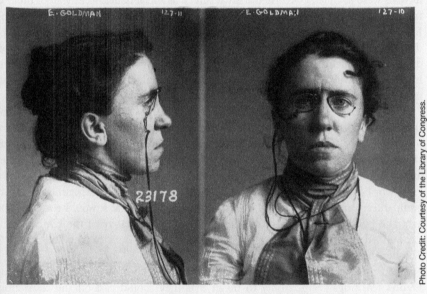

Photo Credit: Courtesy of the Library of Congress.

A "mug shot" of Emma Goldman, 1901. She was arrested so often that she took to carrying a book with her everywhere so that she would have something to read in jail if she were arrested.

The couple moved to New Haven, where Emma started a cooperative dressmaking shop. Then they moved to Springfield, Massachusetts, where, with Berkman's cousin, an artist, they opened a photography studio. When this business failed, they opened an ice cream parlor.

Nearly all immigrants of that period retained their faith in the promise of American life even after they discovered that the streets were not paved with gold. But Emma was so disappointed that she became a radical.

In 1892 when she and Berkman learned of the bloody battle between Pinkertons and strikers during the Homestead steel strike, they closed the ice cream parlor and plotted to assassinate Henry Clay Frick, the archvillain of the Homestead drama. Berkman went to Pittsburgh, where, posing as a representative of an agency that provided strikebreakers, he got into Frick's office. Pulling a pistol, Berkman aimed for Frick's head but the shot went wide and hit Frick in the shoulder. Berkman then stabbed Frick, but still the Homestead boss survived. Convicted of the attempt on Frick's life, Berkman was imprisoned for fourteen years.

The next year Goldman was herself arrested and sentenced to a year in jail for making an "incendiary" speech urging unemployed workers to distrust politicians. Upon her release, Goldman went to Vienna, where she trained as a nurse. When she returned to America, she worked as a midwife among the New York poor, an experience that made her an outspoken advocate of birth control. She also helped organize a theatrical group, managed a touring group of Russian actors, and lectured on theatrical topics. In 1901, Goldman was arrested on charges of inspiring Leon Czolgosz to assassinate President McKinley. Czolgosz had attended one of Goldman's lectures, but there was no direct connection between the two, and the charges against her were dropped.

In 1906 Goldman founded *Mother Earth*, an anarchist journal. When Alexander Berkman was released from prison later that year, she made him its editor. *Mother Earth* denounced governments, organized religion, and private property. By this time Goldman had become a celebrity. "She was considered a monster, an exponent of free love and bombs," recalled Margaret Anderson, editor of a literary magazine.

Now Goldman campaigned for freedom of speech and lectured in support of birth control. In 1915, after Margaret Sanger was arrested for disseminating information on birth control, Goldman did the same in public speeches. She was arrested and spent two weeks in jail.

Goldman regarded the Great War—and especially American entry in it—as a calamity beyond measure. In 1917 Goldman and Berkman were convicted of conspiring to persuade men not to register for the draft. They served two years in federal prison. In 1919 they were deported to Russia. Two years later, disillusioned with the Bolsheviks, Goldman left the Soviet Union.

"Red Emma" Goldman was not a typical American, but she was in many ways a typical American immigrant. She learned English and quickly became familiar with American ways. She worked hard and developed valuable skills. Gradually she moved up the economic ladder. And while she was critical of the United States, she was a typical immigrant also in insisting that she was an American patriot. "The kind of patriotism we represent," she said during her trial in 1917, "is the kind of patriotism which loves America with open eyes."

Questions for Discussion

■ Why did most immigrants, on learning of the gap between the promise of America and its reality, not become radicals?

■ Was Goldman a radical by birth or by acculturation?

Political Reform: Cities First

To most "ordinary" progressives, political corruption and inefficiency lay at the root of the evils plaguing American society, nowhere more obvious than in the nation's cities. Urban life's anonymity and complexity help explain why slavery did not flourish in cities, but also why the previously named vices did flourish. As the cities grew, their antiquated and boss-ridden administrations became more and more disgraceful.

City reformers could seldom destroy the machines without changing urban political institutions. Some cities obtained "home rule" charters that gave them greater freedom from state control in dealing with local matters. Many created research bureaus that investigated government problems in a scientific and nonpartisan manner. A number of middle-sized communities (Galveston, Texas, was the prototype) experimented with a system that integrated executive and legislative powers in the hands of a small elected commission, thereby concentrating responsibility and making it easier to coordinate complex activities. Out of this experiment came the city manager system, under which the commissioners appointed a professional manager to administer city affairs on a non-partisan basis. Dayton, Ohio, which adopted the plan after a flood devastated the town in 1913, offers the best illustration of the city manager system in the Progressive Era.

Once the political system had been made responsive to the desires of the people, the progressives hoped to use it to improve society itself. Many cities experimented with "gas and water socialism," taking over public utility companies and operating them as departments of the municipal government. Under "Golden Rule" Jones, Toledo established a minimum wage for city employees, built playgrounds and golf courses, and moderated its harsh penal code. Mayor Seth Low improved New York's public transportation system and obtained passage of the tenement house law of 1901. Mayor Tom Johnson forced a fare cut to three cents on the Cleveland street railways.

Political Reform: The States

To carry out this kind of change required the support of state legislatures since all munic-ipal government depends on the authority of a sovereign state. Such approval was often difficult to obtain—local bosses were usually entrenched in powerful state machines, and rural majorities insensitive to urban needs controlled most legislatures. Therefore the progressives had to strike at inefficiency and corruption at the state level too.

During the first decade of the new century, Robert M. La Follette, one of the most remarkable figures of the age, transformed Wisconsin. He had served three terms as a Republican congressman (1885–1891) and developed a reputation as an uncompromis-ing foe of corruption before being elected governor in 1900. That the people would always do the right thing if properly informed and inspired was the fundamental article of his political faith. "Machine control is based upon misrepresentation and ignorance," La Follette said. "Democracy is based upon knowledge."

Despite the opposition of railroad and lumbering interests, Governor La Follette obtained a direct primary system for nominating candidates, a corrupt practices act, and laws limiting campaign expenditures and lobbying activities. In power he became something of a boss himself. He made ruthless use of patronage, demanded absolute loyalty of his subordinates, and often stretched, or at least oversimplified, the truth when presenting complex issues to the voters.

La Follette was a consummate showman who never rose entirely above rural prejudices. He was prone to see a nefarious "conspiracy" organized by "the interests" behind even the mildest opposition to his proposals. But he was devoted to the cause of honest government. Realizing that some state functions called for specialized technical knowledge, he used commissions and agencies to handle such matters as railroad regulation, tax assessment, conservation, and highway construction. Wisconsin established a legislative reference library to assist lawmakers in drafting bills. For work of this kind, La Follette called on the faculty of the University of Wisconsin, enticing top-notch economists and political scientists into the public service and drawing freely on the advice of such outstanding social scientists as Richard T. Ely, John R. Commons, and E. A. Ross.

The success of these policies, which became known as the Wisconsin Idea, led other states to adopt similar programs. Reform administrations swept into office in Iowa and Arkansas (1901); Oregon (1902); Minnesota, Kansas, and Mississippi (1904); New York and Georgia (1906); Nebraska (1909); and New Jersey and Colorado (1910). In some cases the reformers were Republicans, in others Democrats, but in all the example of Wisconsin was influential. By 1910, fifteen states had established legislative reference services, most of them staffed by personnel trained in Wisconsin. The direct primary system, in which candidates were selected by voters rather than party bosses, became almost universal.

Some states went beyond Wisconsin in striving to make their governments responsive to the popular will. In 1902 Oregon began to experiment with the initiative, a system by which a bill could be forced on the attention of the legislature by popular petition, and the referendum, a method for allowing the electorate to approve measures rejected by their representatives and to repeal measures that the legislature had passed. Eleven states, most of them in the West, legalized these devices by 1914.

State Social Legislation

The first state laws aimed at social problems long preceded the Progressive Era, but most were either so imprecise as to be unenforceable or, like the Georgia law "limiting" textile workers to eleven hours a day, so weak as to be ineffective. In 1874 Massachusetts restricted the working hours of women and children to ten per day, and by the 1890s many other states, mostly in the East and Midwest, had followed suit. Illinois passed an eight-hour law for women workers in 1893.

As part of this trend, some states established special rules for workers in hazardous industries. In the 1890s several states limited the hours of railroad workers on the grounds that fatigue sometimes caused railroad accidents. Utah restricted miners to eight hours in 1896. In 1901 New York finally enacted an effective tenement house law, greatly increasing the area of open space on building lots and requiring toilets for each apartment, better ventilation systems, and more adequate fireproofing.

Before 1900 the collective impact of such legislation was not impressive. Powerful manufacturers and landlords often succeeded in defeating the bills or rendering them innocuous. The federal system further complicated the task of obtaining effective legislation.

The Fourteenth Amendment to the Constitution, although enacted to protect the civil rights of blacks, imposed a revolutionary restriction on the states by forbidding them to "deprive any person of life, liberty, or property without due process of law." Since much state social legislation represented new uses of coercive power that conservative judges considered dangerous and unwise, the Fourteenth Amendment gave such judges

On March 25, 1911, as scores of young factory girls leaped to their deaths from the eighth, ninth, and tenth stories of the Triangle Shirtwaist Factory in New York City, eighteen-year-old Victor Gatto watched in horror. Thirty-three years later he painted this rendering of his nightmare, the bodies of the dead girls placed in order at the base of the building.
Source: Victor Joseph Gatto (1893–1965), *Triangle Fire: March 25, 1911.* c. 1944 (depicting 1911), oil on canvas, 19 × 28", Gift of Mrs. Henry L. Moses, 54.75. The Museum of the City of New York.

an excuse to overturn the laws that deprived employers of the "liberty" to choose how long their employees should work or the conditions of the workplace.

As stricter and more far-reaching laws were enacted, many judges, fearing a trend toward socialism and regimentation, adopted an increasingly narrow interpretation of state authority to regulate business. In 1905 the U.S. Supreme Court declared in the case of *Lochner v. New York* that a New York ten-hour act for bakers deprived the bakers of the liberty of working as long as they wished and thus violated the Fourteenth Amendment. Justice Oliver Wendell Holmes, Jr., wrote a famous dissenting opinion in this case. If the people of New York believed that the public health was endangered by bakers working long hours, he reasoned, it was not the Court's job to overrule them.

Nevertheless, the progressives continued to battle for legislation to use state power against business. Women played a particularly important part in these struggles.

●─View the Image
Little Spinner in Globe Cotton Mill at **myhistorylab.com**

Sparked by the National Child Labor Committee, organized in 1904, reformers over the next ten years obtained laws in nearly every state banning the employment of young children and limiting the hours of older ones. Many of these laws were poorly enforced, yet when Congress passed a federal child labor law in 1916, the Supreme Court, in *Hammer v. Dagenhart* (1918), declared it unconstitutional.[1]

---

[1]A second child labor law, passed in 1919, was also thrown out by the Court, and a child labor amendment, submitted in 1924, failed to achieve ratification by the necessary three-quarters of the states.

By 1917 nearly all the states had placed limitations on the hours of women industrial workers, and about ten had set minimum wage standards for women. But once again federal action that would have extended such regulation to the entire country did not materialize. A minimum wage law for women in the District of Columbia was overturned by the Court in *Adkins v. Children's Hospital* (1923).

The passage of so much state social legislation sent conservatives scurrying to the Supreme Court for redress. Such persons believed that no government had the power to deprive either workers or employers of the right to negotiate any kind of labor contract they wished. The decision of the Supreme Court in *Lochner v. New York* seemed to indicate that the justices would adopt this point of view. When an Oregon law limiting women laundry workers to ten hours a day was challenged in *Muller v. Oregon* (1908), Florence Kelley and Josephine Goldmark of the Consumers' League persuaded Louis D. Brandeis to defend the statute before the Court.

The Consumers' League, whose slogan was "investigate, agitate, legislate," was probably the most effective of the many women's reform organizations of the period. With the aid of league researchers, Brandeis prepared a remarkable brief stuffed with economic and sociological evidence indicating that long hours damaged both the health of individual women and the health of society. This nonlegal evidence greatly impressed the justices, who upheld the constitutionality of the Oregon law.

Political Reform: The Woman Suffrage Movement

On the national level the Progressive Era saw the culmination of the struggle for **woman suffrage**. The shock occasioned by the failure of the Fourteenth and Fifteenth Amendments to give women the vote after the Civil War continued to embitter most leaders of the movement. But it resulted in a split among feminists. One group, the American Woman Suffrage Association (AWSA), focused on the vote question alone. The more radical National Woman Suffrage Association (NWSA), led by Elizabeth Cady Stanton and Susan B. Anthony, concerned itself with many issues of importance to women as well as suffrage. The NWSA put the immediate interests of women ahead of everything else. It was deeply involved in efforts to unionize women workers, yet it did not hesitate to urge women to be strikebreakers if they could get better jobs by doing so.

See the Map *Woman Suffrage Before the 19th Century* at **myhistorylab.com**

Aside from their lack of unity, feminists were handicapped in the late nineteenth century by widely held Victorian ideals: Sex was a taboo topic, and women were to be "pure" guardians of home and family. Even under the best of circumstances, dislike of male-dominated society is hard enough to separate from dislike of men. Most feminists, for example, opposed contraception, insisting that birth control by any means other than continence would encourage what they called masculine lust.

These ideas and prejudices enticed feminists into a logical trap. If women were morally superior to men—a tempting conclusion—giving women the vote would improve the character of the electorate. Society would benefit because politics would become less corrupt, war a thing of the past. "City housekeeping has failed," said

Another argument in support of woman suffrage claimed that women were intrinsically *better* than men. Note that this woman in the turn-of-the-century poster, crowned by a halo, has her clothes arranged in the shape of a cross.

VOTES for WOMEN

Photo Credit: The Schlesinger Library, Radcliffe Institute, Harvard University.

Jane Addams of Hull House in arguing for the reform of municipal government, "partly because women, the traditional housekeepers, have not been consulted."

By the early twentieth century there were signs of progress. In 1890 the two major women's groups combined as the **National American Woman Suffrage Association (NAWSA)**. Stanton and Anthony were the first two presidents of the association, but new leaders were emerging, the most notable being Carrie Chapman Catt, a woman who combined superb organizing abilities and political skills with commitment to broad social reform. The NAWSA made winning the right to vote its main objective and concentrated on a state-by-state approach. Wyoming gave women the vote in 1869, and Utah, Colorado, and Idaho had been won over to woman suffrage by 1896.

The burgeoning of the progressive movement helped as middle-class recruits of both sexes adopted the suffrage cause. The 1911 referendum in California was crucial. Fifteen years earlier, California voters had rejected the measure. But in 1911, despite determined opposition from saloonkeepers, the proposal barely passed. Within three years, most other Western states fell into line. For the first time, large numbers of working-class women began to agitate for the vote. In 1917, bosses at New York City's Tammany Hall, who had engineered the defeat of woman suffrage in that state two years earlier, concluded that passage was inevitable and threw their support to the measure, which passed. The suffragists then shifted the campaign back to the national level, the lead taken by a new organization, the Congressional Union, headed by Alice Paul and the wealthy reformer Alva Belmont. When President Wilson refused to support the idea of a constitutional amendment granting women the vote, militant women picketed the White House. A number of them were arrested and sentenced to sixty days in the workhouse. This roused a storm of criticism, and Wilson quickly pardoned the picketers. After some hesitation the NAWSA stopped concentrating on the state-by-state approach and began to campaign for a constitutional amendment. Pressure on Congress mounted steadily. The amendment finally won congressional approval in 1919. By 1920 the necessary three-quarters of the states had ratified the Nineteenth Amendment; the long fight was over.

Woman Suffrage, 1896–1914

- States that adopted full woman suffrage, 1869–1896
- States that adopted full woman suffrage, 1910–1914
- States that had not adopted full woman suffrage by 1914

Woman Suffrage Resolution May 21, 1919, House of Representatives

- Yes
- No
- Not voting
- Unsettled
- Boston
- New York City
- Philadelphia
- Baltimore
- Detroit

The Advance of Woman Suffrage In 1869 Wyoming, still a territory, voted to give women the vote. The next year, after Mormon leader Brigham Young endorsed woman suffrage, Utah followed. Then came Colorado (1893) and Idaho (1896), frontier states that sought to attract women settlers. In 1911, by a margin of 3,587 votes, California endorsed woman suffrage, and within three years the remainder of the western states had done so, too. World War I stimulated support for the Woman Suffrage (Nineteenth) Amendment. The May 21, 1919, vote in the House of Representatives shows that most of the opposing votes came from southern congressmen who believed that woman suffrage would be the first step toward securing the vote for blacks.

Theodore Roosevelt: Cowboy in the White House

On September 6, 1901, an anarchist named Leon Czolgosz shot President McKinley during a public reception at the Pan-American Exposition at Buffalo, New York. Eight days later McKinley died and Theodore Roosevelt became president of the United States. His ascension to the presidency marked the beginning of a new era in national politics.

Although only forty-two, by far the youngest president in the nation's history up to that time, Roosevelt brought solid qualifications to the office. Son of a well-to-do New York merchant, he had graduated from Harvard in 1880 and studied law briefly at Columbia, though he did not obtain a degree. In addition to political experience that included three terms in the New York assembly, six years on the U.S. Civil Service Commission, two years as police commissioner of New York City, another as assistant secretary of the navy, and a term as governor of New York, he had been a rancher in the Dakota Territory and a soldier in the Spanish-American War. Politically, he had always been a loyal Republican. He rejected the mugwump heresy in 1884, and during the tempestuous 1890s he vigorously denounced populism, Bryanism, and "labor agitators."

Nevertheless, Roosevelt's elevation to the presidency alarmed many conservatives, and not without reason. He did not fit their conception, based on a composite image of the chief executives from Hayes to McKinley, of a president. He seemed too undignified, too energetic, too outspoken, too unconventional. It was one thing to have operated a cattle ranch, another to have captured a gang of rustlers at gunpoint; one thing to have run a metropolitan police force, another to have roamed New York slums in the small hours to catch patrolmen fraternizing with thieves and prostitutes; and one thing to have commanded a regiment, another to have killed a Spaniard personally.

Roosevelt worshiped aggressiveness and was extremely sensitive to any threat to his honor as a gentleman. When another young man showed some slight interest in Roosevelt's fiancée, he sent for a set of French dueling pistols. His teachers found him an interesting student, for he was intelligent and imaginative, if annoyingly argumentative.

Few individuals have rationalized or sublimated their feelings of inferiority as effectively as Roosevelt and to such good purpose. And few have been more genuinely warmhearted, more full of spontaneity, more committed to the ideals of public service and national greatness. As a political leader he was energetic and hard-driving. Conservatives and timid souls, sensing his aggressiveness even

Theodore Roosevelt addressing a crowd in Evanston, Illinois, in the early 1900s.

Photo Credit: Getty Images.

when he held it in check, distrusted Roosevelt's judgment. In fact his judgment was nearly always sound; responsibility usually tempered his aggressiveness.

When Roosevelt was first mentioned as a running mate for McKinley in 1900, he wrote, "The Vice Presidency is a most honorable office, but for a young man there is not much to do." As president it would have been unthinkable for him to preside over a caretaker administration devoted to maintaining the status quo. However, the reigning Republican politicos, basking in the sunshine of the prosperity that had contributed so much to their victory in 1900, distrusted anything suggestive of change.

Had Roosevelt been the impetuous hothead that conservatives feared, he would have plunged ahead without regard for their feelings and influence. Instead he moved slowly and often got what he wanted by using his executive power rather than by persuading Congress to pass new laws. His domestic program included some measure of control of big corporations, more power for the Interstate Commerce Commission (ICC), and the conservation of natural resources. By consulting congressional leaders and following their advice not to bring up controversial matters like the tariff and currency reform, he obtained a modest budget of new laws.

The Newlands Act (1902) funneled the proceeds from land sales in the West into federal irrigation projects. The Department of Commerce and Labor, which was to include a Bureau of Corporations with authority to investigate industrial combines and issue reports, was established. The Elkins Railroad Act of 1903 strengthened the ICC's hand against the railroads by making the receiving as well as the granting of rebates illegal and by forbidding the roads to deviate in any way from their published rates.

Roosevelt and Big Business

Roosevelt soon became known as a trustbuster, and in the sense that he considered the monopoly problem the most pressing issue of the times, this was accurate to an extent. But he did not believe in breaking up big corporations indiscriminately. Regulation seemed the best way to deal with large corporations because, he said, industrial giantism "could not be eliminated unless we were willing to turn back the wheels of modern progress."

With Congress unwilling to pass a stiff regulatory law, Roosevelt resorted to the Sherman Act to get at the problem. Although the Supreme Court decision in the Sugar Trust case (*E.C. Knight* [1895]) seemed to have emasculated that law, in 1902 he ordered the Justice Department to bring suit against the Northern Securities Company.

He chose his target wisely. The Northern Securities Company controlled the Great Northern, the Northern Pacific, the Chicago, the Burlington, and the Quincy railroads. It had been created in 1901 after a titanic battle on the New York Stock Exchange between the forces of J. P. Morgan and James J. Hill and those of E. H. Harriman, who was associated with the Rockefeller interests. In their efforts to obtain control of the Northern Pacific, the rivals had forced its stock up to $1,000 a share, ruining many speculators and threatening to cause a panic.

Neither side could win a clear-cut victory, so they decided to put the stock of all three railroads in a holding company owned by the two groups. Since Harriman already controlled the Union Pacific and the Southern Pacific, the plan resulted in a virtual monopoly of western railroads. The public had been alarmed, for the merger seemed to typify the rapaciousness of the tycoons.

The announcement of the suit caused consternation in the business world. Morgan rushed to the White House. "If we have done anything wrong," he said to the president, "send your man to my man and they can fix it up." Roosevelt was not fundamentally opposed to this sort of agreement, but it was too late to compromise in this instance. Attorney General Philander C. Knox pressed the case vigorously, and in 1904 the Supreme Court ordered the dissolution of the Northern Securities Company.

Roosevelt then ordered suits against the meat packers, the Standard Oil Trust, and the American Tobacco Company. His stock among progressives rose, yet he had not embarrassed the conservatives in Congress by demanding new antitrust legislation.

The president went out of his way to assure cooperative corporation magnates that he was not against size per se. At a White House conference in 1905, Roosevelt and Elbert H. Gary, chairman of the board of U.S. Steel, reached a "gentlemen's agreement" whereby Gary promised "to cooperate with the Government in every possible way." The Bureau of Corporations would conduct an investigation of U.S. Steel, Gary allowing it full access to company records. Roosevelt in turn promised that if the investigation revealed any corporate malpractices, he would allow Gary to set matters right voluntarily, thereby avoiding an antitrust suit. He reached a similar agreement with the International Harvester Company two years later.

There were limits to the effectiveness of such arrangements. Standard Oil agreed to a similar détente and then reneged, refusing to turn over vital records to the bureau. The Justice Department brought suit against the company under the Sherman Act, and eventually the company was broken up at the order of the Supreme Court. Roosevelt would have preferred a more binding kind of regulation, but when he asked for laws giving the government supervisory authority over big combinations, Congress refused to act.

Roosevelt and the Coal Strike

Roosevelt made remarkable use of his executive power during the anthracite coal strike of 1902. In June the United Mine Workers (UMW), led by John Mitchell, laid down their picks and demanded higher wages, an eight-hour day, and recognition of the union. Most of the anthracite mines were owned by railroads. Two years earlier the miners had won a 10 percent wage increase in a similar strike, chiefly because the owners feared that labor unrest might endanger the election of McKinley. Now the coal companies were dead set against further concessions; when the men walked out, they shut down the mines and prepared to starve the strikers into submission.

The strike dragged on through summer and early fall. The miners conducted themselves with great restraint, avoiding violence and offering to submit their claims to arbitration. As the price of anthracite soared with the approach of winter, sentiment in their behalf mounted.

Roosevelt shared the public's sympathy for the miners, and the threat of a coal shortage alarmed him. Early in October he summoned both sides to a conference in Washington and urged them as patriotic Americans to sacrifice any "personal consideration" for the "general good." His action enraged the coal owners, for they believed he was trying to force them to recognize the union. They refused even to speak to the UMW representatives at the conference and demanded that Roosevelt end the strike by force and bring suit against the union under the Sherman Act. Mitchell, aware of the immense prestige that Roosevelt had conferred on the union by calling the conference, cooperated fully with the president.

Table 1   **Major Supreme Court Rulings during the Progressive Era**

Northern Securities Case	1904	Upheld antitrust ruling against railroad conglomerate
Lochner v. New York	1905	Overturned (progressive) New York law restricting the hours bakers could work; invoked the Fourteenth Amendment to protect bakers' "right" to work as long as they wished
Muller v. Oregon	1908	Affirmed the right of Oregon to limit the hours worked by women in laundries

The attitudes of management and of the union further strengthened public support for the miners. Even former president Grover Cleveland, who had used federal troops to break the Pullman strike, said that he was "disturbed and vexed by the tone and substance of the operators' deliverances." Encouraged by this state of affairs, Roosevelt took a bold step: He announced that unless a settlement was reached promptly, he would order federal troops into the anthracite regions, not to break the strike but to seize and operate the mines.

The threat of government intervention brought the owners to terms. A Cabinet member, Elihu Root, worked out the details with J. P. Morgan, whose firm had major interests in the Reading and other railroads. The miners would return to the pits and all issues between them and the coal companies would be submitted for settlement to a commission appointed by Roosevelt. Both sides accepted the arrangement, and the men went back to work. In March 1903 the commission granted the miners a 10 percent wage increase and a nine-hour workday.

To the public the incident seemed a perfect illustration of the progressive spirit—in Roosevelt's words, everyone had received a **Square Deal**. In fact the results were by no means so clear-cut. The miners gained relatively little and the companies lost still less. The president was the main winner. The public acclaimed him as a fearless, imaginative, public-spirited leader. Without calling on Congress for support, he had expanded his own authority and hence that of the federal government. His action marked a major forward step in the evolution of the modern presidency.

TR's Triumphs

By reviving the Sherman Act, settling the coal strike, and pushing moderate reforms through Congress, Roosevelt ensured that he would be reelected president in 1904. Despite his resentment at Roosevelt's attack on the Northern Securities Company, J. P. Morgan contributed $150,000 to the Republican campaign. Other tycoons gave with equal generosity. Roosevelt swept the country, carrying even the normally Democratic border states of Maryland and Missouri.

Encouraged by the landslide and the increasing militancy of progressives, Roosevelt pressed for more reform legislation. His most imaginative proposal was a plan to make the District of Columbia a model progressive community. He suggested child labor and factory inspection laws and a slum clearance program, but Congress refused to act. Likewise, his request for a minimum wage for railroad workers was rejected.

Early in the twentieth century, when malnutrition was common, companies such as this one advertised that its pills could make people fatter. The Pure Food and Drug Act of 1906 fined manufacturers who made false claims for their products. A century later, in 2010, the *Seattle Post Intelligencer*, under the headline "Too Fat to Fight," reported that over a fourth of eighteen to twenty-four-year-old potential army recruits were rejected as unfit.

GET FAT
ON LORINGS
FAT-TEN-U
AND
CORPULA
FOODS.

Photo Credit: © CORBIS All Rights Reserved.

With progressive state governors demanding federal action and farmers and manufacturers, especially in the Midwest, clamoring for relief against discriminatory rates, Roosevelt was ready by 1905 to make railroad legislation his major objective. The ICC should be empowered to fix rates, not merely to challenge unreasonable ones. It should have the right to inspect the private records of the railroads since fair rates could not be determined unless the true financial condition of the roads were known.

Because these proposals struck at rights that businessmen considered sacrosanct, many congressmen balked. But Roosevelt applied presidential pressure, and in June 1906 the Hepburn bill became law. It gave the commission the power to inspect the books of railroad companies, to set maximum rates (once a complaint had been filed by a shipper), and to control sleeping car companies, owners of oil pipelines, and other firms engaged in transportation. Railroads could no longer issue passes freely—an important check on their political influence. In all, the **Hepburn Act** made the ICC a more powerful and more active body. Congress also passed meat inspection and pure food and drug legislation. In 1906 Upton Sinclair published *The Jungle*, a devastating exposé of the filthy conditions in the Chicago slaughterhouses. Sinclair was more interested in writing a socialist tract than he was in meat inspection, but his book, a best seller, raised a storm against the packers. After Roosevelt read *The Jungle* he sent two officials to Chicago to investigate. Their report was so shocking, he said, that its publication would "be wellnigh ruinous to our export trade in meat." He threatened to release the report unless Congress acted. After a fight, the meat inspection bill passed. The Pure Food and Drug Act, forbidding the manufacture and sale of adulterated and fraudulently labeled products, rode through Congress on the coattails of this measure.

●●─Read the Document

"Inside the Packinghouse" from Upton Sinclair's *The Jungle* at **myhistorylab.com**

To advanced liberals Roosevelt's achievements seemed limited when placed beside his professed objectives and his smug evaluations of what he had done. How could he be a reformer and a defender of established interests at the same time? Roosevelt found no difficulty in holding such a position. As one historian has said, "He stood close to the center and bared his teeth at the conservatives of the right and the liberals of the extreme left."

Roosevelt Tilts Left

As the progressive movement advanced, Roosevelt advanced with it. He never accepted all the ideas of what he called its "lunatic fringe," but he took steadily more liberal positions. He always insisted that he was not hostile to business interests, but when those interests sought to exploit the national domain, they had no more implacable foe. **Conservation** of natural resources was dear to his heart and probably his most significant achievement as president. He placed some 150 million acres of forest lands in federal reserves, and he strictly enforced the laws governing grazing, mining, and lumbering.

As Roosevelt became more liberal, conservative Republicans began to balk at following his lead. The sudden panic that struck the financial world in October 1907 speeded the trend. Government policies had no direct bearing on the panic, which began with a run on several important New York trust companies and spread to the Stock Exchange when speculators found themselves unable to borrow money to meet their obligations. In the emergency Roosevelt authorized the deposit of large amounts of government cash in New York banks. He informally agreed to the acquisition of the Tennessee Coal and Iron Company by U.S. Steel when the bankers told him that the purchase was necessary to end the panic. In spite of his efforts, conservatives insisted on referring to the financial collapse as "Roosevelt's panic," and they blamed the president for the depression that followed on its heels.

Roosevelt, however, turned left rather than right. In 1908 he came out in favor of federal income and inheritance taxes, stricter regulation of interstate corporations, and reforms designed to help industrial workers. He denounced "the speculative folly and the flagrant dishonesty" of "malefactors of great wealth," further alienating conservative, or Old Guard, Republicans. When the president began criticizing the courts, the last bastion of conservatism, he lost all chance of obtaining further reform legislation. As he said himself, during his last months in office "stagnation continued to rage with uninterrupted violence."

William Howard Taft: The Listless Progressive, or More Is Less

But Roosevelt remained popular and politically powerful; before his term ended, he chose William Howard Taft, his secretary of war, to succeed him and easily obtained Taft's nomination. William Jennings Bryan was again the Democratic candidate. Campaigning on Roosevelt's record, Taft carried the country by well over a million votes, defeating Bryan 321 to 162 in the Electoral College.

Taft was intelligent, experienced, and public spirited; he seemed ideally suited to carry out Roosevelt's policies. Born in Cincinnati in 1857, educated at Yale, he had served as an Ohio judge, as solicitor general of the United States under Benjamin Harrison, and

Photo Credit: The Granger Collection.

"GOODNESS GRACIOUS! I MUST HAVE BEEN DOZING!"

A hapless Taft is entangled in governmental yarn, while a disapproving Roosevelt looks on. "Goodness gracious! I must have been dozing," reads the caption, a reference to Taft's penchant for naps.

then as a federal circuit court judge before accepting McKinley's assignment to head the Philippine Commission in 1900. His success as civil governor of the Philippines led Roosevelt to make him secretary of war in 1904.

Taft supported the Square Deal loyally. This, together with his mentor's ardent endorsement, won him the backing of most progressive Republicans. Yet the Old Guard liked him too; although outgoing, he had none of the Roosevelt impetuosity and aggressiveness. His genial personality and his obvious desire to avoid conflict appealed to moderates.

However, Taft lacked the physical and mental stamina required of a modern chief executive. Although not lazy, he weighed over 300 pounds and needed to rest this vast bulk more than the job allowed. Campaigning bored him; speech making seemed a useless chore. The judicial life was his real love; intense partisanship dismayed and confused him. He was too reasonable to control a coalition and not ambitious enough to impose his will on others. He supported many progressive measures, but he never absorbed the progressive spirit.

Taft honestly wanted to carry out most of Roosevelt's policies. He enforced the Sherman Act vigorously and continued to expand the national forest reserves. He signed the Mann-Elkins Act of 1910, which empowered the ICC to suspend rate increases without waiting for a shipper to complain and established the Commerce Court to speed the settlement of railroad rate cases. An eight-hour day for all persons engaged in work on government contracts, mine safety legislation, and several other reform measures received his approval. He even summoned Congress into special session specifically to reduce tariff duties—something that Roosevelt had not dared to attempt.

But Taft had been disturbed by Roosevelt's sweeping use of executive power. "We have got to work out our problems on the basis of law," he insisted. Whereas Roosevelt had excelled at maneuvering around congressional opposition and at finding ways to accomplish his objectives without waiting for Congress to act, Taft adamantly refused to use such tactics. His restraint was in many ways admirable, but it reduced his effectiveness.

In 1910 Taft got into difficulty with the conservationists. Although he believed in husbanding natural resources carefully, he did not like the way Roosevelt had circumvented Congress in adding to the forest reserves. He demanded, and eventually obtained, specific legislation to accomplish this purpose. The issue that aroused the conservationists concerned the integrity of his secretary of the interior, Richard A. Ballinger. A less than ardent conservationist, Ballinger returned to the public domain certain waterpower sites that the Roosevelt administration had withdrawn on the legally questionable ground that they were to become ranger stations. Ballinger's action alarmed Chief Forester Gifford Pinchot, the darling of the conservationists. When Pinchot learned that Ballinger intended to validate the shaky claim of mining interests to a large tract of coal-rich land in Alaska, he launched an intemperate attack on the secretary.

In the Ballinger-Pinchot controversy Taft felt obliged to support his own man. The coal lands dispute was complex, and Pinchot's charges were exaggerated. It was certainly unfair to call Ballinger "the most effective opponent the conservation policies have yet had." When Pinchot, whose own motives were partly political, persisted in criticizing Ballinger, Taft dismissed him. He had no choice under the circumstances, but a more adept politician might have found some way of avoiding a showdown.

Breakup of the Republican Party

One ominous aspect of the Ballinger-Pinchot affair was that Pinchot was a close friend of Theodore Roosevelt. After Taft's inauguration, Roosevelt had gone off to hunt big game in Africa, bearing in his baggage an autographed photograph of his protégé and a touching letter of appreciation, in which the new president said, "I can never forget that the power I now exercise was a voluntary transfer from you to me." As soon as he emerged from the wilderness in March 1910, bearing more than 3,000 trophies, including nine lions, five elephants, and thirteen rhinos, he was caught up in the squabble between the progressive members of his party and its titular head. Pinchot met him in Italy, laden with injured innocence and a packet of angry letters from various progressives. TR's intimate friend Senator Henry Cabot Lodge, essentially a conservative, barraged him with messages, the gist of which was that Taft was lazy and inept and that Roosevelt should prepare to become the "Moses" who would guide the party "out of the wilderness of doubt and discontent" into which Taft had led it.

Roosevelt hoped to steer a middle course, but Pinchot's complaints impressed him. Taft had decided to strike out on his own, he concluded. Taft sensed the former president's coolness and was offended. He was egged on by his ambitious wife, who wanted him to stand clear of Roosevelt's shadow and establish his own reputation.

Perhaps the resulting rupture was inevitable. The Republican party was dividing into two factions, the progressives and the Old Guard. Forced to choose between them, Taft threw in his lot with the Old Guard. Roosevelt backed the progressives. Speaking at Osawatomie, Kansas, in August 1910 he came out for a comprehensive program of social legislation, which he called the **New Nationalism**. Besides attacking "special privilege" and the "unfair money-getting"

Read the Document

Roosevelt, *The New Nationalism*
at myhistorylab.com

practices of "lawbreakers of great wealth," he called for a broad expansion of federal power. "The betterment we seek must be accomplished," he said, "mainly through the National Government."

The final break came in October 1911 when Taft ordered an antitrust suit against U.S. Steel. He was prepared to enforce the Sherman Act "or die in the attempt." But this initiative angered Roosevelt because the lawsuit focused on U.S. Steel's absorption of the Tennessee Coal and Iron Company, which Roosevelt had unofficially authorized during the panic of 1907. The government's antitrust brief made Roosevelt appear to have been either a proponent of the monopoly or, far worse, a fool who had been duped by the steel corporation. Early in 1912 he declared himself a candidate for the Republican presidential nomination.

Roosevelt plunged into the preconvention campaign with typical energy. He was almost uniformly victorious in states that held presidential primaries, carrying even Ohio, Taft's home state. However, the president controlled the party machinery and entered the national convention with a small majority of the delegates. Since some Taft delegates had been chosen under questionable circumstances, the Roosevelt forces challenged the right of 254 of them to their seats. The Taft-controlled credentials committee, paying little attention to the evidence, gave all but a few of the disputed seats to the president, who then won the nomination on the first ballot.

Roosevelt was understandably outraged by the ruthless manner in which the Taft "steamroller" had overridden his forces. When his leading supporters urged him to organize a third party, and when two of them, George W. Perkins, formerly a partner of the banker J. P. Morgan, and the publisher Frank Munsey, offered to finance the campaign, Roosevelt agreed to make the race.

In August, amid scenes of hysterical enthusiasm, the first convention of the Progressive party met at Chicago and nominated him for president. Announcing that he felt "as strong as a bull moose," Roosevelt delivered a stirring "confession of faith," calling for strict regulation of corporations, a tariff commission, national presidential primaries, minimum wage and workers' compensation laws, the elimination of child labor, and many other reforms.

Watch the Video

Bull Moose Campaign Speech at **myhistorylab.com**

The Election of 1912

The Democrats made the most of the opportunity offered by the Republican schism. Had they nominated a conservative or allowed Bryan a fourth chance, they would probably have ensured Roosevelt's election. Instead, they nominated Woodrow Wilson, who had achieved a remarkable liberal record as governor of New Jersey.

Although as a political scientist Wilson had criticized the status quo and taken a pragmatic approach to the idea of government regulation of the economy, he had objected strongly to Bryan's brand of politics. In 1896 he voted for the Gold Democratic party candidate instead of Bryan. But by 1912, influenced partly by ambition and partly by the spirit of the times, he had been converted to progressivism. He called his brand of reform the **New Freedom**.

The federal government could best advance the cause of social justice, Wilson reasoned, by eradicating the special privileges that enabled the "interests" to flourish. Where

1912: Divided Republicans, Democratic Victory In 1912, when Theodore Roosevelt chose to run as a Progressive, he took away millions of votes from the Republican Taft. This ensured Democrat Woodrow Wilson's landslide election.

1912

Democratic (Wilson)
Progressive (T. Roosevelt)
Republican (Taft)

Roosevelt had lost faith in competition as a way of protecting the public against monopolies, Wilson insisted that competition could be restored. The government must break up the great trusts, establish fair rules for doing business, and subject violators to stiff punishments. Thereafter, the free enterprise system would protect the public from exploitation without destroying individual initiative and opportunity.

Roosevelt's reasoning was perhaps theoretically more sound. He called for a New Nationalism. Laissez-faire made less sense than it had in earlier times. The complexities of the modern world seemed to call for a positive approach, a plan, the close application of human intelligence to social and economic problems.

But being more in line with American experience than the New Nationalism, Wilson's New Freedom had much to recommend it. The danger that selfish individuals would use the power of the state for their own ends had certainly not disappeared, despite the efforts of progressives to make government more responsive to popular opinion. Any considerable expansion of national power, as Roosevelt proposed, would increase the danger and probably create new difficulties. Managing so complicated an enterprise as an industrialized nation was sure to be a formidable task for the federal government. Furthermore, individual freedom of opportunity merited the toleration of a certain amount of inefficiency.

To choose between the New Nationalism and the New Freedom, between the dynamic Roosevelt and the idealistic Wilson, was indeed difficult. Taft got the hard-core Republican vote but lost the progressive wing of the GOP to Roosevelt. Wilson had the solid support of both conservative and liberal Democrats. As a result, Wilson won an easy victory in the Electoral College, receiving 435 votes to Roosevelt's 88 and Taft's 8. The popular vote was Wilson, 6,286,000; Roosevelt, 4,126,000; and Taft, 3,484,000.

If partisan politics had determined the winner, the election was nonetheless an overwhelming endorsement of progressivism. The temper of the times was shown by the 897,000 votes for Eugene Debs, who was again the Socialist candidate. Altogether, professed liberals amassed over 11 million of the 15 million ballots cast. Wilson was a minority president, but he took office with a clear mandate to press forward with further reforms.

Wilson: The New Freedom

No one ever rose more suddenly or spectacularly in American politics than Woodrow Wilson. In the spring of 1910 he was president of Princeton University; he had never held or even run for public office. In the fall of 1912 he was president-elect of the United States. Yet if his rise was meteoric, in a very real sense he had devoted his life to preparing for it. As a student he became interested in political theory, dreaming of representing his state in the Senate. He studied law solely because he thought it the best avenue to public office, and when he discovered that he did not like legal work, he took a doctorate at Johns Hopkins in political science.

For years Wilson's political ambitions appeared doomed to frustration. He taught at Bryn Mawr, then at Wesleyan, and finally at his alma mater, Princeton. He wrote several influential books, among them *Congressional Government* and *The State*, and achieved an outstanding reputation as a teacher and lecturer. In 1902 he was chosen president of Princeton and soon won a place among the nation's leading educators. In time Wilson's educational ideas and his overbearing manner of applying them got him in trouble with some of Princeton's alumni and trustees. Although his university career was wrecked, the controversies, in which he appeared to be championing democracy and progress in the face of reactionary opponents, brought him at last to the attention of the politicians. Then, in a great rush, came power and fame.

Wilson was an immediate success as president. Since Roosevelt's last year in office, Congress had been almost continually at war with the executive branch and with itself. Legislative achievements had been few. Now a small avalanche of important measures received the approval of the lawmakers. In October 1913 the **Underwood Tariff** brought the first significant reduction of duties since before the Civil War. To compensate for the expected loss of revenue, the act provided for a graduated tax on personal incomes.

Two months later the **Federal Reserve Act** gave the country a central banking system for the first time since Jackson destroyed the Bank of the United States. The measure divided the nation into twelve banking districts, each under the supervision of a Federal Reserve bank, a sort of bank for bankers. All national banks in each district and any state banks that wished to participate had to invest 6 percent of their capital and surplus in the reserve bank, which was empowered to exchange paper money, called Federal Reserve notes, for the commercial and agricultural paper that member banks took in as security from borrowers. The volume of currency was no longer at the mercy of the supply of gold or any other particular commodity.

The nerve center of the system was the Federal Reserve Board in Washington, which appointed a majority of the directors of the Federal Reserve banks and had some control over rediscount rates. The board provided a modicum of public control over the banks, but the effort to weaken the power of the great New York banks by decentralizing the system proved ineffective. Nevertheless, a true central banking system was created.

When inflation threatened, the reserve banks could raise the rediscount rate, discouraging borrowing and thus reducing the amount of money in circulation. In bad times it could lower the rate, making it easier to borrow and injecting new dollars into the economy. Much remained to be learned about the proper management of the money supply, but the nation finally had a flexible yet safe currency.

In 1914 Congress passed two important laws affecting corporations. One created the Federal Trade Commission (FTC) to replace Roosevelt's Bureau of Corporations. In addition to investigating corporations and publishing reports, this nonpartisan board could issue cease-and-desist orders against "unfair" trade practices brought to light through its research. The law did not define the term *unfair*, and the commission's rulings could be taken on appeal to the federal courts, but the FTC was nonetheless a powerful instrument for protecting the public against the trusts.

The second measure, the **Clayton Antitrust Act**, made certain specific business practices illegal, including price discrimination that tended to foster monopolies; "tying" agreements, which forbade retailers from handling the products of a firm's competitors; and the creation of interlocking directorates as a means of controlling competing companies. The act exempted labor unions and agricultural organizations from the antitrust laws and curtailed the use of injunctions in labor disputes. The officers of corporations could be held individually responsible if their companies violated the antitrust laws.

The Democrats controlled both houses of Congress for the first time since 1890 and were eager to make a good record, but Wilson's imaginative and aggressive use of presidential power was decisive. He called the legislators into special session in April 1913 and appeared before them to lay out his program; he was the first president to address Congress in person since John Adams. Then he followed the course of administration bills closely. Administration representatives haunted the cloakrooms and lobbies of both houses. Cooperative congressmen began to receive notes of praise and encouragement, whereas recalcitrant ones received stern demands for support, often pecked out on the president's own portable typewriter.

Wilson explained his success by saying, only half humorously, that running the government was child's play for anyone who had managed the faculty of a university. Responsible party government was his objective; he expected individual Democrats to support the decisions of the party majority, and his idealism never prevented him from awarding the spoils of office to city bosses and conservative congressmen, as long as they supported his program. Nor did his career as a political theorist make him rigid and doctrinaire. In practice the differences between his New Freedom and Roosevelt's New Nationalism tended to disappear. The FTC and the Federal Reserve system represented steps toward the kind of regulated economy that Roosevelt advocated.

Table 2   Progressive Legislation (Federal)

Newlands Act	1902	Funneled revenues from sale of public lands to irrigation projects
Elkins Act	1903	Strengthened the ICC by making it illegal for railroads to deviate from published rates, such as by granting rebates
Hepburn Act	1906	Gave ICC the power to fix rates of railroads and other corporations involved in interstate commerce (such as corporations operating oil pipelines)
Pure Food and Durg Act	1906	Prohibited the fraudulent advertising, manufacturing, and selling of impure foods and drugs
Mann-Elkins Act	1910	Empowered ICC to suspend rate increases for railroads or telephone companies
Underwood Tariff	1913	Lowered tariff rates; introduced graduated tax on personal incomes
Federal Reserve Act	1913	Established federal supervision of banking system
Sixteenth Amendment	1913	Authorized federal income tax
Clayton Antitrust Act	1914	Exempted labor unions from antitrust laws and curtailed injunctions against labor leaders
Nineteenth Amendment	1920	Established woman suffrage

There were limits to Wilson's progressivism. He objected as strenuously to laws granting special favors to farmers and workers as to those benefiting the tycoons. When a bill was introduced in 1914 making low-interest loans available to farmers, he refused to support it. He considered the provision exempting unions from the antitrust laws equally unsound. Nor would he push for a federal law prohibiting child labor; such a measure would be unconstitutional, he believed. He also refused to back the constitutional amendment giving the vote to women.

By the end of 1914 Wilson's record, on balance, was positive but distinctly limited. The president believed that the major progressive goals had been achieved; he had no plans for further reform. Many other progressives thought that a great deal more remained to be done.

The Progressives and Minority Rights

On one important issue, race relations, Wilson was distinctly reactionary. With a mere handful of exceptions, the progressives exhibited strong prejudices against nonwhite people and against certain categories of whites as well. Many were as unsympathetic to immigrants from Asia and eastern and southern Europe as any of the "conservative" opponents of immigration in the 1880s and 1890s.

American Indians were also affected by the progressives' racial attitudes. Where the sponsors of the Dawes Act (1887) had assumed that Indians were inherently capable of adopting the ways of "civilized" people, in the progressive period the tendency was to write Indians off as fundamentally inferior and to assume that they would make second-class citizens at best. Francis Leupp, Theodore Roosevelt's commissioner of Indian affairs, put it this way in a 1905 report: "If nature has set a different physical stamp upon different races of men it is fair to assume that the variation . . . is manifested in mental and moral traits as well. . . . Nothing is gained by trying to undo nature's work." A leading muckraker, Ray Stannard Baker, who was far more sympathetic to blacks than most progressives, dismissed Indians as pathetic beings, "eating, sleeping, idling, with no more thought of the future than a white man's child."

In 1902 Congress passed the Dead Indian Land Act, which made it easier for Indians to sell allotments that they had inherited, and in 1906 another law further relaxed restrictions on land sales. Efforts to improve the education of Indian children continued, but most progressives assumed that only vocational training would help them. Theodore Roosevelt knew from his experiences as a rancher in the Dakota Territory that Indians could be as energetic and capable as whites, but he considered these "exceptional." As for the rest, it would be many generations before they could be expected to "move forward" enough to become "ordinary citizens," Roosevelt believed.

To say that African Americans did not fare well at the hands of progressives would be a gross understatement. White southerners, furious at Populist efforts to unite white and black farmers, imposed increasingly repressive measures after 1896. Segregation became more rigid, white opposition to black voting more monolithic. In 1900 the body of a Mississippi black was dug up by order of the state legislature and reburied in a segregated cemetery; in Virginia in 1902 the daughter of Robert E. Lee was arrested for riding in the black section of a railroad car.

On May 15, 1916, after deliberating for one hour, an all-white jury in Waco, Texas, found seventeen-year-old Jesse Washington guilty of bludgeoning a white woman to death. A mob rushed him out of the courtroom, chained him to a tree, and burned him to death. The story was chronicled by Patricia Bernstein in *The First Waco Horror* (2005).

Many progressive women, still smarting from the insult to their sex entailed in the Fourteenth and Fifteenth Amendments and eager to attract southern support for their campaign for the vote, adopted racist arguments. They contrasted the supposed corruption and incompetence of black voters with their own "purity" and intelligence. Southern progressives of both sexes argued that disfranchising blacks would reduce corruption by removing from unscrupulous white politicians the temptation to purchase black votes!

The typical southern attitude toward the education of blacks was summed up in a folk proverb: "When you educate a Negro, you spoil a good field hand." In 1910 only about 8,000 black children in the entire South were attending high schools. Despite the almost total suppression of black rights, lynchings persisted; between 1900 and 1914 more than 1,100 blacks were murdered by mobs, most (but not all) in the southern states. In the rare cases in which local prosecutors brought the lynchers to trial, juries almost without exception brought in verdicts of not guilty.

Booker T. Washington was shaken by this trend, but he could find no way to combat it. The times were passing him by. He appealed to his white southern "friends" for help but got nowhere. Increasingly he talked about the virtues of rural life, the evils of big cities, and the uselessness of higher education for black people. By the turn of the century a number of young, well-educated blacks, most of them Northerners, were breaking away from his accommodationist leadership.

Read the Document
"Events in Paris, Texas," from Ida B. Wells, *A Red Record* at myhistorylab.com

Black Militancy

William E. B. Du Bois was the most prominent of the militants. Du Bois was born in Great Barrington, Massachusetts, in 1868. His father, a restless wanderer of Negro and French Huguenot stock, abandoned the family, and young William grew up on the edge of poverty. Neither accepted nor openly rejected by the overwhelmingly white community, he devoted himself to his studies, showing such brilliance that his future education was ensured by scholarships: to Fisk University, then to Harvard, and then to the University of Berlin. In 1895 Du Bois became the first American black to earn a PhD in history from Harvard; his dissertation, *The Suppression of the African Slave Trade* (1896), remains a standard reference.

Like Washington, Du Bois wanted blacks to lift themselves up by their own bootstraps. They must establish their own businesses, run their own newspapers and colleges, and write their own literature; they must preserve their identity rather than seek to amalgamate themselves into a society that offered them only crumbs and contempt. At first he cooperated with Washington, but in 1903, in the essay "Of Mr. Booker T. Washington and Others," he subjected Washington's "attitude of adjustment and submission" to polite but searching criticism. Washington had asked blacks to give up political power, civil rights, and the hope of higher education, not realizing that "voting is necessary to modern manhood, that . . . discrimination is barbarism, and that black boys need education as well as white boys." Washington "apologizes for injustice," Du Bois charged. "He belittles the emasculating effects of caste distinctions, and opposes the higher training and ambitions of our brightest minds." Du Bois deemed this totally wrong: "The way for a people to gain their reasonable rights is not by voluntarily throwing them away."

Du Bois was not an uncritical admirer of the ordinary American black. He believed that "immorality, crime, and laziness" were common vices. He blamed the weaknesses of blacks on the treatment afforded them by whites, but his approach to the solution of racial problems was frankly elitist. "The Negro race," he wrote, "is going to be saved by its exceptional men," what he called the "talented tenth" of the black population. Whatever his prejudices, Du Bois exposed both the weaknesses of Washington's strategy and the callousness of white American attitudes. Accommodation was not working. Washington was praised, even lionized by prominent southern whites, yet when Theodore Roosevelt invited him to a meal at the White House they exploded with indignation, and Roosevelt, although not personally prejudiced, meekly backtracked, never repeating his "mistake." He defended his record by saying, "I have stood as valiantly for the rights of the negro as any president since Lincoln." That, sad to relate, was true enough.

Watch the Video

The conflict between Booker T. Washington & W.E.B Du Bois at **myhistorylab.com**

Not mere impatience but despair led Du Bois and a few like-minded blacks to meet at Niagara Falls in July 1905 and to issue a stirring list of demands: the unrestricted right to vote, an end to every kind of segregation, equality of economic opportunity, higher education for the talented, equal justice in the courts, and an end to trade-union discrimination. This **Niagara movement** did not attract mass support, but it did stir the consciences of some whites, many of them the descendants of abolitionists, who were also becoming disenchanted by the failure of accommodation to provide blacks with real opportunity.

In 1909, the centennial of the birth of Abraham Lincoln, a group of these liberals, including the newspaperman Oswald Garrison Villard (grandson of William Lloyd Garrison), the social worker Jane Addams, the philosopher John Dewey, and the novelist William Dean Howells, founded the **National Association for the Advancement of Colored People (NAACP)**. The organization was dedicated to the eradication of racial discrimination. Its leadership was predominantly white in the early years, but Du Bois became a national officer and the editor of its journal, *The Crisis*.

A turning point had been reached. After 1909 virtually every important leader, white and black alike, rejected the Washington approach. More and more, blacks turned to the study of their past in an effort to stimulate pride in their heritage. In 1915 Carter G. Woodson founded the Association for the Study of Negro Life and History; the following year he began editing the *Journal of Negro History*, which became the major publishing organ for scholarly studies on the subject.

This militancy produced few results in the Progressive Era. Theodore Roosevelt behaved no differently than earlier Republican presidents; he courted blacks when he thought it advantageous, and turned his back when he did not. When he ran for president on the Progressive ticket in 1912, he pursued a "lily-white" policy, hoping to break the Democrats' monopoly in the South. By trusting in "[white] men of justice and of vision," Roosevelt argued in the face of decades of experience to the contrary, "the colored men of the South will ultimately get justice."

The southern-born Wilson was actively hostile to blacks. During the 1912 campaign he appealed to them for support and promised to "assist in advancing the interest of their race" in every possible way. Once elected, he refused even to appoint a privately financed commission to study the race problem. Southerners dominated his administration and Congress; as a result, blacks were further degraded.

These actions stirred such a storm that Wilson backtracked a little, but he never abandoned his belief that segregation was in the best interests of both races. "Wilson . . . promised a 'new freedom,'" one newspaperman complained. "On the contrary we are given a stone instead of a loaf of bread." Even Booker T. Washington admitted that his people were more "discouraged and bitter" than at any time in his memory.

Du Bois, who had supported Wilson in 1912, attacked administration policy in *The Crisis*. In November 1914 the militant editor of the *Boston Guardian*, William Monroe Trotter, a classmate of Du Bois at Harvard and a far more caustic critic of the Washington approach, led a delegation to the White House to protest the segregation policy of the government. When Wilson accused him of blackmail, Trotter lost his temper, and an ugly confrontation resulted. The mood of black leaders had changed completely.

By this time the Great War had broken out in Europe. Soon every American would feel its effects, blacks perhaps more than any other group. In November 1915, a year almost to the day after Trotter's clash with Wilson, Booker T. Washington died. One era had ended; a new one was beginning.

Many of the young Americans who had participated in the various crusades of the "age of reform" would soon embark on another crusade—but one of a very different character.

Milestones

1890	National American Woman Suffrage Association is founded	1908	*Muller v. Oregon* upholds law limiting women's work hours
1900	Robert La Follette is elected governor of Wisconsin		William Howard Taft is elected president
	McKinley is reelected president	1909	NAACP is founded
1901	McKinley is assassinated; Theodore Roosevelt becomes president	1910	Ballinger-Pinchot Affair deepens Roosevelt–Taft rift
1902	Roosevelt helps settle anthracite coal strike	1911	Roosevelt gives New Nationalism speech
	Oregon adopts initiative system for proposing legislation	1912	Roosevelt runs for president on Progressive ticket
1904	Northern Securities case revives Sherman Antitrust Act		Woodrow Wilson is elected president
	National Child Labor Committee is established	1913	Sixteenth Amendment authorizes federal income taxes
	Theodore Roosevelt is elected president		Seventeenth Amendment provides for direct election of U.S. senators
1905	Anticapitalist Industrial Workers of the World (IWW) is founded		Underwood Tariff Act reduces duties and imposes personal income tax
1906	Hepburn Act strengthens Interstate Commerce Commission		Federal Reserve Act gives the United States a central banking system again
	Upton Sinclair exposes Chicago slaughterhouses in *The Jungle*	1914	Federal Trade Commission is created to protect against trusts
1907	U.S. Steel absorbs Tennessee Coal and Iron Company		Clayton Antitrust Act regulates business
1908	Theodore Roosevelt convenes National Conservation Conference	1920	Nineteenth Amendment guarantees women the right to vote

✓•⌐[**Study** and **Review** at **www.myhistorylab.com**

Review Questions

1. The introduction to this chapter compares volunteers today to young reformers early in the twentieth century. What were the similarities and differences?

2. List the ideas of the various progressive-thinking leaders and their movements. What attitudes and values did they share? Were these sufficiently coherent to constitute a "Progressive movement"?

3. How did the attitudes of the reformers and political activists compare with those of the people whose lives they meant to improve? How did immigrants, Native Americans, and workers respond to Progressive reforms?

4. In what ways was the Progressive Era especially challenging for African Americans?

5. How did the relationship between business and government change during the presidencies of Roosevelt, Taft, and Wilson? Did business oppose government regulation or favor it as a means of controlling competition and weakening radicalism?

Key Terms

Ashcan School
Clayton Antitrust Act
Conservation
Federal Reserve Act
Hepburn Act
Industrial Workers of the World (IWW)

muckraker
National American Woman Suffrage Association (NAWSA)
National Association for the Advancement of Colored People (NAACP)

New Freedom
New Nationalism
Niagara movement
Progressivism
Square Deal
Underwood Tariff
woman suffrage

From Isolation to Empire

From Chapter 22 of *American Destiny: Narrative of a Nation*, Combined Volume, Fourth Edition.
Mark C. Carnes and John A. Garraty. Copyright © 2012 by Pearson Education, Inc. Published by
Pearson Prentice Hall. All rights reserved.

From Isolation to Empire

((•─[Hear the Audio at myhistorylab.com

Can you find Afghanistan on a map?

During the presidential campaign of 2000, Republican candidate George W. Bush chastised the Clinton administration for sending troops to Haiti and the Balkans. "If we don't stop extending our troops all around the world in nation-building missions," Bush declared, "then we're going to have a serious problem coming down the road."

Few could have imagined that within two years, following the 9/11 attacks on the World Trade Center and the Pentagon, thousands of American troops would be patrolling the high mountains of the Hindu Kush, fighting enemies at places named Tora Bora and Mazar-e Sharif, and working to install a new government in Afghanistan. A National Geographic Society survey found that nearly half of Americans aged 18 to 24 knew that the fictional island for the *Survivor* TV series was located in the South Pacific, but five in six could not find Afghanistan on a map.

Yet by the summer of 2010, President Barack Obama had increased American troops in Afghanistan to nearly 100,000. "If I thought for a minute that America's vital interests were not at stake here in Afghanistan," he told American soldiers, "I would order all of you home right away." These vital interests in many ways originated during the late nineteenth and early twentieth centuries.

Until then, Americans had given little thought to foreign affairs. In 1888 Benjamin Harrison articulated a widely held belief when he said that the United States was "an apart nation" and should remain so.

But sentiment was shifting. Intellectuals and many others cited "Darwinian" principles, such as "survival of the fittest," to justify American expansion abroad. Missionaries called on Americans to help impoverished and ill-educated peoples elsewhere in the world. American businessmen, increasingly confident of their own powers, craved access to foreign resources and markets. Such factors converged in Cuba, prompting the United States to go to war with Spain.

In 1898 tens of thousands of American troops were dispatched to Cuba and, within a year, to the Philippines. For years thereafter, Americans at home would struggle to locate on globes and in atlases battle sites in places such as Balangiga, Pulang Lupa, and Kandahar. They still do.

Isolation or Imperialism?

If Americans had little concern for what was going on far beyond the seas, their economic interest in Latin America was great and growing, and in East Asia only somewhat less so. Whether one sees isolation or expansion as the hallmark of American foreign policy after 1865 depends on what part of the world one looks at.

The disdain of the people of the United States for Europe rested on several historical foundations. Faith in the unique character of American civilization—and the converse of that belief, suspicion of Europe's supposedly aristocratic and decadent society—formed the chief basis of this **isolationism**. Bitter memories of indignities suffered during the Revolution and the Napoleonic Wars and anger at the hostile attitude of the great powers toward the United States during the Civil War strengthened it. In an era before airplanes, the United States was virtually invulnerable to European attack and at the same time incapable of mounting an offensive against any European power. In turning their backs on Europe, Americans were taking no risk and passing up few opportunities.

Origins of the Large Policy: Coveting Colonies

The nation's interests elsewhere in the world gradually increased. During the Civil War, France had established a protectorate over Mexico, installing the Archduke Maximilian of Austria as emperor. In 1866 Secretary of State William H. Seward demanded that the French withdraw, and the United States moved 50,000 soldiers to the Rio Grande. While fear of American intervention was only one of many reasons for their action, the French pulled their troops out of Mexico during the winter of 1866–1867. Mexican nationalists promptly seized and executed Maximilian. In 1867, at the instigation of

Midway Island, an inhospitable atoll acquired in 1867, was valuable as a military base located midway between Pearl Harbor, another naval station, and East Asia. The acquisition of a Pacific empire during these years was a reason why Pearl Harbor and Midway became pivotal during the war in the Pacific in World War II.

Photo Credit: REUTERS/Hugh Gentry/ Landov.

Seward, the United States purchased Alaska from Russia for $7.2 million, ridding the continent of another foreign power.

In 1867 Seward acquired the Midway Islands in the western Pacific. He also made overtures toward annexing the Hawaiian Islands, and he looked longingly at Cuba. In 1870 President Grant submitted to the Senate a treaty annexing the Dominican Republic. He applied tremendous pressure in an effort to obtain ratification, thus forcing a "great debate" on extracontinental expansion. The distance of the Dominican Republic from the continent and its population of what one congressman called "semi-civilized, semi-barbarous men who cannot speak our language" made annexation unattractive. The treaty was rejected.

The internal growth that preoccupied Americans eventually led them to look outward. By the late 1880s the country was exporting a steadily increasing share of its agricultural and industrial output. Exports, only $450 million in 1870, passed the billion-dollar mark early in the 1890s. Imports increased at a rate only slightly less spectacular.

The character of foreign trade was also changing: Manufactures loomed ever more important among exports until in 1898 the country shipped abroad more manufactured goods than it imported. By this time American steelmakers could compete with producers anywhere in the world. When American industrialists became conscious of their ability to compete with Europeans in far-off markets, they took more interest in world affairs, particularly during periods of depression.

Shifting intellectual currents further altered the attitudes of Americans. Darwin's theories, applicable by analogy to international relations, gave the concept of manifest destiny a new plausibility. Darwinists like the historian John Fiske argued that the American democratic system of government was so clearly the world's "fittest" that it was destined to spread peacefully over "every land on the earth's surface." In *Our Country* (1885) Josiah Strong found racist and religious justifications for American expansionism, again based on the theory of evolution. The Anglo-Saxon race, centered now in the United States, possessed "an instinct or genius for colonization," Strong claimed.

The completion of the conquest of the American West encouraged Americans to consider expansion beyond the seas. "For nearly 300 years the dominant fact in American life has been expansion," declared Frederick Jackson Turner, propounder of the frontier thesis. "That these energies of expansion will no longer operate would be a rash prediction." Turner and writers who advanced other expansionist arguments were much influenced by foreign thinking. European liberals had tended to disapprove of colonial ventures, but in the 1870s and 1880s many of them were changing their minds. English liberals in particular began to talk and write about the "superiority" of English culture, to describe the virtues of the "Anglo-Saxon race," to stress a "duty" to spread Christianity among the heathen, and to advance economic arguments for overseas expansion.

European ideas were reinforced for Americans by their observation of the imperialist activities of the European powers in what would today be called underdeveloped areas. "While the great powers of Europe are steadily enlarging their colonial domination in Asia and Africa," James G. Blaine said in 1884, "it is the especial province of this country to improve and expand its trade with the nations of America." While Blaine emphasized commerce, the excitement and adventure of overseas enterprises appealed to many people even more than the economic possibilities or any sense of obligation to fulfill a supposed national, religious, or racial destiny.

Finally, military and strategic arguments were advanced to justify adopting a "large" policy. The powerful Union army had been demobilized rapidly after Appomattox; in the 1880s only about 25,000 men were under arms, their chief occupation fighting Indians in the West.

Half the navy, too, had been scrapped after the war, and the remaining ships were obsolete. While other nations were building steam-powered iron warships, the United States still depended on wooden sailing vessels. In 1867 a British naval publication accurately described the American fleet as "hapless, broken-down, tattered [and] forlorn."

Although no foreign power menaced the country, the decrepit state of the navy vexed many of its officers and led one of them, Captain Alfred Thayer Mahan, to develop a startling theory about the importance of sea power. According to him, history proved that a nation with a powerful navy and the overseas bases necessary to maintain it would be invulnerable in war and prosperous in time of peace. Applied to the current American situation, this meant that in addition to building a modern fleet, the United States should obtain a string of coaling stations and bases in the Caribbean, annex the Hawaiian Islands, and cut a canal across Central America. A more extensive colonial empire might follow, but these bases and the canal they would protect were essential first steps to ensure America's future as a great power.

Mahan attracted many influential disciples. One was Congressman Henry Cabot Lodge of Massachusetts, a prominent member of the Naval Affairs Committee. Lodge had married into a navy family and was close with the head of the new Naval War College, Commodore Stephen B. Luce. In 1883 he helped push through Congress an act authorizing the construction of three steel warships, and he consistently advocated expanding and modernizing the fleet. Elevated to the Senate in 1893, Lodge pressed for expansionist policies, basing his arguments on the strategic concepts of Mahan. Lodge's friend Theodore Roosevelt was another ardent supporter of the "large" policy, but he had little influence until McKinley appointed him assistant secretary of the navy in 1897.

View the Image

Uncle Sam Teaching the World at **myhistorylab.com**

Toward an Empire in the Pacific

The interest of the United States in the Pacific and East Asia began in the late eighteenth century, when the first American merchant ship dropped anchor in Canton harbor. After the Treaty of Wanghia (1844), American merchants in China enjoyed many privileges and trade expanded rapidly.

The Hawaiian Islands were an important way station on the route to China, and by 1820 merchants and missionaries were making contacts there. As early as 1854 a movement to annex the islands existed, although it foundered because Hawaii insisted on being admitted to the Union as a state. Commodore Perry's expedition to Japan led to the signing of a commercial treaty (1858) that opened several Japanese ports to American traders.

American influence in Hawaii increased steadily; the descendants of missionary families, most of them engaged in raising sugar, dominated the Hawaiian monarchy. While they made no overt effort to make the islands an American colony, all the expansionist ideas of the era—manifest destiny, Darwinism, Josiah Strong's racist and religious assumptions, and the relentless force of American commercial interests—pointed them in that direction. In 1875 a reciprocity treaty admitted Hawaiian sugar to the United

The Course of Empire, 1867–1901 China was the focus of American imperial visions: Missionaries, most of them women, flocked into China, and American manufacturers craved access to the huge China market.

States free of duty in return for a promise to yield no territory to a foreign power. When this treaty was renewed in 1887, the United States obtained the right to establish a naval base at Pearl Harbor. In addition to occupying Midway, America obtained a foothold in the Samoan Islands in the South Pacific.

During the 1890s American interest in the Pacific area steadily intensified as a result of the situation in Hawaii. The McKinley Tariff Act of 1890, discontinuing the duty on raw sugar and compensating American producers of cane and beet sugar by granting them a bounty of two cents a pound, struck Hawaiian sugar growers hard, for it destroyed the advantage they had gained in the reciprocity treaty.

The following year the death of King Kalakaua brought Queen Liliuokalani, a determined nationalist, to the throne. Placing herself at the head of a "Hawaii for the Hawaiians" movement, she abolished the existing constitution under which the white

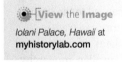

Iolani Palace, Hawaii at **myhistorylab.com**

minority had pretty much controlled the islands and attempted to rule as an absolute monarch. The resident Americans then staged a coup. In January 1893, with the connivance of the U.S. minister, John L. Stevens, who ordered 150 marines into Honolulu, they deposed Queen Liliuokalani and set up a provisional government. Stevens recognized their regime at once, and the new government sent a delegation to Washington to seek a treaty of annexation.

In the closing days of the Harrison administration such a treaty was negotiated and sent to the Senate, but when Cleveland took office in March, he withdrew it.

The new president disapproved of the way American troops had been used to over-throw the monarchy and attempted to restore Queen Liluokalani. But by now the new regime, backed by American businessmen, was firmly entrenched. Cleveland found himself unable to do anything.

Finally, in July 1898, after the outbreak of the Spanish-American War, Congress annexed the islands by joint resolution, a procedure requiring only a simple majority vote.

Toward an Empire in Latin America

Most of the arguments for extending American influence in the Pacific applied more strongly to Central and South America, where the United States had much larger economic interests and where the strategic importance of the region was clear.

As early as 1869 President Grant had come out for an American-owned canal across the isthmus of Panama, in spite of the fact that the United States had agreed in the Clayton-Bulwer Treaty with Great Britain (1850) that neither nation would "obtain or maintain for itself any exclusive control" over an inter-oceanic canal. In 1880, when the French engineer Ferdinand de Lesseps organized a company to build a canal across the isthmus, President Hayes announced that the United States would not permit a European power to control such a waterway.

When Cleveland returned to power in 1893, the possibility of trouble in Latin America seemed remote, for he had always opposed imperialistic ventures. Yet scarcely two years later the United States was again on the verge of war in South America as a result of a crisis in Venezuela, and before this issue was settled Cleveland had made the most powerful claim to American hegemony in the hemisphere ever uttered. The tangled borderland between Venezuela and British Guiana had long been in dispute, Venezuela demanding more of the region than it was entitled to and Great Britain making exaggerated claims and refusing to submit the question to arbitration. What made a crisis of the controversy was the political situation in the United States. With his party rapidly deserting him because of his stand on the silver question, and with the election of 1896 approaching, President Cleveland desperately needed a popular issue.

There was considerable anti-British feeling in the United States. By taking the Venezuelan side in the boundary dispute, Cleveland would be defending a weak neighbor against a great power, a position certain to evoke a popular response.

In July 1895 he ordered Secretary of State Richard Olney to send a near ultimatum to the British. By occupying the disputed territory, Olney insisted, Great Britain was invading Venezuela and violating the Monroe Doctrine. Unless Great Britain responded promptly by agreeing to arbitration, the president would call the question to the attention of Congress.

The note threatened war, but the British ignored it for months. They did not take the United States seriously as a world power. The American navy, although expanding, could not hope to stand up against the British, who had fifty battleships, twenty-five armored cruisers, and many smaller vessels. When Lord Salisbury, the prime minister and foreign secretary, finally replied, he rejected outright the argument that the Monroe Doctrine had any status under international law and refused to arbitrate what he called the "exaggerated pretensions" of the Venezuelans.

Cleveland was furious. On December 17, 1895, he asked Congress for authority to appoint an American commission to determine the correct line between British Guiana and Venezuela. When that had been done, he added, the United States should "resist by every means in its power" the appropriation by Great Britain of any territory "we have determined of right belongs to Venezuela." Congress responded at once, unanimously appropriating $100,000 for the boundary commission. Popular approval was almost universal.

In Great Britain government and people suddenly awoke to the seriousness of the situation. No one wanted a war with the United States over a remote patch of tropical real estate. In Europe, Britain was concerned about German economic competition and the increased military power of that nation. The immense potential strength of the United States could no longer be ignored. Why make an enemy of a nation of 70 million, already the richest industrial power in the world?

Great Britain agreed to arbitrate the boundary, and the war scare subsided. When the boundary tribunal awarded nearly all the disputed region to Great Britain, whatever ill feeling the surrender may have occasioned in that country faded away. Instead of leading to war, the affair marked the beginning of an era of Anglo-American friendship. It had the unfortunate effect, however, of adding to the long-held American conviction that the nation could get what it wanted in international affairs by threat and bluster—a dangerous illusion.

The Cuban Revolution

On February 10, 1896, scarcely a week after Venezuela and Great Britain had signed the treaty ending their dispute, General Valeriano Weyler arrived in Havana from Spain to take up his duties as governor of Cuba. His assignment to this post was occasioned by the guerrilla warfare that Cuban nationalist rebels had been waging for almost a year. Weyler, a tough and ruthless soldier, began herding the rural population into wretched **"reconcentration" camps** to deprive the rebels of food and recruits. Resistance in Cuba hardened.

The United States had been interested in Cuba since the time of John Quincy Adams and, were it not for Northern opposition to adding more slave territory, might well have obtained the island one way or another before 1860. When the Cubans revolted against Spain in 1868, considerable support for intervening on their behalf developed. Hamilton Fish, Grant's secretary of state, resisted this sentiment, and Spain managed to pacify the rebels in 1878 by promising reforms. But change was slow in coming—slavery was not abolished until 1886. The worldwide depression of the 1890s hit the Cuban economy hard, and when an American tariff act in 1894 jacked up the rate on Cuban sugar by 40 percent, thus cutting off Cuban growers from the American market, the resulting distress precipitated another revolt.

Public sympathy in the United States went to the Cubans, who seemed to be fighting for liberty and democracy against an autocratic Old World power. Most newspapers supported the rebels; labor unions, veterans' organizations, many Protestant clergymen, a great majority of American blacks, and important politicians in both major parties demanded that the United States aid their cause. Rapidly increasing American investments in Cuban sugar plantations, now approaching $50 million, were endangered by the fighting and by the social chaos sweeping across the island.

In April 1896 Congress adopted a resolution suggesting that the revolutionaries be granted the rights of belligerents. Since this would have been akin to formal recognition, Cleveland would not go that far, but he did exert diplomatic pressure on Spain to remove the causes of the rebels' complaints, and he offered the services of his government as mediator. The Spanish rejected the suggestion. For a time the issue subsided. The election of 1896 deflected American attention from Cuba, and then McKinley refused to take any action that might disturb Spanish-American relations. In Cuba General Weyler made some progress toward stifling rebel resistance.

American expansionists, however, continued to demand intervention, and the press kept resentment alive with tales of Spanish atrocities. McKinley remained adamant. Although he warned Spain that Cuba must be pacified, his tone was friendly and he issued no ultimatum. A new government in Spain relieved the situation by recalling Weyler and promising partial self-government to the Cubans. In a message to Congress in December 1897, McKinley urged that Spain be given "a reasonable chance to realize her expectations" in the island.

His hopes were doomed. The fighting in Cuba continued. When riots broke out in Havana in January 1898, McKinley ordered the battleship *Maine* to Havana harbor to protect American citizens.

Shortly thereafter Hearst's *New York Journal* printed a letter written to a friend in Cuba by the Spanish minister in Washington, Dupuy de Lôme. The letter had been stolen by a spy. De Lôme, an experienced but arrogant diplomat, failed to appreciate McKinley's efforts to avoid intervening in Cuba. In the letter he characterized the president as a *politicastro*, or "small-time politician," which was a gross error, and a "bidder for the admiration of the crowd," which was equally insulting though somewhat closer to the truth. Americans were outraged, and de Lôme's hasty resignation did little to soothe their feelings.

Then, on February 15, the *Maine* exploded and sank in Havana harbor, 260 of the crew perishing in the disaster. Interventionists in the United States accused Spain of having destroyed the ship and clamored for war. The willingness of Americans to blame Spain indicates the extent of anti-Spanish opinion in the United States by 1898. No one has ever discovered what actually happened. A naval court of inquiry decided that the vessel had been sunk by a submarine mine, but it now seems more likely that an internal explosion destroyed the *Maine*. The Spanish government could hardly have been foolish enough to commit an act that would probably bring American troops into Cuba.

Watch the Video
Burial of the *Maine* Victims
at **myhistorylab.com**

With admirable courage, McKinley refused to panic; but he could not resist the wishes of millions of citizens that something be done to stop the fighting and allow the Cubans to determine their own fate. Spanish pride and Cuban patriotism had taken the issue of peace or war out of the president's hands. Spain could not put down the rebellion, and it would not yield to the nationalists' increasingly extreme demands. The Cubans, sensing that the continuing bloodshed aided their cause, refused to give the Spanish regime room to maneuver. After the *Maine* disaster, Spain might have agreed to an armistice had the rebels asked for one, and in the resulting negotiations it might well have given up the island. The rebels refused to make the first move. The fighting continued, bringing the United States every day closer to intervention.

The president faced a dilemma. Most of the business interests of the country, to which he was particularly sensitive, opposed intervention. Congress, however, seemed

The explosion of the *Maine* in Havana harbor, killing 260 men, caused much speculation in the newspapers and across the nation. Many Americans accused Spain of destroying the ship, a reaction that typified American sentiment toward the Spanish in 1898. What really caused the explosion remains unknown.
Source: ICHi-08428/Kurz & Allison/Chicago History Museum.

determined to act. When he submitted a restrained report on the sinking of the *Maine*, the Democrats in Congress, even most of those who had supported Cleveland's policies, accused him of timidity. Vice President Garret A. Hobart warned him that the Senate could not be held in check for long; should Congress declare war on its own, the administration would be discredited.

Finally, early in April, the president drafted a message asking for authority to use the armed forces "to secure a full and final termination of hostilities" in Cuba.

At the last moment the Spanish government seemed to yield; it ordered its troops in Cuba to cease hostilities. McKinley passed this information on to Congress along with his war message, but he gave it no emphasis and did not try to check the march toward war. To seek further delay would have been courageous but not necessarily wiser. Merely to stop fighting was not enough. The Cuban nationalists now insisted on full independence, and the Spanish politicians were unprepared to abandon the last remnant of their once-great American empire. If the United States took Cuba by force, the Spanish leaders might save their political skins; if they meekly surrendered the island, they were done for.

The "Splendid Little" Spanish-American War

On April 20, 1898, Congress, by joint resolution, recognized the independence of Cuba and authorized the use of the armed forces to drive out the Spanish. An amendment proposed by Senator Henry M. Teller disclaiming any intention of adding Cuban territory to the United States passed without opposition. Four days after passage of the **Teller Amendment**, Spain declared war on the United States.

Photo Credit: The Granger Collection, New York.

Sailors on the USS *Oregon* watch the destruction of the Spanish cruiser, *Cristobal Colon*, during the Battle of Santiago, Cuba, July 3, 1898.

The Spanish-American War was fought to free Cuba, but the first action took place on the other side of the globe, in the Philippine Islands. Weeks earlier, Theodore Roosevelt, at the time assistant secretary of the navy, had alerted Commodore George Dewey, who was in command of the United States Asiatic Squadron located at Hong Kong, to move against the Spanish base at Manila if war came. Dewey had acted promptly, drilling his gun crews, taking on supplies, giving his gleaming white ships a coat of battle-gray paint, and establishing secret contacts with the Filipino nationalist leader, Emilio Aguinaldo. When word of the declaration of war reached him, Dewey steamed from Hong Kong across the South China Sea with four cruisers and two gunboats. On the night of April 30 he entered Manila Bay, and at daybreak he opened fire on the Spanish fleet at 5,000 yards. His squadron made five passes, each time reducing the range; when the smoke had cleared, all ten of Admiral Montojo's ships had been destroyed. Not a single American was killed in the engagement.

Dewey immediately asked for troops to take and hold Manila, for now that war had been declared, he could not return to Hong Kong or any other neutral port. McKinley took the fateful step of dispatching some 11,000 soldiers and additional naval support. On August 13 these forces, assisted by Filipino irregulars under Aguinaldo, captured Manila.

Watch the Video

Roosevelt's Rough Riders
at **myhistorylab.com**

Meanwhile, in Cuba, the United States had won a total victory. When the war began, the U.S. regular army consisted of about 28,000 men. This tiny force was bolstered by 200,000 hastily enlisted volunteers. Aggressive units like the regiment of "Rough Riders" raised by Theodore Roosevelt, who had resigned his Navy Department post to become a lieutenant colonel of volunteers, scrambled for space and supplies, shouldering aside other units to get what they needed.

Since a Spanish fleet under Admiral Pascual Cervera was known to be in Caribbean waters, no invading army could safely embark until the fleet could be located. On May 29 American ships found Cervera at Santiago harbor, on the eastern end of Cuba, and established a blockade. In June a 17,000-man expeditionary force landed at Daiquiri, east of Santiago, and pressed quickly toward the city. The Americans sweated through Cuba's torrid summer in heavy wool winter uniforms, ate "embalmed beef" out of cans, and fought mostly with old-fashioned rifles using black powder cartridges that marked the position of each soldier with a puff of smoke whenever he pulled the trigger. On July 1 they broke through undermanned Spanish defenses and stormed San Juan Hill, the intrepid Roosevelt in the van.

With Santiago harbor in range of American artillery, Admiral Cervera had to run the blockade. On July 3 his black-hulled ships, flags proudly flying, steamed forth from the harbor and fled westward along the coast. Five American battleships and two cruisers, commanded by Rear Admiral William T. Sampson and Commodore Winfield Scott Schley, ran them down. In four hours the entire Spanish force was destroyed. Damage to the American ships was superficial; only one American seaman lost his life in the engagement.

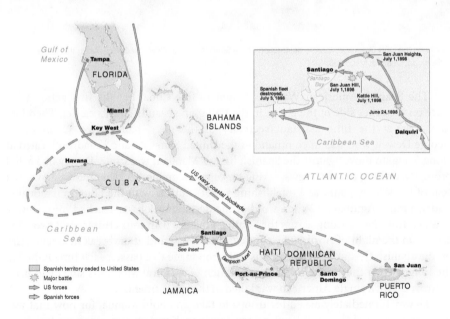

Spanish-American War: Caribbean Theater, 1898 After boarding in Tampa, American soldiers landed near Santiago, Cuba. They swiftly overran Spanish fortifications on the heights to the east of the city. When U.S. troops came within artillery range of Santiago Bay, the Spanish fleet fled. Soon the Spanish ships were intercepted and destroyed by the American navy.

The end then came abruptly. Santiago surrendered on July 17. A few days later, other U.S. troops completed the occupation of Puerto Rico. On August 12, one day before the fall of Manila, Spain agreed to get out of Cuba and to cede Puerto Rico and an island in the Marianas (Guam) to the United States. The future of the Philippines was to be settled at a formal peace conference, convening in Paris on October 1.

Developing a Colonial Policy

Although the Spanish resisted surrendering the Philippines at Paris, they had been so thoroughly defeated that they had no choice. The decision hung rather on the outcome of a conflict over policy within the United States. The war, won at so little cost militarily, produced problems far larger than those it solved.[1] The nation had become a great power in the world's eyes. European leaders had been impressed by the forcefulness of Cleveland's diplomacy in the Venezuela boundary dispute and by the efficiency displayed by the navy in the war. The annexation of Hawaii and other overseas bases intensified their conviction that the United States was determined to become a major force in international affairs.

But were the American people determined to exercise that force? The debate over taking the Philippine Islands throws much light on their attitudes. It was titillating for Americans to think of a world map liberally sprinkled with American flags and of the economic benefits that colonies might bring, but most citizens were not prepared to join in a worldwide struggle for power and influence. They entered blithely on adventures in far-off regions without facing the implications of their decision.

Since the United States had abjured any claim to Cuba, even though the island had long been desired by expansionists, logic dictated that a similar policy be applied to the Philippines. But expansionists were eager to annex the entire archipelago. Even before he had learned to spell the name, Senator Lodge was saying that "the Phillipines [sic] mean a vast future trade and wealth and power," offering the nation a greater opportunity "than anything that has happened . . . since the annexation of Louisiana."

President McKinley adopted a more cautious stance, but he too favored "the general principle of holding on to what we can get." A speaking tour of the Midwest in October 1898, during which he experimented with varying degrees of commitment to expansionism, convinced him that the public wanted the islands. Business opinion had shifted dramatically during the war. Business leaders were now calling the Philippines the gateway to the markets of East Asia.

The Anti-Imperialists

The war had produced a wave of unifying patriotic feeling. It greatly furthered reconciliation between the North and the South. But victory raised new divisive questions. An important minority objected strongly to the U.S. acquisition of overseas possessions.

The anti-imperialists insisted that since no one would consider statehood for the Philippines, it would be unconstitutional to annex them. It was a violation of the spirit of

---

[1]More than 5,000 Americans died as a result of the conflict, but fewer than 400 fell in combat. The others were mostly victims of yellow fever, typhoid, and other diseases.

Photo Credit: Courtesy of the Library of Congress.

While the good children (the states) sit at their seats, with the Indian off to the side, the unruly blacks—"Cuba," "Puerto Rico," "Hawaii," and "Philippines"—are lectured by Uncle Sam. Racist anti-imperialists argued, as did this cartoon in *Puck* in 1899, that the inclusion of other peoples would weaken the American nation.

the Declaration of Independence to govern a foreign territory without the consent of its inhabitants, Senator George Frisbie Hoar of Massachusetts argued; by taking over "vassal states" in "barbarous archipelagoes" the United States was "trampling . . . on our own great Charter, which recognizes alike the liberty and the dignity of individual manhood."

McKinley was not insensitive to this appeal to idealism and tradition, which was the fundamental element in the anti-imperialist argument. But he rejected it for several reasons.

Public opinion would not sanction restoring Spanish authority in the Philippines or allowing some other power to have them. That the Filipinos were sufficiently advanced and united socially to form a stable government if granted independence seemed unlikely. Senator Hoar believed that "for years and for generations, and perhaps for centuries, there would have been turbulence, disorder and revolution" in the islands if they were left to their own devices.

The president searched the depths of his soul and could find no solution but annexation. The state of public feeling made the decision easier, and he probably found the idea of presiding over an empire appealing. Certainly the commercial possibilities did not escape him. In the end it was with a heavy sense of responsibility that he ordered the American peace commissioners to insist on acquiring the Philippines. To salve the feelings of the Spanish the United States agreed to pay $20 million for the archipelago, but it was a forced sale, accepted by Spain under duress.

The peace treaty faced a hard battle in the U.S. Senate, where a combination of partisan politics and anticolonialism made it difficult to amass the two-thirds majority necessary for ratification. McKinley had shrewdly appointed three senators, including one

Democrat, to the peace commission. This predisposed many members of the upper house to approve the treaty, but the vote was close. William Jennings Bryan, titular head of the Democratic party, could probably have prevented ratification had he urged his supporters to vote nay. Although he was opposed to taking the Philippines, he did not do so. To reject the treaty would leave the United States technically at war with Spain and the fate of the Philippines undetermined; better to accept the islands and then grant them independence. The question should be decided, Bryan said, "not by a minority of the Senate but by a majority of the people" at the next presidential election. Perplexed by Bryan's stand, a number of Democrats allowed themselves to be persuaded by the expansionists' arguments and by McKinley's judicious use of patronage; the treaty was ratified in February 1899 by a vote of fifty-seven to twenty-seven.

The Philippine Insurrection

The national referendum that Bryan had hoped for never materialized. Bryan himself confused the issue in 1900 by making free silver a major plank in his platform, thereby driving conservative anti-imperialists into McKinley's arms. Moreover, early in 1899 the Filipino nationalists under Aguinaldo, furious because the United States would not withdraw, took up arms. A savage guerrilla war resulted, one that cost far more in lives and money than the "splendid little" Spanish-American conflict.

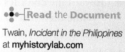

Read the Document

Twain, *Incident in the Philippines* at **myhistorylab.com**

Neither side displayed much regard for the "rules" of war. Goaded by sneak attacks and instances of cruelty to captives, American soldiers, most of whom had little respect for Filipinos to begin with, responded in kind. (See American Lives, "Frederick Funston".) Civilians were rounded up, prisoners tortured, and property destroyed. Horrifying tales of rape, arson, and murder by U.S. troops filtered into the country, providing ammunition for the anti-imperialists.

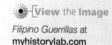

View the Image

Filipino Guerrillas at **myhistorylab.com**

In fact, far more than 8,000 Filipinos lost their lives during the conflict, which raged for three years. More than 70,000 American soldiers had to be sent to the islands before the resistance was crushed, and about as many of them lost their lives as had perished in the Cuban conflict.

In 1900 McKinley sent a commission headed by William Howard Taft, a federal judge, to establish a government. Taft took an instant liking to the

Emilio Aguinaldo, shown here with his young son, commanded Filipino insurgents who worked with Commodore Dewey to help overthrow Spanish rule of the Philippines in 1898. He later took up arms against the United States in a brutal three-year struggle when President McKinley opposed granting independence to the islands.

Photo Credit: © Bettmann/CORBIS All Rights Reserved.

Filipinos, and his policy of encouraging them to participate in the territorial government attracted many converts. In July 1901 he became the first civilian governor of the Philippines.

Actually, the reelection of McKinley in 1900 settled the Philippine question so far as most Americans were concerned. Anti-imperialists still claimed that it was unconstitutional to take over territories without the consent of the local population. Their reasoning, while certainly not unsound, was unhistorical. No American government had seriously considered the wishes of the American Indians, the French and Spanish settlers in Louisiana, the Eskimos of Alaska, or the people of Hawaii when it had seemed in the national interest to annex new lands.

Cuba and the United States

Nevertheless, grave constitutional questions arose as a result of the acquisitions that followed the Spanish-American War. McKinley acted with remarkable independence in handling the problems involved in expansion. He set up military governments in Cuba, Puerto Rico, and the Philippines without specific congressional authority. The Supreme Court, in what became known as the "insular cases," granted Congress permission to act toward the colonies much as it pleased.

While the most heated arguments raged over Philippine policy, the most difficult colonial problems concerned the relationship between the United States and Cuba. Despite the desire of most Americans to get out of Cuba, an independent government could not easily be created.

The insurgent government was feeble, corrupt, and oligarchic, the Cuban economy in a state of collapse, and life was chaotic. The first Americans entering Havana found the streets littered with garbage and the corpses of horses and dogs. All public services were at a standstill; it seemed essential for the United States, as McKinley said, to give "aid and direction" until "tranquillity" could be restored.

The problems were indeed knotty, for no strong local leader capable of uniting Cuba appeared. Even Senator Teller, father of the Teller Amendment, expressed concern lest "unstable and unsafe" elements gain control of the country. European leaders expected that the United States would eventually annex Cuba; and many Americans, including General Leonard Wood, who became military governor in December 1899, considered this the best solution. The desperate state of the people, the heavy economic stake of Americans in the region, and its strategic importance militated against withdrawal.

In the end the United States did withdraw, after doing a great deal to modernize sugar production, improve sanitary conditions, establish schools, and restore orderly administration. In November 1900 a Cuban constitutional convention met at Havana and proceeded without substantial American interference or direction to draft a frame of government. The chief restrictions imposed by this document on Cuba's freedom concerned foreign relations; at the insistence of the United States, it authorized American intervention whenever necessary "for the preservation of Cuban independence" and "the maintenance of a government adequate for the protection of life, property, and individual liberty." Cuba had to promise to make no treaty with a foreign power compromising its independence and to grant naval bases on its soil to the United States.

The Cubans, after some grumbling, accepted this arrangement, known as the **Platt Amendment**. It had the support of most American opponents of imperialism. The amendment was a true compromise: It safeguarded American interests while granting to the Cubans real self-government on internal matters. In May 1902 the United States turned over the reins of government to the new republic. The next year the two countries signed a reciprocity treaty tightening the economic bonds between them.

Read the Document
The Platt Amendment at myhistorylab.com

True friendship did not result. Although American troops occupied Cuba only once more, in 1906, and then at the specific request of Cuban authorities, the United States repeatedly used the threat of intervention to coerce the Cuban government. American economic penetration proceeded rapidly and without regard for the well-being of the Cuban peasants, many of whom lived in a state of peonage on great sugar plantations. Nor did the Americans' good intentions make up for their tendency to consider themselves innately superior to the Cubans and to overlook the fact that Cubans did not always wish to adopt American customs and culture.

The United States in the Caribbean and Central America

If the purpose of the Spanish-American War had been to bring peace and order to Cuba, the Platt Amendment was a logical step. The same purpose soon necessitated a further extension of the principle, for once the United States accepted the role of protector and stabilizer in parts of the Caribbean and Central America, it seemed desirable to supervise the entire region.

The Caribbean and Central American countries were economically underdeveloped, politically unstable, and desperately poor. Most of the people were uneducated peasants, many of whom were little better off than slaves. Rival cliques of wealthy families struggled for power, force being the usual method of effecting a change in government. Most of the meager income of the average Caribbean state was swallowed up by the military or diverted into the pockets of the current rulers.

Cynicism and fraud poisoned the relations of most of these nations with the great powers. European merchants and bankers systematically cheated their Latin American customers, who in turn frequently refused to honor their obligations. Foreign bankers floated bond issues on outrageous terms, while revolutionary governments in the region annulled concessions and repudiated debts with equal disdain for honest business dealing.

In 1902, shortly after the United States had pulled out of Cuba, trouble erupted in Venezuela, where a dictator, Cipriano Castro, was refusing to honor debts owed the citizens of European nations. To force Castro to pay up, Germany and Great Britain established a blockade of Venezuelan ports and destroyed a number of Venezuelan gunboats and harbor defenses. Under American pressure the Europeans agreed to arbitrate the dispute. For the first time, European powers had accepted the broad implications of the Monroe Doctrine. By this time Theodore Roosevelt had become president of the United States, and he quickly capitalized on the new

American Lives

On the night of March 22, 1901, as rain battered his campsite in the deep jungles of Luzon Island in the Philippines, Frederick Funston pondered what awaited him the next day. Ten miles to the north lay his prey, Emilio Aguinaldo, President of the Philippine Republic. For two years, the American army had been trying to capture Aguinaldo. But repeatedly Aguinaldo had slipped away. This time Funston was close. His ruse was working.

It had been a wild idea, something out of a boy's adventure story. He conceived it after capturing a Filipino messenger carrying coded documents. Funston's interrogation of the courier had been successful. The courier confirmed that Aguinaldo's secret headquarters was located in a remote area of Luzon.

Funston had chosen eighty Filipino scouts from the Macabebes, a tribe hostile to Aguinaldo. He outfitted them in the uniforms of Aguinaldo's army and trained them to pretend to be Filipino nationalists. These "nationalists" would escort five American "prisoners" (including Funston) for presentation to Aguinaldo.

Funston longed to be a hero. Ever since he was a child, he worried that he failed to measure up to his father. Edward "Foghorn" Funston had been an artillery officer during the Civil War and a fiery Republican congressman afterward. At six feet two and 200 pounds, he was regarded by all as an exemplar of nineteenth-century manhood. But Frederick, born in 1864, was only five feet four and slightly built. He compensated with bravado displays of martial manliness. He craved a military career, but though his father was a congressman, West Point rejected him: His grades were mediocre, and he was too small.

In 1886 he enrolled at the University of Kansas but didn't fit in. He devoted himself to the pursuit of the most desirable women on campus, all of whom spurned him. Increasingly he retreated from social situations, preferring to drink alone in his room, periodically bursting out in a drunken rage.

He dropped out of college. First, he explored an unmapped section of Death Valley in California. Then he volunteered to gather botanical samples in Alaska for the Department of Agriculture. When the department proposed that he command an entire expedition for the purpose, he flatly turned them down. Alone, he trekked into the frigid wastes of northern Alaska and remained there for the better part of a year. When he ran out of food he ate his sled dogs.

During those long, silent nights, Funston realized that he could hardly prove that he measured up if no one were around to take the measurements. He decided to become a soldier, not caring much against whom he fought. In 1895 he contacted a recruiter for the cause of Cuban independence and accepted a commission as an artillery officer in the rebel army.

In Cuba he was given command of a Hotchkiss cannon; he made up for his lack of gunnery skill by sneaking his cannon absurdly close to Spanish fortifications at night, often within 400 yards. As the sun rose, the Spaniards, aghast at what was sitting on their doorstep, fired everything they had at Funston's cannon. Funston calmly adjusted the sights, pulled the lanyard, and climbed upon the parapet, shouting

Frederick Funston: hero or antihero?

Photo Credit: © Bettmann/CORBIS All Rights Reserved.

"Viva Cuba libre!" He was repeatedly wounded; once, a bullet pierced his lungs. When a severe hip wound became infected, he returned to the United States for medical assistance.

But he was not done with war. In 1898 Funston was given command of the Kansas regiments that had volunteered against Spain. To his dismay, they were sent to the Philippines, where the Spaniards had already ceased fighting. But after President McKinley decided to annex the Philippines, war broke out between the Americans and the Filipino nationalists. Funston finally got what he craved: sweeping charges, glorious victories, and newspaper feature stories. Yet the jokes persisted. Behind his back, his men called him the "Bantam General." The *New York Times,* in its coverage of a battle in which he won a Congressional Medal of Honor, ran the headline: "Daring Little Colonel Funston." The opening paragraph attributed Funston's courage to the fact that he was too small to hit.

But now, if he captured Aguinaldo, Funston, the little man, would become a great one.

On March 23, 1901, Funston's Macabebes and their five American "prisoners" met up with a contingent of Aguinaldo's army. Deceived, Aguinaldo's troops escorted Funston's band into the town of Palanan. Aguinaldo watched from a window above. When shots rang out, thinking the troops were firing a salute, he shouted, "Stop that foolishness. Don't waste ammunition!"

Then Funston burst into Aguinaldo's compound: "I am General Funston. You are a prisoner of war of the Army of the United States of America."

Dazed, Aguinaldo replied, "Is this not some joke?" Funston seized Aguinaldo, dragged him through the jungle to the coast, where the USS *Vicksburg* was waiting. It took them to American headquarters in Manila.

After being subjected to intense pressure by American officials, Aguinaldo renounced the Filipino revolution, swore allegiance to the United States, and called on his followers to do likewise. The Philippine-American conflict was virtually over. Frederick Funston had almost single-handedly won the war.

For a time, Funston was a sensation. He was promoted to brigadier general. Newspaper editors and politicians championed him for governor of Kansas or for vice president on a ticket headed by Theodore Roosevelt in 1904. But within a few years Funston all but vanished. Anti-imperialists pointed out that Funston's men had surrendered and then fired their weapons, and that the Macabebes had been wearing enemy uniforms; both actions violated international law. Worse, several reporters and some of his soldiers claimed that Funston had ordered the execution of Filipino prisoners. He was ordered to an inconse-quential command in San Francisco.

One hundred years after Funston's capture of Aguinaldo, U.S. troops would again be tracking a rebel fugitive: Osama bin Laden, mastermind of the September 11, 2001, attacks on the World Trade Center and Pentagon. That virtually no one recalled Funston's single-handed pursuit and capture of Aguinaldo was one measure of how completely he had slipped from view.

But Funston's name resurfaced in 2010, after major earthquakes had triggered widespread looting in Haiti and Chile. The *New York Times* observed that when the 1906 earthquake destroyed much of San Francisco, General Frederick Funston had immediately marched his troops into the city and taken charge; sometimes, the *Times* noted, leaders must act decisively.

Question for Discussion

■ To catch Aguinaldo, Funston employed tactics of doubtful legality. A century later Americans have been accused of using torture and other unsavory methods to win "the war on terror." Are such techniques morally or legally wrong? Why or why not?

The United States in the Caribbean and Central America Puerto Rico was ceded by Spain to the United States after the Spanish-American War; the Virgin Islands were bought from Denmark; the Canal Zone was leased from Panama. The ranges of dates shown for Cuba, the Dominican Republic, Haiti, Nicaragua, and Panama cover those years during which the United States either had troops in occupation or in some other way (such as financial) had a protectorate relationship with that country.

European attitude. In 1903 the Dominican Republic defaulted on bonds totaling some $40 million. When European investors urged their governments to intervene, Roosevelt announced that under the Monroe Doctrine the United States could not permit foreign nations to intervene in Latin America. But, he added, Latin American nations should not be allowed to escape their obligations.

The president did not want to make a colony of the Dominican Republic. He therefore arranged for the United States to take charge of the Dominican customs service—the one reliable source of revenue in that poverty-stricken country. Fifty-five percent of the customs duties would be devoted to debt payment, the remainder turned over to the Dominican government to care for its internal needs. Roosevelt defined his policy, known as the Roosevelt Corollary to the Monroe Doctrine, in a message to Congress in December 1904. "Chronic wrongdoing" in Latin America, he stated with his typical disregard for the subtleties of complex affairs, might require outside intervention. Since, under the Monroe Doctrine, no other nation could step in, the United States must "exercise . . . an international police power."

In the short run this policy worked. Dominican customs were honestly collected for the first time and the country's finances put in order. The presence of American warships in the area provided a needed measure of political stability. In the long run, however, the Roosevelt Corollary caused a great deal of resentment in Latin America.

⊙ See the Map

Activities of the United States in the Caribbean at **myhistorylab.com**

The Open Door Policy in China

The insular cases, the Platt Amendment, and the Roosevelt Corollary established the framework for American policy both in Latin America and in East Asia. Coincidental with the Cuban rebellion of the 1890s, a far greater upheaval had convulsed the ancient empire of China. In 1894–1895 Japan easily defeated China in a war over Korea. Alarmed by Japan's aggressiveness, the European powers hastened to carve out for themselves new spheres of influence along China's coast. After the annexation of the Philippines, McKinley's secretary of state, John Hay, urged on by business leaders fearful of losing out in the scramble to exploit the Chinese market, tried to prevent the further absorption of China by the great powers.

For the United States to join in the dismemberment of China was politically impossible because of anti-imperialist feeling, so Hay sought to protect American interests by clever diplomacy. In a series of "Open Door" notes (1899) he asked the powers to agree to respect the trading rights of all countries and to impose no discriminatory duties within their spheres of influence.

The replies to the Open Door notes were at best noncommittal, yet Hay blandly announced in March 1900 that the powers had "accepted" his suggestions! Thus he could claim to have prevented the breakup of the empire and protected the right of Americans to do business freely in its territories. In reality nothing had been accomplished; the imperialist nations did not extend their political control of China only because they feared that by doing so they might precipitate a major war among themselves. Nevertheless, Hay's action marked a revolutionary departure from the traditional American policy of isolation, a bold advance into the complicated and dangerous world of international power politics.

Within a few months of Hay's announcement the **Open Door policy** was put to the test. Chinese nationalists, angered by the spreading influence of foreign governments, launched the so-called Boxer Rebellion. They swarmed into Peking and drove foreigners behind the walls of their legations, which were placed under siege. For weeks, until an international rescue expedition (which included 2,500 American soldiers) broke through to free them, the fate of the foreigners was unknown. Fearing that the Europeans would use the rebellion as a pretext for further expropriations, Hay sent off another round of Open Door notes announcing that the United States believed in the preservation of "Chinese territorial and administrative entity" and in "the principle of equal and impartial trade with all parts of the Chinese Empire." This broadened the Open Door policy to include all China, not merely the European spheres of influence.

Hay's diplomacy was superficially successful. But once again European jealousies and fears rather than American cleverness were responsible. When the Japanese, mistrusting Russian intentions in Manchuria, asked Hay how he intended to implement his policy, he replied meekly that the United States was "not prepared . . . to enforce these views." The United States was being caught up in the power struggle in East Asia without having faced the implications of its actions.

In time the country would pay a heavy price for this unrealistic attitude, but in the decade following 1900 its policy of diplomatic meddling worked fairly well. Japan attacked Russia in a quarrel over Manchuria, smashing the Russian fleet in 1905 and winning a series of battles on the mainland. Japan was not prepared for a long war,

Photo Credit: Courtesy of the Divinity School Library, Yale University.

Grace Service, a YMCA missionary, explained that these porters worked at the base of Mount Omei in Szechwan, China, a favorite site for Buddhist pilgrims. Upper-class Chinese women's feet were bound to keep them small. The deformities that resulted limited the distance they could walk, so they hired men such as these to carry them to the summit.

however, and suggested to President Roosevelt that an American offer to mediate would be favorably received.

Eager to preserve the balance of power in East Asia, which enabled the United States to exert influence without any significant commitment of force, Roosevelt accepted the hint. In June 1905 he invited the belligerents to a conference at Portsmouth, New Hampshire. At the conference the Japanese won title to Russia's sphere around Port Arthur and a free hand in Korea, but when they demanded Sakhalin Island and a large money indemnity, the Russians balked. Unwilling to resume the war, the Japanese settled for half of Sakhalin and no money.

The Treaty of Portsmouth was unpopular in Japan, and the government managed to place the blame on Roosevelt, who had supported the compromise. Ill feeling against Americans increased in 1906 when the San Francisco school board, responding to local opposition to the influx of cheap labor from Japan, instituted a policy of segregating Asian children in a special school. Japan protested, and President Roosevelt persuaded the San Franciscans to abandon segregation in exchange for his pledge to cut off further Japanese immigration. He accomplished this through a "Gentlemen's Agreement" (1907) in which the Japanese promised not to issue passports to laborers seeking to come to America. Discriminatory legislation based specifically on race was thus avoided. However, the atmosphere between the two countries remained charged. Japanese resentment at American racial prejudice was great; many Americans talked fearfully of the "yellow peril."

Roosevelt did not appreciably increase American naval and military strength in East Asia, nor did he stop trying to influence the course of events in the area, and he took no step toward withdrawing from the Philippines. He sent the fleet on a world cruise to demonstrate its might to Japan but knew well that this was mere bluff. "The 'Open Door' policy," he advised his successor, "completely disappears as soon as a powerful nation determines to disregard it." Nevertheless he allowed the belief to persist in the United States that the nation could influence the course of East Asian history without risk or real involvement.

The Panama Canal

In the Caribbean region American policy centered on building an interoceanic canal across Central America. The first step was to get rid of the old Clayton-Bulwer Treaty with Great Britain, which barred the United States from building a canal on its own. In 1901 Lord Pauncefote, the British ambassador, and Secretary of State John Hay negotiated an agreement abrogating the Clayton-Bulwer pact and giving the United States the right to build and defend a canal connecting the Pacific Ocean with the Caribbean Sea.

One possible canal route lay across the Colombian province of Panama, where the French-controlled New Panama Canal Company had taken over the franchise of the old De Lesseps company. Only fifty miles separated the oceans in Panama. The terrain, however, was rugged and unhealthy. While the French company had sunk much money into the project, it had little to show for its efforts aside from some rough excavations. A second possible route ran across Nicaragua. This route was about 200 miles long but was relatively easy since much of it traversed Lake Nicaragua and other natural waterways.

President McKinley appointed a commission to study the alternatives. It reported that the Panamanian route was technically superior, but recommended building in

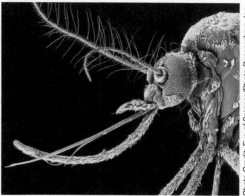

An electron microscopic photo of a mosquito that carried yellow fever. Major Walter Reed of the U.S. army proved that yellow fever was not spread directly among humans, but from the bites of infected mosquitoes. The virus then multiplied in the human bloodstream. Headache, backache, fever, and vomiting ensued. Liver cells were destroyed, resulting in jaundice—thus the name "yellow fever." American surgeon William Crawford Gorgas worked to eliminate yellow fever by destroying the breeding grounds of these mosquitoes. The last yellow fever outbreak in the United States struck New Orleans and parts of the South in 1905.

Photo Credit: Eye of Science/Photo Researchers, Inc.

The U.S. Panama Canal Following many negotiations, construction of the Panama Canal began in 1904. After many delays and hardships, it was completed in 1914.

Nicaragua because the New Panama Canal Company was asking $109 million for its assets, which the commission valued at only $40 million. Lacking another potential purchaser, the French company lowered its price to $40 million, and after a great deal of clever propagandizing by Philippe Bunau-Varilla, a French engineer with heavy investments in the company, President Roosevelt settled on the Panamanian route.

In January 1903 Secretary of State Hay negotiated a treaty with Colombia. In return for a ninety-nine-year lease on a zone across Panama six miles wide, the United States agreed to pay Colombia $10 million and an annual rent of $250,000. The Colombian senate, however, unanimously rejected this treaty. It demanded $15 million directly from the United States, plus one-fourth of the $40 million U.S. payment to the New Panama Canal Company.

A little more patience might have produced a mutually satisfactory settlement, but Roosevelt looked on the Colombians as highwaymen who were "mad to get hold of the $40,000,000 of the Frenchmen." When Panamanians, egged on by the French company, staged a revolution against Colombia in November 1903, he ordered the cruiser *Nashville* to Panama. Colombian government forces found themselves looking down the barrels of the guns of the *Nashville* and shortly thereafter eight other American warships. The revolution succeeded.

Roosevelt instantly recognized the new Republic of Panama. Secretary Hay and the new "Panamanian" minister, Bunau-Varilla, then negotiated a treaty granting the United States a zone ten miles wide in perpetuity, on the same terms as those rejected by Colombia. Within the Canal Zone the United States could act as "the sovereign of the territory . . . to the entire exclusion of . . . the Republic of Panama." The United States guaranteed the independence of the republic. The New Panama Canal Company then received its $40 million, including a substantial share for Bunau-Varilla.

Historians have condemned Roosevelt for his actions, and with good reason. It was not that he fomented the Panamanian revolution, for he did not. Separated from the government at Bogotá by an impenetrable jungle, the people of Panama province had long wanted to be free of Colombian rule. He sinned, rather, in his disregard of Latin American sensibilities. He referred to the Colombians as "dagoes" and insisted that he was defending "the interests of collective civilization" when he overrode their opposition to his plans.

If uncharitable, Roosevelt's analysis was not entirely inaccurate, yet it did not justify his haste in taking Panama under his wing. Throughout Latin America, especially as nationalist sentiments grew stronger, Roosevelt's intolerance and aggressiveness in the canal incident bred resentment and fear.

Table 1 Path to Empire, 1885–1901

Josiah Strong, *Our Country*	1885	Applied social Darwinism—"survival of the fittest"—to justify American expansion
A. T. Mahan, *The Influence of Seapower upon History*	1890	Endorsed naval power to ensure prosperity and national security
United States helped sugar planters depose Queen Liliuokalani	1893	Major step toward annexation of Hawaii
United States intervened in British dispute with Venezuela over land claims	1895	Reaffirmed the Monroe Doctrine claim to American supervision of Latin America
USS *Maine* exploded in Havana harbor	1898	Generated public pressure for war against Spain
Defeat of Spain	1898	Opened former Spanish colonies to U.S. annexation and economic penetration
U.S. annexation of Philippines	1899	United States became formal empire
"Open Door" Policy	1899	United States asserted trading rights in China
Roosevelt intervened on behalf of Panamanian independence	1903	Advanced expansive rights in Central America
Roosevelt Corollary	1904	Asserted U.S. right to military intervention in Latin America
Taft's Dollar Diplomacy	1909–1913	Encouraged U.S. government-supported investment abroad
Panama Canal opened	1914	Allowed U.S. warships to travel swiftly between Atlantic and Pacific

The first vessels passed through the canal in 1914—and American hegemony in the Caribbean expanded. Yet even in that strategically vital area there was more show than substance to American strength. The navy ruled Caribbean waters largely by default, for it lacked adequate bases in the region. In 1903, as authorized by the Cuban constitution, the United States obtained an excellent site for a base at Guantanamo Bay, but before 1914 Congress appropriated only $89,000 to develop it.

The tendency was to try to influence outlying areas without actually controlling them. Roosevelt's successor, William Howard Taft, called this policy **dollar diplomacy**, his reasoning being that economic penetration would bring stability to underdeveloped areas and power and profit to the United States without the government's having to commit troops or spend public funds.

Under Taft the State Department won a place for American bankers in an international syndicate engaged in financing railroads in Manchuria. When Nicaragua defaulted on its foreign debt in 1911, the department arranged for American bankers to reorganize Nicaraguan finances and manage the customs service. Although the government truthfully insisted that it did not "covet an inch of territory south of the Rio Grande," dollar diplomacy provoked further apprehension in Latin America. Efforts to establish similar arrangements in Honduras, Costa Rica, and Guatemala all failed. In Nicaragua orderly administration of the finances did not bring internal peace. In 1912, 2,500 American marines and sailors had to be landed to put down a revolution.

Economic penetration proceeded briskly. American investments in Cuba reached $500 million by 1920, and smaller but significant investments were made in the Dominican Republic and in Haiti. In Central America the United Fruit Company accumulated large holdings in banana plantations, railroads, and other ventures. Other firms plunged heavily into Mexico's rich mineral resources.

Imperialism without Colonies

If one defines imperialism narrowly as a policy of occupying and governing foreign lands, American imperialism lasted for an extremely short time. With trivial exceptions, all the American colonies—Hawaii, the Philippines, Guam, Puerto Rico, the Guantanamo base, and the Canal Zone—were obtained between 1898 and 1903. In retrospect it seems clear that the urge to own colonies was only fleeting; the legitimate questions raised by the anti-imperialists and the headaches connected with the management of overseas possessions soon produced a change of policy.

The objections of protectionists to the lowering of tariff barriers, the shock of the Philippine insurrection, and a growing conviction that the costs of colonial administration outweighed the profits affected American thinking. Hay's Open Door notes marked the beginning of the retreat from imperialism as thus defined, while the Roosevelt Corollary and dollar diplomacy signaled the consolidation of a new policy. Elihu Root summarized this policy as it applied to the Caribbean nations in 1905: "We do not want to take them for ourselves. We do not want any foreign nations to take them for themselves. We want to help them."

Yet imperialism can be given a broader definition. Although the United States did not seek colonies, it pursued a course that promoted American economic penetration of underdeveloped areas without the trouble of owning and controlling them. American statesmen regarded American expansion as beneficial to all concerned. They genuinely believed that they were exporting democracy along with capitalism and industrialization.

Dollar diplomacy had two main objectives, the avoidance of violence and the economic development of Latin America; it paid small heed to how peace was maintained and how the fruits of development were distributed. The policy was self-defeating, for in the long run stability depended on the support of local people, and this was seldom forthcoming.

By the eve of World War I the United States had become a world power and had assumed what it saw as a duty to guide the development of many countries with traditions far different from its own. The national psychology, if such a term has any meaning, remained fundamentally isolationist. Americans understood that their wealth and numbers made their nation strong and that geography made it virtually invulnerable. Thus they proceeded to do what they wanted to do in foreign affairs, limited more by their humanly flexible consciences than by any rational analysis of the probable consequences. This policy seemed safe enough—in 1914.

See the **Map**

World Colonial Empires, 1900 at **myhistorylab.com**

Milestones

1850	Britain and United States sign Clayton-Bulwer Treaty concerning interoceanic canal	1898	Theodore Roosevelt leads Rough Riders at Battle of San Juan Hill
			United States annexes Hawaii
1858	Commercial treaty with Japan opens several ports to American trade	1899	Hay's Open Door policy safeguards United States' access to China trade
1867	United States buys Alaska from Russia		United States annexes Philippines and becomes an empire
1871	Treaty of Washington settles *Alabama* claims	1900	Platt Amendment gives United States naval stations and right to intervene in Cuba
1875	Reciprocity treaty increases U.S. influence in Hawaii		
1885	Josiah Strong justifies expansionism in *Our Country*	1901	Hay-Pauncefote Treaty gives United States rights to build interoceanic canal
1890	A. T. Mahan fuels American imperialism in *The Influence of Sea Power*		Supreme Court's insular cases give Congress free reign over colonies
1893	United States helps sugar planters depose Queen Liliuokalani of Hawaii	1902	Europeans accept Monroe Doctrine during Venezuela bond dispute
1895	United States supports Venezuela in European border dispute over British Guiana	1904	Roosevelt Corollary to Monroe Doctrine gives United States "international police power"
1898	*Maine* explodes in Havana harbor		
	Spanish-American war breaks out	1907	"Gentlemen's Agreement" curtails Japanese immigration
	Dewey defeats Spanish fleet at Manila Bay	1914	Panama Canal opens

✓•⌐Study and Review at www.myhistorylab.com

Review Questions

1. The introduction to this chapter holds that American soldiers are fighting in Afghanistan in part because of American imperialism after 1890. Could Americans then have avoided imperial expansion? What factors impelled them to support imperialism?

2. On what issues did the anti-imperialists and the imperialists agree? And how did they differ?

3. How did American involvement in the Caribbean differ from the United States' approach to China and East Asia?

4. Why did McKinley choose to annex the Philippines? Was his decision a wise one?

5. How did the Roosevelt Corollary modify the Monroe Doctrine? How did Taft's policies differ from those of Roosevelt?

6. Was American imperialism from 1890–1910 chiefly beneficial or harmful to other nations? To the United States?

Key Terms

dollar diplomacy
isolationism
Open Door policy

Platt Amendment
"reconcentration"
    camps

Teller Amendment